THE GODS' MACHINES

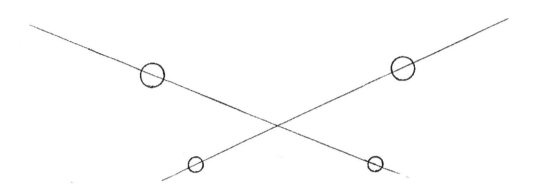

The Gods' Machines
were built according to
a universal rule:
an angle of 135 degrees,
explicitly shown by
the four Station Stones
of Stonehenge

THE GODS' MACHINES

FROM STONEHENGE TO CROP CIRCLES

WUN CHOK BONG

Frog Books
Berkeley, California

Published by Frog Books

Frog Books' publications are distributed by
North Atlantic Books
P. O. Box 12327
Berkeley, California 94712

Cover design by Maxine Ressler
Book design by Wun Chok Bong
Printed in the United States of America

The Gods' Machines: From Stonehenge to Crop Circles is sponsored by the Society for the Study of Native Arts and Sciences, a nonprofit educational corporation whose goals are to develop an educational and cross-cultural perspective linking various scientific, social, and artistic fields; to nurture a holistic view of arts, sciences, humanities, and healing; and to publish and distribute literature on the relationship of mind, body, and nature.

North Atlantic Books' publications are available through most bookstores. For further information, call 800-733-3000 or visit our website at www.northatlanticbooks.com.

Library of Congress Cataloging-in-Publication Data

Wun, Chok Bong.
    The gods' machines : from Stonehenge to crop circles / Wun Chok Bong.
        p. cm.
    Includes bibliographical references.
    ISBN-13: 978-1-58394-207-9 (trade pbk.)
    1. Electric power plants—History—To 1500. 2. Antiquities, Prehistoric.
3. Megalithic monuments. 4. Curiosities and wonders. 5. Earth currents.
6. Storage batteries. 7. Stonehenge (England) I. Title.
    TK1005.W87 2008
    930.1'4—dc22
                                2008007817

1 2 3 4 5 6 7 8 9 Versa 14 13 12 11 10 09 08

Table of Contents

Acknowledgments

Many thanks to:

C. E. W. Porritt BA, Johnny Cheng, and Grace Chu for proofreading the manuscript.

Colin Andrews, Ian Armit, Burl Aubrey, Michael Balfour, Stan Beckensall, Percy Brown, Martin Byrne (and carrowkeel.com), Christopher Chippindale, Michael D. Coe, Zef Damen, Michael Dames, Erich von Däniken, Stuart Dike and Mark Fussell (and cropcircleconnector.com), George Eogan, Susan Toby Evans, A. Hardy, Claude Jacques, Eleanor Mannikka, Donattello Mazzeo and Chiari S. Antonini, G. Michell, Andreas Muller, Michael O'Kelly, Stuart Piggott, Mike Pitts, Chris Scarre, Freddy Silva, Richard H. Wilkinson, Zecharia Sitchin, and cropcircle-archive.com, for the many inspirations.

Andy K. S. Cheng and M. H. Chu for their technical support, and Philip Smith of North Atlantic Books for editorial assistance.

Introduction

"God knows what their use was! They are hard to tell, but yet may be told."

—Samuel Pepys, 11 June 1668, from
Michael Balfour, *Stonehenge and Its Mysteries*

The Irish called them the *Tuatha De Danann*. The British called them *Cernunnos* and they were known to the ancient Sumerians as the *Anunnaki*. The Mayans named them *Quetzalcoatl* and *Kukulkan,* whereas they were the *Shiva* and *Vishnu* in ancient Cambodia. Neolithic megalithism marks their history on Earth, leaving us clusters of mysteries. A planet-sized house containing rooms of riddles.

Starting from the New Stone Age, around 4000–3000 B.C., while our ancestors were still using primitive tools to eke out a living, a mysterious race appeared and reappeared for thousands of years, constructed awe-inspiring monuments and then left, leaving modern investigators with little or no idea as to the purpose behind their actions. They established themselves first in the northwest of France, building large tumuli and stone alignments across the land. Several centuries passed and their infrastructure expanded to the rest of the European continent. From Orkney to the Malta Islands of the Mediterranean, passage graves, stone dolmens, monoliths, henges and enclosures, as well as standing stone circles, have been deciphered as simple burial tombs.

The Neolithic Era/Bronze Age also marks the beginning of farming, through the introduction of metal equipment. For centuries, these mysterious structures have been regarded as icons of this epoch. These monuments symbolize our ancestors' advances in culture and technology. It was the same period when our Mesolithic forebearers suddenly abandoned their hunting-and-gathering ways and decided to settle down, beginning the most risky period of our civilization's development, investing in the bare lands where crops could only be harvested months afterward, not to mention attacks from animals, risk of pestilence, and the unpredictability of weather. Agriculture was a great leap forward, both technologically and mentally. It would transform the face of civilization forever.

Again, it was at this critical moment that our ancestors established permanent settlements such as the ancient cities of Babylon and Ur of the Two Rivers. Why did these particular areas, apart from arable land and adequate water supplies, attract our ancestors? At this time humans also began to manipulate stone tools for hunting and farming, inventing woven-fabric textiles as well as metallurgy. Who guided mankind in the dawn of civilization? Should we believe humans stumbled upon this knowledge by chance? After thousands of years of hunting and gathering, did we wake up one morning and decide to change and giving up everything we knew and owned, and experiment with entirely unknown forms of food production and toolmaking?

Humans are blessed with curiosity, but we are also creatures of habit. If something works we don't suddenly introduce an uncertain element. We generally loathe change. Contrary to human nature, this is exactly what we did. We changed the very fabric of our society. These were not cosmetic changes, moving from one place to another or discovering a certain stone that made a better flint. This was a complete upheaval of everything we knew. Something big and influential must have happened to shake our world view so completely and effectively: Someone higher gave us civilization.

Even with such advancements in social and technological living, why did the monument builders, after spending hundreds of years in planning and building them, stay for such a short time and then disappear, leaving only clusters of silent structures, as suggested by the experts? Unfortunately no accounts exist, as the first written language, usually not deciphered, was not invented until a thousand years later.

"World mysteries" do exist for a reason, a very practical one. And they were all bounded by a universal formula. A rule not only helped to disclose the real function behind these monuments, but also evidenced the repeated visits of their advanced masters to Earth, and why they were and are still here. The flourishing of our civilization was just a by-product, unfortunately.

Humans watched the activities of this starfaring civilization with tremendous awe and little understanding. They deified them.

A message from these super beings has been waiting for us for millennia. Stored in megalithic safes. Carved onto stone slabs. Placed inside ancient temples. Waiting silently down the long stretch of human history until we possessed the knowledge to decipher the secrets.

This book traces this civilization on Earth. The findings are as solid as those Neolithic stones. Newgrange was not a tomb. Stonehenge and Egyptian temples were not Gods' mansions. Mayan pyramids and Angkor gopuras were in no way the temples of divinities. Together with modern-day crop circles, they were simply the power-generating machines of the Gods.

Chapter 1
Houses of Mystery

Stonehenge, 2006

An Enigma?

"No one has been able to discover by what mechanism such vast masses of stone were elevated, nor for what purpose they were designed."

—Henry of Huntingdon,
A.D. 1129

Stonehenge in Wiltshire, England, is described as "a giant ring dropped by the demon before the dawn of mankind." While it is indisputable that Stonehenge is a Neolithic product, few markings or carvings have been found inside the monument. The earliest record comes from the twelfth century, with no word of its origin. The only certainty is that it has been standing there for thousands of years. Stonehenge has played different roles in different epochs. It once served as a venue for the witches' sabbath, a symbol for fostering love and health, an altar for religious ceremonies, a cemetery for human skeletal remains, a setting for rites, a prehistoric observatory, a Druidic temple and, presently, a tourist attraction. None of these roles reflect the true function of Stonehenge. From the mid twentieth century onward, archaeologists, mathematicians, astronomers and sexologists have voiced their interpretations of Stonehenge. However, none of them are right. The complexity of the monument makes many people believe that the henge must have a specific function that has so far defied all attempts to explain it. Its enomorous stones, even though past their most glorious days, still pose a challenge to our intelligence. Its monumental doorways only lead open our ignorance. Stonehenge has always been regarded as "an enigma that cannot be solved."

Inside Stonehenge

Stonehenge has stood on Salisbury Plain in southern England for over a hundred generations. It is a ceremonial complex, surrounded by huge earthwork enclosures and long barrows of the mid-Neolithic period and the round barrows and henges of the early Bronze Age. Stonehenge is the best known prehistoric monument in Europe. It is the most sophisticated and mysterious structure among nine hundred stone circles in England and Ireland. What tourists see today is actually the third incarnation of Stonehenge—Stonehenge III. It consists of massive blocks of gray sarsen meticulously carved into upright stones and topped by horizontal slabs, creating a circle with narrow openings or lintel doorways. But in around 3000 B.C., long before the construction of this inner ring, a circle of ditch and bank was built at the site marking the initial circumference. This "henge" is about a thousand years older than the inner rings. The builders further enhanced the monument by introducing a double semicircle of bluestones five to eight hundred years later. They demolished them afterward. Stonehenge as it stands today was completed in 1800 B.C. A total of 1,200 years was invested in its construction. Stonehenge must have been extremely important to this ancient society, a society believed to possess only simple tools and social organization.

3

The tour of Stonehenge starts with its most neglected feature. The henge was built with a round enclosure formed by an external shallow ditch and an internal embankment. In order to reach its sacred center, there are two entrances. One opens to the northeast and the other to the south. The wider one to the northeast forms an avenue—the northeast causeway—12m wide with a bearing of 50 degrees. A large sarsen stone, probably showing the entrance to the structure, sits in the middle. This is the Heel Stone—"stone of the rising sun" (from classical Greek). It is 77.3m from the center of the circle and 4.7m above the ground, with another 1.2m extending below ground level, making it altogether 5.9m long. It weighs thirty-five tons and is surrounded by a ditch of its own. This demonstrates its sacred status among the other megaliths nearby. It has stood like a watchman overlooking the henge for several millennia.

Just inside the bank are the fifty-six Aubrey Holes (AHs) discovered in 1666 by John Aubrey (who actually identified only five of them). Even though half of these Holes are still buried in their original places, they are regarded as one of the main mysteries of Stonehenge. Each of these steep-sided Holes borders the embankment (diagram 1.1). Each is 1m deep and 1.5m in diameter. Strangely, these Holes were filled again immediately after being dug. Experts believe that these Holes must have a special function, as no wooden or megalithic uprights were ever erected in them (despite their having been carefully measured and excavated).

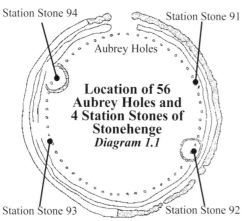

Station Stone 94
Station Stone 91
Aubrey Holes
Location of 56 Aubrey Holes and 4 Station Stones of Stonehenge
Diagram 1.1
Station Stone 93
Station Stone 92

Four other rough sarsens, the Station Stones nos. 91–94, stood smartly along the AH circumference forming a rectangle just inside the bank. For centuries these were overlooked because their original design is no longer apparent. Stone 91 has fallen and Stone 93 has been truncated. Stones 92 and 94 have been removed altogether and replaced by oval mounds, possibly as compensation or substitution. Experts believe the diagonals of the Station Stones were used to determine the center of the stone circles of the later period. Others believe that they are aligned to astronomical settings. The shorter sides of the rectangle were oriented to sunrise and sunset on the longest day of the year (John Smith) whereas the longer side indicates the northernmost position of the setting moon (C. A. Newham). However, their location along the AH circumference suggests they may have had a similar function as the AHs. The sarsen stones may also reflect being erected in the last stage of Stonehenge, around 1800 B.C.

In the eyes of modern tourists, the shallow enclosure and refilled Aubrey Holes are not one of the highlights of the monument. In the center of the monument, an impressive circle of sarsen stones is erected (diagram 1.2). The circle consisted of thirty rectangular stones, capped at the top, numbered 1–30, each measuring 4m × 2m × 1m and weighing twenty-five tons. There were thirty lintels, numbered 101–130, on top of the sarsen circle and they were held in place by the tongue-and-groove method, in which the V-shaped projection at the end of one lintel fits neatly into the V-shaped cavity at the end of its partner. The lintels are curved inward and outward so as to make a smooth circle. The columns and beams also have mortice and tenon joints. Some important functions had to be served beyond simply showing off the builder's sophisticated skills. This three-dimensional stone circle gave Stonehenge its uniqueness in the megalithic world and made it the champion among all comparable examples. It would have looked like thirty giants holding hands to form a circle protecting something beyond our imagination and so important it has illuminated our civilization ever since.

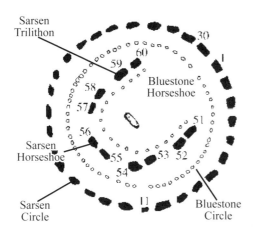

Inner Megalithic Structures of Stonehenge
Diagram 1.2

Further inside is another stone ring made of bluestone. This is an igneous rock, rectilinear in shape and smaller in size than the sarsen. The average bluestone is 2.4m long, 0.6m wide and 0.6m thick. Unlike the gray sarsen, which is of sandstone, the bluestones are mostly dolerite, rich in quartz. Each stone weighs about three to six tons. What amazed the people are not the complexity or the sizes of these bluestones, but the area where they came from. The origin of the bluestones remains a mystery, as the nearest possible source of these stones is over a hundred kilometers away, in the Preseli Mountains southwest of Wales. Originally there were about sixty of them, but now only six remain upright. A few of the bluestones show a deliberate smooth dressing of the natural coarse surface of rock.

The builders kept challenging their own abilities as well as ours by erecting two more semicircles of horseshoes inside the two concentric stone circles (diagram 1.3). Resulting from the arrangement of five trilithons, each is formed by two uprights with a lintel on top to form a doorway, constructed with an opening to the northeast. These five great sarsen trilithons, each composed of two pillars, weighing fifty tons each and capped with a lintel weighing ten tons, are arranged in a horseshoe shape 14m wide and 13.1m deep. They vary in height and are set northeast-to-southwest from its open mouth to its apex. They are the tallest stones of the monument and the sarsen trilithon in the middle marks the highest point of Stonehenge.

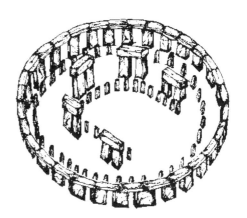

Stonehenge During Its Heyday, 2000 B.C.
Diagram 1.3

Matching the great trilithon horseshoe is an inner horseshoe of nineteen small bluestones. Like the outer ring of the bluestone circle, the horseshoe bluestones are carefully selected, dressed and arranged into square-section pillars. The shortest is less than 1.8m high, and, like the sarsen horseshoe, they increase in size towards the southwest to a maximum of about 2.4m. Both sarsen and bluestone horseshoe arrangements fall symmetrically across the northeast-southwest axis of the monument. Structurally, a vast open space is formed in the center with another forecourt at its northeast, suggesting it might be a prehistoric temple.

The final features of Stonehenge III were the introduction of two more rings of pits, the thirty Y and Z holes They lie in an open space between the Great Sarsen Circle and the fifty-six Aubrey Holes (diagram 1.4). The reason for their existence is unknown.

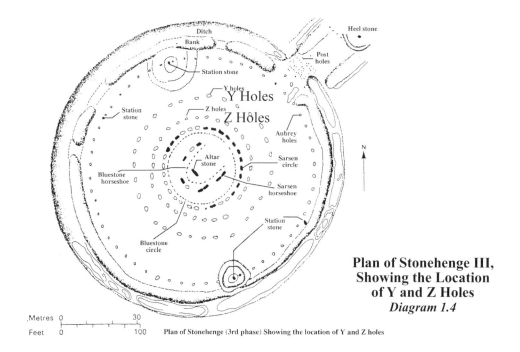

**Plan of Stonehenge III,
Showing the Location
of Y and Z Holes**
Diagram 1.4

Plan of Stonehenge (3rd phase) Showing the location of Y and Z holes

The general layout and formation of the monument is clear. However, the purpose is unknown. Here are some theories:

1. Memorial: To the Britons slaughtered by the Saxons in the Middle Ages.
2. Astronomical: Indicating the midsummer sunrise and midwinter sunset line. Some experts suggest the sarsen circle was a calendar, or even an astronomical temple.
3. Ceremonial: Wooden buildings and circles of timbers were once set in the middle of the monument.
4. Extraterrestrial: Some think it was a landing station for alien spacecraft.

What makes Stonehenge an enigma is that, unlike other megalithic sites, there are few carvings or markings left on the stones, given that the site was so important to the people of the ancient world. Could this signify reluctance on the part of the local people to leave their mark on this sacred site? As a result, the answer to its mystery may not lie in Stonehenge.

The Newgrange Answer

"Many years ago the Giants transported them [enormous stones] from the farthest ends of Africa and set them up in Ireland at a time when they lived in that country."

—Geoffrey of Monmouth, early-twelfth-century historian

Ironically, the carvings to understanding Stonehenge do exist; however, they are not found in England, but hundreds of kilometers away, in Ireland. The word "sarsen" comes from "Saracen," meaning "eastern from Arabic"—this suggests the prehistoric people believed the monument was a product of distant lands. Although the two countries are separated by the Irish Sea, similar megalithic monuments are found in both places.

Following the last Ice Age, in around 10,000–5000 B.C., the Grooved Ware People, a society advanced in architecture and astronomy, suddenly appeared and dominated the extreme edges of the continent. These megalith-loving people possessed sophisticated organization and architectural prowess, erecting thousands of stones, each weighing several tons, afterwards placing even heavier stones across the tops. The experts assume these megalithic sites were tombs for the dead. However, are we supposed to believe they were intended to house the dead in the equivalent of a stone age five-star hotel while no other permanent settlements were built in the same areas? Where did the living dwell? The Grooved Ware People possessed advanced knowledge but left no records of their own. It seems their sole purpose was to construct this megalithic infrastructure, after which they simply faded into the canvas of prehistory.

The local Irish, having lived among these sites their entire lives, might disagree with the tomb theory the experts purport. Having listened to bedtime stories from their fathers, they have their own explanation for these monstrous structures, such as the droppings of devils to the beds or tables of Giants. These Neolithic tombs not only housed the dead, but also contained the secrets of their own ancestry. Unfortunately these structures have fulfilled the role of keeping their secrets too effectively. Time will tell, the old saying goes, but this time, the stones do the talking.

Newgrange: A Prototype Stonehenge

Fifty kilometers north of Dublin in the Boyne Valley sits the most famous megalithic structure in Ireland—the passage mound of Newgrange. Newgrange lies on the highest point of an elongated ridge and was constructed around 3200 B.C., fully 1,000 years before the introduction of the inner megaliths into Stonehenge and 3,000 years before the arrival of the first Celts to Ireland.

In 1993, Newgrange, together with its two sister mounds, Knowth and Dowth, was designated a World Heritage Site by UNESCO due to the outstanding legacy of its infrastructure. It has long been an important monument in the region and marked the geological and architectural advancement of its ancient builders. According to legends, the great mound of Newgrange was built by a group of "invaders" who "came from the sky" or from the "south islands of the world." They were said to have emerged from a dense cloud and brought with them magical tools, including a large deep pot that could restore the dead to life. Another piece of Irish literature mentions that the mound was associated with supernatural creatures or the Sun God, the Lord of Light.

Archaeologists classify Newgrange as a passage tomb, probably originated from Spain. But for the builders, the site was ritual and spiritual, a house for their deities and ancestors. It was until the arrival of the Beaker people who turned it into living house and a focal point for ritual gathering. During the Middle Ages, the land became a new grange (outlying farm) of the Mellifont Abbey, giving the tomb its modern name. The site was rediscovered in 1699 in the course of removal of material for road building (Knowth.com), but it was not until 1962 that the first major excavation of the site began.

Today, most people come to Newgrange and its sister mounds for their artistry (diagram 1.5). Many slabs are decorated with the swirling patterns of passage grave art. The single most celebrated design is a group of spirals appearing on a large kerbstone blocking the entrance to the mound. This carving is a key to unlock the ultimate secret of Newgrange.

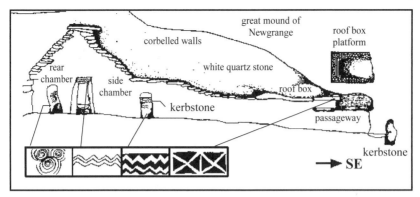

Cross-section of Newgrange, with Location of Some Famous Carvings
Diagram 1.5

Newgrange is believed to be made from 200,000 tons of stones, most of which are greywacke. It is also believed the top of the southeast sector of the cairn was once covered with white quartz stones, making it shine like a pearl during the day as well as on a moonlit night. The tomb passage opens into the southeast of the mound and runs northwest in a slight S-shaped curve for 18.95m, ending in a corbelled stone chamber 3.6m high at the entrance and 7m high in the middle, with an average height of about 1.5m. There are twenty-two orthostats on the left side and twenty-one on the right, with the tallest stones near the chamber. There are three side chambers, each cruciform in shape, one opening at the end and the two on the sides (diagram 1.6). Each of these recesses contains a carved round-bottomed stone basin.

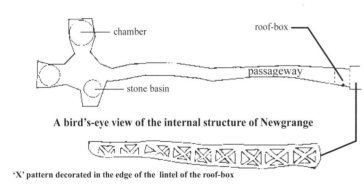

A bird's-eye view of the internal structure of Newgrange

'X' pattern decorated in the edge of the lintel of the roof-box

Cruciform Tomb of Newgrange
Diagram 1.6

Ornamentation of unknown significance is found on many of the roof slabs and their supporting corbels. The most interesting structure is a rectangular opening above the passage entrance known as the "roof box." Its roof-stone is meticulously ornamented on the forward-facing edge. Some archaeologists believe the mound builders used this opening to allow the spirits of the dead to enter or leave the tomb. Historians think the specially designed roof box of Newgrange and other chambered tombs of this period have alignments allowing the sun's rays into the rear end of the mound—a carefully designed way to glorify their sacred solar god and goddess. In 1972 a survey found that the internal structures of the mound, with its long and curved passage, were constructed with such sophistication they accurately align with the sun's rays and maximize the length of the beam entering the chamber at the spring and autumn solstice. This is why the mound is regarded as the world's oldest solar observatory. However the passage is narrow and the sun can reach into the chamber for only a few minutes each year (probably lasts for 17 minutes, from 8:58 a.m. to 9:15 a.m.). If the site was originally used as a tomb, then the sole observers were the dead inside! It is hard to imagine that these people spent generations building these massive structures merely to observe the sun and moon for a few short minutes each year. Today, more than 27,000 apply for just 100 places to see winter solstice sunrise inside this prehistoric time-telling device.

Newgrange was originally built around 3200 B.C. Today it is in a restored form. The mound and its passageway were first built with large stone slabs. The mound is just over 13m high with an average diameter of 107.6m. This is slightly bigger than the 97.5m of Stonehenge. Ninety-seven kerbstones are arranged end to end, forming a circle at the base of the mound and covering about 4,047 square meters. Once there was a circle of monoliths surrounding the

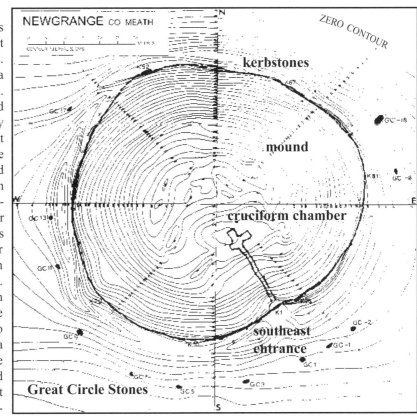

Cross-section of the Mound of Newgrange and Its Great Stone Circle (after O' Kelly 1986)
Diagram 1.7

mound, but now only twelve remain. Three of the largest monoliths (GC3, GC-8, and GC-10) are sandstone while the others, 2m high, are igneous rock. GC3 and GC-10 (2.4m high) were found lying prone, and were re-erected afterwards. Archaeologists believe that the standing stones were erected at the very final stage of construction (diagram 1.7).

Newgrange and Stonehenge: A Mirror Image

Although Stonehenge and Newgrange are separated by hundreds of kilometers of land and sea and a thousand years in time, they share many consistencies in their surrounding layouts and internal structures:

1. Both are circular megalithic monuments of the late Neolithic era;
2. Both monuments lie in a Neolithic complex and each has a cursus (parallel banks measuring 100m in length and 20m wide) to the northeast. Each site has a river running to its south;
3. Both are centered with sarsen stones. Newgrange's chamber walls and Stonehenge's stone circle and horseshoe are made of harder sarsen with quartz grains;
4. The structure of the long passage of Newgrange is more or less equivalent to the elongated horseshoe of Stonehenge. Each is characterized by a long gallery of standing stones—orthostats in Newgrange and the bluestone horseshoe of Stonehenge—which form a chamber or recess at one end and an entry or opening at the other (diagram 1.8);

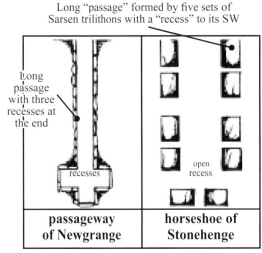

Long "passage" formed by five sets of Sarsen trilithons with a "recess" to its SW

Long passage with three recesses at the end

recesses

open recess

passageway of Newgrange

horseshoe of Stonehenge

Internal "Causeways" of Newgrange and Stonehenge
Diagram 1.8

5. The entrances to the passage of Newgrange and horseshoe of stonehenge, with their spacious forecourts similarly cut across the circular cairn and the bluestone circle (diagram 1.9).

6. The corbelled chamber of Newgrange and the sarsen trilithon (Sarsens 55+56) of Stonehenge (diagram 1.10) dominate the center of each monument and are the highest points respectively;

7. Each monument is abundant in quartz-rich minerals. The southeast portion of the Newgrange cairn is covered by a sheet of white quartz stones a few meters high. The center of Stonehenge is encircled by crystallized sarsens and bluestones, 4m high (diagram 1.9);

8. The corbelled chamber of Newgrange is surrounded by a structural circle of kerbstones forming a mound, and another circle of twelve greywacke sandstones, named the "Great Stone Circle," stand at the outskirt. A similar design is also found in Stonehenge, as two circles of sarsens (red sandstones) and bluestones encircle the great trilithon horseshoe at the inner section of Stonehenge;

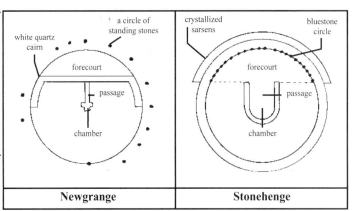

white quartz cairn

a circle of standing stones

forecourt

passage

chamber

crystallized sarsens

bluestone circle

forecourt

passage

chamber

Newgrange

Stonehenge

Forecourts of Newgrange and Stonehenge
Diagram 1.9

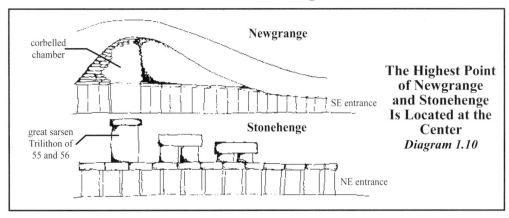

Newgrange

corbelled chamber

SE entrance

great sarsen Trilithon of 55 and 56

Stonehenge

NE entrance

The Highest Point of Newgrange and Stonehenge Is Located at the Center
Diagram 1.10

9. The most striking similarity between the two monuments is their basic construction plan. As indicated in diagram 1.11, the main axis of both monuments aligns to their marker stones—the bisector of an angle formed by the interception of the four marker stones. The layout of Stonehenge has features precisely the same as those of the earlier Newgrange; it could be said to be a refined copy of Newgrange. In the case of Newgrange, if a straight line is drawn to connect the standing stone (GC1) at the entrance with the slab (K52) at the back of the cairn, the line will pass through the corbelled chamber as well as the passageway of the mound. At the same time, if two lines are drawn from the standing stones of GC11 and GC7 (the marker stones) of the Great Circle that surrounds the mound, they will intercept at the center of the corbelled chamber (diagram 1.11). In other words, the standing stones GC11 and GC7 of Newgrange become the "Station Stones" (corresponding to SS91 and SS92 of Stonehenge). An angle of 135 degrees is formed by the two chords. In the case of Stonehenge, the same angle is formed by the interception of two straight lines formed by Station Stones 91 and 93, 92 and 94 respectively (diagram 1.12).

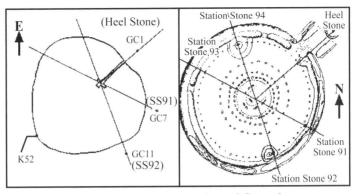

**Layouts of Newgrange (*left*) and Stonehenge
Are Both Subjected to Their Station Stones**
Diagram 1.11

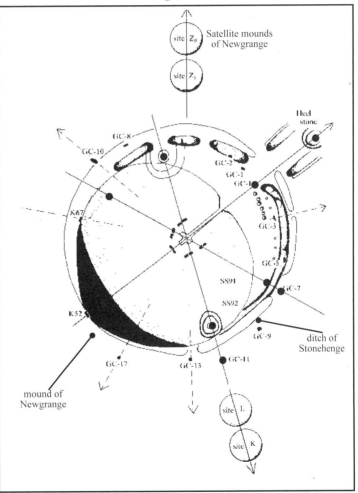

**Newgrange (Rotated 90°) Superimposed on
Stonehenge**
Diagram 1.12

Secrets behind the Passage Grave Art

Like all tourists, I am attracted to the intricate carvings of Newgrange. Familiar shapes such as spirals, concentric circles, cups, zigzag lines, and lozenge designs were skillfully decorated with a unified theme on the slabs and blocks inside and outside the mound. The entrance stone (K1) with its spiral carvings is the most famous (diagram 1.13).

Another slab, forming the recess wall, was ornamented with a triskelion, the icon of Newgrange (diagram 1.14). This comprises simple spirals and was apparently carved using simple tools, but some suggest a lunar and solar connection. Altogether ninety-seven blocks decorated with the same geometric motif lie around the mound. It is hard to believe that the intricacy and intensity of the patterns was the work of Stone Age people, possibly under the influence of herbal hallucinogens, trying to carve them in the dark.

"Icon" of Newgrange—the Famous Carved Kerbstone K1 of Newgrange
Diagram 1.13

Triskelion
Diagram 1.14

It is conceivable that the artists might have been exposed to advanced instruments that showed electric currents on monitors and screens. The zigzag pattern could resemble the nodes and antinodes of frequency waves. The spiral and concentric circles are the movement of radio or microwaves. In any event, these carvings were not simply a leisurely pursuit (diagram 1.15). They might have more "practical" meaning instead.

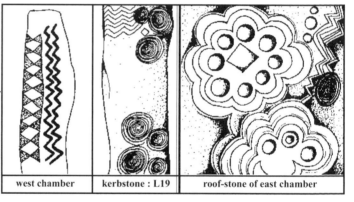

west chamber | kerbstone : L19 | roof-stone of east chamber

Diagram 1.15

In his fantastic book *Newgrange: Archaeology, Art and Legend,* Professor Michael J. O'Kelly goes to great lengths to explore the mound and describe its structure and design. His many drawings of the best-known ornamented stones and slabs are fascinating. High levels of intricacy convince me the Neolithic people did leave us a message, which probably provides an indication of the real function of the mound. According to Professor O'Kelly, a slab (Co.1/C7) inside the mound's chamber was excavated in 1965 (O'Kelly 1965, figure 82; diagram 1.17). In his book there are the usual spirals, concentric circles, and zigzag lines. The most striking patterns are carved at the southwestern corner of the slab (O'Kelly, p. 172; diagram 1.18). Consisting of a circle in the center with radiating lines, these carvings are regarded as images of the solar god and goddess. They are cited as evidence to prove that Newgrange and its sister mounds were used as solar observatories in the third millennium B.C.

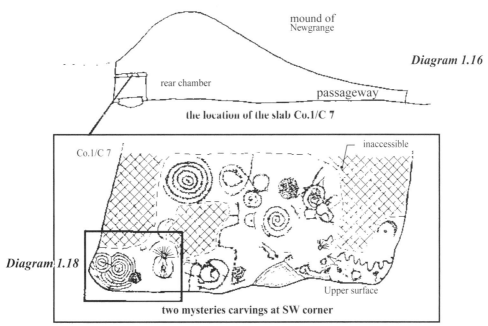

Diagram 1.16

mound of
Newgrange

rear chamber

passageway

the location of the slab Co.1/C 7

Co.1/C 7

inaccessible

Diagram 1.18

Upper surface

two mysteries carvings at SW corner

Carvings on Co.1/C7, Capstone of the Rear Chamber
(after O'Kelly) *Diagram 1.17*

Solar God of Slab Co.1/C7

I have named the pattern below the "Solar God" of slab Co.1/C7. It is made up of two semicircles of different sizes (diagrams 1.18 and 1.19). The smaller circle at the lower end is elongated to form a horseshoe, whereas the upper one is the arc of a larger circle. The diameters of the two circles are parallel with the semi-circumferences facing outward. Since the upper semicircle is larger than the lower horseshoe circle, they form a unique pattern on the slab, whereas most circles representative of Neolithic art are spiral. In the upper semicircle, twelve straight lines radiate from another smaller circle at its center. Experts think this represents a Solar God. Most interestingly, these straight lines are not directly connected to the circumference of the upper semicircle. Instead, they stop at another semicircle formed by an arc of small dots carved just inside (diagram 1.20).

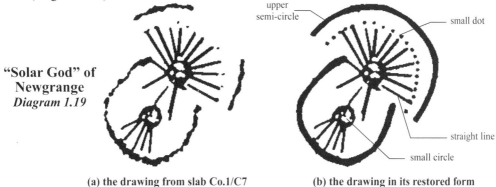

upper
semi-circle

small dot

**"Solar God" of
Newgrange**
Diagram 1.19

straight line

small circle

(a) the drawing from slab Co.1/C7

(b) the drawing in its restored form

Diagram 1.20

Another small circle the same size as the upper "Solar God" is engraved in the center of the lower horseshoe. Five straight lines project downward. Like those in the upper semicircle, these lines stop a few millimeters before touching the lowest ebb of the horseshoe. The two small circles, supposedly representing two Neolithic gods, are connected by another straight line. This defines the typical Solar God carving of the Neolithic time. Archaeologists say many carvings with a similar motif are found all over the Boyne Valley, proving the whole area was once a very important religious region in Neolithic Ireland. I think the answer to unlock this enigma was deliberately placed here five millennia ago.

Another interesting carving is on the left of the Solar God (diagram 1.21a). It is made up of two sets of concentric circles, the one on the right being larger than the one on the left. Some parts are overlapping. The sizes of the two circles in the center are identical with the two Solar Gods of Co.1/C7. This suggests the two drawings are related to each other. Attention is also drawn to a straight line connecting the two circles and passing through their centers. Another line runs from the center of the larger set of concentric circles to their circumference. This kind of pattern of straight lines within concentric circles is rarely found in the region. This means the two drawings may be unique in the whole of the Boyne Gallery (diagram 1.21b,c,d).

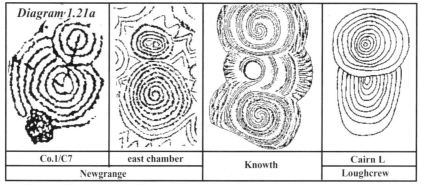

Co.1/C7	east chamber	Knowth	Cairn L
Newgrange			Loughcrew

Of the Different Concentric Circles Pattern of Carvings among the Region, Only the One on Co.1/C7 Has Straight Lines Passing through the Centers
Diagram 1.21a, b, c, d

Kerbstone K6

A similar carving is found on one of the kerbstones surrounding the mound: no. K6 in Professor O'Kelly's book (diagram 1.22). According to Professor O'Kelly, "the ornament is at the bottom and has been covered by earth for many years. It was unearthed in a thorough excavation in the 1980s." The carvings of K6 consist of two sets of semi-concentric circles, each formed by four rows of small dots. On the right of the drawing, a set of straight lines radiate from the center of the semicircles. It is suggested the carving was a Neolithic sundial.

But like the Solar God of Co.1/C7, the straight lines stop just before touching these dots. On the left of the drawing, under the dotted semicircle, the artist carved another small circle with a dot in the center. Carved under the dotted semicircles, the design on the right of the stone is a U-shaped pattern, instead of a complete circle. The two are carved side by side with the same theme. Carving these patterns as sundials was not an easy task, and are they really sundials? If so, why bury a sundial underground? Perhaps they were motifs of the Sun God and Goddess of the worshippers? In my opinion, K6, together with those on the slab Co.1/C7, illustrates the builders using their advanced technology.

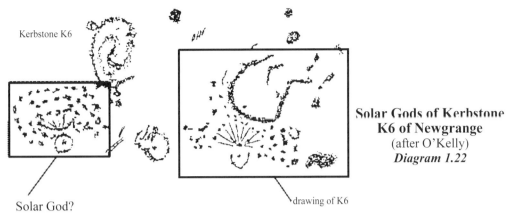

Kerbstone K6

Solar God?

Solar Gods of Kerbstone
K6 of Newgrange
(after O'Kelly)
Diagram 1.22

drawing of K6

The "Sundial" Slabs of Knowth

When it comes to Neolithic sundial slabs, one that should not go unmentioned is found in the mound of Knowth. The site is a passage mound next to Newgrange. Knowth, regarded as one of the oldest passage graves in Ireland, has two separate passages that lead to two chambers opposite each other. What makes Knowth extraordinary is the sixteen to eighteen smaller satellite mounds encircling the main mound (Site 1). Twelve of them have passageways and chambers inside.

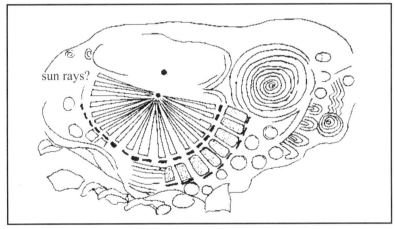

sun rays?

K15, the Famous "Sundial" Slab of Knowth
(after Mohen 1999, p.78) *Diagram 1.23*

Knowth is also famous for its passage grave art. One of the slab carvings—Kerbstone 15—inside the mound is said to have served as a solar clock tracking the movement of the sun, showing that Knowth was an observatory (diagram 1.23). Some say its long passage is illuminated at sunrise on the equinoxes. K15 is thought to be a sundial because of the straight lines radiating from the center to surrounding elongated dots forming a semicircular pattern. The "dot" is a hole carved deep into the rock surface, which is believed to have once held a pole to cast a shadow indicating the approximate time of day. Its cresent-shaped carvings may also be interpreted as a lunar calendar. The so-called solar clock is a semicircle with two centrally placed dots or holes (one off-center). So it is highly unlikely it is an instrument for telling time. Their formation must have had special meaning beyond holding a pole. There are nineteen radiating lines carved into the surface. This matches the number of bluestones inside the horseshoe of Stonehenge (diagram 1.24)! There is an obvious relationship between the two monuments. No archaeologist has tested the Knowth "sundial." Therefore its function for recording solar movement is pure speculation.

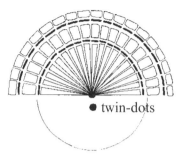

twin-dots

Sundial Drawing Restored
Diagram 1.24

Another similar "sundial" is found on another kerbstone of Knowth (diagram 1.25). However, Anthony Murphy, author of the website *www.mythicalireland.com* states that "this sundial will never work now because it is hidden from the sun due to an overhanging concrete ledge which protects the kerbstone from rain." In Murphy's illustration, what caught my attention were the four sets of elongated dots forming a set of semi-concentric circles on the slab. These match the four rows of small dots in Professor O'Kelly's illustration of the K6 carving. Like the famous sundial slab of the same mound, there are two dots carved deeply into the center. What is the real meaning of these "sundials" encircled with semi-concentric rings and centered with twin dots?

Stone Age Snapshots

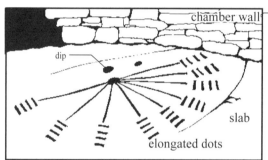

chamber wall

dip

slab

elongated dots

Another Sundial Slab inside the Mound of Knowth
Diagram 1.25

I can't help being skeptical about these so-called "sundial" slabs with bi-centric semicircles of small dips. Some are hidden from the sun and their assumed function has not yet been tested. Are we missing the real meaning behind these carvings? Let's re-examine them in their right perspective.

Going back to the Solar God of Co.1/C7 (diagram 1.20), the larger, upper semicircle with a smaller horseshoe pattern below reminds me of the inner megalithic structure of Stonehenge. Firstly, the upper semicircular pattern of the Solar God of Co.1/C7 is part reflection of the stone ring made by the thirty sarsens capped with lintels inside Stonehenge. Secondly, the larger lower half of the sarsen ring was not drawn onto the Solar God slab because the carver thought that the lower part of the sarsen stone circle was not important. Undoubtedly, the horseshoe drawing of the Solar God represents the five great sarsen trilithons erected at the center of Stonehenge. The individual bluestones of Stonehenge were even indicated by the small dots just inside the larger semicircular carving. Thick and complete lines were used to represent the sarsen circle (upper) and trilithons (lower) because both of these rings are formed by enormous sarsens with lintels on top. The bluestones, from a structural perspective, stand individually like dots on a piece of paper when we view them from above. It is quite obvious to me that the Solar God of Co.1/C7 describes the workings of Stonehenge thousands of years ago. As illustrated in the Solar God of Co.1/C7, there should be two other small circular objects, one placed in the center and the other at the forecourt of Stonehenge. But records of their location, probably left by their mysterious masters, are still available. What are these radiating lines that connect the two circular objects with the surrounding dots?

Chapter 2

The Real Stonehenge

"Much of what has been written about Stonehenge is derivative, second-rate or plain wrong."
—Christopher Chippindale, *Stonehenge Complete*

Two Mysterious Small Circles

It is no surprise that the Newgrange builders had designed and constructed Stonehenge. They might have drafted their master plan onto the stones in the Boyne Valley, probably showing the secret mechanism of Newgrange and Stonehenge. In my opinion, the Solar motif of Co.1/C7 drawing is not the "Solar God" of the Neolithic Irish. Apart from the patterns of semicircles and the U-shaped horseshoe that constitute the basic megalithic structures of Stonehenge, there are two small complete circles placed inside the semicircle and horseshoe of the Solar God of Co.1/C7. Surrounding them are radiating lines, fourteen from the upper circle, and five from the lower (diagram 2.1). It seems these lines are produced from the two small circles in the centers and come into contact with the surface of the surrounding small dips. Like the sundial of Knowth, there are nineteen radiating lines altogether in the Solar God of Co.1/C7.

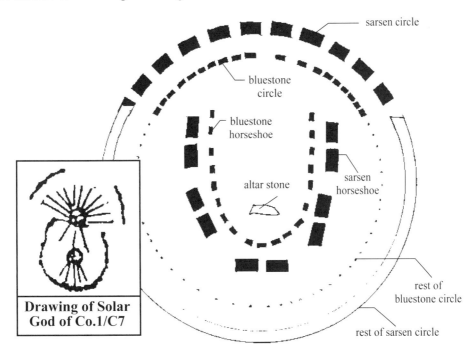

Inner Structure of Stonehenge (Partially Emphasized)
Diagram 2.1

What do the two small circles in the centers of the upper semicircle and lower horseshoe represent? If part of a plan of Stonehenge the two circles cannot depict megaliths, as each would weigh over 100 tons and they should still be in their original place today. Were they wooden objects and the radiating lines wooden poles? Did the Stone Age people practice some kind of rite here 5,000 years ago? Did they indicate measuring Stonehenge to build another one for themselves in Ireland? Were the two mysterious circles some kind of sundisks—circular mirrors of polished metal—like those placed inside Egyptian temples for sun and fire worship, as they helped to catch and reflect the rays into the interior of the buildings? What exactly were these two circles for?

Furthermore, the two circles couldn't be megaliths because the carver used strong dark lines and dots to represent the stones in the sarsen circle and bluestone horseshoe. These two small circular objects were intended to be drawn with a "blurred and shadowy" surface (as shown in Professor O'Kelly's drawing). The following are two important clues:

1. They were probably spherical or even conical in shape.
2. They were made of metal because their surface reflected the surrounding light. This required in a shiny surface as represented by the shadowy surface in the drawing.

What were these two circular metal objects that could generate radiating lines to the surrounding bluestones (diagram 2.2a)? What was the purpose of these radiating lines? The answer is in another famous Neolithic passage grave located in France.

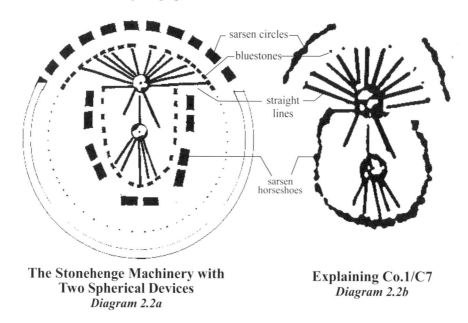

sarsen circles
bluestones
straight lines
sarsen horseshoes

The Stonehenge Machinery with Two Spherical Devices
Diagram 2.2a

Explaining Co.1/C7
Diagram 2.2b

"Conical Motif" of Gavrinis and the Conical Device

Like Ireland, Brittany of France is regarded as the "Disneyland" of Megalithism. Experts estimate there are hundreds of Neolithic monuments in the region, from rectangular tumuli to menhirs. The most impressive infrastructure of the Stone Age is the passage grave of Gavrinis. This site, a contemporary of Newgrange, is formed by a long passage leading to a rectangular corbelled chamber consisting of ten standing stones. The grave is significant due to the number of carvings. Among all these carved slabs, the one below—I have named it the "conical motif" (diagram 2.3)—clearly represents a conical object with horizontal rims. Two rows of dagger-like objects are carved on the right-hand side, apparently produced by the conical motif and pointing at another elongated motif above. This elongated motif is commonly found in megalithic Brittany. Experts call it the "shield." Obviously the conical motif of Gavrinis is depicting an unknown device that was once common in the Neolithic world. As shown in the drawing, a super-advanced conical device, once placed next to a standing stone (monolith), projected two rows of light beams (which I have named "megalights") onto the surfaces of the stones.

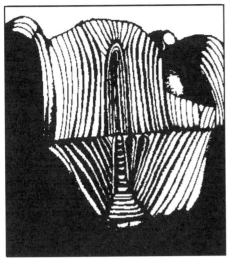

Pillar 16 of Gavrinis: A Conical Motif Was Carved under an Elongated Object with a Pair of Dagger-like Objects to Its Right.
(after M. Balfour 1979)
Diagram 2.3

Monolith of Punchestown: The Oldest Generator in Ireland

Experts say there are about 600 standing stones in the southwest of Ireland. These monuments have stood like signposts to sacred regions for more than 5,000 years. The most famous monolith around the region is the Longstone of Punchestown Great, located in a field near the Punchestown racecourse. At seven meters high, the tall granite stone is the highest in Ireland and weighs about nine tons. It was re-erected in 1934. At its base an empty stone cist sat devoid of burial goods. Experts speculate that the monolith was a memorial marker of a Bronze Age burial site. However, with the message from the "conical motif" of Gavrinis, the Punchestown monolith was a power generator in 4500 B.C. A conical device placed inside the burial cist projected two rows of megalights onto the standing stone of Punchestown. This generated power. This is what the conical motif of Gavrinis and the Solar God of Newgrange describes.

This device is not a product of my imagination. Similar conical or hat-shaped relics of the Late Neolithic to Early Bronze Age period are not new to archaeologists. The object below is generally called the "Gold Hat of Priest King" because experts speculate that it represents one once used as the ceremonial hat of a powerful priest in northern Europe during the Early Bronze Age period. With the inspiration of the "conical motif" slab of Gavrinis, the gold hat is a replica of the conical device of the megalithic builders. It is this powerful device that will help us unlock the enigma of the megalithic world and provide us with a better understanding of our own civilization. The same conical devices were once placed inside most of the megalithic sites on our planet around 4000–2500 B.C., and generated power (diagram 2.4).

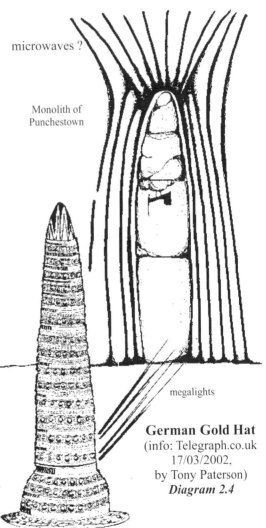

microwaves ?

Monolith of Punchestown

megalights

German Gold Hat
(info: Telegraph.co.uk
17/03/2002,
by Tony Paterson)
Diagram 2.4

Clues from the Hills of Loughcrew

Another well-known complex in Ireland is the Loughcrew Cairns/Passage Graves. It is one of the four largest passage tomb cemeteries of Ireland (the other three being Carrowmore, Carrowkeel, and the Boyne Valley site). The Loughcrew cemetery, lying on the hilltops of Sliabh na Caillighe, is close to the Boyne Valley. The word "Loughcrew" probably refers to a small local lake. Sliabh na Caillighe—hill of the witch—tells an ancient story of Cailleach Bhearra, a witch who leapt from hill to hill and formed cairns by dropping stones from her apron (O Crualaoich 1988). Evidence suggests the Loughcrew site once served as burial chambers and predates Newgrange by a thousand years. Excavations show the site to be a rich archaeological landscape once containing a stone circle, a henge monument, standing stones, and a possible cursus monument (Colin Shell and Corinne Roughley). All the features in the complex are similar to those around Newgrange and Stonehenge.

Remains of approximately thirty cairns are still visible at Loughcrew today. They were built southwest to northeast along a ridge, with four summits more than 244m above sea level. At least one large cairn is found on each of the other two, and a few remains of smaller cairns are found along the crest of the ridge. Cairn T is the best preserved mound of Loughcrew. Like Newgrange, the cairn might have once been covered with white quartz, as three circles of quartz grains were uncovered outside its entrance (E. C. Rotheram, 1985).

The wall of Cairn L, another tomb, is skillfully carved with a "cup and ring" pattern (diagram 2.5). This style of carving is commonly found all over northern Europe; particularly in the north

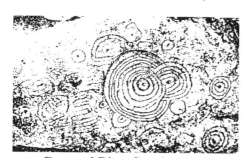

Cup and Ring Carving inside Cairn L, Loughcrew
Diagram 2.5

of Scotland. In my opinion, the carving of Cairn L is just another expression of the Solar God of Co.1/C7 in Newgrange. A set of large concentric circles dominating the chamber wall represent the sarsen circle of Stonehenge. The sarsen horseshoe is clearly indicated by the "cup" pattern of the carving. Once again, the carver of Loughcrew, like those in the Boyne Valley and Brittany of France, wanted to record the function of the exotic technology that once powered these ancient sites.

Secrets Behind the "Dagda Skirt" Carving of Patrickstown

The engraved slab "Solar Goddess Sunray Skirt" (or Calendar Stone) that I refer to as the "Dagda Skirt" (diagram 2.6) is 1.2m in diameter and found in the passage Cairn X1, Patrickstown Hill of Loughcrew. The wonderful drawing below, which was produced by G.V. du Noger in the 1860s, shows the marvelous pattern of that slab (information from: http://www.carrowkeel.com/sites/loughcrew.html). Archaeologists believe the stone carving was produced by the Neolithic Irish to describe an important Irish-Celtic god—Dagda, the god of aristocracy—the *Tuatha De Danann,* also known as the Sons or Lords of the Light. According to legend, they were among the earliest invaders of Ireland, defeating the demon Fomorians, the aboriginal inhabitants. Dagda—the "father of all," or leader of the Tuatha—possessed a club that could kill nine men with one blow. The same club could also revive them. He had a bottomless cauldron. He is the God of Magic and Time, the ruler over life and death, and possesses superhuman strength. The Tuatha later retired to the sidhs, halfway states between this world and the otherworld where any wound can be cured.

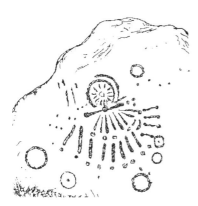

**Dagda Sunray Skirt Slab
from Patrickstown,
Loughcrew**
(after M. Dames 1996)
Diagram 2.6

Experts interpret the engraving by explaining the central rayed circle as the solar goddess with her dress on! They state the circles surrounding the central goddess are stars or planets. However, instead of viewing the slab drawing as presented by Noger, I look at the carving upside down. After such an inversion it is no longer an expression of a fashionable skirt or a Neolithic calendar, but of the famous Stonehenge-like monument of the Late Neolithic and Early Bronze Age! It is the same old "story" which was lost and forgotten for more than 5,000 years.

The Dagda Skirt carving of Loughcrew actually describes the function of Stonehenge in great detail, like the pattern on the Solar God of Co.1/C7 in Newgrange. In order to have a better understanding of the slab, I have simplified the carving with the removal of the surrounding small circles (diagram 2.7). The drawing consists of two sets of semi-circles. The lower one, with two concrete U-shaped curves, represents the double horseshoes, most likely of sarsens and bluestones. There is a circle of the dagger-like beams that I call megalights radiating from the small dot in the center of the horseshoe and then projected onto the horseshoe. The same story is told in the Solar God of Co.1/C7 of Newgrange and sundials of Knowth.

An Irish Stonehenge from an Earlier Time

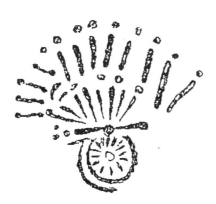

**Dagda Sunray Skirt Inverted,
with the Removal of Circular
Decorations**
Diagram 2.7

The most remarkable part of the drawing is its upper portion formed by several arcs of small dots. A similar design is found on a carved slab (K6) of Newgrange. If there was really an Irish Stonehenge, albeit in a different form (four sets of semi-concentric circles made of standing stones instead of two stone rings of sarsen and bluestone) erected 1,000 years before Stonehenge III, the Dagda Skirt of Loughcrew might record that megalithic machinery. It is interesting to point out that there are four rings of megalithic structures in the center of Stonehenge as well. Starting from the center, after the sarsen trilithons come the bluestone circle, the sarsen circle topped with lintels, and the Y and Z holes. Let's assume that if the sarsen lintels of Stonehenge were erected inside these Y and Z holes instead of acting as lintels of the sarsen circle, there would be four sets of concentric circles in the center of Stonehenge—the exact layout that was described by the Dagda Skirt carving. Or did the builder simply rearrange the four arcs into a complete circle of bluestones in Stonehenge?

As shown in the Irish "Stonehenge" carving, megalights radiate from the center of the forecourt and project onto the first arc of small dots of the upper semi-concentric patterns. At the same time, several thick elongated lines were carved, connecting the second arc of small dots (stones) to the third arc (of stones).

Comparing the Dagda Skirt drawing with the Solar God of Co.1/C7 of Newgrange (diagrams 1.2 and 2.7), we see these dagger-like objects are the megalights produced by the conical devices no. 1 and no. 2 set in the center of the Stonehenge-like machine. The megalights were projected onto the surface of the standing stones—probably the bluestones—of the stone circle and the horseshoe. The conical motif of Gavrinis, France, also replicates this exactly. The megalights, as shown in the Dagda Skirt drawing, have penetrated the first arc of bluestones. This has produced another set of elongated objects, light beams or microwaves, connecting the second arc with the third. Interestingly, the light beams are no longer in a dagger-like pattern; rather, they are scribed as thick lines. They resemble air bubbles connecting the stones. So what is the principle behind all this? Was their Neolithic-age-old technology more advanced than ours today?

If an Irish Stonehenge did exist, it had to be thousands of years older than Stonehenge III. Since the idea of an Irish Stonehenge is mainly inspired by the Dagda Skirt and the two carvings on slab K6 of Newgrange, I strongly believe the Irish Stonehenge was once erected in east Ireland, a place between the mountains of Loughcrew and the Boyne Valley. The most likely area would be the site of Newgrange. The builders demolished the outdated Irish Stonehenge, and used the standing stones to build the passageways and chambers of Newgrange and Knowth. That's why many orthostats of Newgrange and Knowth were carved and decorated with a solar god pattern and concentric circles. They probably memorialized an old legend originating from the first building. Most strangely, some of these orthostats were carved with their inner faces hidden or below surfaces.

Dr. Eogan, in *Antiquity* 72 (1988), suggests there may have been an earlier tomb, probably the first of the great tombs in the Boyne Valley, because many decorations on Knowth's slabs do not extend all over their faces and it may be assumed that they originally served as orthostats with the undecorated portions being in the socket. "When they were re-used as orthostats, most were placed upside-down in relation to their former positioning." By suggesting a possible location of that earlier tomb, Dr. Eogan speculates that "as (decorated) stones from it have been found both at Newgrange and Knowth its location had to have been some place in Brugh na Boinne (the Boyne), but as the greatest number occur at Knowth it may have been there that the tomb stood. Its location could have been on the hill-top; there would have been ample room to accommodate it in the area now covered by the large mound, extensive portions of which remain unexcavated." I agree with Dr. Eogan's theory, but with ideas inspired by the Dagda Skirt carving, an earlier Irish Stonehenge-like monument consisting of a double horseshoe on one end with a set of four semicircles of standing stones on the other becoming the later decorated orthostats of Knowth and Newgrange seems more likely than an earlier passage tomb.

In my opinion the great mounds of Knowth and Newgrange may be the upgraded models of this lost Irish Stonehenge. With the introduction of the twin-device mechanism, these two stations served as powerful generators. They were also used as megalithic safes to house the builders' secrets and messages which I will discuss in the next chapter.

What do these dagger-like pattern objects of the Dagda Skirt and the megalights of the Solar God in Newgrange stand for? Though Stonehenge III lacks Neolithic carvings, in 1953 Professor Richard Atkinson did photograph a hilted dagger, now called the Atkinson's Dagger, carved on the inner surface of Stone 53 of the Great Trilithon Horseshoe. Another dagger-like carving was discovered on Stone 23 by a journalist a year later. Some cup marks were found on Stone 9b. These "Stonehenge" carvings—dagger and cup patterns—constitute the main element of the Dagda Skirt drawing. Could they be the alphabet of the advanced builders? The carvings reveal a direct relation between Stonehenge of England and the mound of Loughcrew where the Dagda Skirt stands.

Electromagnetic Accelerator and the Microwave Beamed Technology

"Every age gets the Stonehenge it desires, or deserves."

—Jacquetta Hawkes, archaeologist

Diagram 2.8 shows the inner megalithic structure of Stonehenge with the inspiration of the Solar God of Co.1/C7 in Newgrange and a modification of the Dagda Skirt of Loughcrew. The two main parts of the machinery are highlighted: the upper consisting of two arcs of sarsen and bluestones forming part of the two rings, and the lower, formed by the two megalithic horseshoes. Together they create an elongated open space in the center connecting to another forecourt to the northeast. This is the secret of Stonehenge III. In 2000 B.C., when the machine was constructed, two conical devices were placed at the center and the forecourt respectively. They are in the exact locations suggested and described by the Solar God of Newgrange and Dagda Skirt of Loughcrew. These two powerful devices were capable of generating rows of megalights to the surrounding stones. As indicated in the Irish carvings mentioned above, conical device no. 1, placed at the center of the site with the interception point marked by the four Station Stones, projected rows of megalights to the bluestone horseshoe nearby. At the same time, conical device no. 2, being placed in the middle of the northeast forecourt, would project rows of megalights to the bluestone ring nearby.

The "Solar God" motif (diagram 1.19) of Newgrange is telling us the work of Stonehenge 4,000 years ago. Two conical devices were once installed in the very center of the arena and were connected by a beam of light (slab Co.1/C7). It actually resembles how electricity is created by magnetism, the modern concept of energy generation.

These two devices act exactly like two polarities of an electromagnet, with one end being North and the other being South (or, in the case of a modern battery, one end positive and the other negative). They were connected by a row of megalights, which served as an electric wire, and generated a magnetic field in the center of Stonehenge. In a bar magnet, the magnetic field runs from the North to the South poles.

Two radial megalights, each from the two devices, were then projected onto the surfaces of the bluestones, adding heat and stress on these iron-rich dolerites. According to the principle of electro-magnetism, protons and electrons, which make up atoms, can be accelerated and emitted by the magnetic field to high energy because of their different charges. It is exactly what the "conical motif" slab of Garvinis, Brittany, is trying to say (diagrams 2.3 and 2.4). Large numbers of these subatomic particles, in the form of an electrical current, flew outside of the bluestone circle and horseshoe.

The high-energy current, generally known as electromagnetic radiation (such as gamma rays), was then further magnified by the quartz-rich sarsen stones nearby. That's why the Newgrange carver drew another motif with two concentric circles just next to the "Solar God" motif of Co.1/C.7 (diagram 1.21a). In this way, Stonehenge was once a gigantic powerhouse. Who really needed to recharge in our Stone Age world with the use of such advanced technology?

High-energy particles inside the bluestones were accelerated by the megalights

Quartz inside the sarsens helped to contain and magnify the microwave being generated by the bluestones nearby

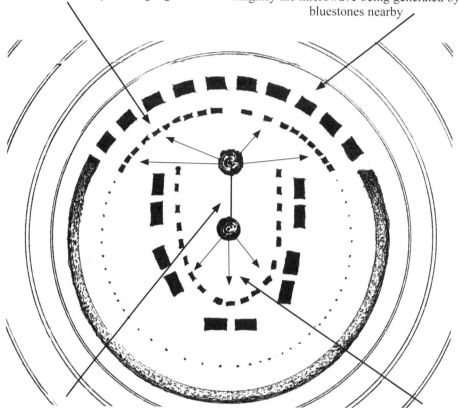

Devices no. 1 and 2 were connected by a megalight to form a magnetic field in the middle of Stonehenge III

Megalights, functioning like electric wires, heated up the surrounding bluestones

The Electromagnetic Accelerator, ca. 2000 B.C.
Diagram 2.8

"The significance is that beamed energy propulsion is the first demonstration of a new propulsion method, truly twenty-first century, that can reach speeds far beyond the rocket."

—Jim Benford, president, Microwave Sciences, Lafayette, California

"My own view is that laser-propelled vehicles will be the first to attain orbit, but in 15–25 years, microwave propulsion will ultimately take over."

—Leik Myrabo, associate professor of engineering physics, Rensselaer Polytechnic Institute, Troy, New York

Space travel is very much a twenty-first century pursuit. Business enterprises are competing for space flight, as multimillionaires are applying for lift-off. But still, space travel demands tremendous power and velocity to launch the spacecraft out of the Earth's atmosphere and for interplanetary travel. In the meantime, solid and liquid fuels are far too expensive and dangerous while the use of solar radiation is immature and unreliable. That's why the NASA researchers are experimenting on microwave propulsion for high-speed space exploration.

Today, some geo-orbiting spacecrafts are actually starting to use electric propulsion (Wikipedia). Scientists suggest the possibility of using electromagnetic forces to accelerate particles so as to generate high power for navigation. In theory, high-powered microwaves could be fired by superconductors, or the so-called high-power particle accelerator, which are constructed directly from the surface of a planet near one of its magnetic poles, repelling itself from the planet's magnetic field.

Similar to the transmission of radio waves into space in the past fifty years, high-power energy in the form of microwave will be beamed from a local power station. Instead of carrying bulky fuels by itself, the spaceship, being equipped with microwave antenna, receives and collects beamed energy directly from the station below. The flight, according to the scientists, is driven by particles of energy generated by electromagnetic radiation (NASA/JPL news release July 6, 2000).

In 2003, scientists started to beam microwave energy to a Russian rocket called Cosmos 1. Sponsored by NASA, a small-sized "Lightcraft" has already been shot high into the air over the White Sands, New Mexico desert (Leonard David, 2002). Scientists from the University of Tokyo also succeeded in using a pulsed microwave beam to propel a 9.5g object two meters into the air. Another Japanese energy research institute, by using a one-megawatt microwave-producing device, could propel an object weighing half a kilogram to a height of about 10 meters (Paul Kallender, 2003). According to Japanese scientist Kimiya Komurasaki, a one-gigawatt pulsed microwave beam could in theory propel a 100-kilogram craft to a velocity of 8,000 meters per second. It is generally agreed that microwave-based beamed propulsion system may prove easier and less costly than conventional chemical rockets. He further suggests that microwaves have the added benefit of not losing their energy as rapidly as laser light as they travel through the atmosphere. This was exactly how Stonehenge functioned in 2000 B.C.

Stonehenge Exits and the Aubrey Holes

The Sarsen Circle and the Great Trilithons draw much attention from archaeologists and experts who have spent years interpreting them. Firstly, I want to direct the readers' attention to the henge structure, the ditch and bank of the enclosure of Stonehenge I, much neglected because its ditch is now more or less silted. It is the earliest formation of the monument. The most striking part of Stonehenge, the megaliths, weren't erected until a thousand years later. Experts estimate that 2,700 cubic meters of chalk rubble was dug and filled in again. The depth of the ditch varies from 1.4m to 1.8m; whereas the bank is about 1.8m high, with a diameter of 97.5m. There is a causeway entrance opening to the northeast and another small one to the south. It is important to note that there are other smaller exits along the bank (diagram 2.9). Before the construction of a pair of parallel banks and the southern exit, there is an outlet near Station Stone 94 (E3), another one between the northeast exit and Station Stone 94 (E2), two more exits in the northwest (E4 and E5), two possible exits in the southwest formed by refilling the ditch with earth and mud (E6 and E7), one next to the southern exit (E8), and one near Station Stone 91 (E9). Finally, the one between the northeast exit (E1) and Station Stone 91 is labeled E10 (diagram 2.9).

The Stonehenge Generator, 2000 B.C.
Diagram 2.9a

Experts believe these exits were constructed long before the erection of the bluestone and sarsen circles and horseshoes. Together with the fifty-six Aubrey Holes, they constitute the first stage of Stonehenge. I believe that the real function of Stonehenge I is closely related to its ditch, bank, and various exits. This may be disclosed by the Dagda Skirt, carved 6,000 years ago.

The real function of the fifty-six Aubrey Holes has long been an enigma. Dr. Gerald Hawkins suggests they are the "solar and lunar observers" (eclipse predictors). Professor Hoyle suggests that the circle formed by the Aubrey holes is a model of the sky and markers for the movement of the sun and moon. Few experts are certain about the role of these holes, which were dug and refilled with chalk rubble. Experts conclude the henge builders suddenly changed their original plan and therefore abandoned these holes. Others suggest the holes were once used as cremation pits in the Early Bronze Age. After examining their relation with the ditch and bank, I venture to explain the real function of these holes.

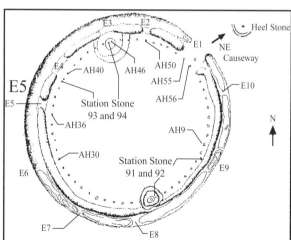

Small Openings of Stonehenge
Diagram 2.9b

As previously mentioned, the holes were dug beside the bank of the enclosure, probably during the same period. This is why the builders constructed an internal bank—a rare design, as most of the Neolithic henges were built with an external bank enclosing an internal ditch housing these holes. This draws my attention to the relation between the bank, together with the various exits and the Aubrey Holes. Take exit E3 as an example. Aubrey Hole no. 46 (AH46) faces E3 and is next to Station Stone 94. Choosing any exit hole (also an Aubrey Hole) as the starting point (no. 1), after counting ten Aubrey Holes from either side (the tenth being the exit hole), you will find another exit. For example, counting ten Aubrey Holes from AH46 you will stop at AH55 clockwise and AH36 counterclockwise (diagram 2.9). These two holes—the tenth Aubrey Hole from either side of AH46 (i.e., AH55 and AH36)—are also the exit holes of the exits E1 and E5 respectively (diagram 2.10). Take another example: AH50 is facing the exit E2. After counting ten holes clockwise, it stops at AH4, the exit hole of E10. By moving counterclockwise, it stops at AH40, the exit hole of E4. The same situation happens in other exits.

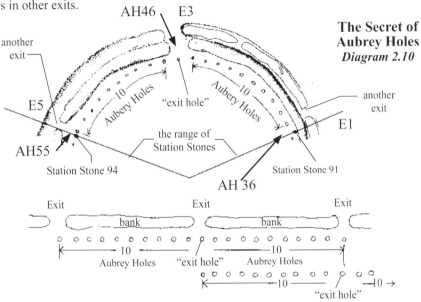

The Secret of Aubrey Holes
Diagram 2.10

As a result, the Aubrey Holes could act as location markers with a specific formula. The relation between the exits of Stonehenge and its fifty-six Aubrey Holes can be read and understood as the following rule:

$$10 \text{ AHs} + \text{the "exit hole" (also an AH)} + 10 \text{ AHs}$$

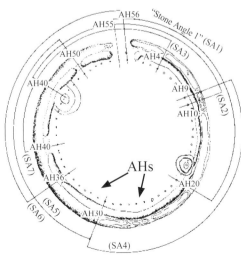

The Relation between the Ditch and Bank and the Aubrey Holes
Diagram 2.11

The above formula includes twenty-one Aubrey Holes out of a total of fifty-six. If two lines connect the center, marked by the interception of the four Station Stones of Stonehenge (i.e., with two Aubrey Holes of the two far ends of the above formula), an angle of 135 degrees is produced. The same angle results in joining SS91 and SS94 with the center of Stonehenge (the interception point between SS91–SS93 and SS92–SS94). The Aubrey Hole in the middle of the above formula becomes the bisector of that angle of 135 degrees. Why did the Stonehenge I builders construct the ditch and bank, together with fifty-six Aubrey Holes, with this formula? (The answer will be provided in Chapter 6.)

The Transmission Angle

The Station Stones (SS91–SS94) are sarsens believed to have been erected in around 2500 B.C. during the phase of Stonehenge III. They are the most insignificant and neglected monoliths of the monument. Experts state they were erected in their present positions to form a rectangle 80m long at its southeast and northwest sides and 32.7m to 34.2m at its shorter sides so as to demarcate the center of the later stone circles. Why did the builders not choose to set out a simple square? Some suggest that the two longer parallel sides of the rectangle indicate the midsummer sunrise as a solar temple, while the other two show the moonrise and moonset at the major standstill as a lunar temple.

Using the Dagda/Stonehenge diagram I have superimposed the Dagda Skirt diagram on the plan of Stonehenge (diagram 2.12) to explain the real function of these Station Stones. Two straight lines are drawn to connect the four Station Stones, Stones 91 and 93, 92 and 94 with their interception point in the middle of the horseshoe where device no. 1 was positioned. As shown in the Dagda carving, the megalights generated by conical device no. 2 fall within the boundary formed by Station Stone 94 (SS94)—device no. 1 (center of Stonehenge)—Station Stone 91 (SS91). In other words, the "SS94 and SS91" boundary marks the angle or spectrum of transmission of the megalights from device no. 2 (gray area). The angle is 135 degrees. This is why a rectangle instead of a square is formed by the Station Stones.

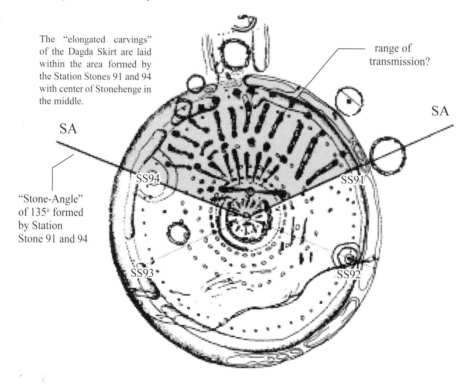

"Dagda Skirt" Carving Superimposed upon Stonehenge
Diagram 2.12

The Golden Rule

The Station Stones are so precisely sited inside the inner bank as to be away from the more densely populated sarsen and bluestone circles and horseshoe formations at the center. The builders deliberately selected a Heel Stone standing outside the henge and housed inside a small ditch to bisect the SA. This bisector is further emphasized by an avenue formed of two parallel earthen banks. The placement of these Station Stones and the Heel Stone might be the ultimate theme of Stonehenge. The builders wanted to demonstrate to future generations how to activate this earth power machine. An exact arc is formed by SS91 and SS94, with the center of Stonehenge in the middle. It consists of twenty-one AHs with an angle bisector pointing northeast. The megalight generated would not pass beyond this boundary while the conical device pointed to the Heel Stone. This was the golden rule the builders followed. As mentioned earlier, I have named the spectrum of megalight the SA (diagram 2.13). All the experts seem to have ignored the relative importance of these high-profile standing stones. I believe the SA is the key to unlocking all the mysteries of the megalithic world.

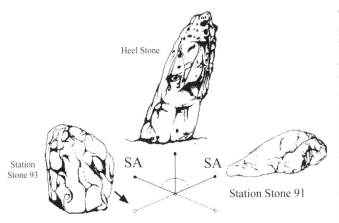

SA: The Golden Rule of Megalithism
Diagram 2.13

To the Chinese, feng shui permeates life and business. They believe specific locations have certain qualities of air and water that affect our health and wealth. Modern western architects came up with the idea of simplicity and environmental protection because they need to reduce the consumption of our Earth's resources as they become increasingly scarce. What about the mysterious megalithic people? Experts suggest they were solar worshippers because most of the main exits and entrances of their "tombs" are aligned to the sun. Take the thirty cairns of Lougcrew as an example: over 90% are oriented to the east or southeast. Secondly, there are carvings supposed to be solar patterns: circles with radiating lines, zig-zags, and spirals. All are found inside these "tombs."

The standard explanations of these carvings are based on authors' own perceptions and our limited understanding of an ancient world void of records. Under the assumption that prehistoric people were more superstitious than we are, experts conclude that the megalithic people, by building these sites, wanted to glorify the sun and the moon as they advanced to the agricultural age. This is why Stonehenge is believed to have been built as an early Bronze Age temple to worship the sun god. But has this Solar Divinity concept been manufactured by modern academics? Or did our Neolithic ancestors encounter a starfaring civilization? There is an extremely advanced architectural theory underlying these monuments for some unimaginable purpose. What constitutes the ultimate enigma of Megalithism is that some advanced intelligence superimposed their cosmic technology onto our Stone Age world. Using the SA formula, we are able to trace the footprints of that unknown civilization and better understand why they came here. Ironically, our Neolithic world was not as primitive as the experts would have us believe.

Chapter 3
Neolithic Ireland

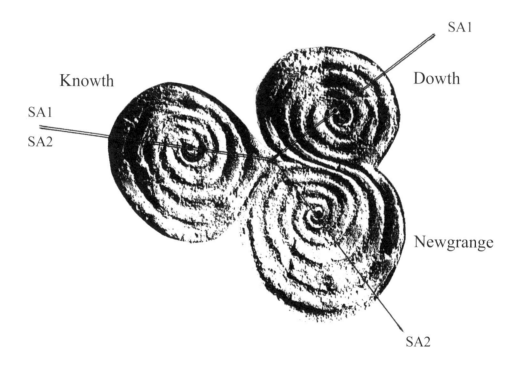

Knowth

SA1

SA2

SA1

Dowth

Newgrange

SA2

Triskelion of the Boyne
A triple spiral design, 30cm in diameter,
on a chamberstone in the rear recess of Newgrange
is probably the most famous Irish megalithic symbol.
It represents the three great mounds of the region
(Newgrange, Knowth, and Dowth)
connected by two SAs.

Neolithic Loughcrew: The Original Power Generator

"At (Neolithic) Loughcrew, animals, hills, lakes and springs, glacial boulders, quartz pebbles and ancestral spirits may have been taken as powerful, immanent forces interconnected with designers and other human actors engaged with their world."

—Jean McMann, "Forms of Power: Dimensions of an Irish
Megalithic Landscape," *Antiquity* 68 (1994)

In the minds of the Stonehenge builders, the transmission range of the megalights must have been so important they erected two stones (SS91 and SS94) between AH10–AH11 and AH45–AH46. I believe this is the real function of the Station Stones. If the Dagda Skirt carving, symbolizing the real function of Stonehenge, is found on an engraved slab at Patrickstown, Loughcrew, can it also help to explain the secret behind all the Neolithic monuments of Ireland? Diagram 3.1 shows the geographical layout of the famous Loughcrew chambered cairns cemetery and standing stones totalling forty monuments. They are located 40km west of Newgrange on three summits along the 200m contour line. The so-called Mountain of the Witch is formed by three Storied Hills: Carnbane West, Carnbane East, and Patrickstown. They are believed to be older than Newgrange, dating back to 4000–3500 B.C.

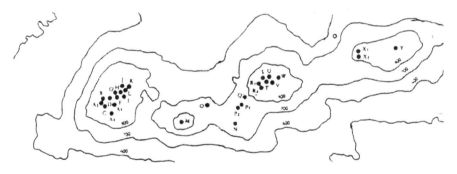

Distribution of Various Neolithic Settlements of Loughcrew
Diagram 3.1

Among the earliest "tombs" around the region, the Loughcrew cairns and portal dolmens on the summits are small, free-standing stone chambers formed by upright stone slabs called orthostats roofed with capstones. The rectangular chamber was usually formed by two portal slabs, with a third one blocking the entrance. Finally, the tomb chamber was covered with dirt and rubble in the shape of a mound (diagram 3.2).

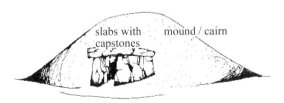

**Neolithic Cairn: The Builders'
Dry Cell Battery**
Diagram 3.2

I believe the cemetery lies on an interception node of an underground energy stream of the type often referred to as "Ley lines." This stone-inside-rubble formation of the Neolithic cairns would primarily emit energy, acting as dry cell batteries, or serve as conductors to transmit the energy from below when heated.

The SA of Loughcrew

The Tomb of Ollamh Fodhla, or Cairn T of Loughcrew, is one of seven monuments on the central and highest peak with a roof covered in white quartz (diagram 3.3b). There are fifteen monuments on the western hill and Cairn D is the largest of them (diagram 3.3a). The eastern hill of Patrickstown is badly eroded and damaged. The artist G. V. du Noger visited the site and recorded many of the decorated stones. Since his visit many of the engravings have weathered greatly and some have disappeared. His drawing of the Dagda Skirt from Cairn X at Patrickstown may help us unlock this ancient mystery.

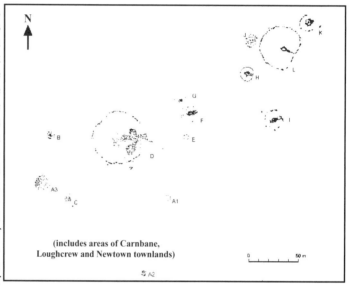

(includes areas of Carnbane, Loughcrew and Newtown townlands)

Cairns on Carnbane West (after McMann 1994)
Diagram 3.3a

The remnant of Cairn M, 20m in diameter, stands 244m above sea level atop its own hill. The hill of Carraigbrack lies about halfway between the western and eastern hills. If we apply the SA to that region, we find a perfect match. With Cairn M as the center of a circle, and with two "Station Stones"—Cairns T and D of the central and western hills—to indicate the angle of transmission (diagram 3.4). Coincidentally, a cluster of standing stones or circles is located north of Cairn M and within its range of transmission. Do they help transfer the microwave signals or power as depicted in the Dagda Skirt drawing? That may explain why the Dagda Skirt carving is found close by, in Patrickstown.

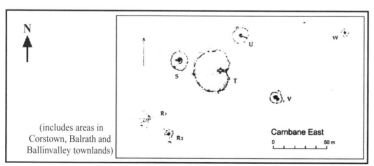

(includes areas in Corstown, Balrath and Ballinvalley townlands)

Carnbane East

Cairns on Carnbane East
(after McMann)
Diagram 3.3b

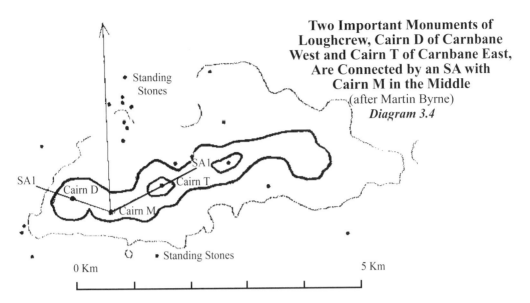

Two Important Monuments of Loughcrew, Cairn D of Carnbane West and Cairn T of Carnbane East, Are Connected by an SA with Cairn M in the Middle
(after Martin Byrne)
Diagram 3.4

There shows something more that makes Loughcrew an important site in Ireland. Diagram 3.5a is the general layout of the cairns on Carnbane West with the SA imposed. It is important to note that one of the passage "tombs," Cairn F (in the middle of the diagram), forms at least three sets (SA1, SA2, and SA3) with the surrounding cairns (E, G, H, and L). Other SAs can also be spotted in the diagram (information from Jean McMann, "Forms of Power: Dimensions of an Irish Megalithic Landscape," *Antiquity* 68 [1994]); for example, passage tomb D forms two sets (SA4 and SA5) with the surrounding cairns (A, B, C, and E) (diagram 3.5a).

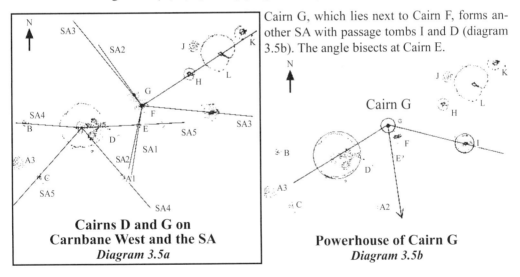

Cairn G, which lies next to Cairn F, forms another SA with passage tombs I and D (diagram 3.5b). The angle bisects at Cairn E.

Cairns D and G on Carnbane West and the SA
Diagram 3.5a

Powerhouse of Cairn G
Diagram 3.5b

In addition, if we magnify the sites of Loughcrew (from Martin Byrne's website, http://www.carrowkeel.com), there are seven cairns on the central peak and eight remains on the western peak. If Cairn M between the two peaks is the center, six sets of SAs can be derived from the site (diagram 3.5c). In addition, a cairn which lies to the northeast of the central peak also forms seven sets of SAs with the surrounding sites.

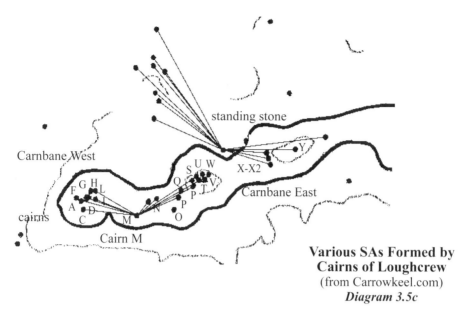

Various SAs Formed by Cairns of Loughcrew
(from Carrowkeel.com)
Diagram 3.5c

The Cup and Ring of Cairn L

A famous carving of Loughcrew is found on the chamber wall of Cairn L on Carnbane West. Archaeologists agree that the carving is a cup and ring. It includes a large set of concentric circles carved to the left of the wall and bordering a "cup" shape, not dissimilar from a horseshoe shape, to its right. The marking is decorated and surrounded by smaller concentric circles with deepening dips in the middle. Experts suggest that the carving, like those inside mounds such as Newgrange, Knowth, and Tara Hill, was a way of expressing worship to their sun gods. Before unlocking the real meaning of these carvings, I would like to point out that several sets of SAs are formed by these small circles with the "cup" as the center and the "ring" in the middle respectively (as shown in diagram 3.6). This arrangement concerning the SA is the main theme. The "solar god symbol" is a misunderstanding by our archaeologists of what the builders intended to demonstrate. To me, they are messages left by the builders recording an advanced technology used to siphon power from our Earth in the distant past, the knowledge of which is lost to us today (diagram 3.7).

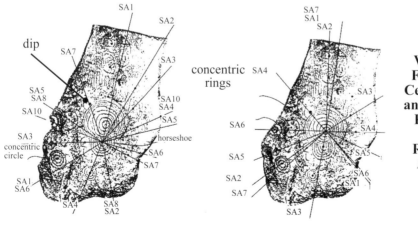

Various SAs Formed with Centers of Cup and Concentric Rings in the Middle, Respectively
Diagram 3.6

Cairn L and Its Satellites

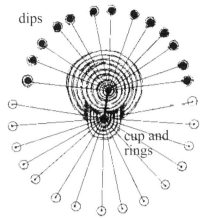

Twin-device Energy Mechanism of Carving in Cairn L
Diagram 3.7

Cairn L is the second largest mound, after Cairn D, on Carnbane West. This cordiform cairn, with a passage opening to the southeast, leads to a central cruciform chamber formed by orthostats. Like the famous mound of Newgrange, the entrance of the cairn was deliberately truncated to form a forecourt. Four satellite cairns were constructed around Cairn L: Cairn K sits northeast of Cairn L, Cairn J is to its west, Cairn H to its southwest, and Cairn I to its south. Like Cairn L in the middle, Cairns K, H, and I are passage tombs, all opening to the east.

I believe these megalithic cairns were not tombs of the Grooved Ware people, at least in their preliminary stage. Diagram 3.8a shows the general layout of Cairn L and its satellites with the application of the SA. Note the entrances of Cairn K and Cairn I form an SA with the cruciform chamber of Cairn L in the middle. In addition, the truncated forecourt of Cairn L forms another SA with the chambers of Cairn K and H. The "Equinox Stone" of Cairn T shows three large sunwheels connected by the SA may actually suggest the real function of Cairn L and its satellites (diagram 3.8c). The message is similar to that of the Solar God of Co.1/C7 and the Dagda Skirt of Loughcrew.

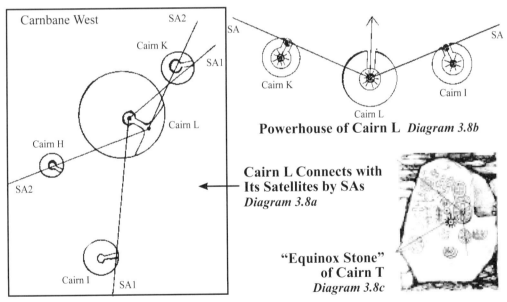

Powerhouse of Cairn L *Diagram 3.8b*

Cairn L Connects with Its Satellites by SAs
Diagram 3.8a

"Equinox Stone" of Cairn T
Diagram 3.8c

Real Function of the Passage

Cairns K and I both acted as dry cell batteries. Again I stress that conical devices placed inside the two chamber mounds projected rows of megalights onto the surfaces of the orthostats to generate power (diagram 3.8b). A much more powerful generator was built by connecting the two satellites, mini power stations: Cairns K and I, with two rows of megalights, forming an angle of 135 degrees and projected by another conical device placed inside the cruciform chamber of Cairn L. The axis of the angle bisector, point of power recharging, lies exactly along the passage of Cairn L. These passages of Loughcrew cairns were constructed for the megalights and the energy they carried.

Stone Age Batteries

Most of the internal formations of the Loughcrew cairns are cruciform in shape—a central chamber which is formed by orthostats is subdivided into cells. These orthostats are erected according to the SA formula (diagram 3.9). Investigators wonder why holes are carved into the surface of these orthostats, especially on orthostats L5 and R5 in Cairn T, R4 in Cairn L, and C3 in Cairn T (McMann 1994). Similar depressions are also found on the kerb and interior stones of Newgrange and Knowth (O'Kelly 1986). Dr. McMann continues to say that these mysterious depressions with surface diameters ranging from 1cm to 8.5cm "seem to have been deepened by repeated contact," probably by the megalights during the energy mechanism process.

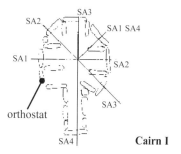

Cairn I

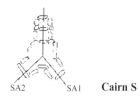

Cairn S

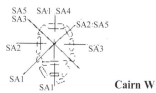

Cairn W

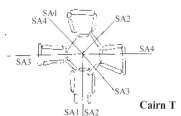

Cairn T

Ground Plan of Chambers of Loughcrew Mounds, with Orthostats Aligned to the SA
(after William Frazer 1893)
Diagram 3.9

(Illustration shows how rows of megalights connected various cairns of Loughcrew)

Unlocking the Secret of Cairn F, Loughcrew
Diagram 3.10

Unlocking the Secret of Cairn F

Basing my impressions on the Neolithic site map of the Loughcrew cemetery, I think the cup and ring decoration of Cairn L has a hidden secret. If we compare it with a local map, the "cup" carving actually represents Cairn F, southwest of Cairn L, a kerbed mound about 15m in diameter (diagram 3.10). It forms three sets of SAs with the surrounding cairns (diagram 3.11):

SA1: Cairn G and Cairn I
SA2: Cairn E and Cairn H
SA3: Cairn E and Cairn G

This is exactly what the cup and ring pattern inside Cairn L describes.

One thing that puzzles me is the pattern of concentric circles (the "ring") in the middle of the carving of Cairn L. When we compare it with the distribution of cairns in

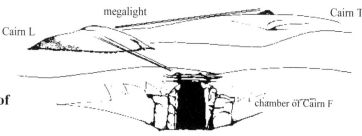

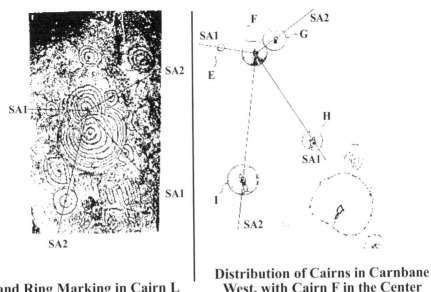

Cup and Ring Marking in Cairn L

Distribution of Cairns in Carnbane West, with Cairn F in the Center

Diagram 3.11

Carnbane West, it many refer to an object once parked outside Cairn F to the southwest, and Cairn H to the northeast. What do these concentric circles stand for? Do the cup and ring carvings found all over northern Europe serve the same function?

Cairn D: Megalithic Generator on Carnbane West

Cairn D is the largest cairn surrounded by kerbstones. A cruciform passage with three re-

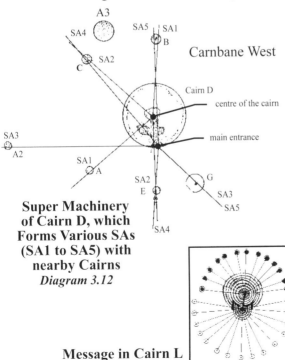

Super Machinery of Cairn D, which Forms Various SAs (SA1 to SA5) with nearby Cairns
Diagram 3.12

Message in Cairn L
Diagram 3.12a

cesses opens to the east. As shown in the location plan, it is further encircled by a number of smaller cairns such as Cairns C, A3, and B to the west, Cairn A2 to the south, and Cairns E, F and, G to its east. Inspired by the cup and ring carving of Cairn L, it appears there were two devices once placed in the cairn, one inside the rear recess and the other just outside the cairn (diagram 3.12). In order to produce power they projected several rows of megalights to satellite cairns that stored energy. Five sets of SAs can be derived from Cairn D, connecting and activating the surrounding cairns.

This is exactly what the cup and ring marking of Cairn L explains (diagram 3.12a). It was also the same twin-device energy mechanism that worked inside Newgrange when the builders replaced earthen mounds with standing stones. Is this the key to the secret of Loughcrew?

Mound H is another passage cairn lying northeast of Cairn F (diagram 3.13a). As shown in diagram 3.14, it forms an SA with the surrounding cairns (I and J).

Diagram 3.13b is a bone slip with Iron Age decoration excavated from Cairn H (Information from the "Sacred Island"). It may tell us the real secret of Cairn H.

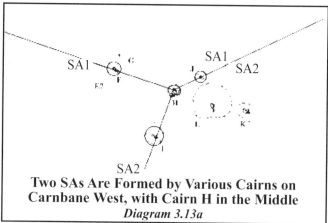

Two SAs Are Formed by Various Cairns on Carnbane West, with Cairn H in the Middle
Diagram 3.13a

Bone Slip with Iron Age Decoration from Cairn H

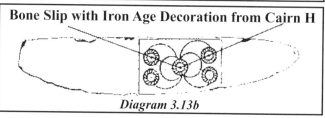

Diagram 3.13b

Power Generator of Cairn H
Diagram 3.14

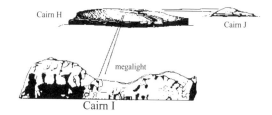

SAs on Carnbane East

Like Cairn T, Cairn U, center of diagram 3.15, is a cruciform tomb with a passage opening to the east. The entrance forms SA1 with the center of Cairn W and the chamber of Cairn T. The angle bisects at the center of Cairn V. Other cairns, such as Cairns R1 and V, form SA2 with Cairn R2 in the middle. At the same time, the angle bisects at Cairn S.

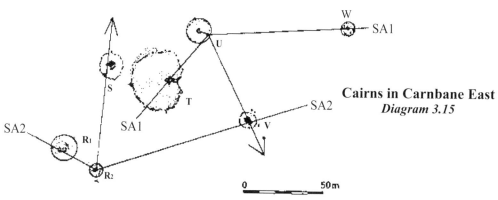

Cairns in Carnbane East
Diagram 3.15

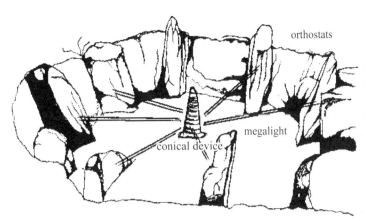

Installation of the Conical Device: Cairn I, Loughcrew
Diagram 3.16

With all these SAs in mind, I speculate that the orthostats erected inside the cairns of Loughcrew acted as batteries capable of converting and transfusing earth energy to the machinery of the Neolithic builders (diagram 3.16) when they were activated by the conical device. For example, Cairns V and S, which lay at the bisector, acted as refueling stations that collected power from the two generators nearby.

Applying the SA formula to the region, it is logical to suggest rows of megalights traveled from place to place in order to obtain the powerful magnetic energy contained in our planet. Since the cairns and other megalithic sites are scattered around the area, each of these cells was purposefully constructed on the energy stream underneath. The builders had identified a mysterious form of energy in our planet. This brought them to our blue planet so long ago. The illustration below shows how a Loughcrew power station operates. Power-generating devices are placed inside the chambers formed by orthostats: the dry cell batteries. The three charged mounds will then be connected by two rows of megalights, allowing energy to transfer to the central mound.

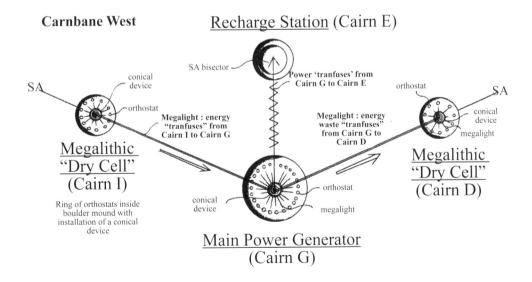

Energy-generating Mechanism of Neolithic Loughcrew
Diagram 3.17

Loughcrew Power Nodes

It is strange to find that the Neolithic Irish built their passage tombs along the ridge and on the highest points of the Loughcrew hills instead of the more sheltered areas of the valley below. Perhaps construction on high ground secured their sacred tombs from the backward inhabitants of Stone Age Ireland, or perhaps it was to protect our ancestors from these highly charged and dangerous power nodes. The view from these cairns is impressive and the high land is an ideal landing place for their vehicles. Experts state that many cairns of Loughcrew are intervisible (Cooney 1990). This is a clear indication they could be connected by rows of megalights (diagram 3.18). Dr. McMann further concludes that six of the Loughcrew cairns "face points within eight degrees of the passage tomb site at Fourknocks which is intervisible with Loughcrew" (McMann 1994). Another six cairns bore within 10.5 degrees of Newgrange (Patrick 1975). The cemetery of Loughcrew and Fourknocks forms an SA with the Dowth, the sister mound of Newgrange, in the middle. Loughcrew forms another SA with Carrowmore cemetery at its northwest point and with the cemetery of Carrowkeel in the middle. In other words, Loughcrew connected the eastern end of Ireland with the westernmost point by the SA.

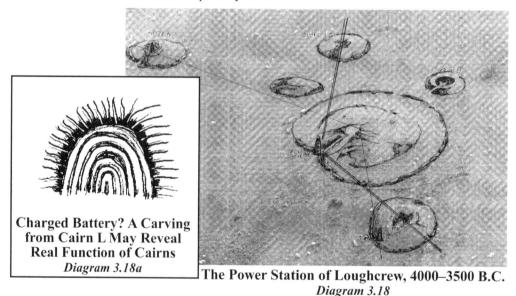

Charged Battery? A Carving from Cairn L May Reveal Real Function of Cairns
Diagram 3.18a

The Power Station of Loughcrew, 4000–3500 B.C.
Diagram 3.18

Passage-tombs are regarded as a clear example of monumental architecture in Neolithic Europe. Academics predict the openings of these cairns and the main axis of passages are oriented to the sun. However, the application of the SA onto Loughcrew cemetery, namely Cairn L and its satellites, shows that these passages were actually opened to the megalights rather than the sunrays. Only in this sense are the experts correct. That's why these tombs were always regarded as homes of Irish solar gods—the Lords of Light. With the inspiration from the Loughcrew powerhouses, it seems that our ancient visitors knew more about our planet more than we do.

Cairn L, together with its satellite cairns, acted as a power station. They are evolved models that replaced the earlier monoliths, such as Punchstown. They were capable of generating large amounts of energy by using smaller size orthostats inside earthen mounds. Another common type of carving is the "shield" in Cairn L (diagram 3.18a). It probably describes the real function of these stations when they were activated by the megalights. Imagine the builders' vehicles parked outside these Loughcrew stations, connected by way of a light beam to the conical device inside the tomb.

Stone Age Metropolis

The Boyne passage-grave cemetery lies on a major interception point of energy streams. New-grange and its two sister mounds Knowth and Dowth, together with other megalithic monu-ments, including circular embanked enclosures, standing stones, and earthen cursus, are located on similar power nodes (diagram 3.19a). Think of them as the power outlets in your house. The SA formula once fits the region. The mounds of Knowth and Dowth form a perfect angle of 135 degrees (SA1) with an enclosure/henge R in the middle (diagram 3.19b); whereas the mounds of Knowth and Newgrange form SA2 with the same henge in the middle.

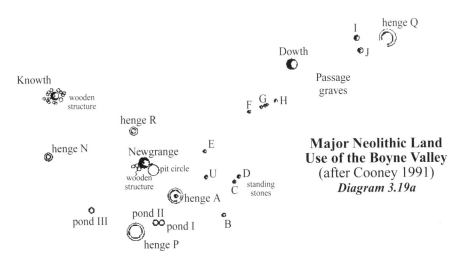

Major Neolithic Land Use of the Boyne Valley
(after Cooney 1991)
Diagram 3.19a

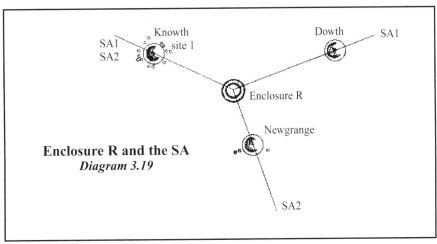

Enclosure R and the SA
Diagram 3.19

Knowth and Its Satellites

"A four-feet granite stone basin in the Eastern passage of Knowth may be engraved with a map of the city of Atlantis, as Plato described it. The three concentric circles match the three concentric lakes of Atlantis…."

—Anthony Murphy, *the mythicalireland homepage*

satellite mounds

Site 1 of Knowth

carved kerbstones

Site 1 and Its Satellites
Diagram 3.20

Like Newgrange, the mound of Knowth, one of the grandest mounds of the Boyne Valley, is famous for its long passageways and Neolithic art. Dr. George Eogan has conducted complete excavations since 1962. Consequently we now understand the mound better. The bi-passages at the central mound (Site 1) (diagram 3.20) of Knowth face east and west, directed towards the spring and autumn equinoxes as suggested by the experts. The eastern passage is 40.4m in length and the longest in Europe. Like Newgrange, the cruciform east chamber of Site 1 is the largest in Ireland. Its corbelled roof, more than 7m above the floor, is the highest capstone found in Ireland (diagram 3.21). The eighteen satellite passage-tombs, constructed around Site I, are generally oriented toward the main mound (Eogan 1986).

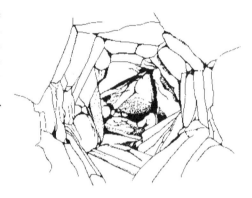

Corbelled Ceiling of Knowth
Diagram 3.21

The layout of the main mound (Site 1) of Knowth with its eighteen smaller satellites is also subject to the SA. For example, satellite mound 6 forms an SA with satellite 15. The rear recess of Site 1 of Knowth is in the middle and the angle bisects mound 12 (diagrams 3.22 and 3.23). How exactly did the powerhouse of Knowth function in 3000 B.C.? Interestingly, the manual of the powerhouse has already been written inside and outside of Knowth.

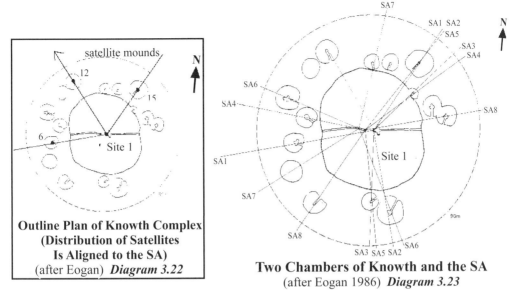

Outline Plan of Knowth Complex (Distribution of Satellites Is Aligned to the SA)
(after Eogan) *Diagram 3.22*

Two Chambers of Knowth and the SA
(after Eogan 1986) *Diagram 3.23*

An engraving on kerbstone no. 5 of Site 1 gives us a tantalizing glimpse of what occurred at Knowth (diagram 3.24). The carving consists of three drawings. A large spiral carved in the center and flanked by two "cup" motifs, and a straight groove engraved inside both of the cups. It seems that the two cups are connected to the spiral in the middle by the grooves. The engraving can be understood in the following way: a large central mound (spiral), probably Site 1 of Knowth, projected two rows of megalights (straight grooves) to two surrounding satellite mounds ("cup" motifs—passage cairns with openings). This activated the whole system by generating some kind of spiral effect from energy or electric waves. The mound's high corbelled ceiling may probably facilitate the transmission process. This is exactly what the mound functioned 5,000 years ago.

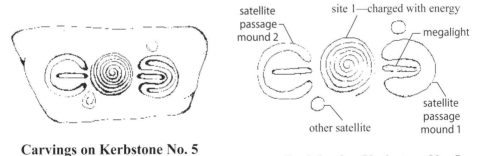

Carvings on Kerbstone No. 5 of Knowth

Deciphering Kerbstone No. 5

Diagram 3.24

As described by Martin Byrne, the orthostats under the corbelled roof of the east chamber of Knowth are decorated with a range of angular and curved-linear motifs, which I believe represent energy waves. Although many will consider this idea sheer fantasy, one thing for sure is these Boyne mounds are not the "god-worshippers' temples" or "solar observatories" experts claim them to be.

Role of the Stone Basin

Let's examine another drawing found nearby. It was copied from the wall of the chamber inside the great mound of Knowth. Like other mounds in the Boyne Valley, there was a stone basin laced inside its recess. Luckily, the stone basin of Knowth is still in perfect condition (diagram 3.25). The round-bottomed base of the container facilitates rotation and the concave surface enables the placement of objects inside. However, archaeologists suggest the stone basin was used for holding water in the winter, as it could be used as a gigantic cup.

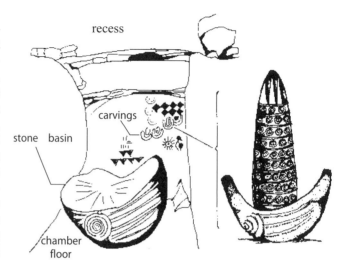

The Round-bottomed Base of the Stone Basin Facilitates Rotation (*left*: Mohen 1999, p. 77) **and the Concave Surface Permits the Placing of Objects Inside**
Diagram 3.25

What is the logic in a round-bottomed cup? Are we to assume that because these people lived in the Stone Age they were complete idiots? If we can explain the function behind this stone basin in Knowth, we may also solve the mystery of Newgrange. Stone basins are found at both mounds. Anthony Murphy questioned that this "giant stone bowl (four feet in diameter) in the northern recess of the eastern chamber presents a real mystery about how the site was constructed. The stone cauldron is too big to be moved in or out of the passage, and so many have concluded that it must have been in situ when construction of the passageway began." (The mythicalireland homepage.)

Like those bowls in Newgrange and Dowth, patterns of a lozenge and a radiating sun decorate the walls of the recess of Knowth as shown in diagram 3.25. What makes Knowth stand out is the famous "cup" patterns on the upper right corner of the wall. There is a blurred elongated object found inside each of the cups. What are these objects? Do they symbolize the placing of a device inside these stone basins as shown in the diagram? The answer might lie in the circular devices in Solar God of Newgrange, the Dagda Skirt drawing. and the sundials of Knowth.

Diagram 3.25 also shows the well-preserved Great Basin of Knowth found in the right recess of the East Chamber. The stone basin is known as "Dagda's Cauldron," the traveling machine of the legendary Irish God. According to Martin Byrne the basin, measuring 1.2m in diameter, is carved from a huge lump of sandstone. The surface of the basin is heavily engraved with Neolithic style carving—a cup and ring (diagram 3.26a). The focal point of the carving is a circular motif with two smaller circles in the center. One is encircled with three "cups" (a nest of arcs—Martin Byrne) and the other is decorated with a solar design radiating into twelve grooves, six at each side. Newgrange is encircled by twelve (GC) stones. Another series of seven grooves run around the basin. Martin Byrne suggests that the motif represents the meeting of the sun and the moon, the two small circles of the carving, at Knowth on a specific date.

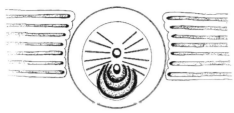

Solar Carvings on the Great Basin of Knowth (after Byrne)
Diagram 3.26a

However, I regard the carving as a message from the builders telling us about a lost technology that once used by a mysterious race in the Boyne Valley. It also explains the real function of the Great Mound of Newgrange (next to Knowth) as well as Stonehenge of the later period. The markings on the basin tell us two exotic devices, represented by the two small circles in the carving, placed in Newgrange and Stonehenge, activated a machine that tapped energy from the Earth (diagram 3.26b). A layout of the mound of Newgrange and Stonehenge is placed side by side with the carving of the Knowth basin in order to show their similarities (diagram 3.26c).

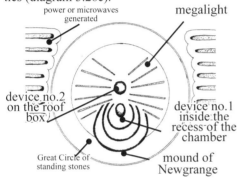

Deciphering the Stone Basin Carvings of Knowth
Diagram 3.26b

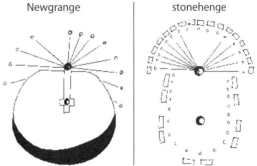

Applying Stone Basin Carving into Newgrange and Stonehenge
Diagram 3.26c

Phallus and Pillar Stones of Knowth

Diagram 3.27

Another artifact helping unravel the enigma is a stone ornament excavated by George Eogan inside the mound of Knowth (diagram 3.27). A similar object was also found in the great mound of Newgrange. According to Martin Byrne, it is a 25cm long sandstone with a groove on one side and ribs along the other terminating in a headpiece with three engraved ovals (The Sacred Island—Guided Tours of Ireland's ancient sites). Martin Byrne further suggests the relic may have been used as a sight piece for making astronomical observations, a measuring device, or for holding a stringed pendulum that calculated the lunar movements. Anthony Murphy further suggests that some of the engravings on the object are repeated on the kerbstones at Knowth.

I believe it is a replica of the device (the golden hat/cone) once placed inside the mounds of Knowth, Newgrange, and Stonehenge, capable of generating power. One should note the basic form and design of the phallus stone of Knowth and the golden cone of Switzerland are the same: both are conical in shape with a pointed top. The ribs of the phallus directly respond to those decorated horizontal zones of the Golden Cone. The oval carvings at the

Pillar-like Standing Stone outside Knowth
Diagram 3.28

bottom of the stone refer to the concentric circles and disks of the Cone. Therefore both ornaments actually describe the same object—a missing device once placed at the heart of these megalithic monuments to generate megalights to the surrounding standing stones. The same devices were used at the great cemetery of Loughcrew, the Neolithic complex of Knowth and other sites aligned to the SA.

As a matter of fact, there are two pillar-like standing stones erected at the two entrances of the mound (diagram 3.28). They are also replicas of the missing conical device. The place where they were found most likely marks the exact location where it once projected a line of light beams into the mound, connected to another device inside to start up the energy mechanism.

The Art of Knowth: A Message from the Builders

In his article "Knowth before Knowth" (*Antiquity* 72, 1998), Dr. George Eogan says Knowth contains at least 200 decorated stones, and at least 300 for the whole site. During excavations in 1996, many new decorated stones emerged. Many rectangular orthostats and capstones averaging 1.5m in length and 70cm in breadth, picked with chevrons, spirals, and zigzag motifs wholly or partially hidden from sight (diagrams 3.29). Some of the slabs were decorated only at the end, designed to be inserted into the socket. One stone, C10, has decoration on two faces. Eogan speculates that the slabs, used in an earlier tomb nearby, were all recycled. He further suggests that in comparison with similar carvings in Newgrange, "this art must have served a specific purpose and, therefore, constitutes a group in its own right." Unfortunately the theme of these works still remains a mystery.

After studying the illustrations produced by Eogan, I discovered most of the spirals are aligned to the SA (diagram 3.30). The typical slabs of C.10, or Or.18, Corbel 10F, and C.20, show the spirals deliberately picked or arranged so they form an angle of 135 degrees.

Zigzag and Concentric Carvings of Knowth
(after Eogan) *Diagram 3.29*

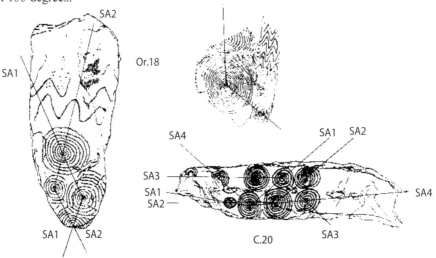

Spiral and Concentric Carvings of Knowth and the SAs
(after Eogan) *Diagram 3.30*

The builders might be trying to show us the real function of these monuments through messages contained in the carvings. Diagram 3.31 illustrates how the central mound of Knowth, projecting two rows of megalights, formed a Neolithic power station with her surrounding mounds (diagram 3.31).

A kerbstone outside the great mound of Knowth shows at least three sets of SAs (diagram 3.32).

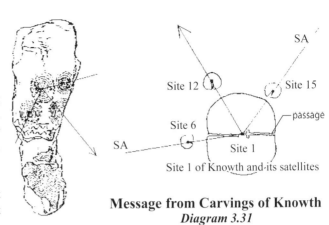

C.10 of Knowth

Message from Carvings of Knowth
Diagram 3.31

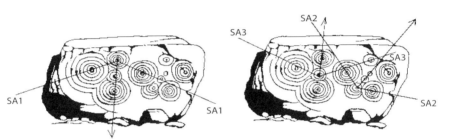

Kerbstone of Knowth *Diagram 3.32*

A decorated slab (L19) with a similar theme and style is also found in Newgrange (O'Kelly 1982). The upper portion of the slab was decorated with the famous "Triskelion" surrounded by chevron patterns. What caught my attention are the four spirals carved on the lower portion of the slab just above the ground level. Like those slabs of Knowth, three of the spirals form a perfect SA and the angle bisector points to another spiral on the bottom left (diagram 3.33). Did Newgrange also serve the same function as her sister mound?

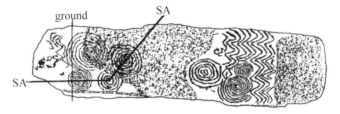

L19 of Newgrange and the SA (after O'Kelly)
Diagram 3.33

The Radiating Suns of Dowth and Knowth

The tomb of Dowth is a bi-passageway mound famous for its "radiating suns" pattern. The "Stone of the Seven Suns" (kerbstone 51) is regarded as one the most beautiful Neolithic carvings in Ireland (diagram 3.34). It describes suns or stars with rays coming out from the center. Naturally, archaeologists think that kerbstone 51 is an astronomical stone.

George Coffey, who explored the site, termed these stellar symbols "stars and discs," and claimed

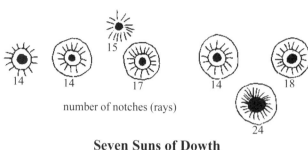

number of notches (rays)

Seven Suns of Dowth
Diagram 3.34

they were "inherently astronomical, probably representing a symbol of the sinking or
rising sun." After studying the
drawings in Newgrange and
Knowth, I believe the artists of
Dowth were trying to describe
a circle of megalights projected
from the chamber in the center
of the mound, such as Site 1 of
Knowth, to surrounding satellite
mounds. Is this a true description
of the mounds of Knowth when the SA machine was activated?

In a recess of Knowth, there is a drawing of twelve radiating sunrays. There are eighteen satellite mounds around Knowth but only twelve of them have passageways and chambers. If we
compare the radiating sun drawing with the layout of Knowth, we can see a connection between
the two. Did the artist try to imply that a circle with twelve straight lines—megalights—was
projected to the surrounding satellites (diagram 3.35)? Let's not forget that the megalights could
penetrate solid bluestones as described by the Dagda Skirt drawing. What do these megalights
stand for? Are they sunrays, light beams, or microwaves?

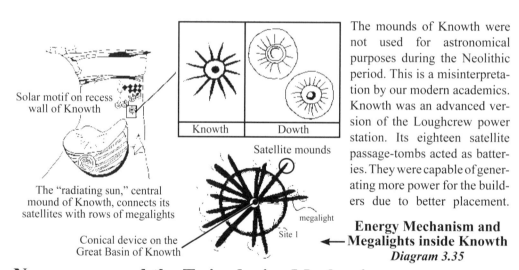

Solar motif on recess
wall of Knowth

Knowth | Dowth

Satellite mounds

The "radiating sun," central
mound of Knowth, connects its
satellites with rows of megalights

megalight

Site 1

Conical device on the
Great Basin of Knowth

The mounds of Knowth were
not used for astronomical
purposes during the Neolithic
period. This is a misinterpreta-
tion by our modern academics.
Knowth was an advanced version of the Loughcrew power
station. Its eighteen satellite
passage-tombs acted as batteries. They were capable of generating more power for the builders due to better placement.

**Energy Mechanism and
Megalights inside Knowth**
Diagram 3.35

Newgrange and the Twin-device Mechanism

*"The Tuatha de Danann, who were also known as the Lords of Light, were very closely associ-
ated with Ireland's Boyne Valley megalithic complex, and were believed to be able to control
the light of the sun. At the first Battle of Moytura they won by smothering the land in darkness
and hiding the light of the sun."*

—Christopher Knight and Robert Lomas, *Uriel's Machine*

*"The many mysteries of Newgrange—who built it? What was its purpose? What do the spirals
mean?—have prompted a variety of theories about its origin and purpose. Newgrange is especially revered by New Age adherents, who believe it to be a place of great energy and mystical
power."*

—sacred-destinations.com

Newgrange is believed to be the home of the Tuatha de Danann. As shown in the diagram below, the basic layout of the mound is determined by the pair of Great Circle Stones of GC 11 and GC 7, acting as the Station Stones of the structure, whereas another monolith (GC1) acts as the Heel Stone, an angle bisector, of Newgrange. If three straight lines are drawn from the three GC Stones they will intercept at the corbelled chamber of the cairn (diagram 3.36), forming an SA with the bisector passing through the long passage and pointing to the entrance at the platform of the roof box. Surely this is no coincidence. It shows a purpose and design beyond what we expect from our Stone Age people.

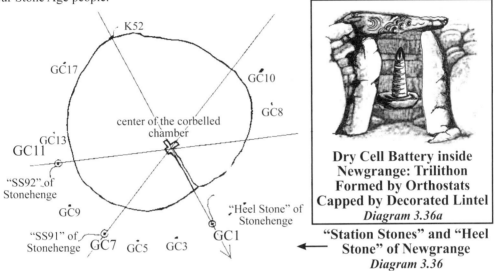

Dry Cell Battery inside Newgrange: Trilithon Formed by Orthostats Capped by Decorated Lintel
Diagram 3.36a

"Station Stones" and "Heel Stone" of Newgrange
Diagram 3.36

Most visitors recognize twelve standing stones surrounding the cairn. With inspiration from the power generator of Cairn D of Loughcrew and the cup and ring carving inside Cairn L, the general layout of these standing stones (GC of Newgrange) is aligned to the SA formula too. With the chamber of the mound as the center, SAs develop with the following pairs of standing stones: GC-2 and GC11 (SA1), GC-10 and GC13 (SA2), GC17 and GC3 (SA3), GC5 and GC-8 (SA4), GC5 and K52 (SA5), GC1 and K67 (SA6), GC9 and K67 (SA7) (diagram 3.37).

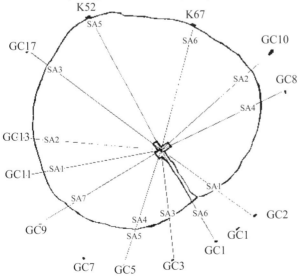

Corbelled Chamber and the Great Circle Stones of Newgrange
Diagram 3.37

When we take the entrance of the mound, the exact location of the roof box, as the center (diagram 3.38), a series of SAs are formed by the following pairs of standing stones: GC17 and socket GC2 (SA8), GC1 and GC13 (SA9), GC-1 and GC9 (SA10), GC-2 and GC7 (SA11), GC5 and socket GC-3 (SA12), GC-8 and socket GC2 (SA13), GC3 and K52 (SA14), GC5 and K67 (SA15). Why did the builders incorporate this angle into their construction? Was it necessary to employ this angle in tapping the earth energy needed to power their technology?

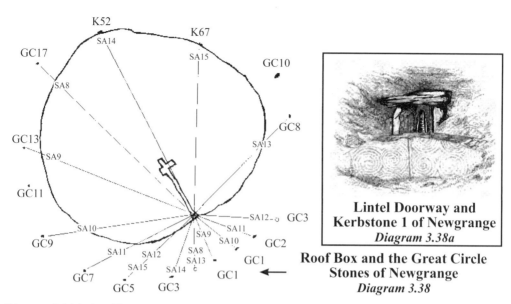

Lintel Doorway and Kerbstone 1 of Newgrange
Diagram 3.38a

Roof Box and the Great Circle Stones of Newgrange
Diagram 3.38

Diagram 3.39 below illustrates my conception of what Newgrange was like 5,000 years ago.

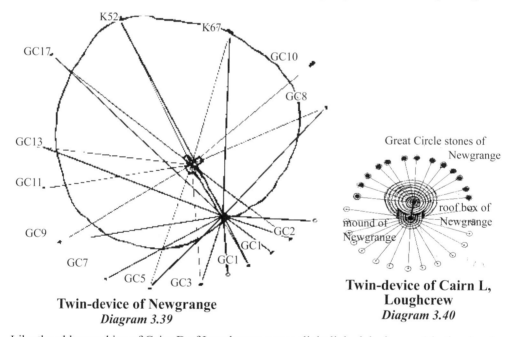

Twin-device of Newgrange
Diagram 3.39

Twin-device of Cairn L, Loughcrew
Diagram 3.40

Like the older machine of Cairn D of Loughcrew, a megalight linked device no. 1 in the chamber of Newgrange with device no. 2 of the roof box (diagrams 3.39 and 3.40). When the Newgrange power station was activated, a machine needing to be refueled or recharged would be parked outside its entrance at the southeastern part. A circle of postholes was excavated, and experts suggest that there was a timber henge constructed southeast of Newgrange. The timber henge forms an SA with the roof box and the corbelled chamber of Newgrange. The machine would project a megalight to the second device located on the platform of the roof box, which in turn would activate another device (no. 1) under the corbelled wall of the chamber. Energy would be generated, amplified, and transmitted to the machine inside the timber henge ready for recharging (diagrams 3.41 and 3.42). Newgrange is a megalithic power station.

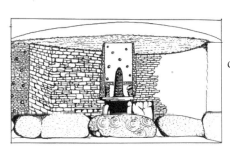

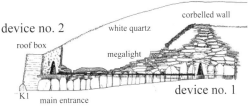

**Conical Device No. 2 inside
Roof Box, Newgrange**
Diagram 3.41

Twin-device Installed, Newgrange
Diagram 3.42

Another interesting feature of the mound of Newgrange is its long passageway (extending for 18m). Why did the builders construct such a long S-shape passage? Today, there are three stone basins lying quietly inside each of the three recesses. If the SA is applied to the internal structure of the mound, the angle bisector formed by the two opposite basins leans slightly to the right towards the slabs at the eastern wall of the passage. This explains why the four slabs are heavily carved with spiral patterns. This also explains why the long passage slightly leans to the right when it reaches the corbelled chamber.

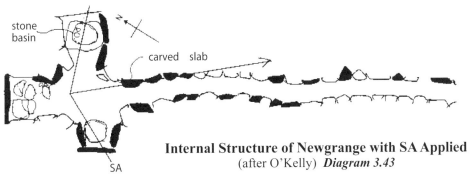

Internal Structure of Newgrange with SA Applied
(after O'Kelly) *Diagram 3.43*

The Irish Triple Spirals

What was Newgrange? Author Chris O'Callaghan suggests "there is not the faintest evidence that Newgrange had ever been as any sort of dedicated repository for bodies, bones, burial artifacts or ashes" (mythicalireland.com). If the cairn was not used as a burial site, then what was its real function? Is it logical to believe the Grooved Ware Culture, with an average lifespan of twenty-five to thirty years, spent hundreds of years constructing Newgrange simply to look at a ray of sunlight on a wall for a few minutes each year? And why are so many mysterious patterns carved both inside and outside the cairn? Is it enough to attribute everything our Stone Age predecessors did to the movements of the sun and moon? Why do we assume they were so different from us? The truth is they were every bit as intelligent as we are today. Civilization has demonstrated countless times it is no benchmark of intelligence. The people of antiquity may have been superstitious, but they weren't stupid. Survival was tough in those days. They simply didn't have time to sit around looking at the stars and building elaborate stone mansions to house tiny squares of reflected light. Something else of a completely different nature has gone on here.

As mentioned before, I believe Neolithic carvings such as the tri-spiral orthostats of Knowth (Eogan 1998) and the cup and ring slab of Loughcrew are messages from the builders. Newgrange is a center of megalithic art and contains similar messages.

The most famous icon of the Newgrange carvings is the Triskelion, the famous triple spiral carvings on the slab C10 (the Threshold Stone) in the rear recess of the mound and K1 at the entrance. The symbol is so famous that it has become an object for pilgrims from all over the world. Again, no one knows the real meaning behind these spirals. Some believe it depicts a Stone Age deity, or the three spirals represent life, death, and eternity. Others think that it only records the Neolithic holy man's visions after taking herbal drugs. These experts possibly neglected the environmental evidence around the mound, which might help to solve the mystery. I am aware that the mound of Newgrange consists of three recesses. For me,

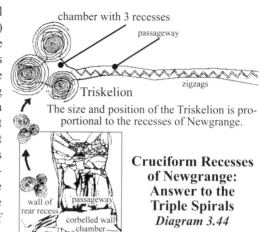

Cruciform Recesses of Newgrange: Answer to the Triple Spirals
Diagram 3.44

the famous triple spirals are just a reflection of what happened inside the three recesses of the mound. If we rotate the three spirals to match the layout and direction of the three recesses, (diagram 3.44) with the large spiral on the top, the smaller one at the bottom right, and the smallest spiral at the bottom left, the sizes and positions of the three spirals match perfectly with the three chambers of the mound. This is no coincidence. The artist was recording what actually happened inside the mound when this ancient machinery was at work.

Antediluvian Televisions

The Stone Age people didn't understand what they were seeing when the machines were operating (diagrams 3.45a, b, and c). They engraved zigzag patterns to represent the light beams and the three spirals to represent microwaves on the slabs of the mound. They even carved the builders' instruments with a Visual Display Unit onto the Newgrange kerbstone 52. There is another oddly shaped stone at Cairn T in Knowth (known as the "Hag's Chair"). There is also a trapezium shape with uncommon straight lines carved in the middle, looking eerily similar to the control panel of a television.

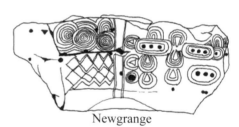

The Famous Kerbstone 52 with Its Wonderful Carvings and Strange Shape
Diagram 3.45a

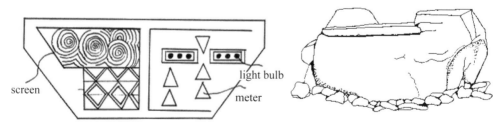

A Neolithic VDU
Diagram 3.45b

The "Hag's Chair" Slab of Loughcrew, of Similar Shape as K52
Diagram 3.45c

Slab K52 and the Hag's Chair are replicas of this missing machine. It once lay at the back of the mounds of Newgrange and Loughcrew so as to detach the reaction of electric charge inside the mound.

Prof. O'Kelly's "Solar God" slab of Co.1/C7 inspires my idea the most. It demonstrates a circular device projecting light beams onto the surrounding stones in Stonehenge. Could this have happened in the mound of Newgrange? Archaeologists conclude that the mound was deliberately designed to allow the sun to pass through the specially designed roof-box set deep into the rear chamber. It seems that the builders were not expecting natural sunlight; rather, they deliberately generated a line of megalights from the device placed on the roof-box platform (diagram 3.46) and let it penetrate the passageway, as illustrated by the zigzag patterns carved on the kerbstones along the passageway into the rear chamber where another device (no. 1) was waiting. A circular device (no. 1) projected a row of light beams onto the surrounding bluestones inside the smaller horseshoe of Stonehenge. But what was the reason for projecting a single line of light beam into the rear chamber of Newgrange? Did it serve the same function as Stonehenge 1,000 years later?

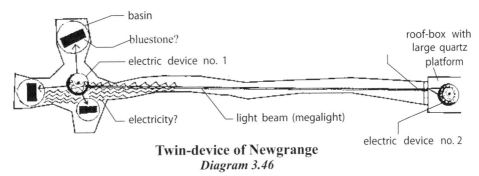

Twin-device of Newgrange
Diagram 3.46

Newgrange: An Early Model of Stonehenge

I believe that the mound of Newgrange is a prototype of Stonehenge. Diagram 3.47 illustrates the same mechanism of the two Neolithic machines as they stood 4,000 to 5,000 years ago. As previously mentioned, the structures of the two monuments are roughly the same. The long passageway of Newgrange shares the same function as the horseshoe structure of Stonehenge. Both galleries end with a high chamber in the center.

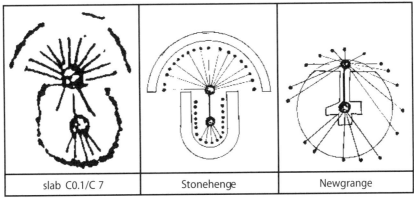

Twin-device Mechanism of Stonehenge and Newgrange
Diagram 3.47

Stonehenge's chamber is formed by the three largest trilithons, acting as stone walls, with narrow gaps in between. A device placed inside the high chamber projected megalights to the surrounding bluestones. Another device (no. 2) would then be placed outside the truncated roof-box of the oval shaped mound of Newgrange and at the northeast entrance of the horseshoe structure of Stonehenge waiting for signals from the megalight device (diagram 3.48). Such a design optimizes the amount of megalights from device no. 2, projected to the Great Circle stones of Newgrange and bluestone circle of Stonehenge. When the two devices (nos. 1 and 2) were connected, winding spirals of electricity were generated inside the three recesses of Newgrange, as described by the Triskelion and the trilithons of Stonehenge, as the megalight touched the surface of the bluestones. The spirals were further magnified by the quartz-rich stone structures—the layer of white quartz at the southeast of the cairn of Newgrange and the Great Trilithons of Stonehenge with a northeast opening. These spirals then reacted with the standing stones of the Great Circle of Newgrange as well as the sarsen and bluestone circle of Stonehenge, resulting in rings of concentric circles—microwaves—as depicted on Professor O'Kelly's Solar God slab of Co.1/C7 (diagram 3.48a).

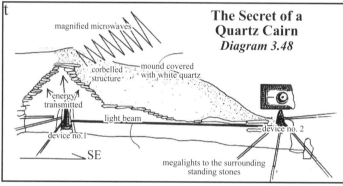

The Secret of a Quartz Cairn
Diagram 3.48

magnified microwaves

corbelled structure — mound covered with white quartz

energy transmitted

light beam

device no. 1

device no. 2

SE

megalights to the surrounding standing stones

According to Irish legends, the masters of these structures—the Tuatha de Danann—were also known as the Lords of Light. The Neolithic carvings in Newgrange, the engraved slabs in Loughcrew, and the bizarre patterns in Gavrinis may be a record of their use (diagram 3.49).

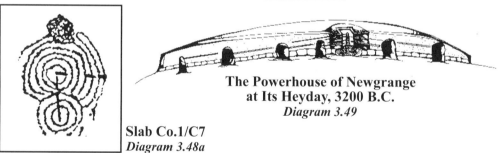

The Powerhouse of Newgrange at Its Heyday, 3200 B.C.
Diagram 3.49

Slab Co.1/C7
Diagram 3.48a

Sockets, Site Z, and Timber Circle

According to the excavation report of Professor O'Kelly, there is an arc of three sockets at the southern part of the site along the same circumference as the Great Stone Circle. Experts speculate that they once held stones like those of the stone circle, so they are named GC4, GC6, and GC8. At the same time, satellite passage mound Site Z, with a small chamber at the end, was built at the east of the great mound. The socket GC4 forms an SA1 with the chamber of Site Z, with the roof box of Newgrange in the middle. Interestingly, socket GC8 forms another SA2 with the chamber of Site Z; this time, the corbelled chamber of Newgrange occupies the middle (diagram 3.51).

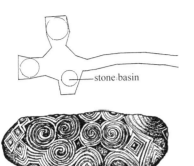

**Cruciform Passage of Newgrange
and the Five Spirals of K1**
Diagram 3.50

Sweetman (1985) discovered concentric arcs of pits forming part of a large circular enclosure at the eastern area of the mound. It is suggested there was once a domestic building constructed next to the mound of Newgrange dating back to the late Neolithic period. The center of this timber circle forms an SA3 with the corbelled chamber of Newgrange, with the roof box in the middle. It also forms an SA4 with socket GC6 of Newgrange, the roof box of the passage grave is in the middle. Newgrange is more complicated than we previously imagined.

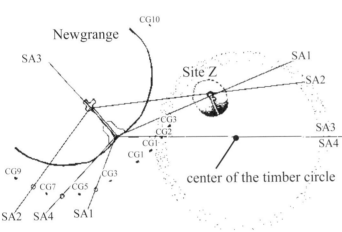

Newgrange and Its Timber Circle
Diagram 3.51

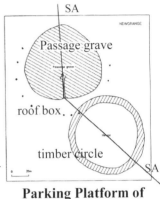

**Parking Platform of
Newgrange**
(after O'Kelly 1982,
Sweetman 1985; diagram
from Richard Bradley, *The
Significance of Monuments*,
p. 103)
Diagram 3.51a

Patterns of the Newgrange Concentric Circles

Like Knowth, Newgrange is also famous for its carvings. The following engraved slab (Stone 55 from O'Kelly) lies at the west junction of the passage and chamber roofs. The slab is fully covered with ornaments such as squared dots, small circles, spirals, and concentric circles. Once again the drawings appear to be randomly scattered on the slab without any setting. However, using the SA, we can see they are systematically arranged (diagrams 3.52a, b, and c).

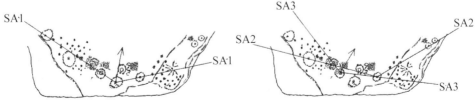

Stone 55 of Newgrange and the SA
(after O'Kelly) *Diagram 3.52a*

Nearly all the ornaments, including the black dots/ dips that represent the standing stones and the concentric circles representing cairns and henges, are aligned to the SA. Another orthostat, L19, is carved with spirals that are likewise consistent with my SA formula. It seems the mound build-ers were recording or

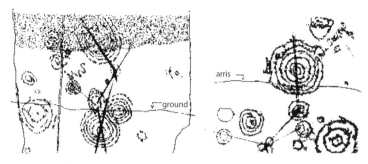

Carvings from Newgrange (after O'Kelly)
Diagram 3.52b   *Diagram 3.52c*

drafting their projects onto the slab, or perhaps they wanted to show us the secret behind all these Neolithic monuments. If it really was a record of the workings of these sites, the heavily carved recess-roofs of Newgrange are an important map of their ancient activities. I would like to examine other curious ornaments, produced by Prof. O'Kelly, and how they are aligned to the SA formula.

Kerbstone K52 and the Capstone of the East Recess

Kerbstone 52, located at the northwest side of the great kerb diametrically opposite the entrance stone K1, is one of the trademarks of Newgrange. The finest decorated slab is richly patterned with spirals, cup-and-ring designs, and zigzags. Double lines are carved at the center. Experts discovered that these lines, together with another line from the center of Kerbstone K1, demar-cate the entire mound into two halves. Other ornaments on K52 are shallow dips that almost seem unintentionally carved. Most of these dips represent standing stones and are aligned to the SA, with the spiral carving representing the mound in the middle (diagram 3.53). Is K52 also a message left by the Tuatha de Danaan?

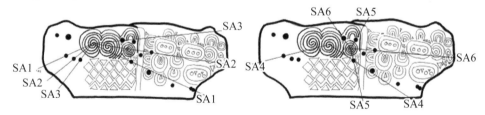

K52 and the SA
Diagram 3.53

I have modified diagram 3.54 after one of Prof. O'Kelly's illustrations of the capstone carvings in the eastern recess of Newgrange. The massive block is heavily carved with concentric circles, spirals, zigzags, and other bizarre lines and patterns. Most researchers think they are simply pas-sageway decorations, but I believe differently. It is not hard to see that the spiral in the center of the carving represents the great mound of Newgrange and the set of concentric circles lying at its southeast refers to the henge monument recently excavated. Besides, there are two enclosures (A and P) represented by two flower patterns on the capstone lying further southeast of the henge. The mound of Newgrange is surrounded by several satellite mounds, indicated by smaller circles in the carving.

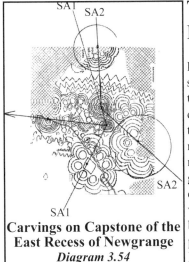

Carvings on Capstone of the East Recess of Newgrange
Diagram 3.54

The Twin-devices of Newgrange and Knowth

If we apply the SA formula to the two Boyne Valley passage graves, Knowth and Newgrange, we find their function identical. Twin-device placed under the corbelled walls of the eastern and western chambers of Knowth, as well as the chamber and roof box of Newgrange, projected rows of megalights onto the surrounding standing stones and satellite mounds tapping energy from the earth's magnetic core (diagrams 3.55 and 3.56). These two conical devices were then connected by another row of megalights necessary to activate the energy mechanism. The same mechanism can also be applied to Stonehenge when the twin conical devices are placed inside the bluestones horseshoe and the sarsen circle. It is shown in the Solar God of Newgrange and Loughcrew's Dagda Skirt carving. Both passage graves once acted as powerhouses for an advanced Neolithic race. The Newgrange station was probably an improved model of Knowth, as the builders used a circle of monoliths to replace and improve the more time-consuming satellite mounds of Knowth.

What makes the region so remarkable is that the two powerhouses each lie on energy grids commonly referred to as Ley Lines. They are further connected by enclosure R with an SA, acting like a recharging platform for the builders' vehicle, forming a mega-power generator in the valley (diagram 3.57). The

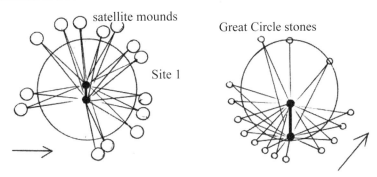

Twin-device Mechanism of Knowth (*left*) and Newgrange
Diagrams 3.55 and 3.56

same case is also applied to the passage grave of Dowth, as it forms another SA with Knowth.

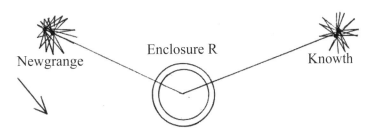

Mega Generator of Boyne Valley
Diagram 3.57

White Quartz Wall of Newgrange and Bipolarization

The diagram below is a bipolar transistor. It controls the flow of electrical current through a device called a voltage-controlled semiconductor. This transistor is a three-terminal, three-layer device—an emitter, a base, and a collector (diagram 3.58a). The basic function is to modulate the current flowing through the base from the emitter to the collector. A properly biased signal injected into the quartz base will result in an amplified signal appearing at the collector terminal. This creates an amplifier.

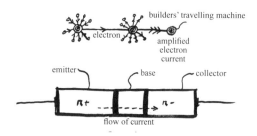

A Bi-polar Transistor
Diagram 3.58a

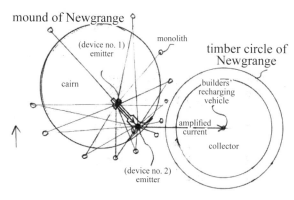

A Bi-transistor (Semiconductor) Mechanism Applied to Newgrange and Its Timber Circle
Diagram 3.58b

The conical devices of the megalith builders act in a similar way. Device no. 1 acts as an emitter of the bipolar transistor, projecting rows of megalights to the surfaces of the surrounding monoliths tapping energy underneath. An electron current will then travel from the emitter (device no. 1) to the central base (device no. 2) of the transistor. In Newgrange this is the roof box, which is deliberately placed and surrounded by white quartz for modulating and amplifying the electron current. This is well illustrated by spiral carvings inside the mound. The fully charged base will project another light beam of amplified current, functioning like electric wire, to the collector section of the transistor. In Neolithic Ireland, the receiver of this amplified electron current is some form of machine most likely used for transportation. Most importantly, if the golden rule of the builders' advanced technology were applied, the conical devices nos. 1 and 2 and the landing platform of the builders' transport (the east timber circle of Newgrange) had to align to the SA (diagram 3.58b).

Dowth: The Oldest Power Generator of the Boyne Valley

Lying 2km east of Newgrange, the unexcavated mound of Dowth is regarded as the oldest monument in the region. It stands at the highest point of a ridge, 87m above sea level. The cairn, bound by 100 kerbstones, is 85m in diameter and 15m in height. There are two entrances opening to the west, where a kerbstone engraved with a cup and ring marking lies across its mouth (diagram 3.59). Dowth's main passage chamber is cruciform in shape with three main recesses. The southern recess extends to a few smaller recesses. Like the cruciform tombs in the Loughcrew cemetery, the chamber of Dowth North, formed by large orthostats, is also aligned to the SA (diagram 3.60).

In addition, there are passage graves surrounding the mound (diagram 3.61), probably satellites acting as dry cell batteries of Dowth. They form several sets of SAs, with Dowth in the center. This makes Dowth a carbon copy of the Loughcrew power station.

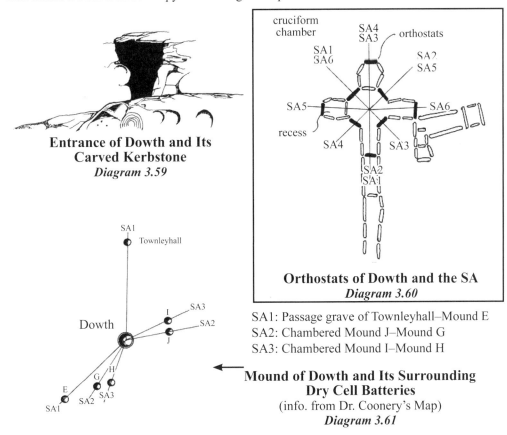

Entrance of Dowth and Its Carved Kerbstone
Diagram 3.59

Orthostats of Dowth and the SA
Diagram 3.60

SA1: Passage grave of Townleyhall–Mound E
SA2: Chambered Mound J–Mound G
SA3: Chambered Mound I–Mound H

Mound of Dowth and Its Surrounding Dry Cell Batteries
(info. from Dr. Coonery's Map)
Diagram 3.61

Boyne Valley Metropolis

"There is a story that the Tuatha De Danann came to Ireland in flying ships but could not land as Danann's rival enemies, the Fomorians, had set up a great energy field they could not penetrate. So they had to circle Ireland nine times before finding a breach in the energy field and setting down on Sliabh an Iarainn (The Iron Mountains) in Co. Leitrim."

—Shee-Eire.com

The Boyne Valley ritual landscape is one of the most complex Neolithic sites in Ireland. The three most outstanding mounds are Knowth, Newgrange, and Dowth. Each dates back to between 3500 and 3000 B.C. Numerous ancient monuments around the region have been excavated, including two timber henges built outside Knowth and Newgrange, a number of small passage graves along the ridge of the low hill, large henge enclosures surrounding Newgrange, several artificially created ponds, and a number of standing stones. Experts speculate that the valley had been an important ritual landscape of the Grooved Ware culture.

I believe the entire Boyne Valley complex was built over varying time periods. The first period initiated the construction of the three passage graves of Knowth, Newgrange, and Dowth. They acted individually as the local power generators and regional communication centers. The great mound of Knowth emitted rows of megalights to her satellites. Dowth was also a regional communication center between Loughcrew and Fourknocks. Carvings show us Newgrange also projected the daggerlike megalights onto the surrounding standing stones (GC), generating power and refueling the builders transport machines.

The above system of passage tombs ran for several hundred years until the introduction of the earthwork enclosures around the early Bronze Age. Henge R was constructed and strategically placed between the three passage graves. Naturally SA1 is formed with the mounds Knowth and Dowth, and SA2 with the mound of Knowth and Newgrange. The enclosure acted as a landing platform once the builders' vehicles connected and activated the surrounding three powerhouses.

Henges and Timber Circle of Newgrange

The large henges, such as Site M to the west, Site P to the south, Site A to the southeast, Site V to the north, and Site Q to the northeast of Newgrange, probably other platforms, were constructed later. A timber circle, known as pit circle, of Newgrange was constructed just southeast of the great mound of Newgrange. It forms an SA with the roof box and corbelled chamber of Newgrange. Six large henges were the focal points of the builders, as they are connected by the SAs with the timber circle of Newgrange in the center (diagram 3.62). If the timber circle was once the refueling platform of the builders, then these surrounding henges had to be its dry cell batteries in 2500 B.C.

The third phase started with the introduction of artificial ponds into the region. Like the southeast timber circle of Newgrange, they served to connect the Boyne powerhouses in the form of the SA alignment (diagram 3.63).

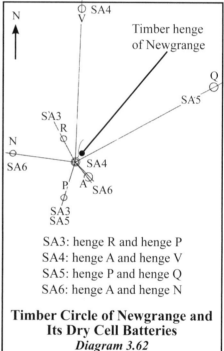

SA3: henge R and henge P
SA4: henge A and henge V
SA5: henge P and henge Q
SA6: henge A and henge N

**Timber Circle of Newgrange and
Its Dry Cell Batteries**
Diagram 3.62

SA7: SW wooden structure of Newgrange–timber circle of Newgrange–henge A
SA8: henge A–pond I–henge P, bisects at Knowth
SA9: henge P–pond III–Knowth, bisects at Newgrange
SA10: Knowth–henge N–pond III, bisects at henge R
SA11: pond III–Knowth–pond IV, bisects at Site F
SA12: Knowth–pond IV–passage grave of Townleyhall, bisects at Site G
SA13: Knowth–timber circle of Newgrange–pond I, bisects at pond III
SA14: Knowth–Newgrange–pond II, bisects at the wooden structure of Newgrange
SA15: henge V–pond IV–henge P, bisects at henge Q

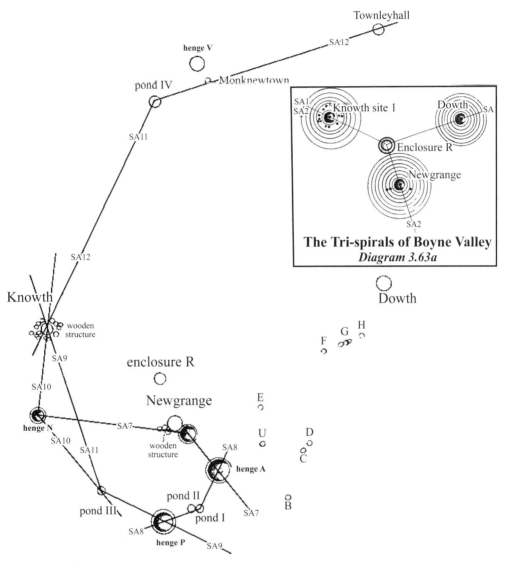

The Tri-spirals of Boyne Valley
Diagram 3.63a

**Boyne Neolithic Metropolis,
Showing the Role of Artificial Ponds**
(after Dr. Cooney's Map)
Diagram 3.63

Interestingly, all the powerhouses of the third phase form a spiral pattern originating from the mound of Newgrange. The diagram echoes the famous spirals of Newgrange. The site of Newgrange, obviously extremely important for the builders, probably lies above a major energy stream. Although Newgrange was built on a slope, the builders overcome this by introducing a roof box, constructed on the same horizontal level as the central chamber, so that megalight, instead of sun rays, could reach the rear recess when the energy mechanism was activated.

Tara Hill Power Station

The word *Tara* means a "place of great prospect" or "the place with a wide view," as the site enjoys a commanding view of more than ten counties in Ireland. Experts consider the hill one of the most sacred sites in Irish history and crucial to Irish culture. Legend has it 142 kings have reigned on the hill. Others believe it was the entrance to the otherworld. Around 500 B.C., it was believed that whoever ruled Tara was the High King standing upon a Stone of Destiny, the Lia Fail, and had right of supremacy over all Ireland's kings.

Mound of the Hostages
Diagram 3.64

About thirty barrows, earth enclosures and megaliths cluster around a 154m high hilltop. To the northwest the brilliant white quartz mound of Newgrange can be seen. The monuments were built over a period of 4,000 years. The earliest and most prominent monument on the hill is a small passage grave called the Mound of the Hostages (diagram 3.64). Archaeologists suggest an enclosure was first built around 3000 B.C. and a passage tomb was constructed at a later period. The tomb is 3m long and 1m wide and divided by rows of stones into three sections. Just inside the entrance sits a large decorated orthostat with cup and ring markings and it actually explains the real function of the mound (diagram 3.65). According to legends, the mound was once used for taking and holding hostages from other provinces in order to symbolize their submission to the Irish king.

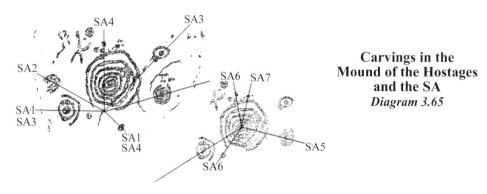

Carvings in the Mound of the Hostages and the SA
Diagram 3.65

On the Hill of Tara lie the remains of many Iron Age earthworks (diagram 3.66). The Royal Enclosure (2), consisting of a bank and ditch, lies south of the Mound of the Hostages (6). Inside stand two ringed forts (the Royal Seat and the Forradh) (3 and 4). In the center of this smaller banked enclosure, the Forradh or Cormac's House, lies a phallic-shaped monolith called Lia Fail, the Stone of Destiny (5).

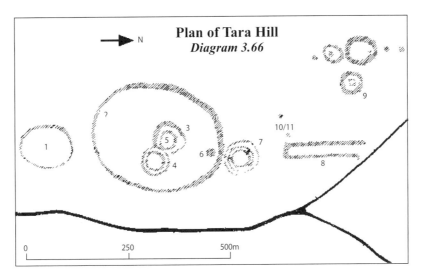

Plan of Tara Hill
Diagram 3.66

N

1
2
3
4
5
6
7
8
9
10/11

0   250   500m

This is an ancient fertility pillar and the inauguration stone of the kings—it roared three times when a would-be king stood on it (diagram 3.67). According to legends, the stone was a sacred object brought to Ireland by the Tuatha De Danann—the Lords of Light. Can it be a replica of the builders' megalight device? Another ringfort with three banks is the Rath of the Synods. This monument is famous for its excavation by a group of British-Israelities searching for the Biblical Ark of Covenant, another powerful device believed hidden in a secret tomb at Tara by the prophet Jeremiah in 583 B.C. The legend stated that Jeremiah was finally buried in Cairn T at

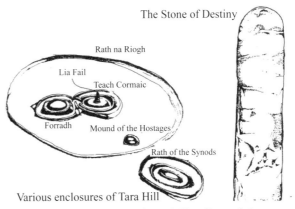

The Stone of Destiny

Rath na Riogh
Lia Fail
Teach Cormaic
Forradh
Mound of the Hostages
Rath of the Synods

Various enclosures of Tara Hill

The Stone of Destiny: A Replica of the Builders' Conical Device, Revealing the Real Function of These Enclosures
Diagram 3.67

Loughcrew. Generally, these circular enclosures were not royal palaces, as few artifacts were unearthed and no entrances were constructed. These rings make poor defensive structures. They are too small to garrison a force of any size, and the banks are too shallow to stop a determined enemy. It is time to abandon theories which on the surface are satisfying explanations, but examined further fall apart, all for the sake of convenience. All for the sake of consensus. After all, who is going to rewrite all those textbooks delivering false impressions and explanations of these sites?

The earliest phase of the Hill of Tara was constructed in the same period as those found in the Boyne Valley. The layout of the Hill of Tara aligns perfectly with the SA formula. In diagram 3.68 below, three sets of SAs are formed by these earth enclosures in three different time periods, with Rath of the Synods as their centers—an "enclosure to enclosure" type of connection forms. As a result, I speculate the Lia Fail standing stone, like the golden hat cones of Western Europe, is a replica of the missing conical device. Its location might mark the exact position to place this device: in the center of these circular earthen enclosures.

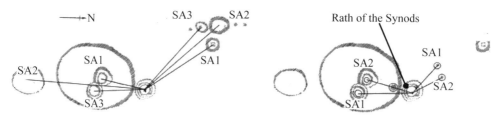

"Enclosure to Enclosure" (*right*)
and "Mound to Enclosure" Power Stations of Tara Hill
Diagrams 3.68 and 3.69

The enclosure of Rath of the Synods also serves as the center for another two sets of SAs with earth mounds nearby (diagram 3.69). SA1 is formed by the enclosure of Teach Cormaic and a plow-out mound where traces of a burial mound were found northeast of Rath. Another SA is formed by the enclosure of Forradh and another plow-out mound northeast-to-east of Rath.

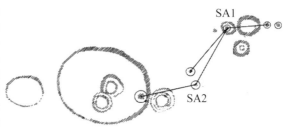

"Mound to Mound" Power Station of
Tara Hill
Diagram 3.70

As shown in diagram 3.70, north of the main site is another set of plow-out mounds around the enclosure of Rath Grainne. SA1 and SA2 form with the other plow-out mounds.

Indications from Tara Hill

Although the layout of these monuments is complicated, the SA can decipher them. A mysterious conical device, like the one on the roof box of Newgrange, was placed at the center of this three-banked enclosure (the Rath), projecting two beams of energy to the two other conical devices erected in the center of the surrounding earthen enclosures (diagram 3.71). These earthen enclosures replaced the cumbersome barrows for generating power. The Rath of the Synods probably lies on the main energy stream around the region. The construction of an earth ring and the installation of a conical device helped to tap the mysterious Earth energy underneath and contained it within a restricted area. According to the builders' energy mechanism, energy waste had to be discharged from the center conical device to other devices on either side, explaining why several enclosures were constructed around the Rath of the Synods.

Why did the builders construct three different sets of SAs over a limited space with a single center—the Rath of the Synods? Does it imply that only the tiny space enclosed by the Rath of the Synods on Tara Hill could provide the mysterious earth energy? If these three sets of SAs were constructed in three different periods of time, does it suggest the megalithic power station would eventually exhaust its supply, necessitating another substitute in the form of a pair of enclosures around the corner? Did the builders construct three sets of megalithic power stations in a row, with their center at Rath of the Synods, to produce a greater energy output? Is there a more rational and scientific explanation for these complex monuments apart from tragic love tales or legends of high kings?

Navan Fort

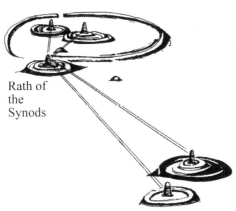

Rath of
the
Synods

**Conical Devices Were Placed inside
the Enclosures Connected with
Megalights to Generate Power; the
Famous Standing Stone (Lia Fail) Is
Just a Replica of the Conical Device**
Diagram 3.71

Navan Fort or *Emhain Macha* ("the twin goddess") is situated in County Armagh, the ancient
capital of Ulster. It is the subject of legendary stories known as the Ulster Cycle. Like Tara Hill, it
has long been identified as a mystic site of ancient
kings and heroes. The circular hill-fort has been
regarded as the fortress-palace, home or seat of the
Gaelic Kings of Ulster. The large enclosure, with
an external bank 15m wide and 4m high outside
a ditch 4m deep, lies on a prominent hilltop with
a commanding view. Such an "external bank and
internal ditch" design indicates the structure was
not used for defensive purposes but to stop people
leaving the enclosure instead of entering it.

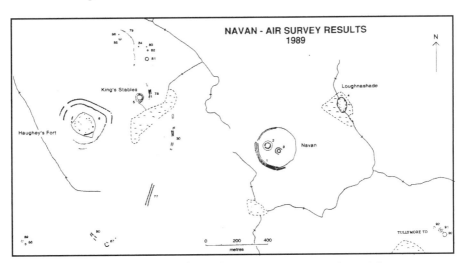

Plan of Navan Complex (*Current Archaeology* 134)
Diagram 3.72

Inside the enclosure is a large barrow, 3,000 years old, containing a ring-ditch 40m in diameter.
Another stone cairn southeast of the barrow was built in a later period (diagram 3.72) (source:
"Navan Fort: New Light on the Irish Epics," *Current Archaeology* 134). According to legend,
this "Macha's twins" was founded by Macha, the wife of the landowner of Ulster, as her palace
and refuge. It is also the place where Deirdre committed suicide after seeing her lover Naoise.
Experts suggest that the stones of the cairn came from a chambered tomb of an earlier period.
A survey shows the circular enclosure has two openings, one to the northwest and one to the
southeast. Another magnetic survey around the site shows a wide earth ring of 30m in diameter surrounding the small mound at the geographical center of the Navan hilltop (Kenneth L.
Kvamme).

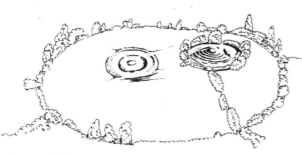

Icon of Navan Fort: A Large Barrow (*left*) and Stone Cairn inside a Large Enclosure
Diagram 3.73

Navan is more complicated than it looks, as many prehistoric earthworks are concentrated around the enclosure. At least two sacred pools lie northwest and northeast of the fort. The first, Lough na Shade, is a small artificial lake dating back to the early Iron Age. Another ritual pool is the King's Stables, a small boggy hollow surrounded by an uneven bank. Excavation in the 1970s revealed it was an artificial pool 25m in diameter and 3m deep. It is interesting to note the two ritual pools act like Station Stones 91 and 94 of Stonehenge, forming SA1 with the barrow of Navan Fort in the middle (diagram 3.74) (*Current Archaeology* 134). The northwest opening of the Navan enclosure is also aligned to that angle.

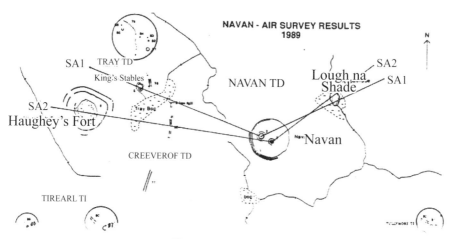

Navan and the SA
Diagram 3.74

Aerial photographs inform us another famous prehistoric site, Haughey's Fort—a ploughed-out bank and ditch lying west of Navan—is actually a three-ditched enclosure. There are pole-holes and pits inside the fort. Artifacts excavated, including some pottery of the Late Bronze Age and a stone with cup and ring markings, bear messages from the Neolithic builders (diagram 3.75).

An SA2 is produced by the waterlogged Haughey's Fort enclosure and the artificial pool of Lough na Shade, with the stone cairn of Navan in the middle (diagram 3.74). The Fort forms SA3 with the barrow and stone cairn of the Navan Fort, aligning with the artificial lake of King's Stables occupying the middle (diagram 3.76). The northwest entrance of the Navan enclosure is also aligned to the SA.

Cup and Ring Carving Stone of Haughey's Fort: The Builders' Message
Diagram 3.75

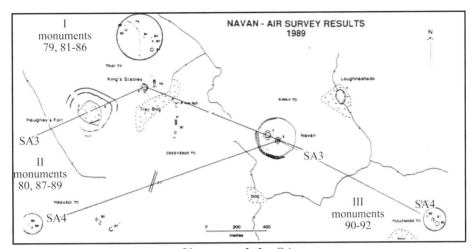

Navan and the SA
Diagram 3.76

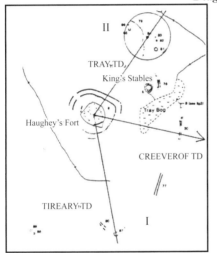

Diagram 3.76a

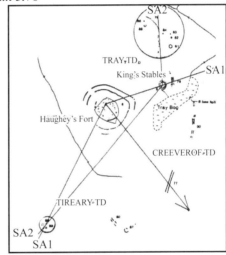

Diagram 3.76b

According to the results of the air survey in 1989, clusters of barrows and crop marks were found to the northwest (monuments 79, 81–86), southwest (monuments 80, 87–89) and southeast (monuments 90–92) of Navan Fort (numbered I, II, and III). Two groups of monuments (southeast and southwest) are located at an exact SA (SA4), with the barrow and stone cairn of Navan in the middle (diagram 3.76).

In diagram 3.76a, an SA is formed by monument 87 (number II of southwest) and monuments 81–86 (number I of northwest), with Haughey's Fort in the middle. It bisects at a parallel earthen bank (monument 30).

In diagram 3.76b, SA1 is formed by the artifical lake of King's Stables and monuments 88–89 (number II of southwest), with the Haughey's Fort in the middle. It bisects at another set of parallel earthen lines (77). SA2 is formed by monuments 81–86 (number I of northwest) and monuments 88–89 (number II of southwest), with the lake of King's Stables in the middle. Based on the number of SAs formed, the Navan Complex must have been an important region.

Lintel Recess of Fourknocks

The Fourknocks mound, Naul, County Meath, lies nine miles southwest of Newgrange. The site sits on a ridge running east-west and dates back to 2400 B.C. It consists of three main cairns, of which the mound of Fourknock I is the best preserved and most famous. It has an oval chamber 41m in size with three small recesses and a passage linking the entrance and the chamber. A post-hole occupies the center of the floor (diagram 3.79). Surprisingly, the 1950 excavation suggests the site was roofless. Most experts believe the mound has never been used for burial purposes; rather, it once served as a meeting place for ritual practices. Like other mounds in the area, the chambers of Fourknocks are decorated with Neolithic patterns. Most of the carvings—by now familiar zigzag and lozenge patterns—are concentrated and skillfully expressed on the lintel of capstones set in the recesses. Experts believe they represented the rising of the "W"-shaped constellation of Cassiopeia during Stone Age (Martin Dire, 2004). But to my understanding, the three small recesses, with their decorated lintels, actually contain the secret of Fourknocks.

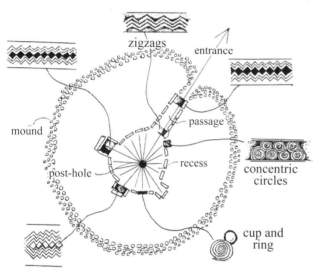

Plan of Fourknocks with Location of Various Carved Lintel Slabs
Diagram 3.79

Like the mound in Newgrange, Fourknocks was once used as an energy recharging station. As illustrated in diagram 3.80, a conical device was placed in the posthole in the middle of the chamber. It then projected rows of light beams onto the orthostats that form the chamber walls of Fourknocks. The orthostats acted as dry cell batteries. Power devices were probably installed inside the three recesses as well, acting as small dolmens (i.e., two standing slabs covered with another capstone), for power. Energy would be generated when light beams heated the dolmens, as depicted by the zigzag and lozenge patterns on their capstones.

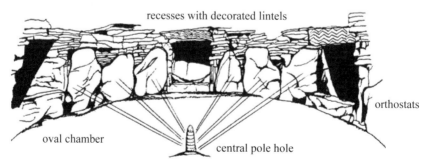

The Fourknocks Powerhouse
Diagram 3.80

The cup and ring carving found inside the mound intimates the real purpose of the site: the roof-less Fourknocks was a Neolithic service station (diagrams 3.81 and 3.82). The question is what kind of machinery needs refueling in late Stone Age Ireland?

Finally, the mound of Fourknocks and the cemetery of Loughchew form an SA with the great mound of Dowth of the Boyne Valley in the middle.

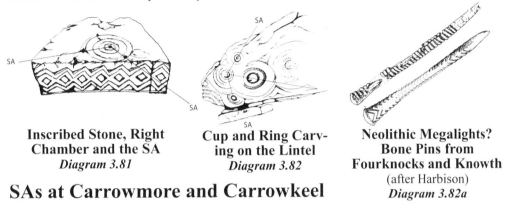

Inscribed Stone, Right Chamber and the SA
Diagram 3.81

Cup and Ring Carving on the Lintel
Diagram 3.82

Neolithic Megalights? Bone Pins from Fourknocks and Knowth
(after Harbison)
Diagram 3.82a

SAs at Carrowmore and Carrowkeel

The cemeteries of Carrowmore of the Cuil Irra peninsula and Carrowkeel of northwest Ireland, together with the Neolithic sites of Loughcrew and the Boyne Valley, are regarded as the four most important ancient sites of Ireland. Each is over 6,000 years old. Carrowmore lies at the heart of the Cuil Irra peninsula in County Sligo. Cuil Irra, when translated, approximates to "The Remote Angle of the Moon." This region hosts the largest Neolithic village in the country, containing many ring forts and earthworks, and surrounded by a range of mountains and the sea. The 321m-high mountain of Knocknarea ("Hill of the Moon") to the west, the chain of the Ox Mountains to the south, a low double hill called Cairns Hill to the east, and Sligo Bay in the north. Neolithic cairns have been constructed on the summits of these mountains overlooking Carrowmore to the north (diagram 3.83).

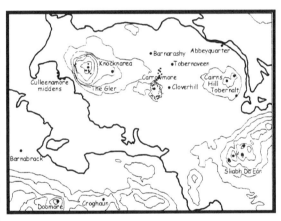

The Cemetery Complex of Carrowmore
(carrowkeel.com) *Diagram 3.83*

Carrowmore is a Neolithic complex with about 120 sites, of which twenty-seven Stone Age monuments remain, including boulders, circles, dolmens, and stone cairns. It boasts the largest collection of Stone Age monuments in the British Isles. Most are situated on a sloping plateau with the large central cairn of Listoghil (Portal Tomb) in the middle. The layout of the cairns of Carrowmore are simple, with a central chamber consisting of a fat capstone supported by typical five uprights surrounded by a circle of boulders. The chamber was then covered by a mound to form a cairn. As shown in diagram 3.84, the Carrowmore boulders of Tomb 3, acting like the kerbstones, align to the SA.

Boulder Circle of Tomb 3 and the SA
(after Herly)
Diagram 3.84

Trilithon Chamber of Listoghil:
The Builders' Dry Cell Battery
Diagram 3.85

The history of the region dates back to 5400 B.C., when the Mesolithic hunter-gatherers evolved into Neolithic farmers. The most remarkable monument of Carrowmore is Listoghil (Cairn 51) (diagram 3.85). This site contains a chamber quite different from the others, carefully constructed with square slabs of stone and a massive roof-slab decorated with incised markings similar to those of the Boyne Valley (information: www.carrowkeel.com).

SAs of the Cuil Irra Peninsula

Studying the Carrowmore cemetery on a regional map, several sets of SAs are apparent. The most prominent (SA1) is formed by the great cairn of Queen Maeve's occupying the summit of the Knocknarea Mountain to the west of Carrowmore and the great stone circle of Abbeyquarter northeast of the peninsula. The large cairn of Listoghil of Carrowmore lies in the middle (diagram 3.86).

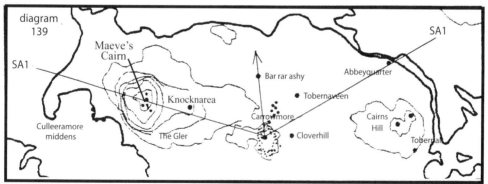

Carrowmore and the SA
Diagram 3.86

According to local legend, the cairn is the final resting place of the Iron Age Queen Maeve of Connaught. Queen Maeve is one of the major figures in the Irish saga. She led her people to war against Ulster. The cairn is known as Misgaun Maeve, and is one of the most well-preserved monuments around the region. It was built between 4000 and 3000 B.C. (diagram 3.87). The cairn is 60m in diameter, 10m high, and 55m across and is made of 40,000 tons of small stones. It is situated on the highest point of a flat-topped limestone plateau, 327m above sea level, on Knocknarea Mountain (diagram 3.87). It can be seen 40km away.

**Queen Maeve's Cairn with a
Neolithic Ruin in Foreground**
Diagram 3.87

Around the cairn are a number of tombs, including a passage tomb with a cruciform central chamber on the ridge to the north, and the remains of three other cairns to the south, including an enclosure and a stonewall. Acting like a gigantic dry battery, Queen Maeve once received rows of megalights from the nearby cairn of Listoghil of Carrowmore (diagram 3.88).

**Knocknarea with Queen
Maeve's Cairn over
Carrowmore Tomb 27**
Diagram 3.88

Listoghil, acting as the center of the builders' machine, would project another row of megalights to the Abbey-quarter Stone Circle in the northeast. This is a boulder circle standing on a knoll and is believed to contain a cruciform structure at the center. The power generator of Listoghil bisects at another Neolithic site, Barnara-shy Stone Circle in the north.

Researchers believe there may originally have been five monuments at Barnarashy, but only two remain. The first is the stone of a large cairn with a cruciform

Barnarashy Stone Row
Diagram 3.89

chamber and the second is a stone row with four large boulders (diagram 3.89). The other two monuments may have been cairns or boulder circles. However, SA1 constitutes only part of the story of the Cuil Irra peninsula.

The story continues with SA2 formed by the Barnarashy Boulders Circle and Stone Row to the north and the Neolithic cairn of Sliabh Da Ear, a 15m diameter cairn built from quarried local gneiss rock and constructed on the highest point of the hilltop (263m high), to the southeast. The cairn of Listoghil occupies the middle. Coincidentally, the angle bisects at the Stone Circle of Abbeyquarter (diagram 3.90).

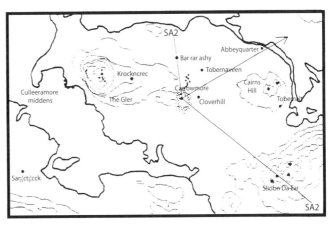

Carrowmore and the SA
Diagram 3.90

At the same time, SA3 is formed by Barnarashy to the north and the cairn of Doomore, situated on the summit of the Ox Mountain at an altitude of 272m, to the southwest of the peninsula with the cairn of Listoghil of Carrowmore lying in the middle. The angle bisects at the Great Cairn of Queen Maeve of Knocknarea (diagrams 3.91 and 3.92).

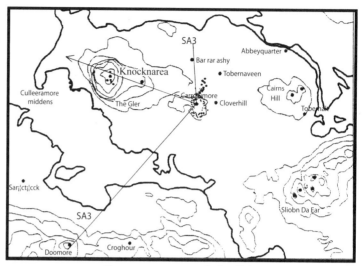

Carrowmore and the SA
Diagram 3.91

Looking Northeast from Doomore Cairn across Ball Sodare Bay to Knocknarea
Diagram 3.92

The Fourth SA (SA4) is formed along the range of the Ox Mountain between the boulder circle of Barnabrack, located on a low hill above Beltra to the west, and the Neolithic cairn of Silabh Da Ear to the southeast. Another Neolithic cairn, Croghour, located on a cone-shaped peak 170m high on the Ox Mountains with a small cairn of 7m in diameter, lies in the middle (diagram 3.93). It bisects at a cairn lying on the eastern shoulder of the Knocknarea Mountain (source: carrowkeel.com).

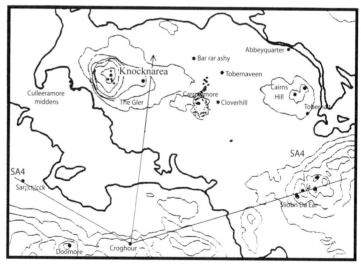

SA over Carrowmore
Diagram 3.93

The Great Cairn of Queen Maeve of Knocknarea and the large central cairn of Listoghil of Carrowmore form another SA with the Neolithic cemetery of Carrowkeel.

Carrowkeel and the SA

The cemetery of Carrowkeel is another sacred center of ancient Ireland with monuments situated along the limestone plateaus of the Bricklieve Mountains. The Carrowkeel cairns are made of local limestone and like other famous sites of the island, they occupy commanding positions. There are at least fourteen cairns on several ridges. Each cairn is identified by a different letter (diagrams 3.94 and 3.95) (from carrowkeel.com).

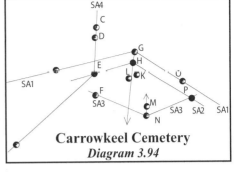

Carrowkeel Cemetery
Diagram 3.94

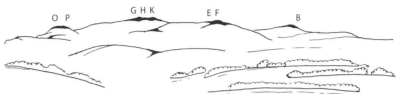

Looking to Carrowkeel, with Various "Stations" over the Horizon
Diagram 3.95

Some do not appear to have any kind of structure under the cairn. Freestanding orthostats are found inside most of the cairns (diagram 3.96) and they probably served as dry cell batteries to the builders. Some of the cairns are passage tombs. Two of them, like the mound of Newgrange and Knowth, are classic cruciform-chambered passage tombs with corbelled roofs.

Evidence suggests the cemetery was built between 3800 and 3300 B.C. Cairn G contains an excellent intact chamber and a Newgrange roof box structure at the entrance (diagram 3.97). Does it imply that the cairn once served the same function as Newgrange?

Orthostats inside Cairn G: Neolithic Dry Cell Batteries
Diagram 3.96

Roof-slab of Cairn K, Carrowkeel: As with the Great Mound of Newgrange, the Opening Allowed Megalights to Travel In and Out of the Cairn
Diagram 3.97

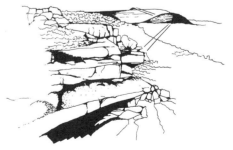

Cairn K with Roof-slabs, Viewing Cairn L (Cairn B on the Horizon with Megalight Connection)
Diagram 3.98

The relation among Carrowmore, Carrowkeel, Loughcrew, and the Boyne Valley can be understood with the application of the SA. Diagram 3.99 shows that Queen Maeve's cairn of Knocknarea and Carrowkeel form SA1 with Carrowmore in the middle. The cemetery of Carrowmore and Loughcrew form SA2 with Carrowkeel in the middle. Loughcrew and the burial chamber of Fourknocks form SA3 with the Boyne Valley in the middle. Tara Hill lies close to their angle bisector. With so many important stations here, was ancient Ireland the capital of our Stone Age super civilization?

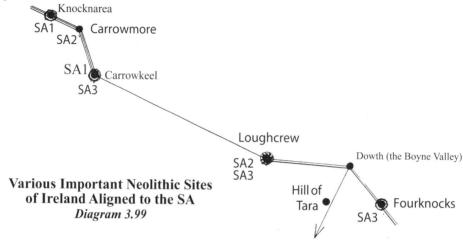

**Various Important Neolithic Sites
of Ireland Aligned to the SA**
Diagram 3.99

Court Tombs of Creevykeel

Of all the Neolithic monuments, court tombs are the earliest type of stone tomb found in Ireland. It is generally believed they were built 500 years earlier than those of Boyne Valley. There are more than 400 court tombs in the county of Silgo, North Ireland. The cairn has a rounded forecourt leading to a flat-roofed gallery. Most of the court tombs are 25m long and 15m wide. The internal chambers and court are made of upright orthostats with a lintel across the top. The court walls are further strengthened by sections of dry-walling from a post-and-panel construction. Such a forecourt might contain special acoustical properties important in rituals (megalithic.co.uk).

There are two central stones guarding the internal gallery and compartments. Burials are found inside these compartments but experts suggest they were deposited secondarily (Harbison 1988). The primary function for these 400 tombs remains a mystery for the archaeologists. What the experts do know is these tombs are three miles apart from each other.

The three ancient graves of Creevykeel are impressive examples of the court tombs dotted around the region. Diagram 3.100 illustrates the general layout of a typical court cairn containing a large forecourt linked to two burial chambers through a large gallery.

The cairn is trapezoidal in shape and is retained by a dry stone wall of upright slabs 1m to 2m high. These lining stones vary in length. The entrance to the main court is an orthostat-lined passage 1m wide and 4.5m long. The oval-shaped court is 15m × 9m and is lined with upright orthostats. About fifty people can stand in the court area. This is why experts speculate the building was once a ritual center. Near the center of the court is a shallow sand-filled pit. A gallery of standing stones, 9m long and 3m wide, connect the forecourt and the two compartments. The front compartment is 4.5m across and the rear one is about 3.5m. Three subsidiary compartments are found on the north and south sides of the cairn. There are pits inside the two chambers of the court cairn. Three subsidiary chambers are found on the north and south sides of the cairn.

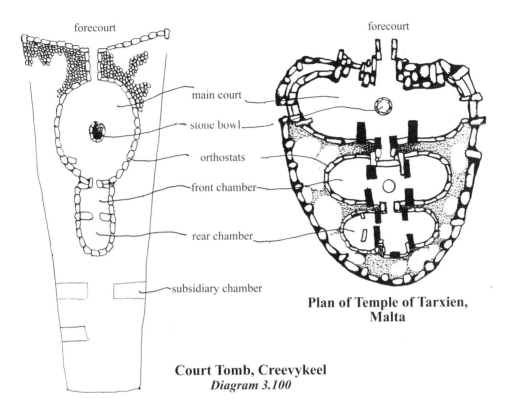

forecourt

main court

stone bowl

orthostats

front chamber

rear chamber

subsidiary chamber

Plan of Temple of Tarxien, Malta

forecourt

Court Tomb, Creevykeel
Diagram 3.100

With regard to the special layout of the court cairn, the cup and ring carvings on the Knowth stone basin and on slab Co.1/C7 of Newgrange come to mind. To a certain extent, the basic design of the court cairns of Creevykeel is the same as the two carvings mentioned above (diagram 3.101). The difference is the absence of two circular objects carved inside the drawings. The two circular dots represent two conical devices the builders once placed in the shallow pit of the court and the gallery between two burial chambers. Like the other missing devices, they projected rows of megalights to the surrounding orthostats. The builders' machinery recharged outside the façade, to the southeast.

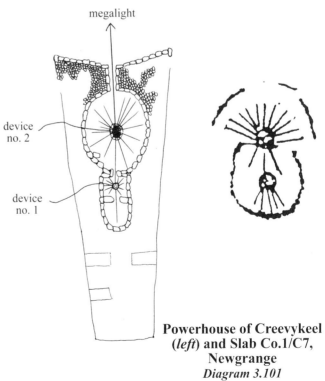

megalight

device no. 2

device no. 1

Powerhouse of Creevykeel (*left*) and Slab Co.1/C7, Newgrange
Diagram 3.101

Center-court Tombs and the SA

Power Generator of Ballyglass
Diagram 3.102

Ballyglass of County Mayo is a typical example of a center-court tomb of Ireland (diagram 3.103a and b). The tomb is 27m long with a western entrance leading to an elongated central court 12m long by 7m wide. A pair of twin-chambered galleries, formed by standing slabs and lintels, has been constructed at each end. The two rear side chambers form a perfect SA with the western entrance of the tomb. Similar planning has been found inside the temples of Malta, with trilithon altars and curved walls (discussed in Chapter 5).

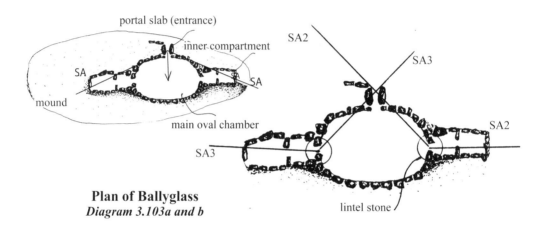

Plan of Ballyglass
Diagram 3.103a and b

Other types of court tombs are shown below. The single court tomb at Browndod, County Antrim, and dual court tomb at Ballywholan, County Tyrone, are another two versions of power stations. Conical device no. 1 was placed inside the compartments of these tombs and conical device no. 2 was put at the center of the forecourt outside the tomb (diagram 3.104a and b). Megalights were produced to generate energy from standing slabs nearby.

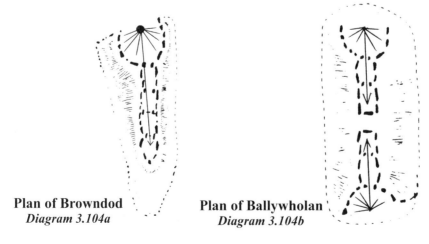

Plan of Browndod
Diagram 3.104a

Plan of Ballywholan
Diagram 3.104b

The full end court at Malinmore, County Donegal, is the most complicated court tomb around the region. A pair of portal stones opens the tomb from the east and connects to an oval chamber. Two compartments have been constructed at the eastern part of the chamber, one at each side of the portal entrance. Another two pairs of twin-compartmented galleries have been built at the far west of the chamber. Several sets of SAs make Malinmore one of the most sophisticated court tomb–type powerhouses in my study (diagrams 3.105a and b).

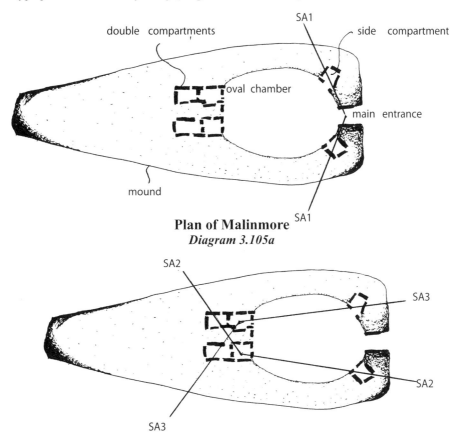

Plan of Malinmore
Diagram 3.105a

SAs Formed by Various Compartments, Malinmore
Diagram 3.105b

Beaghmore Megalithic Complex

"Mysteries exist at Beaghmore…. The distorted circles are enigmatic, their interrelated circles, cairns and rows having no obvious patterns."

—Aubrey Burl, 2000

Beaghmore Complex overlooks a wide valley to the northeast in County Tyrone, Northern Ireland. The county is replete with stone monuments. Almost all its sixty-one known circles are arranged in pairs or multiples of cairns and stone rows. The most famous example is at Beaghmore, with a total of seven semicircles with a mean diameter of 13.2m (Burl 2000), six of which are paired along with many cairns and stone rows within an area 21m in diameter. As shown in the site plan (diagram 3.106), three small cairns lie sandwiched between a pair of irregular rings. These unusual rings are composed of more than fifty stones. Bronze Age urns and food vessels have been excavated here. Stone rows fan out from the cairn, running from southwest to northeast, believed to be used for recording the movement of celestial bodies. However Archie Thom, who had examined these rows, suggested that they offered no astronomical alignments.

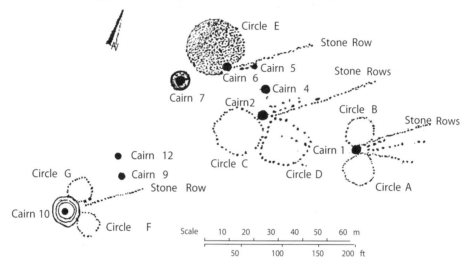

Plan of Beaghmore Megalithic Complex
Diagram 3.106

Cairn 1 lies between the two rings (Circle A and B) 11m and 10m in diameter respectively. Four stone rows radiate from Cairn 1 towards the northeast, followed by another short row of stones. Another medium row lies to the south and finishes in a low row of stones (diagrams 3.107a and b).

Circle A (*left*) and Circle B, with Cairn 1 in the Middle and Four Stone Rows in Different Sizes in the Foreground (Looking West)
Diagram 3.107a

The Secret of Cairn 1: Power Generator of the Builders
Diagram 3.107b

Cairn 2 lies west between Ring C and D along an east-west axis. It is similar to Cairn 1 and its two rings. The cairn contains an empty cist. Circles C and D are 18m and 16m in diameter, respectively. Two stone rows, one short and high and the other long and low, run from the cairn towards the northeast, guiding visitors away from the centre of this mystic zone.

Cairn 10

Circle F (*right*), with a Pair of Huge Portal Slabs, and Circle G, with Cairn 10 Lying in the Middle (Looking West)
Diagram 3.108

The final pair of rings (Circles F and G) lies southwest of the site, with Cairn 10 in the middle (diagram 3.108 and 3.109). The cairn, surrounded by a ditch and an external bank, has an empty cist inside. A single, long row of low stones run northeast from the cairn. These stone circles appear rather irregular and experts agree they were erected according to geometric principles.

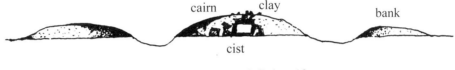

cairn   clay   bank

cist

Cross-section of Cairn 10
Diagram 3.109

Carbon dating of the hearths and cists place them around 2900–2600 B.C. The real function of the complex is still a mystery, but it is suggested the site could have been a focal point for religious or social purposes. Others speculate it was an ancient observatory in which the stone rows correspond to a point on the horizon where a star rose or fell on some significant day. Other suggestions include an attempt to restore fertility to the area, with the embryo stone circle sided with phallic stone rows.

The cairns of the complex, especially the three sandwiched between the stone rings (numbered 1, 2, and 10), form a perfect SA (SA1) as shown in diagram 3.110. It is my speculation that each of these cairns, reacting with its two sandwiched rings, forms an individual power generator. A larger and probably more powerful one was constructed by linking the three cairns by megalights.

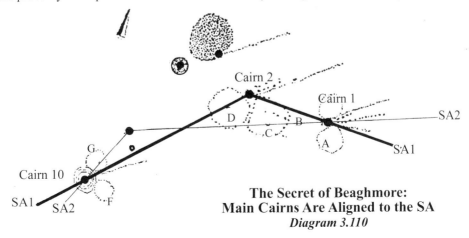

Cairn 2   Cairn 1   SA2

D   B

C   A

G   SA1

Cairn 10

SA1   SA2   F

**The Secret of Beaghmore:
Main Cairns Are Aligned to the SA**
Diagram 3.110

Cairn 1 appears to have some importance, as it forms several SAs (SA1 to SA4) with the surrounding cairns and rings (diagram 3.111).

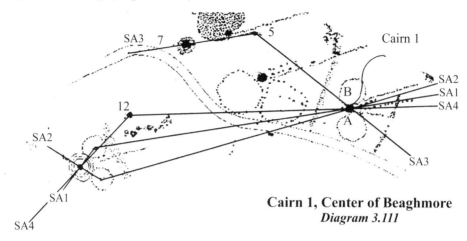

Cairn 1, Center of Beaghmore
Diagram 3.111

In addition, other cairns and stone rings form several SAs within the complex (diagrams 3.112a to e):

SA4: Cairn 9 and Cairn 10 form an SA with Circle G in the middle. The angle bisector is between two large portal slabs (diagram 3.112a). Can it be a coincidence?
SA5: Cairn 1 and Cairn 7 form an SA with Cairn 5 in the middle. It bisects at the center of Circle D (3.112b).
SA6: Cairn 4 and the center of Circle C with Cairn 2 in the middle. A stone row lies exactly on the angle bisector (3.112c).
SA7: Cairn 10 forms an SA with the stones from Circle F and G. Again, a stone row lies exactly on the angle bisector (3.112d).

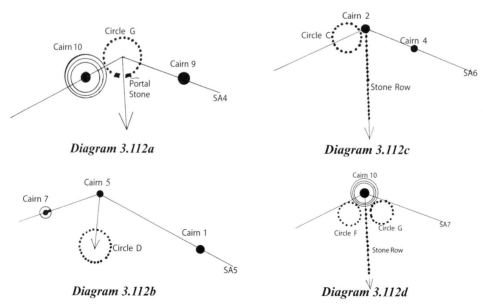

Diagram 3.112a

Diagram 3.112c

Diagram 3.112b

Diagram 3.112d

An SA is formed by Circles C, D, and F, and Circles A, C, and F, respectively (3.112e).

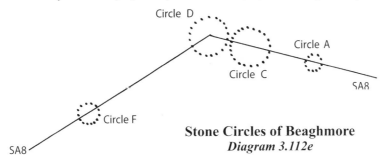

Stone Circles of Beaghmore
Diagram 3.112e

The Ballynahatty Complex and the SA

The Ballynahatty Complex is located on an irregular plateau of the Lagan Valley in Northern Ireland just under 7km from the center of Belfast. The main features of the site include a large earthen enclosure called the Giant's Ring. A partially destroyed passage grave lies close to the center. Two timber circles stand to the north, and an isolated standing stone sits to the northwest. Cemeteries dot the region (diagram 3.113). Believed to be an important ritual or cult center, it became a popular venue for horse races during the eighteenth century.

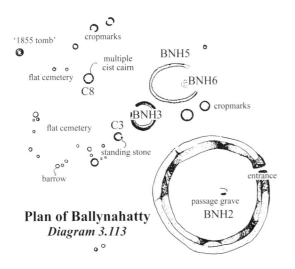

Plan of Ballynahatty
Diagram 3.113

The enclosure is spacious enough to house all the inner rings of Stonehenge. But to everyone's surprise, inside the ring lies a tiny mound (BNH2) with five orthostats forming a chamber of 1.5m across (Barrie Hartwell). These stones must have been deliberately brought to the site, as they are not commonly found around the region. A passage orientated to the northwest was constructed at the site. Experts suggest the passage tomb was the earliest structure of the site and can be dated back to the late Neolithic age.

Two circles (BNH5 and BNH6) of timber post holes for palisaded enclosures are situated on the edge 100m north of the ring. Ballynahatty 5 consists of an enclosure of timber posts 100m × 7m. There is a sub-rectangular chamber 80cm by 40cm excavated in the center of the enclosure. Another circle, BNH6, formed by rings of timber holes with a diameter of 16m lies at the eastern end of BNH5. Barrie Hartwell strongly suggests they were once mortuary structures with ritual and ceremonial functions (Barrie Hartwell, "The Ballynahatty Complex" in *Prehistoric Ritual and Religion,* ed. Alex Gilson and Derek Simpson, pp. 32–44). The complex also included two flat cemeteries with stone cists in the middle. Excavators found a cemetery mound (C8) containing five stone cists with urns and other grave goods. A standing stone was placed at the eastern periphery of another mound (C3). Several SAs are derived from the passage tomb of the Giant's Ring (diagram 3.114):

SA1: northwest entrance of the passage grave–tomb C1–multiple cist cairn of C8
SA2: northwest entrance of the passage grave–tomb C2–center of BNH5 and tomb C5
SA3: northwest entrance of the passage grave–center of BNH5–tomb C4
SA4: northwest entrance of the passage grave–tomb C3–tomb C2, it bisects at the timber circle of BNH6

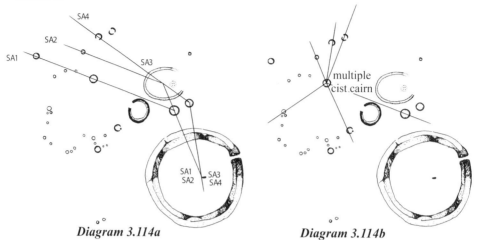

Diagram 3.114a   *Diagram 3.114b*

The multiple cist cairn (C8), which was also an important structure, was deliberately placed at the intersection of several sets of SAs (diagram 3.114b):

SA5: tomb C3–tomb C6
SA6: tomb C2–tomb C7
SA7: tomb C1–tomb C4
SA8: tomb C2–tomb C7

Lough Gur: Sacred Home of Gods and Goddesses

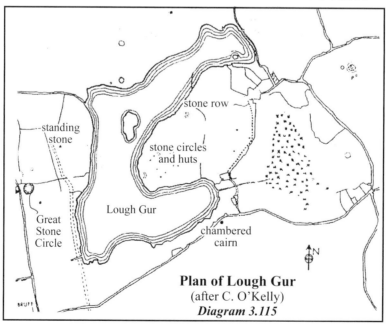

Plan of Lough Gur
(after C. O'Kelly)
Diagram 3.115

Lough Gur, a late Neolithic and early Bronze Age complex, lies southeast of Limerick. There are over thirty ancient sites and monuments in the area comprising stone circles, standing stones, ring forts, and megalithic wedge-tombs dating back to 2000 B.C. Lough Gur is a small horseshoe-shaped lake (lough) nestled among limestone hills. Oral tradition tells us the lake was under the protection of the goddess Aine who made it. According to the legend, Aine looked at the water and caused it to sparkle to facilitate her entry into another "world." The lough is her divine blood and the world is her extended body (Michael Dames, *Mythic Ireland*, 1996).

There is a large triangular peninsula known as Knockadoon lying east of the lake. A great concentration of prehistoric remains were found here. According to Professor C. O'Kelly, sites A, B, and C are probably Neolithic houses with postholes and a central hearth. Site D is a stone circle and megalith E is multiple stone avenues forming an SA. Site J is another stone circle 30 m in diameter with two concentric rings of standing stones. Site K is the largest stone circle in Knockadoon with an overall diameter of 31m. It is made up of two concentric rings with an east entrance (C. O'Kelly 1985). Other monuments (sites F, G, H, I, L, M, and 10, 11, and 12) are unknown.

The Giant's Grave or Bed of Dermont and Graney, lying south of Knockadoon, is one of the most well preserved wedge-tombs of about 400 in total concentrated mainly in northwest Ireland. They are believed to have been built between 2000 to 1500 B.C. and originated from Brittany in France. The rectangular main chamber still retains the roof stones and the double walling remains intact. The tomb with the northeast–southwest orientation has a 9m portico at the southwest end. The chamber is no more than 70cm tall at the northeast end, rising to 1.2m at the southwest. It is set into a wedge-shaped cairn bound by standing stones serving as kerbstones. Some stones are cup-marked. Another semicircle of low-lying stones was constructed in front of the main entrance.

**Wedge-tomb of the Giant's Grave,
Lough Gur (From Behind)**
Diagram 3.116

Obviously, a structure formed by a doubled horseshoe on one hand and a semicircle on the other is the master plan of a power house clearly shown in the Solar God carving of Co.1/C7 at Newgrange. I believe it reveals the mystery of the wedge tombs. The diagram below is the layout of Island court tomb in County Cork. Its design mirrors Stonehenge but is smaller in size. The outer ring of timber holes directly corresponds to the lintel sarsen stone circle of Stonehenge (diagrams 3.117 and 3.118).

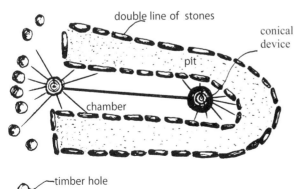

double line of stones

conical device

pit

chamber

timber hole

**Wedge-tomb at Island and
the Twin-device Energy
Mechanism**
Diagram 3.117

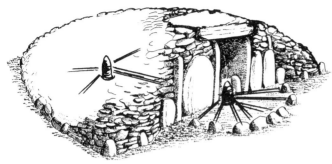

Reconstruction of the Wedge-tomb at Island, County Cork
Diagram 3.118

There are more than 200 stone circles in Ireland and most of them are concentrated in the southwestern counties of Cork and Kerry. The Great Stone Circle of Lough Gur, sometimes known as the "race course," lies west of the sacred lake. The circle is the largest in Ireland with a diameter of 55–60m surrounded by a bank 4m deep and 2m high. An entrance passage, guarded by two giant slabs, opens to the northeast and cuts through the embankment (diagram 3.119). The circle, ringed by 113 megaliths, was erected round 2500 B.C. Burl suggests that ten spots for uprights 1.9m in height were marked in order to construct the Great Circle with short slabs (1m). Four of the upright slabs actually served as the Station Stones (91 to 94) of Stonehenge, bisecting at the main entrance (northeast).

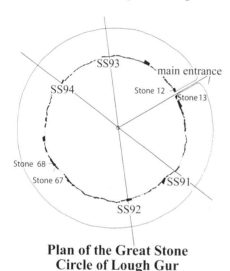

Plan of the Great Stone Circle of Lough Gur
Diagram 3.119

Portal Tombs: Dry Cell Batteries of the Gods

Portal tombs, probably the simplest form of grave, dating back to 4000 B.C., are the most widespread monuments in Ireland. These tombs consist of three to seven uprights covered by an enormous roofing capstone that slopes downward to the back. For centuries, these freestanding monuments have been regarded as stone tables and altars. Today it is generally accepted they were used for burial purposes. Occasionally the portal stones had a further stone flanking them externally, acting like a small forecourt in front of the tomb entrance (Harbison 1988).

A Megalithic Calendar

It appears these strange visitors knew more about our planet than we do. Our Earth is a gigantic power station emanating powerful magnetic energy. Our mysterious visitors knew this. This is why they came here. This is why megaliths dot our planet.

Using their sophisticated technology, they identified specific points of concentrated energy running through the Earth. Places such as the cemeteries of Loughcrew, the Boyne Valley, and Tara Hill are powerful nexus points of these energy streams. In order to tap this power, a wide variety of megalithic structures serving as power conductors were erected on these nexus points. Like some God-sized plug fitting into a wall socket, with great precision the power was released.

Instead of housing dead bodies, those passage-chambered mounds, tabled dolmens, and earthen enclosures were once equipped with orthostats (Neolithic "dry cell batteries") and advanced conical devices capable of generating megalights to heat up the surrounding stones. Thousands of years later our forebears stumbled upon these abandoned megaliths and used them to house their dead. Megalithism continues as an unsolved enigma when most of our modern-day archaeologists and historians, deeply conditioned by scientific training and problem solving techniques, are actually misled by the silent remains of these ancient structures. The so-called "nothing but tombs" theory became the main stream of academic thought for more than a century. However, when the SA is applied to megalithism, a curious pattern emerges. It's time to revise our concept of prehistory.

The late Neolithic is a period decisive in the development of human civilization. However, it left us nothing but a vast variety of megalithic structures. The portal tombs (4000–3000 B.C.), court tombs (3800–3500 B.C.), wedge tombs (3300–2500 B.C.), passage mounds (3300–2500 B.C.), stone circles (Lough Gur, 2500 B.C.), the earth enclosures (Navan, 1000–700 B.C.) were all constructed in Ireland, the last land colonized by humans in Neolithic times. Unknown to our distant ancestors, these power houses served as a calendar, recording the builders' repeated visits to our planet over different periods of time.

passage mound 1: dry cell battery of the builders?

passage mound 3: major powerhouse of the builders?

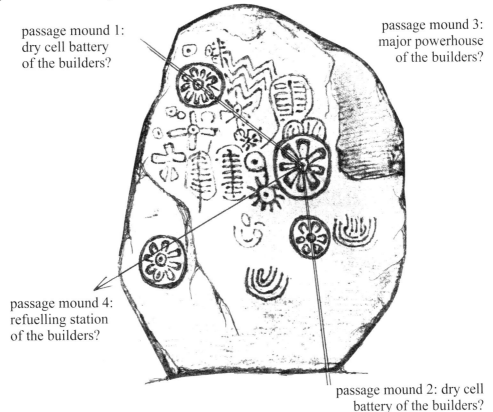

passage mound 4: refuelling station of the builders?

passage mound 2: dry cell battery of the builders?

The "Equinox Stone"
The highly decorated backstone (Stone 14) at the innermost recess of Cairn T, Loughcrew, shows the real secret of the site. Three large "sunwheels," probably symbolizing passage graves such as Cairns D, G, and I, form an SA. Its angle bisects at Cairn E.
(drawing from John Michell, 1989, p. 96)
Diagram 3.120

NEOLITHIC IRELAND

Explaining the Dagda Skirt Slab of Loughcrew
Diagram 3.121a and b

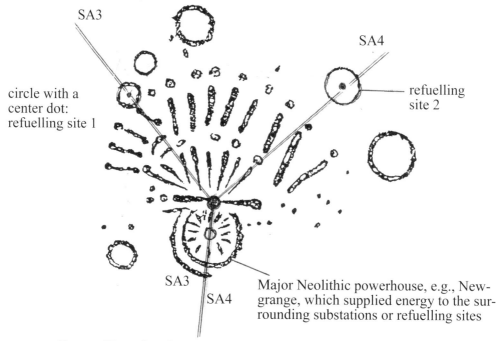

SA3

SA4

circle with a
center dot:
refuelling site 1

refuelling
site 2

SA3

SA4

Major Neolithic powerhouse, e.g., Newgrange, which supplied energy to the surrounding substations or refuelling sites

Energy Transfers from Newgrange to nearby Refuelling Sites
Diagram 3.121a

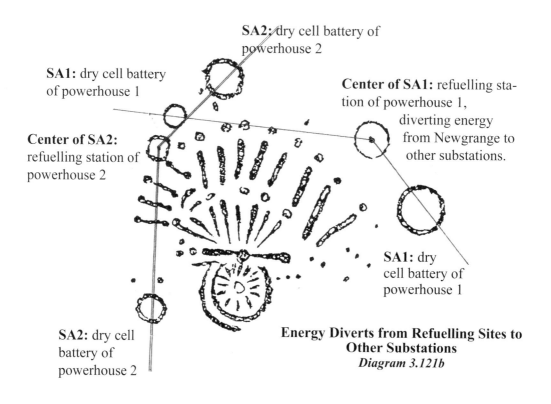

SA2: dry cell battery of
powerhouse 2

SA1: dry cell battery
of powerhouse 1

Center of SA1: refuelling station of powerhouse 1,
diverting energy
from Newgrange to
other substations.

Center of SA2:
refuelling station of
powerhouse 2

SA1: dry
cell battery of
powerhouse 1

SA2: dry cell
battery of
powerhouse 2

**Energy Diverts from Refuelling Sites to
Other Substations**
Diagram 3.121b

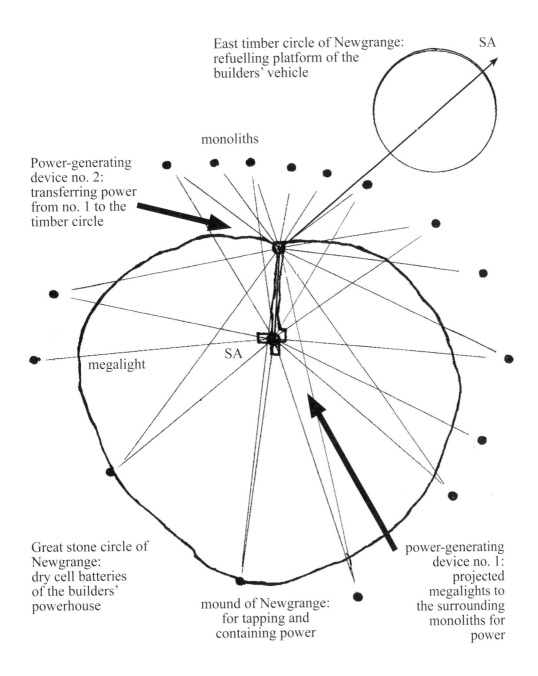

East timber circle of Newgrange:
refuelling platform of the
builders' vehicle

SA

monoliths

Power-generating
device no. 2:
transferring power
from no. 1 to the
timber circle

megalight

SA

Great stone circle of
Newgrange:
dry cell batteries
of the builders'
powerhouse

power-generating
device no. 1:
projected
megalights to
the surrounding
monoliths for
power

mound of Newgrange:
for tapping and
containing power

**The Twin-device Powerhouse of
Newgrange, 3200 B.C.**
(after O'Kelly)
Diagram 3.122

Chapter 4
Neolithic Brittany

Its Celtic Origin

"(Brittany is) a province of the supernatural...."

—Breton poet Xavier Grall

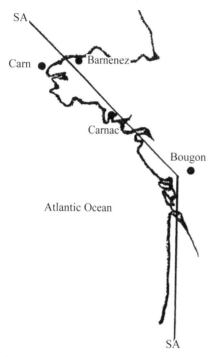

Major Prehistoric Sites of Brittany
Diagram 4.01

Brittany of France, covering an area of around 34,000 sq km, is regarded as the "wonderland of megalithism" (Burl 1985) not because of the scale of its monuments, but because of the high concentration and vast varieties of such monuments within a relatively small area. Brittany is located at the extreme west of France and is isolated from the rest of the country by its rocky peninsula, measuring 250km long and 100km wide. Its history is closely related to the Celts, the first immigrants who raised megaliths throughout the region. Even today, the indigenous language of Brittany is Breton, a Celtic language closely related to Welsh; and its textiles are decorated with Celtic art. The Festival Interceltique, the biggest cultural festival in the whole of France, celebrates music and dance of Celtic origin.

The Stone Age people of Brittany certainly found the most suitable place and materials to build their masterpieces, as the interior plateau of Brittany is made of ancient rocks such as schists, quartzites, and sandstones. Around 6000–2000 B.C., these megalith builders, with an average life expectancy of no more than thirty years, surpassed their rivals by erecting huge monoliths, some of which weigh more than 300 tons—the largest and heaviest in Europe. Lying next to them are smaller freestanding stones, thousands in number and lined up in several rows, several hundreds meters wide and some thousands of meters long. Like Newgrange, Brittany is also dotted with passage graves formed by mysterious carved slabs.

The function of these megalithic structures, which is parallel to that of contemporary Ireland, has aroused controversy among the experts. Theories ranging from astronomical purposes, religious practices, to serving as territorial markers are suggested but only result in greater controversy. But the principle of SA can perfectly explain these monuments. Undoubtedly, Neolithic Brittany, with the construction of all these powerhouses, certainly used to be an important center of the unknown travelers.

Long Tumuli: First Power Generators

In the middle of the fifth millennium B.C., millennia before the first pyramid, Neolithic builders in Brittany and west-central France were constructing huge tumuli with manmade ditches. Most of the tumuli are long and low structures, rectangular or trapezoidal in shape, built of earth mixed with stones and bordered by a line of slabs on the ground (diagram 4.02). All the tumuli are more or less oriented towards the east. Some contain one or two tombs with coffers or cists to form subterranean graves. Coffers vary in size and shape in different regions. It might have been due to the materials available in different regions. Some are built of wood, others earth, flint, or drystone to form corbelled ceilings. Experts speculate that they are the transitional models from the simple grave to the first passage grave.

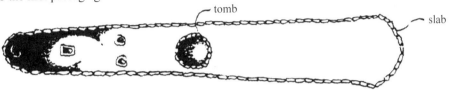

Keriescan Tumuli, Carnac
Diagram 4.02

In some earlier tumuli which have no entry passages, like that of St-Martin-la-Rivière (Vienne, France), coffers are built into a pit below the ground. Others, like the tumulus complex of Les Fouillages (Guernsey), the long tumuli of St-Michel and Moustoir at Carnac (Morbihan), Manè-er-Hroeck and Manè-Lud (Locmariaquer), and Tumiac (Arzon), have coffers built at ground level and protected by mounds surrounded by large blocks. In tumuli of the later period, like the tumulus of Barnenez, round burial chambers made of large slabs with a passageway accessible to the outside replace the coffers. Diagram 4.03 shows the distribution of the main Neolithic tumuli in France at the end of the fifth millennium B.C. (Boujot and Cassen 1993).

Distribution of the Main Neolithic Tumuli in Northwest France, 5000 B.C. (Boujot and Cassen 1993)
Diagram 4.03

The most spectacular tumuli around the region is located at the Passy site, about seventy miles southeast of Paris, which has been carbon dated to between 4463 and 4279 B.C. They are wedge in shape, 15m to 36m long. The longest one is monument 5, which consists of two parallel ditches 6m apart, each more than 257m long (diagram 4.04). One end of the ditches terminates in a circular area some 45m in diameter.

Monument 5 of Passy
Diagram 4.04

In the Gulf of Morbihan, the most famous earth mound is the Saint-Michel tumulus with an impressive size of about 113m long, 45m wide, and 9m high. Further to the south are other large, elongated stone mounds. The one in the community of Tuson measures 136m long, 18m wide, and almost 4m high.

The tumulus of Bougon (Deux-Sèvres) which dates from around 5000 B.C., and occupies about five acres of land, consists of five juxtaposed monuments built over the centuries. At the tumulus of Petit Mont (Arzon), the initial monument is a mound with a central ditch 53m in length and dates from around 4500 B.C. A rectangular cairn was built on the ditch afterwards. The Locmariaquer complex in Brittany is about 500m long; if the extended, angled chamber of Pierres Plates is included, the length amounts to 1515m.

These major megalithic complexes characterized by exceptionally long earth mounds form three sets of SAs with La Motte-des-Justices in the center (diagram 4.05). Instead of housing their owners, the central cists of these powerhouses were installed with some superior technology for energy.

Long Tumuli of La Motte-des-Justices
Diagram 4.05

SA1 with Petit Mont, Carnac, Locmariaquer Complex, and Passy site; with Rots Complex along the angle bisector (diagrams 4.06 and 4.07).

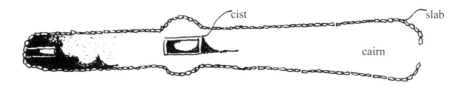

cist

slab

cairn

Long Tumuli of Rots
Diagram 4.06

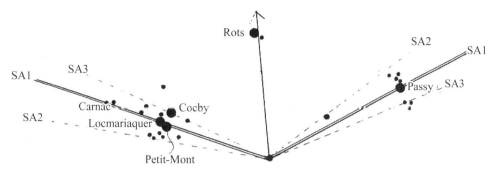

Major Prehistoric Sites of France, with La Motte-des-Justices as the Center
Diagram 4.07

SA2 with La Tombe de Demoiselle, Les Moindreaux Complex, and Rots Complex; with Tumiac, Petit Mont, Carnac, and Locmariquer complexes along the angle bisector (diagrams 4.08 and 4.09).

Long Tumuli of Les Moindreaux
Diagram 4.08

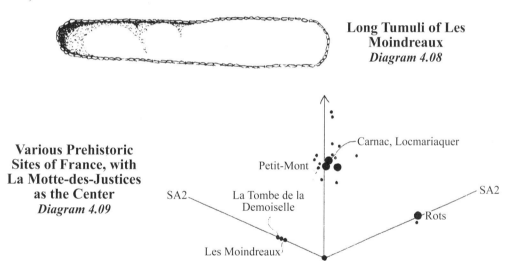

Various Prehistoric Sites of France, with La Motte-des-Justices as the Center
Diagram 4.09

SA3 with Passy site and Le Planti, Le Bernet Complex, with St Martin-la-Riviere along the angle bisector (diagram 4.10).

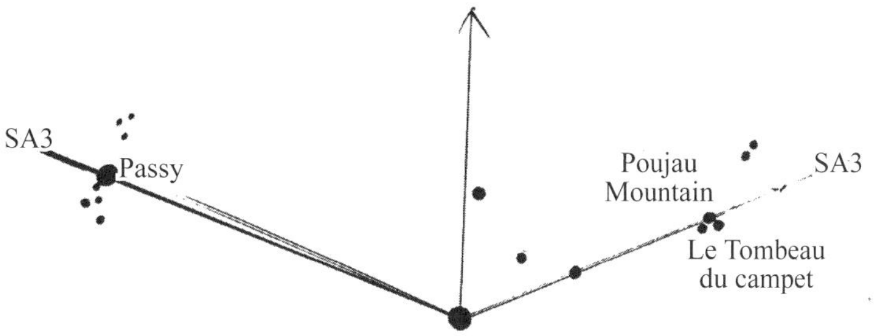

Various Prehistoric Sites of France, with La Motte-des-Justices as the Center
Diagram 4.10

Ultimate Function of Passage Graves and Messages of Gavrinis

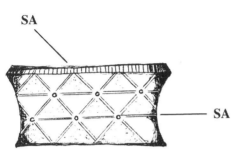

Passage-grave Pottery of Chassey: "Multiple Triangles" Style
Diagram 4.11

Passage graves were regarded as the direct successors of the long tumuli. Probably inspired by and improved from the tumuli, they have drystone-walled long passages, which are capped with heavy flat slabs. The passage leads to a central circular corbelled chamber. According to Burl (1985), most of the graves were deliberately constructed on crests or high places with an entrance facing southeast, which suggests an astronomical purpose. Many graves are decorated with mysterious carvings such as axes with triangles, zigzags, and meanders, both along their long passages and inside their chambers.

According to Burl (1985), there is a lot of Neolithic pottery found inside these passage-graves. They consists of shouldered, round-bottomed bowls decorated with grooved and dotted geometrical patterns of triangles, lozenges, squares, and semicircles. The so-called "multiple triangles" decorations (Burl 1985), which form several angles of 135 degrees, actually describe the builders' energy mechanism in which rows of megalights were generated for power (diagram 4.11).

Art Gallery of Gavrinis

"That the men who carved them must have associated them with some idea, a meaning, and that this is more than just an ornament, appears to me beyond any doubt; but as for the meaning, who today can hope to discover it?"

—Prosper Mérimée, *Notes on a Monument on the Isle of Gavrinis* (1858)

Gavrinis passage grave, one of Brittany's hundreds of megalithic monuments, is certainly the finest of them all. It is located on a small island in the Gulf of Morbihan with a history of about 6,000 years. Experts suggest Gavrinis was connected with Carnac and Locmariequer—the very heart of Megalithism when it was first completed (S. Dyer). Like other mounds in Northern Europe, Gavrinis is piled up with large slabs to form a truncated step-like pyramid, surrounded by inward-bending drystone walls, and then covered with earth (diagram 4.12). The mound is now about 50m in diameter by 7m in height with a quadrangular cairn in the center.

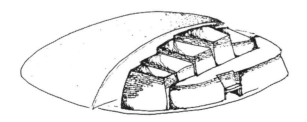

Passage-grave of Gavrinis
Diagram 4.12

Its passage is about 0.8m width and 1.5m high, consisting of twelve pillars on the northeast side and eleven on the southwest side. Nine lintels rest on the drystone walling where the passage floor is slabbed. Being the longest in Brittany and having an entrance on the southeast, it has a single-chambered passage that is probably aligned to the midwinter sunrise (diagram 4.13). As a matter of fact, the rays of sunlight are blocked off by the entrance lintel before reaching the very rear of the chamber, suggesting no real "astronomical" positioning (after Z. Le Rouzic).

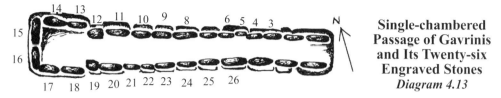

Single-chambered Passage of Gavrinis and Its Twenty-six Engraved Stones
Diagram 4.13

What makes Gavrinis special is its spectacularly carved stones that line the interior passageway and rear chamber. Twenty-three out of the twenty-nine uprights have been heavily carved with motifs in the shape of rainbows, crooks, axe-heads, bucklers, serpents, spirals, suns, zigzags, shields, daggers, and the letter "V," so no empty space is left between them. Similar carvings are found in Boyne Valley of Ireland, which suggests a connection between them. Given that these mysterious symbols have similar styles with united themes, experts speculate they bear messages from the megalithic builders.

Similar to Newgrange, Gavrinis is a selection of quartz stones deliberately placed inside a passageway and chamber. Carvings are found not just throughout the whole interiors, including both the passageway and the chamber, but also on the reverse sides of the stones, hidden from view. It proves that these slabs were carved before being placed inside to form the walls of Gavrinis. It's strange but logical to say the builders might probably construct the mound solely to house and display these slabs with their messages, as the square chamber is surprisingly small (2.55m × 2.4m) for dwelling (culture.gouv.fr). The mound was so meticulously built that it is still waterproof. It is a superb megalithic safe housing a secret waiting for someone to open.

The carvings are bizarre with their regularity and unusual arrangements. Some consider these a series of inscriptions in cuneiform characters. Its phallic iconography suggests the emblems of male power and female deity. No matter what the meaning behind these carvings is, Gavrinis certainly represents the peak of Morbihan art.

With what happened in Neolithic Ireland, I suggest that the carvings of Gavrinis actually tell and explain the energy mechanism of an advanced intelligence, which once took our planet as their center of power supply around 5,000 years ago. They are simply messages left by that civilization for unknown reasons. Why did they deliberately store their advanced technology inside the mound? Was it knowledge left for our future generations or for theirs?

Megalights inside Gavrinis

Inside the Dagda Skirt slab of Loughcrew and the Solar God of the Co.1/C7 slab, the twin-device and the surroundings stones are connected by rows of dagger-like objects which I call megalights. These light beams, described as round-bottomed at one end and pointed at the other, are produced and projected by a mysterious conical device. They probably serve as electric wires for tapping and transferring energy under our Earth. What actually are these daggerlike objects that seem to have dominated the whole picture of the Neolithic drawings? The answer has been kept in Gavrinis for more than 5,500 years.

On its carved slab no. 21 (diagram 4.14), there are a number of elongated triangular pattern carvings, like wedges, Celtic axes (which have a round bottom at one end and a pointed one at the other), or axes with pointed handles and wide blades. These wedges point in two opposite directions. Some point to upward while others point downward. Many are paired. As shown in the slab, these round wedges are produced or projected by a set of concentric circles below. Carved in such large numbers and intensity, these wedge patterns are rarely found in Brittany. Without doubt, the carved slab becomes the icon of Gavrinis. Interpreted as solar rays, they further strengthen the astronomical hypothesis of the site.

Dagger-like Carvings of Gavrinis: The Neolithic Megalights (Mohen 1999, p. 96)
Diagram 4.14

But the wedges of Gavrinis are no different from the daggerlike carvings of Neolithic Ireland, as both are designed with a round base and a pointed tip. The two small mysterious dots in the Dagda skirt and Solar God—the twin-device capable of generating megalights—are now expressed in the form of a set of concentric circles in Gavrinis. It is a true description of the conical device when viewed horizontally. This famous Gavrinis slab actually describes a mysterious device projecting rows of megalights to a slab nearby, probably onto the iconic wedge slab itself. As with the Solar God of Newgrange, there are nineteen wedges/daggers carved on the Gavrinis slab, and the same number of bluestones forms the horseshoe of Stonehenge. These powerful light beams were supposedly generated by a mysterious circular device that was once placed inside all these megalithic powerhouses. What actually was this device that tapped our energy and turned our Earth into the power station of a præternatural intelligence? To many people's surprise, the image of this mysterious super device can be found all over our prehistoric world.

Conical Motif and the Builders' Device

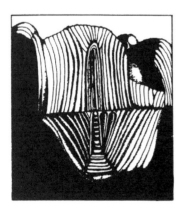

Conical Motif, Slab No. 16 of Gavrinis
(after M. Balfour)
Diagram 4.15

Diagram 4.15 shows another carving slab (no. 16), which bears the "conical motif" of Gavrinis. The slab stands at the left side of the rear of chamber (diagram 4.13), suggesting its relative importance. According to the experts, the slab can be made out from the entrance when it is lit up (culture.gouv.fr). The carving can be divided into two parts. The central figure of the upper part is a so-called "shield motif" surrounded by and decorated with layers of parallel and vertical lines, like radiance generated by that shield. This style of carving, similar to those of Loughcrew, Ireland, is commonly found inside Gavrinis. The lower part of the slab is decorated and centered with a conical figure bearing parallel lines horizontally carved on its surface. Horizontal carved lines were rare in Gavrinis and they must be a distinctive feature of the conical object. Two daggers are engraved next to the cone, which probably discloses the real function of the device.

The shield motif is unique to Gavrinis. Obviously, its elongated shape presents a tall standing stone, a menhir which is commonly found around the region. As intimated by the slab, waves of mysterious energy are emitted from these standing stones in the form of radiance.

As shown in the slab, two rows of megalights which activate the menhir nearby are produced from a brim-based conical device decorated with horizontal lines similar to a witch's hat. Four mysterious hat-shaped gold relics of the early Bronze Age are found in central and west Europe. They are all engraved with horizontal parallel lines with dozens of small round and concentric circles on the body of each ring. Judging from the design of these golden cones, which seem to have no practical uses, it is highly possible that they are replicas of the real ones of the advanced civilization (diagram 4.16). Megalights were probably generated by the device, piercing through the light holes on its rings and reaching the stones nearby.

Where is the menhir that once served as the builders' powerhouse 5,500 years ago? The capstone of Gavrinis may provide us with an important clue. In fact, that huge capstone came from a famous Neolithic menhir weighing 200 tons and once stood up to 14m in height! Is that why the builders selected a portion of their power generator to cover up their messages in Gavrinis? The mound certainly contains a lost message, a technology beyond our understanding.

German Gold Cone
Diagram 4.16

Grand Menhir Brise: The Neolithic Dry Cell

Indisputably, the most famous monolith/standing stone around the region is the Le Grand Menhir Brise. It lies at Morbihan of Locmariaquer, just 5km east of Gavrinis (diagram 4.17). The monolith, now broken into four huge fragments, originally measured about 21m long and weighed 300 tons and is the largest of its kind. This gigantic post is presumed to have once been used as an astronomical calendar for foresighting the sun for worshipping. It might also have served as a regional marker for defining territories of the Neolithic people. It certainly took tremendous effort and courage to erect a menhir of this size.

If we try to understand the menhir in the Gavrinis way, it was a gigantic dry cell battery of the builders in 4500 B.C. The builders erected the stone on a selected place, probably on the main junction of energy streams underground. According to the conical motif of Gavrinis, a conical device was placed next to the menhir, which projected two rows of megalights directly onto its surface for power. The full picture may be illustrated in the following diagram (diagram 4.17). The carver of the slab tries to explain the effect of his energy mechanism by drawing parallel and radiant lines around the menhir, which possibly represents the energy or microwaves being generated.

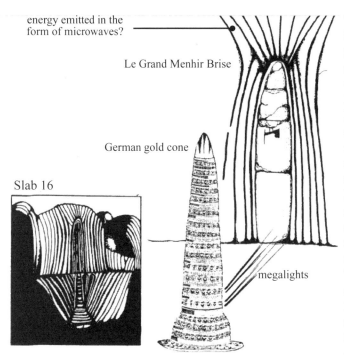

energy emitted in the form of microwaves?

Le Grand Menhir Brise

German gold cone

Slab 16

megalights

The Neolithic Power Generator, Ultimate Secret of Gavrinis: A Conical Device Once Projected Megalights to a nearby Menhir
Diagram 4.17

The capstone of Gavrinis itself, weighing nineteen tons, has once been part of another large monolith which once stood next to Le Grand Menhir Brise. It was then pulled down deliberately and broken into three parts. All of them were later reused as capstones of three famous Neolithic sites around the region, namely the passage grave of Gavrinis, the tomb of Er-Grah, built next to the original site, and the Table des Marchand, 4km away. The original monolith, which is 14m high and weighs 200 tons, is heavily decorated with ox and axe plow carvings, and they probably stand for the traveling machines of the builders (diagram 4.18).

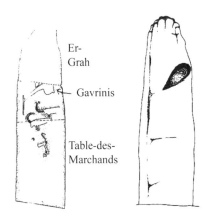

Er-Grah

Gavrinis

Table-des-Marchands

Monolith of Brittany: The Builders' Dry Cell Battery
Diagram 4.18

Kerdeslvas Menhir
Diagram 4.19

Quartz Menhirs

Menhirs are one of the earliest and simplest megalithic monuments that were erected in Brittany. There are around 1,200 isolated menhirs in the region and most of them are large, rough, undressed, and unshaped, without any surface design. The name "menhir" is derived from the Breton language: *men* = stone, *hir* = large. However, the overwhelmingly huge size, some up to 10m high, has long been an enigma. Experts suggest they were land markers (Hibbs 1983; Burl 1985; Bender 1986; Patton 1993); some think these standing stones are closely associated with the sources of spring and water courses (Giot 1979); others speculate that the stones are aligned to the movements of the sun and the moon (Le Pontois 1929), or their elongated and phallic shapes might be associated with fertility (Giot 1988). These pillar-shaped standing stones once stood around the Neolithic woodland like the skyscrapers dotting Manhattan, posting one of the most spectacular sites in the megalithic world. Only the passage graves could be compared with them.

Most of these menhirs are made of the same local granite, which is coarse-grained with reddish pink quartz crystals (Tilley 2004). Some are fine-grained with densely packed white quartz crystals. The inherent properties of the white quartz correspond with the materials formed inside at the southeast external wall of Newgrange, while the stone circles and horseshoes of Stonehenge were also conspiratorially selected with quartz-enriched sarsens and bluestones. Some of these menhirs are even carved with axe-shaped inclusion, another expression of the megalights. Similar messages are also discovered on the eastern face of Stone 4 of Stonehenge. Crystal-enriched megalith, with its special property, was selected and erected as the builders' power supplier in 4500 B.C.

An Electric Charged Menhir

The menhir of La Bretelliere with zigzag carving (diagram 4.20) is discovered by Chris Scarre and Paul Raux (*Antiquity* 74 [2000]: 757–8). According to Scarre, the 6.2m high standing stone is made of local granite. The vertical zigzag motif, which recalls those inside the great mound of Newgrange, has a total length of 5.5m.

Menhir of La Bretelliere: It Could Be Described as a "Charged" Menhir with Zigzag Carving (Discovered by Chris Scarre and Paul Raux)
Diagram 4.20

Menhir and Stone Basin

Being the tallest standing stone of Brittany, the Menhir du Champ-Dolent is 9.5m high. According to legends, this granite fell from the sky. There is a basin-like slab lying just in front of the giant stone, which may mark the location of the builders' conical device (diagram 4.21). According to Burl (1985), there is a half-buried flat stone pitted with cavities lying near another 2.9m-high menhir at L'Aiguille de Gargantua. This flat-lying stone also marks the location of the conical device.

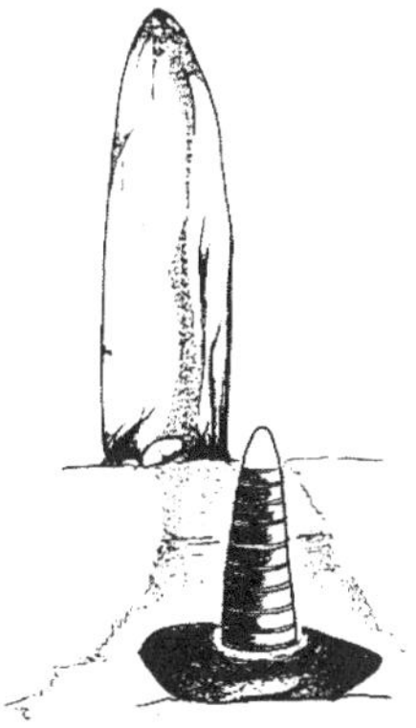

Menhir du Champ-Dolent and Stone Basin
Diagram 4.21

Orthostats: A Substitute for Menhirs

A row of shields is another typical design inside Gavrinis (diagram 4.22). The shields must be the central theme of the carving, as they are placed in the center. If an individual shield represents a charged menhir of the builders, then a row of them may stand for a row of standing stones like the famous stone alignment of Carnac. Besides, the chambers of most passage graves of Brittany, including Gavrinis, are formed by a circle of orthostats and further strengthened with flat slabs to form corbel vaults (diagram 4.23). To a certain extent, these orthostats can be understood as a circle of small menhirs housed inside an earth mound, similar to those inside the cemetery of Loughcrew. They acted as dry cell batteries for the builders' conical device. The new design of a circle of orthostats inside a corbel chamber might have replaced the enormous monolith standing on an open space.

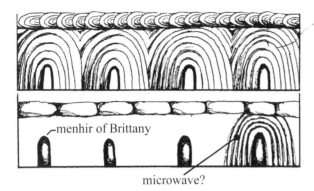

"shield" of
Gavrinis

menhir of Brittany

microwave?

**Shield Carvings inside
Gavrinis (*above*) and the
Menhirs of Brittany**
Diagram 4.22

corbelled wall

**Orthostats inside
a Typical Passage
Grave of Brittany**
Diagram 4.23

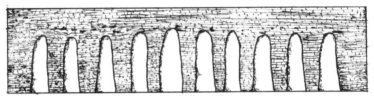

The diagram below shows the floorplan of the famous passage-grave at Ile Longue. The grave is open to the east-southeast with an 11.5m long and 1.5m high passage, which leads to a q-shaped chamber measuring 3m square. The corbelled chamber, consisting of ten granite orthostats, forms a quadrilateral. These orthostats are arranged according to the SA, as a total of six sets of SAs are derived if a conical device is placed in its center. With inspiration from Gavrinis, we can visualize concentric circles of microwaves once generated, most probably spiraling around under its corbel vault and ultimately turning the passage mound into the builders' powerhouse. A row of megalight is projected along the angle bisector of the SA1 and it passes through the passage and main entrance of Ile Longue outside (diagram 4.24).

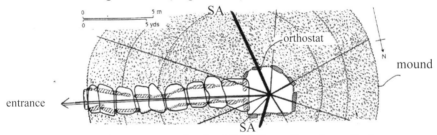

SA

orthostat

mound

entrance

N

SA

Layout of Ile Longue in the Morbihan, Southern Brittany

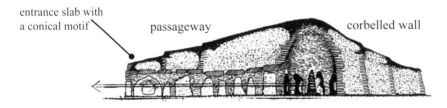

entrance slab with
a conical motif

passageway

corbelled wall

Ile Longue with the Installation of the Conical Device
(info: Barry Cunliffe, *The Oxford Illustrated Prehistory of Europe* [1994], p. 179)
Diagram 4.24

The illustration below (diagram 4.25) demonstrates the work of a conical device inside the passage grave of Les cous at Bazoges-en Pareds (information from *Dolmens for the Dead* by Roger Joussaume).

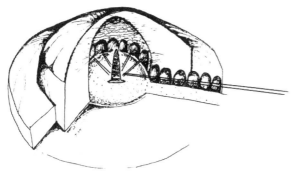

Powerhouse of Les Cous
Diagram 4.25

Diagram 4.26 shows the findings of surface surveys of Late Neolithic monuments in the region of St Nicholas-du-Pelem in central Brittany. An *allée couverte,* also known as trilith passage grave, lies in the center of several menhirs. SA1 is formed by two menhirs, namely M1 and M2, with the allée couverte in the middle. At the same time, SA2 is formed by two other menhirs, M3 and M4. Undoubtedly the miraculous Neolithic formula of SA is applicable to these Neolithic monuments.

Like the passage cairns of Loughcrew, the passage grave of St Nicholas can be explained by the twin-device energy mechanism (diagram 4.26). Twin-device no. 1 is placed inside the passage grave for tapping Earth energy, whereas another device is placed at its entrance projecting rows of megalights onto the menhirs nearby for discharging. The two conical devices are further connected by another row of megalight so as to complete the energy generating process.

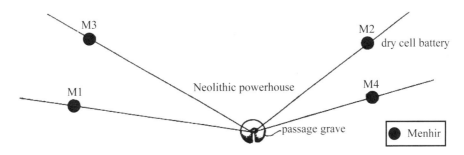

**Passage Grave of St. Nicholas-du-Pelem Connects with
Menhirs nearby to Form a Neolithic Powerhouse**
Diagram 4.26

A Neolithic Manual

Carving no. 8 below (diagram 4.27) is probably the most impressive and elaborate slab in Gavrinis. It is famous for its intensity and complexity and it is quite obvious that it has embraced a lost message that could not be deciphered. The contents of the slab can be divided into three superimposed parts: the lowest part occupies about one-fourth of the carving while on its bottom left is a set of concentric circles, or a "shield," with two daggers on its right. It is the same as the conical motif slab found inside Gavrinis. It describes the conical device viewed from above. Three standing snakelike motifs are found at right. The upper left shows two stone basins with conical devices on top.

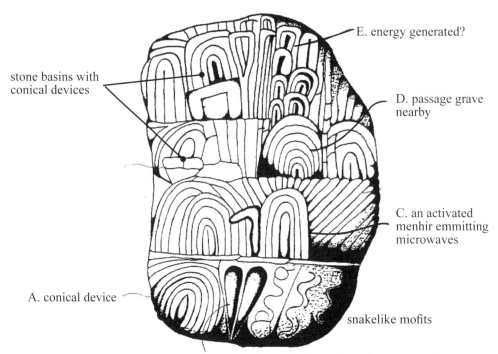

stone basins with conical devices

E. energy generated?

D. passage grave nearby

C. an activated menhir emmitting microwaves

A. conical device

snakelike mofits

B. two rows of megalights projected onto a menhir nearby

Slab No. 8 of Gavrinis: A Manual of the Builders' Energy Mechanism
Diagram 4.27

Two daggers of megalights are projected onto a shield in the second layer, the middle part of the slab. That shield, as mentioned above, stands for a menhir generating parallel radiant lines, or "hair," to the semiconcentric objects above and carved in the third and upper layer. Another shield to the left seems to be intertwined with the "hair" of the first. Do these semicircular objects represent other menhirs which help magnify the power received? It is the same energy mechanism mentioned on the Dadga Skirt of Loughcrew, where daggerlike objects change its appearance to elongated thick lines when they "transfuse" from the inner arc of monoliths to the second arc.

Or do these semicircular objects refer to the passage graves of a similar shape? These passage graves, when housed with orthostats, are capable of generating microwaves. They may also act as relay power stations, displayed as a succession of superimposed shields at the top right corner of the slab, to transfer microwaves from one station to another. On the top left of the slab, the picture of a passage grave clearly indicates a conical device being placed on a stone basin, which is exactly what happened inside the mounds of Newgrange and Knowth in the same period. This wonderful slab captures the entire energy mechanism of the advanced civilization. It probably explains the reason why they were here in 4000 B.C. The mystery of Neolithic Ireland is answered effectively by the rock art of Gavrinis.

Similar messages are also indicated by another carved slab, known as no. 4, of Gavrinis (diagram 4.28). The carving is full of shield motifs, each representing individual passage graves connected together by wave patterns at the upper part of the diagram. The slab may be describing two passage graves once connected by microwaves. Did these Neolithic graves of Brittany serve as the builders' powerhouses and communication centers, like those of the Boyne Valley?

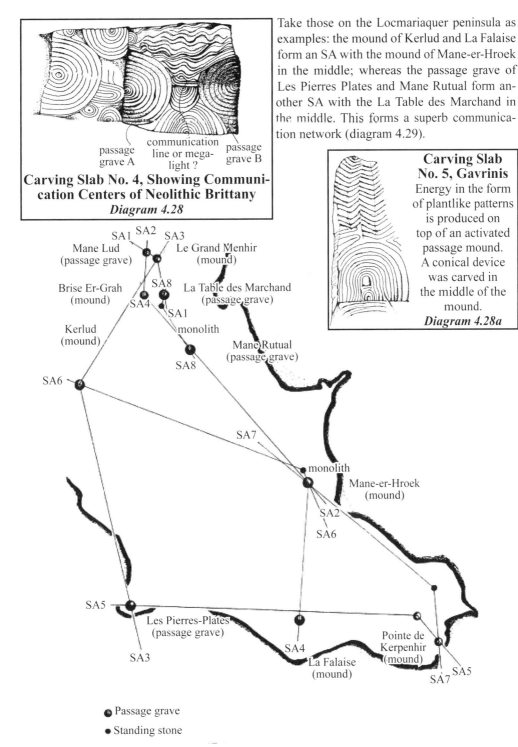

passage grave A

communication line or mega-light ?

passage grave B

Carving Slab No. 4, Showing Communi-cation Centers of Neolithic Brittany
Diagram 4.28

Take those on the Locmariaquer peninsula as examples: the mound of Kerlud and La Falaise form an SA with the mound of Mane-er-Hroek in the middle; whereas the passage grave of Les Pierres Plates and Mane Rutual form another SA with the La Table des Marchand in the middle. This forms a superb communication network (diagram 4.29).

Carving Slab No. 5, Gavrinis
Energy in the form of plantlike patterns is produced on top of an activated passage mound. A conical device was carved in the middle of the mound.
Diagram 4.28a

SA1 SA2 SA3

Mane Lud (passage grave)

Le Grand Menhir (mound)

Brise Er-Grah (mound)

SA8

La Table des Marchand (passage grave)

SA4

SA1

Kerlud (mound)

monolith

Mane Rutual (passage grave)

SA8

SA6

SA7

monolith

Mane-er-Hroek (mound)

SA2

SA6

SA5

Les Pierres-Plates (passage grave)

SA3

SA4

La Falaise (mound)

Pointe de Kerpenhir (mound)

SA7 SA5

⦿ Passage grave

● Standing stone

Passage Graves of the Locmariaquer Peninsula Are Interconnected by the SA
(info: Scarre 1998, p. 60)
Diagram 4.29

101

Allée Couverte

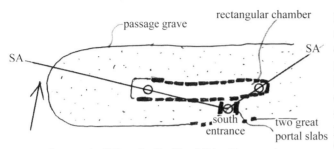

passage grave

rectangular chamber

SA

SA

south entrance

two great portal slabs

Layout of Crech-Quille Allée Couverte
Diagram 4.30

In Neolithic Brittany, there is another type of chambered tomb called "allée couverte," with shorter and lateral passage opening to a right-angled rectangular chamber. Crech-Quille is one of the most important and well-preserved ones. A south lateral entrance formed by two great slabs, a kind of portal stones, leads to a 3m long passage and further connects to a large rectangular compartment, measuring 16.2m long and 1.8m wide, formed by impressive orthostats (Burl 1985). The two ends of its inner compartment form an SA with the two portal slabs of the entrance in the middle (diagram 4.30). It reveals the secret of these allées couverte. Most of the standing stones inside these passage graves are quartzite slabs, which further suggests their relations with power generation.

Two Passage-graves at Mousseaux

The site, measuring 24m × 20m, is located at the head of a slope with its two passages and chambers constructed of sandstone and puddingstone (Burl 1985). A façade is constructed at the southeast with two entrances leading to two parallel passage-graves (diagram 4.31). The southern passage leads to a pair of side cells and ends at a large rear chamber. The northern one has been constructed with a single side cell and ends with another rear chamber. According to Burl, cup-marks are found on the portal stone on the right of the northern tomb (Burl, p. 100), which throws light on the real function of the portal entrance. This portal slabs with a lintel on top forms SA1 with the rear chamber of the northern tomb, with the single side cell in the middle (diagram 4.31). SA2 and SA3 are formed by the lintel portal entrance of the southern tomb and the one leading to the rear chamber with the two side cells in the middle respectively. Acting like dolmens or trilithons, conical devices were once placed inside these lintel doorways of Mousseaux for power.

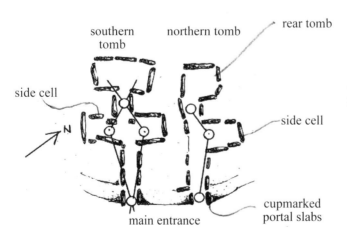

southern tomb

northern tomb

rear tomb

side cell

N

side cell

main entrance

cupmarked portal slabs

Powerhouse of Les Mousseaux with Its Trilithon Doorways Aligned to the SA
(after Burl)
Diagram 4.31

Loire Dolmen at Esse

This interesting monument is formed by thirty-two huge dark-red schist slabs, some weighing up to forty tons. Burl (1985, p. 83) regards it as one of the megalithic wonders of Brittany. According to Burl, the dolmen opens at the southeast with two squatting slabs and a lintel and leads to a short antechamber 1m high. Two transverse slabs separate the antechamber from the main chamber, which measures 14.3m long and 4m wide. The area is then subdivided by three projecting stones into four cells of 2.6m, 1.7m, 2.4m, and 5.4m long (diagram 4.32). The two internal doorways, each formed by a pair of transverse slabs, form an SA with a side cell. The site is nothing but a power station where energy was once generated by the surrounding huge schist stones.

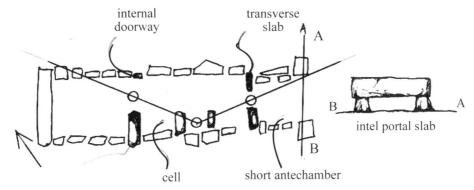

Layout of Esse (after Burl)
Diagram 4.32

Angled Passage-grave at Pierres-Plats and its "Figurines"

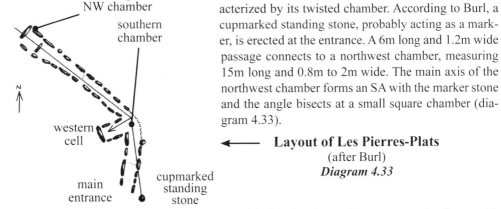

This Middle Neolithic grave was once rebuilt and is now half-buried. The monument is characterized by its twisted chamber. According to Burl, a cupmarked standing stone, probably acting as a marker, is erected at the entrance. A 6m long and 1.2m wide passage connects to a northwest chamber, measuring 15m long and 0.8m to 2m wide. The main axis of the northwest chamber forms an SA with the marker stone and the angle bisects at a small square chamber (diagram 4.33).

← **Layout of Les Pierres-Plats**
(after Burl)
Diagram 4.33

The grave is also famous for its anthropomorphic figurine denoted by a rectangular frame with two "horns" and further decorated with "breasts" and arcs inside (diagram 4.34). The horned figurine carving actually represents a passage-grave with a façade formed by two horns at its entrance. Two conical devices, as described by the slab, were once found inside according to the SA.

Alignments of Carnac

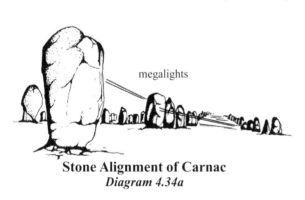

The most famous and mysterious megalithic monuments of Carnac are the stone alignments which are arranged in rows like an army and stretching remorselessly in straight lines across the landscape. Some regard them as marking a mass cemetery, while others relate them to astronomy. Some of the stone alignments are deliberately sited close to the earlier burial mounds. For example, the Kermario alignments are constructed on the Manio I long mound; whereas the Kerlescan alignments have their origin in the Kerlescan long barrow (Alex Gibson and Derek Simpson). These "sacred" sites had to be extremely important to the builders, as they were deliberately selected and reused.

Mound-shaped "Figurine" on Stone 13, Les Pierres-Plats
Diagram 4.34

Stone alignments at Le Menec, which consist of 1,050 standing stones, are arranged in ten rows stretching almost a mile long. Its eastern end spreads 60m wide while the western one has a breadth of 100m. The Kerlescan alignments are formed by thirteen stone rows running from WNW to ESE, and end at a roughly rectangular enclosure known as the Kerlescan West cromlech and a long mound (Chris Scarre). Experts speculate that these alignments are related to the ritual ceremonies of the Neolithic people.

A slab carving "figurine" on Stone 12 of a passage-grave at Les Pierres-Plats (Burl 1985) may suggest what actually happened among these stone rows in 4500 B.C. (diagram 4.35). Rows of megalights are once travelled around these standing stones for power, which is the same energy mechanism inside the Dagda Skirt of Loughcrew (diagram 4.36).

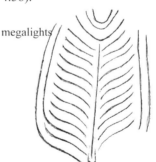

megalights

"Figurine" on Stone 12, Les Pierres-Plats
Diagram 4.35

megalights

Stone Alignment of Carnac
Diagram 4.34a

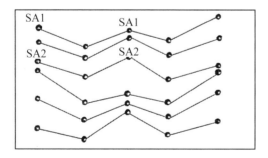

Stone Alignment of Carnac
Diagram 4.36

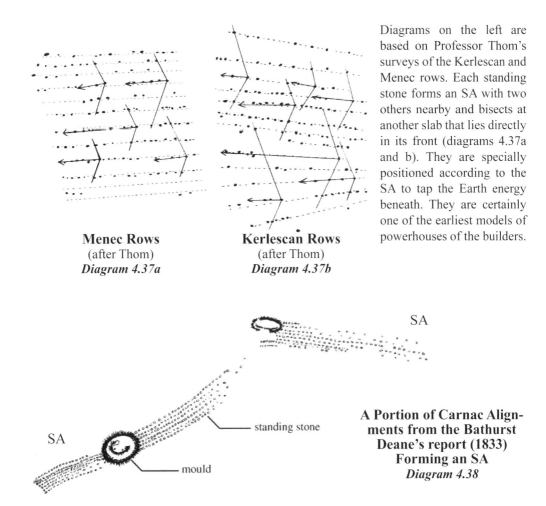

Diagrams on the left are based on Professor Thom's surveys of the Kerlescan and Menec rows. Each standing stone forms an SA with two others nearby and bisects at another slab that lies directly in its front (diagrams 4.37a and b). They are specially positioned according to the SA to tap the Earth energy beneath. They are certainly one of the earliest models of powerhouses of the builders.

Menec Rows
(after Thom)
Diagram 4.37a

Kerlescan Rows
(after Thom)
Diagram 4.37b

SA

SA

standing stone

mould

A Portion of Carnac Alignments from the Bathurst Deane's report (1833) Forming an SA
Diagram 4.38

Barnenez Chamber Cairns

Barnenez stepped cairn lies on the northern end of the peninsula of Kernelehen with a history of more than 6,700 years. The eleven-passage grave, oriented from east to west, was built in two distinct stages. The eastern tombs are slightly older than the western ones (diagram 4.39). Typical Neolithic and Bronze Age ornaments such as beakers, pottery, daggers, and arrowheads are excavated from these tombs. Tomb H is the most eye-catching and complicated megalithic structure with chambers formed by large orthostats. The two chambers are separated by two septal slabs that act like portals, and are covered with a huge capstone on top. One of the septal slabs and four orthostats inside the main chamber have been carved with axes, wavy lines, and zigzags—messages from the builders. An orthostat at the entrance of Tomb A is also engraved with seven "wavy" symbols (Giot 1958). The capstone of tomb J is also engraved with classic megalithic art of southern Brittany.

Huge monoliths are also erected inside these tombs; for example, a carved granite is placed at the entrance of Tomb G, another stands near the chamber of G1 and one along the corridor of tomb J. Tombs A and B are built with enormous orthostats. All these megalithic fittings are deliberately positioned, probably according to the SA (diagram 4.39). SA1 and SA2 are formed by the orthostats and monoliths inside the east tombs.

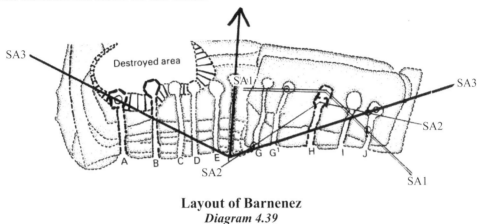

Layout of Barnenez
Diagram 4.39

For some reason, after these eastern powerhouses of Barnenez had been used for more than 500 years the builders decided to extend it by constructing the western part of the site with six more passage tombs. A conical device was placed outside the entrance of Tomb F, the longest tomb, and then it produced two rows of megalights that reached the chambers of Tombs A and J, the two with the shortest passageways, to form SA3. The angle bisects at the chamber of Tomb F.

The Long Mound of Saint-Michel: A Gigantic Powerhouse

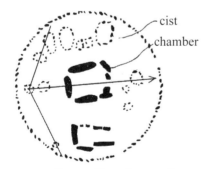

Inner Structures of Saint Michel
Diagram 4.40

This enormous long tumulus, measuring 125m by 60m with a height of 10m, lies northwest of Carnac. The site is so huge that a chapel has been built on its summit. Under the mound, a circle of stones is constructed along the long axis with a small burial chamber measuring 2.5m × 2m × 1m in the middle (diagram 4.40). The central chamber is further surrounded by a circle of small cists underneath a huge pile of stones and clay. These cists are aligned to the SA, with their angle bisectors pointing to the central burial chamber.

There are a number of finely polished axes found inside the chamber of Saint-Michel, probably for ceremonial use as they are still in excellent condition. They are hypothesized as symbols of power for the prehistoric rulers. Like the conical gold hats, these enigmatic and precious jadeite axes are actually the replicas of the mysterious megalights generated inside the cists for power.

The following diagram shows the relation between the mound of Saint-Michel and her neighboring monuments as they are aligned to the SA (diagram 4.41).

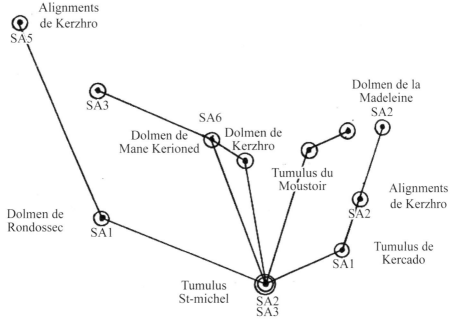

Saint-Michel and Neighboring Sites
Diagram 4.41

Brittany of France, especially the region along the Gulf of Morbihan can lay claim to being the world's earliest settlements of the mysterious advanced civilization. Why did they erect huge standing stones, large tumuli, and passage graves there? Was the region lying at the heart or junction of the so-called Ley line?

Curved Stones Horseshoe

There are some late Neolithic monuments in Brittany, where an arc or semicircle of close-set stones are set up to form a curved spacious ring termed a "cromlech." Most of these horseshoe settings are no less than 50m across. The following diagram shows the cromlech at Kergonan with an arc of horseshoe formed by thirty-six tall menhirs, varying from 2m to 3.5m in height. It opens at the southeast end. The builders' conical device was placed at the center of the horseshoe for power (diagram 4.42).

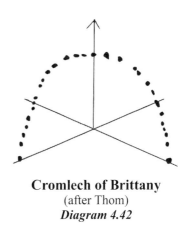

Cromlech of Brittany
(after Thom)
Diagram 4.42

At Carnac, cromlechs and stone rows are associated with the cromlech standing on the higher ground and the stone rows leading uphill towards the ring (Burl). The Mence West cromlech, measures 91m × 71m, forms an egg-shaped enclosure with seventy close-set stones. The Kerlescan West cromlech, a loaf-shaped horseshoe enclosure, opens to the true north. Acting likc stone circles, a conical device was once placed in the center of each of these cromlechs for power (diagram 4.43).

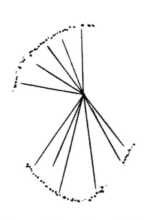

Menec West Cromlech
(after Thom)

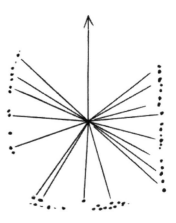

Kerlescan West Cromlech
(after Thom)

Diagram 4.43

Stone Rectangle of Brittany

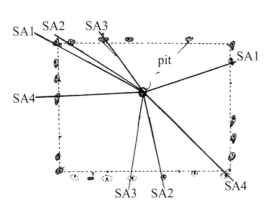

Crucuno of Plouharnel is rich in megalithic monuments. The Crucuno Dolmen is one of the best-known in the whole of Brittany, with a chamber of 1.8m in height and an area of 3.4m × 3.5m. Its capstone is 7.6m in length and weighs about 40 kg. Another rectangular cromlech once lay nearby but has suffered the ravages of time. Its standing stones are aligned to the SA (diagram 4.44).

Plan of the Stone Rectangle at Crucuno
Diagram 4.44

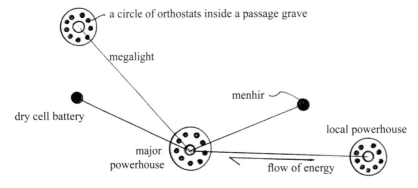

a circle of orthostats inside a passage grave

megalight

dry cell battery

menhir

local powerhouse

major powerhouse

flow of energy

A Typical Powerhouse of Brittany, 3500 B.C.
Diagram 4.45

Tustrup Power Station of Denmark

Agriculture was first introduced in Denmark circa 3900 B.C. The earliest farmers, generally known as the Beaker Culture, were energetic builders who constructed large assembly areas surrounded by palisades. The one in Sarup on Funen is a typical example. In around 2800–2400 B.C., another mysterious group, the Single Grave Culture, succeeded and replaced the previous one. They abandoned subsistence strategy in agriculture by building the oldest stone burial monuments, the dolmens and the passage graves around the region, with endless ambitions. Today, thousands of them have been preserved in Denmark.

The Late Neolithic site of Tustrup in east Denmark is another excellent example to demonstrate how the builders' power station functioned thousands of years ago. The megalithic complex, first discovered in 1954, features several monuments set in a semicircle within a radius of 15m (diagram 4.46). A polygonal burial mound with a set of two concentric circles of rough boulders lies at the northeast of the complex while a horseshoe-shaped sanctuary temple with a central oval pit of sand is found next to the mound. Another round barrow with a burial chamber is constructed next to the temple. Today, only a circle of stones is left behind. Further northwest of the complex is a fallen capstone lying in the open. A passage grave known as "jaettestue" ("Giant's Tomb") is formed by a rectangular chamber measuring 10m × 1.8m, and it is linked up with another side chamber off the back wall at the southeast corner by a deep stone passage.

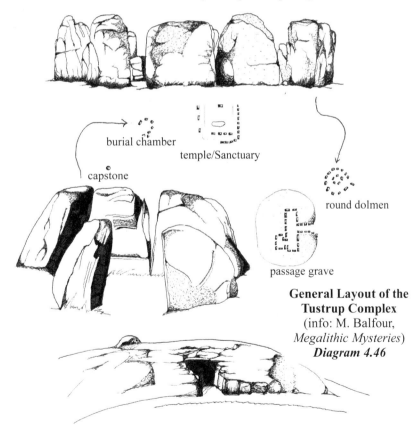

burial chamber

temple/Sanctuary

capstone

round dolmen

passage grave

**General Layout of the
Tustrup Complex**
(info: M. Balfour,
Megalithic Mysteries)
Diagram 4.46

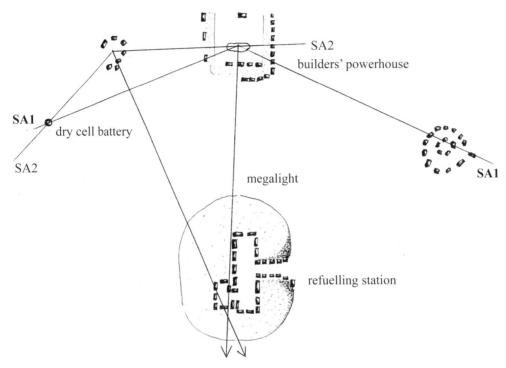

Powerhouses of Tustrup, Denmark, circa 3000 B.C. (after M. Balfour 1992)
Diagram 4.47

The sanctuary temple, which is supposed to be the center of the complex, is enclosed by a stone wall in the shape of a horseshoe, forming an area of 5m × 5.5m with an opening to the northeast. The wall, 0.5 to 1.5m thick and about 1m high, is formed by standing slabs. There is a niche 2m wide and 0.8m deep at the northern wall, which includes a stone-filled oval pit about 0.8m in depth. This central pit may probably mark the location of the builders' conical device, as it forms SA1 with a concentric round barrow to its right and the capstone to its left (diagram 4.47). The angle bisects at the lintel passage that connects the main and side rectangular chambers of the passage grave. It must be a deliberate plan of the builders as a stone circle, located left of the sanctuary, forms SA2 with the oval pit of the sanctuary and the capstone; again, the angle bisects at the side chamber of the passage grave. SA3 is derived from the oval pit of the sanctuary and the lintel passage of the passage grave with its main entrance in the middle.

A conical device was once placed in the temple's pit and the stone circle nearby for tapping Earth energy. The capstone may be there for discharging while the double-chambered passage grave, which lies south of the complex, once functioned as a refuelling house for the builders' machinery. No theory can explain Tustrup more effectively and convincingly than the SA. SA2 is probably a substitute for the dried-out SA1.

The Builders' Secret

An "activated" monolith—builders' dry cell battery

conical device—German gold hat

megalights

The Energy Mechanism of the Builder
**Slab no. 16—the "conical motif" of Gavrinis, Brittany of France—showing
two rows of megalights being projected into the surface of a
monolith by a power-generating device below.**
(Picture 4.48 from Michael Balfour, *Stonehenge and Its Mysteries*)

Chapter 5
The Megalithic Powerhouses of Malta

Stone Bowl of Tarxien and the Conical Device
Diagram 5.01

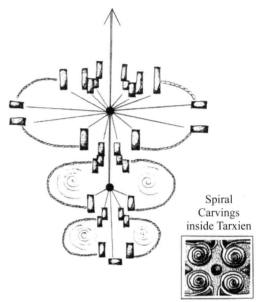

Spiral
Carvings
inside Tarxien

The Powerhouse of Tarxien, 3000–2500 B.C.
Diagram 5.02

"As civilizations go theirs was an enviable one—yet they remain frustratingly out of our grasp."

—Richard Rudgley, *Secrets of the Stone Age*

The Malta archipelago is located in the western Mediterranean and is regarded as the bridge between Europe and Africa. The area mainly consists of two islands: Malta (245.5 sq. km) and Gozo (67 sq. km). Geologically speaking, the Malta islands are part of the European continent. Archaeological evidences suggest the first wave of Maltese settlers came from Sicily during the Stone Age and lived a peaceful nomadic life of fishing and hunting there.

Malta is definitely not an ideal place for starting a civilization. The island lies in the middle of a vast inland sea that has hindered inter-continental trading (especially during the period of the relatively backward seaborne transportation of the Neolithic period). Its rock plateau is fringed with deep cliffs up to hundred meters high, which discourage coastal fishing. Most surfaces of the island are covered with hard and porous limestones that are infertile and retain rainwater with difficulty. This, together with limited rainfall in the summer, makes conditions highly unfavorable for the practice of agriculture. Besides, vegetation is fairly sparse and reptiles such as lizards and snakes are more numerous than mammals, which further makes even the simplest way of hunting and gathering on the island impossible.

However, against all odds, a cluster of massive megalithic infrastructures constructed by skilful and sophisticated techniques shows that an unknown culture once flourished on the islands in 4000–2500 B.C. This culture, probably contemporary with the Grooved Ware people of Neolithic Europe, built huge stone temples out of simple stone tools to worship their mother goddess. These impressive and overwhelming temples were constructed with a unified theme and became one of the oldest large-stone structures in the world, a thousand years before the pyramids in Egypt. Some of the erected stones are 14 to 16m high. Instead of being constructed on the accessible central flatland of the island, most of them are conspiratorially placed on coastal plateaus, over the 100m-high cliff top, with their entrances facing the ocean. Apart from these gigantic temples, the culture left no other infrastructures, making the region merely a temple-island.

After more than 1500 years of peace and achievements, this megalith-loving culture, like their comrades in northwest Europe, suddenly vanished for unknown reasons, and left the empty islands with their sacred temples buried in sand. The sudden disappearance of a culture is always an enigma. Today, people generally agree that a devastating epidemic or a catastrophic drought was a possible cause. This culture repeatedly rebuilt their temples for more than 1,500 years, but left no writings or descriptions. Not even a signature. Instead, familiar Neolithic carvings such as spirals and zigzag patterns, parallel to those of the Boyne Valley and Brittany, are carved in high relief, displayed in huge sizes and placed at the most sacred places inside their temples. Without doubt, they reveal the function of these megalithic buildings again.

There were over forty Neolithic temples on the islands of Malta and Gozo, with twenty-three remaining. Temples at Skorba and Xewkija are the oldest, which can date back to 4500–3800 B.C., whereas the latest (of 3500–2800 B.C.) is found at Mnajdra. It was the time when Newgrange of Ireland and long barrows of the British Isles were built and used. These Malta temples outplayed their counterparts by being the first freestanding megalithic buildings in the world. Built with hard coralline limestone and soft globigerina stone, the temples are famous for their iconic curved apses made of orthostats. Their entrances and doorways are expressed by massive dressed trilithons which certainly demonstrate their supremacy. Occasionally, mysterious stone basins or slabs with sockets are placed on the floor.

Temple at Mgarr

Mgarr Temple is one of the oldest temples, dating back to 3600–3500 B.C. It has a trefoil (clover-leaf) layout, with three apses opening off a central passage (diagram 5.03). This central passage is connected by massive doorways in the form of megalith trilithons, each leading to a pair of apses at its two sides. These kidney-shaped apses are in the form of horseshoes made of limestone orthostats with one or two more layers of horizontal slabs on top of them. In theory, Neolithic high priests once passed through the massive entrances to the "Holy of the Holies," the rear apse of the temple, to perform their ritual ceremony. Shallow cavities and stone bowls, which function as libation holes, are found on the floor. It suggests that the building was probably used as a Neolithic temple.

With the SA applied, the building of Mgarr was more than a temple. SA1 and SA2 can be derived by the rear apse and the trilithon of the main entrance with each of the two doorways of the side apses in the middle (diagram 5.03).

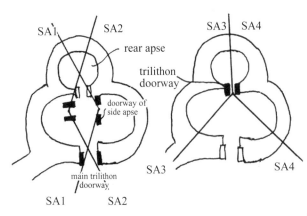

**Temple at Mgarr with its Major Trilithon
Doorways Aligned to the SA**
Diagram 5.03

At the same time, SA3 and SA4 are produced by the rear apse and the two side apses with the two inner doorways of the apses in the middle respectively. Acting like two horseshoes of orthostats, the two oval-shaped side apses are connected by megalights and used for generating power for the builders. The builders' twin-devices are placed, one in each of the two apses, to activate the energy mechanism. The third device is probably installed inside the trilithon doorways to activate the two conical devices above. Interestingly, large spiral carvings are found on the slabs of the temples, probably revealing its power generation function.

Temple of Mnajdra

Mnajdra lies in the cliffs on the southern coast of Malta, just 500m from another important temple, Hagar Qim. The design of the temple of Mnajdra is the best example to show how different megalithic fittings inside the complex are aligned to the SA. The complex consists of three adjoining temples connected with one another but sharing a common forecourt floored with stone slabs. It suggests they were built in the same period. The East Temple, the smallest and the first to be built, dates back to 3500 B.C. Only one or two megaliths survive today while the rest has now been reconstructed (diagram 5.05). The most impressive and finest is the West Temple which believed to have been constructed in the early Tarxien phase, 3150–2500 B.C. Its masonry demonstrates excellent building techniques and workmanship.

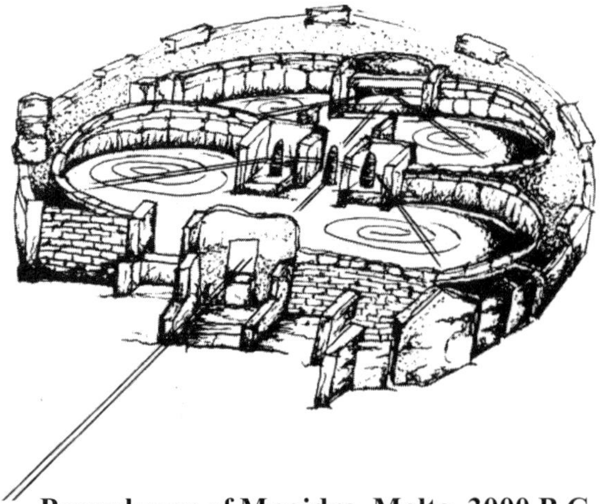

The Central Temple, the largest one, is enclosed with horseshoe-shaped outer walls formed by large slabs of harder coralline limestone. It enters through a large window stone in the form of a trilithon. The temple consists of two kidney-shaped chambers with curved walls of 1m high orthostats in the form of two opposite horseshoes.

The inner doorway of the temple is flanked by two low-lying slab altars 30cm high. They form an SA and bisect at the main entrance (diagram 5.06). It probably constitutes the earliest power generator of the temple. A similar setting is also found in the other two temples.

Powerhouse of Mnajdra, Malta, 3000 B.C.
Diagram 5.04

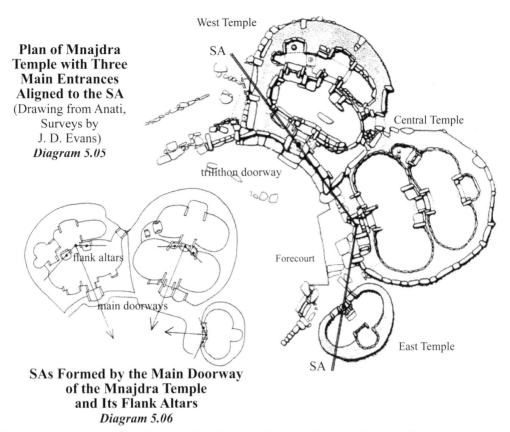

Plan of Mnajdra Temple with Three Main Entrances Aligned to the SA
(Drawing from Anati, Surveys by J. D. Evans)
Diagram 5.05

West Temple

SA

Central Temple

trilithon doorway

flank altars

main doorways

Forecourt

East Temple

SA

SAs Formed by the Main Doorway of the Mnajdra Temple and Its Flank Altars
Diagram 5.06

The horseshoe-shaped West Temple, the older one, has a semicircular façade with bench altars in front of it. A trilithon entrance leads to the main chamber. Another series of bench altar, window stone, and trilithons is found on its southern apse, and its northern apse is also constructed with three small trilithon recesses. Like the Central Temple, there are two low-lying slab altars sandwiched in its inner doorway, and they are aligned to the SA.

Apses and Trilithons of Mnajdra: The Temple's Secret

As shown in the diagram below, the massive trilithon doorway of the Central Temple, carved with spiral carvings, forms SA1 with its rear altar and the one from the East Temples. There are three conical devices, one of which is placed under the trilithon doorway and the other two in the centers of the rear altars of the Central and the East Temples. They act like two horseshoes and are installed with the twin-device for energy (diagram 5.07). That is how the energy mechanism of a Maltese powerhouse works. Interestingly, all these so-called altars, with no statues found, are connected to the rear chamber of the East Temple by SA2 to SA4.

Besides, these rear altars also form various SAs with the apses of the Central and Western Temples (diagram 5.08). It explains why all the temples are constructed with curved walls, functioning structurally as horseshoes, and are connected by trilithon doorways, the dry cell batteries of the builders.

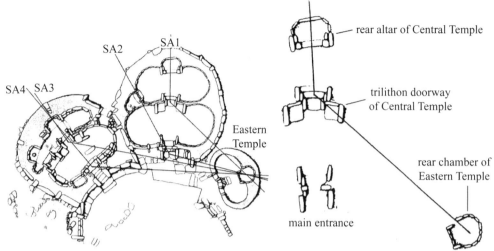

Altars and Trilithon Doorways of Mnajdra Connected by the SA
Diagram 5.07

How the Builders Play Their Game: A Trilithon Doorway, Containing the Conical Device, Connects Two Apses or Horseshoes of Standing Stones
Diagram 5.08

Extensions of the Central and West Temples

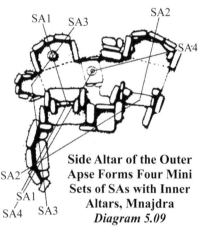

Side Altar of the Outer Apse Forms Four Mini Sets of SAs with Inner Altars, Mnajdra
Diagram 5.09

The megalith builders decided to expand their station with additional altar horseshoes constructed at the west curved walls of the inner apse, both in the Central and West Temples (diagram 5.09). Coincidentally, they form four more sets of SAs: SA1 to SA4, connecting the altar horseshoes with the trilithons in between.

The following diagram shows the trilithon doorway of the West Temple of Mnajdra complex (Julien Ries, *The Origins of Religions* [1994], p. 59, illustration 76a). As Ries illustrates, "there is a (stone) bowl with a cylindrical stone fit into it which is a symbol related to fertility." Obviously, the cylindrical stone is a replica of the conical device (diagram 5.10).

Location of the Stone Bowl with a Cylindrical Stone →
Diagram 5.10

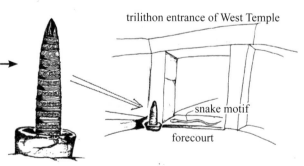

Temple of Hagar Qim

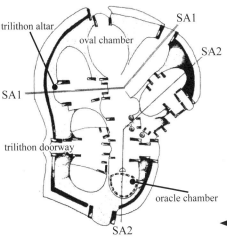

The diagram at left is the plan of Hagar Qim in south Malta, dating back to 3000–2500 B.C. The complex originally consisted of three temples but only the central one is well preserved. Hagar Qim is believed to have been built for worshiping the mother goddess, as female statues have been found inside. A 3.5m high massive outer wall encloses a six-chambered temple. A stone slab with holes is lying just outside its main entrance. Its floor plan seems less regular and is different from other symmetrically designed temples. But the two main axes of the temple are aligned to the SA (diagram 5.11).

← **Main Axis of Hagar Qim**
(after Baedeker) *Diagram 5.11*

Like other Maltese temples, the apses inside the temple are formed with curved walls of large slabs and connected by trilithon doorways (diagram 5.12). Sometimes, tall trilithon altars are built along its curved walls. The oval apses are connected to a main chamber which has a small rear apse at the end. A unique oracle chamber at the east end of the main axis is formed by eighteen orthostats and each measures 1.5m high. They are placed in the form of a stone circle.

The Trilithon Doorway of Hagar Qim
Diagram 5.12

Altar tables and niches are all over the apses, which are believed to hold the Gods' statues. The most famous ones are the three mushroom-shaped altars with beautiful carving and dressing at the four sides (diagram 5.13a) where sacrificial animals were placed. The decorated carving of the mushroom altar, in form of a plantlike object, is actually a description of the builders' conical device.

Mushroom Altars of Hagar Qim with the Builders' Conical Device
(after Rudgley, 2000)
Diagram 5.13a

"plant altar"

carvings on the altar

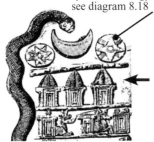

symbol of energy mechanism:
see diagram 8.18

Heaven-god of Mesopotamia, 3000 B.C.?
Anu with horned headdress, three conical shape objects
placed on top of the altars, is the overlord of the ancient
Sumerian gods and the creator of mankind.
Diagram 5.13b

The three mushroom altars of Hagar Qim form an SA with its angle bisecting at another trilithon altar nearby (diagram 5.14). There are two massive lintel doorways formed at the outer entrances at the two sides of the temple and constructed perpendicular to its main axis. Functioning as dry cells, the two massive-sided doorways form an SA with the entrance slab of the oracle stone circle in the middle. Its SA bisects at the west entrance of the temple. Conical devices are placed on these trilithons and the stone circle for generating power (diagram 5.15). Obviously, the locations of the doorways, tall platforms, altar tables, and niches inside Hagar Qim also align to the SA. Some of them are shown below.

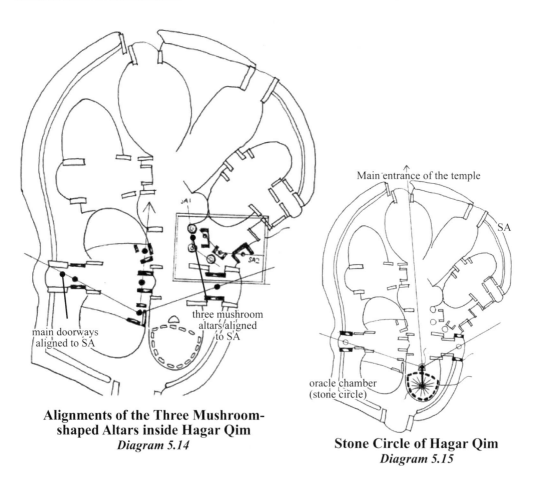

main doorways
aligned to SA

three mushroom
altars aligned
to SA

Main entrance of the temple

SA

oracle chamber
(stone circle)

**Alignments of the Three Mushroom-
shaped Altars inside Hagar Qim**
Diagram 5.14

Stone Circle of Hagar Qim
Diagram 5.15

Temple of Ggantija, Gozo

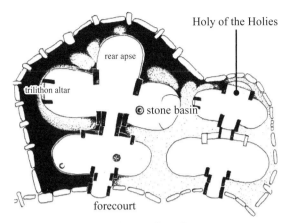

Plan of Ggantija, Gozo
Diagram 5.16

The Maltese temple of Ggantija, meaning "Giant's Tower," is located on the edge of a plateau in the middle of Gozo. According to local legend, it was built by a group of giants with the help of magic powers in 3600 B.C. It is formed by two five-lobed limestone temples, lying side by side and sharing a common outer wall with the main axis oriented to the southeast (diagram 5.16). A semicircular open forecourt is constructed outside the horseshoe-shaped temple. Each of the two temples consists of a central courtyard, side apses, lintel niches, altar tables, and large upright orthostats. Mysterious stone basins and depressions, probably serving as libation, are found inside the apses of the trefoil-shaped court.

However, the temple can be explained and interpreted by the SA. The lintel doorways and trilithon altars of the temples form various sets of SAs with a stone basin or sacrifice hole in the middle (diagram 5.17 a, b, c, and d).

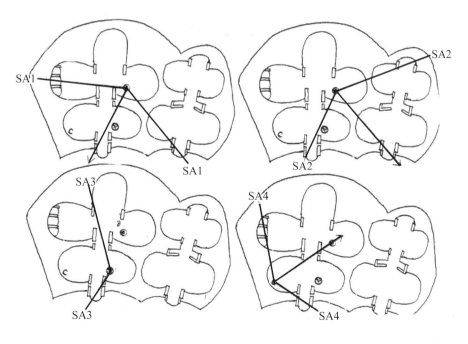

SAs Formed by the Lintel Doorways and Trilithon Altars of Ggantija
Diagram 5.17 a, b, c, and d

Temple of Tarxien: The Perfect Power Generator

The concept of SA is best expressed by the temples in Tarxien. The complex is probably the most famous and well-preserved one. The plan of Tarxien shows three temples—the Southern, Central, and Eastern temples—constructed in different periods. The Southern and Eastern Temples, which share the same alignment, were constructed in 3000–2500 B.C. and the right apse of the Southern Temple was later dismantled for the Central Temple (diagram 5.18).

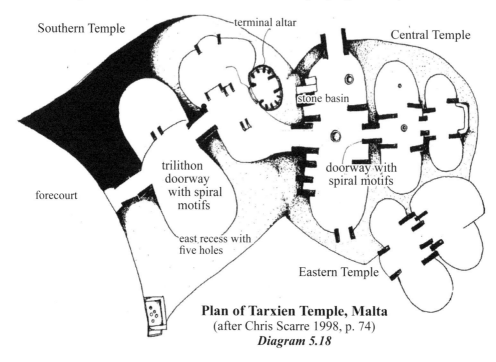

Plan of Tarxien Temple, Malta
(after Chris Scarre 1998, p. 74)
Diagram 5.18

Spiral Doorways

The Southern Temple, probably the oldest, has a con-cave façade of massive coralline limestone slabs framed by bench altars and connected to an outer bay of the horseshoe-shaped building. The eastern apse of the outer bay is decorated with abstract designs of scrolls and running spirals in raised relief, similar to those inside the mound of Newgrange. It suggests a connection between the two contemporary Neolithic infrastructures which probably served the same function as well. These enigmatic spirals might be a direct answer to the curved walls where they are located (diagram 5.19). The op-posite western apse is accessed by a passage flanked by two uprights.

Where the Secret Lies: Gigantic Spiral Carvings at the Doorways of the Southern Temple
Diagram 5.19

Altars formed by large blocks are decorated with a pair of running spirals and placed on both sides of the passage. Again, the builders put a mark on the spot where conical devices had once been placed to generate energy in the form of spirals (diagram 5.20a, 5.20b).

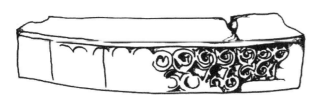

Carved Stone Bench with Running Spirals
Diagram 5.20a

Spiral Carvings on Slabs
Diagram 5.20b

Stone Circle of the Southern Temple

The biggest secret of the Southern Temple is its terminal niche. The specially carved niche, also known as the Holy of the Holies, is framed by curved stone benches with enormous standing orthostats in between. Its low-lying entry altar is carved with running spirals, and they are deliberately arranged to show the SA (diagram 5.21). This terminal niche once functioned as a stone circle where a device was installed in its center. It must be the master plan of the builders.

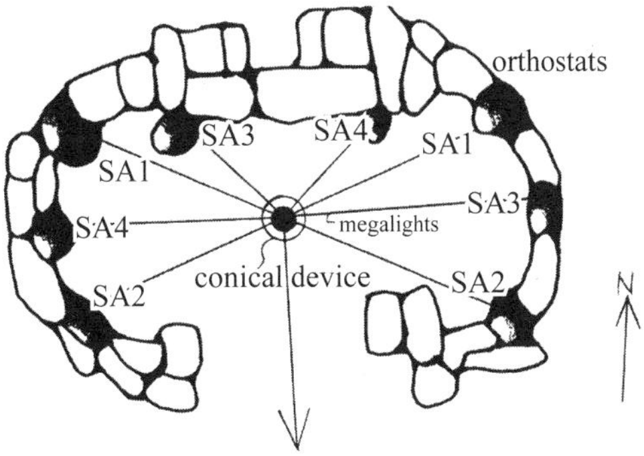

Orthostats Forming the Terminal Altar, the Holy of the Holies of the Southern Temple: A Built-in "Stone circle"
Diagram 5.21

As suggested above, the curved apses of the Maltese temples once functioned like orthostats horseshoes. The following illustration shows how an SA connects the two horseshoes: the terminal niche and right/left apse of the outer bay of the Southern Temple, with the heavily decorated trilithon doorway in the middle (diagram 5.22). Three carved stone phalli, cylindrical with horizontal lines, are found inside the terminal niche, which further suggests that a conical device was once placed inside for generating power.

SA Formed by Two "Stone Circles" of Southern Temple with the Carved Doorway Trilithon in Middle
Diagram 5.22

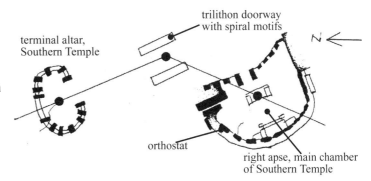

A large square recess with five holes is found outside the Southern Temple (diagram 5.23). The recess forms SA1 and SA2 with the terminal niche and the trilithon altar at the west apse of the inner bay respectively. Therefore, the holes of the recess probably mark the location of the conical devices.

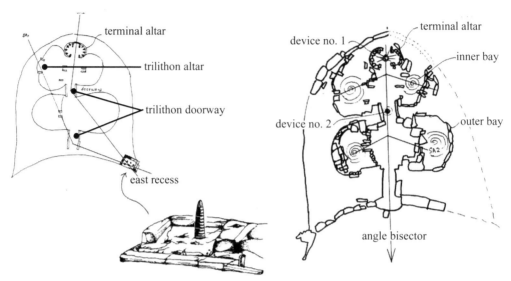

Square Recess with Conical Device Connecting Terminal Altar by Megalights
Diagram 5.23

Megalithic Generator of Southern Temple, Tarxien, 3000 B.C.
Diagram 5.24

Central Temple: Real Soul of the Builders' Generator

The use of the SA inside Tarxien is further proved by the Central Temple, the youngest temple on the island. In order to make way for the Central Temple, the eastern apse of the Southern Temple was deliberately or inevitably dismantled. It further suggests that the whole structure could not have been a sacred temple, as such an additional construction would be sacrilege to their goddess in the first place, and destabilize the entire infrastructure in the second. This was probably an inevitable move for the Central Temple builders in order to connect the power cells of the two neighboring temples. The diagram below shows how the three trilithon doorways of the three Tarxien temples are connected by the SA (diagram 5.25). Besides, the main axis of the Central Temple forms another SA with the terminal niche of the Southern Temple.

Three Major Temples of Tarxien Connected by the SA
Diagram 5.25

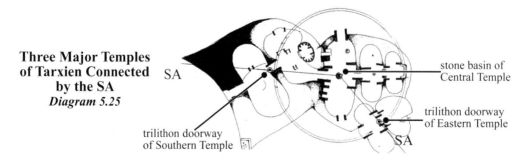

Trilithon Doorway and the Conical Device

The Central Temple of Tarxien is famous for its massive doorways. A pair of huge standing stone blocks forms a trilithon with an even larger slab on top (diagram 5.26). These doorways are heavily dressed and carved with iconic spiral patterns. Structurally, they function like the dolmens of Neolithic Europe and probably supplied power for the builders. What they need is the power activator, the builders' conical device.

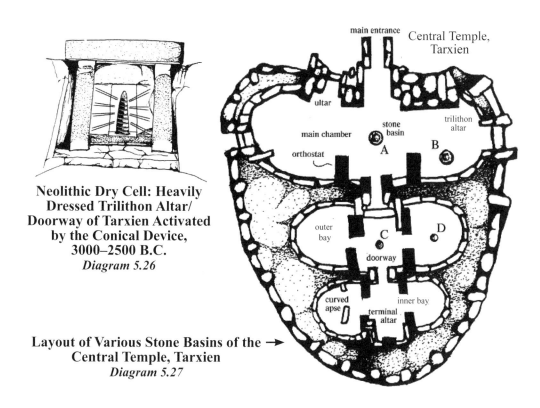

Neolithic Dry Cell: Heavily Dressed Trilithon Altar/ Doorway of Tarxien Activated by the Conical Device, 3000–2500 B.C.
Diagram 5.26

Layout of Various Stone Basins of the → Central Temple, Tarxien
Diagram 5.27

The Secret of the Stone Basins

What makes the Central Temple of Tarxien so interesting is the mysterious circular stone basins, designated A, B, C, and D, placed in the center of the temple apses. They are magnificently set into a huge megalithic floor-stone. They once served as markers for the conical devices and were placed according to the SA. For example, stone basin C forms an SA with the terminal niche of the Southern Temple with stone basin A in the middle. The angle bisects at stone basin B (diagram 5.28). Besides, another SA is formed by stone basin C and the terminal niche, with stone basin B in the middle. Again, the angle bisects at stone basin A. They further suggest that the terminal niche of the Southern Temple, working as a power supplier, provided energy not only for the Southern Temple but also for the Central Temple. That explains why the Central Temple was deliberately constructed and placed in such an odd location.

Spiral Carvings of Tarxien

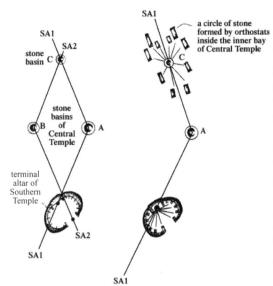

SAs Formed by Various Stone Bowls of Central Temple
Diagram 5.28

The real function of these megalithic monuments is repeatedly told by the temples' spiral carvings. Our journey starts with a slab with four enormous spirals carved on the sillstone. It stands in the narrow passageway that connects the outer and inner bays of the Central Temple (diagram 5.29). As shown in the carving, the four huge and eye-catching spirals are carved in high relief enveloping a circle of dots. They are all placed inside a "quadra-curve" diagram, with each spiral placed at the four corners of that diagram. There are two openings which are probably exits carved at both sides of the "quadra-curve" diagram, as suggested by the empty space between two carved lines.

The artist is trying to capture what happened inside the temple 5,000 years ago. The "quadra-curve" diagram is actually a bird's-eye view of the four-apse temple with trilithon doorways at the two ends. A conical device, represented by the central dot-circle, lies in the middle doorway and connects the curved apses—the stone horseshoes of the Central Temple—with megalights (diagram 5.30). When the mechanism is activated, energy in the form of spinning spirals would be generated inside these four apses. And this is the whole story of Tarxien.

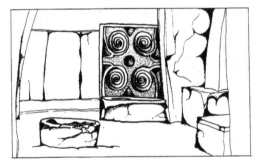

Magnificent Spiral Carvings in the Inner Bay of Central Temple with Stone Bowl A nearby
(Source: David Hatcher Childress, *Lost Cities of Atlantis, Ancient Europe and the Mediterranean,* p. 213)
Diagram 5.29

The Quadra-curve and the Four-apse Central Temple of Tarxien
Diagram 5.30

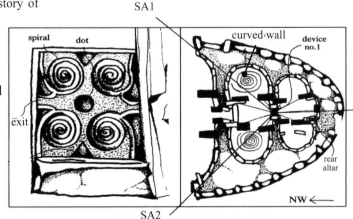

The same mechanism can be applied to Newgrange, where three spirals, the famous Triskelion, are generated in its recesses. A rock carving found inside a Neolithic tomb in County Clare of Ireland perfectly explains the mechanism of the Maltese powerhouse (diagram 5.31). It clearly describes the layout of the Central Temple of Tarxien where two oval-shaped chambers are connected by central doorways ending with another rear chamber. Two cone-shaped objects are carved predominantly in the center of the two oval chambers, the exact location of stone basin A, and they probably represent the builders' conical devices.

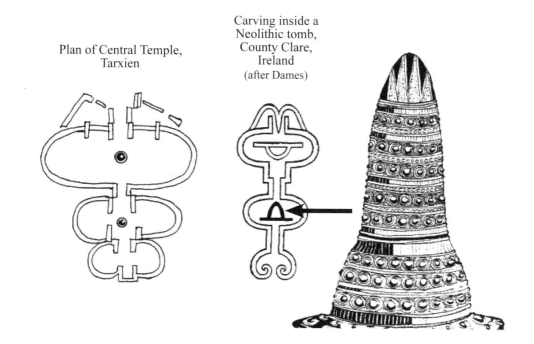

Plan of Central Temple, Tarxien

Carving inside a Neolithic tomb, County Clare, Ireland (after Dames)

Hints from a Rock Carving in a Neolithic Tomb, County Clare, Ireland (*center*), and Its Similarities in Layout with the Temple of Tarxien
Diagram 5.31

Obviously, the two-sided trilithon altars of the outer bay form an SA with the lintel passageway of the Central Temple. It could not be coincidental as these passages are decorated with running spirals (diagram 5.32). Different Maltese models with identical functions are placed side by side for comparison (diagram 5.33).

Power Generator of the Central Temple, Tarxien, 2500 B.C.
Diagram 5.32

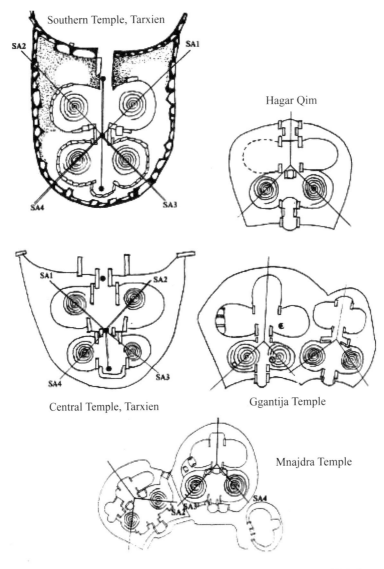

Spirals Showing the Real Function of the Temples of Malta
Diagram 5.33

Great Goddess Motif of Mycenae

The following ideogram of the Great Gods, also known as the sectioned egg motif, was written by a Mycenaean who had a direct link to the first civilization—the Sumerians of the Near East—in 3000 B.C. Sitchin describes the symbol as the eye slots or goggles of the ancient travelers from the stars. This divine being continues to dominate the art of not only Asia Minor but also the early Greeks during the Minoan and Mycenaean periods. The ideogram can be divided into three main parts: an elongated object placed inside a rectangle which separates two semioval objects embraced with a radiance of dagger-like objects. These dagger-like objects are then connected to another semioval circumference formed by small circles (diagram 5.34).

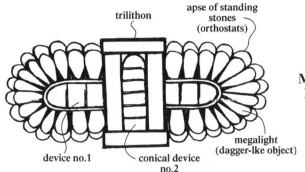

apse of standing
stones
(orthostats)

trilithon

**Messages behind the Goddess
Motif of the Ancient Greeks**
Diagram 5.34

megalight
(dagger-lke object)

device no.1

conical device
no.2

**A Neolithic Dry Cell:
Conical Device inside the
Trilithon Doorway of a
Maltese Temple**
Diagram 5.35

The ideogram actually describes the energy mechanism of the builders, with the elongated object referring to the conical device as we can tell from its round top, flat bottom, and the horizontal lines on its body. The artist places the device inside a trilithon doorway, denoted by three rectangular bars that surround an elongated object. It is a typical dry cell battery of the builders. The dry cell battery is further flanked by two conical devices, each placed in the center of a horseshoe-shaped stone circle. Rows of dagger-like objects are projected from these two devices onto the surface of the surrounding monoliths. That is exactly how the Maltese temples work: two "activated" apses are connected by a trilithon dry cell battery by megalights (diagrams 5.35, 5.36).

**Goddess of Greeks Applied
to the Powerhouse of
Tarxien**
Diagram 5.36

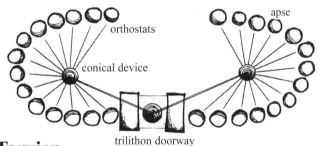

orthostats

apse

conical device

trilithon doorway

Megalithic Phalli of Tarxien

The following diagram shows a group of phalli made of globigerina limestone. According to the excavators, the three phalli stand on a triangular base which is cut to resemble a carved slab in the front. The statuette is 12.3cm high and 6.5cm wide and was found at the terminal niche, the power supplier of the Southern Temple (diagram 5.37). The conical or cylindrical shape of these phalli echoes another stone phallus found in the great mound of Knowth and the gold cones of Western Europe. They are replicas of the builders' conical device and as a matter of fact, it takes three to form an SA!

←**"Phalli" of Tarxien—Replicas of the Conical Device**
Diagram 5.37

Skorbe Temples

The site, which is in the northwest of Malta comprises two temple remains, each of which is a typical three-apsed temple. The temples are made of globigerina limestone from a mile away. The earlier West temple has a stone-paved doorway leading to the inner apse (ca. 3600 B.C). The irregularity of the floors, the absence of hearths, and the excavation of a group of figurines in the northern room suggest that the building had a religious, rather than domestic, function around 3100 B.C. A second temple was added to the east one, which originally consisted of four apses and a central niche (Heritage Malta 2003). The diagram below shows two SAs are derived from the trilithon doorways of the temples (diagram 5.38).

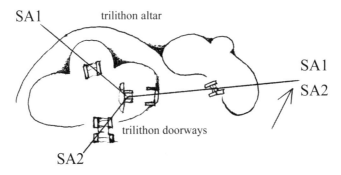

Plan of Skorba, 3600–3000 B.C.
Diagram 5.38

Kordin III Temples

Kordin III is the best-preserved of the trefoil structures, which can date back to 3600–3000 B.C. A forecourt leads to a stone-paved entrance with a passage leading to the central court. The whole structure is made of hard limestone brought from over 2km away (megalithic.co.uk). The diagram below shows that SA1 connects the main entrances of the three Kordin temples. SA2 is formed by the doorway to the rear apse and the main entrance of the central temple together with the entrance of the western temple (diagram 5.39).

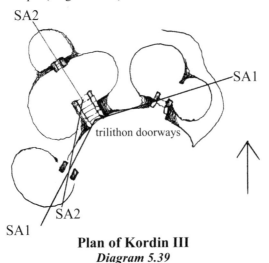

Plan of Kordin III
Diagram 5.39

Spirals of the Hypogeum

The most mysterious Neolithic monument on Malta is the Hypogeum of Hal Saflieni, an underground complex of chambers, passages, and stairways. It is believed to be a rock-cut temple turned into a tomb, and dates back to 3800 B.C. This three-level structure consists of thirty-three oval or circular chambers and recesses and is carved out of solid rock. There are twenty chambers that contain numerous shallow post-holed niches and altars serving unknown purposes.

Chambers 18 and 20 have ceilings carved with running spirals in red paint. The diagram below comes from one of the paintings of the Hypogeum, with the red dots forming various sets of SAs (diagram 5.40). It is fair to conclude that the underground site which is equipped with circular chambers, trilithon entrances, Stone Angled drawings, and spiral decorations, is just another center of that lost civilization.

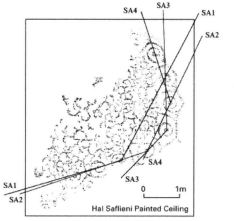

Famous Red-painted Spiral Carvings of Hypogeum (from Christopher Tilley and Wayne Bennett, *The Materiality of Stone*)
Diagram 5.40

Mysterious Trilithon Altar inside Hypogeum
Diagram 5.41

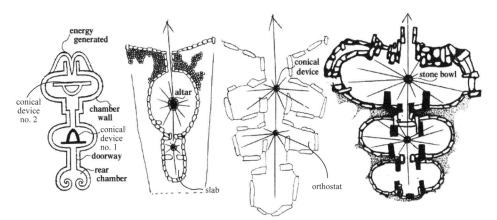

Twin-devices Mechanism: The Ultimate Trick of the Temple Builders
(from left: an Irish Neolithic carving; chambered cairn in Ireland; West Kennet long barrow of Britain; and Central Temple of Tarxien)
Diagram 5.42

Menhirs, Dolmens, and Stone Circle of Malta

The Maltese Islands certainly constitute one of the centers of the Neolithic builders. Apart from the twenty-three sophisticated temple powerhouses, other megalithic structures are commonly found around the region. Like those from contemporary Europe, there are eight standing stones, recognized as menhirs (Evans 1971, Trump 1990) located at the southern part of the two islands. Most of them are made of coralline or globigerina limestone. The tallest menhir at Qala has a height of 3.3m. However, experts find no significant orientation with these monoliths (Malta Homepage).

Ta' Hammud is the only dolmen excavated on the Maltese islands which could date back to the Early Bronze age. It consists of a horizontal slab of coralline limestone lying on a number of supporting stones.

One of the famous megalithic infrastructures is the Xaghra Circle, also known as the Brochdorff Circle after two watercolor paintings describing the site left behind by Charles de Brochorff in 1824. According to the artwork, several trilithon altars were once erected at the center of the circle, which probably reveals the real function of the construction. Experts suggest that the Circle had been used since 4100–3800 B.C.

Tiny Model of a Megalithic Temple from Ta' Hargrat Temple. Energy Shown as Horizontal Bars Carved above Trilithon Doorways.
Diagram 5.43

Carving on the "Plant Altar" of Hagar Qim, Showing Microwaves above Trilithon Doorways
(Rudgley, p. 28)
Diagram 5.45

Carving inside Mnajdra Showing Horizontal Lines of Energy above an Activated Maltese Trilithon Doorway
Diagram 5.44

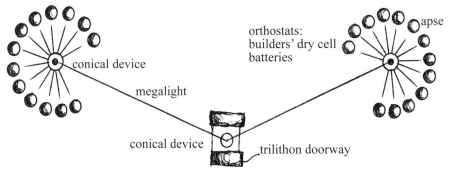

A Typical Powerhouse of Malta
Diagram 5.46

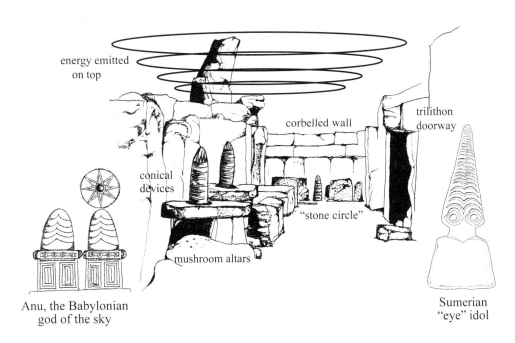

energy emitted
on top

corbelled wall

trilithon
doorway

conical
devices

"stone circle"

mushroom altars

Anu, the Babylonian
god of the sky

Sumerian
"eye" idol

The Powerhouse of Hagar Qim, 3000 B.C.:
Conical Devices on Top of Mushroom Altars
Diagram 5.47

The dry cell
battery of
Tarxien

Sculpted Pair of Phalli Found in a Temple Niche, Tarxien, Malta
(info: Marija Gimbutas, *The Language of the Goddess*)
Diagram 5.48

Chapter 6
Neolithic Britain

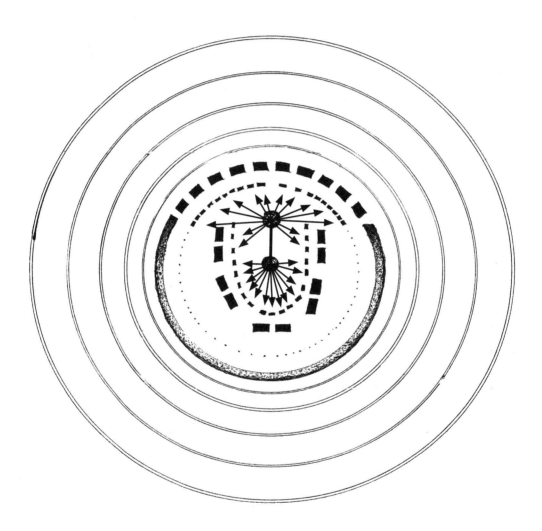

Twin-device Energy Mechanism of Stonehenge Powerhouse, ca. 2000 B.C.
A power-generating machine consisting of upper (ten sarsens + nineteen bluestone circles) and lower (ten sarsens + nineteen bluestone horseshoes) parts.

Mystery of the Long Barrow

Dating back to 4000–3000 B.C., the megalithic long barrows are regarded as one of the oldest human-made structures in England and Wales. There are 260 long barrows, which can be divided into unchambered and chambered barrows. The unchambered or earthen long barrows have a longer history than the chambered ones. Most of the earthen long barrows are rectangular or trapezoidal in shape and about 20–120m long with almost vertical walls or banks of chalk and earth (Lesley and Roy Adkins) along their sides (diagram 6.01). Their unusually long earthen tails, which constitute more than seven-eighths of the whole structure, seem to serve no apparent purpose other than display. That is why

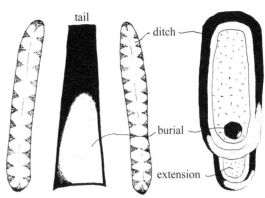

Plan of an Unchambered Long Barrow (*left*) and the West Rudham Long Barrow
(after Hogg)
Diagram 6.01

they are built on the slopes rather than the crests of the ridges. Some are constructed with stone mortuary chambered mounds in one end where skeletons are seldom found. Their mystery is no less than that of Stonehenge. One of the famous earthen long barrows around the region is the Horslip long barrow, which is found on the southern side of Windmill Hill.

The diagram below shows the distribution of ten unchambered earthen long barrows around Stonehenge. They form at least seven sets of SAs. They probably acted as the builders' dry cell batteries for tapping energy in 4000 B.C.

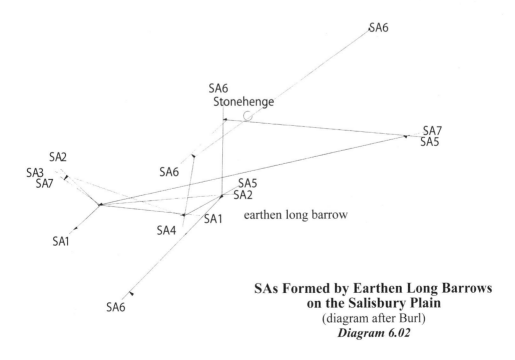

SAs Formed by Earthen Long Barrows on the Salisbury Plain
(diagram after Burl)
Diagram 6.02

Long Barrows and the Cursus of Stonehenge

The Salisbury Plain is densely populated with Neolithic structures of different kinds. The Stonehenge Great Cursus, another kind of extremely long and narrow monument, is also regarded as one of the megalithic enigmas. It is probably the most neglected around the region. This 5,000-year-old structure that lies north of Stonehenge and extends from west to east is characterized by a pair of almost exactly parallel earthen banks of 3km in length and 100m in width. It covers an area of 280,000 square meters and required 1,250,000 man-hours to build (Rodney Castleden 1993). The two ends of the Great Cursus lie on higher ground between the valley of Salisbury, which makes the two ends inter-visible. Its function as an ancient racecourse is questionable. Its intimate links with the surrounding earthen long barrows, no fewer than a dozen in the region, suggests that it once worked as a parade track for Neolithic funerals (diagram 6.03).

By applying the SA to the monument, one can easily see that the track of the Cursus lies exactly on the intercepting point(s) of the surrounding pairs of long barrows. In other words, any point along the track would become an angle bisector of a set of SAs with the long barrows on two sides. The Cursus may be a landing place for refueling the builders' machines.

On the other hand, the chambered earthen long barrows are constructed with stone chambers, an antechamber, and a passage at one end (diagram 6.04). Some, like those in Nutbane, were rebuilt and enlarged with their front walls turned into a forecourt by adding a pair of large posts at each end. They are deliberately positioned on rising ground so as to be visible from a long distance, with a preference for an east-west orientation. Like the unchambered ones, they were not simply burial places but some kind of territorial markers for astronomical purposes.

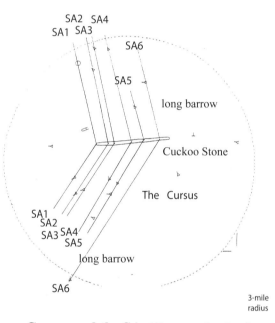

Cursus and the SA (diagram after Burl)
Diagram 6.03

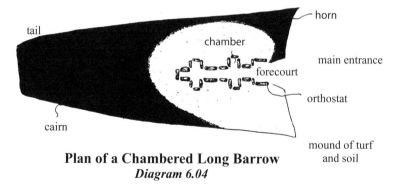

Plan of a Chambered Long Barrow
Diagram 6.04

The West Kennet Long Barrow

The West Kennet long barrow is certainly the most famous and dramatic, and one of the largest, stone-chambered earth mounds dating back to 3600 B.C. It is located on a prominent chalk ridge, about 2km south of the great henge of Avebury. It is about 104m in length with the widest opening (23m) in the east. A semicircular open forecourt is skillfully constructed with huge sarsen slabs at the eastern entrance. The forecourt leads to the main passage, along which two sarsen chambers open on each side, and another larger polygonal chamber, which is 2.3m high is at its west end. These five chambers only constitute one-eighth of the whole barrow's length. A long tail of earth extends to the west. The barrow has two long ditches on its sides. It had been used as a ceremonial place continuously for more than 1,000 years before becoming a major burial site (huge numbers of skeletons are found inside its chambers). It is also said to be a temple for worshipping the Great Goddess (Dames). Local legends say the tomb is visited by a ghost priest and a large white hound on Midsummer's Day, which probably suggests its astronomical function.

Structurally speaking, the design and arrangement of the chambers of the West Kennet long barrow are similar to those of the Maltese temples in Tarxien and Ggantija (diagram 6.05). They were built between 3500 and 3000 B.C. In West Kennet, a forecourt leads to a passage with two pairs of recesses adjacent to each other and ending with another rear recess. Such a design is found in most of the Maltese temples, where two pairs of apses are constructed at two sides and end with a rear recess—the holy of the holies. Like West Kennet, a huge forecourt is formed by gigantic limestone blocks outside the trilithon entrance of the Maltese temples. Both of these two mysterious Neolithic infrastructures, which are both installed with five stone circles of orthostats connected by trilithon doorways—the dry cell batteries—were probably the earliest version of Stonehenge III.

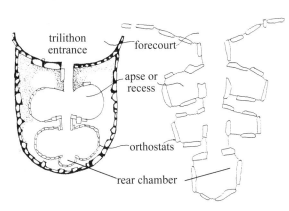

trilithon entrance
forecourt
apse or recess
orthostats
rear chamber

Plan of Southern Temple, Tarxien, 3500–3000 B.C.

Plan of West Kennet long barrow, 3500 B.C.

"Stone Circles" inside the Tarxien Temple and West Kennet Long Barrow
Diagram 6.05

The West Kennet long barrow was certainly built for housing the conical devices, as we can tell by the special design of its four side chambers (diagram 6.06a). Instead of paralleling the main entrance, the orthostats of the two outer chambers, together with the two inner ones, are conspiratorially placed to lean towards the rear recess to form an SA. In exactly the same pattern as the Tarxien powerhouse, two conical devices were once placed inside the two chambers. Device no. 1 projected megalights and tapped energy from a circle of orthostats nearby, whereas device no. 2 was responsible for discharging. The third device, which was placed in the middle of that SA, connected and activated the twin-device energy mechanism by megalights. The polygonal chamber at the rear marks the angle bisector. The same process repeated itself inside the two inner chambers of West Kennet, and this is exactly what the "Mycencaean Goggle" tries to tell us. It constitutes the first stage of the West Kennet powerhouse in 3500 B.C.

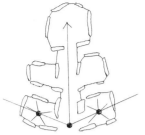

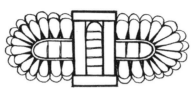

The Twin-device Energy Mechanism inside West Kennet
Diagram 6.06a

Goddess Motif of Greece
Diagram 6.06b

Powerhouse of West Kennet
Diagram 6.06c

Another important chambered long barrow is Wayland's Smithy, which is found on a high ridge. It was constructed in at least two phases. The first phase includes an oval structure that contains a wooden mortuary house lying between two pits of tree trunks. A pavement of sarsens was laid on the chalk, and the central tomb was placed inside a horseshoe-shaped wall of sarsen slabs up to 1m high with an opening to the south. A forecourt-like structure was constructed just outside the horseshoe. The tomb was finally covered with chalk rubble (diagram 6.07).

Wayland's Smithy Long Barrow (Frontal View)
Diagram 6.07

The horseshoe-like structure of phase I of Wayland's Smithy echoes the drawing of the Solar God of Newgrange, and their designs are basically the same. As suggested by the twin-device mechanism, the two timber posts inside the tomb of Wayland probably mark the locations for placing the twin-device, which projected megalights to the surrounding sarsen horseshoe for power (diagram 6.08). Another long barrow in a similar design is the Fussell's Lodge, and I would like to compare their internal structure with the drawing of the Solar God of Newgrange (diagrams 6.09a and b).

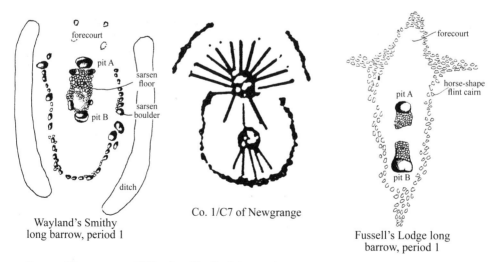

Wayland's Smithy
long barrow, period 1

Co. 1/C7 of Newgrange

Fussell's Lodge long
barrow, period 1

Inner Structure of Wayland's Smithy and the Twin-device Mechanism
Diagrams 6.08 (left) and 6.09a and b

The long barrow of Way-
land's Smithy was then
further enlarged by a 55m-
long trapezoidal mound,
which is surrounded by
kerbstones (diagram
6.10a). It is tapered from
about 14m wide at its
southern end to less than
6m at its northern. Similar
to the bluestone horse-
shoe of Stonehenge III,
the elongated circle of
kerbstones of Wayland
was once heated up by the
twin-device. A cruciform
chamber is built at its
wider end, which proba-
bly marks the angle bisector of the powerhouse.

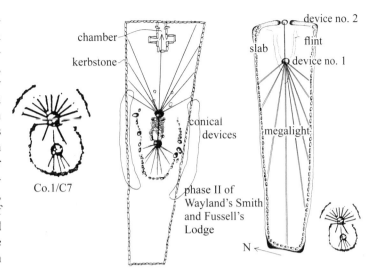

**Powerhouse of Wayland's
Smithy II mechanism**
Diagram 6.10a

**Fussell's Lodge II and the
Twin-device**
Diagram 6.10b

Long and Round Barrows

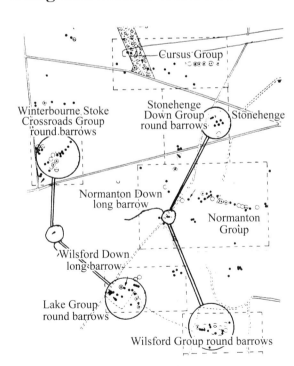

**Cemetery Groups Round Barrows around
Stonehenge** (diagram after M. Balfour)
Diagram 6.11

The secret of the long barrows is certainly
more than this. The map on the left shows
the distribution of the various long and
round barrows on Salisbury Plain (diagram 6.11). Each of the long barrows has
its own territory, a rectangular strip of
land of about 1.5 square miles with one of
them on the high ground of the plain (Aubrey Burl 1987). There are two clusters
of barrow groups near Stonehenge: the
Winterbourne Stoke Crossroads Group in
the north and the Lake Group in the south.
They are separated by two long barrows,
namely, LB1: Wilsford Down long barrow
and LB2: Normanton Down long barrow.
Out of interest, I applied the SA formula
to the region and discovered that any selected pair of round barrows, one from
the Winterbourne Stoke Group and one
from the Lake Group, forms an SA with
the Wilsford Down long barrow, LB1, in
the middle. In the same way, nine sets of
SAs are derived with LB1 in the middle
(diagram 6.12). This pattern repeats itself
in two other groups of round barrows, the

Stonehenge Down Group in the north and the Wilford Group in the south, with the Normanton Down long barrow, LB2, in the middle. They form eight pairs of SAs (diagram 6.13).

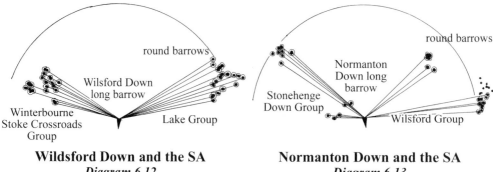

Wildsford Down and the SA
Diagram 6.12

Normanton Down and the SA
Diagram 6.13

In other words, the long and round barrows are connected by the SA to form a gigantic power station (diagram 6.14). Unlike the West Kennet long barrow in Wiltshire where the dry cell batteries were housed inside its chambers, the builders' substituted it with clusters of round earthen barrows. They could certainly generate a huge amount more energy, as they occupy a vast area of land.

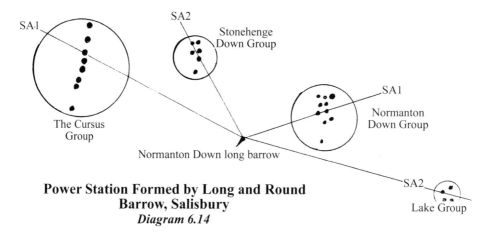

Power Station Formed by Long and Round Barrow, Salisbury
Diagram 6.14

After the construction work, twin device no. 2 would be placed at the entrance of the long barrow and project a radiance of megalights to the surrounding round barrows for energy. At the same time, device no. 1 would be placed inside the long barrow for discharging, and a line of megalight would connect the two devices to complete the twin-device energy mechanism (diagram 6.15).

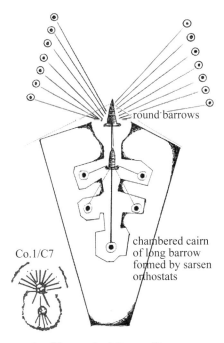

Co.1/C7

round barrows

chambered cairn
of long barrow
formed by sarsen
orthostats

**An Upgraded Long Barrow
Powerhouse Activated by Round
Barrows**
Diagram 6.15

During the energy generating process, local materials such as flint and chalk inside the long barrow helped to transfer energy wastes from device no.1 to the ground. At the same time, the round barrows, which acted as dry cell batteries, were heated up by device no.2 and helped to tap energy underneath. What exactly were these round barrows?

Experts suggest there are about 30,000 to 40,000 round barrows of early Bronze Age over England and Wales. In most cases they consist of a circular, in bowl, bell, disc saucer and pond shaped turf-covered mound or a cairn of earth or boulders, and sometimes with kerbs of stones around its edge (diagram 6.16)

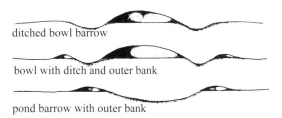

ditched bowl barrow

bowl with ditch and outer bank

pond barrow with outer bank

Various Types of Round Barrows
Diagram 6.16

The Bush Barrow is certainly the most famous round barrows on Salisbury Plain where important gold and jade artifacts are unearthed inside its central chamber (diagram 6.17). It is a typical design of a builders' dry cell battery in which sarsen orthostats were placed and covered by earth and flint. And this must be the secret of their energy mechanism.

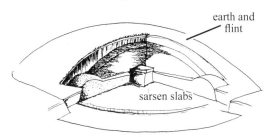

earth and flint

sarsen slabs

**Cross-section of the Bush Barrow, a
Typical Dry Cell Battery of the Builders**
Diagram 6.17

David R. Cowan and Chris Arnold, in their book *Ley Lines and Earth Energies,* suggest the concave surfaces of the burial round barrows helped to focus radiation into a very small area due to the fact that "the angle of incidence for incident light, sound and radiation equals the angle of reflection" (p. 56) (diagram 6.18). Therefore, with the installation of sarsen boulders, which are rich in quartz grains, it is possible that these barrows, clustered over old Wessex—probably a major concentration field of the Earth energy—were there to generate power. Cowan concludes "we are left with the possibility that the barrow was acting as a battery and generating a current, or alternatively, a capacitor, capable of storing energy. If the barrow had been built over a seismic source which emitted infra-red or geothermal energy, however, then the trap of that barrow, comprised perhaps of earth, flint, organic and inorganic matter would emit thermal energy" (p. 210). Burke and Halberg suggest that some man-made British Bronze Age mounds were electromagnetically highly active (2005, p. 39). To sum up, what connected and activated these dry cell batteries were the light beams generated by the builders' conical devices.

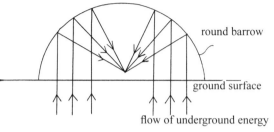

A Neolithic Round Barrow—Dry Cell Battery of the Builders—and the Focus of Energy
(idea from Cowan and Arnold)
Diagram 6.18

round barrow

ground surface

flow of underground energy

Round Barrows and the Cursus

To further modify their power station, the builders replaced the long barrows with the round barrows around ca. 3000–2500 B.C. The drawing on the right shows the relationship between Stonehenge Great Cursus and its surrounding round barrows. It clearly indicates that the two round barrows on both sides of the Cursus form an SA. There are several sets of SAs with their centers or angle bisectors along the Cursus (diagram 6.19).

round barrows

Round Barrows and the Great Cursus
(after Burl) *Diagram 6.19*

Lesser Cursus and the SA

Half a mile northwest of the Stonehenge Great Cursus lies another cursus-like monument, a pseudo long barrow known as the Lesser Cursus, in the shape of a lobster. The monument is 400m long with its two parallel banks reaching out to the northeast like a pair of claws. Its west end forms several sets of SAs with the surrounding long and round barrows respectively (diagram 6.20). That is to say, the Lesser Cursus was also once a power station of the builders.

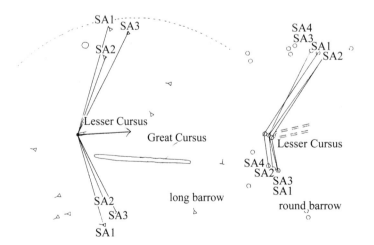

Long and Round Barrows, and the Lesser Cursus Power Station
(after Burl)
Diagram 6.20

Long Barrows on the Wiltshire Plain

The alignment of monuments to the SA on Salisbury was not a unique experiment of the builders. The county of Wiltshire, the favorite sacred precinct of the Neolithic world, contains 148 out of 260 Britain's long barrows. Diagram 6.21 shows the distribution of the long barrows around the great henge of Avebury. The long barrow of Millbarrow, also known as Winterbourne Monkton, lies in its north, and the East Kennet Long Barrow in its south. These long barrows form at least nine sets of SAs with the neighboring monuments (diagram 6.21):

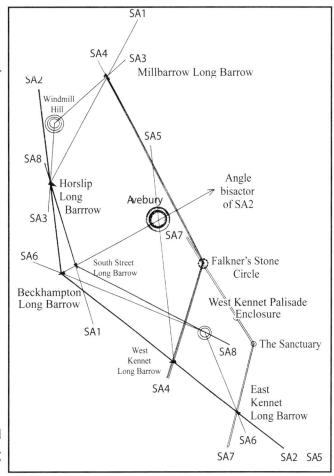

**Long Barrows around
Avebury and the SA**
Diagram 6.21

SA1 Millbarrow Long Barrow–Horslip Long Barrow–South Street Long Barrow
SA2 Horslip Long Barrow–Beckhampton Long Barrow–West Kennet Long Barrow and East Kennet Long Barrow
SA3 Millbarrow Long Barrow–Windmill Hill–Horslip Long Barrow
SA4 Millbarrow Long Barrow–Falkner's Stone Circle–West Kennet Long Barrow
SA5 Avebury–West Kennet Long Barrow–East Kennet Long Barrow
SA6 Beckhampton Long Barrow–West Kennet Palisade Enclosure–East Kennet Long Barrow
SA7 Falkner's Stone Circle–The Sanctuary–East Kennet Long Barrow
SA8 Horslip Long Barrow–South Street Long Barrow–West Kennet Palisade Enclosure
SA9 Falkner's Stone Circle–West Kennet Palisade Enclosure–West Kennet Long Barrow

Long Barrows and Enclosures of Wiltshire

SA1 is formed by the henge of Windmill Hill and the West Kennet long barrow, with the Beckhampton long barrow in the center. The angle bisects at the great henge of Avebury (diagram 6.22 below). It is important to clarify that the SA mentioned is only formed by a (solid) line passing through the center of Windmill Hill on one side, and the other line touching the tail or west end of the West Kennet long barrow. If the golden rule of 135 degrees is strictly observed, it will be impossible for a line to touch the center of Windmill Hill if another line is drawn to the east entrance of the West Kennet long barrow.

The powerhouse of Beckhampton once connected the West Kennet long barrow, one of the many dry cell batteries, with the Windmill Hill. Twin-device no. 2, placed at the entrance of Beckhampton, projected a row of megalight to the tail of West Kennet, tapping energy. Another row of megalight transferred the energy from Beckhampton to Windmill Hill.

Sanctuary Stone and Wood Circle and the SA

At the same time, SA2 is formed by the henge of the Sanctuary and the Beckhampton long barrow, with the West Kennet long barrow in the center. This angle can only be formed when one line passes through the center of the Sanctuary, and the other to the tail, not the entrance of Beckhampton long barrow, with the east facing entrance of the West Kennet long barrow in the middle. The line in no way touches the center of the Sanctuary if the other line reaches the forecourt of the Beckhampton long barrow (diagram 6.22). In this case, West Kennet long barrow functioned in exactly the same way as Beckhampton, which also connected a long barrow and a dry cell battery on one end and an enclosure on the other.

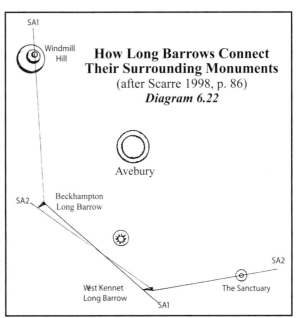

How Long Barrows Connect Their Surrounding Monuments
(after Scarre 1998, p. 86)
Diagram 6.22

Avebury Standing Stone Circles and the SA

As shown in the same regional map, the West Kennet long barrow also forms SA3 with the East Kennet long barrow and the henge of Avebury. Once again, the angle is only formed when a line is projected from West Kennet to the center of Avebury, and the other one to the tail of the East Kennet long barrow (diagram 6.23). An SA is formed according to the following principle: a long barrow and a henge connected by another long barrow. It could be applied to the Windmill Hill causeway, the Sanctuary Circle, and the great henge of Avebury. What about the largest man-made stepped pyramid of Europe—the Silbury Hill?

Powerhouse of Silbury Hill

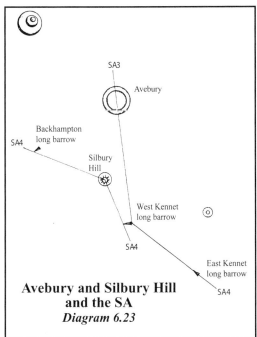

**Avebury and Silbury Hill
and the SA**
Diagram 6.23

Experts point out that all the Neolithic sites on the plain have line-of-sight communication with Silbury Hill, around which they form a ragged circuit (Paul Devereux). This gigantic pyramid of Europe is 183m around the base and stands 55m high. Like the henge and avenues of Avebury as well as Stonehenge I, Silbury Hill was built in the same period, around 2900 B.C. Experts estimate that it took 4,000,000 man-hours (40–50 years of full-time work) to move 250,000 cubic meters of chalk to the site.

Instead of imitating a natural giant mound, the structure of Silbury Hill is more complicated than expected. The artificial mound was constructed in three stages, each filled with local rubble and chalk to form a sort of stepped cone. According to R. J. C. Atkinson, the innermost layer of Silbury Hill (S1) is a small core of clay covered by a circular stack of turf to form a mound 3.5m in height and 20m in diameter. The mound is further enclosed by four successive layers of chalk and gravel to form S2. The S2 chalk mound is then surrounded by a circle of sarsen stones and a circular burial ditch (diagram 6.24a). The last phase—S3—comprises six concentric steps or terraces of chalk, forming a cone-shaped mound.

Silbury: The Gigantic "Dry Cell Battery," 2500 B.C.

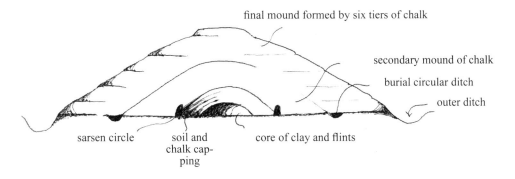

Internal Structure of Silbury Hill, Wiltshire
(info: R. J. C. Atkinson and Stonehenge-avebury.net)
Diagram 6.24a

"Like Wilhelm Reich's orgone accumulator chambers, [Silbury] seems to be some sort of battery storage cell. … It is thought to be an attractor and transducer of energy."

—Barbara Lamb and Judith Moore, *Crop Circles Revealed*

Its flat summit is 40m high and 30m wide, the same diameter as the great sarsen circle of Stonehenge. According to Meaden (1999, p. 11): "Silbury is more than a well-built high mound of quarried loose chalk stored and secured within drum-like walls of chalk blocks, because at its center is a lesser first-stage mound of turves around whose perimeter lies a primitive ring of sarsens—effectively a stone circle inside the hill."

Its complexity is certainly not for decoration. But experts still have no idea as to the real function of the largest pyramid of Europe. It is suggested that the hill might be built on a stone circle. Excavations show it is not a burial tomb of an ancient ruler. Another explanation argues that it could have been used as a solar observatory, as the fabulous view of its surroundings suggests astronomical purposes. Michael Dames has suggested that the hill is a huge symbolic model of the ancient Mother Goddess and probably functioned as a sacred precinct in the prehistoric times.

Some even relate the hill to a "natural earth battery," as the three layers of the structure resemble a modern day battery. It is probably a kind of Chinese *feng shui* mound erected upon the path of the dragon line. Ley hunters suggest that the hill is a center for alignments of straight prehistoric tracks and of standing stones. A ley line even connects Silbury with the church of Avebury and the stone circle at Winterbourne Abbas. Today, mysterious crop circles are also found around the hill.

As shown in diagram 6.23 above, Silbury Hill forms SA4 with the tails of two long barrows nearby, namely Beckhampton and West Kennet. Megalights were once projected to the tails of these two dry cell batteries from the center of the flat hilltop. In my opinion, this gigantic flat-topped hill served as a landing platform for the builders' traveling machine. The diagram below shows several sets of SAs formed by local barrows and Silbury Hill (diagram 6.24b).

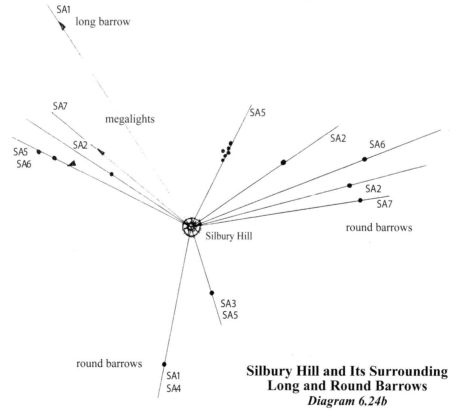

**Silbury Hill and Its Surrounding
Long and Round Barrows**
Diagram 6.24b

Stone Circles of Avebury

People always mention Avebury before turning to Stonehenge, not because the former is 500 years older than the latter, but because its ditch and megaliths are far superior to those of Stonehenge. The monument lies in the heart of old Wessex with some world-class prehistoric monuments such as the West Kennet long barrow, Silbury Hill, and the enclosure of Windmill Hill, forming the most sacred prehistoric precinct in Britain, if not the whole of Europe. Today, Avebury is one of fourteen World Heritage Sites in the country.

Its ditch, with only a third of its original depth remaining today, is the largest and deepest of its kind in the world. Inside, it is estimated there are 184 stones of different sizes (Meaden 1999), ranging from twenty to sixty tons in weight, forming a diameter of 350m, making it the largest stone circle in Europe. Recent excavations at the site discovered a megalithic stone that stands 4.4m above and at least 2.2m below the ground surface and weighs around 100 tons.

To people's surprise, the monument was so huge and old that it was finally "discovered accidentally" by John Aubrey after returning from a day's hunting in 1648. Experts estimate the great stone circle would have taken 1.5 million man hours to gather and erect. It is so huge that a village is built within it. Its entire circumference, an unbelievable 1.3km, is formed by a truly enormous bank and ditch with four entrances. And as expected, these entrances are accurately open at the cardinal compass points (diagram 6.26). However, its irregularity rules out any astronomical function.

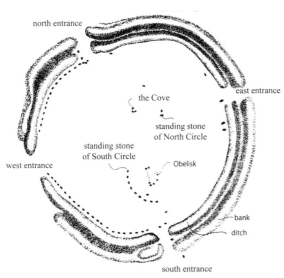

north entrance

the Cove

east entrance

standing stone of North Circle

standing stone of South Circle

Obelisk

west entrance

bank

ditch

south entrance

Plan of Avebury
Diagram 6.26

Today, a road (A4361) splits each quadrant of the circle and practically brings this spiritual and mysterious monument into our secular world. But in ancient times it was an avenue of stones of different sizes, probably acting like a gigantic megalithic serpent, passing through Avebury towards Overton Hill a mile and a half away, forming a traditional alchemical symbol, which only enhanced the site's mystery (sacredsites.com).

Unlike Stonehenge, which is restricted to its center, Avebury is open to pilgrim tourists as well as local sheep. Neo-pagans openly perform their rituals, hoping to recapture the once dominant but now lost natural and spiritual energy of the site. The monument is certainly rich in local folklore and legends. As the story goes, people can summon up natural powers by running 100 times counterclockwise round the Devil's Chair, one of the massive stones of the circle. Women used to come on the eve of May Day and sit on a rock in the shape of a chair and make a wish. A forty-ton stone known as the Diamond Stone is said to be able to cross over to the other side of the road at midnight. Small figures have been seen in the stones in the moonlight. Human faces are frequently identified on the surfaces of the sarsens by Avebury experts. They probably are the sole silent witnesses of the mysterious monument. Visitors today still feel the mythical atmosphere when walking around the site.

In their book *Seed of Knowledge, Stone of Plenty,* John Burke and Haj Halberg believe that the ancient henges are highly electric. As earth currents travel near their surfaces, cutting the ground by a deep circular ditch helped to contain the block and flow.

Ley hunters explain Avebury as part of a vast network of Neolithic sites such as Glastonbury Tor and St. Michael's Mount, which are arranged along a 200-mile "sacred line" stretching across southern England (Hamish Miller). Others further elaborate that two important magical ley lines known as Michael and Mary cross the stones in the southern part of Avebury. It is my suggestion that this ancient energy and wisdom around the region still prevails today, which is evidenced by another mystery of the twentieth century (which will be discussed in Chapter 11).

Inside the henge are a series of stone settings: an immense stone circle with several smaller rings inside. Together with those erected along the Kennet and Beckhampton Avenues, the sixty stones of Sanctuary, and twelve from the Falkner's Circle, the total number of megaliths around the Avebury Complex would have reached about 600 (Meaden 1999). The largest ring is the outer circle, which originally consisted of ninety-eight undressed sarsen stones, some of which weigh over fifty-five tons. Within this largest ring are three smaller stone circles (the northern, southern, and northeast circles), each of which is believed to be formed by two concentric circles or stone arrangements within. Only a few standing stones are now left in the north and south circles; no stones survive in the northeast circle. Many of them were buried, burned, and hammered for religious and economic reasons. The missing stones are marked by small obelisk-shaped posts. The henge complex was built between the late Stone Age and early Bronze Age in around 2800–2600 B.C. and continued to operate until 1500 B.C. Then the whole complex was abandoned and forgotten for more than 3,000 years.

Compared with Stonehenge, Avebury is less explored. John Aubrey described it as "the Scene where the Giants fought with stones against the Gods." People suggest it was built as a temple (of the Sun as well as the Moon), a monument built by the British or Danes, a ruin of the Romans, a place for the funeral rite of the dead, a symbol for fertility, and even a landing site built by aliens and is related to a Martian formation name Cydonia (Deseret News Pub. Co. 2005).

SAs inside Avebury

There has been recent excavation around Avebury, and with the application of geophysics to the site, a two-ringed monument, believed to be a timber henge, was found to the northeast of the North Circle. This timber henge forms SA1 with the center of the South Circle, while the North Circle lies in the middle. The angle bisects at two pairs of portal (standing) stones, one at the east circumference of the North Circle, and the other at the east arc of the great outer ring (diagram 6.27). Were the two stone rings, the South and the North, a substitute for, or a new version of the builders' power machine to replace the long barrow dry cells? A row of megalight once connected the two powerhouses and supplied power to the timber henge nearby.

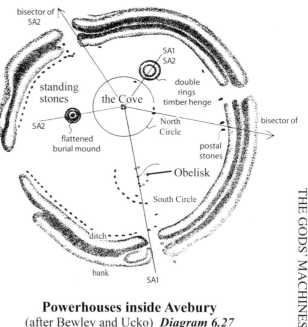

Powerhouses inside Avebury
(after Bewley and Ucko) *Diagram 6.27*

Besides, another prehistoric monument, believed to be a flattened burial mound, lies to the west of the North Circle. It forms SA2 with the missing timber circle of the northeast, and the North Circle lies in the middle. The angle bisects at the north entrance of the henge of Avebury. This time, a round barrow may possibly replace the long barrow to supply energy to that timber henge as well.

Avebury: Phase I

Inside the North Circle of Avebury, a Cove of three colossal stones of hard sandstone form three sides of an open rectangular space (Aubrey and Stukeley). It is like a restricted horseshoe megalithic structure with an east opening. The back stone, the largest of the three, is 4.9m wide and 4.4m high. Another surviving stone is 4.9m high (John North 1996). If there was once a capstone on top, it formed a classic Neolithic dolmen. There are four other standing stones in the northeast, east, and southeast periphery of the North Circle, facing the opening of the Cove (diagram 6.28).

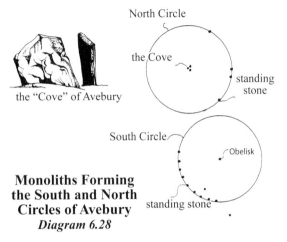

the "Cove" of Avebury

**Monoliths Forming
the South and North
Circles of Avebury**
Diagram 6.28

Lying south of the North Circle is an arc of nine standing stones, forming the southwest periphery of the South Circle. The most eye-catching monolith in the South Circle must be the Obelisk, a tall pillar 6.4m high, standing very close to the center of the circle. There are two more stones, one placed at the south-southwest just inside the southwest arc of the circle and the other erected outside the ring alone at the south-southeast. These standing stones, not forming a complete circle, were there for a definite purpose.

These monoliths were erected according to the SA. For example, the two most impressive features, the Cove of the North Circle and the Obelisk of the South Circle, form an SA (diagram 6.29a). A conical device, which was once placed inside the Cove, projected two rows of megalights, one to a northeast standing stone of the North Circle and the other to the Obelisk of the South Circle. A pair of portal standing stones of the North Circle marks the angle bisector.

A monolith that lies southeast of the North Circle forms another SA with the Cove and the Obelisk (diagram 6.29b). The Obelisk itself forms an SA with the Cove to its north and the isolated monolith lying south-southwest inside the South Circle to its south (diagram 6.29c).

More SAs are probably formed by the rest of the standing stones of the two circles (diagram 6.29d). Were the two inner circles of Avebury the earliest power stations of the builders? Or, were they simply the testing ground of a more elaborate model, like the one standing on the Salisbury Plain 3km away? The answer may be found from its outer stone ring.

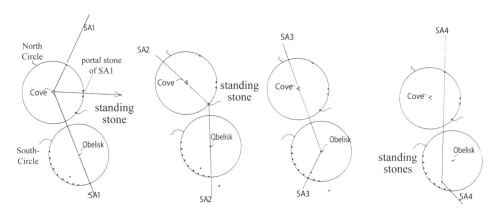

Monoliths of the North and South Circles inside Avebury and the SAs
(diagram after North) *Diagram 6.29a, b, c, and d*

Avebury: Phase II

Diagram 6.30 is a carving found on a rock surface at Old Bewick, Northumberland (John Mitchell, *Megalithomania,* p. 146). It is a typical cup and ring carving with a set of predominantly large concentric circles in the center. A straight line connects its center and a smaller circle at its southeast corner. A row (arc) of nine dots is carved at the northwest corner of the concentric circle. There is a line from each dot connecting the periphery of the circle. It is likely that the artist wanted to tell us the full story of Avebury through the carving.

The Avebury builders intended to upgrade their powerful station. As suggested in the diagram below, the Cove and the Obelisk, functioning like a pair of Station Stones (92 and 93), determine the location of the conical device at point A of Avebury (diagram 6.31). The point marks the true center of the upgraded power station.

Twin-device no. 1, placed at point A, would then project nine rows of megalights onto the standing sarsen stones of the northwest arc of the outer stone circle. At the other end, nine other rows of megalights would also be projected onto the southwest arc of the South Circle for tapping energy (diagram 6.32).

At the same time, another device, no. 1, would have been placed at the center of the South Circle for discharging. It is the same story reflected by the Old Bewick carving, in which a line connects the bigger concentric ring with the south circle. The dramatic modification of Avebury powerhouse from the inner ring to the outer ring echoes the one in Stonehenge, which I will talk about later. It also signifies how a single-SA powerhouse was upgraded to a multi-SA one.

Rock Carving at Old Bewick, Northumberland
Diagram 6.30

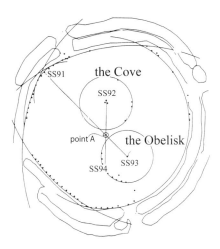

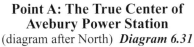

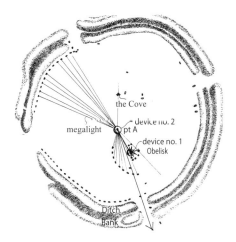

**Point A: The True Center of
Avebury Power Station**
(diagram after North) *Diagram 6.31*

How Avebury Generator Works
Diagram 6.32

Avebury (AV) is the center of the following SAs:

SA1 Horslip Long Barrow–AV–Manton Down Long Barrow
SA2 Windmill Hill–AV–West Kennet Long Barrow
SA3 Horslip Long Barrow–AV–West Kennet Enclosure 2
SA4 Roughridge Hill Long Barrow–AV–Devil's Den Chambered Tomb
SA5 Shelving Stone (circle)–AV–The Sanctuary
SA6 Shelving Stone (circle)–AV–Roughridge Hill Long Barrow
SA7 Monkton Down–AV–Knap Hill
SA8 Oldbury Hill–AV–West Woods Long Barrow
SA9 Rybury–AV–Temple Bottom Enclosure
SA10 Horslip Long Barrow–AV–Longdean Stone Circle
SA11 Hemp Knoll Round Barrow–AV–Clatford (Broadstones) Stone Circle
SA12 Beckhampton (Longstones) Long Barrow–AV–West Overton
SA13 Monkton Down–AV–South Street Long Barrow
SA14 Falkner's Circle–AV–Avebury Trusloe
SA15 Windmill Hill–AV–Devil's Den Chambered Tomb

The famous West Kennet Avenue, which connects the great henge of Avebury and the Sanctuary, runs for 2.5m. Experts suggest that there were originally 100 pairs of stone pillars spaced 24m apart. But today, only the first half of the avenue, lying just outside the southeast exit of Avebury, still survives. Interestingly, this part of the avenue formed by pairs of sarsens, from no. 1 to no. 18, forms an SA (diagram 6.32a). It has to be the same old message from that unknown intelligence.

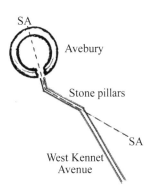

The West Kennet Avenue
Diagram 6.32a

Falkner's Stone Circle and the SA

This small stone circle lies southeast of Avebury and northwest of the Sanctuary. According to Meaden (1999), the single monolithic circle was first discovered and mentioned by Mr. Falkner of Devizes in 1840. It originally consists of twelve stones, forming an circle of 36m in diameter. As shown in diagram 6.33, four sets of SAs are derived from the circle and its surrounding prehistoric monuments:

SA1 two barrows nearby, and the angle bisects at Silbury Hill

SA2 Windmill Hill and Avebury causewayed enclosure–West Kennet palisade enclosure

SA3 round barrow (south-southwest of the circle)–Avebury G55 round barrow (southwest of the circle) and bisects at another barrow in the west

SA4 Millbarrow Long Barrow–West Kennet Long Barrow

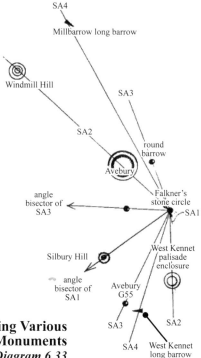

Falkner's Stone Circle Forming Various SAs with Surrounding Monuments
Diagram 6.33

The Sanctuary Stone and Wood Circle

What Stukeley regarded as a "Temple on Overton Hill" sanctuary had consisted of four rings of timber posts and two rings of sarsen stones. As shown in diagram 6.34, two station stone holes can be identified inside the Sanctuary circle. Like Station Stone 93 of Stonehenge, one of them is southwest of the small circle while the other lies, like Station Stone 92 of Stonehenge, in the northeast of the outer larger circle. Another pair of stone holes lies in the northwest of the large circle, probably indicating the angle bisector. As suggested above, it forms an SA with the long barrows of West Kennet and Beckhampton.

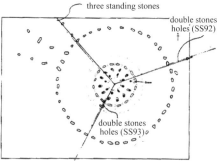

Plan of Sanctuary and Its Station Stones (after Cunnington)
Diagram 6.34

The Function of Woodhenge

Woodhenge is a late Neolithic henge to the northeast of Stonehenge. It has a diameter of 50m with a single entrance at the northeast. The henge is made of timber, earth, and chalk. Its bank is made of chalk from the ditch nearby. Inside it are six concentric elliptical settings of wooden, instead of stone, postholes. Special deposits or objects made of friable chalk including "cups," plaques or discs, and axes have been found in these postholes (diagram 6.35) (Aubrey Burl).

Experts suggest that the arrangements of the postholes are connected with astronomical alignments and conclude that the ritual nature of Woodhenge cannot be doubted. Atkinson speculates the site was once a sacred place for human sacrifice in prehistoric Britain. As shown in the diagram, postholes with special deposits are represented by black dots. Interestingly, dot no. 1, the center of the henge, and dot no. 4 form a wonderful SA. The same pattern occurs in sighting-post (b) and dot no. 5. There are seven postholes filled with chalk fragments, four of which align to an SA. Is this coincidence? Or was it deliberately planned by the henge builders? Was it another laboratory for generating power and did the wooden

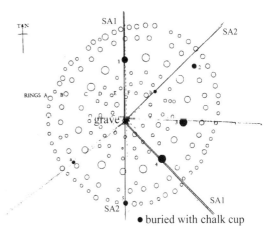

Two SAs and the Plan of Woodhenge
(after Burl)
Diagram 6.35

● buried with chalk cup

construction make it easier to adjust? Was Woodhenge a pre-model of Stonehenge nearby, as the layout of its six concentric settings is similar to those of Stonehenge?

SA of the West Kennet Complex

A large number of prehistoric sites are found in the area around Avebury and the West Kennet Long Barrow; as many still survive as earthworks. However, the ancient significant precinct of Wiltshire is certainly more complicated and congested than it appears. Ring mark traces of a number of new sites were recorded with the introduction of aerial reconnaissance photography. In his article, "A Late Neolithic Complex at West Kennet, Wiltshire, England" (*Antiquity* 65 [1991]), Alasdair Whittle suggests that these new sites include two large palisade enclosures, (numbered 1 and 2 on diagram 6.36), built of massive timbers. Evidence of associated fence lines and several double circular timber structures are found inside enclosure 2.

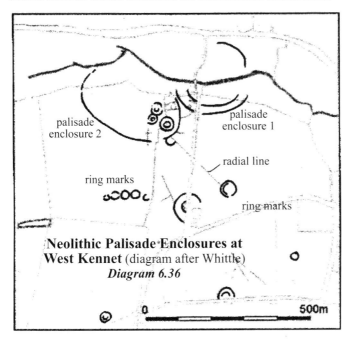

Neolithic Palisade Enclosures at West Kennet (diagram after Whittle)
Diagram 6.36

Enclosure 1 lies southeast of Silbury Hill and northeast of the West Kennet long barrow with two concentric ditches 1 to 2m deep. Oak posts about 30cm in diameter have been found in the base of these ditches, which date back to between 2400 and 2000 B.C. Enclosure 2, which is located just southwest of enclosure 1, is oval in shape and 180m in diameter. Like its sister, the ditch of enclosure 2 is around 2m deep and 2m wide. It has several smaller double-rings within it.

As shown in a Whittle's map below, SA1 is formed by the great henge of Avebury and the Sanctuary, with the center of enclosure 1 in the middle (diagram 6.37). SA2 can be drawn between the Sanctuary and enclosure 2, with the center of enclosure 1 in the middle. As a result of the masterly plan of the builders, extra sets of SAs are derived from enclosure 1 and its surrounding long barrows, the builders' dry cell batteries. My thesis is that the enclosure was used as a landing platform for the builders' vehicles circa 2500 B.C. It is certainly not the end of the story of the West Kennet complex, as more discoveries surfaced with the introduction of aerial reconnaissance and magnetometer technology in the 1990s.

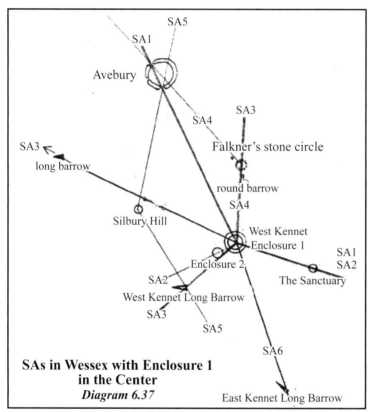

SAs in Wessex with Enclosure 1 in the Center
Diagram 6.37

With the aerial photography technique, three ring marks I have numbered R1, R2, and R3, over 40m in diameter and lying southeast inside enclosure 2 of the double concentric ring type, have been identified (diagram 6.36) (Whittle 1991 and 1997) and indicated in diagram 6.38a. Another cluster of ring marks (R4, R5, R6, R7, and R8) line up the 200m upslope to the south of enclosure 2. Three more rings (R9, R10 and R11) lie further south (400m) away from the two large enclosures. Whittle further suggests that the palisade enclosures can be regarded as sacred precincts, defensive strongholds or stockades around prominent settlements while Parker Pearson and Ramilisonina (1998) speculate that the complex, which was built of wood rather than stone, is a modified and smaller version of Avebury with its surrounding monuments.

As shown in diagram 6.38a below, timber rings R4 and R1 form a "semi SA," which bisects another timber ring at R8. In addition, R5 and R2 form a "semi SA," which also bisects at R8. The same pattern repeats itself with R6 and R3. Another possible "semi SA" is formed by R12 and a semicircular ring marked R13 and the angle also bisects at R8. Whittle continues to suggest that there are radial lines (darker lines in diagram 6.36) found inside and outside these timber enclosures. He especially points out a southeast radial line that develops over 200m and terminates at ring mark R8. In diagram 6.38b, this radial line lies on the exact axis of SA1 formed by the ring marks R2 and R10, with the ring mark R8 in the middle. Interestingly, this angle bisects at the center of the ring marked R7. SA2 is formed by the rings marked R2 and R11, with R7 in the middle. SA3 is produced by R3 and R9, with R7 in the middle, the angle bisects at R4 and R5. The Neolithic complex of West Kennet was certainly more than a ritual site. Like many mysterious monuments around the region, these timber enclosures and rings were once used as cell batteries, with the conical devices probably placed in their centers, for generating energy.

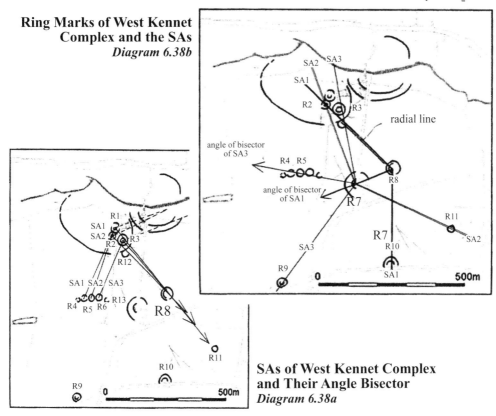

Ring Marks of West Kennet Complex and the SAs
Diagram 6.38b

radial line

angle of bisector of SA3

angle of bisector of SA1

SAs of West Kennet Complex and Their Angle Bisector
Diagram 6.38a

Experts suggest that the Avebury complex was used continuously throughout the Neolithic and Early Bronze Age (i.e., for around 2,300 years), and made the temple of Avebury the hottest and the most significant sacred site in all of Britain. But people still have no idea of its use. Even today, this sacred area is still the place of pilgrimage not of the Stone Age people, but of mysterious crop circles (discuss in Chapter 11). Since 1986, the Avebury complex, which encloses an area of 22.5 square kilometers around the six key prehistoric monuments including Avebery Henge and Stone Circle, Windmill Hill, Silbury Hill, West Kennet Long Barrow, West Kennet Avenue, and the Sanctuary, has become a World Heritage Site (WHS) managed by the National Trust. A volunteer group known as the Avebury Guardians is in charge of the complex. They also aim to help bridge the gap between the archaeological and historical interpretation and the spiritual one of Avebury.

The Stonehenge Powerhouse

Stonehenge III, 2000 B.C.
Diagram 6.39

"They only guess. They could compare it to other large buildings they knew well, such as medieval cathedrals or ancient Egyptian pyramids. But they had no local, contemporary context for the stones. They had no idea what history of construction lay behind the present ruins, and only a hint of when the work took place. There were no other stone circles or similar remains elsewhere that they could claim, with supporting evidence, to have been built by the same people. It was all a complete mystery."

—Mike Pitts, *Hengeworld*

"What is Stonehenge? It is the roofless past."

—Siegfried Sassoon

"To me, Stonehenge is the physical manifestation of the ingenuity, the determination, the spirituality and the genius of our prehistoric ancestors."

—Julian Richards, archaeologist

"The building of Stonehenge is … unlikely to have been the expression of the common will, but rather the fulfillment of a purpose imposed from above."

—Atkinson 1960:166

See how people are obsessed with Stonehenge:

• More than a million tourists visit the site each year.

• In 1985, 30,000 people rushed to Stonehenge during the Midsummer Festival.

• Over 50,000 web pages about Stonehenge are found in the internet.

• A full-size replica of Stonehenge was erected in Washington State as a war memorial. A smaller one is located on the campus of the University of Missouri, and another at East Stroudsburg University, Pennsylvania.

• A modern-day astronomical observatory known as Stonehenge Aotearoa was constructed by New Zealanders for educational purpose (astronomynz.org.nz).

• U.S. artists have built American Stonehenges—one of cars and another from an adobe-like material. The Germans used ex-Soviet tanks to build theirs to memorize the collapse of the Berlin Wall. In New Mexico, a replica was constructed out of junked refrigerators. (info: stonehenge. co.uk)

The glory days of Stonehenge are gone. It is only partially restored—not because we don't know what it looked like, but because few of its stones survive. Everything must have an identity before we can explain its function. Egyptian pyramids are royal tombs. The Mayans built temples to worship their serpent gods. The Great Wall of China defended the Hans from the northern barbarians, the Mongols. What about Stonehenge? It is an unidentified standing object, a mysterious monument sinking into the earth under the weight of its own secret history.

Today, people who visit Stonehenge may be disappointed, as they are fenced off from entering the very center of the site. And that was certainly what happened in prehistoric times, since very few human artifacts have been excavated within the circle. The people of Stonehenge built and rebuilt the monument for 1,200 years but did not intend to use it, or even get close to it. Legends held that Merlin the wizard built the monument by magically transported it from Mount Killaraus in Ireland. Others suggested it was the work of the Devil.

In around A.D. 1129, Stonehenge was regarded as the Second Wonder of Britain, surpassed only by a peak where "swirling winds howled." Perhaps, the "hanging stones" of its five great trilithons reminded people of the mediaeval gibbets used for executions. Even during the Christian Era, rumors suggested Stonehenge was a massacre ground of Druids by the Romans. In the mid seventeenth century, Stonehenge was hypothesized as a Roman Temple dedicated to the Greek sky-god Ouranos (stonehenge.co.uk). It was a forbidden room opening exclusively for its real masters.

It was not until 1640 that Stonehenge was measured and drawn by John Aubrey for the first time. He suggested the monument was the work of Druids. Even today, Stonehenge is a place of pilgrimage for neo-druids. An order was passed in 1905 allowing Druidic practices inside the site. A Druid activist group runs the Loyal Arthurian Warband website dedicated to protection of the stone circle.

Apart from seeing the prehistoric building as some sort of temple, a tool to predict the movements in heaven or a sacred precinct, today a new theory suggests that Stonehenge could constitute an open-sky temple dedicated to the worship of the Earth Mother, in which its concentric sarsen and bluestone circles and horseshoe-shaped trilithons represent her womb. It says that only on the longest day of the year, the rising sun will penetrate the middle-arch of the "womb" to illuminate the internal Goddess Stone—the Heel Stone—symbolizing the Earth Mother and Sky Father coming together to beget the world (Stonehenge-Avebury.net).

Professor Tim Darvill suggests that Stonehenge was a source and center for healing rather than a place for the dead. "Was it [Stonehenge] perhaps a fortress, a temple, an astronomical device, or a ring of ancestors turned to stone? None of these explained the need for such a gargantuan effort of trans-shipment [of the bluestones, which originated hundreds of kilometers away]. What was it about Wales that Wiltshire could not offer?" He suggests, "it was believed that the bluestones had many healing properties because in Preseli, there are many sacred springs that are considered to have health-giving qualities." "What drew people to Stonehenge must been specific, a reputation for relief from disease and disability. Stonehenge was a hospital." (Simon Jenkins 2006). Donna Rosenburg also supports the view, suggesting that the stones were paganish healing rocks from Africa from whence giants brought them to Ireland for their demonic healing properties (stonehenge.co.uk).

Stonehenge is not alone on the Salisbury plain as other less captivating structures are scattered about. Apart from those long barrows with strange tails and racetrack-like Cursuses, there are several groups of round barrows of Early Bronze Age construction encircling Stonehenge. Their existence suggests Stonehenge was an important sacred precinct in prehistoric times.

The history of Stonehenge is much more complicated than its kaleidoscopic inner structures. Experts generally believe the development of the site can be divided into three phases over a period of 1,200 years. More than fifty generations of Stone Age people worked on it. No written records are known to transmit their knowledge.

Stage One: The Henge and Its Exits, 3000–2800 B.C.

The name "Stonehenge" doesn't accurately describe the structure in its first incarnation, as no stones were used. About 3000–2800 B.C., when the earthen long barrows and Cursuses had passed their heyday, the builders cleared a vast area of woodland and constructed a circular ditch and bank: Stonehenge I, with several exits formed by removing the earth from the bank and refilling the ditch. The henge was certainly not the most impressive example of its kind around the region, as its contemporary, Avebury, was the largest henge in the world at that time. It is Stonehenge's unique exits rather than the henge itself that underline its real function.

Each pair of exits of Stonehenge I forms an SA with its center. Even today, the two causeways, one opening to the northeast and the other to the south, can be seen to be aligned to the SA (diagram 6.40). The following diagram shows the relationship between the two exits and the Aubrey Holes

(AHs) of Stonehenge I with the removal of the inner megalithic rings. The northeast causeway forms an SA with the South entrance and with the true center of the henge, marked by the interception of SS91–93 and SS92–94. If the SA/Megalight hypothesis is correct, then the two entrances were once open for the megalights generated by a conical device in the center. But what was it that waited outside Stonehenge I in 2800 B.C. to receive the power from these lights?

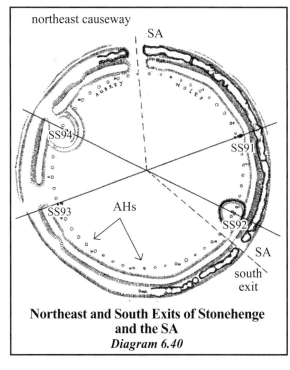

northeast causeway

SA

SA

south exit

SS94

SS91

SS93

AHs

SS92

Northeast and South Exits of Stonehenge and the SA
Diagram 6.40

Aubrey Holes (AHs): Barrow Markers

"…and why there should have been an unusual rectangle of four (station) stones around the circle."

—Aubrey Burl, *Great Stone Circles*

The four Station Stones were deliberately placed along the circumference formed by the fifty-six AHs, but not on a large open space between the circle of AHs and the central megaliths. The four Station Stones were not directly placed inside the AHs. They would have been easier to erect if the holes were already dug; rather they were deliberately located between the AHs.

The Station Stones are indicators for the SA. Their locations, on the same circumference as the AHs, imply the AHs might have served the same function as the Station Stones—to indicate the SA. As the true center of Stonehenge I was derived by the interception of the four Station Stones, each AH forms a perfect SA with another one (diagram 6.40). Thus the AHs measure the builders' sacred angle.

Each megalight would pass through an AH, or the exit, before leaving Stonehenge I. For example, AH20 and AH55 mark an SA for the northeast and the south causeways. They show the direction where the megalights were projected. That also explains why, when the measurement of SAs and the construction of the builders' dry cell batteries around and outside Stonehenge I were completed, the AHs were immediately refilled.

The exits and AHs of Stonehenge I definitely served as markers for the megalights generating power. But what were the dry cell batteries that tapped and transferred Earth energy to the conical device inside the henge? In 2800–2500 B.C., the Salisbury Plain was still woodland devoid of human-built structures. Stonehenge's builders learned their experiences in Loughcrew and the Boyne Valley of Ireland.

The following diagram may provide an answer. It shows the relationship between Stonehenge and its surrounding barrows. These early Bronze Age round barrows, with a radius of 1km and usually with sarsen slabs placed inside, form a rough circle around Stonehenge I. There is a cluster of barrows in the northeast as well as the south of the henge. Inspired by the Irish, the builders constructed their British version of the great mound of Knowth, in which earth barrows were constructed and served as dry cell batteries. Two rows of megalights were produced and projected onto the two round barrows nearby. The AHs ensured that they did not miss their targets (diagram 6.41).

The Secret of the Aubrey Holes

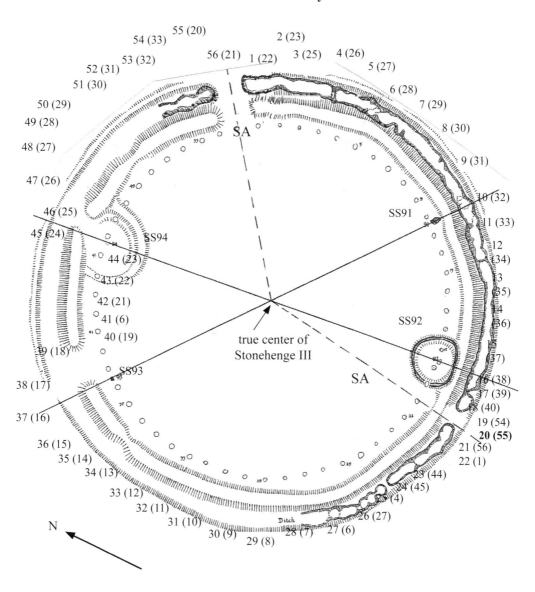

Each Pair of AHs Forms an SA with the Center of Stonehenge in the Middle
Diagram 6.40a

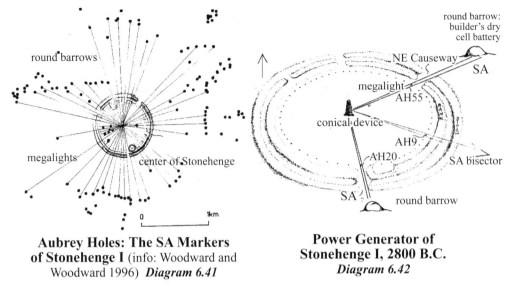

Aubrey Holes: The SA Markers of Stonehenge I (info: Woodward and Woodward 1996) *Diagram 6.41*

Power Generator of Stonehenge I, 2800 B.C. *Diagram 6.42*

The fifty-six enigmatic AHs once served as barrow markers for the builders' conical device. The following illustration is a full picture of the power station Stonehenge I. The builders knew Stonehenge lies at the junction of subterranean earth energy lines. Between 3000–2800 B.C., a henge with an internal bank and an external ditch was built to indicate the recharging platform. Its special formation may have helped to tap the energy below. A conical device was placed inside. With the help of the indicators, the round barrows lying outside AH20 and AH55 would be heated and activate the process of power generation. Another conical device, no. 2, was placed in AH9, the SA bisector, for recharging. This is why the AHs, like a typical Neolithic pit, were dug into steep-sided and flat-floored ground (Rodney Castleden): to house the conical device.

The following was the basic formula of the builders' power station of Stonehenge I:

one exit–nine AHs–the SA bisector–another nine AHs–another exit

The primitive model of Stonehenge I must have been used for more than 500 years, until the arrival of the bluestones when the builders had developed better technology (diagram 6.43).

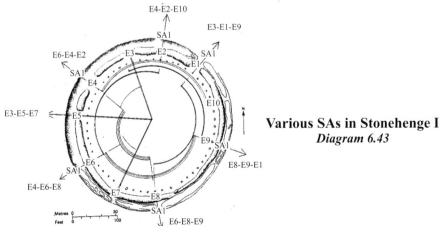

Various SAs in Stonehenge I *Diagram 6.43*

Stonehenge Avenue

Experts speculate that the 11m-wide northeast avenue of Stonehenge was used for hauling the bluestones up from the bank of the river during the later period. This causeway was formed by digging out the soil and

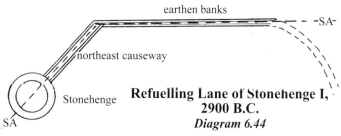

Refuelling Lane of Stonehenge I, 2900 B.C.
Diagram 6.44

chalk rubble of the two side ditches and piling the material up to make two internal banks. It first leads away from the center of Stonehenge in the general direction of the Greater Cursus for 240m before turning eastward from the Stonehenge Bottom. After another 200 meters, it curves and heads south to the river. Researchers wonder why the builders suddenly changed the course of the causeway in such a dramatic way. Was it for hauling the bluestones up from the riverbank, or did it have another function before the arrival of the megaliths? The curving of the avenue forms an SA, as shown in the diagram above. It was part of the Stonehenge powerhouse in 2900 B.C. (diagram 6.44).

Stage Two: The Bluestone Generator, 2500 B.C.

For reasons unknown, the builders redesigned Stonehenge by introducing an additional arc of elongated bluestones from some 250km away into the center of the henge around 2500 B.C. This is Stonehenge II. Excavators found two arcs of bluestone holes, known as the Q and R holes, surrounding the center. These double-diameter bluestone circles are actually in the form of horseshoes, with their openings to the west (diagram 6.45).

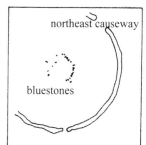

Bluestones Excavated inside Stonehenge *Diagram 6.45*

Some of the bluestones might even have had lintels above them to form a bluestone trilithon. The arrival of the bluestones made Stonehenge more complete as the empty compartment finally found its inhabitants after a long wait of hundreds of years.

Rodney Castleden suggests that the double bluestone circles characterizing Stonehenge II look like the sunrays that Neolithic people often carved on the slabs and walls of their mounds (diagram 6.46).

Typical Neolithic Solar God *Diagram 6.46*

Castleden believes a circle with short radial rays, or a set of radial rays on their own, symbolized the sun in the minds of the Neolithic people. It captured and materialized their gods inside the temple in the same way as the Cross is found in the layout of every Christian Church.

However, these carvings of the Neolithic solar gods actually represent the work of the builders' powerhouse. The sun god in the center in the form of radiant lines is actually the missing conical device that projected megalights. Two arcs of small dots, regarded as surrounding stars, and two horseshoes of monoliths also constitute the main design in the Solar God of Newgrange and the Dagda Skirt of Loughcrew (diagram 6.47).

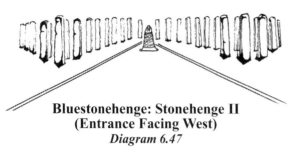

**Bluestonehenge: Stonehenge II
(Entrance Facing West)**
Diagram 6.47

The double bluestone horseshoes of Stonehenge II were just one of the many Neolithic power generators. Its standing stones were erected according to the SA and they served as dry cell batteries in the builders' lost energy mechanism. According to the descriptions of the Solar God carving of Newgrange, device no. 1 was placed inside Bluestonehenge whereas device no. 2 was placed at its west entrance. In theory, the first conical device was responsible for tapping energy from the surrounding bluestones. It then projected an extra row of megalights to device no. 2 for discharging and completing the energy loop.

The map on the right shows the distribution of some of the more than 400 Neolithic round barrows on Salisbury Plain. They are classified into eight main cemetery groups according to their locations. Nobody actually believes all these barrows are the tombs of Geoffrey of Monmouth's warriors. These 3-to-5m–high mounds usually have a crematorium in a burial cist covered with sarsen stones and further covered with layers of chalk, flints, and a soft mound. The Bush Barrow of the Normanton Group, which lies south of Stonehenge, is famous for its gold artifacts. Three groups of round barrow cemeteries lie west of Stonehenge: the Cursus Group in the north, the Stonehenge Down Group in the middle, and the Normanton Group in the south. Normanton Cemetery, 1km from Stonehenge, clusters along the ridges of a barren plain to stand out against the sky with mounds of various types and shapes. In a local map, these barrows look as if they were randomly constructed and scattered all over the plain, but the relatively linear distribution of the Cursus and Normanton Groups Cemeteries tells

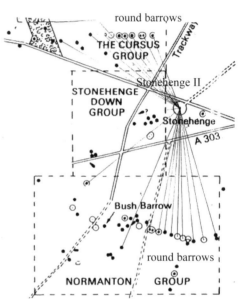

Round Barrows of Salisbury: Dry Cell Batteries of the Twin-device Energy Mechanism (diagram after M. Balfour) *Diagram 6.48*

a different story. The location of these barrows was deliberately selected, and lined up on the two sides west of Stonehenge for one purpose. They were part of the builders' Bluestonehenge power generator.

We can prove this by applying the SA formula to the area. If we pair up one of the round barrows of the Cursus Group with one of the Normanton Group, they form a perfect SA with the center of Stonehenge in the middle. In this particular setting, ten sets of SAs are formed, equivalent to ten power stations of Stonehenge I (diagram 6.48). It means that these earthen mounds were used for discharging power from the lost twin-device mechanism. It was a tremendous breakthrough in the builders' technology as their power capacity was expanded ten times in Stonehenge II.

Implication of the Solar God and the Dagda Skirt Carving

The missing device that powered Bluestonehenge is drawn in the Solar God carving of Newgrange. As shown in the carving, the upper part, formed by discontinuous lines, stands for the western bank of Stonehenge. An exit is open to the west. Just inside these discontinuous lines is another arc of small dots, representing an arc of AHs. A conical device placed at the entrance of the double bluestone horseshoes projects megalights in the direction of the AHs aiming at the round barrows outside the henge.

The builders carved their master design of Bluestonehenge onto the slab of Newgrange before erecting it in Stonehenge. Bluestonehenge was an improved model of Newgrange. It combined the building techniques of the great mounds of both Newgrange and Knowth. The construction of double-bluestone horseshoes reflects the idea from the Great Circle outside Newgrange. The inspiration of using round barrows as dry cell batteries might probably have derived from Knowth and its satellite mounds. Perhaps the medieval historian Geoffrey of Monmouth was correct about the origin of the enormous stones of Stonehenge II. The bluestones were quarried in Ireland before being transported to the Salisbury Plain and erected there.

Why did the builders of Stonehenge II erect two arcs of bluestone horseshoes instead of one, and in concentric formation, supposing the megalights would only heat up the inner one? The introduction of an extra outer horseshoe, doubling the builders' effort, must have its purpose. The Dagda Skirt carving of Loughcrew, in which there is a double horseshoe, may provide an answer.

Experts speculate that the Loughcrew cemetery, where the Dagda Skirt carving is located, had been used for ceremonial and burial purposes for more than a thousand years, ending in around 2500 B.C. This was probably the time when the Stonehenge II inhabitants started to plan and erect their structures. Diagram 6.49a is a modified drawing of G.V. du Noger's, with the surrounding decorations (circles) being removed. Its design parallels the Solar God carving of Newgrange. The double arcs of Bluestonehenge are clearly shown by the two concentric horseshoes constituting the lower part of the drawing. The radiance of megalights was projected onto their surfaces. This central motif has always been misinterpreted as a prehistoric solar deity.

A Modified Dagda Skirt, Loughcrew *Diagram 6.49a*

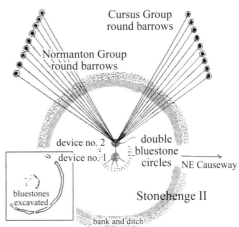

Bluestonehenge Power Station *Diagram 6.49b*

What makes the Dagda Skirt so special is the upper part, which describes the function of the builders' machine in great detail. In the drawing, the upper part is formed by four concentric arcs of standing stones. Rows of dagger-like megalights are projected onto the first and inner arc of monoliths. In the case of Bluestonehenge, these dots represent the round barrows used for discharging energy waste and sitting outside the west of the henge (diagram 6.49b). If these batteries were heated and activated, according to the Dagda Skirt, elongated thick lines of light were produced, replacing the dagger-like megalights. It connected the second arc of barrows with the third one, as indicated by the carving. What did these elongated lines stand for? What was the purpose of connecting these barrows? Was Stonehenge II built not just for generating power but also for communicating messages between barrows? Or, do the mysterious cup and ring carvings suggest a communication station that generated concentric circles of microwaves? Did the unknown intelligences recharge their machinery in the form of these microwaves?

Stage Three: The Perpetual Powerhouse, 2000–1500 B.C.

The second phase lasted for hundreds of years until the builders redesigned and re-erected an even more advanced model. Instead of constructing and using bulky round barrows as their dry cells, the builders employed a more effective but simpler design that required less time and less space. The double bluestone horseshoes were dismantled and re-erected in a different layout, at a different location and orientation.

Before putting their master plan into effect, they built an experimental model of gigantic size in Avebury, 25km north of Stonehenge. Taking Stonehenge II—a west-facing double horseshoe connected with two rows of round barrows—as a reference, the builders eventually replaced the barrows with two rows of huge sarsen stones inside the great ditch of Avebury, at its northwest and southwest edges. As mentioned before, a conical device connected the northwest sarsen arc with the monoliths of the inner South Circle for generating power. Replacing barrows with monoliths required less time, less effort, and less space to house the dry cell batteries. In order to contain and magnify the energy generated, the Avebury builders constructed a henge, probably the largest in the Neolithic world, around its circular powerhouse. The purpose was to replace the corbelled walls of the passage cairns of the Boyne Valley and the Orkney Islands. But in the case of Stonehenge III, the builders came up with an even more effective way to magnify their energy.

After finishing their Avebury experiment, they put their design into practice. As shown in Stonehenge III, the bluestone horseshoe was rearranged in the very center and reoriented to the northeast. It is further encircled by another circle of bluestones. As shown in the Solar God carving, the twin-device placed at their center was the ultimate secret of Stonehenge. Tapping energy from megaliths was an ageless activity of the builders. Orthostats, the dry cells, were installed inside the passage graves of Loughcrew and the Boyne Valley of Ireland. They were also found inside the Orkney tombs in the form of lintel trenches. They were rearranged as apses and trilithons inside the Tarxien temples, the oldest man-made structures found on Earth, not to mention more than 900 stone circles scattered all over northwest Europe.

The following diagram shows bluestones 62 and 63 of the bluestone circle, in which only six out of an original total of sixty bluestones are still standing upright (diagram 6.50a). Their elongated shapes actually echo the large menhirs erected in Brittany, France. Interestingly, the famous shield-motif carvings of the passage mound of Gavrinis seem to illustrate the function of these elongated dry cells of Stonehenge III (diagram 6.50b).

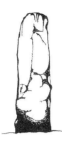

**Bluestones 62 and 63,
Stonehenge III**
Diagram 6.50a

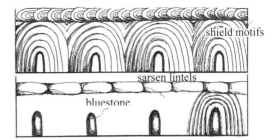

**"Shield Motifs" of Gavrinis (*above*)
and Bluestones of Stonehenge III**
Diagram 6.50b

What makes Stonehenge superb is not the human sized bluestones, but the sarsen infrastructure. According to Aubrey Burl, the sarsen circle, the outermost ring of the inner megaliths, had been dressed and pounded to produce smooth inner faces. The lintels were curved to the line of the circle as well. Structurally and functionally speaking, the sarsen circle, acting like a circular wall with narrow gaps in between, was built to replace the gigantic henge of Avebury and certainly the corbelled walls of the passage mounds.

These huge sarsens were strategically placed next to the bluestones, not just embracing the bluestone circle, but also the horseshoe as well. They were constructed not to protect the smaller elongated bluestones, but to react with the dry cells when they were charged. Their skillfully dressed surfaces were probably measured to reduce friction or interruption when generating power. The sarsen circle is a circle of thirty gigantic doorways. The lintel doorways, in the form of dolmens, trilithons, and lintel trenches, were the basic structure for generating power. It certainly performed the same function in Stonehenge III.

A small forecourt at the northeast part of the inner megaliths, formed by two overlapping bluestone circles, became the sacred precinct of the builders. This tiny little area was probably the most powerful place in the Neolithic world. It was a forbidden room to any but the restricted few.

The Hidden Forecourt

People are impressed by the inner structure of Stonehenge III even though less than half of these stones survive in ruin. A secret is hidden inside these giant stones, a lost technology from another time, but now the truth is within our grasp.

The soul of Stonehenge III is a small T-shaped forecourt lying at the center. The lower part of the powerhouse consists of a double horseshoe of sarsen and bluestone in which its northeast opening is connected with the upper part. The upper part comprises two small arcs of sarsen and bluestone derived from the two stone circles of Stonehenge III (diagram 6.50c). Basically, the inner ring of this forecourt is formed by a horseshoe of nineteen bluestones and another arc of nineteen bluestones. This inner ring is then further framed by ten sarsens in the form of a horseshoe, with a lintel in each pair to form five great sarsen trilithons. They connect with another arc of ten sarsens topped by lintels. In terms of function, the area can be understood as two overlapping stone circles, each formed by nineteen bluestones and ten sarsens. The forecourt once housed and connected two conical devices. This was the driver's seat.

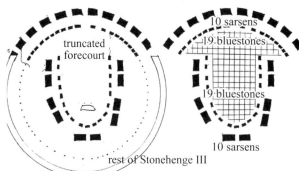

truncated forecourt

10 sarsens
19 bluestones
19 bluestones
10 sarsens

rest of Stonehenge III

The Forecourt Formed by Twin Stone Circles of Stonehenge III
Diagram 6.50c

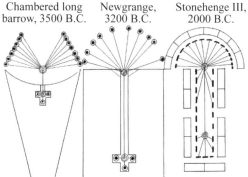

Chambered long barrow, 3500 B.C.   Newgrange, 3200 B.C.   Stonehenge III, 2000 B.C.

Various Truncated Forecourts of the Builders' Powerhouses
Diagram 6.51

The truncated forecourt of Stonehenge III is just one of the many powerhouses of the builders. Similar designs are found in the long barrows of southern Britain, where a semicircular wall of orthostats is erected outside the multi-recess chamber, same as the truncated roof box found just outside the passage mound of Newgrange. Most of the court and wedge tombs of Ireland were built with a semicircular forecourt of boulders (diagram 6.51).

The T-shaped forecourt also constitutes a compressed and elaborate form of its predecessor—the Bluestonehenge (diagram 6.52). Ten pairs of round barrows of Stonehenge II were replaced by nineteen bluestones, nearly doubling the capacity of the powerhouse from ten sets of SAs in Bluestonehenge to nineteen sets in Stonehenge III. In Stonehenge II, power had to be generated through the earthen round barrows with the sarsen stones installed. But in Stonehenge III, sarsen stones were explicitly erected in open space with lintels on top. Their polished surfaces helped to magnify and reflect the energy generated by the bluestones nearby.

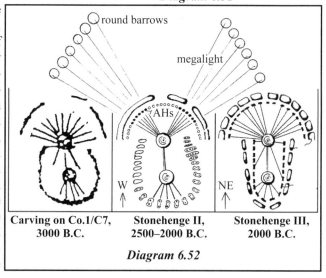

round barrows

megalight

AHs

W ↑

NE ↑

Carving on Co.1/C7, 3000 B.C.   Stonehenge II, 2500–2000 B.C.   Stonehenge III, 2000 B.C.

Diagram 6.52

The evolution of Stonehenge paralleled the development of the builders' technology, from a single-SA powerhouse in 3000 B.C. to the barrow-stone horseshoe version in the Bluestonehenge period to the final "stone circle to stone circle" model of Stonehenge III in 1800 B.C. Even though they differ structurally, they were all built for housing the twin-device, the key to the whole energy-generating machine.

The Mechanism at Work

This specially designed forecourt is composed of the northeast arc of the bluestone and sarsen stone circles and the double horseshoes in the southwest. The nineteen bluestones of the horseshoe match perfectly with another nineteen bluestones of the circle. The ten sarsens forming the horseshoe correspond with the ten sarsens from the circle.

With reference to the early Bronze Age gold hats, the conical device, a megalight generator and energy capacitor, consisted of several horizontal rings. More than two dozen light holes, as suggested by the solar motif carved on the body of the gold cone, were installed in each of these rings. Each pair of light holes in the ring produced two rows of light beams, as shown in the conical motif of Gavrinis, forming an SA. Each horizontal ring is adjustable to the surrounding stones. The number of solar motifs on the gold cone suggests that each ring could produce more than a dozen sets of megalights at one time. If there were more than ten rings in each conical device, more than one hundred sets could be generated.

Bronze Shield Found at Lough Gur, Co. Limerick (after Harbison) (*left*) **and Gold "Sun-disc" from Tedavnet, Co. Monaghan, Showing the Pointed Star atop the Conical Device (after Harbison)** 27 to 35cm in diameter—too small to wear for protection. They may have had a ceremonical use. Two similar disc brooches were found below the turf outside Newgrange. (O'Kelly)
Diagram 6.53

The Conical Device and the Neolithic Gold Discs

The megalights, acting like electric wires, aimed at heating up the surrounding bluestones. Earth energy under the stone would be tapped through the megalight and stored inside the conical device. When the device was fully charged, energy in the form of microwaves, portrayed as concentric circles in many Neolithic carvings, would be generated.

Deep inside the sacred precinct of Stonehenge III, conical device no. 1 was placed at its very center, formed by the intersection of SS91–93 and SS92–94. Conical device no. 2 was placed in the middle of the horseshoe entrance. The twin-devices were now in their standard positions. With the signal from their master, rows of light beams were projected onto the stones nearby, both in the northeast arc of the bluestone circle and the southwest bluestone horseshoe (diagram 6.54). The energy mechanism is explicitly presented in the Solar God motif of Newgrange.

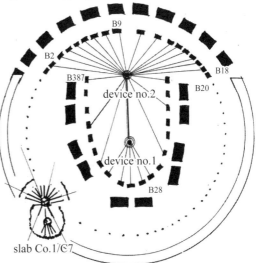

An Activated Stonehenge III
Diagram 6.54

As illustrated in diagram 6.54, bluestones B2 and B12 would form an SA with conical device no. 2 in the middle. B3 and B13 would form another SA. SAs were formed by B4–B14, B5–B15 and B6–B16. At first, five stones in the middle of the bluestone arc, namely B7, B8, B9, B10, and B11, could not form their SAs. The builders adjusted the design with an elongated bluestone horseshoe to its southwest and overcame the above inconsistency. In other words, bluestone B7 in the northeast arc would form an SA with B20, first on the right arm of the bluestone horseshoe. Other sets of SAs could be formed as a result of this adjustment. Thus, additional sets of SAs were derived from the following pairs of bluestones: B8 and B32, B9 and B22, B10 and B25, B11 and B38.

As suggested by the Solar God motif of Newgrange, twin-device no. 1 was connected with device no. 2 by a megalight beam. It also projected five rows of megalights onto the stones at the lower ebb of the horseshoe, probably for discharging. These five megalights correspond to the five recesses in the West Kennet long barrow and the apses inside the temples of Malta. Fully activated, Stonehenge III is the Solar God motif of Newgrange. Coincidentally, a total of ten sets of SAs were generated in Stonehenge III, the same number as formed by the barrows and the bluestones in Stonehenge II.

Special Arrangements of Stonehenge III

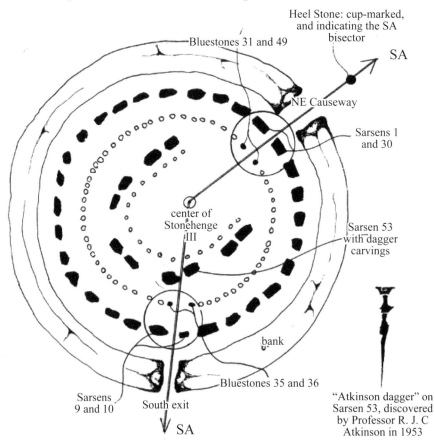

Special Arrangements inside Stonehenge III
Diagram 6.55

Diagram 6.55 above shows the general distribution of sarsens and bluestones inside Stonehenge III. It consists of two megalithic circles and two horseshoes. The pair of northeast-facing sarsens 1 and 30 of the lintel-stone circle is deliberately widened, like stones 31 and 49 of the bluestone circle lying just inside them. Experts suggest they not only symbolized but also formed ceremonial doorways leading from the outside to the inner altar. Similar arrangements could be found in the two rings at the southern sector, in which sarsen stone 10 is deliberately dwarfed as compared with the neighboring sarsens 9 and 11. At the same time, the pair of bluestones just inside the two sarsens mentioned above (no. 35 and 36) also has a wider gap (diagram 6.56).

Megalithic Causeway for the Megalights: Widened Doorways inside Stonehenge III
Diagram 6.56

Experts believe the two wider doorways at the northeast and the south were a direct response to the two causeways that run from the center to the outside. This is one reason why Stonehenge was believed to be a religious center in 3000–1500 B.C. The sacred precinct at the very center, supposed to be protected and hidden by rings of megaliths, was only accessible to the high priest.

The northeast and southern causeways form a perfect SA with the center of Stonehenge III in the middle. These two openings were designed for the megalights that would provide power for the builders, instead of the Bronze Age high priests and their sacrifices. The pair of sarsen trilithon uprights, nos. 53 and 54 (diagram 6.57), are famous for the ancient dagger-

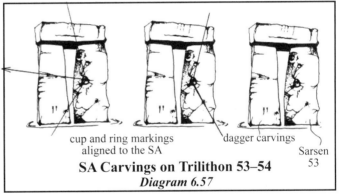

SA Carvings on Trilithon 53–54
Diagram 6.57

like engravings on their lower surfaces (diagram 6.58a). It suggests that megalights once traveled in and out of Stonehenge through this doorway of Trilithon 53–54. It seems that our Neolithic and Early Bronze Age artists were describing how this amazing machine worked.

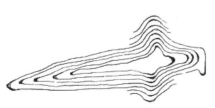

The Famous Dagger-like Carving on Sarsen 58
Diagram 6.58a

Shallow Pits on Sarsen 53 and the SA
Diagram 6.58b

Between the inner stone rings of Stonehenge III and the Heel Stone lies another stone known as the Slaughter Stone. It is heavily carved with deep hollows (diagram 6.60). Archaeologists speculate that the stone was once used for holding the blood of the sacrifice. However, these round hollows might have acted like the mysterious stone bowls inside the Tarxien temples and were used for holding the builders' conical device.

In order to make the recharging point stand out, the builders erected an eye-catching monolith, the Heel Stone, as the SA bisector. Interestingly, two dagger-like markings on the stone form an SA with a Cursus-like marking in the middle (diagram 6.59). Two pairs of Station Stones, SS91 to SS94, were erected on the embankment. The builders even encircled these standing stones—the Heel Stone and Station Stones 92 and 94—with earthen mounds so that they would not be overlooked. To whom are these megalithic reminders supposed to be given? And why?

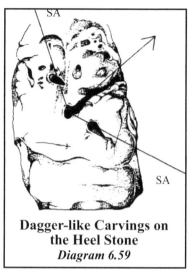

Dagger-like Carvings on the Heel Stone
Diagram 6.59

I further suggest the heavily carved Slaughter Stone, lying along the SA bisector of Stonehenge III, is probably a landing platform for the builders' vehicle (diagram 6.60).

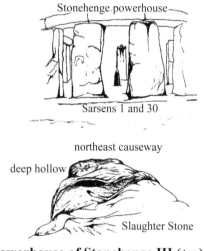

Powerhouse of Stonehenge III (*top*) and the Slaughter Stone: A Landing Platform of the Builders' Traveling Vehicle
Diagram 6.60

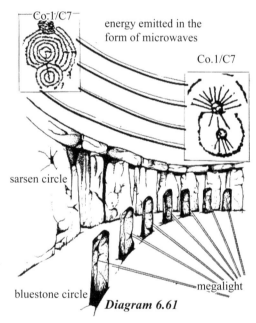

Diagram 6.61

From the construction of a henge in around 3000 B.C., a double arc of bluestones with an opening to the west in around 2500 B.C., and the placement of gigantic stone circles in around 2000–1800 B.C., we can explain why it took 1,200 years to build Stonehenge as it stands today. It has arguably been the longest human project in the history of mankind. Today's Stonehenge is the product of a technology unimaginable to our current level of development (diagram 6.61). The missing devices acted like a semiconductor inside a computer generating unfathomable power. They were the Central Processing Unit of Stonehenge. Without them, the sophisticated machinery of Stonehenge was rendered dumb, silent tombs like the barrows the experts claim to understand.

A Question about the Station Stones

The four Station Stones are the least eye-catching megaliths in Stonehenge III when compared with its massive inner rings. During Stonehenge I, around 3000–2800 B.C., the most important SA indicator was its northeast and south entrances or causeways, more specifically, the SA formed by AH55 and AH20. The four sarsens were not yet in place. In the Bluestonehenge period, it was the enigmatic AHs that formed SAs with the round barrows nearby. Two horseshoes of bluestones were erected in the center with no room for the sarsens. In the final stage, with the arrival of the central megaliths, it was both the bluestones and the sarsens that took up the job of generating power. From the beginning to the end, the four Station Stones and the Heel Stone actually played a very minor role. They seem out of place and, unlike other Stonehenge megaliths, they did not serve as dry cell batteries. Why did the builders deliberately place these seemingly redundant monoliths inside Stonehenge in such a predominant position?

The Station Stones served only one purpose: to indicate the SA. Evidence suggests the four sarsens were erected at the final stage of Stonehenge, in around 1500 B.C., when the builders introduced the sarsen horseshoe and circle into the site. They left their ultimate secret there. Did they foresee that we could one day decipher the secrets of their energy? Was it an attempt to prove their supremacy on our planet 4,000 years ago? Or did they plan to return to our planet and restart the engine?

The Misunderstood Sundial of Knowth

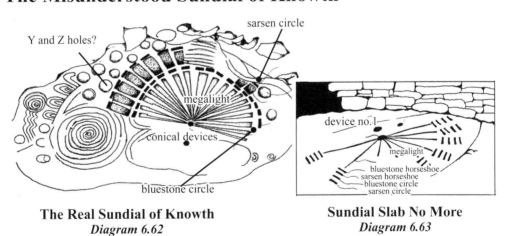

The Real Sundial of Knowth
Diagram 6.62

Sundial Slab No More
Diagram 6.63

Studying the sundial slabs in Knowth (diagrams 6.62 and 6.63), one can imagine the artist seeking to express the bizarre lights he witnessed one night on the Salisbury Plain 4,000 years ago. The two intense dots on the sundial slab, equivalent to the two small circles in the Solar God carving, represent the two conical devices. In the sundial of diagram 6.62, device no. 1 projected nineteen rows of megalights, represented by straight lines, onto the surrounding bluestones, represented by a semicircle of dark and elongated dots. It perfectly matches the number of bluestones installed inside the powerhouse of Stonehenge III. The bluestones are further surrounded by another semicircle of sarsen blocks, represented by a semicircle of rectangular-shaped objects. What makes the Knowth's sundial superb is that the two extra rows of small circles carved outside the two semicircles are equivalent to the Y and Z holes of Stonehenge.

The Amazing Number 19 and the Megalithic Powerhouse

As diagram 6.62 indicates, the Knowth sundial artist explicitly carved nineteen light beams. The twin-device of Newgrange also produced nineteen megalights—fourteen from the upper device and five from the lower one. The sacred forecourt in Stonehenge III is also formed by a south-west horseshoe made of nineteen bluestones and another arc of nineteen bluestones. Why did the builders design a powerhouse of two stone circles, each with nineteen bluestones? Does it imply that they could only generate nineteen sets of SAs in a row—the maximum capacity of their twin-device mechanism? To sum up, the megalithic machine of Stonehenge III consists of three parts:

1. The lower part is formed by a horseshoe of nineteen freestanding bluestones at the very center of Stonehenge. The stones were once used for tapping the energy beneath.
2. The upper part is formed by a semicircle of nineteen freestanding bluestones. They were probably used for discharging energy during the power generating process.
3. A horseshoe of ten lintelled sarsens and another semicircle of ten lintelled sarsens were placed next to and outside of the bluestone horseshoe and semicircle respectively. Their enormous size and carefully dressed surfaces helped to magnify the energy generated from the bluestones nearby.

The rest of the structures seem to play a more subordinate role. The megalithic powerhouse of Stonehenge III was ready in 2000 B.C. but they were waiting for the missing devices to activate the energy generating process. What exactly were these two lost devices? Without our identifying and understanding them, all Stone Age infrastructures are simply the tombs of our ancestors.

The Conical Devices

Even today, their existence seems unimaginable. In the early nineteenth century, excavations were undertaken in the round barrows on Salisbury. Sophisticated burial artifacts were unearthed. Among these treasures are cone-shaped copper ornaments of the early Bronze Age. Their surfaces are decorated with straight lines and zigzag patterns, the favorite designs of the builders. Do these decorations indicate the energy these devices once generated? Are they replicas of the builders' conical devices? The Stone Age people knew the special relationship between these devices and the round barrows, so they put them together hoping to use them in their afterlife.

An object excavated by Fenton in the Bush Barrow south of Stonehenge is believed to be a miniature cup. The artifact is circular with many elongated holes surrounding its circumference (diagram 6.64). Did these holes once allow light beams to pass through and project onto the surrounding bluestones? Was it a prototype of the missing device? What about the device in the small forecourt of Stonehenge III, capable of generating more than ten pairs of megalights at the same time? According to the description on the conical motif of Gavrinis, this device is a conical shape. Was there really a device like that or is it simply speculation? The answer might be found in the Museum of Berlin.

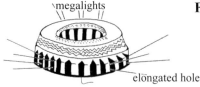

megalights

elongated hole

Fenton's Device: Earliest Model of the Builders' Machine?
(info: Mohen 1998)
Diagram 6.64

The Gold Cones of the King-Priests

"That is, who possessed this hat and which indication could read, that had power to determine the time and predict things."

—Prof. Dr. Wilfried Menghin of the Museum for Pre- and Early History, Berlin

Berlin Gold Hat
Diagram 6.65

Did wizards really wear pointed hats? Professor Gerioff, a German archaeologist and historian, believes that they did, as four golden cone-shaped objects have been unearthed at Bronze Age sites over the past 170 years. The one found in the central west of France is known as the "Avanton of Vienne" and was accidentally discovered when a tree uprooted in Avanton, France, in 1844. Another one was discovered in 1835 in a region between northern Switzerland and the southern Rhineland of Germany and is named the "Golden Hat of Schifferstadt," also known as "golden hat of boat operator city." The Ezelsdorf-Buch cone was excavated on the south hill of Brentenberg, Bavaria, in the spring of 1953. Finally the "Berlin cone," generally known as the "citizen of Berlin hat," is now kept at the Museum für Vor- and Frühgeschichte (Museum for Pre- and Early History), Berlin.

All four conical hats resemble each other in their form, symbolism, and technique. As Wilfried Menghin describes, "the Berlin Gold Hat (cone) [diagram 6.65] consists of a hollow, pointed cone 74.5cm in height, fashioned of hammered gold with no seams. A separate cap and a horizontal brim of paper-thin sheet gold is adorned with twenty-one horizontal zones, consisting of repousse bands with rows of stamped beading, enlivened by embossed ornaments in concentric circles of varying number and size, none of which overlap. A six-pointed star with attenuated arms, between which a regular stamped bead pattern appears, marks the top of the cone. The fourth zone from the top shows a decorative band of horizontally-set half-moons with a central dot and a parallel pattern of ovoids with pointed ends (like eyes). The junction of the cone proper to the cap is marked by a band of parallel vertical grooves. The brim, 5.3cm wide, is marked off from the 10cm high cap by a fold into which a circular strip of bronze is set. The brim is further reinforced by wrapping its rim around a bronze ring (30.7 × 29.5cm in dimension) of twisted metal. With a height of 74.5cm and an average thickness of 0.06mm, the cone, together with the stabilizing bronze base and brim reinforcements, weighs some 490 grams. … the base of the cone has an oval diameter (20.3 × 17.5cm) and the decorative patterns on the underside of the brim are positive." (from "The Berlin Gold Hat: A Ceremonial Head-dress of the Late Bronze Age," in *Gods and Heroes of the European Bronze Age,* ed. Demakopoulou et al.). Menghin further suggests that "all four ceremonial hats were hammered up whole from a single piece of gold. … The decorative zones and ornaments were laid out using a template to mark up the surface: on the gold cone from Ezelsdorf, for example, twenty different punches, six ornamental wheels and a decorative comb were used."

The Ezelsdorf-Buch cone is 88.3cm tall, weighs 310 grams and made of a thin material 0.78mm thick (Tobias Springer, "The Golden Cone of Ezelsdorf-Buch: A Masterpiece of the Goldsmith's Art from the Bronze Age," in *Gods and Heroes of the European Bronze Age*) (diagram 6.69). According to Springer, the most important decorative motifs, like the other three hats, are disks and circles. There is a ten-pointed star crown at the top of the cone and 154 horizontal decorative zones extending to the base. On the 120th zone, a frieze of twenty-one eight-spoked wagon wheels encircle the cone (diagram 6.67). Springer speculates these wheel symbols suggest the movement of the sun, and the cone was believed to be able to transmit the power of the sun to the wearer.

The citizen of Berlin hat was sold by a private art dealer to the Berlin Museum of Archaeology and Early History in 1996 for 1.5 million DM. The golden hat of Schifferstadt is the oldest and the first found, in 1835, among the four. The artifact weighs about 350g, is 29.6cm in height, and has a diameter of 18cm (Wikipedia).

Until now nobody is sure about the real function of these artifacts. Different suggestions have been offered including that of hats, quivers, calendars, containers, objects of unknown function, crowns, and a cult device placed atop a pole. Some experts claim that these mysterious objects originally functioned as ceremonial hats or decorative caps for the powerful king-priests in the Bronze Age, probably a divine object allowing the master to look into the future. The theory as ceremonial caps has gained widespread acceptance.

The Metonic Cycle and the Gold Cone

The gold cones are 3,000 years old, made of paper-thin gold, and originally had brims. They vary from 60cm to 90cm in height. Each is decorated with circles and other motifs representing the sun and the moon. The sun and moon decorations suggest astronomical significance. According to Prof. Dr. Wilfried Menghin and his researchers, the 1739 sun and half-moon symbols, representing the nineteen-year cycle of the moon, match the Metonic cycle invented by Meton, the Greek astronomer in 432 B.C., 500 years after the gold cone was made. The Metonic cycle is composed of 235 lunar months. At the end of the nineteen-year-cycle, the full moon appears on the same day of the year as it did at the beginning of the cycle.

Could the Bronze Age people develop such sophisticated astronomical skills? Where did their knowledge come from? Why did they put the message on a conical object instead of a disk or cylindrical one? What was the main purpose for a primitive agrarian society to make long-term, empirical astronomical observations? Judging from the details of these motif decorations (diagram 6.67), we could say the artist studied the cone before duplicating another one. Instead of predicting the movement of the sun and the moon, these gold cones may serve a more practical function.

Gold Hat of Avanton
(info: Mohen and Eluere 2000)
Diagram 6.66

The Lost Device of the Super-advanced Civilization

The size and decoration of these cones perfectly match the lost conical devices in Stonehenge and other Neolithic sites. The device was once capable of generating rows of dagger-like megalights to its surrounding stones for power. These 75cm high mysterious gold cones are small enough to stand on the roof box platform of Newgrange (diagram 6.68).

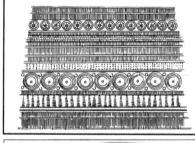

Detail of the Gold Cone
Diagram 6.67

Conical Device on the Roof Box of Newgrange
Diagram 6.68

THE GODS' MACHINES

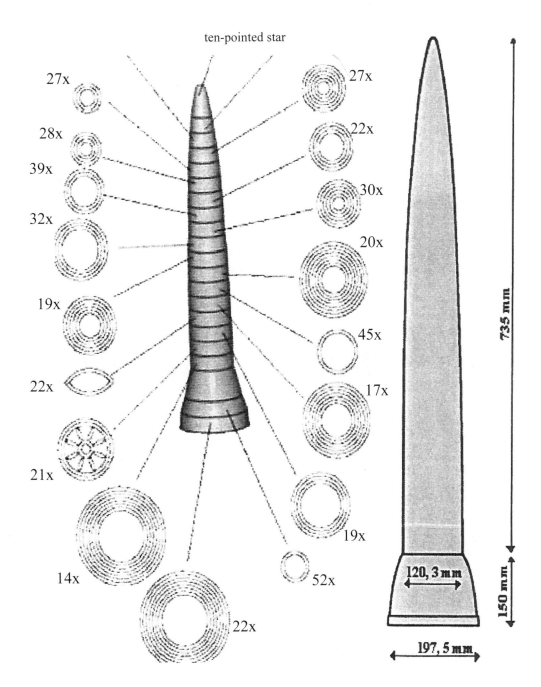

ten-pointed star

27x

28x

39x

32x

19x

22x

21x

14x

27x

22x

30x

20x

45x

17x

19x

52x

22x

735 mm

120, 3 mm

150 mm

197, 5 mm

**Ornamentation Details on the Surface of the
Golden Cone of Ezelsdorf-Buch**
(info: Wikipedia)
Diagram 6.69

Each sector of the cone is installed with light holes. The multistoried device, together with more than 1,000 solar-like symbols on their surfaces, is capable of activating several sets of SAs simultaneously. The picture above shows a gold hat of the king-priest, which has twelve storeys and can generate twelve times more power than the early Fenton model. Its pointed head with the star-like ornament suggest it was an advanced transmitter. Concentric circles of microwaves were generated on top of the device when it was fully charged. It is the same description shown in Professor O'Kelly's drawing of the Solar God Slab of Newgrange. This is the conical device's purpose. That's why experts suggest these gold cones are similar in cultural context to other gold sheet metal crowns discovered since 1692 in southwest Ireland (Comerford Crown) and at the Spanish Atlantic coast (gold sheet metal crown of Axtroki and Rianxo) (Wikipedia). Similar cones have been excavated around the same region. For example, one was unearthed in the early seventeenth century in Ireland and another one (the "Gold Cape of Mold") was unearthed in Wales in 1831.

Gavrinis, Knowth, and the Golden Hats

The builders of Gavrinis did carve the multilayered conical device onto the slab of their Neolithic safe 5,000 years ago (diagram 6.70). The conical motif shows a horizontal-lined device, with brim reinforcements, generating two rows of megalights onto the shield-shaped monolith behind. This carved slab constitutes convincing evidence showing the existence of the builders' advanced machine.

Conical Motif of Gavrinis
Diagram 6.70

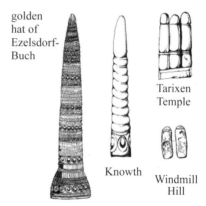

golden hat of Ezelsdorf-Buch

Tarixen Temple

Knowth

Windmill Hill

Phallus of Knowth and Malta Temple
Diagram 6.71

In the great mound of Knowth a long stone was excavated near the entrance of the western passage. The stone has ribs along its body (diagram 6.71). A similar phallus was excavated in Newgrange nearby, and its design was almost identical to the gold hat. According to Byrne, there are three engraved ovals on the headpiece of the ornament, which is probably equivalent to the lowest part of the Ezelsdorf-Buch Hat, also decorated with concentric circles.

The same happens to the stone phalli of Tarxien Temple, Malta (diagram 6.71) as well as other from Wiltshire, Britain (Mike Pitts 2000). They are all replicas of the conical devices and that is why they are found near the Neolithic powerhouses. Our ancestors saw this powerful device and they decided to duplicate one for themselves. They put the manmade conical devices into the powerhouse where they stayed for thousands of years until they were unearthed and misinterpreted as phallic objects. How could these conical devices generate power out of bare stones? What was the technology behind the megalights?

Daggers and Dagger-like Objects

As reflected in the Dagda Skirt carving of Loughcrew and the wedge motif of Gavrinis (diagram 6.72), the megalights were presented as dagger-like objects. The tail points in the direction of the light hole of the conical device where the round top touches the surface of the monolith. The megalight rows function like modern electric wires, allowing power in the form of electricity to move from the stone to the conical device and from the conical device to the stone.

Loughcrew   Gavrinis

Dagger-like Carvings of the Neolithic world
Diagram 6.72

Burial artifacts or offerings in terms of jadeite axes or in dagger-like shapes are commonly found inside many Neolithic passage graves such as Gavrinis and Breton of Brittany (diagram 6.73). In the tomb of Arzon, seventeen axes/daggers are hidden in a single burial site. In Wessex of Britain, a large number of bronze daggers of the mid–second millennium have been excavated inside a round barrow. Most of these blades show no sign of use and experts suggest they are symbols of male power. How did the prehistoric people, predating the Iron Age, come by these metallic objects, and instead of using them as tools or weapons, place them inside their tombs? If the megalithic tombs were actually powerhouses of an advanced civilization, at least primarily, then what were these dagger-like objects used for?

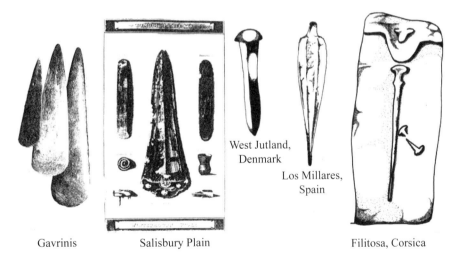

West Jutland, Denmark

Los Millares, Spain

Gavrinis   Salisbury Plain   Filitosa, Corsica

Megalithic Megalights
Diagram 6.73

Starting from the left: jade daggers of Gavrinis; bronze daggers of Wessex;
stone dagger from Tovstrup in West Jutland, Denmark; bronze dagger of Los Millares;
status-menhir from Filitosa, Corsica.

These dagger offerings and carvings are replicas of the mysterious megalights generated by the conical device (diagram 6.74). With their conical replicas in hand, all they needed to activate their version of the energy mechanism was the dagger-like megalights. All they could do was put the replicas into their barrows, where they sat silently in darkness for thousands of years.

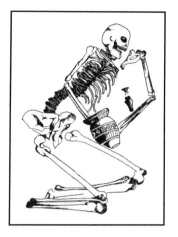

"Energy Mechanism" of our Ancestors:
Beaker and the Dagger
(Symbolizing the builder's conical device
and the megalight it generated)
Diagram 6.74

The Bluestones and the Sarsens

"The stones are enormous and there is no one alive strong enough to move them."

—Merlin, tutor of King Arthur

The sarsen circle and horseshoe are built of red sandstone, which is igneous rock formed by volcanic ash. The quartz sand becomes sandstone, a kind of metamorphic rock, resulting from the effects of pressure and water. The Stonehenge sarsens are tertiary sandstones of fine to medium-size grain, and consist of sub-angular quartz grains strongly cemented together with silica. They are scattered around the Marlborough Downs, north of Stonehenge. Its richness in quartz grains may be the main reason why it is used by the builders.

According to old legends, the bluestone circle and the smaller horseshoe were believed to possess magical properties. They are not homogeneous, though. About 62% of them are hard spotted dolerite while the rest are volcanic ash and rhyolite. Experts generally believe the bluestones of Stonehenge were transported from the Prescelly Mountains in South Wales, 250km away from their present spot. It must have taken more than 200,000 man-days to bring them to Salisbury (Hawkins 1965). Legendary historian Geoffrey of Monmouth even believed the bluestones danced from Ireland. He might be correct as the drawings of the Solar God of Newgrange and the Dagda Skirt of Loughcrew suggest there could have been another Stonehenge-like infrastructure in Ireland long before the one which sits on the Salisbury plain. A bluestone circle had already stood in the Boyne Valley for many years before being transported to England, rearranged and re-erected in the form of Bluestonehenge in 2000 B.C. The builders carefully selected their stones, with special properties for generating power while being heated or stressed. Certain stones with particular properties were transported from a long distance to their selected destinations. For example, the slabs of West Kennet long barrow and Stony Littleton of Somerset were carefully selected. In the passage grave of La Hougue Bie of Jersey, there were stones from nine different sources (Darvill and Malone 2003).

Certain stones had to match particular places, such as the junction of underground energy streams. The builders must have intimate knowledge of our planet. It is the Earth energy rather than the bulky megaliths that brought them here. The question is no longer why they built all these megalithic infrastructures, but how they converted these stones to dry batteries for tapping our Earth energy (diagram 6.75).

Bluestones:
Dry Cell Batteries

Sarsen Trilithon:
Energy Amplifier

Diagram 6.75

The Quartz

"If we accept that electrons can only move via conductors, should we look to an arrangement or alignment of particular kinds of stones for the possible loss-free conduct of electrons? Some are semi-conductors, they store free electrons, and react to micro-waves. For example, manganese trace elements in flint (in sarsen) change their orientation under microwave. Accepting that the principles of scientific biofeedback exist, was it once possible for man to transfer energy to and from some stones…?"

—Michael Balfour, *Stonehenge and Its Mysteries*

Both the sarsen and the bluestone have a main component, quartz, a small, flat but hard glossy mineral consisting of silicon dioxide in crystal form. In theory, quartz will vibrate and generate radio waves when heated. In fact, a large amount of quartz was used in World War II in the chemical apparatus and electrical instruments to detect submarines.

Since both sarsens and bluestones are rich in quartz, if megalights hit their surfaces, as suggested in the carvings, it may result in:

1. The process of piezoelectricity—i.e., electricity produced by mechanical pressure on quartz. This piezoelectric effect of crystals has been widely used in technology, particularly in quartz resonators for frequency control, quartz watches, propagators of ultrasonic wave-trains, etc. In theory, the quartz-rich Stonehenge was a Neolithic powerhouse; or,

2. It also generated microwaves for communication, as shown by Professor O'Kelly's drawing of Co.1/C7 of Newgrange (diagram 6.76).

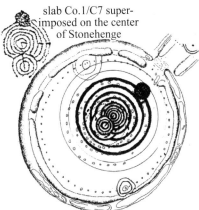

slab Co.1/C7 super-imposed on the center of Stonehenge

The bluestones, full of quartz grains, were once heated up by the megalights of the builders' twin-device, thus tapping underground energy. The energy was also stored inside the conical device then magnified by the crystallized sarsen trilithons in the form of microwaves and transmitted from its pointed top. The builders mastered an advanced technique that we don't understand. The technology was used for their space traveling 5,000 years ago. Our planet possesses certain energy they needed. The flourishing of our civilization was only a by-product of their energy-acquiring activities on earth.

A Microwaved Stonehenge
Diagram 6.76

The Magnificent Horseshoe Design

a. The horseshoe opening effectively shows the direction of refueling in three dimensions.

b. Its giant tuning fork design helps to focus and direct energy and microwaves to the desired destination (diagram 6.77).

c. The step-like structure of the trilithons helps to transmit microwaves in the desired direction or spectrum (diagram 6.78).

d. The inner surfaces of the trilithons were skillfully polished and dressed probably to reduce friction of the generated energy and reflect microwaves (diagram 6.79).

e. The narrow gap between the upright sarsens helps to maximize the reflection effects.

f. The shape of the sarsens is also specially designed. The uprights decrease in thickness toward the top. Experts think the design helps to avoid the optical illusion of the stones "leaning forward" when they are looked at from below. Or, the builders' real intention was to allow the microwaves to travel more effectively in the air.

g. The stones of Stonehenge have acoustic properties and may serve as a gigantic amplifier. Can they also effectively amplify microwaves?

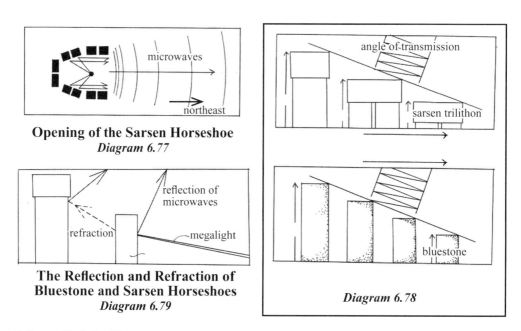

Opening of the Sarsen Horseshoe
Diagram 6.77

The Reflection and Refraction of Bluestone and Sarsen Horseshoes
Diagram 6.79

Diagram 6.78

Megalithic Energy

There are more than 800 stone circles around England, Ireland, and France and they capture the attention of many modern scientists and tourists, who try to unlock the secrets of these magical rings. For many years, researchers have conducted a series of experiments in these circles with modernized instruments such as magnetometer. They conclude that on some occasions, there was more magnetic strength at the top of a megalith. Another group used electronic devices to detect various forms of energy, and they registered changing energy readings at the stone circle around the time of sunrise. They suggest that the megalith builders chose sites that are naturally radioactive (Joyce Robins 1989). Do these experiments offer a glimpse to the secret of these stone circles? How did Stone Age people take radiation readings? Did they use flint Geiger counters?

Some tourists reported that they had experienced electric shocks and all kinds of strange feelings inside the stone circles. Geologists also suggest unknown forces and energies might be generated, as many Neolithic standing stones are in close proximity to geological fault lines. Some stones are magnetic, with iron content, while others have materials that are believed to be capable of enhancing natural radioactivity. For example, granite, which is the most common material in Neolithic construction, contains natural radioactivity and can emit constant streams of gamma radiation.

In their wonderful book *Ley Lines and Earth Energies,* David R. Cowan and Chris Arnold suggest that most of the ancient sites of Britain, such as standing stones, burial barrows, and even churches are deliberately "and carefully positioned over powerful points of Earth energy" (p. 4) where two or more energy currents cross at a node. By using simple equipment of divining rods, they were capable of "picking up a spiral of energy" from a standing stone and they suggest that these stones "were powered by subterranean energies of some sort" (p. 9). They also suggest streams of energy were emitted through the gaps of the stone circle (p. 30). They may have unlocked the secrets of these Neolithic powerhouses and explained why the monuments were built in particular places, not for religious or other rational purposes, but rather for tapping an unknown energy.

Working like gigantic energy conductors, the monoliths, round barrows, and passage cairns with sarsen orthostats inside were used as dry cell batteries for storing and generating power. They were usually erected and built close to the Earth energy streams underneath.

The Stonehenge People: As Mysterious as Their Monuments

Even though the Salisbury Plain was rich in monuments, permanent settlements were scarcely found. The Stonehenge people built huge megalithic infrastructures, such as stone circles and earthen enclosures, that are seemingly uninhabitable. They possessed skillful building technologies but there are no records about them. No diagram or drawing of their masterpieces exists. Stonehenge had taken more than a thousand years to complete. How did the Beakers, with a life span of 25–30 years and having just turned from their traditional hunting and gathering to farming, have time to construct these mammoth structures? Unlike the Grooved Ware people, who practiced collective burial, the Beakers were buried with their weaponry in their own barrows. How could such a selfish community build such constructions? Every mound had a beaker vessel placed next to the owner. It was supposed to be a container, as suggested by the experts, for daily use in the other world. But archaeologists found nothing inside these precious vessels. Did it imply the vessel itself was the most important item for the afterlife? What did these heavily decorated vessels stand for? Why were they so important that their owners had to cradle them in death?

The Beakers' sudden demise is another enigma. Possibly, the numerous and consistent projects drained the wealth of the community, which finally led to its downfall. However, archaeological evidence shows it was the last period of the culture (around 1800 B.C.) that hosted the most breathtaking construction. It was in their heyday when, without a sign, they left forever. No other place in this world would we see any monuments that could compare with Stonehenge until the construction of the Great Pyramid 500 years later. We do know Stonehenge was not built for the Bell Beakers.

Why do the experts know so little about such a remarkable and predominant Neolithic culture even though it left us with such breathtaking artifacts? Is there something wrong in our modern archaeological methodology, or is the appearance of that mysterious culture inconsistent with our accepted history so our experts are not willing to accept it? I believe many formally educated experts will find my ideas too radical.

Interplanetary travel is no longer science fiction. With current rocket technology we can reach the moon in only three days. A trip to Mars, two hundred times farther than the Moon, will take six months. Pluto at its closest approach to Earth is six billion miles away. It constitutes the most fundamental problem of space travel—where can we find or generate such a large amount of energy to propel a spacecraft across these unfathomable distances of space? Batteries are reliable but have a short life span. Solar panels and cells are possible but require constant light—and it is cold and dark in space. A radio isotopic thermoelectric generator, or RTG, takes the heat that is generated from the natural decay of radioisotope materials and converts it into electricity. But they produce a lot of radiation, and are relatively expensive. It took the Cassini unmanned probe, launched in 1997, seven years to get to Saturn by using chemical propulsion. Another alternative being considered is the construction of Space Power Stations (SPS) to launch satellites to collect solar power and transmit energy to earth in the form of microwaves. Production of SPS does not require any kind of fuel and does not create any waste products. Most importantly, solar energy is abundant and free of charge.

If we can leap civilizations with the above Space Power Stations theory to solve our space travel problem, so could other cultures on other planets. Power stations could be erected along their flight paths. They stop and refuel at each of these stations before heading to the next planet until they arrive at their destination. Our planet is probably one of the many power stations. Instead of using the solar energy from our Galaxy, they discovered something even more reliable and abundant: magnetic energy, stored inside the core of our planet. By erecting monoliths that serve as conductors, this energy can be effectively tapped along the junction of the underground power streams.

Advanced conical devices were once introduced into the centers of these power generators—for instance, inside the bluestone horseshoe and circle of Stonehenge. They acted as power collectors by projecting rows of megalights onto the surfaces of the surrounding bluestones. These megalithic conductors heated up and added mechanical stress during the processing of piezo-electricity. The quartz grained stones were capable of generating and emitting energy in the form of microwaves. In order to facilitate transmission, the builders erected the largest sarsen trilithons in the center of Stonehenge. Electrons would then move from one end of the megalight through the conical device in the center to the other end. Earth energy would be stored inside the device in the form of an electric current.

The diagram opposite illustrates how a conical device works. Rings of horizontal rims were ornamented on the hat and further decorated with hundreds of solar motifs. These motifs represent the holes that produced the megalights. What attracts my attention is the starlike ornament at the pointed tip of the gold hat. The tip once functioned as a converter and emitter. When the light holes of the horizontal rings projected megalights to the surrounding stones, electric currents were generated, collected, and stored inside the cone. At the same time, when the device was fully charged, its tip would activate in the form of a five-pointed star and convert the stored electricity into microwaves beamed into the sky above. That's why the builders carved circles inside their power generators. They are microwaves in the form of concentric circles.

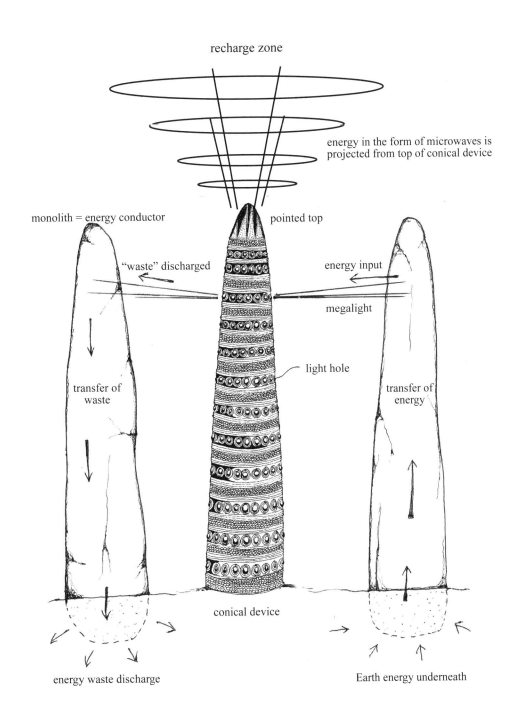

recharge zone

energy in the form of microwaves is
projected from top of conical device

monolith = energy conductor

pointed top

"waste" discharged

energy input

megalight

light hole

transfer of
waste

transfer of
energy

conical device

energy waste discharge

Earth energy underneath

A Megalithic Power Generator, ca. 3000 B.C.
Diagram 6.79

Microwave Beam Propulsion

"Any sufficiently advanced technology is indistinguishable from magic."

—Arthur C. Clarke, *Profiles of the Future*

In 1974, two Cornell University scientists beamed an encoded radio message that included an image of a human figure and the structure of DNA. This was the "Arecibo message," and radio waves sent it hurling toward the great globular cluster M13, 25,000 light years away (space.com). In 1999 and 2003, similar messages were sent out from a radio telescope in Ukraine. Recently, commercial companies beamed the first transmission of a Web site that includes classified listings for jobs and other goods.

NASA scientists are developing experiments on microwave beam propulsion for high-speed space exploration. The modern history of beamed energy propulsion started in 1972, when Arthur Kantrowitz, founder and CEO of the Avco Everett Research Laboratory, first popularized the idea of laser propulsion to aid flights into orbit. It is suggested that beam-boosted sails could be used to propel a spacecraft for interstellar exploration. The spaceship collects beamed energy in massive sails from a solar-powered satellite. The sails are driven by photons, particles of energy in which sunlight and other forms of electromagnetic radiation are emitted. By means of a remote laser or microwave source, beamed energy can be directed toward a space sail (NASA/JPL News Release, July 6, 2000).

The First International Symposium on Beamed-Energy Propulsion was held at the University of Alabama in Huntsville in 2002. The Korean researchers proposed a supersonic air-breathing laser propulsion vehicle. The Japanese team displayed X-ray driven micro-ships. Were these the mode of transport for the henge builders in 3000 B.C.? Was Stonehenge a laser powered launcher capable of emitting concentric circles of microwaves for Space Age technology in our Stone Age world? Microwaves beamed from the pointed tips of the conical devices to such aircraft would be converted to electricity by special antennas inside the craft (information from NASAexplores. com). Stonehenge can only be understood in the light of our twenty-first century technology. What makes the monument an enigma is the fact we are not advanced enough to understand it. Like a child on Christmas Day we are taken in with the packaging, giving little thought to what might lie beneath it.

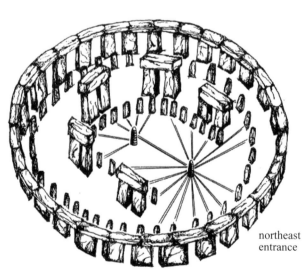

**The Power Generator of
Stonehenge III, 2000 B.C.,
with the Twin-device
Mechanism Installed**
Diagram 6.80

northeast
entrance

The Powerhouse of Stonehenge III, ca. 1800–1500 B.C.

"The preparation of this stone was solely in the hands of the initiates at the time; and the entity was among those who directed the influences of radiation which arouse, in the form of rays that were invisible to the eye but acted upon the stones themselves as in the motivating forces. ... These (aircrafts), then, were impelled by the concentration of rays from the stone which was centered in the middle of the power station, or powerhouse. ... As for a description of the manner of construction of the stone: we find it was a large cylindrical glass; cut with facets in such manner that the capstone on top of it made for centralizing the power or force that concentrated between the end of the cylinder and the capstone itself."

—Edgar Cayce (1933), quoted in D. H. Childress, *Vimana Aircraft of Ancient India and Atlantis*

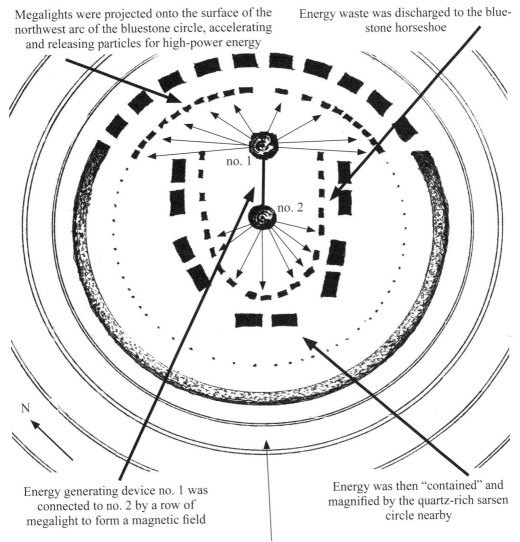

Megalights were projected onto the surface of the northwest arc of the bluestone circle, accelerating and releasing particles for high-power energy

Energy waste was discharged to the blue-stone horseshoe

no. 1

no. 2

N

Energy generating device no. 1 was connected to no. 2 by a row of megalight to form a magnetic field

Energy was then "contained" and magnified by the quartz-rich sarsen circle nearby

High-power microwaves fired from the very center of Stonehenge III

The Twin-device Mechanism of Stonehenge III
Diagram 6.80a

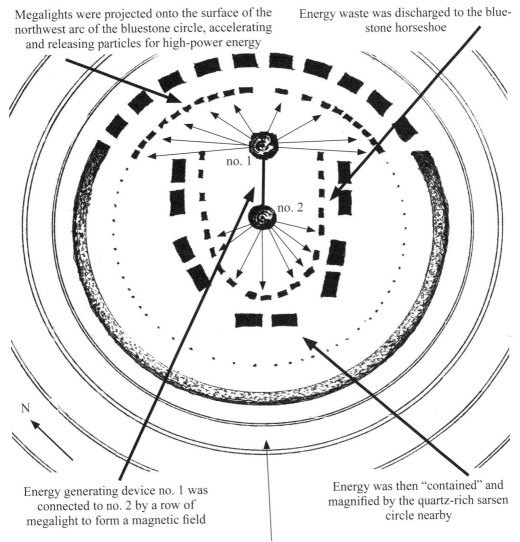

NEOLITHIC BRITAIN

Mycenaean Culture: Treasury of Atreus

"When were the ancient palaces and cities built, and by whom? What function did the various monuments have? Where did these ancient 'Greeks' come from?"

—Heinrich Schliemann, excavation of Mycenae 1876 (info: Coen Vonk)

Today, it is generally agreed that Stonehenge is more than 4,000 years old. However, before the introduction of the radiocarbon revolution of the 1960s and 1970s, experts suggested Stonehenge and its barbaric people originated from a more sophisticated civilization—the Mycenaean of the Near East. The Mycenaean marked the beginning of the first civilization where metallurgy was invented (Renfrew 1973). Burial artifacts from the Early Bronze Age Bush Barrow in Wessex provided archaeological evidences that they were directly imported from the east Mediterranean to Britain in 1500 B.C. In fact, the heyday of Stonehenge III was contemporary with the rise of the Mycenaeans.

The city of Mycenae, certainly one of the wonders of the ancient world, consists of magnificent palaces and colorful houses. The city was built on hilltop and protected by massive fortifications with 6m thick walls. One of the famous archaeological findings around the site is the tomb of the princes. Like those passage graves in Brittany and Ireland, the Mycenaean tholos is approached by a long passage cut out of the rock. Its door is 5m high and tapering inward toward the top with massive lintel blocks. Its interior measures 14.5m across and is 13.2m high with a corbelled dome, a feature of Neolithic passage graves.

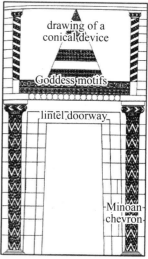

The Treasury of Atreus, dating back to 1350 B.C., is the best-preserved and the most famous tholos of Mycenae. Experts suggest the owner of the tomb must be have been Atreus—the Mycenaean king. An access passage, 35m long and 6m wide, leads to a façade 10.5m high. Its tremendous doorway is most elaborate and is decorated with wonderful painting and carvings. At its two sides stand two tall half-columns of marble carved with Minoan chevron and spiral motifs (Pedley 1993) (diagram 6.81). These motifs echo similar designs in the Boyne Valley and the Malta Islands.

The most striking decoration is the painting on its lintel, which is made of two enormous blocks weighing more than 100 tons each. A cone-shaped object decorated with horizontal rims and filled with spiral motifs is drawn. The object is placed on two painted horizontal strips decorated with another row of spiral motifs and the famous sectioned egg motifs (diagram 6.82a). A conical object with a horizontal base is a perfect description of a brimmed Berlin gold cone, the builders' conical device to be exact. But it is not the end of the Mycenaean story.

Conical Device and the Lintel Doorway of the Treasury of Atreus, Mycenae
(after Taylor 1990)
Diagram 6.81

According to the painting on the lintel, the conical object is flanked by two smaller semi-columns of marble decorated with spiral motifs. Obviously, this smaller pair is a duplicate of the larger pair below that flanks the main doorway of the tholos. The artist probably wanted to show where the genuine conical device lay, i.e., under the lintel doorway of the tholos, the same location where the builders once housed their device on the roofbox of Newgrange and at the northeast entrance of the bluestone horseshoe of Stonehenge III. Readers certainly know the rest of the story. But the secret of the Treasury of Atreus does not simply end here.

Sectioned Egg Motifs and the Twin-device Mechanism

Under the conical painting, a row of so-called sectioned double-egg motifs, icon of Mycenaean culture, is painted in detail (diagram 6.82a). The motif is an ideogram of the Great Goddess of the Mycenaeans. Experts suggest it represents a harmonious combination of germ cell and comic snakes and fawns (Gimbutas 1982). Its prevalance in the region certainly reflects its importance to the Mycenaeans. Similar stylized patterns known as "flower motifs" (diagram 6.82b) are decorated all over the walls of the palace, especially at the three sides of its main doorways, and are of different colors.

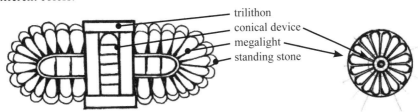

trilithon
conical device
megalight
standing stone

Sectioned Double-egg Motif:
Twin-device of Mycenaean Culture
Diagram 6.82a

Flower Motif: Rosette Design from
Ceiling Pattern at Orchomenos Shows
Conical Device with Megalights
Diagram 6.82b

As in the case of the Maltese temples, the egg ideogram probably describes what once happened inside these Neolithic temples. There were two conical devices placed at the center of the two side apses of the temple, which projected a radiance of megalights to the surrounding orthostats that formed the apses. This is what the egg ideogram of Mycenae tries to convey: the twin-device energy mechanism of the builders. Placed in the center of the motif, the third conical device is drawn inside a lintel trilithon. As proved by the application of the SA, a conical device was once placed inside the trilithon doorway of the Maltese temple and connected two conical devices with megalights.

Interestingly, the egg ideogram can be applied to Stonehenge III as well. If the egg motif is placed vertically, we can see Stonehenge III as the upper sectioned-egg motif that represents the northeast arc of the bluestone circle, while the lower sectioned-egg motif stands for the bluestone horseshoe (diagram 6.83). The conical devices, decorated with horizontal rims, are painted and placed at the center of the two semicircles. A radiance of dagger-like objects was generated from the two conical devices to the two semicircles. It is expressed explicitly by the Solar God slab of Newgrange and the Dagda Skirt of Loughcrew.

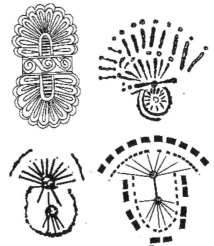

The Builders' Twin-device Energy Mechanism
(*Clockwise from top left*): Great Goddess of Mycenae (after Gimbutas 1982); Dagde Skirt of Loughcrew; Solar God of Newgrange; Twin-device of Stonehenge III
Diagram 6.83

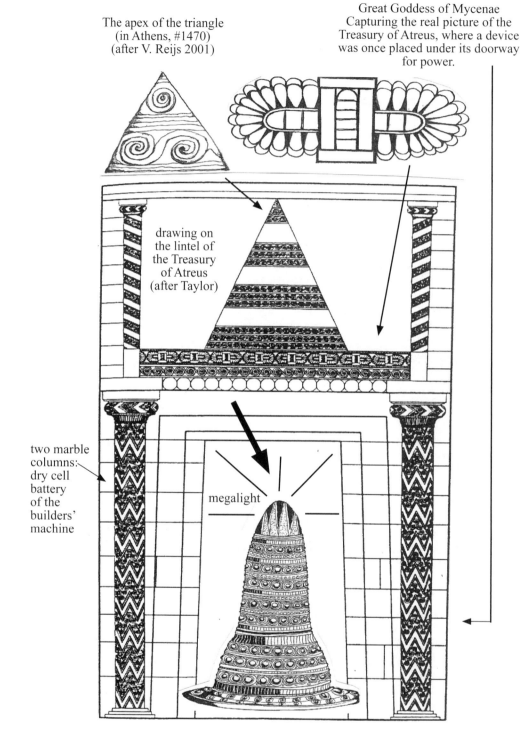

The apex of the triangle
(in Athens, #1470)
(after V. Reijs 2001)

Great Goddess of Mycenae
Capturing the real picture of the
Treasury of Atreus, where a device
was once placed under its doorway
for power.

drawing on
the lintel of
the Treasury
of Atreus
(after Taylor)

two marble
columns:
dry cell
battery
of the
builders'
machine

megalight

Powerhouse of Mycenae, ca. 1350 B.C.
Diagram 6.83a

Lintels of the Treasury of Atreus

Nine tholos that date from 1500 to 1250 B.C have been discovered at Mycenae. The Treasury of Atreus is the most advanced and magnificent monument. Its doorway leads to a huge, round, and corbelled chamber 14.5m across, with the height of the roof at 13m. To create the curve of the vault each course of masonry is made to project beyond the one below. Its design resembles that of the Neolithic passage graves of Brittany and the Boyne Valley. Strangely, another lintel doorway connects it to a small side chamber that measures 8m × 8m and opens to the right of the inner wall of Atreus. The side chamber was not vaulted and a pit, serving an unknown purpose, is found in its central floor.

The Treasury of Atreus is most famous for its sophisticated lintel doorway design. Its lintel is comparatively longer and often survives the relief of pressure exerted by the empty triangular space above it. Its two vertical portal doorways are built of solid ashlar masonry (Taylour 1990). It is these tremendous lintel doorways that hide the secret of the tomb. Like many corbelled tombs of Neolithic Europe, an SA is formed by the doorway of its main entrance and the central pit of its side chamber with the lintel doorway of the side chamber in the middle (diagram 6.84). Conical devices were placed under these lintels to generate energy. Like the passage mounds of Knowth and Maes Howe, the generated energy was further magnified by its corbelled wall. The Treasury of Atreus was just another powerhouse of the builders.

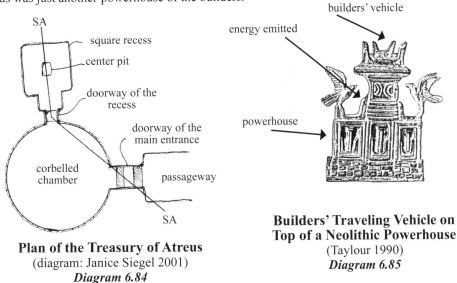

Plan of the Treasury of Atreus
(diagram: Janice Siegel 2001)
Diagram 6.84

Builders' Traveling Vehicle on Top of a Neolithic Powerhouse
(Taylour 1990)
Diagram 6.85

Diagram 6.85 shows a gold ornament from Grave Circle A of Mycenae that probably represents a shrine. Experts suggest deities in the form of columns or pillars are present in these rustic shrines for worship. But the ornament can also be interpreted in the following way: the builders' conical devices, represented by columns, were placed under the lintel doorways and produced power. Energy, in form of concentric circles of microwaves, is expressed by five horizontal lines above the central lintel. A builders' vehicle which appears as a square cabinet under a crown with a horn-like antenna is recharging on top of the powerhouse.

The Power Station of Mycenae, ca. 1350 B.C.

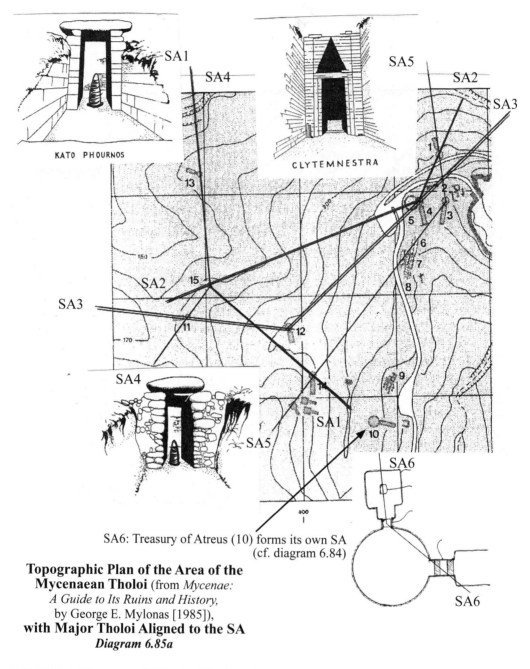

KATO PHOURNOS

CLYTEMNESTRA

SA6: Treasury of Atreus (10) forms its own SA
(cf. diagram 6.84)

**Topographic Plan of the Area of the
Mycenaean Tholoi** (from *Mycenae:
A Guide to Its Ruins and History,*
by George E. Mylonas [1985]),
with Major Tholoi Aligned to the SA
Diagram 6.85a

SA1 13-Kato Phournos + 15 Tomb of the Gennii + 14 Panayitsa
SA2 15 + 4 Klytemnestra + 1 Lion
SA3 11 Cyclopean Tomb + 12 Epano Phournos + 4
SA4 13 + 15 + 11
SA5 14 + 3 Aigisthos + 1

The Mycenaens were obsessed with amber and used it for the manufacture of ornamental objects inside their "tombs." Similar items have been found in Neolithic remains in Denmark and in Bronze Age Britain. Rubbing amber can produce an electrostatic charge. This property is reflected in etymology of the word "electricity" (from the Greek world for amber, *elektron*) (Wikipedia).

The Lion Gate: Builders' Dry Cell Batteries

Today, every visitor has to pass through the Lion Gate before entering the Citadel, the wall city of Mycenae (diagram 6.86). The Gate was built in 1250 B.C., 200 years after the completion of the Treasury of Atreus. Structurally speaking, the design of the Lion Gate is identical to the doorway of Atreus. A massive megalithic trilithon is constructed under a corbelled wall in the form of a relieving triangle. The lintel of the Gate measures 4.5m × 2m × 0.8m, whereas its two jambs are 3m × 1.74m × 0.54m. Its threshold is 4.56m × 2.31m × 0.88m. A triangular slab is placed inside the relieving triangle above the gate. The slab is carved with a relief depicting a pair of lions. A columnar object with circular motifs on top is placed on an altar-like platform and is further flanked by the two lions. Judging from the location of the Gate and its being protected by two fierce creatures, the "column" had to be an extremely important object for the Mycenaeans. Experts speculate that the object, serving as sacred

Lion Gate of Mycenae with Columnar Device on Top
Diagram 6.86

pillar, was a symbol of the might of Mycenae, probably showing their determination to defend their city against enemies.

Since the design of the Gate is identical to the doorway of Atreus, it follows that if the painting of Atreus reveals a conical device being placed at its doorway, the carving of the Lion Gate may also suggest that a columnar device was also placed under the gate. The picture is captured on a gold ornament excavated in Grave Circle A, where three columnar devices are each placed under a lintel doorway (diagram 6.85). With the installation of the builders' device, the Lion Gate once functioned as a dry cell battery.

The great city of Mycenae is famous for its Cyclopean city walls, which were built with large boulders. These 4.6m to 6.7m fortification walls were further strengthened by ashlar masonry. Large symmetrical blocks were dressed by hammer. This first civilization which easily outplayed the others by manipulating metallurgy and being protected by massive walls suddenly came to an end in 1100 B.C. Without archaeological evidence, experts suggest the Mycenaeans were invaded by the Dorians who came from the lower class of society. However, instead of taking the walled city, the Dorians just left and lived in their small houses, abandoning the city of Mycenae. The sudden demise of the city and its civilization is still an enigma for the experts.

power-generating devices under lintel doorways symbol for the twin-device mechanism

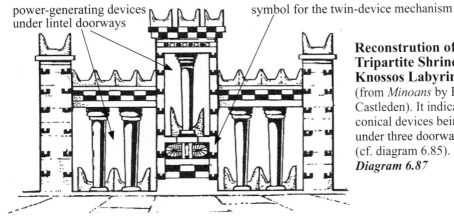

Reconstruction of the Tripartite Shrine in the Knossos Labyrinth
(from *Minoans* by Rodney Castleden). It indicates conical devices being placed under three doorways (cf. diagram 6.85).
Diagram 6.87

Power Stations in Wessex, 3500–3000 B.C.

With its intricate inner megalithic infrastructure, Stonehenge III has overshadowed other Neolithic monuments in Wessex for more than 4,000 years. Actually, the chalkland of Wessex is clustered with numerous Neolithic sites such as causewayed camps and earthen henges that are much older than Stonehenge III. Strictly speaking, Stonehenge I was a henge with a ditch and bank in 3000 B.C.

Windmill Hill and Its Round Barrows

Today, there are about sixty causewayed enclosures, of which the one at Windmill Hill is regarded as the oldest, dating back to 3600–3000 B.C. The Windmill Hill Neolithic site is located at a gentle slope of a hilltop that is 43m above the land of the Winterbourne valley nearby. It is now only possible to trace the lines of three circuits of the enclosure, being divided into more than twenty complete segments of ditches (diagram 6.88a). The most noticable features of Windmill Hill are the early Bronze Age round barrows, most of them being destroyed now. Large quantities of pottery, broken remains of over hundreds of pots, have been found during excavations. As a result, the enclosure is considered to be a great gathering place of the Neolithic people or a center for ritual activities.

Evolution of Power Plants in Wessex

I have discovered that these round barrows around Windmill Hill are aligned to the SA. Four sets of SAs can be derived, as shown in the following diagram. They acted as dry cells of the Neolithic builders, and were used for abstracting the Earth energy inside the enclosure. The causewayed enclosure of Windmill Hill must have functioned like the ditch and bank of Stonehenge I, as the earliest power plant of Wiltshire. It functioned like the crop circles in southern Britain today.

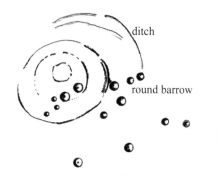

Plan of Windmill Hill Enclosure and Early Bronze Age Round Barrows
Diagram 6.88a

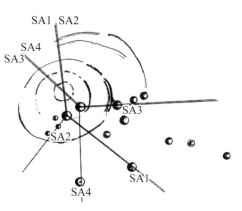

SAs Formed by the Round Barrows and the Center of Windmill Hill
Diagram 6.88b

Durrington Walls and Its Post Hole Circles

The massive circular earth enclosure of Durrington Walls, with a diameter of 520m, dates back to the early and middle Neolithic, around 3000 B.C. Experts believe Durrington Walls, which once had a close relationship with Stonehenge, were its ritual center, since no human activities have ever been found inside Stonehenge. The enclosure lies just 3km to the northeast of Stonehenge, and to the north of another famous prehistoric monument—Woodhenge. Like other causewayed camps, Durrington Walls is an oval enclosure encircled by a ditch and external bank believed to have been built around 3100 B.C. The enclosure has two entrances, one at the southeast, 38m wide, and the other at the northwest, 12m wide. Inside this huge enclosure, there are two main circles, the Southern and Northern Circles, of post-holes or pits which are believed to have been constructed in a later period, around 2500 B.C. But unlike the great henge of Avebury, where two inner stone circles were constructed in the center of the site, the two post-hole circles of Durrington Walls were deliberately placed at the northeast edge inside the enclosure. Various functions have been suggested for the site, including settlement, defense, and a meeting place for trade. However, its real function remains unknown.

According to experts, the Southern Circle, which lies inside the east entrance on a raised platform area, could have been constructed in two phases. Today, the Circle comprises six concentric rings with massive timber uprights (phase 2). A southeast entrance opens to the main eastern entrance of the enclosure. The Northern Circle of post-holes are located 121m north of the Southern Circle with a double circle of pits pointing southward, probably toward the northern end of the Southern Circle. It is important to point out that an SA is formed by the Southern and Northern Circles. The causeway of Northern Circle lies on the exact axis of Station Stone 93 of Stonehenge; whereas the southeast entrance of the Southern Circle lies on the axis of the angle bisector, i.e., the Heel Stone of Stonehenge. A row of megalights could travel northward from the center of the Southern Circle along the southern causeway of the Northern Circle so as to connect another charged device inside the circle. Another row of megalights would travel through the southeast entrance of the Southern Circle and supply power to the builders' machinery parked just outside the main eastern entrance of the Durrington Walls (diagram 6.89a).

The causewayed enclosure of Durrington Walls and the classic henge of Coneybury form an SA, with the Woodhenge in the middle (diagram 6.89b). The classic henge of Coneybury with a single northeast entrance is a small henge measuring 40m along its greatest axis (Richards 1990) and lying southeast of Stonehenge. The Woodhenge is another classic henge with a single northeast entrance.

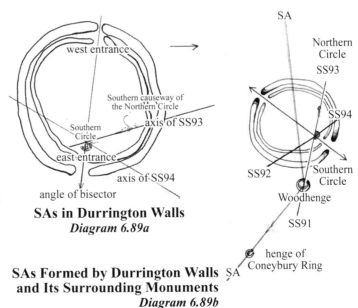

SAs in Durrington Walls
Diagram 6.89a

SAs Formed by Durrington Walls and Its Surrounding Monuments
Diagram 6.89b

Marden and Its Round Barrows

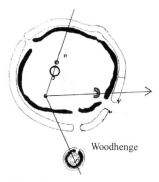

SA of Durrington Wall
Diagram 6.89c

The Neolithic earthwork of Marden lies 16km northwest of the Durrington Walls enclosure and 11km southwest of Avebury. Marden is located on a floodplain with an internal ditch, 16m wide and 2m deep, inside a bank 13m wide and 1m high. The site stretches 530m from north to south and 360m from east to west and forms a rough oval shape. There are two entrances to the earthwork. The north entrance is 15m wide while the east is 19m. There are traces of the Hatfield Barrow, a huge barrow with a diameter of 160m and a height of 7m to the east of the east entrance (diagram 6.90a). Another unknown circular enclosure of 60m in diameter has been found south of the Hatfield Barrow. Potteries have been excavated inside several pits, and post-holes have also been found along the entrance causeway, which evidences the early Neolithic builders' occupation of the region.

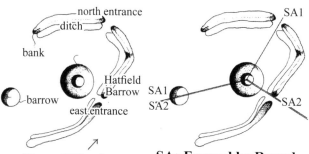

Plan of Marden Enclosure and Its Barrows
Diagram 6.90a

SAs Formed by Round Barrows and Entrances East and Northeast of Marden Enclosure
Diagram 6.90b

The relationship between the causewayed ditches and the barrows inside can be revealed by applying the SA to the site. As shown in the diagram, if the two barrows, Hatfield and the South Enclosure, are connected with a straight line passing through their centers, SA1 and SA2 will be formed by the two causewayed entrances, north and east, of Marden, with the center of Harfield Barrow in the middle (diagram 6.90b). The Marden causewayed camp is just another version of the Windmill Hill. The two barrows acted as the builders' dry cells and helped to abstract the Earth energy of the site for power. The circular ditch and bank also helps to tap and store the Earth energy in the Wessex chalkland.

Mount Pleasant and the SA

Mount Pleasant, a modest hill, lies across a ridge on the eastern edge of Dorchester. It is formed by a single bank, 16m wide, with an internal ditch 17m wide in a rough oval shape. The dimensions measure 370m from west to east and 320m from south to north. There are four entrances, north, east, southeast, and southwest, formed by the gaps of the ditches and banks (diagram 6.91). Experts suggest it was built during the late Neolithic and early Bronze period and had been in use for over a thousand years.

Plan of Mount Pleasant Enclosure and the Location of the Timber Circle
Diagram 6.91

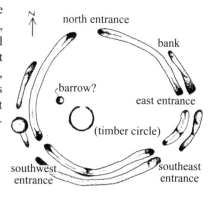

As revealed in the excavation report, Site IV, a timber monument of a large ring ditch 45m in diameter, 2.6 to 4.6m wide and 2m deep, and only traces of its bank, is located on the southwestern ridge, but not at its summit of the enclosure. The ring ditch contains five concentric rings of post-holes, from 12.5m to 38m in diameter, together with several stones and pits found inside (diagram 6.92). The general layout of all these stones and pits is aligned to the SA, as shown in the diagram. The location of Site IV might have indicated the availability of the Earth energy inside and under Mount Pleasant. The same situation is found in Durrington Walls, where two post-hole circles were constructed close to the northeast edge of the enclosure.

Besides, Site IV has a single causeway/exit to the north, directly opposite the north entrance of Mount Pleasant enclosure. Interestingly, several sets of SAs are formed by this northern causeway of Site IV and the surrounding round barrows and entrances of Mount Pleasant. A conical device no. 1 of the builders must have been placed in the pit A of Site IV to generate Earth energy; whereas device no. 2 must have been put along the northern exit of Site IV (diagram 6.93). The latter on the one hand projected a megalight to connect conical device no. 1 in the center of Site IV for power. On the other hand, it also projected two other rows of megalights, one connecting the Conquer Barrow for discharging; and the other one projected onto the builders' machine which was probably parked outside the southeast entrance of Mount Pleasant.

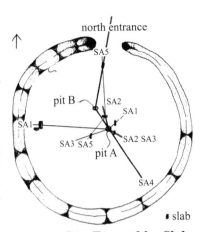

Various SAs Formed by Slabs of the Timber Circle, with Pit A in the Middle
Diagram 6.92

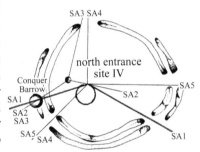

Plan of Mount Pleasant Enclosure and the Application of SA
Diagram 6.93

Knowlton Henge Complex

The complex of the late Neolithic and early Bronze Age monuments at Knowlton is an important enclosure complex in Wessex. It consists of four earthworks: the Church Circle, North Circle, Southern Circle, and the Old Churchyard (diagram 6.94) (info: Steve Burrow). There is a huge round barrow—Great Barrow—lying east of the Church Circle. Being over 6m high and having a diameter of 40m, it is the largest round barrow in Dorset. These earthworks are surrounded by a large number of smaller barrows. The whole complex consists of massive earthwork enclosures up to 480m across. Experts suggest that the complex was used for domestic and ritual purposes.

The Southern Circle is the largest henge in the complex with a ditch, 5.7m in depth, and a bank, forming an enclosure of 228m in diameter. However, the focus of the complex is the Church Henge, where the ruins of a Roman church stands. It lies in the middle of the whole Neolithic complex. The earthwork comprises a 2m high bank with a 2m deep ditch. What makes this henge special is that, by applying the SA to the site, it becomes the center of the Neolithic Knowlton. As shown in diagram below, SA1 is formed by three enclosures: the Old Churchyard in the north, the Southern Henge in the south, with the Church Henge in the middle. Interestingly, there are two round barrows, A and B, lying on the exact axis of the SA. The SA bisects at a small barrow E at the southwest. Like the evolution of power plants I discussed before, the builders constructed the three Stone Angled enclosures first, during the late Neolithic period, and they replaced the enclosures with the two round barrows probably in the early Bronze Age.

Besides, SA2 is formed by round barrow C and South Barrow Henge, as well as barrow B in between, with Church Henge in the middle. The SA bisects at barrow D, east of the Church Henge (diagram 6.95)

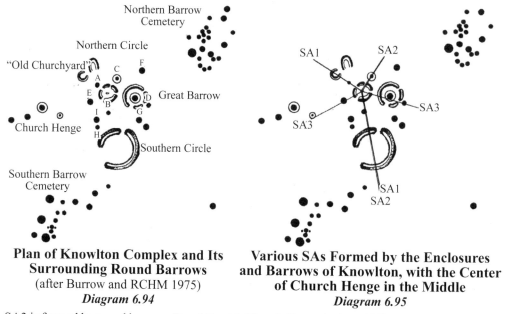

Plan of Knowlton Complex and Its Surrounding Round Barrows
(after Burrow and RCHM 1975)
Diagram 6.94

Various SAs Formed by the Enclosures and Barrows of Knowlton, with the Center of Church Henge in the Middle
Diagram 6.95

SA3 is formed by round barrows D and E, with Church Henge in the middle, and the SA bisects at barrow B. Therefore, all round barrows clustering around Church Henge are deliberately placed to align to the SA formula. This complex must have been a dominating feature 5,000 years ago.

Furthermore, Great Barrow forms SA4, with two surrounding round barrows B and F, and the SA bisects at Northern Henge (diagram 6.96).

Northern Henge, on the other hand, forms SA5 and SA6, with the surrounding barrows and the angles bisect at the center of Church Henge and Southern Henge respectively (diagram 6.97).

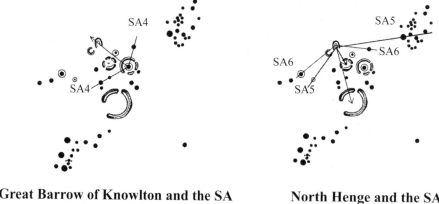

Great Barrow of Knowlton and the SA
Diagram 6.96

North Henge and the SA
Diagram 6.97

Great Barrow and Old Churchyard form SA7, with the small round barrow C in the middle. The angle bisects at the center of Church Henge.

Great Barrow and Southern Henge form SA8, with round barrow G in the middle. The angle bisects at round barrow B to the west.

The following Bronze Age round barrows around the region also form various SAs (diagram 6.98):

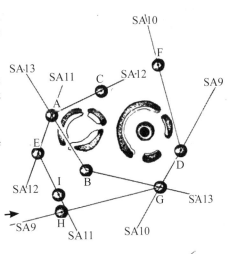

SAs Formed by Barrows around Church Henge and Great Barrow of Knowlton ➤
Diagram 6.98

SA9 Round barrows D–G–H and the angle bisects at barrow C
SA10 Round barrows F–D–G and the angle bisects at Church Henge
SA11 Round barrows A–E–I and the angle bisects at barrow H
SA12 Round barrows C–A–E and the angle bisects at Church Henge

Furthermore, there are two groups of barrows, Northern and Southern Barrow Cemeteries, located at the northeast and southwest of the site, which are also aligned to the SA, with the center of Church Henge in the middle (diagram 6.99).

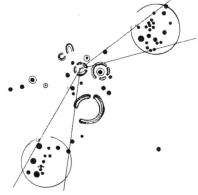

Two Barrow Cemeteries Aligned to the SAs
Diagram 6.99

Rock Art at Knowlton

In the year 2000, a stone decorated with concentric rings—a message from the Neolithic builders—was ploughed out of Southern Henge at Knowlton (diagram 6.100). The rectangular stone, 60cm wide and 105cm long, appears to be a hearthstone of iron-rich sarsen (see Helen Lewis, Charles French, and Martin Green, "A Decorated Megalith from Knowlton Henges, Dorset, England" in *Past* 35 [2000]). A drawing of four concentric rings is engraved into the centre of the stone, which must have been deliberately left by the builders to show the real function and the importance of the Knowlton henges.

A Message from Neolithic Builders: A Stone Decorated with Concentric Rings in Southern Henge, Knowlton
Diagram 6.100

The Thornborough Project

"Thornborough was a sacred landscape, a place of religious worship, and the most important prehistoric site between Stonehenge and the Orkneys."

—Dr. Jan Harding, Senior Lecturer in Archaeology at Newcastle University

The Thornborough Complex lies on the low-lying gravel plateau between the central Pennines and Hambleton. Experts suggest that it is a triple super-henge monument that is believed to have been constructed around 3000 B.C. The three almost identical henges, each 240m in diameter and defined by a massive ditch and bank with the same northwest and southeast alignment, are placed approximately 550m apart, making the whole complex extend for nearly 1.7km ("Historical Studies—Welcome to the Thornborough Project" by Dr. Jan Harding, University of Newcastle) (diagram 6.101). The complex is made up of many monuments, including cursuses, enclosures, burial barrows, settlements, and pit alignments. Once again, experts have no idea of the function of all these monuments. Some speculate that the complex had served as an important place for spiritual and ritual activities for more than 4,000 years (Jan Harding).

According to the "Friends of Thornborough", the monuments at Thornborough were aligned to astronomical orientations. "A giant cursus appears to have been deliberately oriented towards the midsummer solstice sunrise, to the east, and towards the setting of the constellation of Orion's Belt. The entrances of the three henges frame the rising of Sirius."

The application of the SA to the complex helps us to understand the complex better. For example, Northern Henge, actually lying at the northwest, forms two sets of SAs with the surrounding round barrows in Nosterfield (diagram 6.102), whereas Central Henge forms an SA with a barrow at the west and another barrow at southeast. The SA bisects at a barrow in the south. The Southern Henge forms an SA with a barrow at the southwest and another at the southeast. They were once power generators of the builders, like all those megalithic sites around the region. Conical devices were placed inside these henges around 2500 B.C. and they projected rows of megalights to the surrounding round barrows, the Neolithic dry cells, for energy.

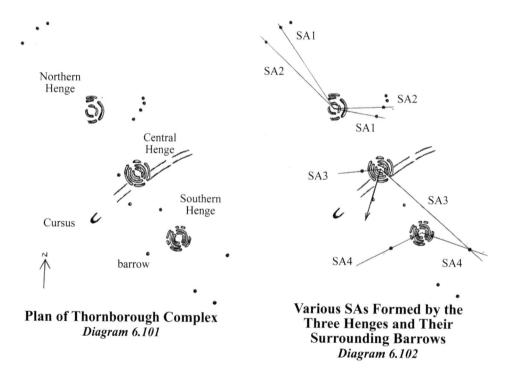

Plan of Thornborough Complex
Diagram 6.101

Various SAs Formed by the Three Henges and Their Surrounding Barrows
Diagram 6.102

Dr. Harding and his team suggested Central Henge is constructed on an earlier cursus, which is 1.1km long and 44m wide. The diagram at right shows the earlier phase of Thornborough with the removal of Central Henge. It is important to note that an SA is formed by the Northern and Southern Henges, with the Thornborough cursus in the middle. The main axis of this ritual walkway lies precisely along the SA bisector of the two henges. It reminds me of Stonehenge Cursus, which once served as the recharging platform and forms various sets of SAs or power generators along the causeway with the surrounding long and round barrows. Therefore, the whole complex has nothing to do with the alignment to the stars whatsoever.

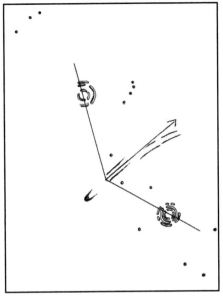

Relation between the Thornborough Henges and Cursus
Diagram 6.103

Stone Circles: The Builders' Local Power Stations

"Stone circles fascinate. They perplex. They seldom satisfy."
—Aubrey Burl, *Great Stone Circles* (1999)

"In their (megalithic temples') sitting, orientation and inter-relationships, these structures are generally related to the pattern of the heavens, but they have many features which cannot be explained astronomically. Their secrets lie not merely in the stars, but on the same ground which their builders trod."
—John Michell, *A Little History of Astro-Archaeology* (1989)

There are about 800 or more stone circles, including Avebury and Stonehenge, around the British Isles and Northern France. There should have been more because archaeological and local histories evidenced that a handful of them were destroyed for religious reasons or reused as building materials. Others are still lying quietly in local bushes or deep valleys hiding from people. These monuments certainly pose an enigma for the experts, as they are believed to be 3,500 to 5,000 years old, an age when no related records are found. For millennia, these circles have embraced not only standing stones, but also local rumors, mysteries, and legends.

Most of these stone rings consist of six to over sixty stones, with Avebury being the outer ring composed of 100 stones. They are fixed to the ground to enclose a circular central area where ring cairns or burial cists are commonly found. Many are erected in rough circles but some of them are perfect ones. Most of the stones, carefully selected and of different sizes and colors, are not dressed or shaped but some are decorated with cupmarks on their surfaces. Many of them were built on open spaces, along mountain ridges or on top of the hill, but some of them were deliberately placed deep inside the valley or under the trees.

There are many interpretations of these circles. According to local tales, they were people turned into stones, while there were rumors that they were the homes of the witches, and children were warned not to go near them. Besides, some circles were believed to possess special forces or powers, such as raising fertility and curing diseases. Archaeologists suggest that they might have been used for measuring solar positions, religious ceremonies, social gatherings, or simply as burial places. But once again, no theory has been put to test. Haunted shadows and modern scientists are still wandering around these rings of mystery.

It is true that most of the rings are located on the upland areas with little forestry and an excellent view of the surroundings. Some people suggest that many of these circles lie at the nodes of the energy lines that are believed to concentrate and redirect potent Earth energy to enable the people to live in fulfillment and abundance. With a view to exploring the real functions of Newgrange, Avebury, and Stonehenge, I have always wondered: were these stone circles, which might also function as dry cells batteries, used to tap the Earth energy and at the same time transfer this energy to the builders' conical devices?

Northeast Circle

Great Circle

Stanton Drew
Diagram 6.104

Stanton Drew "Redevelopment Program"

The name Stanton is derived fron the Anglo-Saxon *stan* ("stone") *tun* ("farm"). No excavations are recorded, nor have any modern surveys been made until 1998. The circles was first noted by John Aubrey in 1664 and planned by William Stukeley in 1776. Legend says the stones represent the members of a wedding party and its musicians, lured by the Devil to celebrate on the Sabbath. Others suppose the impossibility of counting the stones.

The Stanton Drew Neolithic Complex consists of three stone circles, two avenues, and two sets of standing stones (diagram 6.105), which could date back to 3000 B.C. The central feature of the complex is the central ring of Great Circle of twenty-seven standing limestones. It has a diameter of 115m, the second largest in Britain.

This major circle is underappreciated. The experts, using electromagnetism in a geophysical survey conducted by the Ancient Monuments Laboratory of English Heritage, uncovered a very huge buried enclosure ditch inside the great circle. Its diameter measures 135m and has a series of concentric rings of pits inside (diagram 6.106). The limestones of the Great Circle form several sets of SAs with the central pit holes. Extended from this circle is a short and disrupted avenue of six stones, 33m long and 8.5m wide, which leads northeast towards the River Chew.

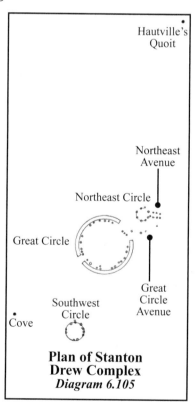

Hautville's Quoit

Northeast Avenue

Northeast Circle

Great Circle

Great Circle Avenue

Southwest Circle

Cove

Plan of Stanton Drew Complex
Diagram 6.105

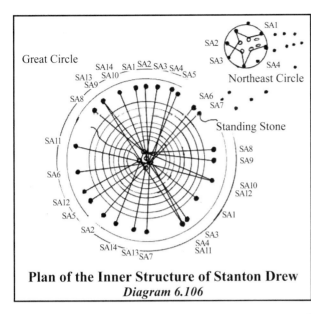

Plan of the Inner Structure of Stanton Drew
Diagram 6.106

The Northeast Circle is a small ring of eight stones with a diameter of 29.6m. The electromagnetic survey shows four pits inside the circle and they form several sets of SAs with the surrounding stones. An eight-stoned avenue about 9m wide extends northeastward from this small circle. A less impressive stone circle, known as the Southwest Circle formed by ten small and lying stones, is 44m in diameter. No avenue is found.

Three large standing stones made of dolomitie breccia, known as "the Cove," are located southwest of the Great Circle. It comprises two upright stones and a third one, now fallen. A single large flat standing sandstone called Hautville's Quoit, 3.2m long, is found at the northeast of the Great Circle lying high on a ridge.

The whole Stanton Drew complex fits perfectly in the SA formula. The site could be divided into three phases. The first phase is the simplest and most primitive one, which includes the Cove, the Hautville's Quoit, the Northeast stone circle, and its east avenue. SA1 is derived from the monolith of Hautville's Quoit and the southwest entrance of the Great Circle at the south, with the center of the Northeast Circle in the middle (diagram 6.107).

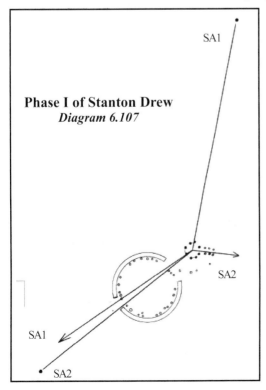

Phase I of Stanton Drew
Diagram 6.107

At the same time, SA2 is formed by another set of standing stones—the Cove and the avenue of the Northeast Circle, with the center of the Circle in the middle. The Northeast Circle became the focus point of Phase I of Stanton Drew.

In the second phase, the Great Circle was the center of the builders' powerhouse. The circle forms SA3 with the avenue of the Northeast Circle where the center of the Northeast Circle lies in the middle. Twin-device no. 1 was placed inside the Great Circle, and projected rows of megalights onto the surrounding standing stones to tap the energy underneath. Another device, twin-device no. 2, was probably placed inside the center of the Northeast Circle for discharging.

The third phase started with the introduction of the Southwest Circle to replace the monoliths of Hautville's Quoit and the Cove (diagram 6.108). As shown in the diagram, the centers of the two rings form an SA with the northeast avenue. The complex was in no way a ritual site, an astronomical landscape, or a place for wedding party. It was simply a powerhouse of the builders.

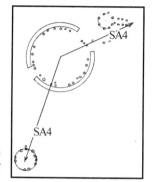

Stanton Drew and the Southwest Circle
Diagram 6.108

Clava Cairns of Scotland

The Clava Cairns group is one of the most notable and prettiest prehistoric sites in Scotland. The complex consists of thirty passage tombs, with three of them, the so-called Clava type, being the most impressive. They have round chambers and are built in drystone walling with a high corbel roof. The central cairn is surrounded by a stone circle, usually 3m to 5m from the kerbstones.

Three Clava tombs are located at Balnuaran with heavily kerbed ring-cairns and passage-graves (diagram 6.109). The Northeast Cairn stands 3m high and is surrounded by a circle of eleven monoliths. The Southwest Cairn has a passage leading to a chamber 4m in diameter and is surrounded by a circle of twelve monoliths. The Central Ring-cairn has no passage but it has a stone circle of nine monoliths that surrounds a small kerb-circle of fifteen boulders. Another remarkable feature of the Central Ring-cairn is a unique arrangement of three stone causeways of thin earth banks leading from the edge of the cairn to the three standing stones surrounding it.

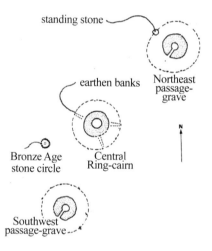

Clava Cairns
(after M. Balfour)
Diagram 6.109

Like other cairns around the British Isles, quartz pebbles are found inside these Clava cairns. Two kerbstones, one from the Northeast cairn and one from the Southwest cairn, are heavily carved with cup or cup and ring marks. Experts suggest these carvings represent the symbol of fertility (Burl 2000), but to me, they probably show the real function of these megalithic powerhouses.

The standing stones of the northeast and southwest stone rings are aligned to the SA when the twin-device energy mechanism is applied (diagram 6.110). Conical device no. 1 was placed inside the cairn, and projected megalights onto the surrounding kerbstones for tapping power. Twin-device no. 2 was located at the entrance of the cairn for discharging by heating the standing stones nearby.

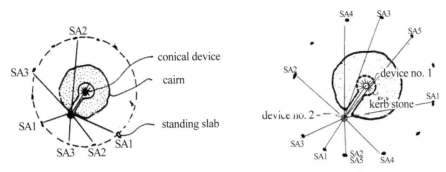

Southwest Cairn (*left*) and Northeast Cairn of Balnuaran
Diagram 6.110

But the most wonderful design of the builders' powerhouse is the Central Ring-cairn. The cairn is surrounded by nine monoliths and three of them are carefully placed and attached to the central cairn by three thin earthen banks (diagram 6.111). These banks are generally described as mini causeways, as no one understands their function. Each of these banks, or parallel lines, lies precisely on the axis of the angle bisector formed by a pair of standing stones. The same setting is found not only in its eastern bank, but also in the western and southern banks. The builders skillfully and cautiously show us their magic.

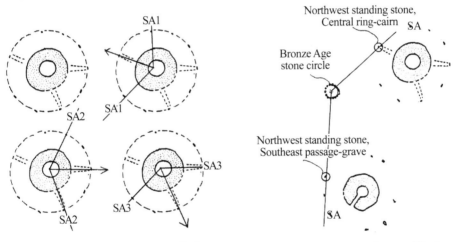

Earthen Banks of Central Cairn and the SA
Diagram 6.111

Bronze Age Stone Circle and the SA
Diagram 6.112

A small Late Bronze Age stone circle, probably a small kerb-cairn with a diameter of 3.7m, is architecturally related to the Clava family (Burl 2000) (diagram 6.112). Most of the stones in the oval-shaped circle have fallen but they bear cup and ring markings. Scattered fragments of white quartz are also found inside the circle. Interestingly, the center of this small circle together with two standing stones nearby form an SA. Was this Bronze Age stone circle a temporary station or an extension? The energy generated might be magnified by the white quartz minerals inside the ring.

Corrimony Chambered Cairn

Corrimony chambered cairn of Inverness, a Clava type, has a stone circle of large pebbles surrounding a central burial chamber of stone measuring 15.5m × 14.5m. A stone-lined passage leads to the east-northeast. Like the central cairn of Clava, Corrimony has a corbelled chamber 4m across (Burl 2000). A cupmarked stone lying on the top of the cairn suggests that Corrimony might have been another powerhouse of the Neolithic builders (diagram 6.113).

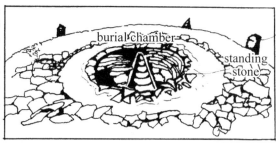

Corrimony Powerhouse
Diagram 6.113

The Magnificent SA of Callanish

Callanish Neolithic monument is probably the most famous and elaborate prehistoric site of Scotland. It actually refers to a complex of Stone Age megaliths including stone circles, stone alignments, standing stones, and chambered cairn. The stone circle, the earliest and most complicated megaliths of Callanish I, is believed to have been constructed around 3000 B.C. Professor Alexander Thom suggested that the alignment of the stone avenue pointed to the setting of midsummer full moon. Local tradition says that giants who lived on the island refused to be converted to Christianity and were then turned to stone as a punishment (answers. com). "The stones were brought to the island in ships and erected by black men under the direction of priests, according to the legend" (Gerald Ponting).

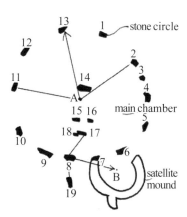

Central Ring of Callanish I
(megalithic.co.uk)
Diagram 6.114

Callanish I includes a central setting—a ring of thirteen standing stones and a central chambered cairn with four to five monoliths forming a horseshoe (diagram 6.114). The central obelisk is the tallest, at 4.75m. The ring stones are all Lewissean gneiss with fine lines of quartz.

Callanish I is superb for its four stone alignments that originate and develop from the center stone circle. The longest one is the north-northeast avenue, 83m long, formed by two parallel stone rows with a total of sixteen standing stones on each side. A single row of four stones runs due west for 9m. The third row of five stones runs east-northeast for 15.4m. Running south for a distance of 22m is another row of five stones.

As shown in diagram 6.114, drawn by Boyle T. Somerville in 1909, the center of the stone circle, point A, is formed by its thirteen standing stones (S1 to S13). The center is further framed by five more stones (S14 to S18). A satellite cairn was once constructed at the northeast edge of the circle with point B as the center. And all of these orthostats once served as the dry cells of the builders' energy mechanism. Point A forms sets of SAs with each pair of standing stones and the angle bisects at another stone. For example, standing stones S11 and S2 of the ring form an SA with point A and stone S13 becomes their angle bisector.

Each of the following pairs of standing stones forms an SA with point A in the middle:

S11 + S2 (S13)
S12 + S4 (S1 + S14)
S9 + S13 (S11)
S1 + S16 (S4)
S3 + S9 (S6)
S5 + S10 (S17)
S6 + S11 (S9)
S10 + S1 (S12)
S4 + S18 + S8 (point B)
S17 + S8 + S19 (point B)

Stone circle of Callanish I was a typical power generator of the builders. What makes Callanish I unique is its four stone rows extending from the circle, forming a Celtic cross. These stone rows were simply the extensions of the generator because all stones of these rows were carefully erected according to the SA as well. They all form various sets of SAs with their neighboring partner (diagram 6.115). These standing stones, once serving as dry cell batteries, helped to tap the Earth energy beneath.

Callanish II

Callanish II, locally known as Cnoc Ceann a'Gharraidh, lies a few hundred meters southeast of Callanish I. It is a stone circle with five upright slabs ranging in height from 2m to 3.3m. Two other stones are thought to have been buried (diagram 6.116). The stones are all Lewisean gneiss with the tallest triangular one to the northeast. They form an ellipse of 19m × 21.6m in diameter with the remains of a cairn situated next to the center. Coincidentally, three sets of SAs can be derived from this setting (diagram 6.117).

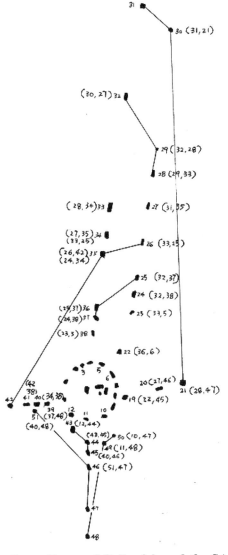

Stone Rows of Callanish and the SA
Diagram 6.115

Callanish II and the Conical Device
Diagram 6.116

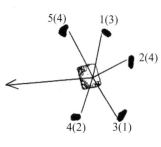

Callanish II
Diagram 6.117

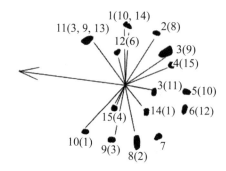

Callanish III
Diagram 6.118

Callanish III

The same pattern can be applied to Callanish III—Cnoc Fillibhir Bheag (diagram 6.118). According to experts, the stone circle was originally a setting of twelve upright and three lying slabs. It consists of two concentric ellipses, one of which measures 13m × 13.7m and is formed by ten stones with an eleventh outlier, while the other one is 10.5m × 6.5m in area. A cairn of 8.5m in diameter lies in the center of the concentric rings. The stones in the outer circle are 1m to 1.7m in height while those inside are taller, ranging from 1.4m to 2.1m in height (diagram 6.119). All the stones are carefully packed at their base with small boulders (in care of Historic Scotland). Several sets of SAs are derived from the stones of Callanish III. Besides, the stone circles of Callanish I, II, and III form an SA, with Callanish II in the middle (diagram 6.120).

Callanish III
Diagram 6.119

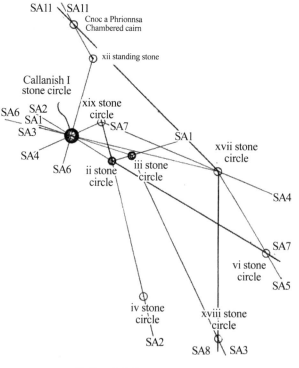

Callanish I and Surrounding Megalithic Monuments
Diagram 6.120

Recumbent Stone Circles of Northeast Scotland

These stone circles are characterized by selected slabs of specific color and texture, graded in height towards the southwest. ("The Stone Circles of Northeast Scotland in the Light of Excavation" by Richard Bradley, Chris Ball, Sharon Croft, and Tim Phillips, *Antiquity* 76 [2002]: 840–8). They were usually constructed on the ring-cairns encircled by a rubble wall of an earlier period. A single large stone, known as the recumbent stone, is deliberately set on its side. The stone is further flanked by two slightly taller upright ones which are just a little higher than the recumbent. Experts suggest that these 4,500-year-old RSCs show the prehistoric people's interest in the rising and setting of the moon in the southern sky.

Loanhead of Daviot of Scotland: Recumbent Stone Circle

There are around 100 Recumbent Stone Circles (RSCs) in Aberdeenshire and many of them were deliberately built on hillside terraces with a commanding view of its surroundings. Loanhead of Daviot is oriented towards the southwest. This well-preserved RSC lies near the summit of a hill with an excellent view of the north. A circle of eleven standing stones with a diameter of 20.5m dates back to 2500 B.C. The recumbent stone measures 1.75m high and 3m long, and its pair of tall flankers that stand south-southwest are set just inside the line of the circle (diagram 6.121). All the stones are graded, with the higher ones closest to the recumbent, probably an indication of the importance of the stone. A group of at least five cupmarks are carved at the inner face of a stone beside the eastern flanker. Inside the circle is an internal low ring cairn of small stones strewn around. A central hearth, about 4m across, is found in the middle of the site. A pair of outlying stones is strategically placed at the west and southeast of the circle. Most strikingly, the edge of the external platform of the circle contains some large blocks of quartz, whereas the huge recumbent stone also contains more quartz than the other parts of the circle (Bradley 2002). These crystallized slabs were carefully selected for their special properties for the builders' power station. A similar quartz setting was deposited on the ground of another RSC at Cothiemuir Wood.

The design of Loanhead is no different from the other hundreds of stone circles around the region when the SA is applied. In diagram 6.121, the two outliers of Loanhead function as two Station Stones (SS91 and SS94 of Stonehenge III) to determine the very center of the power station. Its angle-bisector rests right on the recumbent stone. When the device was introduced, rows of megalights would then be projected onto the surrounding standing stones for power (diagram 6.122).

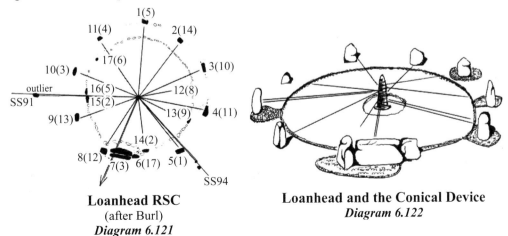

Loanhead RSC
(after Burl)
Diagram 6.121

Loanhead and the Conical Device
Diagram 6.122

NEOLITHIC BRITAIN

As shown in the following diagrams, other RSCs such as Tomnaverie, Castle Fraser, Tyrebagger (their recumbent stones lie in the southwest quadrant and are decorated with cupmarks and quartz pebbles: Burl 2000), and Tomnaverie (Phases I and II) were planned according to the principle of the SA (diagrams 6.123, 6.124 and 6.125).

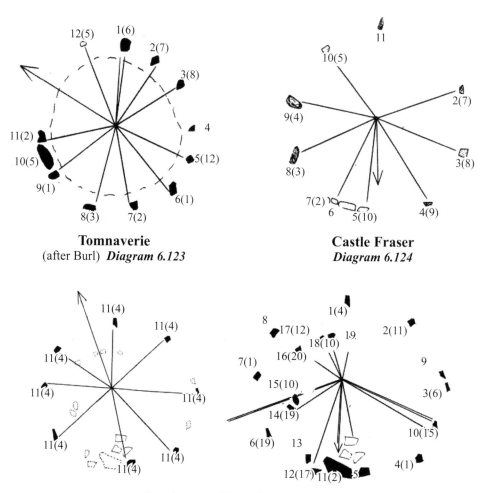

Tomnaverie
(after Burl) *Diagram 6.123*

Castle Fraser
Diagram 6.124

Tyrebagger, Phase I (*left*) and II
(info: RCAHMS) *Diagram 6.125*

RSC of Easter Aquhorthies, Berrybrae, Aikey Brae, and Old Keig

Another example of the RSC is Easter Aquhorthies 3000 B.C. (diagram 6.126). Experts suggest that the recumbent is deliberately framed for lunar observations, as it is found on the crest of hill with wide southerly views. Like Loanhead of Daviot, its eleven standing stones are graded by height with those closest to the recumbent being the tallest. These stones were erected according to the SA.

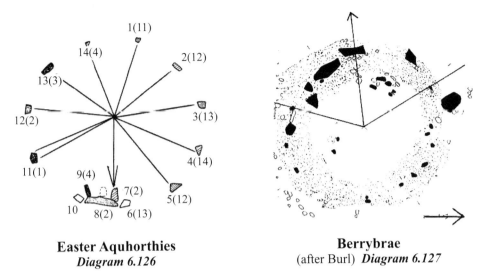

Easter Aquhorthies
Diagram 6.126

Berrybrae
(after Burl) *Diagram 6.127*

Another RSC is the Berrybrae in Aberdeenshire (diagram 6.127). Various sets of SAs are formed by its stones. They all bisect at another slab.

Another group of RSCs is found at the northern limit of northeast Scotland, where Aikey Brae contains a large amount of quartz. The diagram below suggests the RSC of Aikey Brae and Old Keig are aligned to the SA (diagram 6.128).

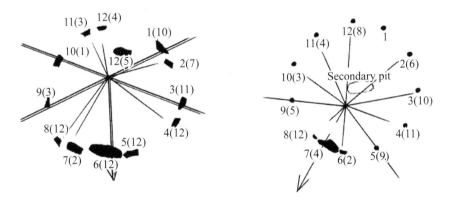

Aikey Brae (*left*) and Old Keig
(after Burl) *Diagram 6.128*

Structurally similar to the RSCs are those found in the southwest of Ireland. Instead of a huge recumbent stone and its two flankers, a large rectangular stone is placed at the southwest frame of the circle. The stone circles of Carrigagulla and Currebeha, County Cork, in southern Ireland are 8m in diameter, formed by sixteen small stones with a quartz boulder in the center. The builders used a pair of tall portal stones to indicate the bisector (diagram 6.129).

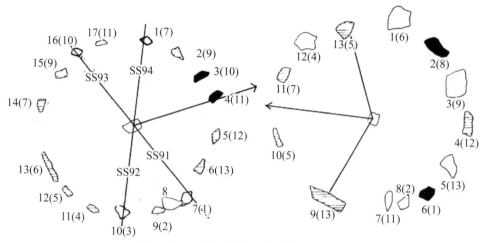

Carrigagulla (*left*) and Currebeha
Diagram 6.129

Cullerlie Stone Circle

Another famous stone circle around the region is Cullerlie of Leucher Moss. The well-preserved stone circle consists of eight red granites that form a circle of 10.1m across (Burl 2000). The stones are graded in height to the north-northwest. Within the circle, there lies a small cairn with eleven kerbstones. Between this central cairn and the ring are seven smaller kerbed cairns. Diagram 6.130a shows the general plan of Cullerlie, in which its internal cairns are arranged according to the SA. In theory, each of the cairns also forms various sets of SAs with the surrounding standing stones (diagram 6.130b).

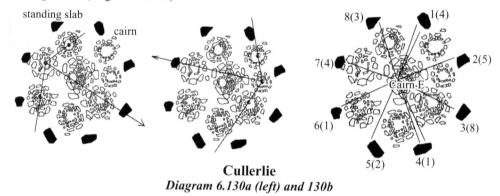

Cullerlie
Diagram 6.130a (left) and 130b

Long Cairn of Slewcairn

The long and trapezoidal cairn of Slewcairn is one of the mortuary enclosures in southwest Scotland. The site is oriented to the north with a forecourt where the walls of its two horns are aligned to the SA (diagram 6.131a). An 8m-long compartment situated south of the two portal stones of its main entrance connects the interior compartments. Further inside is a sub-passage running from the west of the cairn to a setting of four standing stones at the southernmost end. The three ends of the passage—i.e., the paved portal entrance, the southernmost of the southern passage, and the westernmost of the western sub-passage—acting as dry cell dolmens, form a perfect SA (diagram 6.131b).

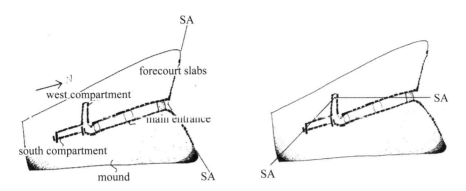

Plan of Slewcairn
Diagram 6.131a (left) and b

Rollright Stones Power Station

The Rollright Stone Circle has stood on a high ridge between Oxfordshire and Warwickshire for thousands of years. It consists of about a hundred standing stones, each weighing less than six tons. They are crudely graded in height and weight. The stone circle has a portal entrance, 5m wide, which opens at the southeast. The Rollright Stones comprise three elements: the monolith known as King's Stone, another group of standing stones called King's Men and the Whispering Knights, and the stone circle itself. According to legends, the King's Stone was a king turned into stone by a witch when he and his soldiers marched over the witch's land. His soldiers became the Circle and some

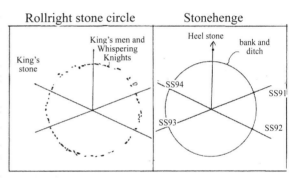

Station Stones of Rollright Stone Circle
Diagram 6.132

distance away, the Whispering Knights were muttering. Others say it is impossible to count the Stones. The man will never live who shall count the stones three times and find the number the same each time, whereas, it is also said that anyone who thrice counts the same number will have their heart's desire fulfilled (Rollright Trust). It has been a traditional meeting place of witches since the Tudor times. The circle has been seen as some kind of prehistoric astronomical observatory. However, experts generally agree that there are very few meaningful alignments represented, with a view of the midsummer sunset being the only one that stands out as potentially significant.

Its famous outlying stones, the King's Stone and the Whispering Knights, function as the Heel Stone and Station Stone 94 of Stonehenge (diagram 6.132) to determine the center of the circle. The standing stones form several sets of SAs with the center of Rollright in the middle (diagram 6.133). In theory, conical device no. 1 was put at its center for power while device no. 2 was placed between the circle and the King Stone at its northeast, precisely where the Heel Stone of Stonehenge lies. Even today, many dowsers have recorded powerful reactions, probably in terms of concentric rings of energy, at Rollright Stones (Rollright Stones website).

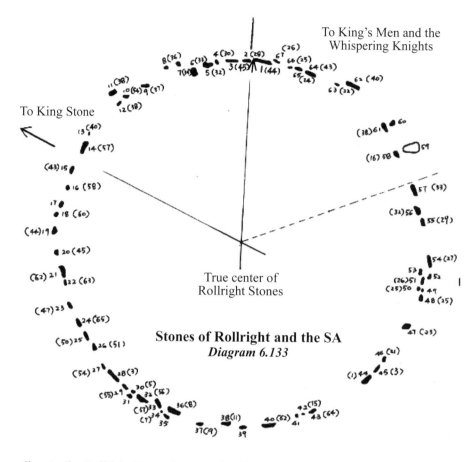

To King's Men and the Whispering Knights

To King Stone

True center of
Rollright Stones

Stones of Rollright and the SA
Diagram 6.133

According to the Rollright Trust, there are ley lines associated with the Rollright Stones that across churches, long barrows, standing stones, and round barrows.

Cornwall and Merry Maidens

The county of Cornwall is a triangular block of land which lies at the southwest tip of England. Experts believe this extreme peninsula had contact with northern France and Spain in the Neolithic. Stone tools, dating back to 4500 B.C., were used by the people in the sparsely populated Cornwall. The county is also rich with unusual and well-preserved ancient sites. Actually, the name "Cornwall" comes from *Cornoviii,* meaning "hill dwellers," and it is the place where famous Neolithic settlements such as Chysauster and Carn Brea are found.

The stone circle of Merry Maidens, also known as the Stone Dance, is probably the most famous monument around Cornwall. It was restored between 1862 and 1869. Standing in a coastal area, 1m from the sea, the nineteen stones form a true circle of 24m in diameter with an eastern entrance. Two standing stones, probably as outliers, lying north of the circle are called the Pipers. Another to the west is known as the Fiddler. Legend has it that nineteen maidens and their musicians were turned into stone there for dancing on a Sunday. It is also believed that the number of stones at Merry Maidens can be counted by a woman but not by a man.

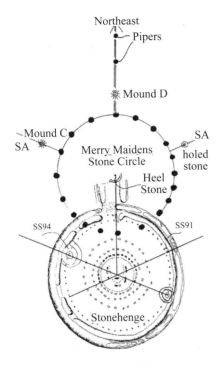

As shown in diagram 6.134, the two outliers Mould C and Holed Stone, standing at the north and east outside the stone circle, serve as the Station Stones to determine the center of the site. They form an SA, probably to show the range of energy transmission. Like Stonehenge, Mound D and the pair of piper stones, which lies northeast of the powerhouse, act similarly to the Heel Stone of Stonehenge and show the point of recharging.

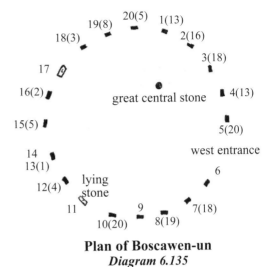

Merry Maidens and Stonehenge
Diagram 6.134

Plan of Boscawen-un
Diagram 6.135

Boscawen-un Stone Circle

This Bronze Age stone circle lies close to Merry Maidens. Like Merry Maidens, Tregeseal East stone circle, and the bluestone horseshoe of Stonehenge III, Boscawen-un is formed by nineteen stones, seventeen of which are still standing and the remaining two lying flat, with a diameter of 25m. The wide gap at the west suggests an entrance or astronomical alignment. The local granite standing stones are evenly spaced, vary from 0.9m to 1.5m in height, with the smooth sides facing the interior of the ring. Only the one in the west-southwest is made of quartz. The stones increase in height towards the western arc. There is a great central menhir of 1.3m standing or leaning near its center, probably pointing towards the midsummer sunrise in the northeast (diagram 6.135). Burl believes it was a way marker. Experts speculate that the circle might once have been used as an observatory or a place of council and gathering. Various sets of SAs are derived from the site.

Other Stone Circles in Cornwall

In *Illustrations of Stone Circles, Cromlehs and Others Remains of the Aboriginal Britons in the West of Cornwall,* several little-known stone circles around the region are introduced by Dr. Borlase. One is known as Dance Maine, which is found in a field at the parish of Burian. It consists of nineteen stones, with sixteen standing, two lying, and one missing, standing at equal distance (Borlase p. 33). Like other circles, most of the standing slabs of Dance Maine are aligned to the SA (diagram 6.136).

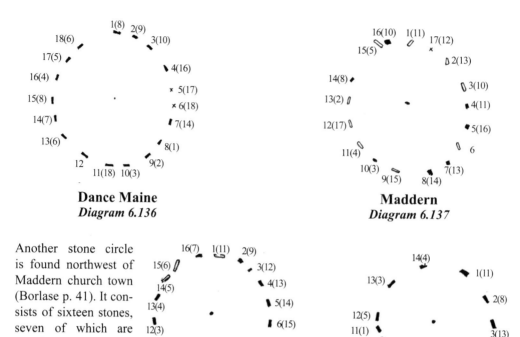

Dance Maine
Diagram 6.136

Maddern
Diagram 6.137

Another stone circle is found northwest of Maddern church town (Borlase p. 41). It consists of sixteen stones, seven of which are standing and nine lying, with a diameter of 21m. Some of the stones are much taller than the others (diagram 6.137).

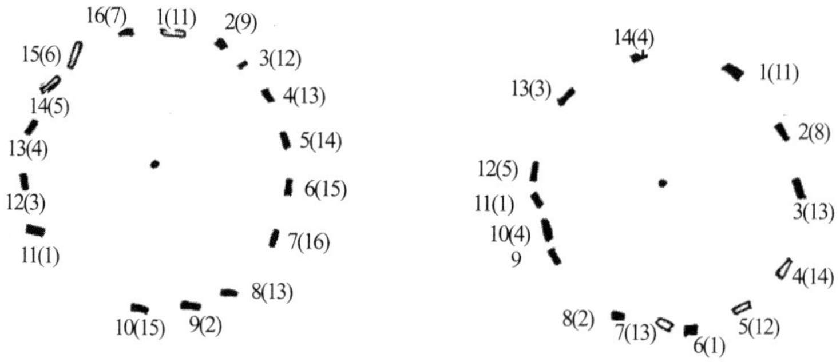

East (*left*) and West Stone Circles of St. Just
Diagram 6.138

Two other stone circles, one with twelve standing stones and the other with ten, are found between two ridges of a hill in the parish of St. Just (Borlase pp. 42–44). Their standing stones also form various SAs with the center of the circle (diagrams 6.138).

Chysauster, Cornwall

Chysauster is the best-preserved house settlement at the westernmost point of England. It is an Iron Age courtyard village, inhabited from around 100 B.C. to A.D. 300, with a group of eight stone huts in pairs and a ninth one within a stone's throw away from the group in the south (diagram 6.139) (James Dyer and Allen Lane, *The Penguin Guide to Prehistoric England and Wales*). According to the experts, the village was probably built by members of the Dumnonii tribe of Cornish Britons. The eight huts, which are oriented on an east-west axis, are adjoined by low stonewalls and have largely similar layouts: about 30m in diameter and oval in shape. Its general design echoes the Neolithic village of Skara Brae, Orkney. Each house of Chysauster has an entrance passage leading into a stone-paved central courtyard surrounded by rooms in different shapes, an open hearth, and a back door. Many houses at the site are built in pairs with circular living rooms and smaller store rooms built into the walls. Stone basins and flat stones with hallow are commonly found in the center of the main rooms. Experts believe the inhabitants of Chysauster survived by farming and livestock raising.

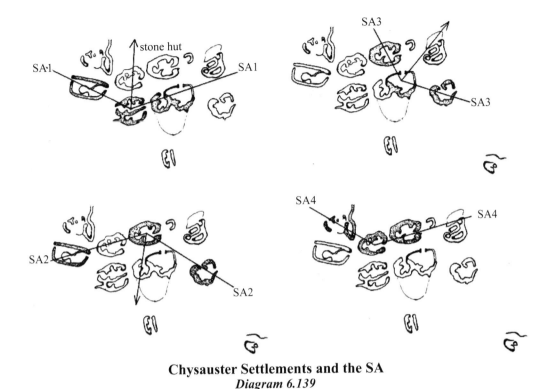

Chysauster Settlements and the SA
Diagram 6.139

The megalithic huts of Chysauster are aligned to the SA. Its circular rooms, open hearths, flat slabs, and round stone basins were once used for placing the builders' conical devices, and megalights were projected onto the surrounding orthostats of the walls for power.

The diagram at left shows another prehistoric earth enclosure in Cornwall, where a cluster of round houses is strategically constructed according to the SA (diagram 6.140).

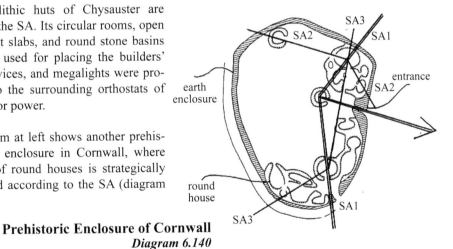

Prehistoric Enclosure of Cornwall
Diagram 6.140

Bosphrennis Bee-hive Hut, Cornwall

The prehistoric village of Bosphrennis lies at the Zennor Down next to Chysauster. The site includes the ruin of a stone circle and several barrows (West Penwith Resource). The most important monument is the Bosphrennis bee-hive hut. The hut consists of two chambers, one circular and the other rectangular (diagram 6.141) (Rev. B. L. Barnwell in the *Archaeologia Cambrensis*, 1862).

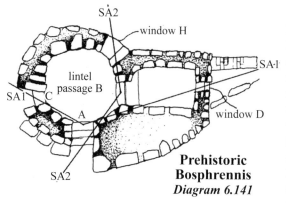

SA2
window H
lintel
passage B
SA1
C
A
SA1
window D
SA2

**Prehistoric
Bosphrennis**
Diagram 6.141

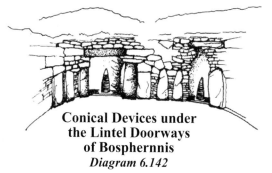

**Conical Devices under
the Lintel Doorways
of Bosphernnis**
Diagram 6.142

Passage A leads to the main entrance, a lintel doorway composed of three slabs of granite, of a circular chamber. There is another smaller lintel doorway C opening to the north-northwest. A hole or window H is found on the eastern wall of the chamber. Another lintel doorway B connects the circular chamber and the rectangular one to its south. A lintel doorway D, opposite to doorway B, is open to the southern wall of the rectangular chamber with a platform E constructed outside.

According to Penwith, the circular chamber is skillfully fit with large granite slabs to form a perfect dome more than 2m in height. Judging from these familiar lintel doorways, structurally equivalent to the dolmens or trilithons, I would say that they once acted as the builders' dry cells with conical devices installed. Two sets of SAs are derived from these lintel doorways, as shown in diagram 6.141.

Row Stones of Dartmoor

Dartmoor of southwest England is characterized by its moorland landscape—a layer of waste fields resulted from the removal of a thin upland soil. There are Bronze Age settlements with hamlets and villages. But it is famous for its seventy stone rows. These rows are single, double, or even triple stone alignments, probably a simplified version of those of Carnac. They are regarded as procession ways in the Bronze Age. The shortest stone row is 32m in length, and others like Stall Moor and Green Hill are over 2km in length. Usually, small stone circles with diameters from 19 to 35m or single large standing stones are found at the end of these stone rows. Many of the stones of these rows are very small, some less than 30cm high. Experts suggest that they might have been used for astronomical purposes as well.

There are lots of stone rows and circles located at the north of the moor. Four sets of SAs are produced by six stone circles around the region (diagram 6.143).

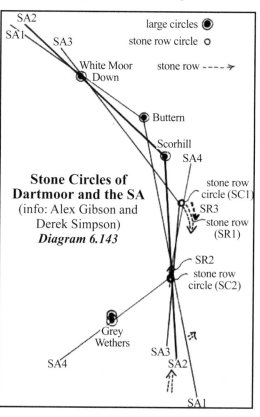

**Stone Circles of
Dartmoor and the SA**
(info: Alex Gibson and
Derek Simpson)
Diagram 6.143

SA2
SA1
SA3
large circles ◉
stone row circle ○
White Moor
Down
stone row ----➤
Buttern
Scorhill
SA4
stone row
circle (SC1)
SR3
stone row
(SR1)
SR2
stone row
circle (SC2)
Grey
Wethers
SA3
SA2
SA4
SA1

The British Isles are rich in various types of Neolithic monuments, such as Cursus, timber circles, earthen enclosures, and cairns. Archaeologists speculate that these Neolithic complexes might have served as ritual and ceremonial centers of the prehistoric people. Those gigantic parallel earthen Cursus are regarded as some kind of processional way, and the circular enclosures might have been sacred precincts for handling dead bodies. However, these mysterious complexes can be "explained" by the application of the SA.

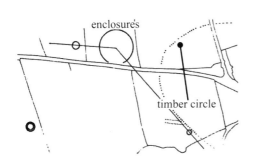

1. Walton
(from *Prehistoric Ritual and Religion*)
Diagram 6.144a

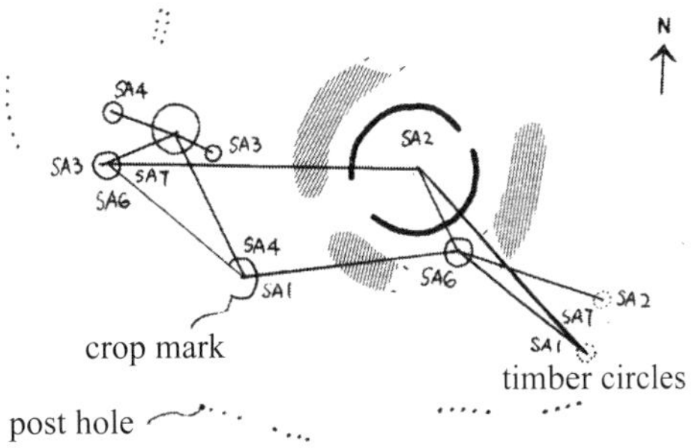

2. Ferrybridge
(from *Stonehenge and Timber Circles*)
Diagram 6.144b

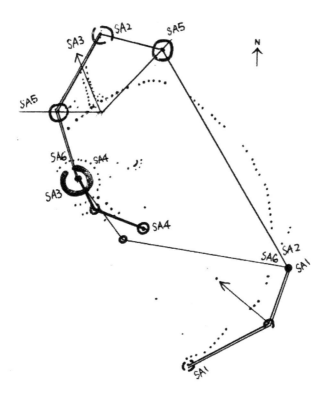

3. Forteviot
(from *Stonehenge and Timber Circles*)
Diagram 6.144c

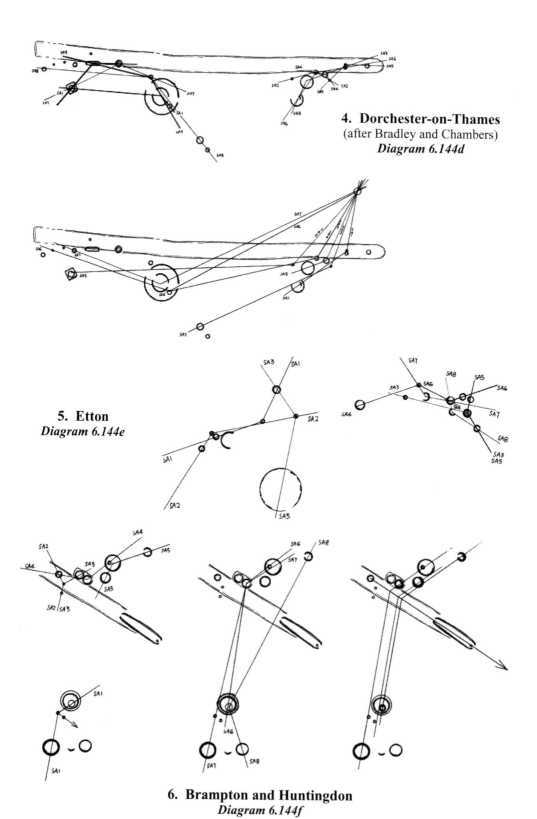

4. Dorchester-on-Thames
(after Bradley and Chambers)
Diagram 6.144d

5. Etton
Diagram 6.144e

6. Brampton and Huntingdon
Diagram 6.144f

Birkrigg Stone Circle of Cumbria

Birkrigg Stone Circle, also known as the Druid's Temple, is located at the base of Appleby Hill of Brikrigg Common. The 3,500-year-old circle is made up of a double ring of stones varied in height and with a paved floor. Its inner ring is 8.4m in diameter and consists of ten limestones whereas the incomplete outer circle measures about 26.5m in diameter with fifteen stones (diagram 6.145a). The whole site is then covered with cobbles.

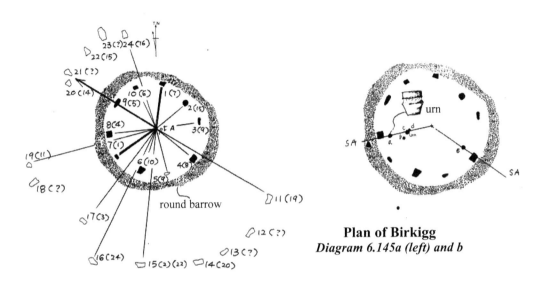

Plan of Birkigg
Diagram 6.145a (left) and b

Point A forms the center of the circle and several sets of SA are derived with the stones in the inner and the outer rings. Interestingly, some of the stones inside the inner ring stand right at the angle-bisector. An SA is formed by two standing stones of the inner ring with another (bracketed) in the middle:

SA1 1–7 (9)
SA2 3–9 (1)
SA3 4–8 (6)
SA4 5–9 (7)
SA5 6–10 (8)

According to Aubrey Burl, there are five Neolithic urns excavated inside the inner circle and it seems that they were carefully placed according to the SA (diagram 6.145b).

Nine Ladies Stone Circle, Derbyshire: No Sex Involved

Nine Ladies, a typical Derbyshire stone circle, consists of nine small standing millstones, mostly shorter than 1m in height lying to form a circle of 9.1m × 7.9m. The circle is further encircled by a small circular bank. Two conspicuously taller portal stones, 1.2m and 2.1m tall respectively, might have been the main entrance to the site. An outlier, the King Stone stands on its own 40m to the west-southwest of the circle (diagram 6.146a). The bank and cairn have disappeared.

According to local folklores, the circle was formed by people being turned into stone for dancing on the Sabbath. The King Stone was said to have been their fiddler. Burl suggests that the stones of Nine Ladies, of different sizes, ranging from 0.9m to 3.4m in height and in pillar and broad shape, are rich in sexual symbolism. But the formation of this circle can be explained by the SA. A pair of opposite SAs, formed by four "Station Stones"—stones 4, 5, 8, and 9—bisect at the two entrances of the enclosure. The southwest bisector even points to the King Stone!

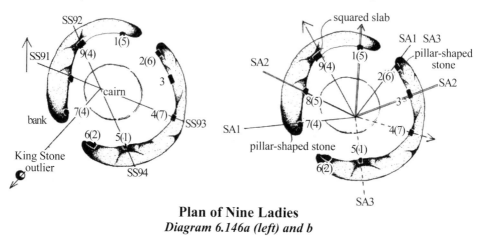

Plan of Nine Ladies
Diagram 6.146a (left) and b

Besides, selection and placements of the pillar-shaped stones and the broad, square slabs of Nine Ladies can be defined by the SA as well. The builders' formula was: a pair of pillar-shaped standing stones was erected according to the SA and their angle bisected at a square slab (diagram 6.146b).

Castleruddery Stone Circle

Another stone circle with a similar design is Castleruddery. The circle was once known as the Druidical Circle and is about 100m in diameter, and consists of forty small granite stones with two selected large white quartz portal stones at the entrance. The stone ring is then encircled by a ditch enclosure and an earthen bank around four feet high (megalithicireland.com) (diagram 6.147). Cup marks are found on one of the stones. But some stones were heavily weathered. Four relatively large standing stones, like the Station Stones of Stonehenge, determine the location of the conical device (point A). Its angle-bisector passes through the two quartz stones framing the entrance of the circle.

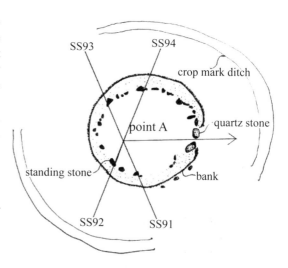

Plan of Castleruddery
Diagram 6.147

Castlerigg Stone Circle of Cumbria

Castlerigg, one of the earliest and finest stone circles in Britain, is located near Keswick on a low hill surrounded by high mountains. Forty-two monoliths form the main ring, measuring 32m × 29m, with a flattened arc. The two largest ones in the north define the originally 4m-wide entrance and are aligned to the cardinal north. There are remains of a small cairn in Castlerigg. A large spiral 48cm in diameter is decorated on one of the stones and it may uncover the true identity of the monument.

Diagram 6.148 below shows the general layout of Castlerigg circle with its center at point A. A conical device was once placed at point A and projected megalights onto its surrounding standing stone for power. According to excavation reports, a pit lying on the northeast axis inside the stone circle might probably hold another conical device for discharging. The same mechanism is also found in the powerhouse of Newgrange.

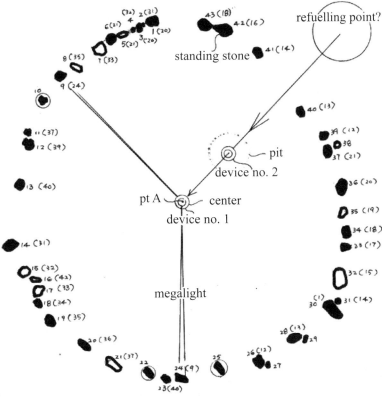

Castlerigg and the SA
Diagram 6.148

Stone Circles on Burn Moor

A stone circle that stands to the west just below Brats Hill knoll measures 32m × 25.9m with forty-two stones. Within the circle are five small cairns, measuring 6.4m to 7.6m in diameter (Burl 2000), and surrounded by stones no more than 0.31m in height. The cairns are now in a ruined state. As shown in the diagram below, the distribution of these cairns is aligned to the SA (diagram 6.149).

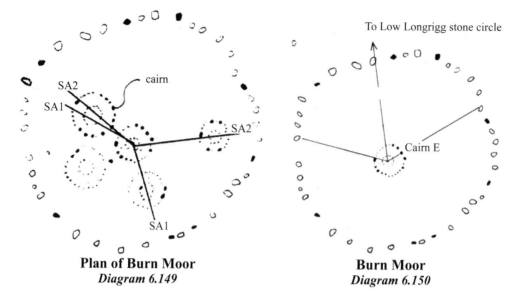

Plan of Burn Moor
Diagram 6.149

Burn Moor
Diagram 6.150

Furthermore, the central Cairn E forms several sets of SAs with the stones of the Great Circle (diagram 6.150). The standing stones of the two sister circles of Burn Moor nearby also constitute various SAs with their central cairn (diagram 6.151).

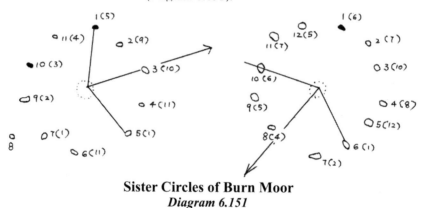

Sister Circles of Burn Moor
Diagram 6.151

Stone Circles with a Central Slab: Hoarstones of Wales

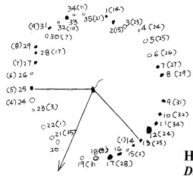

According to Burl (2000), the site has a perimeter of 23m × 19.8m with thirty-eight to forty local dolerite boulders irregularly graded towards the southeast. A tall pillar, 1.1m in height, lies in the center and it forms sets of SAs with its surrounding stones.

Hoarstones of Wales
Diagram 6.152

Rock Art of Long Meg: Regional Map of Neolithic Stations

Long Meg and Her Daughter Standing Stone Circle, Langwathby, Cumbria, is located on a ridge above the east bank of River Eden. The stone circle is the third largest in the British Isles, the sixth largest in the world. It is elliptical in form, measuring 109m × 93m and is edged by about seventy massive igneous boulders (diagram 6.152). The east-west axis entrance aligns to the midwinter sunset. It is believed that there were once two great mounds of later period inside Long Meg and Her Daughters (J. Aubrey 1725).

Long Meg, the most famous stone in the circle, is a 3.7m-high red sandstone pillar, standing outside the stone circle on the highest point of the ridge. The monolith was brought from the bank of the River Eden nearly two miles away. It is a mediaeval term meaning a "long and slender" object. A story suggests the stone was named from a local witch, Meg of Meldon, of the early seventeenth century. The Stone also marks the burial place of monks who died during the Black Death. A legend says that Michael Scott, a wondrous wizard, turned Meg, a local witch, and her coven into stones for their black arts. The stones of the circle are said to be uncountable, and that should one ever reach the same total twice, that the spell would be broken (bbc.co.uk). Another legend claims that the stones of the circle were Meg's daughters or even her lovers. It is believed that Meg would "bleed" if pieces were broken off her body (the monolith of Long Meg). The wondrous wizard also cast a spell on the stones so that no one could count them accurately. One story says a local squire was planning to blow the stone, but before his men could light the powder, a fearful storm suddenly started to rage and the attempt was abandoned (mysteriousbritain.co.uk).

On the northwest face of Long Meg is a series of complex rock art forms: cup and ring marks, spirals, and concentric rings (diagram 6.154). The monolith of Long Meg and another standing stone which lies east of the stone circle of Her Daughters act as a pair of "Station Stones" of the stone circle (diagram 6.153).

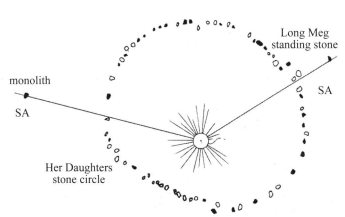

Stone Circle of Long Meg and Her Daughters, and Its Two Station Stones
Diagram 6.153

Furthermore, the cup and ring carvings on Long Meg (after P. Frodsham) match the SA formula. Most strangely, the artist who carved and erected the monolith had deliberately placed it upside down (diagram 6.154). If we compare the carving with a map of the major ancient monuments of the Cumbria County (Damien Noonan, *Castles and Ancient Monuments of England*), one can easily find that the patterns of the two maps are more or less identical. In Cumbria, the stone circle of Long Meg and Her Daughters and the Ambleside fort form an SA with the ruin of Shap Abbey in the middle (diagram 6.155). The alignment of this angle is identical to the Long Meg carving, that is, an SA is formed by two concentric circles: C1 and C2, with C3, a blurred one with double circle, in the middle. The three concentric circles C1, C2, and C4, form a straight line, whereas the stone circle of Long Meg, Ambleside Roman fort, and the Dalton Castle also form a straight line in the map of Cumbria. A triangle is formed by connecting Long Meg, Shap Abbey, and Ambleside.

Another SA is formed by Long Meg and Dalton Castle, with Castlerigg stone circle in the middle (as shown in the Cumbria map). A similar SA is found on the Long Meg carving with an angle formed by C1, C6, and C4. As shown in the Cumbria map, the third SA is formed by Long Meg and Dalton Castle, with Hardknott Fort in the middle.

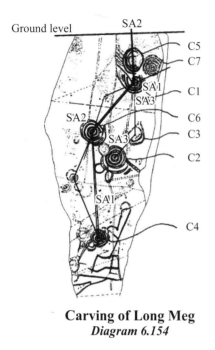

Carving of Long Meg
Diagram 6.154

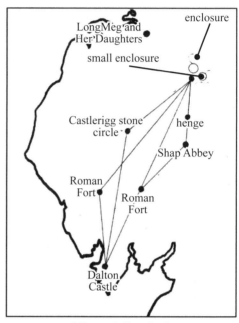

Map of Cumbria
Diagram 6.155

As "told" by the carving, the stone circle of Long Meg and Her Daughters might have been an important regional center as three sets of SAs are derived. The two concentric circles C5 and C7 lie near concentric circle C1, which actually stand for the two enclosures next to Long Meg and Her Daughters in Cumbria. Interestingly, the artist even drew the monolith of Long Meg with an angle of 135 degrees. It also parallels the actual coastal line of the Cumbria County. To the Neolithic builders, the monolith certainly served as a signpost to tell the actual location of their powerhouses.

Another small stone circle, known as the Little Meg, lies less than a kilometer from the Long Meg and Her Daughters. The circle is formed by eleven stones in an irregular ring of diameter 5.9m to 4.8m with a low barrow and central cist in the middle. Its tallest stone is 1.2m high and stands at the north-north-west. Like Long Meg, two stones of Little Meg are decorated with spirals and concentric markings, the message from its Neolithic us-ers (diagram 6.156).

The Powerhouse of Little Meg
Diagram 6.156

SAs in the Neolithic Complex of the Eden Valley

With the RAF air photographs taken in the region in the 1970s, other Neolithic monuments such as ditched enclosures and crop marks are discovered on the flat terrace of the east bank of River Eden in the Hunsonby parish, Cumbria. A remarkable pear-shaped two-entranced ditched Enclosure A is attached to the northern periphery of the Long Meg (source: "New Evidence of Ritual Monuments at Long Meg and Her Daughters, Cumbria" by Grahame Soffe and Tom Clare, *Antiquity* 62, 1988). According to Soffe and Clare, the south entrance of Enclosure A is connected with the north 'exit' of Long Meg and Her Daughters (diagram 6.157) where its southern ditches, flattens the northern periphery of the Long Meg. It indicates a close functional relationship between the stone circle and the enclosure.

Another smaller egg-shaped Enclosure B with a thin ditch lies east of the stone circle. It has two entrances, one opens to the east and the other to the west. The third one, Enclosure C, lying west of Long Meg with a half ditch in a small sub-rectangular shape, is revealed as a crop mark. A single stone is found inside the ditch. The final one, Enclosure D, lies northwest of Long Meg, which is pear in shape with a wide ditch and an east entrance.

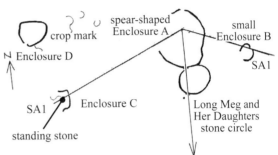

**Long Meg and Her Daughters:
The Recharging Platform of the Builders**
Diagram 6.157

The two small Enclosures B and C, which served as the two Station Stones, form SA1 with the larger Enclosure A in the middle. It bisects right at the south entrance of Enclosure A and the north exit of the Long Meg. In other words, the Long Meg stone circle might have served as a recharging platform in 3000 B.C.

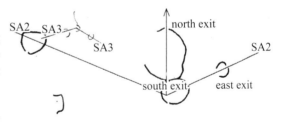

**Enclosure A as the Angle Bisector
of the Builders' Power Station**
Diagram 6.158

In addition, SA2 is derived in the same region when Enclosures B and D form SA2 with the stone circle of Long Meg and Her Daughters in the middle. This time, Enclosure A serves as the angle bisector of the builders' power station (diagram 6.158). As shown in the same diagram, SA3 is formed by three incomplete crop marks which lie between Enclosures A and D.

Soffe and Clare (1988) have also provided a diagram (figure 4) to show the distribution of the decorated stones in relation to Neolithic complexes in Cumbria, and coincidentally, they are aligned to the SA as well (diagram 6.159). Two decorated stones form SA3 with the stone circle of Long Meg while another pair of carved stones forms SA4 with the Mayburgh Enclosure at the south. Did these decorated stones once serve as the builders' dry cell batteries for tapping energy underneath?

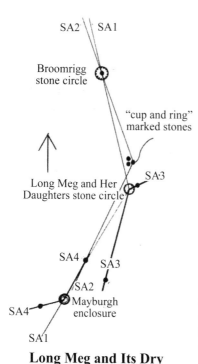

SA2 \ SA1

Broomrigg
stone circle

"cup and ring"
marked stones

Long Meg and Her
Daughters stone circle

SA3

SA4
SA3
SA2
Mayburgh
enclosure
SA4

SA1

**Long Meg and Its Dry
Cell Batteries**
Diagram 6.159

Arbor Low: Stonehenge of the Peak District

Arbor Low is the finest and one of the most interesting stone circles in Derbyshire, north of England. Like Stonehenge, a circle of stones was once erected just inside the enclosure. The site is situated on a high point, 375m above sea level with a stunning view. Its henge, which was built between around 3000 and 2500 B.C., consists of a 2m-high circular bank and a ditch 76m in diameter. It encloses a flat plateau. Inside the circle is a recumbent stone circle of forty-six large and thirteen smaller white weathered limestone blocks, all lying flat now. In the center of the circle is a group of four stones and they may be the remains of a Cove, probably a miniature version of the gigantic trilithon horseshoe of Stonehenge. There are two entrances, one opening to the northwest and the other to the southeast and they were once part of a ceremonial approach and departure of the ritual monument. Besides, Arbor Low is surrounded by a cluster of Late Bronze Age barrows constructed around 1,000 years after the henge was completed. One of the most famous and the largest monuments is known as Gib Hill, lying south of the henge.

Inspired by Stonehenge II, which was contemporary to Arbor Low, I reckon that when two conical devices were placed inside the Bluestonehenge and projected megalights onto the bluestones as well as the neighboring round barrows for power, the round barrows surrounding Arbor Low might have served the same function as well. Conical device no. 1 was placed inside the central Cove for tapping energy from the surrounding stones whereas conical device no. 2 was put at the entrance of the henge and activated the barrows nearby for discharging (diagram 6.160).

barrow

entrance

lying stone

bank

Arbor Low
Diagram 6.160

Key Boulders of the Crick Bell Barrow

The Welsh bell-barrow is situated in the county of Gwent, Southern Britain, 80km northwest of Stonehenge. The site was excavated by Dr. Hubert N. Savory in 1940. According to his report, a circular mound of 31.7m in diameter was built on a stone ring 28m in diameter. The ring is comprised of key boulders of conglomerate sandstone with an average height of 0.7m. These boulders are interspersed with a wall of small stones held together by clayey earth (diagram 6.161) (info: "Astronomical Alignments at the Crick Barrow in Gwent, South Wales" by Martin J. Powell, *Archaeoastronomy* 26 [1995]). The mound is further surrounded by a V-shaped ditch about 3m wide and 1.5m deep. There are two cremations of primary and secondary burials in pits found near its center.

Two key boulders of the ring are heavily carved with numerous circular depressions or cupmarks which have been "proved" to be astronomically aligned. However, these cupmarks are just iconic signature of the Neolithic builders. Take the largest key boulder at the southeast quadrant of the ring as an example. It measures 1.7m long and 0.6m wide with twenty-three cupmarks on its outer face. Interestingly it forms SA1 with another key boulder at the north with the central pit of the primary burial in the middle. The other heavily cupmarked boulder in the northeast forms SA2 with a boulder at the west. Most of the key boulders of the stone ring are aligned to the SA, as shown in diagram 6.161.

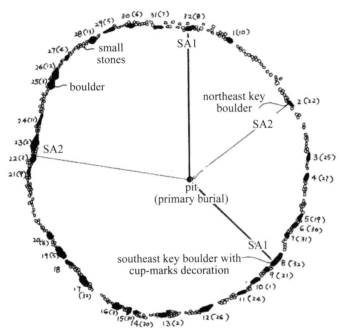

Brick Bell Barrow and Its Cupmarked Boulder
(after M. Powell) *Diagram 6.161*

Crop-mark Enclosures and the SA

Crop-marks are patterns that appear in growing crops as a result of differential growth and ripening patterns. Many of the marks are caused by traces of archaeological features below the plough soil. They are usually only clearly visible from the air. With the plough soil lying over infill ditches or pits, these features will hold additional moisture. A crop will grow more slowly and taller in ditches and pits and it tends to ripen later. This results in different patterns being produced in crops, reflecting the underlying remains (Scottisharchaeology.org.uk). Some crops such as wheat and oats are particular sensitive to soil water content and show marks clearly. Besides, some areas such as northeast Britain are under permanent pasture or lie on clay soils, so crop-marks show up less well than in other parts of the country (pastperfect.info).

Prehistoric crop-mark enclosures can be regarded as henge, or hengiform monuments (i.e., with a bank and a ditch). When air photography is introduced to the prehistoric sites, archaeologists discover their existence and their shape, usually circular or sub-circular. The crop mark enclosures, together with the surrounding group of densely packed ring-ditch cemeteries, form a prehistoric monumental complex.

The following crop-mark complex (diagram 6.162) lies at the fertile bend of River Stour of Essex in southeast England. Dr. Strachan, in his article "Crop-mark Landscape in Three Dimensions," suggests that the site includes a long mortuary enclosure and several ring-ditches, including two dual concentric monuments. These ring-ditches with the surrounding cemeteries probably served ritual purposes. The diagram shows these circular cupmarks form several sets of SAs. The crop-mark lying at the right bottom corner must have been very important, as many SAs are aligned and connected to it.

Crop-marks of Llandegai, Gwynedd

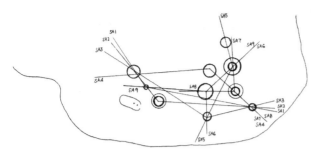

Crop-marks of Essex
(after D. Strachan 1996–7) *Diagram 6.162*

The prehistoric burial and ritual complex at Llandegai is one of the important sites of Wales. The diagram below is from an air photo taken in 1959 by Cambridge University. It shows two large circular henge monuments dating back to 3000 B.C. with a parallel ditch (Cursus) to the right. Several small circular crop-marks are found scattered between the two large henges (Crown Copyright RCAHMW). All megalithic structures of Llandegai are aligned to the SA (diagram 6.163).

The Neolithic complex of Llandegai lies at the very center of the British Isles and Ireland and, as shown in the diagram below, it is connected to the other megalithic complexes by the wonderful SA (diagram 6.164).

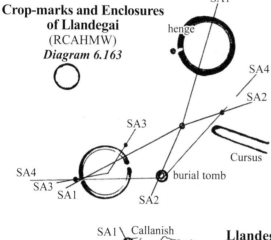

**Crop-marks and Enclosures
of Llandegai**
(RCAHMW)
Diagram 6.163

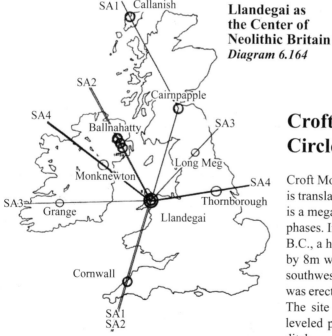

**Llandegai as
the Center of
Neolithic Britain**
Diagram 6.164

Croft Moraig Stone Circle of Scotland

Croft Moraig of Perthshire, Scotland, is translated as the "Field of Mary." It is a megalithic complex built in three phases. In the first phase around 3000 B.C., a horseshoe arrangement of 7m by 8m with an opening to the south-southwest and fourteen wooden posts was erected with a hearth at its center. The site was built on an artificially leveled plateau and surrounded by a ditch.

The second phase includes a similar horse-shaped setting, 6m × 7.5m in diameter, of eight standing stones of graded height, between 0.8m and 1.7m. One of the northeast stones is decorated with cupmarks. A bank encloses the stone setting. To the south-southwest of the bank lies a 2m long stone with twenty-three cupmarks on it.

In the final phase, a 12m-diameter circle of twelve big schist stones, all about 1.7m high, is erected around the horseshoe. Two outlying boulders that lie 5.5m outside the circle mark an entrance of 2.5m apart to the east-southeast. Each pair of the standing stones in the complex forms a set of SA with the central hearth (diagram 6.165).

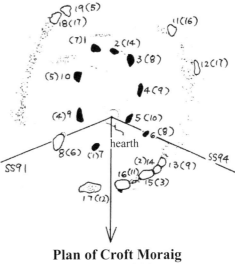

Plan of Croft Moraig
Diagram 6.165

Burial Cairns of Balbirnie, Scotland

The Neolithic site of Balbirnie was built in three phases in around 3000 B.C. The first one includes the erection of ten stones and a small and low rectangular stone enclosure at the center. Several sets of SAs are derived from the surrounding slabs, with the rectangular hearth in the middle. Another stone lies at the angle bisector (diagram 6.166a).

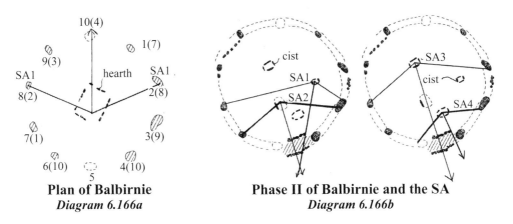

Plan of Balbirnie
Diagram 6.166a

Phase II of Balbirnie and the SA
Diagram 6.166b

Cairnpapple Hill: A 5,000-Year-Old Power Station

The Late Neolithic and Bronze Age sanctuary and burial site on Cairnpapple Hill is situated on top of a 310m-high basalt hill west of Edinburgh, Scotland. It is regarded as one of the most important prehistoric sites in mainland Scotland because different Neolithic monuments such as entranced henges with banks and ditches, stone rings, coves, and burial cairns are found in the same site (diagram 6.167). With reference to the excavations in 1947–8, experts suggest that the construction of the Cairnpapple Hill should have been divided into five phases (information from "The Excavations at Cairnpapple Hill, West Lothian 1947–8" by Stuart Piggott, *Antiquity* 23 [1949]).

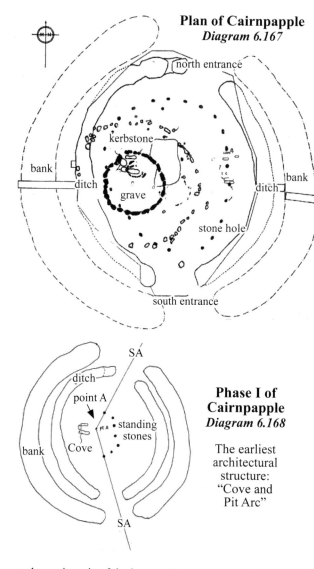

Plan of Cairnpapple
Diagram 6.167

north entrance

kerbstone

bank

ditch

bank

grave

ditch

stone hole

south entrance

**Phase I of
Cairnpapple**
Diagram 6.168

The earliest
architectural
structure:
"Cove and
Pit Arc"

SA

ditch

point A

standing
stones

bank   Cove

SA

In around 3000 B.C., probably just before the people on Salisbury Plain began to build Stonehenge I, the Scot ancestors constructed theirs on the hilltop. Cairnpapple is made up of an internal circular or oval ditch about 1m deep and surrounded by an external earth bank 1.2m high. The double-entranced henge opens to the north and south-southeast, on a line well away from the main axis (Burl 2000).

The first monument erected on the site, as suggested by Piggott (1949), is an irregular arc of seven pits which originally held standing stones and opened to the west-southwest (diagram 6.168). Opposite the opening of the arc are three huge stone-holes which once held large slabs in the form of a cove, with the opening to the east. The setting constitutes Phase I of Cairnpapple. Again, like most of the standing stones and circles around the region, the real function of the Cairnpapple Phase I remains an enigma for the experts.

However, the standing stones at the two ends of the arc form an SA with the central point A. The two axes of the angle lie right at the entrances of the henge. It explains why the two entrances open not according to the main axis of the henge. The same scenario can be found in Stonehenge, as its northeast and Southern Causeways form an SA according to the plan of the builders.

Phase II marks the introduction of an egg-shaped ring with twenty-four large stone holes, 1.2–1.5m high, inside the oval ditch. At the south is a gap of 7.6m, constituting an entrance to the stone setting. There are two single stones erected just inside the perimeter at north-northwest and south-southeast as angled portals for the site (Burl 2000). Within the stone circle there is an oval burial site to the west, probably a Beaker grave, encircled by an outer ring (diagram 6.169). The two angled portals, stones 1 and 14, are strategically placed inside the stone ring. They served as the Station Stones to determine and mark the SA with the Beaker grave. The grave had, therefore, to be constructed offcenter to the west of the circle (Piggott 1949) so as to let two rows of megalights pass through its two entrances. The two arc-ditches of Phase I were deliberately refilled at their ends in order to readjust to the two megalights. As shown in the following diagram, nearly every standing stone of Phase II forms an SA with another stone, like other stone circles around the region.

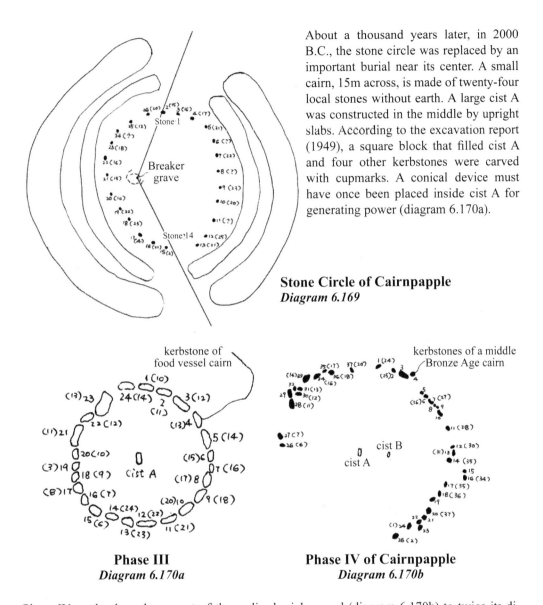

About a thousand years later, in 2000 B.C., the stone circle was replaced by an important burial near its center. A small cairn, 15m across, is made of twenty-four local stones without earth. A large cist A was constructed in the middle by upright slabs. According to the excavation report (1949), a square block that filled cist A and four other kerbstones were carved with cupmarks. A conical device must have once been placed inside cist A for generating power (diagram 6.170a).

Stone Circle of Cairnpapple
Diagram 6.169

Phase III
Diagram 6.170a

Phase IV of Cairnpapple
Diagram 6.170b

Phase IV marks the enlargement of the earlier burial mound (diagram 6.170b) to twice its diameter with the introduction of smaller and rounder stones or boulders (Piggott 1949). The final phase began with the filling of the main site by earth to form a large cairn. The site of Cairnpapple was continuously used by the builders and those who arrived later for over 1,500 years. Like most of the other Neolithic sites, the area was deliberately selected at a place high above the ground, which commands a wide view and is easy to locate. Cairnpapple was certainly an important power station of the builders in 3000 to 2000 B.C.

Clyde Cairns in Southwest Scotland

There are about 100 Clyde megalithic tombs on either side of the Clyde estuary. The most developed and complicated one is the Cairnholy I of Dumfries and Galloway. The name "Cairnholy" may have come from "Carn Ulaidh" which means "treasure cairn." The site was constructed on a gentle slope which overlooks the Wigtown bay. The cairn has an impressive curved façade, an arc of eight tall uprights reaching 3m in height. In front of the entrance is a closing stone. The cairn measures 45m long and 10m wide. A double chamber, with inner and outer compartments, was built in the form of stone boxes. According to the experts, on the southern side of the tomb and behind the façade, there is a cist covered by slab with a large cup and ring carving with at least five concentric rings. Both compartments were then covered by a large trapezoid mound in the later period. The power generator of Cairnholy I is restored in diagram 6.171.

Its neighbor, Cairnholy II, known as King's Galdus' tomb, lies 150m to the north with a double compartment behind a portal slab. A large capstone survives intact over the inner compartment that acts like a lintel trilithon. The cairn measures 22m × 13m. Like Cairnholy I, conical device no. 1 was placed inside the lintel stone box of the inner compartment and connected with conical device no. 2, which was just outside the façade of the structure (diagram 6.172).

**Cairnholy I
Powerhouse
*Diagram 6.171***

**Cairnholy II and the Installation
of the Twin-device
*Diagram 6.172***

SA Alignments of Various Stone Circles

It is interesting to discover that most of the important stone circles around the region are aligned to the SA (SA1 to SA6), as shown in the following diagram (diagram 6.173):

SA1 Callanish–Arbor Low–Stanton Drew (bisects at Grange)
SA2 Callanish–Cairnpapple–Llandegdai + Rough Tor
SA3 Callanish–Croft Moraig–Rough Tor
SA4 Donegore + Lyles Hill + Ballnahatty–Llandegdai–Rough Tor (bisects at Grange)
SA5 Grange–Llandegdai–Long Meg
SA6 Arbor Low–Rollright Stones–Stanton Drew

The Dragon Project and the Ley Hunter

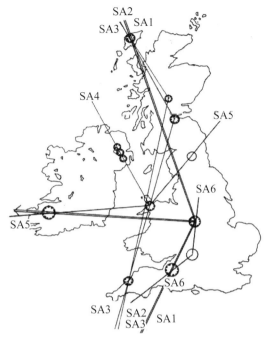

Major Stone Circles and the SA
Diagram 6.173

The Dragon Project was founded in 1977 by Paul Devereux, an expert in anthropology, consciousness studies, ecopsychology, and traditional usage of landscape (environic-foundation.org). It is a research project that employed volunteers from all professions to study various claims and ideas of unusual energies at prehistoric sites. By using various detecting devices from simple dowsers to modernize magnetometers at selected ancient sacred places, they conclude that "there were no strange energies at these places, but that there were strange anomalous effects in known energies. … at many stone circles evidence of anomalies in local geomagnetism and natural background radioactivity" (in *Places of Power* [1990], cited at leyhunter. com). In addition, it was found that the kind of locations favored by megalith builders tended to have a higher than average incidence of unusual light-ball phenomena or "earth lights" (pauldevereux.co.uk). What are these "magnetic and radiation anomalies" as well as "infrared and ultrasonic effects" occasionally found in the stone circles? Were they the energies the megalith builders once generated 5,000 years ago? Was it the magnetism that lay deep inside our planet that attracted them to come from thousands of light years away? Did the so-called "unusual earth lights" refer to the megalights generated by the builders' conical device? No doubt, there are still unusual forces associated with these megalithic rings. They were probably built for tapping energies underneath. Ironically, it is only our relative "backwardness of technological know-how" that really causes the so-called mysteries of megalithism.

Dead men can't speak, and neither can the stone circles. A corpse can tell us the cause of death through autopsy but tell little about its own history. We may know how the Neolithic people erected these megalithic rings but not the reason why. Modern forensic scientists may be able to profile a serial killer if the bodies of the victims are studied. Like an archaeological detective, by using simple mathematics, always a kind of universal language, we may be able to track down the Neolithic suspect and thereby explains those mysterious stone rings.

**The Builders' Message:
Cup and Ring Rock Arts**
(after Dr. Beckensall)
Diagram 6.174

Meaning behind the Cup and Ring Carvings

"It is possible that the spirals are a symbol of the labyrinthine path to the underworld. The concentric circles could be connected with sun worship. The arcs perhaps represent the great Earth Mother, protectress of the dead, and goddess of harvests and fruitfulness. The waves, snakes patterns and zigzags may stand for the sea of the living world, an important force, but they may also evoke the celestial sea of religious meditation."

—Everyman Guides, *Ireland* (1995), p. 197

Ten-thousand-year-old rock paintings and carvings pose no mystery for the experts. These multi-colored masterpieces are usually found inside deep and deserted caves with distinctive and explicit figures such as wild ox and deer. However, for no apparent reason, the late Neolithic artists decided to create their images in a more abstract way.

Many natural rocks and megalithic sites in northern Britain are inscribed with the famous cup and ring markings, which date back to the Late Neolithic and the Bronze Age, with a use over at least 1,000 years. The most common pattern is the cupmark, sometimes called petroglyphs, a small (from 12mm to 15cm across) and simple, roughly circular hemispherical depression carved on stone. But some of the rock surfaces are large. They are placed on gently sloping, horizontal as well as vertical surfaces. They are found on standing stones such as the decorated stones from King's Mountain near Loughcrew, inside the Neolithic coffins, on the standing slabs of stone circles such as the Long Meg, on some natural boulders and rock outcrops in Achnabreck, on the stones of some burial chambers and cists inside Clava cairns, and hidden in caves. A large portion of these decorated rocks are found in the upland open to the sky. They usually enjoy the best views, often on ridges overlooking fertile valleys. Some cannot be seen until you are almost on top of them. Some cists contain reused carvings and others are freshly decorated when building stone cairns (Simon Dension 1998).

Almost all British rock art is abstract. Sometimes several cups are joined together to form an oval depression. Cups are also widely associated with rings that comprise more or less concentric circles with the cup mark at the center (*England: An Oxford Archaeological Guide to Sites from Earliest Time to AD 1600* by Timothy Darvill, Paul Stamper, and Jane Timby). Sometimes a line or groove is inscribed from outside the design to the center of the cup mark, and some experts suggest they were once used for sacrificial purposes. These abstract designs were produced in around 3000 B.C. to A.D. 100 and are found worldwide. Again, the meaning behind these carvings is one of the greatest mysteries of the Neolithic time (diagram 6.175).

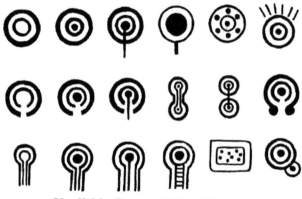

Neolithic Cup and Ring Carvings
(after Darvill, Stamper and Timby)
Diagram 6.175

Recent research suggests that the carving may have been linked to the following uses: seasonal use of the uplands by herders and hunters, maps of sacred places, pathways or access routes, local spots where earth energy is located, land or boundary markers to remind people of their meeting place or to protect their territories, funerary ritual sites of the chiefs, a Neolithic symbol for ancient cosmology, etc. It is also suggested that cups carved into horizontal slabs may have held oil, blood, or holy water whereas the vertical ones may have been a form of exterior decoration. An amateur recorder of rock art, Ronald Morris, listed 104 explanations that had been given for rock art—from musical notation to star charts (Denison 1998). According to Burke and Halberg, the basalt rocks in Petroglyphs National Monuments had electrical charge.

A Universal Message

With the inspiration from the decorated monolith of Long Meg, Neolithic people tried to tell us their secrets through these complicated and mysterious patterns. These carvings in no way, as most of the archaeologists suggest, marked the meeting places or sacred sites of the Stone Age people, nor were they a symbol of fertility. At most, the artists wanted to identify those rocks that could serve as dry cells, with carvings on their surfaces to show that they were suitable for generating Earth energy, like the logo of a local gas station. Besides, they are usually located on treeless high grounds with horizontal or gentle sloping surfaces so as to capture maximum Earth energy. Whether these selected stones can still do the work of tapping and emitting energy nowadays would be the work of the scientists, given that our technology is advanced enough.

I would like to provide some examples of decorated rock outcrop from famous Neolithic sites:

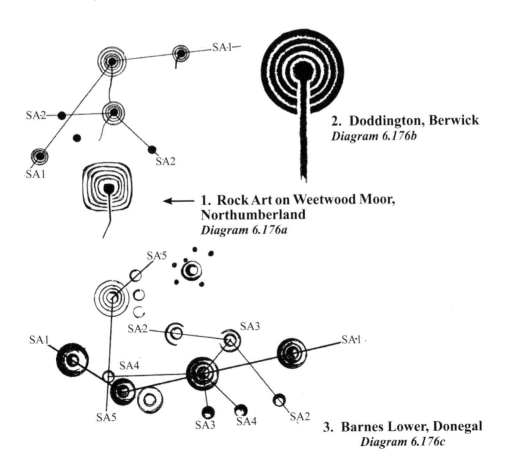

2. **Doddington, Berwick**
Diagram 6.176b

1. **Rock Art on Weetwood Moor, Northumberland**
Diagram 6.176a

3. **Barnes Lower, Donegal**
Diagram 6.176c

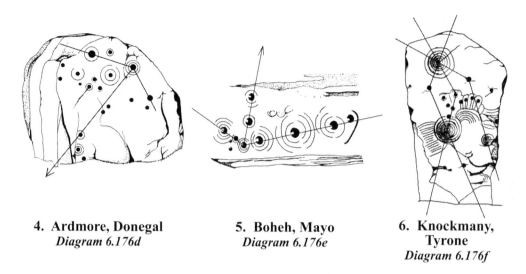

4. Ardmore, Donegal
Diagram 6.176d

5. Boheh, Mayo
Diagram 6.176e

6. Knockmany, Tyrone
Diagram 6.176f

Deciphering the Cup and Ring Marking at Ath An Charbaid, County Kerry

The following decorated stone (diagram 6.177) is found at Ath An Charbaid, County Kerry, Ireland (*Mythic Ireland* by Michael Dames [1996], p. 65). The stone is engraved with dozens of concentric circles or rings of different sizes, and they are surrounded by small dips. No predominant pattern is derived from the diagram but Dames suggests that the carving is "a full-length portrait of the Sun-Moon deity."

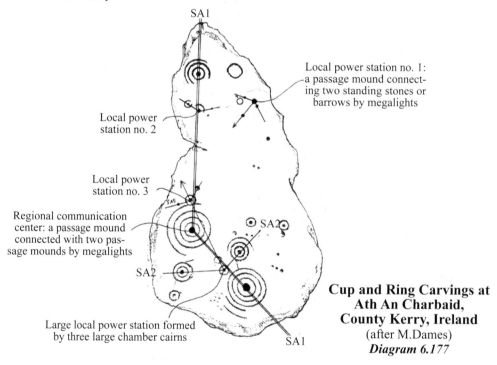

SA1

Local power station no. 1: a passage mound connecting two standing stones or barrows by megalights

Local power station no. 2

Local power station no. 3

Regional communication center: a passage mound connected with two passage mounds by megalights

SA2

SA2

Large local power station formed by three large chamber cairns

SA1

Cup and Ring Carvings at Ath An Charbaid, County Kerry, Ireland
(after M.Dames)
Diagram 6.177

However a clearer and more comprehensive picture of the decorated stone can be observed if the SA is applied to it. SA1 connects the three largest concentric rings which must have been a conspiratorial plan of the builders. I speculate that these three rings represent three important Neolithic centers, as they were deliberately located at some distance apart. They might stand for the ancient sites of Loughcrew, Boyne Valley Group, and Fourknocks, or other sites of Knocknarea, Carrowmore, and Carrowkeel cemeteries, as they are all aligned to the SA. As a matter of fact, SA2 might also represent another regional center of Neolithic Ireland.

Dames's diagram also tells us another message from the builders. Diagram 6.177 shows various sets of SAs formed by the circles and dips engraved in the stone. They probably indicate the power stations of the builders as their angle bisectors point at another circle or dip which might have been the refueling stations. Other possible sets of SAs are illustrated in the diagrams. The small dips that surround the central circle actually represent the standing stones or barrows—dry cells, of the Neolithic period.

If we study the design of all these cup and ring patterns, it is not difficult to find that they share a common theme, i.e., they indicate the energy mechanism of the builders. From my point of view, the cup mark symbol is actually a horseshoe kind of superstructure and represents a fuel station, probably a chambered mound with an opening such as the long passageway of Newgrange, the horseshoe causeway formed by Great Sarsen Trilithons or even the Malta temples with curved apses and horseshoe outer walls. A circle/concentric circles is/are curved just next to the cup, which may represent the builders' machine that was parked outside the station (the cup) waiting for recharging. That's why they are always conjoined by a straight line. Of course, this line represents a row of megalights that is projected by the machine to be recharged (diagram 6.180 right). By the way, was the Neolithic Caltex run by the builders free of charge?

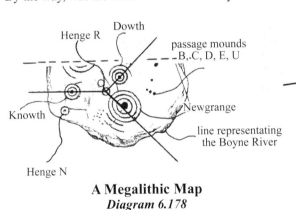

Dowth

Henge R

passage mounds
B,.C, D, E, U

Knowth

Newgrange

line representating
the Boyne River

Henge N

A Megalithic Map
Diagram 6.178

The diagram on the right is an early record of concentric rings carved on a rock surface in the north of England (after J. Y. Simpson's *Archaic Sculpturings* [1867]). As mentioned above, the concentric rings with a straight line drawn from the center represent a charged mound/cairn/barrow that would produce a row of megalight. The small dots among them are the monoliths or barrows that acted as dry cells to transfuse Earth energy to the central mound (diagram 6.179).

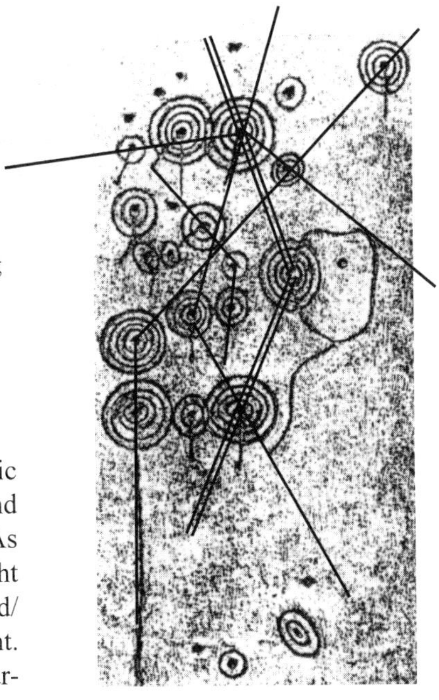

Cup and Ring Carvings
(after Michell, *Megalithomania*)
Diagram 6.179

Did the cup and ring marks found on those monoliths (diagram 6.180 left) (after J. Y. Simpson) indicate whether the stone was suitable for generating power or not? Was it a message for new arrivals?

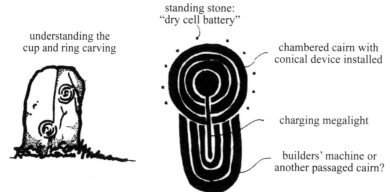

understanding the
cup and ring carving

standing stone:
"dry cell battery"

chambered cairn with
conical device installed

charging megalight

builders' machine or
another passaged cairn?

The Builders' Dry Cell Battery? (*left*) **and the Symbol of a Neolithic Powerhouse**
Diagram 6.180

Another cup and ring carving from Dames's book (diagram 6.181) comes from Derrynalaha of County Kerry, which is described by Dames as "a combining image of staff, ox-horns and copulation." However, it is just another Neolithic carving which indicates the locations and functions of various power stations of the builders. As a matter of fact, I can easily derive at least six sets of SAs from this tiny piece of decorated stone!

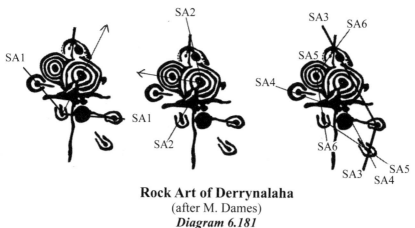

Rock Art of Derrynalaha
(after M. Dames)
Diagram 6.181

Dr. Beckensall and Northumberland Rock Art

"I just hope that somebody who sees a picture of it has seen something like this before and can solve our mystery."

—Dr. Beckensall, making an international appeal for an explanation for a mysterious marking hewn into an isolated sandstone boulder near Wark, Northnumberland (diagram 6.185)

Dr. Stan Beckensall has spent more than forty years on finding, drawing, and recording prehistoric open-air rock carvings in Northumberland, Durham, Cumbria, North Yorkshire, Scotland, and even Ireland. He has recorded over 1,500 carved rocks with life-size rubbings (using newsprint and wax crayon), final drawings, photographs, location information, and descriptive commentary. His Northumberland rock art archive represents the largest and most detailed personal regional rock art archive in Britain. He also publishes several comprehensive surveys of prehistoric rock art panels from Northumberland of Scotland, to Yorkshire, County Durham, Swaledale, and Wensleydale. In 2002, Dr. Beckensall donated his Northumberland rock art archive to the University of Newcastle. The website http://rockart.ncl.ac.uk, which was launched in January 2005, contains 6,000 drawings and photographs with Dr. Beckensall contributing more than 90% of the panels.

There are almost a thousand rock art panels left by Neolithic and Early Bronze Age people in Northumberland in the northeast of England. Most of these mysterious carvings are found on boulders and rocky outcrops. Many British rock art panels are undervalued and understudied. The following drawings of prehistoric rock art are produced by Beckensall (from "The Northumberland Rock Art project team"). Most of the motifs of these carved rocks are aligned to the SA and they are, as a matter of fact, the Neolithic maps of the once-lost builders 5,000 years ago (diagram 6.182).

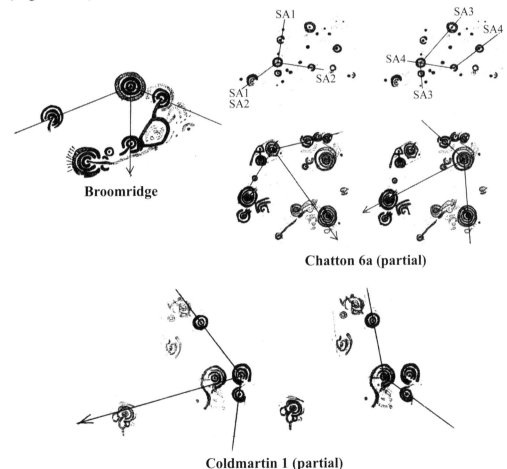

Broomridge

Chatton 6a (partial)

Coldmartin 1 (partial)

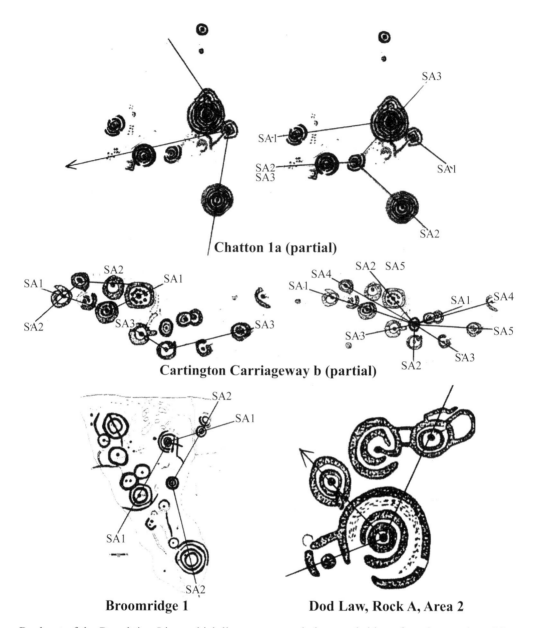

Chatton 1a (partial)

Cartington Carriageway b (partial)

Broomridge 1   **Dod Law, Rock A, Area 2**

Rock art of the Roughting Linn, which lies on a natural elongated ridge of sandstone about 20m long and 12m wide, is the largest and most celebrated decorated rock in northern England. Most of the motifs are based on cup and ring markings. The carvings of the Dod Law have some square and rectangular motifs that are connected to some large rings by long grooves.

The carving below (diagram 6.183) is one of the most elaborate drawings of Dr. Beckensall, and has more than twenty concentric rings and cups pedded together. Some are joined by straight lines through their centers. Other are scattered around the slab without a central theme.

However, it is interesting to note that the four concentric rings in the center of the drawing form an SA. They actually represent the communication between major Neolithic centers or power generators of the builders.

SA1

SA2

SA2

SA1

**Main Axis of the Carving
Is Aligned to the SA**
Diagram 6.183

The largest concentric ring, which lies in the middle of the drawing, had to be one of the most important stations of the builders as nine sets of SAs are formed by the ring with its surrounding circles and dips (diagram 6.184a and b).

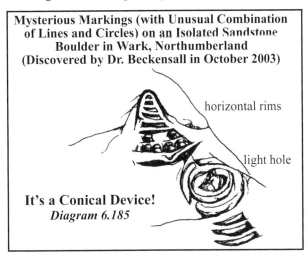

**Mysterious Markings (with Unusual Combination
of Lines and Circles) on an Isolated Sandstone
Boulder in Wark, Northumberland
(Discovered by Dr. Beckensall in October 2003)**

horizontal rims

light hole

It's a Conical Device!
Diagram 6.185

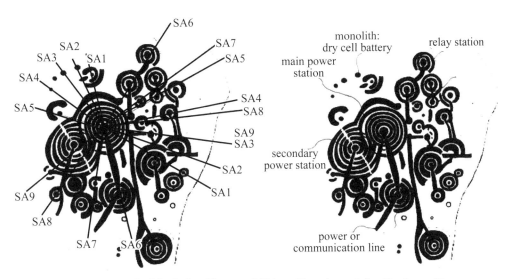

SA6

SA2
SA3 SA1

SA4

SA5

SA7
SA5

SA4
SA8

SA9
SA3

SA2

SA1

SA9

SA8

SA7 SA6

monolith:
dry cell battery
relay station

main power
station

secondary
power station

power or
communication line

Messages behind the Cup and Ring Carvings (after Beckensall)
Diagram 6.184a and b

According to Dr. Beckensall, the big boulder (in diagram 6.184) lies at Bewick CP and overlooks many prehistoric sites such as Blawearie cairns and the Corby Crags hillfort. He describes the block as one of the most interesting ever found. The drawing is mainly divided into two parts by a main central groove, running from top to the bottom. To the right are cups and rings with grooves running from central cups and surrounding rings. To the left, the cups and rings were arranged in a figure-eight pattern. A cup from which a long groove leads down at the centre of five rings and connects to the center of three broken rings below. The lefthand figure has a crowd of motifs below it, cups and rings connected by grooves, some touch the outer arc of the others (from Dr. Beckensall's website).

Rock Art of Traprain Law, Scotland

The Neolithic complex of Traprain Law in East Lothian has been recognized as one of the most important archaeological sites in Scotland (Ian Armit and Margaret McCartney in *Past* 49 [2005]). As mentioned in the article, Traprain Law contains a series of ramparts that served unknown purposes. In the 2004 fieldwork, experts discovered a new rock art panel under the Iron Age deposits. The authors of the article suggest that the marking is in the conventional Atlantic European style which consists of at least five (six to me) cup and ring marks. Three of them are conjoined. As a matter of fact, four of these mysterious cup marks are perfectly aligned to the SA (diagram 6.186).

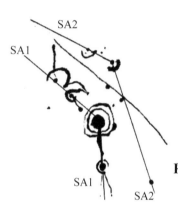

SA2
SA1
SA1
SA2

In his book, David R. Cowan suggests that "the cup-and-ring carvings are no ordinary map, but a pattern of telluric Earth energies, with the petroglyphs transmitting telluric energy between standing stones, stone circles, burial-grounds and homesteads in an astonishingly highly evolved manner" (p. 28). In my opinion, he is correct.

Rock Art of Traprain Law
Diagram 6.186

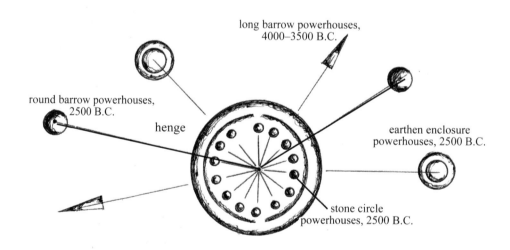

long barrow powerhouses, 4000–3500 B.C.

round barrow powerhouses, 2500 B.C.

henge

earthen enclosure powerhouses, 2500 B.C.

stone circle powerhouses, 2500 B.C.

Various Powerhouses of Neolithic Britain, 4000–2000 B.C.
Diagram 6.187

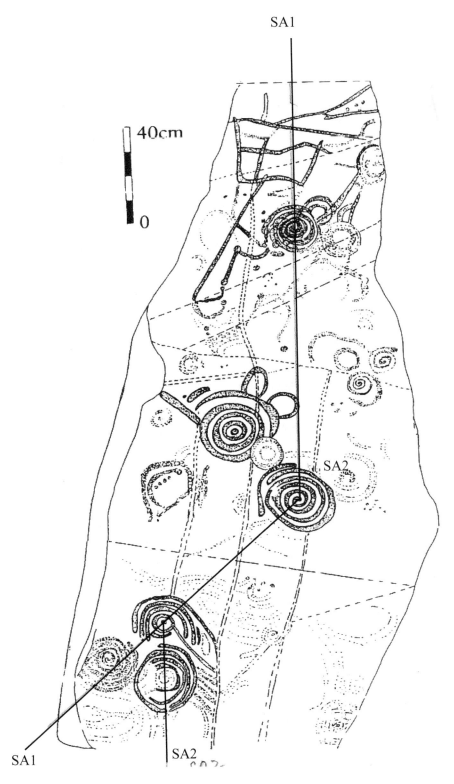

SA1

40cm

0

SA2

SA1

SA2

**Gods' Messages: Carvings on Long Meg, from a Rubbing by
Stan Beckensall, with Major Spirals Aligned to the SA**
(after Darvill, Stamper and Timby 2002)
Diagram 6.188

Chapter 7
Neolithic Orkney

The Ancient Settlements of Orkney

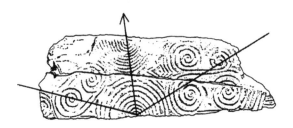

The Pierowell Stone
Diagram 7.01

"...how is it possible to reconstruct something of their world view when no evidence survives of how Neolithic people thought about the world except the material remains?"

—Trevor Garnham, *Lines on the Landscape, Circles from the Sky: Monuments of Neolithic Orkney* (2004)

Orkney, an archipelago of seventy islands located 16km north of the Scottish mainland, is certainly one of the richest regions of Neolithic material remains. Experts suggest that advanced settlers, the so-called Grooved Ware culture, local known as Orcadians, sophisticated with architecture and probably cosmology but leaving no writings, arrived in Orkney early in the fourth millennium B.C., replacing the hunters and gatherers there. Like their European comrades, the Stone Age settlers seemed obsessed with the sky and the dead, displaying endless effort and interest in building numerous breathtaking monuments on the northern tip of the British Mainland. Chambered cairns, basically categorized into two main types with skillfully constructed corbelled walls, were certainly the masterpiece of northwest Europe. Their near-perfect stone circles are scattered around the main island. Seven well-preserved Neolithic settlements are found in Orkney, containing the oldest structural remains of human housing ever built.

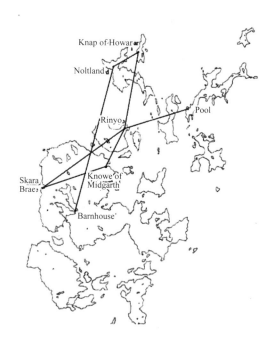

Major Neolithic Settlements in Orkney and the SA
Diagram 7.02

Central Hearths of Skara Brae

Like Chysauster in Cornwall of England, Skara Brae of Orkney was once an important Neolithic village and the largest of the group where the people, probably the elite of wise men or professional priest-astronomers, appear to have lived for 600 years. The village was later abandoned and buried under sand for nearly 4,000 years. The remaining infrastructure consists of the 3m high dry-stone walls of nine huts. These walls are skillfully built with adjacent interlocking passages (diagram 7.03). Inside these square huts were domestic fittings such as beds, shelves, fireplaces, and water tanks formed by thin and flat stone slabs. However, no evidence of roof construction and the absence of wood to keep warm make the life extremely harsh during the extreme winter weather.

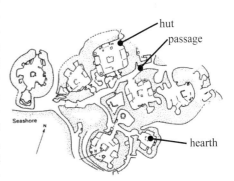

Plan of Skara Brae
Diagram 7.03

The central feature of each hut is the hearth, a square-shaped tray edged by upright stones used for burning dried turfs or animal dung to keep warm in the winter. However, archaeologists are puzzled as the prehistoric Orkney was grassland, where all timber resources had to be imported. If the hearth was not used for burning turf, then what was it used for? Why was it placed in such a central location. A roofed passage, a kind of lintel doorway, links the square houses together. In 1926, distinctive flat-based grooved wares with spiral and lozenge motifs, similar to those in the Boyne Valley and Stonehenge, were found. The following diagrams show the two main axes of Skara Brae; interestingly, they are aligned to the SA (diagram 7.04).

Main Axes of Skara Brae and the SA
Diagram 7.04

Coincidentally, extra SAs can be formed by two of the hearths with a third in the middle (diagram 7.05). For example, hearths H2 and H3 form an SA with H1 in the middle and, H4 lies on their angle bisector. Also, H4 and H5 form their SA with H1 in the middle and H3 lies on the angle bisector. All nine hearths are aligned to the SA.

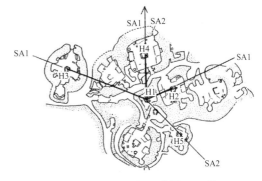

Central Hearths of Skara Brae
Diagram 7.05

Stone balls 6 to 7cm in diameter, carved with lozenge pattern and grooves are found in the site, which could date back to 2700 B.C. (diagram 7.06). Experts still question how the prehistoric people decorated these mysterious balls without the use of metal. These ceremonial objects are similar to those discovered inside the temples of Tarxien. The monuments of Skara Brae and Tarxien are both characterized by curved chambers or apse walls. These stone balls were probably once used for "spinning around" those circular chambers, a tool for generating power 5,500 years ago. Full coverage of the builders' energy mechanism has been clearly and repeatedly depicted on the mysterious spiral carvings in both Tarxien temples and Skara Brae. Located at the far west of the Orkney Islands, the Neolithic settlements of Skara Brae form various SAs with its surrounding monuments (diagram 7.07).

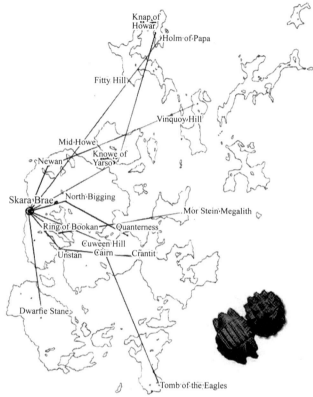

Stone Balls of Skara Brae (*right*)
Diagram 7.06 **and**
Neolithic Settlement of Skara Brae as the Center of the Neolithic Settlement in Orkney
Diagram 7.07

Skara Brae also served as Station Stone for the following SAs:

1. Knap of Howar–Knowe of Yarso
2. Vinquoy Hill Chambered Cairn–Newan Chambered Cairn
3. Mor Stein Megalith–Ring of Bookan
4. Tomb of the Eagles–Cuween Hill Cairn
5. Unstan Chambered Cairn–Crandit Chambered Cairn
6. Midhowe–Newan Chambered Cairn
7. North Bigging Cairn–Quanterness Chambered Cairn

Rinyo of Rousay

Rinyo is another Skara Brae type of Neolithic settlement located at a stone outcrop south of Faraclett Head. Similar to Skara Brae, the Rinyo houses are cruciform in shape with three cells and are built with central hearths and sided with dressers and water tanks. The following diagram is the general layout of Rinyo where its north-south axis is aligned exactly to the SA (diagram 7.08). Besides, several other sets of SAs can be derived from the central hearth of the settlement.

As in Skara Brae, conical devices were once placed on central hearths and projected rows of megalights to the surrounding drystone walls for power.

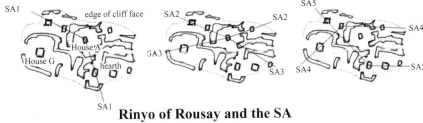

Rinyo of Rousay and the SA
Diagram 7.08

Knap of Howar

A pair of Neolithic houses, House 1 and 2, excavated on the tiny Orkney island of Papa Westray, are believed to be older than those in Skara Brae, making them the oldest remains of human housing in the world. In Knap of Howar, there are also stone cupboards, shelves, and hearths and they had been buried under sand dunes for thousands of years. In one of the houses there is a quernstone which might have been used for grinding grain. But I believe the houses were also used for producing energy 5,500 years ago. House 2 is smaller but better equipped with furnishings and built in cells formed by orthostat drystones (diagram 7.09 and 7.10). These standing stones form several sets of SAs with the central hearth. Similar to the trilithon doorways of the Maltese temples, the lintel doorways served as dry cells connecting the two dry-stone curved houses for power.

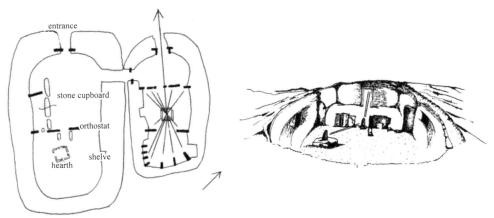

Plan of Houses at the Knap of Howar
Diagram 7.09

House 1, Knap of Howar, and the Conical Device
Diagram 7.10

Mysterious Barnhouse Settlement

One of the sister settlements of Skara Brae is the Barnhouse Settlement, with houses having similar central, kerbed hearths, built-in box-beds, and stone furniture. Excavations show the remains of fifteen small dwellings with round buildings and turf cladding surrounding the outer walls.

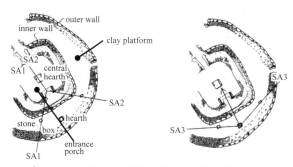

Structure Eight, Barnhouse Settlement
Diagrams 7.11 and 7.12

The most eye-catching building of the settlement is Structure Eight, the largest on the site, with an interior space of 7m × 7m. Constructed with thicker outer walls, it stands out clearly from the other buildings. Experts believe that this building, containing only a hearth, was once used for ceremonial meeting or housing the high priest. Interestingly, the hearth is in the middle of the structure and the entrance porch is flanked by two standing stones, again recalling the trilithon doorways of the Maltese temples.

According to Garnham (2004), there are several elaborate hearths or stone boxes on the clay platform between the inner and outer walls. If a conical device was placed on the flanked porch of the structure, it forms an SA with the central hearth and the stone box (diagrams 7.11 and 7.12). That is exactly the pattern inside the Maltese temples thousands of kilometers apart!

Like the settlements in Skara Brae, the general layouts of the Barnhouse houses are curved and aligned to SA1 and SA2 (diagram 7.13). Besides, the hearths in these small houses constitute five extra sets of SAs, which further indicates the Barnhouse was one of the builders' powerhouses (diagram 7.14).

Diagram 7.15 illustrates how all the hearths inside House Two and Structure Eight form SA1 to SA3 while SA4 to SA8 are formed by the largest site of Structure Eight and its surrounding settlements.

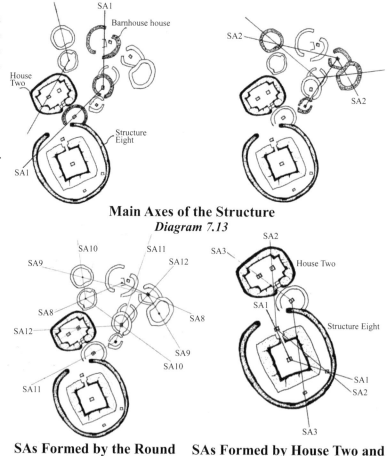

Main Axes of the Structure
Diagram 7.13

SAs Formed by the Round Buildings of Barnhouse
Diagram 7.14

SAs Formed by House Two and Structure Eight of Barnhouse
Diagram 7.15

Ring of Brodgar: Stonehenge II of Scotland

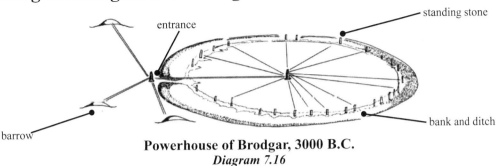

Powerhouse of Brodgar, 3000 B.C.
Diagram 7.16

Another fascinating ruin is the Ring of Brodgar, or "Temple of the Gods," a massive circle of standing stones or henge, erected between 2500 and 2000 B.C. It is one of the most majestic stone circles in the Brodgar peninsula of Scotland. It ranks third in size after the Outer Circle at Avebury and the Great Circle at Stanton Drew. The 100m diameter circle, with an area of 8,435 sq. m is regarded as the finest in Orkney and the largest in Scotland. Besides the twenty-seven exceptionally tall stones (originally sixty), standing inside a bank and a massive ditch, 9m wide and 3m deep, there are also two entrance causeways, one open to the northwest and the other to the southeast. As with many stone circles in Scotland, there is an outlying stone of Brodgar—the Comet Stone—pointing towards the Stones of Stenness, another well-known stone circle of the region. The 4,500-year-old monument is believed to have been a gathering place, a ceremonial center, or a prehistoric observatory, which experts suggest took 80,000 man-hours to build.

According to archaeologists, the circle is surrounded with a complex of burial barrows, cairns and prehistoric earthworks, as shown in the diagram at right. The four large mounds include the Salt Knowe, a 40m diameter barrow southwest of the ring; The Fresh Knowe, 26–38m in diameter and elliptical in shape, northeast of the ring; The South Knowe, 1.8m in diameter and 1.8m tall, south of Brodgar; and the Plumcake Knowe, a barrow 22m in diameter, northeast of the stone circle. These barrows were excavated in the early nineteenth century (www.orkneyjar. com) (diagram 7.17).

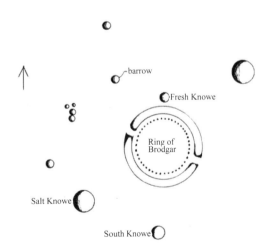

Plan of Ring of Brodgar and Surrounding Prehistoric Barrows
Diagram 7.17

The presence of these barrows shows the Ring of Brodgar was possibly a ceremonial center for treating dead bodies before they were buried in the mounds nearby. However, the Brodgar builders were certainly inspired by the powerhouse of Newgrange and its twin-device mechanism. Like Newgrange, twin-device no. 1 was once placed in the center of the ring, probably inside the Cove and connected with twin-device no. 2 at the northwest entrance of the enclosure (diagram 7.18). This was the design of a typical power generator of the builders.

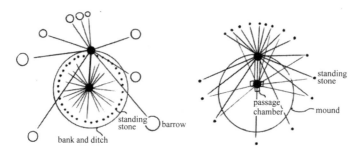

Twin-device Mechanisms of Brodgar and Newgrange
Diagram 7.18

What supports the above idea are the SAs formed by the surrounding barrows with twin-device no. 2. When conical device no. 1 was recharging and collecting energy from the stone circle, another line of megalight together with the energy would then be projected and transferred to device no. 2. At the same time, a radiance of megalights produced by device no. 2 would be projected to the surrounding round barrows for discharging. An energy mechanism activated by twin-device was completed (diagram 7.19).

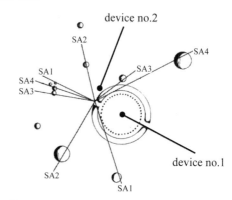

SAs Formed by the Entrance of Brodgar and the Surrounding Barrows
Diagram 7.19

There is runic type inscription on the third standing stone of Brodgar, counting clockwise from the northwest entrance causeway (diagram 7.20). This is known as twig rune because of its twig-like appearance (www.orkneyjar.com). Coincidentally, these runes show the magic angle of 135 degrees! Were they messages from the Vikings, as suggested by the experts, or were they from the advanced builders?

Runes of Brodgar
Diagram 7.20

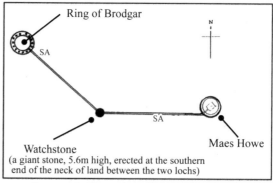

Magnus Spence's Drawing Shows the SA Alignment between the Ring of Brodgar and the Entrance of Maes Howe with the Watchstone in the Middle
Diagram 7.21

Stones of Stenness

Another famous site in the region is the Stones of Stenness. Like the Ring of Brodgar, the site contains four (originally twelve), tall, thin, and interestingly shaped monoliths. Each of them stands at a different angle inside a ditch, 6m wide and 2.4m deep, to form an enclosure 44m in diameter. The tallest is an impressive 5m tall, only Stonehenge exceeds their height. It has a single entrance causeway at the north facing the Neolithic Barnhouse settlement. One of the standing stones is more than six meters high, which makes the monument visible miles away. The stone circle is thought to represent the Temple of the Moon because of its crescent shape. A cove or hearth made of three stones was reconstructed in the center of the circle in the early eighteenth century even though there is no archaeological evidence to suggest the altar was once inside the ring. Experts believe the site was built around 3100 B.C., one of the earliest stone circles in Britain. It has become a tradition for lovers to visit the standing stones, and for women to kneel and pray to the "God Wodden" (orkneyjar.com).

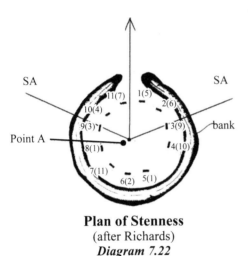

Plan of Stenness
(after Richards)
Diagram 7.22

As illustrated in diagram 7.22, point A, a post hole beside a large hearth, the center of the circle, which is a few meters southwest of the reconstructed central hearth, forms various sets of SAs with the surrounding standing stones. If another conical device, no. 2, was placed at the north entrance of the ring, it would form another SA with the Ring of Brodgar, which has a southeast entrance, on the left, and the famous Neolithic settlement of Maes Howe, with a southeast entrance, on the right. The SA even bisects at another Neolithic settlement—the Barnhouse in the north (diagram 7.23). Thus, the locations and openings of these three monuments are aligned to the SA. By producing megalights, these Stone Age rings were probably used for supplying power to the settlements nearby.

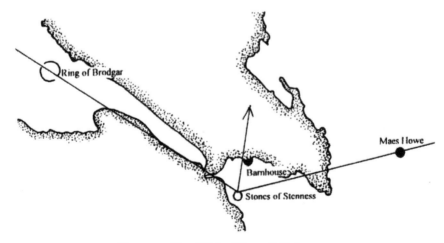

Famous Neolithic Sites of Orkney
(Roy Loveday and Richards 1993)
Diagram 7.23

Chambered Cairns in Orkney

Maes Howe Chambered Cairn
Diagram 7.24

Another type of famous prehistoric monument around many remote areas of the region is the Neolithic Orcadian chambered cairn, built during the Orcadian Neolithic period around 3200 B.C., contemporary to the Great Mound of Newgrange, Ireland. The cairn is built of quarried Caithness flagstone, a kind of sandstone slab. Experts suggest these tombs were used for rituals as well as for burials. Many human bones found inside these Scot cairns were deliberately sorted into type before being taken into the tombs, which suggests that burial was not their primary function. Chambered cairns in Orkney can be divided into two types: the Orkney-Cromarty Group (OC) and the Maes Howe Group (MH) as classified by archaeologists. The MH Group has rectangular chambers with high corbel roofs. In addition, side cells are constructed at each wall of the chamber with accesses formed by lintel trenches (diagram 7.25b), functioning like sets of dolmens and placed inside a corbel chamber; whereas the cairns of OC Group are usually elongated in shape with upright stalls set into the side walls, and structurally speaking, acting like small-scale stone circles inside herringbone walls chamber (diagram 7.25a). There are slab shelves or benches at one or both ends. There is another type called "hybrid" which incorporates the elements of both the OC and MH Groups (diagram 7.25c).

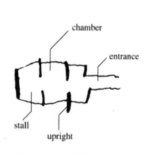

**Knowe of Craie
(OC Group)**
Diagram 7.25a

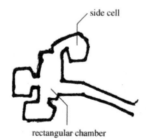

**Wideford Chambered
Cairn (MH Group)**
Diagram 7.25b

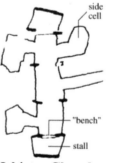

**Isbister Chambered
Cairn: A Hybrid
(OC+MH)**
Diagram 7.25c

Lintel Doorways and Standing Stones of Maes Howe

Chambered Cairn of Maes Howe
Diagram 7.26

The chambered cairn of Maes Howe, probably the finest ancient monument in Britain, is set on a level platform. The cairn is conical in shape and is surrounded by a 2m-deep ditch built around 3000 B.C. On the top of the platform lies a large turf-covered mound over 7m high and 35m across. The whole structure is skillfully designed and tidily constructed. An entrance opening to the southwest leads to a long passage, 1.4m long and less than 1m wide, and made of enormously long stones. There is a lintel recess built into the passage wall, which holds an enormous blocking stone that is suggested to act as a door. The 9m-long passage leads to a high and square chambered mound measuring 4.5m × 4.5m. The four corners of the chamber walls contain huge sandstone upright slabs, probably a stone circle of four standing stones (diagram 7.27). These four massive standing stones that are flat with pointed tops echo those of the Stenness and Brodgar stone circles nearby ("Maes Howe and the Winter Solstice: Ceremonial Aspects of the Orkney Grooved Ware Culture" by Euan W. MacKie, *Antiquity* 71 [1997]: 338–59).

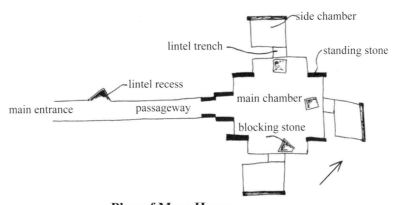

Plan of Maes Howe
(Henshall 1963 and RCAHMS)
Diagram 7.27

As mentioned above, the two famous stone circles of Orkney were power stations of the Neolithic builders, and inside them, rows of megalights were once projected onto the surfaces of these flat-standing slabs with pointed tops for energy. A similar mechanism may also be found on the passage tomb of Maes Howe, as similar slabs were placed inside the cairn. Like the great mound of Newgrange, the passageway of Maes Howe is straight enough to allow natural light to illuminate its chamber, as suggested by astro-archaeologists.

NEOLITHIC ORKNEY

251

What makes Maes Howe superb is that the sandstone slabs were carefully and skillfully fitted together, with the use of masonry, to create a corbelled vault with three recesses set at just above waist height and reached by apertures in the sidewalls. The roof of each recess is formed by a single huge, flat slab to become a lintel-like trench, structurally parallel with a typical Neolithic dolmen. A large stone lies on the floor in front of each of the cells and experts suggest that they were used for blocking the recesses. The site is regarded as an ancient astronomical infrastructure because its entrance passage, again suggested by experts, is aligned to the midwinter sunset when sunrays illuminate the back of the chamber.

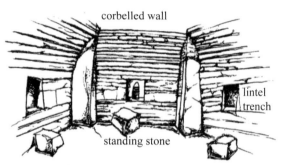

However, after studying the special arrangements inside the tomb, such as the standing slabs, the lintel trenches, and the corbelled walls, I believe Maes Howe once functioned like the great mound of Newgrange and the beehive hut of Bosphrennis, Cornwall. A conical device was once placed on one of these lintel trenches in the three recesses and projected two rows of megalights onto the surfaces of the pointed-top slabs nearby—standing stones placed under the roof, to generate energy (diagram 7.28). Not surprisingly, several sets of SAs are derived from the

**Lintel Trenches and Standing Stones:
Dry Cell Batteries inside Maes Howe**
Diagram 7.28

four uprights with one of the three lintel trenches in the middle (diagram 7.29). Concentric circles of energy or microwaves were then generated spinning around the high, corbelled walls of the chamber (diagram 7.30). The same scenario could also be found in Newgrange, Knowth, and probably inside the temples of Tarxien that were contemporary with Maes Howe. Certainly it must have happened inside the gigantic sarsen trilithons and circle of Stonehenge 1,500 years later.

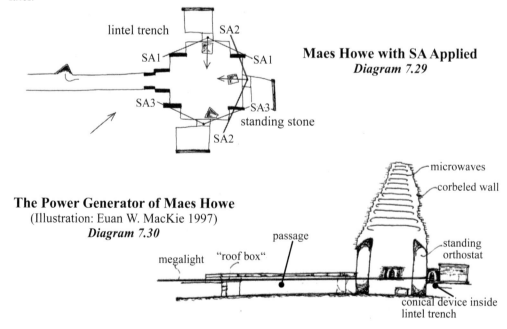

Maes Howe with SA Applied
Diagram 7.29

The Power Generator of Maes Howe
(Illustration: Euan W. MacKie 1997)
Diagram 7.30

Powerhouse of Quoyness

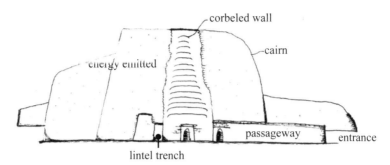

The Powerhouse of Quoyness
Diagram 7.31

Quoyness, which is a Maes Howe-type (MH) cairn, lies on the peninsula of Sanday, in the north of Orkney. As many as twenty-seven cairns of this type are found on the island. According to experts, the site was built on an irregular stony platform 20m across and encircled by an earthen bank. A 9m-long entrance passage connects the central chamber. This rectangular chamber, formed by dry stones, is 4m in length, 2m in breadth, and 4m in height. Six smaller chambers open off from the main chamber with a short trench. Interestingly, any three lintel-trenches of the cairn—acting as the builders' dry cells—form an SA when connected by rows of megalights (diagram 7.32). Therefore, the Quoyness Cairn was once a powerhouse of the Neolithic builders.

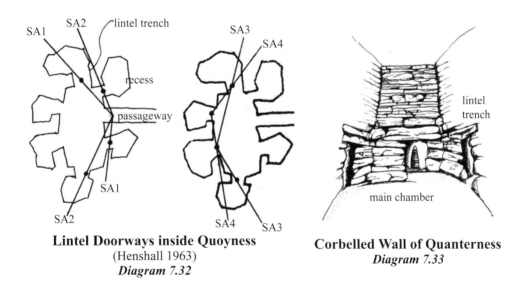

Lintel Doorways inside Quoyness
(Henshall 1963)
Diagram 7.32

Corbelled Wall of Quanterness
Diagram 7.33

Quanterness and Vinquoy Power Generators

What happened in Quoyness also happened in other MH cairns as well. The 4,500-year-old cairn of Quanterness, the finest of its kind, is over 35m in diameter and 3.5m in height. Like Quoyness, a long passage leads to a rectangular chamber that opens to six smaller rectangular side recesses. As shown in diagram 7.34, the lintel entrance to the chamber forms A1 to SA3 with the other lintel trenches of the six recesses (diagram 7.34). That must be the ultimate secret of Quanterness. Besides, three extra sets of SA are derived among these lintel trenches.

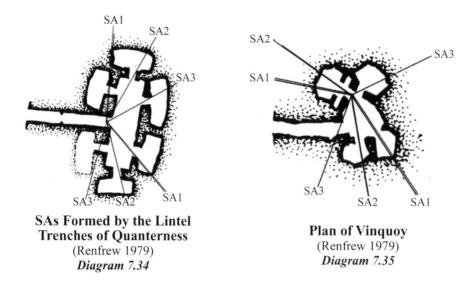

SAs Formed by the Lintel Trenches of Quanterness
(Renfrew 1979)
Diagram 7.34

Plan of Vinquoy
(Renfrew 1979)
Diagram 7.35

The cairn of Vinquoy, a well-preserved chambered tomb, was built on a hilltop with magnificent views over Orkney. Its 4m-long passage opens to the south and leads to a polygonal chamber of 3m in height. The beehive-like chamber opens to four side cells, where several sets of SAs are formed (diagram 7.35).

Cuween Hill Power Station

Another significant monument in the region is the chambered cairn of Cuween Hill. Geographically speaking, the cairn is located at the heart of Orkney overlooking the Bay of Forth. The name "Cuween" meaning "Cattle Pasture" was a local name, "Fairy Knowe." It is also a Maes Howe–type cairn with a passageway, a main chamber, and four side cells dating back to 3000 B.C. A low mound covers the impressive cairn, cut into solid bedrock at the top of a hill. A very low and narrow passage 5.5m long and less than 1m high links a spacious main chamber, more than 2m high, where four smaller recesses opening with lintel doorways branch off from each wall. One of the recesses was extended with a second compartment. Experts suggest that the passageway, like the one inside Maes Howe, is aligned to allow the rays of the rising sun to illuminate the interior of the main chamber. To me, however, it actually opened to megalights of the builders. Conical devices were once placed on the lintel trenches of the recesses for power (diagram 7.36).

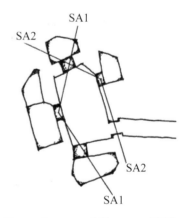

Powerhouse of Cuween Hill
Diagram 7.36

The Cuween Hill Chambered Cairn forms various SAs with its surrounding prehistoric sites:

SA1 Skara Brae–Tomb of the Eagles
SA2 Maesquoy Chambered Cairn–Helliar/Holm Chambered Cairn
SA3 Braeside Chambered Cairn–Unstan Chambered Cairn
SA4 Elsness-Quoyness Chambered Tomb–Maes Howe and Ring of Brodgar
SA5 Wideford Hill–Dwarfie Stane
SA6 Maes Howe–Flaughton Hill Chambered Cairn

Holm of Papa Westray South Chambered Cairn

The tomb lies at the southern end of the uninhabited islet of Holm of Papa Westray, Orkney. It is 38m long, 19.5m wide, and 3m high with a 9m-long entrance passage opening east-southeast. The main chamber measures 20.4m in length with twelve side cells set in the walls. Many slabs' surfaces, especially those of the lintels of the side cells, are decorated with circles, zigzags, eyebrow motifs, dots, and arcs (www.henge.org.uk) (diagram 7.37). Similar designs are found inside the mound of Fourknocks, Ireland.

Zigzag Decoration of the Lintel Doorway, Holm of Papa Westray S.
Diagram 7.37

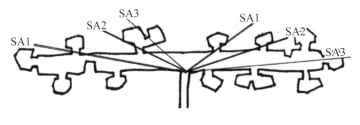

Coincidentally, the lintel doorways of the side cells are aligned to the SA, some doorways forming various sets of SAs with the entrance of the chamber in the middle (diagram 7.38).

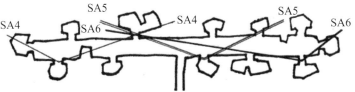

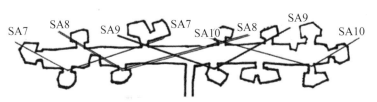

Various SAs Formed by Lintel Doorways of Holm of Papa Westray
Diagram 7.38

Wideford Hill Cairn

Powerhouse of Wideford Hill
Diagram 7.39

Unlike the Holm of Papa Westray South constructed with enormous cells, Wideford Hill has only three small side cells branching off from the rectangular chamber (diagram 7.40). The three lintel doorways of the side cells form a perfect SA, its angle bisector pointing to the main entrance of the chamber. It clearly and undeniably explains the real function of the cairn.

Plan of Wideford
Diagram 7.40

Taversoe Tuick

The chambered cairn of Taversoe Tuick is extraordinary because the site is a two-storied cairn with one OC Group chamber constructed immediately above the other MH Group chamber. The Upper Chamber was built on the top of the burial chamber and accessed by a north-facing passage. The chamber is divided into two round-ended compartments with massive stone lintels lying on the floors. It is interesting to point out that these lintel floors form an SA (diagram 7.41).

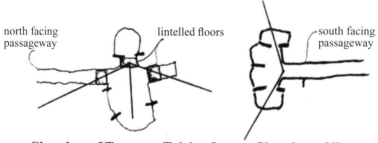

north facing passageway   lintelled floors   south facing passageway

Upper Chamber of Taversoe Tuick   **Lower Chamber of Taversoe Tuick**
Diagram 7.41   *Diagram 7.42*

The Lower Chamber was dug into the hillside and accessed by a narrow southeast-facing passage. The rectangular chamber measures 3.7m × 1.4m and is divided into four compartments. There are shelf slabs constructed into the recesses. The entrances of the two end compartments, formed by pairs of upright slabs, constitute an SA with the main lintel entrance of the chamber in the middle (diagram 7.42). Its meticulous design reveals the whole secret of the Orkney-Cromarty Group (OC) chambered cairns.

Isbister Cairn: A Hybrid Tomb

Isbister cairn, which is also called the Tomb of the Eagles, was built around 3000 B.C. The tomb sits on a spectacular clifftop on the east coast of South Ronaldsay and is special for its hybrid chamber—a mixture of both the stalled compartments of OC and sided cells of MH Groups. The main chamber of the tomb is 8.2m long and 3.5m high, and is rectangular in shape. It is divided into three stalls or compartments built into the walls by pairs of

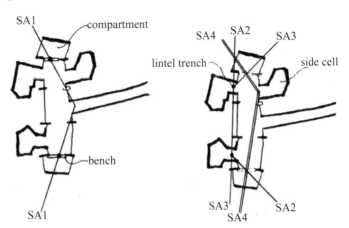

Various SAs inside Isbister
Diagrams 7.43 and 7.44

upright slabs. There are stone benches set into the two end compartments (www.orkney.com). Again, the two benches, structurally like small dolmens, form a perfect SA, with the lintel entrance in the middle (diagram 7.43).

The story of the Isbister continues as experts suggest that the builders extended their OC version with an MH one, as three side cells were constructed in the walls of the chamber. Again, the lintel doorways of these cells form three extra sets of SAs with the benches of the two end compartments (diagram 7.44).

Unstan Cairn, Stenness

Unstan is also a hybrid tomb—a mixture of OC and MH groups. Its internal 8.4m-long rectangular chamber is divided into five stalls by large upright slabs including three central and two shelved end compartments. A side chamber is set in the wall directly opposite the entrance. It is my suggestion that conical devices were once placed at the lintel doorway of the side cell and the benches of the two end compartments because they accurately form an SA (diagram 7.45 and 7.46).

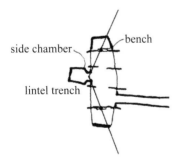

SA inside Unstan
Diagram 7.45

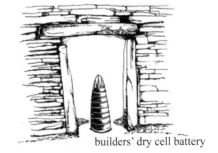

Lintel Trench, Unstan, and the Conical Device
Diagram 7.46

Midhowe Broch and Tombs: The Regional Center

Midhowe chambered tomb lies on Rousay island of Orkney with three other relatively well-preserved chambered cairns, which makes the tomb one of the finest in the region. Experts suggest that this OC group tomb was built about 3500 B.C. The 23m-long tomb consists of twelve compartments/stalls divided by pairs of slabs. Some compartments are fitted with 2.5m-high stone shelves. Conical devices were once placed between the pairs of upright slabs and projected megalights to activate the mechanism (diagram 7.47).

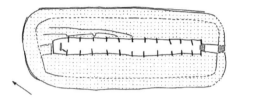

Plan of Midhowe
(Henshall 1963)
Diagram 7.47

The following pairs of ancient sites of Orkney form an SA with Midhowe in the middle:

SA1 Knap of Howar–Birsay standing stone and Crantit Chambered Cairn
SA2 Holm of Papa Westray Chambered Cairns–Wideford Hill Chambered Cairn
SA3 Vinquoy Hill Chambered Cairn–Ring of Brodgar
SA4 Stone of Settler–Ring of Bookan
SA5 Birsay standing stone–Traversoe Tuick Chambered Cairn
SA6 Knowe of Yarso Chambered Cairn–Birsay standing stone
SA7 Holm of Papa Westray Chambered Cairn–Broch of Gurness, an ancient village of six houses and a broch tower, encircled by a triple rampart and Wideford Hill Chambered Cairn

According to experts, there are about sixty Orkney-Cromarty Groups of chambered cairns in the region. Apart from Midhowe, I will show how other OC group tombs are aligned to the SA (diagram 7.48).

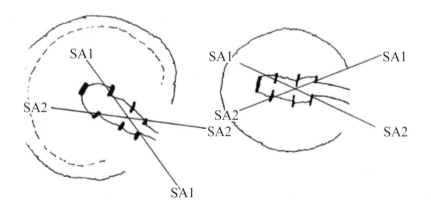

Bigland Round (*left*) and Kierfea Hill (after Davidson)
Diagrams 7.48 and 7.49

Neolithic Powerhouse

Experts estimate there are more than eighty chambered cairns in Orkney. Thus the Islands was one of the highest concentrations of passage graves in Europe. Most of these sophisticated tombs are constructed with standing slabs to form multi-stalls and herringbone pattern walls. Some of the tomb chambers, mainly the MH group, are surrounded by more-than-4m–high corbel walls, rising inward and upward in cone shape. Experts further estimate that most of these tombs required more than 10,000 man-hours to finish, and it is difficult to imagine a small community like Orkney, who settled in one of the most remote regions of Europe, with limited supply of natural resources and food and without the aid of any metal tools, completing the task.

It is my speculation that these chambered cairns were once used for producing and providing power for the builders, as they probably lie on the main junctions or nodes of underground Earth energy streams. By erecting huge standing slabs and constructing lintel doorways, both acting as dry cells of the power station, the builders tapped the mysterious energy that flows deep inside our earth. Conical devices were once placed inside these Neolithic buildings and they activated the energy mechanism. Orkney chambered cairns became gigantic power batteries. Colin Richards suggests that the parallel pairs of orthostats of the OC group of tombs were arranged as the doorway, which spiritually, separated the outside world from the sacred place of communication with the gods and ancestors of Another World. In some ways, these buildings, with their high corbel walls, were capable of communicating with the rest of the archipelago.

Besides, most of these chambered tombs were deliberately built and placed near the Neolithic settlements. For example, the Bigland Round (OC) cairn, 12m across, was set north of the prehistoric village of Rinyo. I believe that the chamber and entrance of Bigland forms an SA with Rinyo, and the tomb probably once provided power for the Rinyo inhabitants around 3000 B.C. Another example would be the Maes Howe powerhouse, which once supplied power to the Barnhouse settlement nearby.

Experts are puzzled by the fact that even though the extremely concentrated ceremonial landscape of Orkneys had taken more than 400 years to build, it was only used for a century. No clear evidence so far has been adduced to explain the reason. It seems that as soon as the complex was created, they abandoned it.

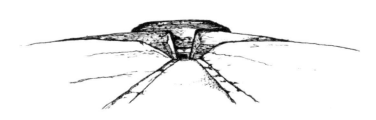

The Powerhouse of Quoyness
Diagram 7.50

Rock Art of Orkney: The Builders' Messages

A. Pierowell Stone

The diagram below shows the famous carved Pierowell Stone, which was excavated from the remains of a Neolithic chambered cairn (MH Group) in Pierowell, Westray—the island's largest settlement (*Lines on the Landscape, Circles from the Sky* by Trevor Garnham [2004], p. 133 diagram 75). The spiral and lozenge design of the stone (ORK72) is the finest of its kind in Scotland. It has been compared with decorated stones at Newgrange, dating back 5,000 years (orkneydigs. org.uk). These mysterious spirals, like all the others around northern and western Europe, are aligned to the SA (diagrams 7.51 and 7.52). Garnham also provides another example of rock art (p. 133), found in the Eday Manse chambered cairn, and its spirals are also aligned to the SA.

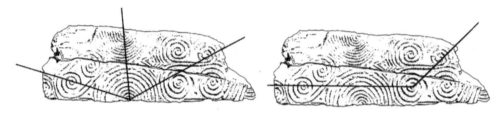

The Pierowell Stone (after Garnham)
Diagram 7.51

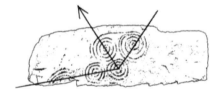

Rock Art in Orkney
(after Garnham)
Diagram 7.52

B. Runes in Orkney

Runes are scratched or engraved symbols, the word meaning "magic signs (Old Norse), formed by modifying Roman or Greek characters to suit carving"—*Concise Oxford Dictionary* (diagram 7.53). Experts believe that the writing was in existence as early as in A.D. 200 and was widely used by Vikings all over Scandinavina, Scottish Ireland, and Ireland for communication or magical practice. Runic inscriptions are commonly found in the chambered cairns of Maes Howe and Unstan, as well as on the surfaces of two stones of the Ring of Brodgar. The angular, straight lines of ancient Runic constitute an angle of 135 degrees. Did they serve the same informative or recording function as those spirals and concentric circles carved on rocks?

Runes in Orkney (orkneyjar.com)
Diagram 7.53

C. Zigzags on Natural Rocks

Archaeologists have always wondered why so many rocks on shorelines across Orkney are decorated with familiar theme patterns, i.e., zigzags, triangles, and lozenges. The drawing at right, which is based on a picture from the wonderful website www.orkneyjar.com, shows the zigzag patterns on the natural rock at Skibigeo, Birsay. These patterns are formed by interceptions of straight lines from different directions and they all probably form an SA. Like the "runes" inside Maes Howe, they are the messages from the builders of an advanced civilization.

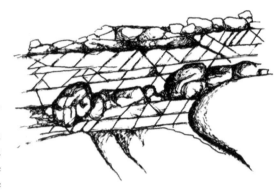

Natural Rock Patterns at Skibigeo, Birsay
Diagram 7.54

Orkney of Scotland and Wiltshire of Britain

It is surprising indeed to learn that a Bronze Age barrow cemetery—Knowes of Trotty, Harray with burial findings of gold discs and amber—has close relationships with those of Wessex, Britain. Both the Orkney and Wiltshire were constructed in roughly the same era, around 3000 B.C. Both contained "Grooved Ware" pottery. The Scottish cemetery consists of sixteen to twenty mounds arranged in two rows along the foot of the western slope in Ward of Redland. In 1858, a local antiquarian uncovered four beautifully crafted gold discs and a selection of amber beads and pendants. Even though the cemetery is heavily damaged by "rabbits and cattles," the alignments of the mounds to the SA are still clearly shown in the following topographic survey conducted by archaeologist Nick Card and a team from the University of Manchester in 2001. The Knowes cemetery is another example of the "Wessex-type" power station—round barrows arranged in SAs.

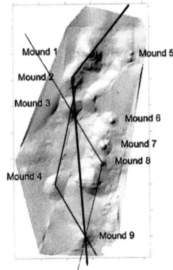

Round Barrows of Orkney and the SA
(after Card 2001)
Diagram 7.55

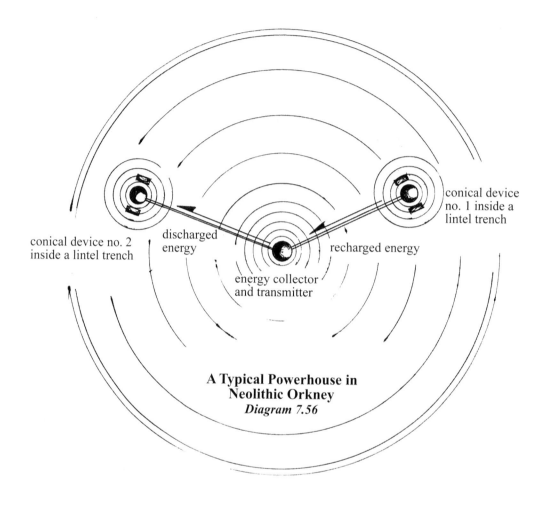

conical device no. 1 inside a lintel trench

conical device no. 2 inside a lintel trench

discharged energy

recharged energy

energy collector and transmitter

**A Typical Powerhouse in
Neolithic Orkney**
Diagram 7.56

Grooved Ware People and the "Cuneiform Inscriptions"

Experts always suggest that most of the megalithic monuments around the world were constructed by the grooved ware people as they were defined by the style of ceramic artifacts, i.e., flat-bottomed pottery with a large number of grooves and lozenge patterns—straight lines sloping outwards—on its surfaces. Archaeologists have always been puzzled by the sudden rise and demise of this culture. Their relics, such as sophisticated monuments and artifacts, are evidence that they were once an advanced civilization that outdid their contemporaries in 3000 B.C. Experts, however, are puzzled by the fact that such an advanced civilization left no writings or any system of inscriptions. How could they communicate with each other or pass on their knowledge to the next generation given that the average longevity of the Neolithic people was around twenty-five to thirty years? In addition, experts have found no evidence of permanent domestic buildings, even though the culture had demonstrated a high degree of architectural and engineering abilities in constructing their ceremonial monuments (Eogan 1986). As Zecharia Sitchin concludes (1993) these "Neolithic people just provided the labor or manpower to construct a complex stone mechanism designed and devised by outsiders with advanced scientific knowledge."

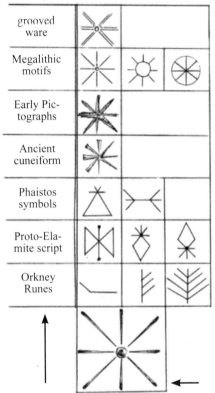

grooved ware			
Megalithic motifs			
Early Pictographs			
Ancient cuneiform			
Phaistos symbols			
Proto-Elamite script			
Orkney Runes			

Various Early Scripts with Their Alignments to SA
Diagram 7.57
(info: J.M. Roberts 2004)

Conical Device Projecting Megalights
Diagram 7.58

Many grooved wares, which have orange brown external surfaces and dark gray internal surfaces and fabrics, were formed by clay with quartz grains, carefully selected for special purposes. The spirals and zigzag patterns on their surfaces might reflect their real function. Some were decorated with solar symbols—a central circle with radiant lines found inside or close to the henge sites suggesting they were used for astronomical purposes as some kind of "ceremonial cult objects." These megalithic symbols became the future "cuneiform writings," a type of logogram script, probably the earliest form of writing where these cuneiform characters were originally simplified drawings (pictograms). Later, they became completely abstract, based on a combination of horizontal, vertical, and diagonal wedges or simply daggerlike patterns (*Ancient History: From the First Civilizations to the Renaissance* by J. M. Roberts, [2004], p. 82). Finally, they evolved and became the first real writing of our civilization.

Diagram 7.57 shows the ancient pictographic symbol of the "star, divinity, and the sky" and actually various sets of SA. To me, the so-called "divine symbol," which was an icon of prehistoric drawing, is clearly a description of the builders' energy mechanism—conical device projecting rows of megalights, represented by the straight and daggerlike lines of the inscriptions, to its surrounding stones for power (diagram 7.58). Therefore, the star or solar symbol, similar to the Goddess motifs of the Mycaene, was a drawing of the magic power of their ancient god.

Interestingly, the oldest cuneiform inscriptions are believed to have originated with the Sumerians, another Middle Eastern culture. They were written on wet clay tablets, on which symbols were drawn with a blunt reed called a stylus. The fresh clay then hardened and a permanent record was created (Richard Hooker). The impressions left by the stylus were wedge shaped, giving rise to the name cuneiform (diagram 7.59a). There are no accurate and reliable records to show their origin. It seems that suddenly, circa 3100 B.C., they were blessed people, developing agriculture, metallurgy, animal breeding, astronomy, and importantly, writing. Many of their texts and tablets mentioned that their knowledge was inherited from their gods who came from heaven and the stars. These gods traveled in superb vehicles and possessed terrible weapons.

Similar stories about an ancient "supernaturals" are found in the Mesoamerican culture such as the Maya, Inca, and Aztec. Is there any possibility that the advanced megalithic builders were actually the gods or wise men of the Sumerians. They probably witnessed their gods traveling in their amazing flying machines. In ancient Chinese, a powerful creature roaring and flying in the sky was described as "the dragon" whereas the ancient Maya called it the "plumed serpent." These traveling machines, probably equipped with jet engines, were capable of projecting daggerlike megalights to the monoliths, earthen barrows, and even the chambered cairns for power. Our Stone Age ancestors, who personally saw the power of these mysterious megalights, were only clever enough to carve their impressions of the builders' magic in form of daggerlike lines on the slab surfaces to record that special occasion, hoping that some day they could repeat the builders' magic themselves. Coincidentally, these megalithic monuments became the first recordings of our civilization.

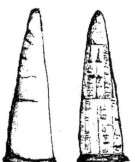

Replicas of the Power-generating Devices
Mysterious conical mud objects with cuneiform inscriptions were "erected" inside many Mesopotamian palaces and temples (source: Bottero and Steve 1993) *Diagrams 7.59a and b*

Cuneiform Inscriptions (after Bottero and Steve)
Diagram 7.59c

megalight —————
conical device —————

Elamite Inscription, One of the Oldest Writings, Originally Described the Builders' Conical Devices and the Megalights They Generated
(info: "Davidian, Mande and Elamite" by Clyde Winters in geocities.com)
Diagram 7.59d

Camster Long Cairn

The huge chambered cairn, an Orkney-Cromarty type in Highlands, is more than 60m long and over 2m high. It is one of the three cairns known as the Grey Cairns of Camster. Experts suggest that the monument was originally a cairn with two adjacent chambers. The space between the chambers was later filled with stones and the site was turned into a single long cairn. Then the builders further extended the southern portion with a horned forecourt. A narrow passage leads to two large chambers. The southern chamber is split into rectangular recesses ("antechambers") by internal megaliths. The larger northern chamber is a single polygon recess formed by large slabs at its back and its sides (diagram 7.60). These large slabs were deliberately placed inside the cairn to form an SA for power generation.

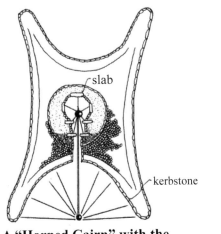

**A "Horned Cairn" with the
Installation of the Twin-device**
Diagram 7.60

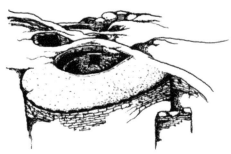

Neolithic Jarlshof, Shetland
Diagram 7.61

Shetland Islands and the SA

The Shetland Islands, Scotland lies at the most northerly part of the British Isle. It comprises over 100 islands with a land area of 1,500 sq km. The Islands have been continuously inhabited for at least 5,500 years as numerous Neolithic and Bronze Age settlements are found all around the region. The most famous site is the Neolithic round house of Jarlshof, located at the southern tip of the island. Like the settlement of Skara Brae in Orkney, the layout of the clustered Jarlshof is aligned to the SA (diagram 7.62).

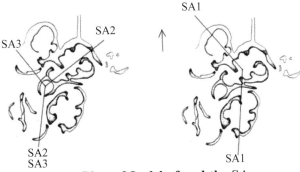

Plan of Jarlshof and the SA
Diagram 7.62

Staneydale and the Twin-device

Staneydale is probably the most mysterious site of Shetland. It lies 5km to the east of Walls, on the west mainland of Shetland. The monument is like a double-sized prehistoric house 4,500 years old. This unique Neolithic building is regarded as a temple but nobody has any idea what it actually was. What we do know is that the site is a large horseshoe-shaped building measuring 12m × 9m with a single entrance passage from the south leading to an oval hall. The diagram below shows that a set of upright stones curves round the southern entrance of the building, forming a façade like that of the heel-shaped cairns (diagram 7.63). Inside this well-preserved house is a main oval chamber from which a small circular compartment runs off at the inner end. Six alcoves separated by stone piers, or orthostats, are in the wall. Interestingly there are two stone-lined sockets at the center serving unknown purposes. The building might have once been a Neolithic hall, the house of a chieftain, a building for rituals, or a community meeting place (from "In Care of Historic Scotland").

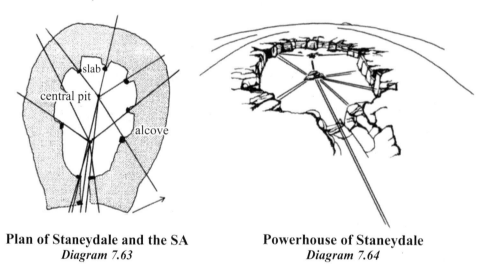

Plan of Staneydale and the SA
Diagram 7.63

Powerhouse of Staneydale
Diagram 7.64

With reference to the general layout of the temple of Staneydale, I am of the opinion that it primarily functioned as a powerhouse. The two empty sockets were once used to house the two mysterious conical devices, twin-devices no. 1 and 2, like those inside the Tarxien temples, and projected megalights to the surrounding standing stone piers—the builders' dry cells. Diagrams 7.63 and 7.64 illustrate how the two devices form various sets of SAs with the stone piers of the temple for power.

In addition, another famous Neolithic and Bronze Age settlement is Scord of Brouster. It is the remains of some oval houses, each of which measures 5m × 7m, constructed with massive orthostats with a hearth in the center. The most striking finding of the site is the discovery of lithic artifacts—nearly 10,000 pieces of struck quartz by Alasdair Whittle in the late 1970s ("Scottish Archaeological Internet Report: Re-examination of the Quartz Artifacts from Scord of Brouster: A Lithic Assemblage from Shetland and Its Neolithic Context" by Torben Bjarke Ballin). The excavation of these mysterious quartz artifacts recalls the white quartz wall of Newgrange as well as the quartz-rich sarsens and bluestones of Stonehenge. Huge prisms of quartz are also found inside the tholos of Spain. These pieces of struck quartz might reveal the real function of the structures (diagrams 7.65 and 7.66).

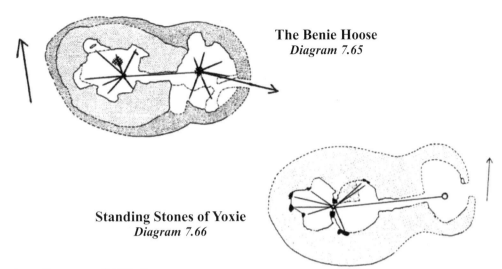

The Benie Hoose
Diagram 7.65

Standing Stones of Yoxie
Diagram 7.66

Anglesey of Wales

Anglesey is the largest island, 276 sq miles, in Wales as well as England, with a population of 71,000. It has a greater concentration of prehistoric sites than anywhere else in Wales. The name Anglesey is of Viking origin, taken from the personal name Ongull, and *ey* meaning "island." There are superb Neolithic burial chambers such as the famous passage graves of Bryn Celli Ddu and Barclodiad y Gawres, and prehistoric villages of the Holyhead Mountain, in South Stack, which is west of the island.

Bryn Celli Ddu Passage Grave of Anglesey

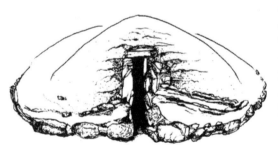

Mound of Bryn Celli Ddu
Diagram 7.67

The grave, known as "the Mound in a Dark Grove," is the best passage grave in Wales. The site was an important ritual center during the Neolithic and Bronze Age periods. It is generally agreed that the site had seen at least two phases of construction. The first phase of the site, around 3000 B.C., consists of a circle of fourteen large standing stones within a henge with an entrance to the east. The henge is 17m in diameter with a bank outside and a 2m deep flat-bottomed ditch inside. Two arcs of standing stones were erected at two sides of the east end to form a façade-like structure (diagram 7.67). Quartz stones of the chamber are arranged so that lines through opposing pairs all intersect at the same point in the center of the henge. The chamber was then covered by two capstones.

**White Stone and Its Location at the Site:
Probably a Replica of the Builders' Device**
Diagram 7.68

There was a 1m diameter and 1.5m deep pit dug at the center of the stone circle before it was turned into a cairn. It was then covered with a flat stone and a large stone that is 2.4m wide with a tall, rounded huge and cylindrical pillar carved with decorations. The carved standing stone was decorated on both sides with long sinuous lines, spiral, and zigzag patterns (diagram 7.69). The cylindrical stone is actually a megalithic replica of the powerful conical device as the grooves on the pillar's surface represented layers of horizontal zones/rings of the super conical device that could produce megalights 5,000 years ago. It probably marks the exact location of the device.

In the later period, around the Bronze Age, a passage grave, which is high and polygonal in shape, was built inside the ditch with a narrow northeast passage, 8.2m long and 0.9m wide, and the mound is further retained by kerbstones. The outer passage, 5m long, was roofed and led to an elaborate forecourt formed by dry-stone walling. The whole passage and the internal grave were then covered by a cairn. The passage and entrance to the tomb was sealed with blocks of stone and rubble in the later period. Besides, there is a row of quartz boulders found on the edge of the blocking earth in

**Inner Pillar of
Bryn Celli Ddu**
Diagram 7.69

the inner passage where another small platform of white quartz pebbles with remains of a hearth had been laid on the forecourt area at the entrance to the outer passage. It was a special setting with selected minerals for generating power.

Near the back of the chamber is a famous standing slab—the White Stone, now re-erected at the entrance of the passage, decorated with a spiraling snakelike motif (diagram 7.68). It might also bear the builders' messages. Experts suggest that the stone was once inside a bigger mound.

During the first phase, the layout of the horseshoe standing stones inside the mound was designed to align to the SA with a ritual pit in the center. Conical device no. 1 is located where the cylindrical standing stone suggested. Another conical device no. 2 was once placed at the main entrance of the grave where the White Stone is located to form a typical twin-device mechanism (diagram 7.70). It is a replica of the great mound of Knowth where conical devices were once placed at the eastern and western entrances.

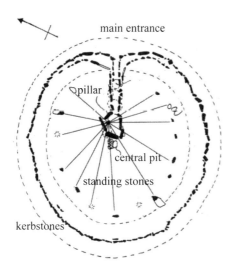

main entrance

pillar

central pit

standing stones

kerbstones

During the early Bronze Age, the builders changed their design by replacing the ritual pit with a burial chamber as the center of the monument. The burial mound of the later period is also horseshoe in shape with its eastern end deliberately truncated to form a façade, same as the great mound of Newgrange of Ireland. The design of Bryn Celli Ddu at the later period is more or less the same as that of the first period.

◄——— SAs in Bryn Celli Ddu
Diagram 7.70

Barclodiad y Gawres Passage Grave

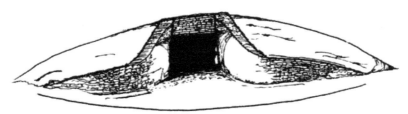

Barclodiad y Gawres Chambered Cairn/Passage Grave
Diagram 7.71

The passage grave lies about 15km west of Bryn Celli Ddu. The grave is the largest of the chambered tombs of Wales with a diameter of 27m (diagram 7.71). The name of the mound is translated as "Giantesses' Apronful" as the legend goes that the grave was created by two giants around 3000 B.C. Like the great mound of Newgrange and Fourknocks, the grave is famous for its carved slabs. On one of the decorated slabs (stone 8) (diagram 7.72), there are at least six large spirals carved on the surface. And three of them are aligned to the SA.

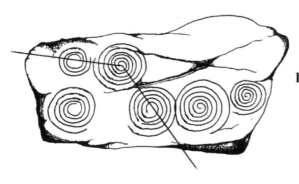

**Decorated Slabs (Stone 8) of
Barclodiad y Gawres**
Diagram 7.72

SAs of Anglesey

The following diagram shows the locations of various Neolithic burial chambers of Anglesey. They form various sets of SAs:

SA1 standing stone at Penryn Mawr–standing stone at Pen-llyn–Bry Celli Ddu burial chamber

SA2 hut circles at South Stack–Presaddfed burial chamber–Bodowyr burial chamber

SA3 hut circles at South Stack–Trefignath burial chamber–Barclodiad y Gawres chambered cairn

SA4 Trefignath burial chamber–Bodowyr burial chamber–Plas Newydd burial chamber

SA5 Din Dryfol burial chamber–Bodowyr burial chamber–Plas Newydd burial chamber

SA6 Ty Newydd burial chamber–Bodowyr burial chamber–Bryn Celli Ddu burial chamber

SA7 Barclodiad y Gawres chambered cairn–Neolithic settlement of Castell Bryn-gwyn–Bryn Celli Ddu burial chamber

SA8 Lligwy burial chamber–Benllech chambered tomb–2.5m high standing stone at Llanddyfnan

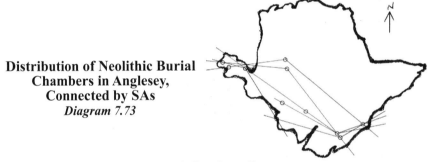

Distribution of Neolithic Burial Chambers in Anglesey, Connected by SAs
Diagram 7.73

Anglesey, British Isles, and Ireland

Geographically, the island of Anglesey is located at the heart of Britain as it is enclosed by the Irish Sea where its southeast coast is separated from the mainland by the Menoi Strait. Then, the island and its inner sea are further embraced by the island of British Isles at its north, east, and south, and Ireland at its west. Various sets of SA are formed by different Neolithic sites around the region, with the island of Anglesey in the middle:

SA1 Carrowmore Neolithic Complex and the Boyne Valley–Yorkshire Region, the angle bisects at Cairnholy, Croft Morgies Stone Circle and Kilmartin Valley Neoithic Complex

SA2 Northern Ireland Region–Arbor Low Complex

SA3 Orkney Islands Neolithic Complex–Avebury of Wessex Region, the angle bisects at Yorkshire Region

SA4 Eastern Scotland Region–Stanton Drew Stone Circle, the angle bisects at Arbor Low

SA5 Grange Complex–Long Meg and Castlerigg Stone Circles, the angle bisects at Ballnahatty Stone Circle

SA6 Grange Complex–Rollright Stone Circle, the angle bisects at Cornwall Neolithic Complex

SA7 Ballnahatty Stone Circle–Cornwall Neolithic Complex, the angle bisects at Lough Gur and Grange Complex

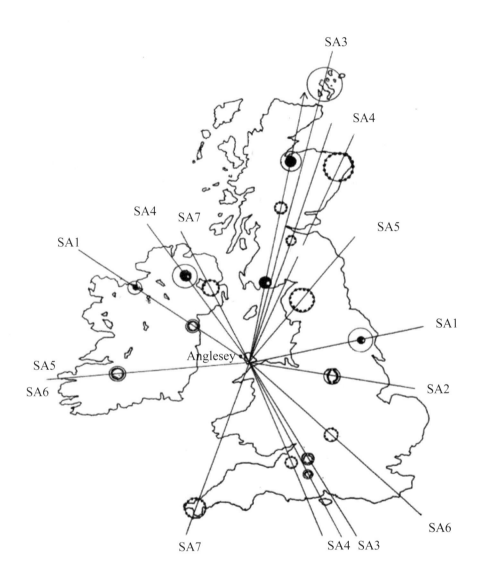

Anglesey as Center of British Isles
Diagram 7.74

Chapter 8
Chalcolithic Spain and Egypt

Iberian Spain and the Chalcolithic Culture

Spain's long prehistory ranges from *Homo erectus* one million years ago to the Neanderthals 30,000 years ago. Archaeological evidence suggests little skill development in this long period of evolution. However, a new species—the Modern man—arrived about 35,000 years ago and soon overrode the others with its fine flint weapons. The grand scale of cave paintings also suggests that Stone Age beings also manipulated comparatively advanced artistic techniques.

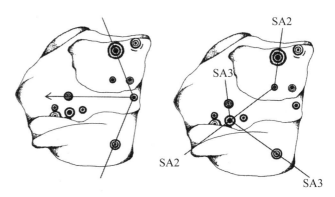

**Teberne Petroglyph of Neolithic Spain
(Rock Carving)**
Diagram 8.01

The Chalcolithic culture or Copper Age of Spain refers to a civilization that flourished from 3500 B.C. to 3000 B.C. Dating back to this period there is evidence of organized societies such as the location of cemeteries outside of settlements and craft specialization in copper tool production. The word "Chalcolithic" is from the Greek for copper (*chalcos*) and stone (*lithos*) (K. Kris Hirst).

El Pozuelo of Spain was one of the centers of the Chalcolithic Culture, as reflected by its complex funerary chambers. The necropolis contains eighteen Neolithic monuments with multiple interior spaces. Usually, the dolmens have a single entrance to two passages, which in turn lead to multiple chambers ("The Megalithic Phenomenon in Andalusia (Spain). An Overview," by Pedro Aguayo de Hoyos and Leonardo Garcia Sanjuan in *Origin and Development of the Megalithic Phenomenon of Western Europe,* ed. Joussaume et al. [2006]). Such a layout of the tombs is aligned to the SA (diagrams 8.02a, b, and c).

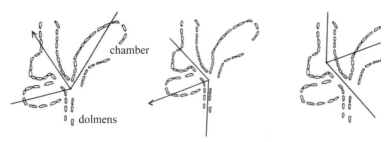

Funeral Chambers of El Pozuelo of Spain
(Source: de Hoyos and Sanjuan)
Diagram 8.02a, b, and c

At Alcaide other kinds of funerary constructions were developed—the so-called "artificial caves," which are tombs excavated in the bedrock with multiple chambers (diagram 8.03) (Hoyos and Sanjuan). Again, these caves are aligned to the SA.

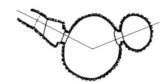

Artificial Caves with Multiple Chambers Aligned to SA
(after Hoyos and Sanjuan)
Diagram 8.03

Beehive-shaped and corbel-roofed graves are known as *tholoi.* The following diagram shows the layout of two intact tholo-type tombs (no. 1 and 3) in La Pijotilla dug into the chalky soil with entrance portals. The plans of these two tholoi are aligned to the SA (diagram 8.04).

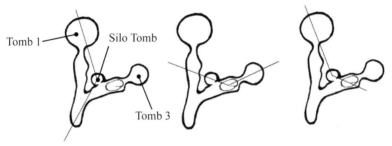

Tholo-type Tombs in La Pijotilla
(after Hurtado 1991) *Diagram 8.04a, b, and c*

Los Millares and the SA

The archaeological site of Los Millares, 17km outside Almeria in the Spanish province of Andalucia, is an example of Chalcolithic culture in around 3025 B.C. It is important to the understanding of the transition from the Neolithic to the Bronze Age as the inhabitants of Los Millares learnt metal work in this particular time. The site is situated on an arid rocky hilltop next to a copper mine. It consists of a settlement which was guarded by numerous outlying forts with sophisticated system of walls and towers of unmortered stones. A great nation probably emerged in this high fort 5,000 years ago. A large cemetery with 100 tholoi were constructed within the successive enclosures, thick walls, and semicircular towers lying northeast of the three Neolithic forts (diagram 8.05).

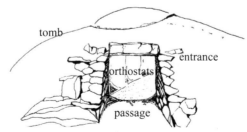

A Reconstructed Tholos at Los Millares
(Source: *Tombs, Temples and Their Orientation* by Michael Hoskin)
Diagram 8.05

These tholoi—chamber dolmens with corbelled covering—are connected with tumuli that were divided by large flat slabs with holes in them. The general structures of these tholoi resemble those of the passage graves of Brittany, in which the orthostats of their chambers were once used as dry cell batteries to tap Earth energy underneath (diagram 8.06).

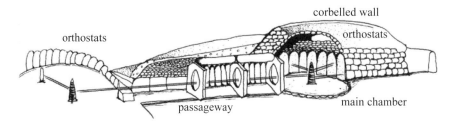

Reconstruction of Corbelled Passage-grave (Tholos) of Los Millares
Diagram 8.06

What attracts my attention is the distribution of the three guarding forts on the high ground, as they form a perfect SA. A similar setting is found in the contemporary Loughcrew cemetery of Ireland, where Cairns D, M, and T form an SA. The Angle, which probably indicates the direction of transmission, covers the northeast of the site, where most of the tholoi lie. Does it imply that the three forts acted as a supplier of power, probably in the form of microwaves, instead of safeguarding these tholoi (diagram 8.07)? The site was famous for its prehistoric copper quarry. Was it the reason why the builder selected and established their center there?

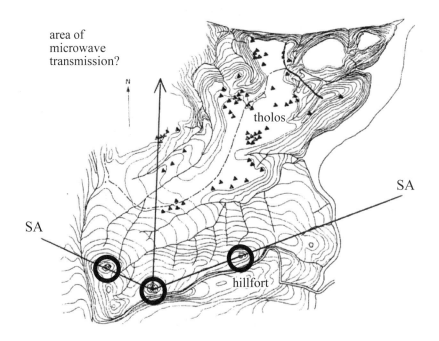

Three Hillforts in Los Millares Forming an SA
(diagram after M. Balfour)
Diagram 8.07

Like Neolithic Ireland and Britain, Iberian Spain was a metropolis of the builders in 3000 B.C. They were probably attracted by the local copper mines. Today, we know copper is a good conductor of electricity—our major source of power. It might also have been important for the Neolithic space travelers as well.

Oculus Motif Plaque: The Megalithic Polaroid

It was perhaps the travelers who informed us that an advanced civilization once visited Spain 5,000 years ago. Megalithic arts and carvings were their means of communication and the Chalcolithic culture was certainly one of them. *Oculus* is the name of a universal motif commonly found on small engraved plaques in Western Europe, mainly in Portugal and Spain. They represent some of the most intriguing prehistoric art. Archaeologists have excavated more than 2,000 engraved slate plaques with a uniform theme. Most of them are recovered from the collective burials, placed on the chest or alongside the body of the owners. Enormous numbers were produced, demonstrating the importance of the artifacts in the eyes of the local prehistoric people.

These plaques are made of slate or schist, trapezoidal, cylindrical, or rectangular in shape, 10–20cm in height and 10cm in width. The classic plaques have a bipartite compositional structure. The upper portion, the narrower one-third top of the plaque, is usually engraved with a triangular face with a pair of circular or spiral eyes, surrounded and radiated by horizontal or vertical stripes. Sometimes separating the top and the base are single horizontal bands decorated with cross-hatching or triangle designs (Katina Lillios). The lower portion of the plaque is made up of two to fourteen horizontal registers of repeating geometric motifs, such as triangles, chevrons, herringbones, zigzags, and checkerboards (diagram 8.08).

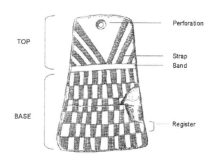

Anatomy of a Classic Iberian Plaque
(after Lillios) *Diagram 8.08*

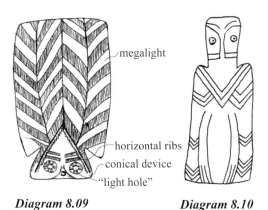

Diagram 8.09   *Diagram 8.10*

Deciphering the Oculus Motif
(info: J. P. Mohen and C. Eluere, *The Bronze Age in Europe: Gods, Heros and Treasures,* p. 38)

Some plaques, clearly with anthropomorphic features engraved (diagrams 8.09 and 8.10), are interpreted as the Mother Goddess who would safeguard the tomb owner in the Other World. But there are only a few of them that unquestionably depict anthropomorphic figures. Lisboa (1985) suggested that these plaques were "meaningful and being used to transmit messages." Experts suggest that the plaques have social and symbolic functions, as some kind of "ethnic identifiers" or heraldic emblems. Some speculate that they once served as symbols of family trees or a kind of textile design. One thing for sure is that they are overwhelmingly consistent and standardized in their basic form, structure, and style, indicating and hiding a very important but lost message.

I believe these intriguing plaques are telling what happened inside these tholoi 5,000 years ago, i.e., a lost energy mechanism was installed to tap energy for the builders. The oculus with an anthropomorphic figure should be received the other way up. In other words, the lower and smaller portion, which is engraved with a triangle, stands for the builders' conical device, in which the two eyes actually refer to the light holes of the device. The two unusually long arms of the Mother Goddess occupying the larger, upper portion of the plaque and decorated with zigzag patterns represent the two rows of light beams generated by the conical device (diagram 8.09).

Other slate plaques with simpler designs reflect a unique story—a conical device generating energy in the form of microwaves—represented by the layers of horizontal registers of the plaque (diagram 8.11). Our Stone Age ancestors certainly witnessed this miracle—the builders' magic. They were reward with the plaques after providing their labor in building the tholoi. To these prehistoric beings, these invaluable identifiers probably served as a ticket to the builders' unknown world. It explains why most of these plaques are generally found in association with undecorated pottery (replicas of the builders' conical devices) and flint blades (megalight?).

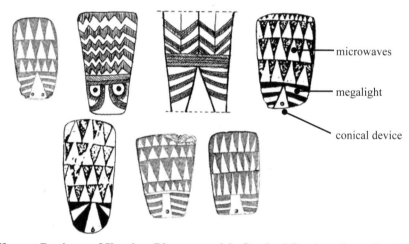

Different Designs of Iberian Plaques, with Conical Devices Inscribed
(info: Hermann Muller-Karpe, Mohen and Eluere 2000, p. 39) *Diagram 8.11*

According to Hoyos and Sanjuan, pieces of minerals such as quartz and rock crystal are commonly found inside these tombs. In the Dolmen de Alberite an exceptional prism, measuring 20 × 7cm, has been discovered (Dominguez-Bella and Morata 1996) (diagram 8.12). Its function probably paralleled the quartz-rich sarsens and bluestones of Stonehenge, quartz deposits in Loughcrew cairns, as well as the white quartz walls of Newgrange which I suggest were once used to magnify the energy.

Crystal Quartz Module from Alberite (Cádiz)
(after Dominguez-Bella and Morata 1996)
Diagram 8.12

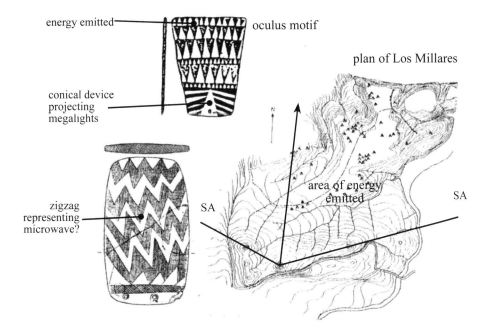

energy emitted

oculus motif

conical device projecting megalights

plan of Los Millares

zigzag representing microwave?

area of energy emitted

SA

SA

Is This What the Oculus Motif Implied?
Conical devices inside the forts on the high ground transmitted
energy or microwaves to the tholoi to the north.
Diagram 8.13

Rock Carving of a Monolith of Spain
Diagram 8.14

The World of Atlantis

In around 355 B.C., the great Greek philosopher Plato (428–348 B.C.) described the existence of a great empire—the Kingdom of Atlantis—with precise architectural and engineering detail in his dialogues *Timaeus* and *Critias*. It is a lost civilization that was fully developed 12,000 years ago in a place rich in precious metals and "stones" (diagram 8.15).

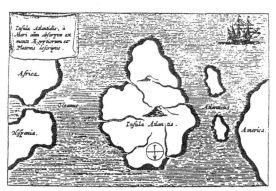

The Island of Atlantis
Diagram 8.15

Plato mentions that this legendary empire is given to the "god of the sea and earthquakes," Poseidon, who then divides the island into ten regions for his descendants. Does it explain why the builders' powerhouses have their unique regional characteristics? For instance, passage tombs are concentrated in eastern Ireland and Brittany of France, whereas court tombs are mostly found in the northern extreme of the island. Besides, stone circles with recumbent are mainly found in northeast Scotland, while rectangular tombs with dry-stone corbelled walls are constructed on the Orkney Islands, the extreme north of Scotland.

Plato further elaborates that the island of Atlantis was fortified with concentric rings—two on land and three in waterways. Are they the island of Anglesey and the "united" continent of the British Isles and Ireland with the Irish Sea in the center, the Celtic Sea in the south of Anglesey, and the North Sea together with the famous English Channel in the south? In his dialogue, the magnificent mountains of the north provide shelter from the strong winds. Is it a description of the Scottish Highlands, which helps to block the cold air currents from the North Pole?

The Atlanteans built their royal palace on a central highland where the great temple of Poseidon was found. According to Plato, the temple was surrounded by a golden wall. Does he refer to the shiny white quartz wall of Newgrange or the dressed surfaces of the sarsen circle of Stonehenge? There are gold pinnacles found inside the temple. Are they the builders' golden conical devices? Inside the temple stands a golden statue of the god in his chariot driving six winged horses. Are the Neolithic builders dressed in metallic spacesuits driving his flying machine for recharging inside the powerhouse? Do their jet bikes look like horses?

In the city, there are both hot and cold springs for the kings, like the Neolithic artificial ponds found in the Boyne Valley and around the Navan Fort. Temples and gardens are built on the two rings on land. Are they the megalithic passage tombs and stone circles around the region? Plato even mentions a racecourse. Could it be formed by the earthen cursus in southern Britain? Were the Egyptian priests who told this true story to the Athenian Solon 200 years before Plato describing what had happened in Neolithic Europe? The only difference is the wording in the descriptions.

Recently, a Swedish geologist claimed that Ireland is the lost island of Atlantis. He compares more than hundreds of possible islands in the world and comes to the conclusion that only the size of Ireland perfectly matches the one Plato describes. Some experts point out the Pillars of Hercules, the main "gateway" to Atlantis and generally known as the Straits of Gibraltar, actually refers to the English Channel. In 1665, the Jesuit scholar Athanasius Kircher published a map of Atlantis that was based on another map stolen from ancient Egypt. It describes an oval-shaped island with rivers (of Paradise) running and radiating from its center. A high ground is drawn in the middle of the island.

Let us "combine" Ireland and the British Isles by taking away the Irish Sea (or by reducing its water level, as it was the case after the last Ice Age) to form a "united island of Britain-Ireland." Geographically speaking, this "united island" is surprisingly similar to the Kircher map in which a series of rivers run and radiate from the center of this "united island."

Furthermore, the submergence of the Irish Sea also allows the reunion of the megalithic sites on both side of the sea. The enclosures or stone circle monuments in the northwest of the British Isles, such as Castlerigg and Mayburgh, match those in the northeast of Ireland, such as Donegore and Ballnahatty. The burial monuments in Anglesey match those in the Boyne Region.

Plato points out that the final downfall of this civilization was due to flooding. Does he mean the formation of the Irish Sea? In *The Atlantis Researches* Paul Dunbavin shares the same view and argues that the level of the Irish Sea was lower 5,000 years ago and the submerged land around the British Isles can be made to fit the description of Plato's Atlantis. He further suggests that the capital city of Atlantis lies submerged in the Irish Sea between Wales, Scotland, and Ireland. Dunbavin describes this "united islands of Britain-Ireland" as a "super-Britain."

"As to describing the manner of construction of the stone, we find it was a large cylindrical glass, as it would be termed today, cut with facets in such a manner that the capstone on the top of same made for the centralizing of the power or force that concentrated between the end of the cylinder and the capstone itself," Edgar Cayce describes the secret and power source of the Atlanteans. The "Sleeping Prophet's" readings of Atlantis have caused great inspiration among his fans.

What further amazes me is Edgar Cayce's description of Atlantis. He states that the Atlanteans were the first developed civilization that "understood the Creative Force" (the Ley lines or Earth energy?). This material civilization could rise to great height (far more advanced than we are today as mentioned by Cayce), with electromagnetic-powered flying machines (flying vehicles powered by vibrations from stones, as described by Cayce), lasers (in the form of rays invisible to the eye, as mentioned by Cayce), and power crystals. They used electricity on well-developed television and radio, amplification of light rays for telescopes, and more advanced systems for heating and lighting. They could even control "various rays."

But the most shocking, at least for me, is the use of the Creative Force by the Atlanteans, or what Cayce describes as the electrical forces made in nature, from the rays of sun caught and reflected by crystals. According to Cayce, there was a mysterious six-sided stone, which is sometimes referred to as the "Tuaoi stone," used for communication with the divine. The priests received and interpreted the "crystalized speech" which Cayce refers to as the "saint realm." In Cayce's words, "the utilization of crystal as a communication device" (such as the white quartz wall of Newgrange or the quartz-rich bluestones and sarsens of Stonehenge) can also be interpreted as evidence showing that the Atlanteans could project beams of light into the air. (*The A.R.E., Search for Atlantis* by Gregory L. Little and Lora H. Little). Is it an apt description of the energy mechanism of the builders?

Furthermore, he mentions an Atlantean substance called firestone which could cause radiation "in the form of rays that were invisible to the eye but act upon the stones themselves." The special power allowed "the aircraft to lift and to guide the more-of-pleasure vehicles to pass along close to the earth." These vehicles "were impelled by the concentration of rays from the stone which was centered in the middle of the power station" (Cayce 1933). And it is also the main theme of my book: an advanced intelligence once came to tap our Earth energy through building megalithic monuments.

Sumerian Cylindrical Seals and the Light Beam– Propelled Vehicle

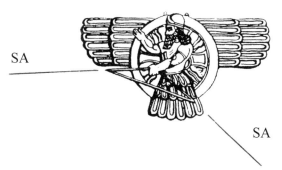

SA

SA

Anshar, a Deity of Babylon, Standing in Front of a Solar Disk and Holding a Hanger-like Object with an Angle of 135°
Diagram 8.16

Who exactly were the megalithic builders that built all kinds of powerhouses with exceptional skills, distinctive purposes, and endless efforts? What kind of sophisticated vehicles were they that "were impelled by the concentration of rays from the stone" as mentioned by Cayce? The following prehistoric relics may provide a possible answer.

The Sumerian of Mesopotamia is regarded as the first civilization that flourished, in around 3000 B.C. Experts still know little about the rise of the culture. They invented the first writing, known as cuneiform characters, for recording by pressing the stylus onto the wet clay at various angles. They also used pictures called "Mesopotamian hieroglyphs" to create scenes depicting anything from financial transactions to divine stories. The negative images of pictures were first carved onto a small cylinder seal made of hard stone. When the carved cylinder was rolled upon the clay, the positive image would be created. Experts find thousands of these clay tablets that can date back to the fourth millennium B.C.

One of the common and important subjects carved and recorded on the Sumerian seal is generally known as the Tree of Life (lower drawings of diagram 8.18). The Tree appears in many different forms, but its structure and design is basically the same. Its main body is a cylindrical tube with a pointed top. The body is subdivided into several segments, sometimes decorated with zigzags or lozenge patterns. Lines of different forms, in the shape of a fan, radiate from the pointed top of the cylindrical tube. The whole device is then webbed by horizontal and diagonal "branches," or criss-crossing lines, to form a conical shape crust. The whole conical crust is further surrounded by daggerlike or leaflike objects, from top to bottom. In ancient beliefs, the symbol is important in nearly every culture. With its branches reaching into the sky, and roots deep in the earth, it dwells in three worlds—a link between heaven, the earth, and the underworld, uniting above and below. In ancient Sumer, god was personified as a tree (info: J. Emick of the Alternative Religions). The Tree is often attended to by Eagle-Headed Gods or Priests (from Wikipedia).

Usually, a flying deity known as the Winged Disk is carved and placed on top of a Sumerian Tree of Life. The disk is in the form of a solar ball with two outstretched wings. Elongated objects that look like landing gears or antennas are found under the ball, whereas anthropomorphic figures are found in the upper part of the disc. They are probably the ancient navigators of the traveling machine. The winged disc tends to be placed atop, or hovering above, a pillar or a Tree of Life (top right of diagram 8.18).

An Energy-generating Device, 3000 B.C. A Fan of Megalights Was Produced on the Top
Diagram 8.17

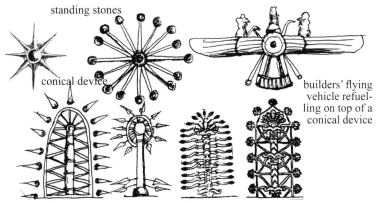

standing stones

conical device

builders' flying vehicle refuelling on top of a conical device

Sumerian "Tree of Life" Forms from Cylindrial Seals, ca. 3000 B.C: A Winged Disk Recharges on Top of an Activated Device (*right*); Two Solar Motifs (*top left*) Show the Secret of the Builders' Energy Mechanism
Diagram 8.18

From my perspective, the pictures of these delicate seals actually record the recharging scene of the builders' vehicle in great detail. Obviously, the Tree of Life is the builders' conical device that is capable for generating power (diagram 8.17). According to the energy mechanism, when the device is charged, energy in the form of microwaves would be projected from the top of the device where a builders' flying vehicle is found. Another solar motif is carved at the top left of the diagram, which throws light on the energy mechanism, i.e., a circle of megaliths are heated up by a conical device in the center.

Anu, Babylonian God of the Sky, with Horned Headdresses on Stylized Thrones (Detail of Babylonian Boundary Stone, 1120 B.C.).
The device objects are usually carved in pairs, revealing the twin-device energy mechanism of the builders. The solar disk of shamash, the sun god of Babylon, is deliberately placed on top of the conical device. Again, the solar motif is a true description of the builders' energy mechanism. A conical device on top of the mushroom altar of Hagar Qim, Malta is shown at right.
Diagram 8.19

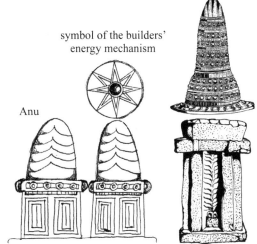

symbol of the builders' energy mechanism

Anu

Plasma physicist Anthony Peratt concludes that the ancient Sumerians witnessed the formation of a "heaven-reaching plasma discharging tube" which was precipitated by a large influx of charged particles from space and it was accurately recorded in the cylindrical seals (thunderbolts.info).

The rival successor of the Sumerians, the Hittites—a great empire with mysterious origins—stretched from Mesopotamia to Syria and Palestine and ended the Old Babylonian empire (1900–1600 B.C.). They spoke an undecipherable language and left few accounts of their history. Ancient scriptures have little to say about them but they were certainly one of the most significant peoples in Mesopotamian history (Hooker 1996). The royal emblem below shows similar themes as the one on Sumerian cylindrical seal. A flying winged disk spreads over the top of five conical objects. All of these energy generating devices are placed inside a basin. Mysterious and weird objects are emitted at their top (diagram 8.20).

energy emitted on top of a powerhouse

conical device under lintel doorway

Hittite Emblem: Seal of Mursil II, King of the Hittites, Ugarit's Overlords from 1400 B.C. (info: *Vanished Civilizations, Reader's Digest 2002*), Showing a Flying Object on Top of the Conical Devices
Diagram 8.20

A Sumerian Carving Showing a Conical Device Placed inside Building with Energy Produced on Top
Diagram 8.21

All these Babylonian seals and emblems are actually telling an extraordinary story, an advanced technology employed by a mysterious intelligence who took our planet as their power supply station in 3000 B.C. Their superb traveling machines, probably propelled by energy light-beams were once parked on top of the conical devices for power. Our prehistoric ancestors certainly witnessed this magical act of god and recorded it explicitly onto their cylindrical seals which indirectly led to the invention of our writings and the start of our civilization.

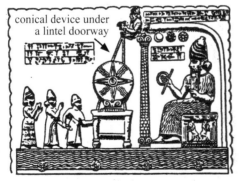

conical device under a lintel doorway

Carving on a Stone Stela from Abu Habba in Mesopotamia Showing a Conical Object Was Placed on Top of an Altar and Under a Roofed Building (the Eye-catching Solar Motif on Its Body Probably Reveals Its Real Function)
(after Sitchin) *Diagram 8.22*

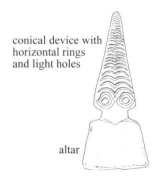

conical device with horizontal rings and light holes

altar

The Sumerian "Eye" Idol Implicating a Conical Device on Top of an Altar
(after Crawford 2004)
Diagram 8.22a

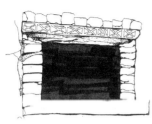

A. Roof Box, Newgrange

B. Cairn K, Carrowkeel

C. Cairn 51, Carrowmore

D. Lanyon Quoit, Cornwall

E. Kit's Coty House, Kent

F. Dolmen de Fonta- naccia, Corsica

G. Chun Quoit, Cornwall

H. Central Temple, Tarxien

I. Hypogeum, Malta

J. Giant's Tombs, Sardinia

K. Caeira 2-anta at Mora, Spain

L. Great Trilithon 53-54, Stonehenge

Builders' Dry Cell Batteries
Diagram 8.23

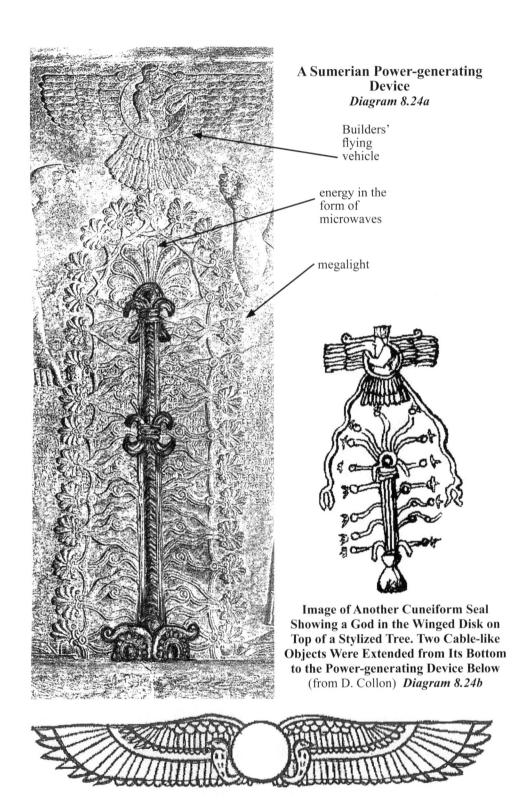

A Sumerian Power-generating Device
Diagram 8.24a

Builders' flying vehicle

energy in the form of microwaves

megalight

Image of Another Cuneiform Seal Showing a God in the Winged Disk on Top of a Stylized Tree. Two Cable-like Objects Were Extended from Its Bottom to the Power-generating Device Below
(from D. Collon) *Diagram 8.24b*

Similar Iconic Solar Disks with Paired Outstretched Wings Are Carved on Top of Many Ancient Egytian Temples. Two Mysterious "Coiling Uraeus-serpents" in Striking Position, Probably Functioning as Recharging Cables, Are Attached to Its Two Sides *Diagram 8.24c*

The Egyptian Stonehenge, 1500–1000 B.C.

builders' vehicle

microwave radiation

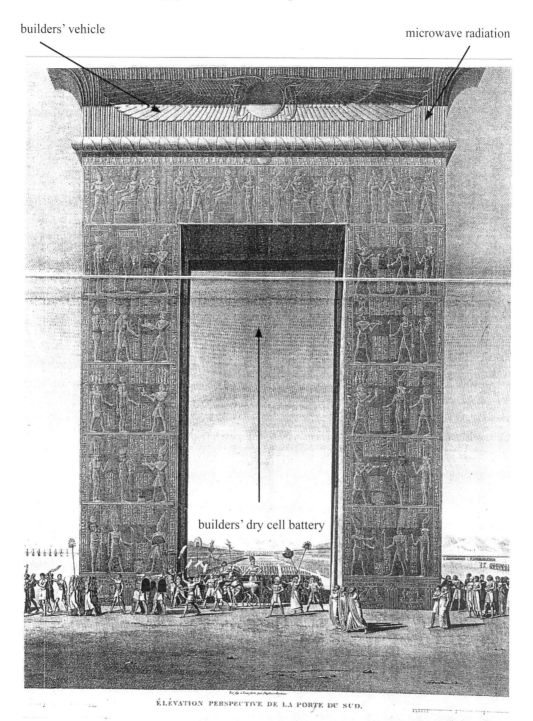

builders' dry cell battery

ÉLÉVATION PERSPECTIVE DE LA PORTE DU SUD.

The Great Propylon to the Temple of Dendera, Thebes
(info: *The Napoleonic Survey of Egypt,* ed. Terence M. Russell [2001])
Diagram 8.25

What Napoleon Bonaparte Told Us

Diagram 8.25: The propylon—"the Gate of the South" to the Temple at Dendera, Thebes, was drawn in a restored version by Napoleon Bonaparte's academics in 1798. The great propylon, together with the south gate at Karnak, built in the form of triumphal arches, were the main entrances to the sacred temples. They are remarkable for the beauty of their proportions and the richness of their decorations. As described in the Napoleonic Survey, the opening of the gateway is one quarter of the proportion of the total height of the construction. The height of the gateway, measuring 21m, is twice that of the opening. The width of the entire edifice is about twice the total height (explanatory texts of Vol. III, Plate 49, of the Napoleonic Survey).

The lintel is yellowish sandstone of very fine grain, decorated with divine sculptures. The most eye-catching ornament of the structure is the cornice, its concave curvature most elegantly proportioned and decorated at the top. A winged globe with fully outstretched wings, ornaments the middle of the cornice and is raised in profile from a channeled background (explanatory texts of Vol. VI, Plate 4). The ceiling of the gateway, under the lintel, is decorated with another winged globe (Vol. III, Plate 49).

The propylon ornamentation is a perfect depiction of the builders' powerhouse, probably revealing the great secret of the Egyptian civilization. As "told" by Napoleon, the great triumphal arch materialized the dry cell battery, which was designed and constructed in the form of lintel and portal. The magnificent cornice ornament symbolizes the energy being generated and emitted from the dry cell battery below. It is further evidenced by the winged globe in the middle—i.e., the builders' flying vehicle recharging on top of the powerhouse.

The Egyptian Powerhouses

"O Egypt, Egypt, nothing will remain of your beliefs but fables, which will seem incredible to future generations, and there will remain only the words on the stones to tell your pious actions!"

—Pseudo-Apuleius, Asclepius, XXIV in
R. A. Schwaller de Lubicz, *The Temple of Karnak*

"Egypt's temples and other monuments of her pharaonic past became as mysterious to the Egyptians themselves as they were to the outside world. Whether covered by drifting sands or standing in full view, Egypt's temples were lost and would have to wait to be rediscovered."

—Richard H. Wilkinson, *the Complete Temples of Ancient Egypt*

The portal-lintel doorway is certainly the best design to house the builders' power generating equipment. Located on top of an energy stream, capable of and designed to tap the power underneath, these megalithic infrastructures became the most advanced power plants ever built. Stonehenge III—a combination of two bluestone circles encircled by another two sarsen trilithons—was the most elaborate and probably the most powerful of its kind. The abandonment of this Salisbury "super ring" in around 1500 B.C. did not mark the end of the builders' adventure on Earth. Their advanced powerhouse reappeared and took the form of a more comprehensive and, particularly a more artistic form. From 1500–1000 B.C., a cluster of unprecedented monumental structures, which still carried the image and soul of Stonehenge, was built on the other side of the Mediterranean.

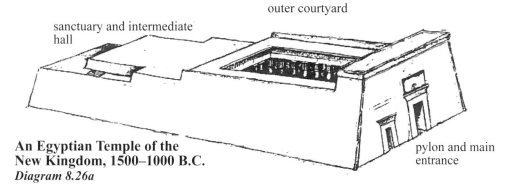

sanctuary and intermediate hall

outer courtyard

pylon and main entrance

An Egyptian Temple of the New Kingdom, 1500–1000 B.C.
Diagram 8.26a

The territory of ancient Egypt was regarded as "gods' land," or at least, a sacred place to display divine "power." Marked by years of wars and disturbances, ancient Egypt became a unified country ca. 3100 B.C. when everything started to change. Governed by a single pharaoh, writing was developed and huge pyramids built. A civilization, probably the first, appeared and flourished on lands repeatedly watered by flooding but gradually eroded by sand dunes. Today, over 95% of Egypt is covered by sand. If money and opulence attract people to the desert city of Las Vegas today, it must have been the acts and blessings of gods that drew the ancient Egyptians to their promised lands.

The modern day "Egyptology rush" was triggered off by Napoleon Bonaparte and his 165 savants and academics when they accompanied 50,000 soldiers in setting sail for Egypt in 1798, in a challenge to another superpower, Great Britain. Although it was a military failure, twenty volumes of the *Description de L'Egypte* were published, carefully describing and recording the noble monuments of ancient Egypt. Unlike modern-day tourists who come to Egypt for the pyramids, the Napoleonic army was first fascinated, then obsessed by its sacred temples as a large number of them were portrayed in great detail (diagram 8.26b). After that, an unstoppable wave of Egyptomania prevailed for more than two centuries. Egypt no longer solely belongs to the Egyptians.

Temple of Esne (from "Napoleonic Survey")
Diagram 8.26b

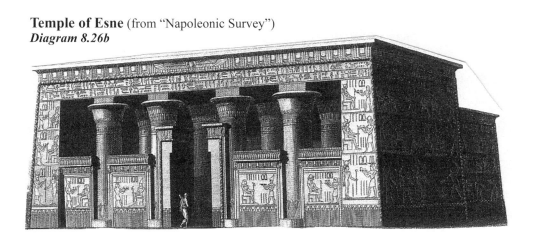

Gods' Mansions

There were hundreds of temples built throughout Egyptian history and most of them, with massive towers and gateways, colossal columns, and pillars decorated with magnificent carvings and inscriptions, dating back to the eighteenth to twentieth dynasties of the New Kingdom (circa 1550–1069 B.C.), still exist.

It was a period of unprecedented success in internal and international affairs, as well as of superb developments in artistic sculpture and architecture. Experts still wonder how all these artistic Egyptian temples, erected with the highest level of perfection, precision, and sophistication, could be made using only primitive tools such as the builders' thread, measuring arms, levers, hard tools, wooden rollers, and ropes (from "Construction in Ancient Egypt by the Egyptian Government"). It was a period of inconsistency, in that social progress did not match the development of technology and knowledge in our ancient past.

According to the experts, these cult temples were dedicated to the worship of the Egyptian gods. The Great Temple of Amun at Karnak is the largest religious structure the world has ever known. It witnessed the supreme power and prosperity of Egypt during the time when the pharaohs controlled many petty states such as Syria-Palestine and Nubia. Constructed with great care and aligned with precise calculation, many of these gods' houses were regularly rebuilt, and enlarged by adding new courts and entrance pylons over hundreds of years. In Elephantine, a succession of temples possibly date from 3100 to 30 B.C. Many temples' sites, abandoned by their pharaohs, were later taken for rebuilding other settlements or simply washed away by floods. Only a handful of survivors, ironically but luckily, were buried by the desert sand and only unearthed with the arrival of archaeologists in the early twentieth century.

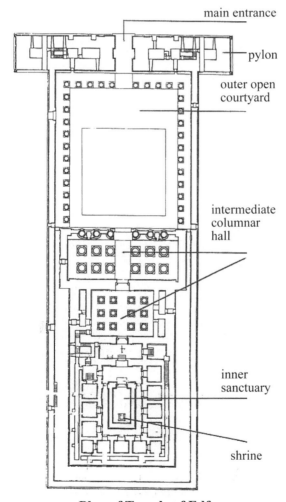

Plan of Temple of Edfu
Diagram 8.27

A Modified Stonehenge

In general, a standard temple of the New Kingdom can be divided into three main sections: outer open courtyard, intermediate columnar hall, and inner sanctuary (diagram 8.27). The entire structure was surrounded and protected by a massive outer enclosure of mud-brick and opened by two massive portal towers or as pylons—broad at the base and narrowed towards the summit—and linked by a central gateway. Like the famous northeast causeway of Stonehenge, most of these pylon entrances were preceded by a processional path.

The pylons, which are exceptionally huge—some up to forty meters wide and eighteen meters high—dominate the whole temple complex, revealing their relative importance. They are built entirely of stone with an outer casing of large blocks. Their surfaces, decorated with raised and sunken reliefs, are surmounted by a grooved cornice, a kind of crowning or overhanging stone fringe. On some, a birdlike creature, probably a sparrowhawk, is placed in the middle of the cornice. An extended-winged solar disk—the emblem of the Egyptian god of heat and light in the ancient cult—is ornately represented on top of the central gateway. Under the cornices, the two pylons and the central gateway are "framed" by a ribbon known as torus molding, that intertwines in a circle and a spiral, imaging bundles of reeds (diagram 8.28).

The Tenth Pylon at Karnak ("The Survey") *Diagram 8.28*

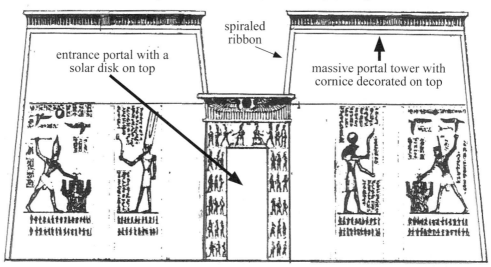

It seems that the ancient Egyptians were obsessed with the above design. A similar theme, i.e., a winged solar disk in the middle of a grooved cornice placed on top of a doorway, is found on precious royal jewels, daily furniture, and even the sacred sarcophagus (diagram 8.29). The solar god was a major deity all over Egypt. Worship of the sun developed with gods of various names throughout their history, from Montu (a local solar god in Upper Egypt) and Ra (the god of the sun) to later Horus (the Egyptian sun god and creator god).

Doorway-styled Jewels and Furniture of Ancient Egypt
Diagram 8.29

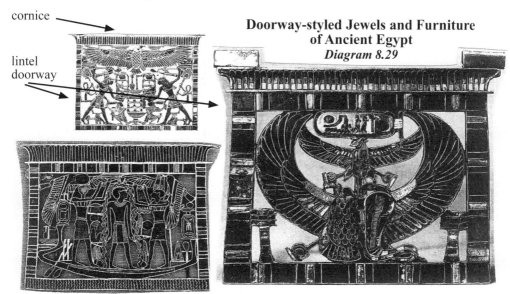

Winged Solar Disk and the Builders' Traveling Vehicles

The aesthetic and artistic ancient Egyptian temples and tombs were dedicated to the sun gods and goddesses, as evidenced by the carvings of the ubiquitous emblematic symbol—a reddish circle or solar-type disk with a pair of outstretched blue multifeathered wings and two coiling uraeus-serpents in striking position attached to its sides—arched over the gateways and doorways (diagram 8.30). In ritual magic it is suspended over the altar in an easterly direction (Murray Hope). Similar religious emblems, atop some tall landmark such as a pillar or a Tree of Life, are found all over the Near East, as in Mesopotamia, Anatolia, and Syria.

The Egyptian Winged Disk *Diagram 8.30*

Importantly, the twin-towering gateway is not just an icon of an Egyptian temple; it also reveals the ultimate function of these buildings. The central gateway, structurally formed by two portals and a lintel, was the dry cell battery of the builders. A power generating device was once placed under the gateway to activate the energy-generating process, as indicated by its decorations. When the powerhouse was "charged," implied by the spiraled ribbon (torus moulding) along the edges of the pylons, energy—shown by the grooved cornice—was generated and emitted on top of the lintel. A builders' traveling vehicle (the winged solar disk) was recharging on top of an Egyptian powerhouse (diagram 8.31)!

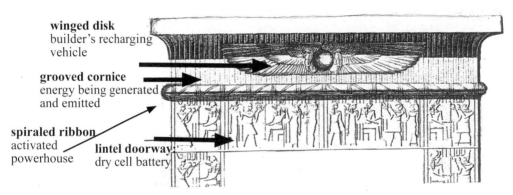

winged disk
builder's recharging vehicle

grooved cornice
energy being generated and emitted

spiraled ribbon
activated powerhouse

lintel doorway
dry cell battery

Builder's Messages on the Entrance of an Egyptian Pylon
Diagram 8.31

Also, erected adjacent to the doorway are two towering pylons or obelisks—elongated, tapering, four-sided shafts, polished, inscribed, surmounted by a sharply pointed pyramidion, standing as high as 30m and weighing hundreds of tons of red granite. According to ancient inscriptions, the Egyptian kings were responsible for the erection of the obelisks in front of the main columned hall. The heads of the obelisks "pierced the sky and illuminated the two lands like the sun disc" (Wilkinson 2000). Like the standing stone erected outside the great mound of Knowth or the one standing inside the earthen enclosure of Tara Hill, the Egyptian obelisks probably symbolize those cylindrical power-generating devices (diagram 8.32). Without doubt, pylons and gateways of the Egyptian temples form several sets of SAs, as discussed later.

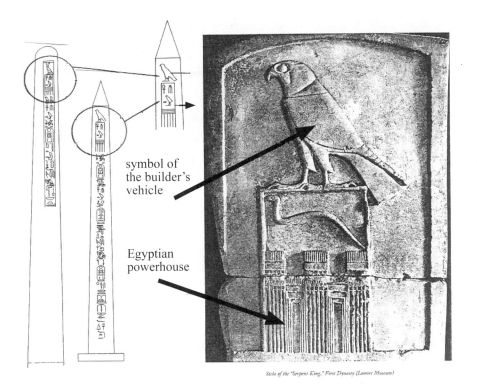

symbol of
the builder's
vehicle

Egyptian
powerhouse

Stela of the "Serpent King," First Dynasty (Louvre Museum)

Egyptian Obelisks with "Refuelling Symbols" on Top *Diagram 8.32*

The Outer Court and the Stone Circle

Beyond the massive gateway lies a large, open peristyle court, partially or wholly surrounded by colonnades. Experts suggest the area served as an interface between the outside world and the sanctified regions deep within the temple (Tehuti Research Foundation). The columns of the colonnade lining the perimeter are shaped like tall bundles of papyrus stalks with lotus blossom capitals (diagram 8.33). They have a square support known as an abacus on top, and above that is the architrave. The whole colossal colonnade forms an ambulatory with a partial roof structure extending from the outer wall of the temple (diagram 8.34). The courtyard was always paved where a great low, table-like offering altar, sometimes with steps leading to the top, was set to one side of the main axis.

The Façade of the Temple of Hathor, Dendara *Diagram 8.33*

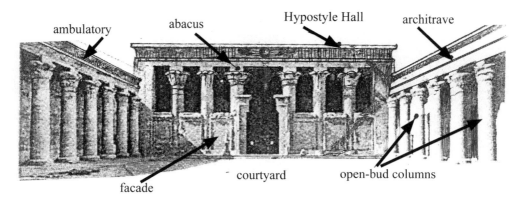

ambulatory   abacus   Hypostyle Hall   architrave

courtyard   open-bud columns

facade

A Typical Egyptian Temple Courtyard *Diagram 3.34*

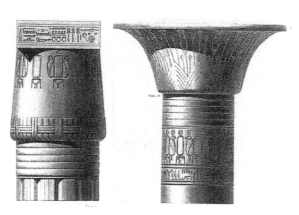

The columns stood on a stone foundation and their shafts were often sculpted with sunk bas-reliefs. Their capitals are decorated differently, some in "bud" style and some in "open-bud" style (diagram 8.35). At the transition of the shaft to the capital, upright rib carvings and five bands of collar may be found. Sometimes, there are images of a solar disk on top of the columns (diagram 8.36).

Capitals of Columns Inside the Temple of Thebes with "Closed" (*left*) and "Open" Styles ("The Survey") *Diagram 8.35*

Solar Disks on Top of the Open-bud Columns
("The Survey") *Diagram 8.36*

The message of the outer court is similar to that of the twin-towering pylons nearby, i.e., emphasizing the energy-generating mechanism of the building. The cylindrical columns symbolize the builders' power-generating device. The "bud-like" capital on top of the horizontal collars is a true reflection of a four-millennia-old conical device, whereas a spreading palm leaf with "open-bud" capital depicts a fully charged device in which energy was generated and emitted on top (diagram 8.37). The energy then "reacted" and was "contained" within the architrave of the hall gallery, structurally, in the form of the lintel design with the solar-disk. Also, grooved cornices on top of the outer court suggest energy being produced by the powerhouse. Architecturally, the colonnade of the temple, the outer courtyard, functioned in the same way as the stone circle in late Neolithic Europe where several sets of SAs radiated from its center (diagram 8.38).

THE GODS' MACHINES

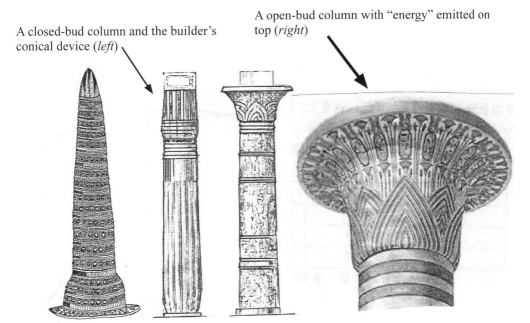

A closed-bud column and the builder's conical device (*left*)

A open-bud column with "energy" emitted on top (*right*)

Egyptian Stylized Columns and the Builders' Conical Device
Diagram 8.37

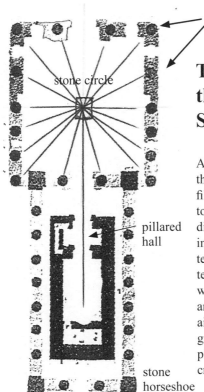

columns

stone circle

pillared hall

stone horseshoe

"Stone Circle" of the Temple of Erment
Diagram 8.38

The Hypostyle Hall and the Bluestone Horseshoe of Stonehenge III

A pillared hall forming a transverse corridor connects the outer courtyard and the inner sanctuary. The hall is filled with tall stone columns, with decorations similar to those of the colonnade, but varying in height and diameter. Their colossal size makes them the most impressive structure of the whole temple. The Karnak temple has 134 columns, some up to twenty-four meters tall. Those lining the axis route—the processional way of the temple—are usually the widest and tallest, are decorated with open-bud capital designs while the aisles have shorter columns with closed buds (diagram 8.39). Experts suggest these columns symbolized plants that were grown around the primeval mound of creation, the sacred landscape where creation began.

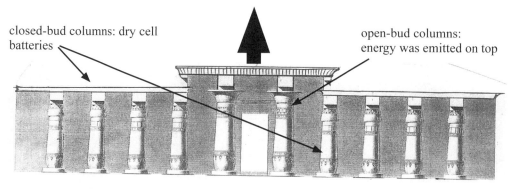

closed-bud columns: dry cell batteries

open-bud columns: energy was emitted on top

Location of the Open- and Closed-bud Columns inside the Temple of Thebes
("The Survey") *Diagram 8.39*

Gods' Barque

The sanctuary, placed precisely at the mound of creation—the home of a deity, according to the Egyptian texts—was a small dark room at the rear of the hall. Sometimes it was represented by a barque shrine, the "Great Seat," an elaborate box probably containing funerary statuary (diagrams 8.40a and b). Another shrine or chapel of the gods' barque, the divine transport vessel as understood by Egyptian experts, was often placed at the rear—the innermost holy chamber, along the main axis of the processional way (diagram 8.41). The shrine, made of hard sandstone and shaped as a doorway surmounted with grooved cornice, was the symbol of the builder's powerhouse.

Shrine of Horus at Edfu
Diagram 8.40a

Pyramid Stela of Amenhotep, 1290 B.C.
Diagram 8.40b

Gods' Barque on Top of an Egyptian Powerhouse (Carvings on the Wall of Interior Shrine, Temple of Karnak)
Diagram 8.41

According to Egyptian mythology, the sun god Re rode in the vessel from the west back to the east at night. Ancient Egyptians also believed the dead accompanied the sun on its daily journey in the Upper Waters around the world by this boat. Hence the images of the gods' barque carved on the sanctuary walls and all over its ceiling (diagram 8.42).

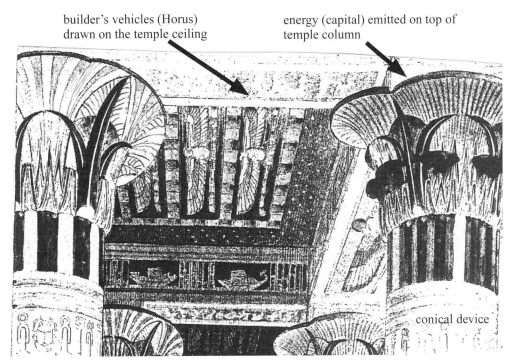

builder's vehicles (Horus) drawn on the temple ceiling

energy (capital) emitted on top of temple column

conical device

Massive Open-bud Columns inside the Portico of Philae with the Builders' Vehicles Recharging on Top *Diagram 8.42*

To the ancient Egyptians, the sanctuary and its Barque Shrine represented the mound of creation and were elevated higher than the rest of the temple. A series of subsidiary rooms, with their lintel doorways opening to and surrounding the central shrine in the form of a horseshoe, were constructed. Structurally speaking, the central sanctuary of an Egyptian temple resembles that of Stonehenge III, in which its "Barque Shrine" was also enclosed by a horseshoe of lintel doorways, most probably repeating from the five Great Sarsen Trilithons of their predecessor (diagram 8.43).

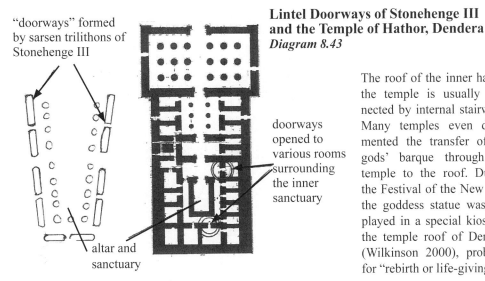

Lintel Doorways of Stonehenge III and the Temple of Hathor, Dendera *Diagram 8.43*

"doorways" formed by sarsen trilithons of Stonehenge III

doorways opened to various rooms surrounding the inner sanctuary

altar and sanctuary

The roof of the inner hall of the temple is usually connected by internal stairways. Many temples even documented the transfer of the gods' barque through the temple to the roof. During the Festival of the New Year the goddess statue was displayed in a special kiosk on the temple roof of Dendera (Wilkinson 2000), probably for "rebirth or life-giving."

It is also suggested that a builders' vehicle landed on the roof for refuelling. It explains the reason why the builder's vehicle was depicted in the center of the sanctuary, instead of their divinities.

CHALCOLITHIC SPAIN AND EGYPT

Structurally and functionally speaking, a standard Egyptian temple (circa 1500–1000 B.C.) mirrored Stonehenge III (circa 2000–1800 B.C.), probably an upgraded model of the latter. The temple's outer courtyard—the colonnade—resembles the outer forecourt of Stonehenge formed by the northeast arc of the bluestone circle and the northeast entrance of the bluestone horseshoe. Its massive outer enclosure wall functioned on the same way as the great sarsen trilithon circle of Stonehenge, a kind of facility for "containing" the energy generated. The two rows of colossal columns of the hypostyle hall and the inner sanctuary of the temple performed the same function as the nineteen bluestones that formed the horseshoe of Stonehenge III. Again, both were "contained" by the temple's thick inner walls as with the five great sarsen trilithon horseshoe of Stonehenge III respectively. The Barque Shrine of the inner sanctuary probably marked the location of the builders' power generating device, the exact position marked by the four Station Stones of Stonehenge (diagrams 8.44 and 8.45).

Stonehenge III and Egyptian Temple
Diagram 8.44

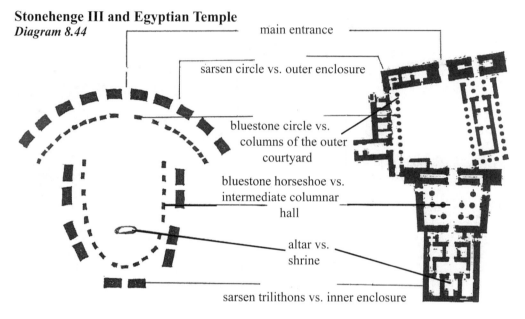

main entrance

sarsen circle vs. outer enclosure

bluestone circle vs. columns of the outer courtyard

bluestone horseshoe vs. intermediate columnar hall

altar vs. shrine

sarsen trilithons vs. inner enclosure

Various Egyptian Temples with "Stonehenge Design" *Diagram 8.45*

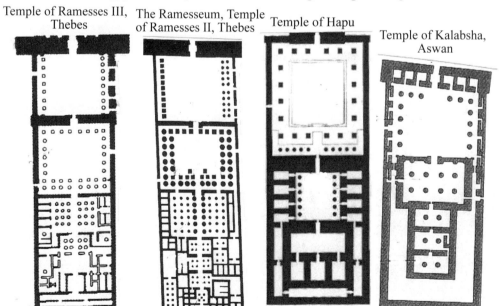

Temple of Ramesses III, Thebes

The Ramesseum, Temple of Ramesses II, Thebes

Temple of Hapu

Temple of Kalabsha, Aswan

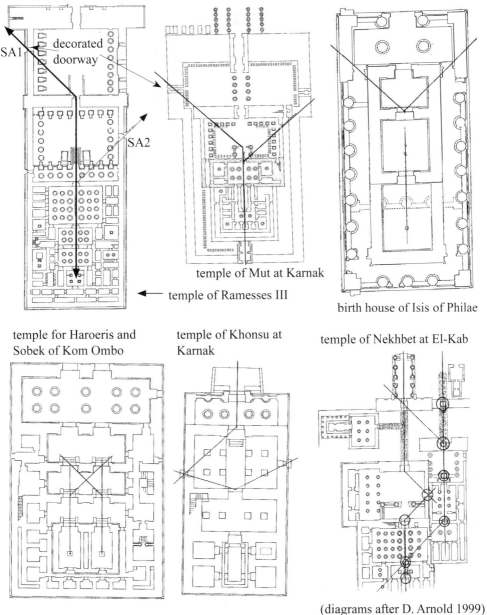

decorated
doorway

SA1

SA2

temple of Mut at Karnak

← temple of Ramesses III

birth house of Isis of Philae

temple for Haroeris and
Sobek of Kom Ombo

temple of Khonsu at
Karnak

temple of Nekhbet at El-Kab

(diagrams after D. Arnold 1999)

SAs of the Egyptian Powerhouses

Usually, the Egyptian temple was surrounded by a number of subsidiary structures such as way
stations and mammises (birth houses). A way station was built along the processional path, only
large enough to allow the entrance of the gods' small portable barque, the experts suggest. It did
not contain anything other than an altar-like base upon which the gods' barque would be set. The
specially designed mammisi was constructed within the temple precinct and was believed to be
a place for the celebration of the birth of a god's offspring. It is a shortened building formed by a
surrounding peristyle with screen-like walls between the columns. These way stations and mammises form SA's with the towering pylons and inner sanctuary of the temple (diagram 8.46). This
explains why during the "Festival of the Beautiful Meeting," celebrated at the temple of Edfu,
the statue of the goddess was placed in the birthplace of the temple for "rejuvenation" (Wilkinson
2000).

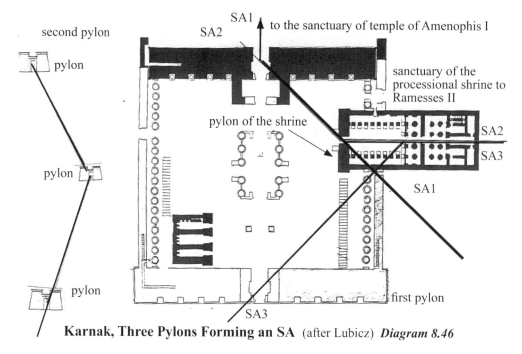

pylon

SA2

SA1

to the sanctuary of temple of Amenophis I

sanctuary of the processional shrine to Ramesses II

pylon of the shrine

SA2

SA3

pylon

SA1

pylon

first pylon

SA3

Karnak, Three Pylons Forming an SA (after Lubicz) *Diagram 8.46*

The sacred temples of Karnak and Luxor of ancient Thebes are the most important archaeological complexes in Upper Egypt. The city was known as "hundred-gated Thebes" (Shaw 2003) probably suggesting the impressiveness of their massive pylons. The whole religious complex of Karnak, covering more than 250 acres, is the largest and best-preserved example of the New Kingdom. Three main sacred precincts, believed to honor the gods of Amun (the sun-god), Mut, and Khonsu, are protected and separated by mid-brick enclosure walls. At the center of the complex is the principal temple of Amun, constructed with an east-west axis. The famous Great Hypostyle Hall of Ramesses II (1290–1224 B.C.) has a west-facing opening, and is extended by a succession of pylons and courtyards built to its west (diagram 8.47). Its southern axis of massive pylons was also extended and connected with the nearby precinct of the goddess Mut. During the reign of Amenhotep IV, a new sun-god, Ra-Horus with one "name" ("the living god who rejoices in the horizon in his identity of light which is in the sun-disc") was honored.

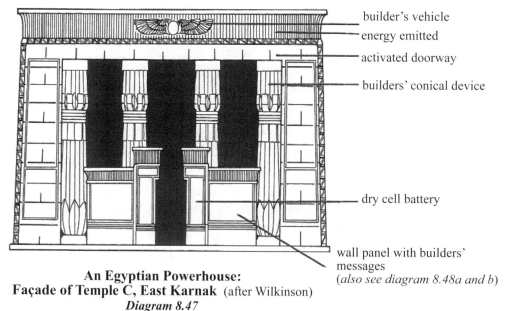

builder's vehicle

energy emitted

activated doorway

builders' conical device

dry cell battery

wall panel with builders' messages
(*also see diagram 8.48a and b*)

An Egyptian Powerhouse:
Façade of Temple C, East Karnak (after Wilkinson)
Diagram 8.47

Wall Panel (Intercolumniation) between Columns of the Inner Temple of Philae
The panel was framed by a cordon of twisted strands (intertwined ribbons). A grooved cornice crowned on top indicates the emission of energy where the builder's vehicle, in the form of a solar disk with extended wings, is recharging in the middle. ("Napoleonic Survey")
Diagrams 8.48a and b

It is these colossal pylons of the temple complex, being designed and carved with the messages from the builders, that reveal the ultimate secret of the whole complex. Its trapezoidal lintel-portal design with cornice on top and a solar disc in the middle clearly suggests it once served as a gigantic dry cell battery for the visitors and why most of the pylons of Karnak are connected by the SA (diagrams 8.49a to e). According to the temple's inscriptions, the powerhouse was finally left in ruins when "the gods had therefore abandoned Egypt and were no longer answering prayers" (Shaw 2003, p. 170).

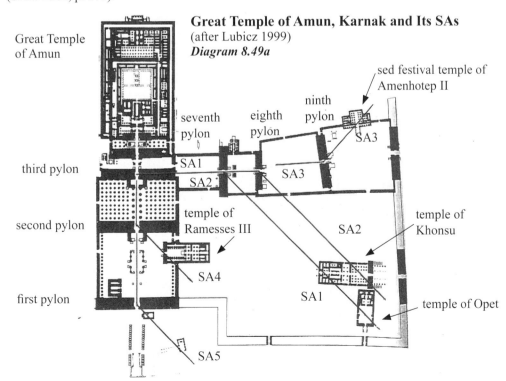

Great Temple of Amun, Karnak and Its SAs
(after Lubicz 1999)
Diagram 8.49a

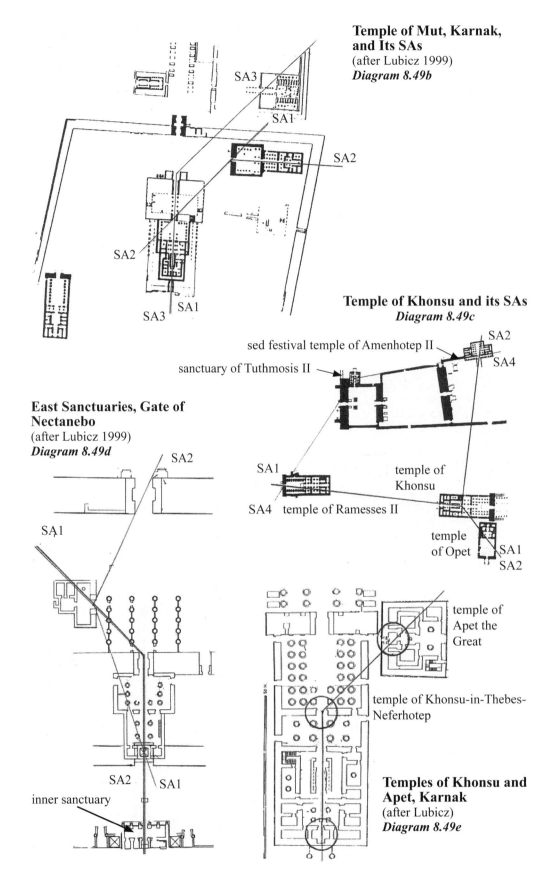

Temple of Mut, Karnak, and Its SAs
(after Lubicz 1999)
Diagram 8.49b

SA3
SA1
SA2
SA2
SA3
SA1

Temple of Khonsu and its SAs
Diagram 8.49c

sed festival temple of Amenhotep II
sanctuary of Tuthmosis II

SA2
SA4

SA1

temple of
Khonsu

SA4   temple of Ramesses II

temple
of Opet
SA1
SA2

East Sanctuaries, Gate of Nectanebo
(after Lubicz 1999)
Diagram 8.49d

SA2

SA1

SA2   SA1

inner sanctuary

temple of
Apet the
Great

temple of Khonsu-in-Thebes-
Neferhotep

Temples of Khonsu and Apet, Karnak
(after Lubicz)
Diagram 8.49e

The temple of Luxor, 2.5km south of Karnak, was also dedicated to the cult of Amun. Its principal temples are perfect examples of how they were designed, modified, and most probably functioned as an Egyptian Stonehenge. After the entrance pylon of Ramesses II from the east is a peristyle court—the First Court with colonnades along its four sides (resembling the bluestone circle of Stonehenge). A huge colonnade consisting of seven pairs of columns with "opening-buds" connects the southern entrance of the First Court to the Second. Its long corridor recalls the bluestones forming the horseshoe of Stonehenge III. The colonnade then leads to another peristyle court—the Second Court (from Amenophis III) with another hypostyle hall—another "bluestone horseshoe" and its sanctuary further south. Generally speaking, the temple of Luxor was formed and extended by two sets of Egyptian "Stonehenges" lying side by side sharing the same inner sanctuary—the "power reactor" of the builders' powerhouse (diagram 8.50).

Temple of Edfu

The magnificent temple of Horus of Edfu is the best-surviving and most impressive post-pharaonic structure (237–57 B.C.). The temple was believed to honour the gods of Horus and Seth—the Divine Winged Beetle or the Falcon of Gold. Again, its massive southern pylon captures the magic moment of the site, keeping its ultimate secret inside (diagram 8.51). The whole temple is surrounded and protected by a stone enclosure wall. The wall created the ambulatory—a long corridor surrounding the rectangular complex, formed by columns along three of its sides. It is an echo of and probably an improvement on the sarsen and bluestone circles of Stonehenge III (diagram 8.52). The erection of the columns at two sides of the two Hypostyle Halls, which run along the main axis, mirrors that of the bluestone horseshoe of Stonehenge III. The sanctuary, built on rising ground, probably marks the exact location of the interception between SS91–93 and SS92–94. Most interestingly, it is enclosed by a "horseshoe" of rooms or shrines with lintel doorways—to function like the five Great Sarsen Trilithons of Stonehenge III. According to experts, the "temple of the sacred falcon," a mammisi with a rectangular structure, was set at right angles to the main temple axis of Edfu (Shaw 2003) and, like those from the temple of Karnak, it forms an SA with the south pylon and sanctuary.

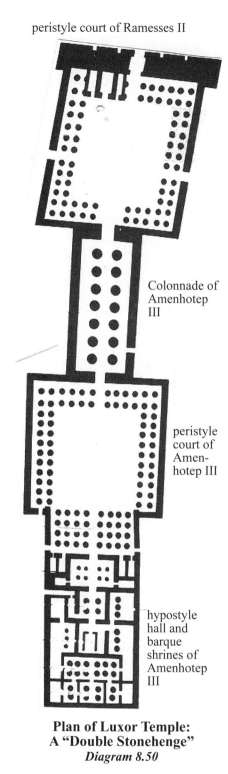

peristyle court of Ramesses II

Colonnade of Amenhotep III

peristyle court of Amenhotep III

hypostyle hall and barque shrines of Amenhotep III

**Plan of Luxor Temple:
A "Double Stonehenge"**
Diagram 8.50

Courtyard of Edfu
("The Survey")
Diagram 8.51

symbol of microwave
radiation and the
builders' vehicle

Powerhouse of Edfu, 237 B.C.: An Evolution of Stonehenge III
Diagram 8.52

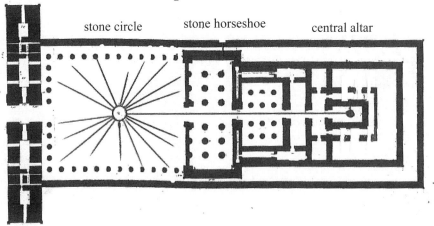

stone circle   stone horseshoe   central altar

Egyptian Temples Were Aligned to the SA
Diagram 8.53a

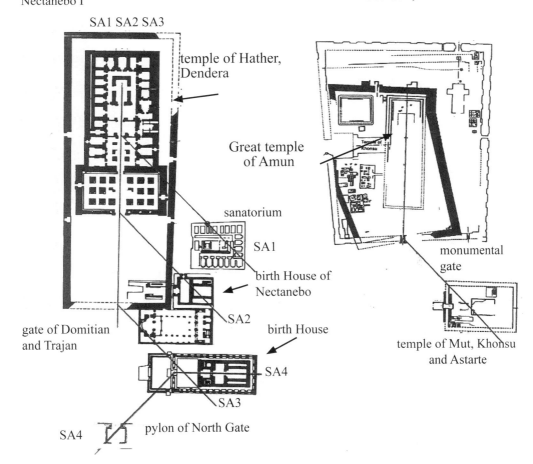

temple of Thoth

SA1

temple of Nekhbet

SA2

birth House

pylon of Ramesses II

SA1

SA3

Roman temple

gate of Nectanebo I

SA3

SA2

Seti I, temple of Millions of Years

SA1

SA2

SA2

Royal Palace

SA1

mortuary temple of Sethos I, Thebes

SA1 SA2 SA3

temple of Hather, Dendera

Great temple of Amun

sanatorium

SA1

birth House of Nectanebo

gate of Domitian and Trajan

SA2

birth House

SA4

SA3

SA4

pylon of North Gate

monumental gate

temple of Mut, Khonsu and Astarte

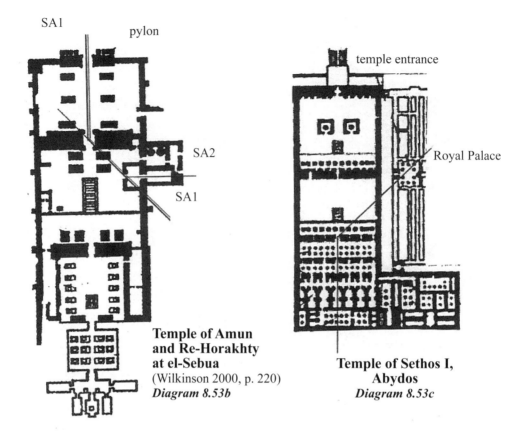

SA1

pylon

SA2

SA1

**Temple of Amun
and Re-Horakhty
at el-Sebua**
(Wilkinson 2000, p. 220)
Diagram 8.53b

temple entrance

Royal Palace

**Temple of Sethos I,
Abydos**
Diagram 8.53c

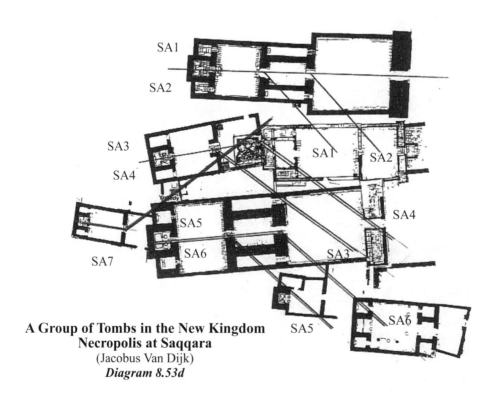

SA1

SA2

SA3

SA4

SA5

SA6

SA7

SA1

SA2

SA4

SA3

SA5

SA6

**A Group of Tombs in the New Kingdom
Necropolis at Saqqara**
(Jacobus Van Dijk)
Diagram 8.53d

THE GODS' MACHINES

Djed Column and the Power-Generating Device

The djed is probably the most recognized symbol of ancient Egypt and could date back to pre-Dynastic times. According to Egyptian theology, the djed pillar represented stability, permanency, and most importantly, strength and regeneration. The mysterious symbol is always depicted as cylindrical in shape, probably a fully round column with a broad base and capital. At the top of the column the capital is divided by four parallel bars with a small protrusion at its very top (diagram 8.54). It was most probably made of gold, as suggested by ancient accounts (Papyrus of Ani, No. 57). The pillar was often painted on the walls of the royal palace and on the coffins of the tombs. Many gold relics and royal jewels were designed in the "powerhouse design" with djed columns decorated under the lintel doorways. On some occasions, mummified Egyptians were discovered with a djed clutched within their hands (Jimmy Dunn).

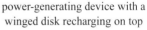
power-generating device with a winged disk recharging on top

Djed Pillar
(info: Jimmy Dunn) *Diagram 8.54*

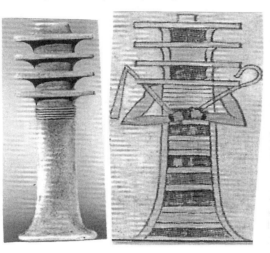

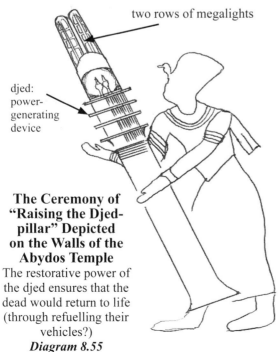

two rows of megalights

djed: power-generating device

The Ceremony of "Raising the Djed-pillar" Depicted on the Walls of the Abydos Temple
The restorative power of the djed ensures that the dead would return to life (through refuelling their vehicles?)
Diagram 8.55

An important ancient festival known as "Raising the Djed Pillar," celebrated as early as the Middle Kingdom (3000 B.C.), symbolized the resurrection and rejuvenation of Osiris and Ptah—the two important gods of ancient Egypt (diagram 8.55). The pillar was described as a human-size object with two elongated objects extending from its top. Could they represent two rows of megalights being emitted for tapping power, or were they the energy generated for their vehicle above? Ptah was always depicted as holding the djed symbol as his staff. According to the texts of the Temple of Horus at Edfu, the djed served its greatest purpose "at the ending of one world age and the beginning of another" (Moira Timms).

Carvings on a Temple Wall Showing Solar Disk (Symbolizing Builders' Vehicle) Recharging on Top of an Egyptian Powerhouse *Diagram 8.56*

According to various ancient Egyptian texts, their deities often possessed creative powers and embodied natural forces. And at the beginning of time, during the creation of the world, a mound of earth, at the center of the temple, rose from the water of existence where a great hawk or falcon (probably the builders' flying vehicle) appeared and settled on a reed (a power-generating conical device). The gods' mansions, or the Egyptian temples, like thousands of other megalithic structures worldwide, were built to generate and maintain energy for the benefits of mankind. "They were places in which the cosmic energy, god came to dwell and radiate their energy to the land and people" (Rediscover Ancient Egypt with Tehuti Research Foundation).

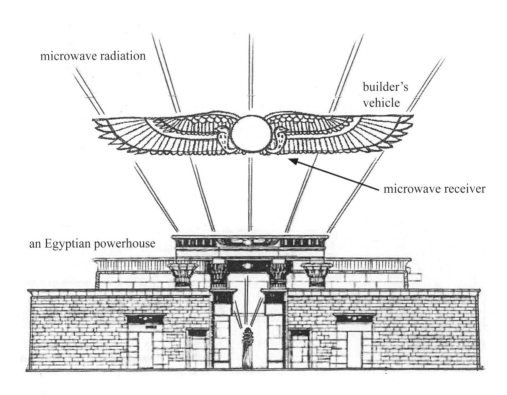

An Egyptian Powerhouse with Power-generating Device (Djed Pillar) Installed
Diagram 8.57

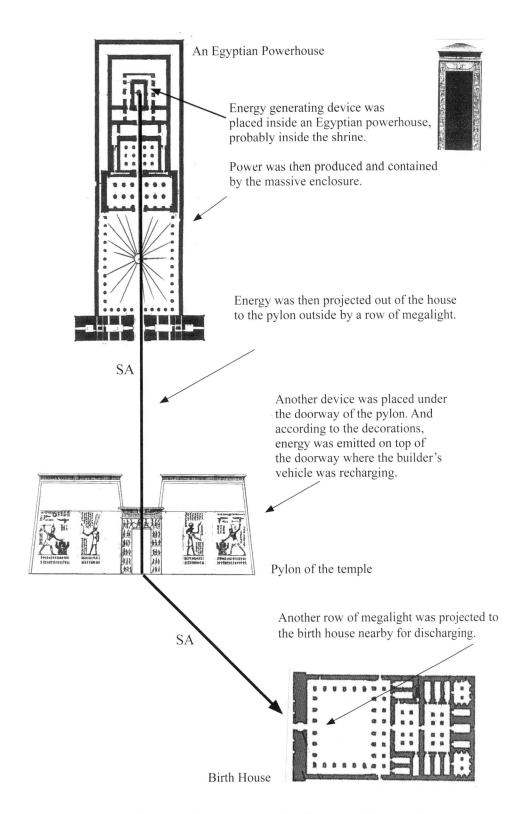

An Egyptian Powerhouse

Energy generating device was placed inside an Egyptian powerhouse, probably inside the shrine.

Power was then produced and contained by the massive enclosure.

Energy was then projected out of the house to the pylon outside by a row of megalight.

SA

Another device was placed under the doorway of the pylon. And according to the decorations, energy was emitted on top of the doorway where the builder's vehicle was recharging.

Pylon of the temple

Another row of megalight was projected to the birth house nearby for discharging.

SA

Birth House

How an Egyptian Power-generating Complex Operated
Diagram 8.58

Chapter 9
Iron Age Powerhouses

Roman Hill Forts

According to the experts, there are about 2,000 Iron Age hill forts in southern Britain. Constructed in 1000–300 B.C., the earliest hill forts are varied in form. Generally, like the mysterious stone circles around the region, most of the hill forts are roughly circular in shape. They are formed by layers of ramparts, in the form of slight banks and ditches of earth, with gateways or entrances in between. These ramparts are composed of rocks and stones/dry-stones, and some are faced with large stones. Usually, a vertical-walled rampart is fronted by a ditch so as to provide necessary space to separate two ramparts.

Again, no one knows who built these forts and what they were used for. Their name—Roman Hill Fort—probably originates from the time these monuments were constructed. To the experts' surprise, little human activities and artifacts were found inside these monuments. Besides, the slight banks and ditches could not be used for defense. However, experts speculate that some of them were once used secondarily as forts for defense purposes during the Iron Age when the inhabitants lived in a period of aggression, unrest, and uncertainty (Timothy Darvill 1987). That's why they are supposed to have functioned as hill forts. The most well-known ones include Maiden Castle, Hambledon Hill, and Danebury.

If the cup and ring carvings were made to deliver the builders' secret, then the weird carving below may probably reveal the real function of the Iron Age hill forts. It is a rock art on a boulder at Dod Law, Doddington, Northumberland (drawing by Stan Beckensall), a favorite tourist site famous for its impressive hill forts. The western hill fort of Dod Law is a D-shaped structure with a pair of concentric ramparts. There are at least ten circular houses inside. Another eastern hill fort is sub-rectangular in plan with a bank and outer ditch.

If a typical circular cup and ring pattern shows the work of the builders' powerhouses, the Dod Law rock art, with square patterns decorated and encircled by large dots and angular lines (diagram 9.1), may be a perfect description of the hill forts nearby. The carving was discovered at Doddington CP, Bewick-upon-Tweed, Northumberland, in 1865. According to Tate, who found and drew the rock, "it was almost entirely covered over and preserved with turf and peat. There are three levels of rock. Some cups and rings have eroded where older motifs was removed by new motifs." According to the rock art, conical devices were once placed inside these square structures, which then projected megalights to the surrounding round houses for power. Like the corbelled walls of Newgrange and the sarsen circle of Stonehenge, drystone rampants of the hill forts may help to shield and contain the energy generated in the form of microwaves. This may be the real message behind the rock art of Dod Law.

**Rock Art on a Boulder at
Dod Law, Doddington,
Northumberland**
(after Beckensall and Darvill 1987)
Diagram 9.1

There is another example in the "Roman Gask Project," which was led by D. J. Woolliscroft and B. Hoffmann and funded by Historic Scotland. The team conducted a series of excavations at the multi-period site of East Coldoch, near the Roman fort of Doune in 2002 and 2003 (www.roman-gask.org.uk). According to their findings, the Roman site shows many superimposed structures such as palisaded enclosures, round barrows and houses, and a heavy penannular ditch. Similar settings were once found in West Kennet of Wiltshire.

The map below is the result of their geophysical surveys (2003) of the Cargill Roman fort, north of Perth. The fort was first discovered from the air during the Second World War. It is rectangular in shape with an opening, probably a gate at the south. The report shows that there are significant clusters of Iron Age sites, a total of ten roundhouses both within and outside the Cargill fort. Four of them were excavated inside the fort and they are aligned to SA1 and SA2. An angle bisector points to the southern gate of the fort (diagram 9.2).

Another group of three large round houses formed by heavy ditches stands to the south and southwest of the fort enclosure (diagram 9.3). They are also aligned to the SA (SA3). Three more ring features were constructed west of the fort enclosure and are aligned to the SA (SA4). Cargill Roman hill fort probably lies at one of the junctions of the underground Earth energy fields and

so the builders constructed circles of drystone rampants in order to trap and contain the energy. After hundreds of years of evolution in the builders' energy technology, the bulky megalithic infrastructures such as passage graves and stone circles were replaced by round houses and drystone walls. The Romans, the latecomers to these powerhouses, did check in and alter their functions when the advanced builders' decided to redesign and relocate their powerhouses in a completely different form.

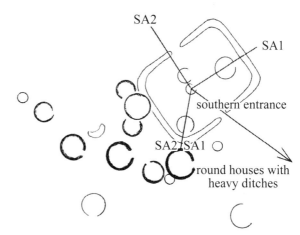

SA Applied to Cargill Roman Fort
(Roman Gask Project 2003)
Diagram 9.2

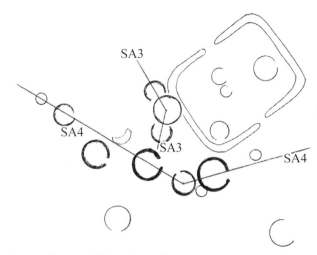

SA3

SA4

SA3

SA4

**SA Applied to Round Houses
Outside the Fort**
Diagram 9.3

Brochs of Scotland

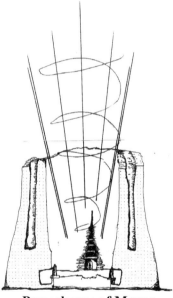

**Powerhouse of Mousa,
100 B.C.** (after Darvill 1987)
Diagram 9.4

Broch comes from the Norse word that means "fort." These 2,000-year-old monuments are round, tapering drystone towers and fort-like buildings that are regarded as a wonder of European architecture. They are found only in western and northern Isles, around Orkney and Shetland, and on the mainland of Caithness and Sutherland, the least-populated areas of Scotland. There are around 700 brochs, which date from the earliest roundhouse structures in Bu of Navershaw, Pierowall, and Tofts Ness of 700 B.C. to the latest, such as Lockie or Buchlyvie of A.D. 500 (Lynn). Even without evidences, experts suggest there is a direct relation between the Roman roundhouses (1800 B.C. to A.D. 200) and the Scot brochs. Mousa in Shetland, Dun Carloway in Lewis, Dun Dornaigil in Sutherland, and Duns Troddan and Telve in Glenelg are well-preserved survivors.

The term "broch" refers to a round windowless and featureless tower with unusual massive inner and outer stone walls. Most of them occupy more than half of the space of the total structure. For example, the two walls of Mousa take up 65% of the total structure, making it difficult to house sufficient garrisons against attack, but its wall was certainly far too massive to block the enemies. It seems that the builders' attention was focused on the massive concentric walls rather than the space created inside.

The broch has only one small and narrow entrance open to the outside. The entrance is usually marked by a lintel doorway in which Armit suggests considerable attention was paid to the selection of good quality lintels. For example, the 7m-high broch of Culswick has a spectacular massive triangular lintel over its doorway. Very often, cells and shrines were constructed within its ground-level walls whereas winding stairs were built within and connected between the inner and outer walls. Experts discover that these stairs rarely show any signs of wear, which suggests that they are seldom used. Some upper galleries are even impassable and their function is still unexplained.

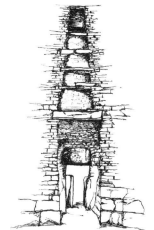

Void of Dun Telve Directly Placed above the Massive Lintel Entrance
Diagram 9.5

Whether these tapering towers had roofs is also the subject of debate. The ground floor of the broch is formed by irregular outcrop of rock, implying that it is not the main focus of the structure (Armit 2004). Besides, its unusual massive walls make an upper floor uneconomical.

Most brochs are a few meters high and are built on bedrock or a platform of boulder clay. Many of them stand on seashore and often on rugged outcrops or inaccessible islets. Some of them once stood 9m in height and 20m in diameter, which made it visible from a far distance. But experts wonder why the brochs were constructed in stark, which is a big contrast to the previous domestic architectural tradition of small, simply constructed stone and turf dwellings (Pearson, Sharples, and Mulville 1996). Some suggest the broch was built as a fort of defense against maritime enemies. However, most of their sole entrances were deliberately built facing the ocean, which made them vulnerable to attack.

They are often found on the types of terrain where earlier Neolithic chambered tombs were constructed. Several brochs, such as Quanterness in Orkney, were actually built on top of chambered tombs (Carter 1984, Hingley 1993, and Mike Parker Pearson, Niall Sharples, and Jacqui Mulville 1996). The broch of Howe was constructed over the site of a 2,500-year-old Neolithic chamber cairn. At Pierowall, an Iron Age roundhouse had been constructed directly above a Maes Howe–type cairn. These impressive towers are remarkably uniform in design but their real function is still an enigma. A subject of "broch-ology" emerges with numerous questions about their existence. Who actually built them? Why on the most deserted areas of British Isles? Did the broch builders want to hide something of importance inside these dramatic infrastructures with high, thick, tapered, and windowless walls, but an opening on top? And why should they later abandon them?

A Perfect Iron Age Powerhouse

The most famous and well-preserved is the broch of Mousa on Shetland, which stands on a rocky headland of Mousa Sound (diagram 9.6). The tower is 13m in height, forming a near-perfect circle with an external diameter of 15m. An entrance which opens to the west leads directly into the interior central chamber, which is 5.5m across. It seems that the two massive inner and outer walls of Mousa, which are constructed in the form of two concentric rings and constitute more than two-thirds of the total structure, were the prime concern of the builders.

There are three large cells with tiny wall-cupboards all set in the thickness of the inner wall. Six galleries or winding stairs, each large enough for a person to pass, are superimposed between the inner and outer walls. The wall surface is also broken by vertical window-like lintel openings called voids, set above the cell entrance. Again, the real function of these distinctive settings is unexplained. Experts suggest that the wall voids may have been there to reduce the weight of stone over the lintel trenches. However, others disagree by arguing that they seem to have created points of weakness in the whole structure. Architecturally speaking, these 2,000-year-old wall voids bear resemblance to the lintel trenches of Maes Howe–type chambered cairns of Orkney constructed in 3000 B.C. Most importantly, like the MH cairns, these lintel doorways and voids of Mousa are aligned to the SA (diagram 9.7).

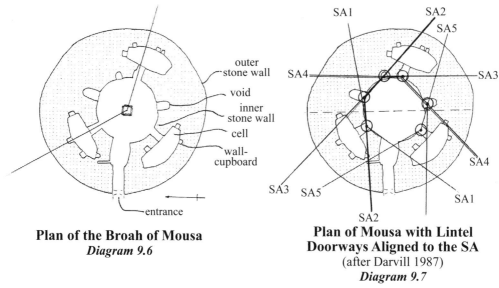

Plan of the Broah of Mousa
Diagram 9.6

Plan of Mousa with Lintel Doorways Aligned to the SA
(after Darvill 1987)
Diagram 9.7

As suggested before, conical devices were once placed inside the lintel trenches of the chambered cairns of Orkney for power in 3000 B.C. Similar settings can be found inside Mousa. SA1 is formed by two inner cells with the central hearth of Mousa in the middle (diagram 9.8). Each lintel doorway of the two cells forms another set of SA with two lintel voids nearby. In other words, a power emitter, device no. 2, was once placed in the middle of Mousa and it connected an energy collector, device no. 1, which was placed under the lintel cell for recharging. At the same time, a row of megalight connected another conical device in the opposite lintel cell, probably for discharging (diagram 9.9).

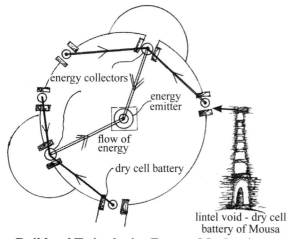

Builders' Twin-device Energy Mechanism Applied to the Powerhouse of Mousa
Diagram 9.8

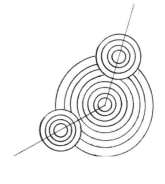

Cup and Ring Pattern Generated upon Activation of the Powerhouse of Mousa
Diagram 9.9

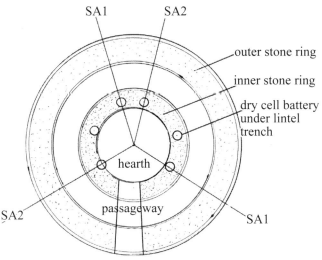

SA1   SA2

outer stone ring

inner stone ring

dry cell battery
under lintel
trench

hearth

passageway

SA2   SA1

**Simplified Illustration Showing a Symmetrical
Design of the Broch of Mousa**
Diagram 9.10

That's why Mousa was constructed with tall and tapering towers, structurally parallel with the corbelled roofs of Newgrange and the MH chambered cairns of Orkney. Its concentric inner and outer walls probably reflect the structure and function of the great sarsen trilithons and sarsen stone circle of Stonehenge, respectively (diagram 9.10). Its lintel trenches and mysterious voids might have worked like the five great lintel trilithons of Stonehenge. Dyker describes these windowless conical infrastructures as "electricity cooling-towers," while Turner suggests Mousa could potentially have become a perfect furnace. But without doubt, the broch of

Mousa together with the rest around the region, was the powerhouse of the builders, and was probably a substitute for the Bronze Age Stonehenge (diagram 9.11).

Dating back to 200 B.C. and 100 B.C., the Broch of Gurness is a tapering tower standing around 8m high with an internal diameter of 20m. The site is surrounded by a series of small stone dwelling houses, each of which contains a central hearth and stone furniture, probably a copy of Skara Brae, Orkney. The diagram below shows the general layout of the complex. A lintel entrance that opens to the northeast-east connects a causeway in the eastern side of the settlement. Another short path is clearly shown in the northwest. It forms a perfect SA with the northeast-east causeway with the center of the broch in the middle (diagram 9.12).

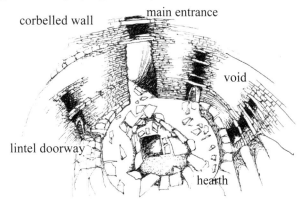

corbelled wall   main entrance

void

lintel doorway

hearth

Internal Structure of the Broch of Mousa
Diagram 9.11

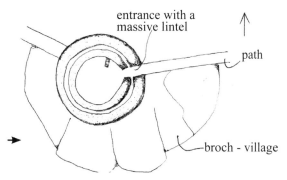

entrance with a
massive lintel

path

broch - village

**Plan of Gurness, Showing Its
Two Paths Aligning to the SA** ➔
Diagram 9.12

Clickimin is another famous and well-preserved broch situated on a peninsula on the south side of the Loch of Clickimin at Lerwick, Shetland (diagram 9.13). It was first built on a late Bronze Age farmstead in around 700–500 B.C. And during the later period, a ditch was dug and a wall was erected to protect the area. A large stone gatehouse was erected around 100 B.C. (diagram 9.14). The construction of most striking feature, the broch, began around A.D. 200 before the finish of the blockhouse. It consists of a tower 20m in diameter and is originally up to 12–15m high with compartments, galleries, and winding stairs formed by drystone walls. There is much debate as to whether it was roofed. One would not be surprised that it once served as the builder's powerhouse when the SA was applied to the structure (diagram 9.15). Similar Iron Age brochs with compartments aligned to the SA are provided below (diagrams 9.16a to h).

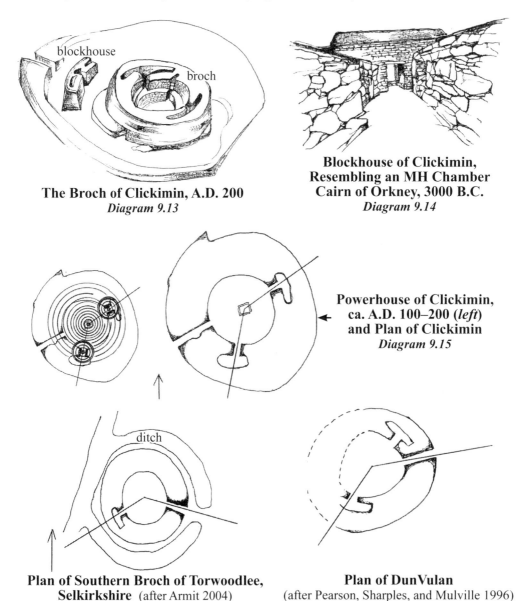

The Broch of Clickimin, A.D. 200
Diagram 9.13

Blockhouse of Clickimin, Resembling an MH Chamber Cairn of Orkney, 3000 B.C.
Diagram 9.14

Powerhouse of Clickimin, ca. A.D. 100–200 (*left*) and Plan of Clickimin
Diagram 9.15

Plan of Southern Broch of Torwoodlee, Selkirkshire (after Armit 2004)
Diagram 9.16a

Plan of DunVulan
(after Pearson, Sharples, and Mulville 1996)
Diagram 9.16b

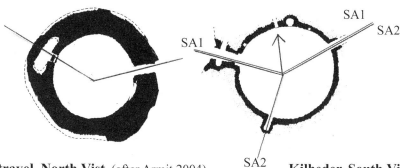

Clettravel, North Vist (after Armit 2004)
The site is 7.5m in diameter with a 2m thick
and 1.2m high wall
Diagram 9.16c

Kilheder, South Vist
(after Armit 2004)
Diagram 9.16d

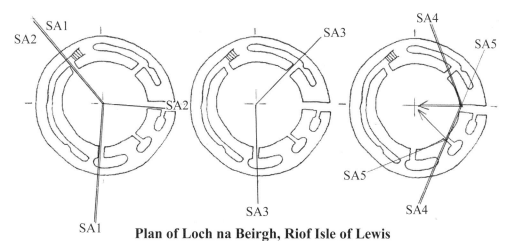

Plan of Loch na Beirgh, Riof Isle of Lewis
A well-preserved multiphase roundhouse structure with intramural galleries,
occupied continuously from A.D. 200–900
Diagram 9.16e

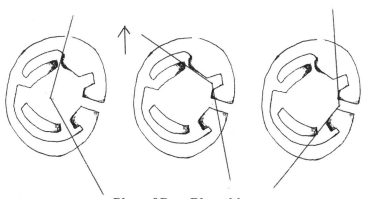

Plan of Dun Bharabhat
An Iron Age Atlantic roundhouse constructed on a small and steep
rocky island in a freshwater lake on Great Bernera
Diagram 9.16f

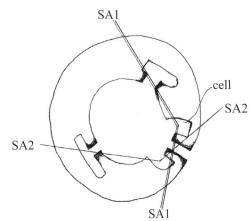

SA1

SA2

SA2

cell

SA2

SA1

Plan of Howe
The broch measures 9m in diameter with
a wall less than 3m thick standing 3m tall.
The outer and inner walls are separated with
passageways and winding stairs connecting
the two walls. Its two cells, which open from
the entrance passage, form separate SAs with
lintel doorways nearby (after Armit 2004)
Diagram 9.16g

The "Semi-broch" of Dun Ardtreck in Skye
This D-shaped enclosure stands on the cliff edge
on the south of Loch Bracadale. Its wall survives
to a maximum height of 2m to form an enclosed
area of 10 x 13m (stonepages.com). There are two
intramural galleries on both sides of the entrance
and they are aligned to the SA (after Armit 2004)
Diagram 9.16h

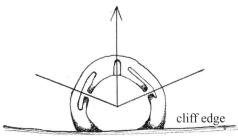

cliff edge

Wheelhouses: The Builders' Powerhouse

Wheelhouses, right after the demise of brochs, are found mainly in Outer Hebrides. Many wheel-houses were semi-subterranean in which the builders dug a large cylindrical pit lined with dry-stone walling. Progressive inward corbelling of the roofing was formed by putting the smaller stones at the bottom and the larger stones at the top. These circular houses are divided into bays by internal stonewalls arranged like the spokes of a wheel. Each of these bays was capped by a corbelled stone roof. The inner end of each of these stone walls is usually lined with a 1m high standing slab to form a stone circle right in the middle of a circular stone-built house. Again, it echoes the OC chambered cairns of Orkney, in which standing stones were erected inside a cor-belled chamber for power. A stone hearth was constructed in the open central area of the wheel-house. In aisled wheelhouses, the piers are freestanding but connected to the wall by stone lintels. Wheelhouses are undergoing a reassessment, as they are seen as contemporaries with the brochs, and going through their own sequence of development.

The diagram below is the layout of the wheelhouse at Middlequarter, Sollas, North Uist. Its central chamber, with a diameter of 9m, is connected to a long and funnel-shaped passage. The chamber is then divided into twelve compartments or storerooms by internal stonewalls. On the northeast side of the room, a lintel doorway leads to an additional oval side chamber. Again, the spoke-like stone walls and its orthostats form various sets of SAs with the central hearth (diagram 9.17a). As suggested by the diagram, the lintel entrance and doorways of Middlequarter were con-structed according to the SA (diagram 9.17b). It has to be the universal formula of the builders, a clue to explain their real function. Other wheelhouses around the region with their spoke-like internal stonewalls are also aligned to the SA (diagram 9.18).

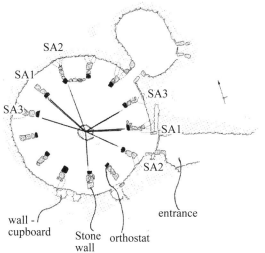

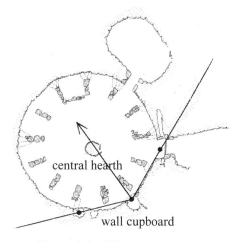

Plan of the Wheelhouse at Middlequarter, North Uist
(after Atkinson, Darvill 1987)
Diagram 9.17a

Plan of the Wheelhouse at Middlequarter with Wall-cupboards Aligned to the SA
(after Atkinson, Darvill 1987)
Diagram 9.17b

Clettraval, North Uist

Kilpheder, South Uist
Diagram 9.18

Cnip, Lewis

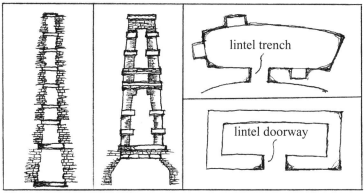

void of Mousa

roof-comb of a Mayan temple-pyramid

cell of Mousa (*above*) and long house of the Maya

"The Maya Connection": Settings of the Broch of Mousa Resemble Mayan Architectural Characteristics
Diagram 9.19

Chapter 10
Mesoamerican Powerhouses and the Builders' Jet Craft

"Maya—the name evokes mystery, engima, adventure. A civilization that was, and is gone, vanished though its people have remained. Incredible cities abandoned intact, swallowed by the green jungle canopy; pyramids that reach sky high, aiming to touch the gods; and monuments, elaborately carved and decorated, that speak out in artful hieroglyphs whose meaning is still mostly lost in the mists of time."

—Zecharia Sitchin, *The Lost Realms* (1990), p. 65

"Where had this civilization come from? How could the Maya have sustained themselves so successfully in such a supposedly inhospitable environment? What catastrophes had overwhelmed their abandoned cities?"

—Robert J. Sharer, *The Ancient Maya* (fifth edition, 1994), p. 3

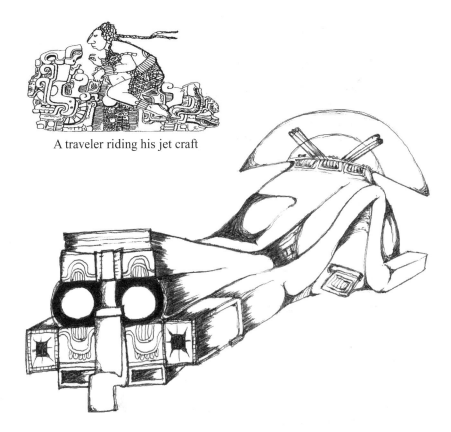

A traveler riding his jet craft

A Jet-propelled Superbike, ca. A.D. 200

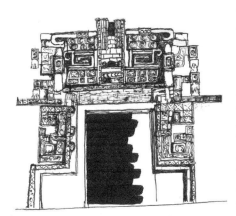

**Masked Doorway of the
West-facing Lower Temple
of the Magician, Uxmal**
Diagram 10.1

The megalithic infrastructures such as brochs and wheelhouses probably mark the last of the builders' megalithic power stations in Europe. Around 1000 B.C., a cluster of mysterious civilizations including the Olmec, the Aztec, and the Maya, and generally known as the Mesoamerican Culture, developed in isolation deep inside the tropical rainforests of central and southern America. Vast plazas with decorated houses at their sides and sky-scraping pyramids with corbel-roofed temples on top were constructed, not on vast open space accessible by roads, but in one of the most difficult environments of the world.

The Maya, one of the principal Mesoamerican cultures, lived in the region extending from the desert of northern Mexico to the eastern third of Honduras and El Salvador. Their history is basically divided into three periods: Preclassic (1500 B.C.–A.D. 200), Classic (A.D. 200–910), and Postclassic (A.D. 910–1524). There were more than sixty kingdoms or city-states in the Classic period, the heyday of the culture.

The rock from lowlands has little earth. The tropical soils there quickly decline in fertility and become unworkable, as a layer of brick-like laterite develops on the surface. Therefore, many Maya lowland areas are and were unsuitable for raised fields or for terracing (Coe). By practicing shifting cultivation, only a small and very unproductive yield of maize cobs was allowed. How could it able to sustain a huge population of millions? Without the use of metal, even today, Mayan villages were only made up of thatched-roof houses.

Most Maya infrastructures were built on solid lime-based artificial platforms constructed of rubble hearting with a cut-stone façade. Most of them are accessed by a medial staircase with three-dimensional sculpture or stucco masks decorated on its side façades. The most striking monumental Mayan structures built on top are the temple-pyramids. They were narrow interior spaced temples built on terraced pyramidal platforms which give them an average height of over 30m. Many temple-pyramids are further extended with roof-combs, probably serving as a kind of free-standing sculptural landmark that could be seen from a considerable distance (Foster 2002). There are radial ladders on all four sides of the steep-sloping pyramids. The temple on top was accessed by one to five large doorways. Its rooms are usually constructed with corbelled vaults, not more than 3m wide, high above its ceilings. Wall niches, altars, and shrines are commonly found at the rear of the temple.

The walls of the Mayan pyramid-temple are usually thicker than the width of its inner rooms, which results in a relatively restricted interior space. This indicates that the elevation of the building was the prime concern of the builders. In addition, many temple-pyramids are further increased in height with the addition of parapets and the massive roof-combs. Again, these extensions were vaulted (diagram 10.2). The doorway and entrance to the pyramid-temple itself provide the largest interior space and its lintel is usually decorated with giant stucco deity ornaments.

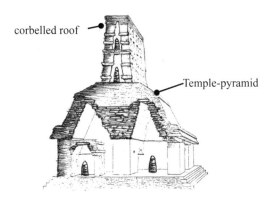

corbelled roof

Temple-pyramid

**Vaulted Extension of Temple of the
Cross, Palenque, and Conical Devices**
(Coe 1999, p. 133)
Diagram 10.2

**Mayan Artifact Showing a
Cone-shaped Object under the
Lintel Doorway of a Temple**
(Evans 2004, p. 284)
Diagram 10.3

Plazas or ceremonial courtyards are icons of Mayan buildings. They are levelled and paved with lime-based plaster at open areas rectilinear in shape. Low-rise building compounds made of clay with rubble-core mounds or platforms are constructed at their four sides (diagram 10.4). It was the paved open plaza rather than the restricted building interior that was the focus for the ancient Maya, and that could be why the exterior of the massive walls of the surrounding buildings are heavily decorated. The most famous Mayan example is Copan, where small satellite plazas cluster around the city center.

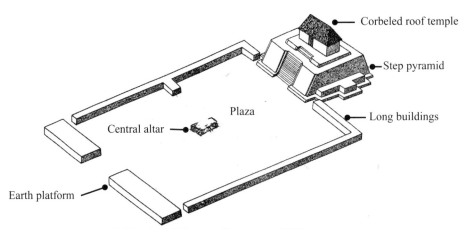

Corbeled roof temple

Step pyramid

Plaza

Long buildings

Central altar

Earth platform

A Typical Mayan Courtyard/Plaza
(after Andrews 1965)
Diagram 10.4

Another basic "accessory" of the Maya were the stelae—standing stones carved with ruling figures and inscriptions. Most of these stelae are in groups at the plaza center. Each stela is usually accompanied by another heavily carved stone altar in front (diagram 10.5).

Can we apply the golden rule of the SA to the Mesoamerican Culture to reveal its history? Experts suggest there were different civilizations flourishing in different times and places over Central and South America. The Olmec and the Classic Maya of the early time dominated the tropical lowlands. The Mixtecs, Zapotecs, and highland Maya flourished in highland Mesoamerica whereas Central Mexico was once the home of the Aztecs. The fact that these Mesoamerican buildings are built according to the SA simply implies that the Mesoamerican culture was just another station of the ancient builders.

Stela 10, Serbal Ruler Ah-Bolon-Abte and His Ceremonial Bar
(drawing by John Montgomery 1988)
Diagram 10.5

Temple-Pyramids of Uxmal and the SA

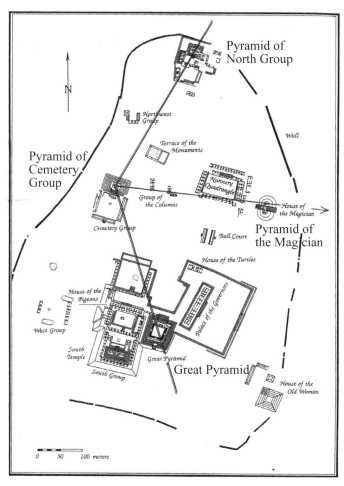

Uxmal is probably the finest ancient city in Maya. It was built on a small area, measuring 700m by 800m in northern Yucatan. Dating back to the Preclassic period, it emerged as the dominant city-state between A.D. 850 and 900 when its terraced Great Pyramid and the House of the Magician were built. The Great Pyramid, decorated with Chac masks suggesting it was a temple to the sun, is 30m high, its nine levels suggesting it might have been constructed in nine phases. Like other Mayan infrastructures, a temple with ornate carvings stands on top. Similar stepped pyramids were constructed around the region, positioned according to the SA (diagram 10.6).

Plan of Uxmal with Main Pyramids Aligning to the SA
(Coe 1994)
Diagram 10.6

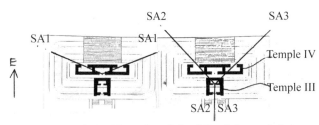

Plan of the Temple of the Magician with Doorways Aligning to the SA
Diagram 10.6a

The most outstanding monument of Uxmal is the Pyramid of the Magician, northeast of the Great Pyramid. Begun in around the sixth century A.D., it was added to over the next 400 years. It rises 38m from the ground, making it the tallest building of the city. According to local legend, the pyramid was built by a magician in one night. Its west stairway is extremely steep but climbers can enjoy a spectacular view over the whole site from its top, where two corbel-roofed temples stand. The upper and east facing temple has three doorways opening to three separate rooms. Incidentally, its lintel doorways form an SA, probably revealing the actual function of the building (diagram 10.6a). Furthermore, the doorways of the lower and west-facing temple form two extra sets of SAs with the east temple. Its single doorway is crowned and carved with the iconic god mask in the most elaborate and conspicuous way (diagram 10.1). What is the significance of this symbolic deity and why is it so prominent on the builders' powerhouse?

The pyramids and buildings of Uxmal are constructed according to the SA:

SA1 is formed by three pyramids: the Great Pyramid and the pyramid of the North Group, with the pyramid of the Cemetery Group in the middle (diagram 10.6). The angle bisects at the Pyramid of the Magician.

SA2 is derived from the pyramid of the North Group and the Jaguar Throne (stone altar) of the Governor's Palace, with the Pyramid of the Magician in the middle. The angle bisects at the plaza of the Cemetery Group. The builders' traveling machine, once parked at this plaza, could have projected a row of megalights to the western doorway of the Temple of the Magician to activate the power mechanism (diagram 10.7).

SA3 is formed by the Jaguar Throne, the Pyramid of the Magician and the South Temple of the Pigeon's Quadrangle. The angle bisects at the plaza of the Cemetery Group.

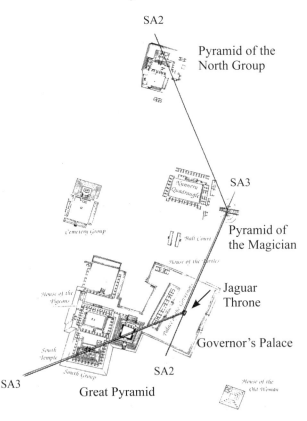

SA2 and SA3 of Uxmal
(after Coe)
Diagram 10.7

Long Houses of Uxmal: The Builders' Dry Cell Batteries

Apart from the terraced pyramids, Uxmal is also famous for its superb houses of assembly in the Puuc architectural style (Sharer 1994). One of these is the Governor's Palace, the largest single structure of its kind, situated west of a triple platform 15m high covering two hectares of ground. It is lined by three main building blocks connected by some small cells, making it 100m long, 12m wide, and 8m high. The central block is the largest with three doorways opening to the main double-chambered compartment. Its doorways are again aligned to the SA (diagram 10.8) and, structurally and functionally, it is similar to the Temple of the Magician.

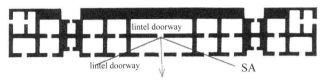

lintel doorway

lintel doorway   SA

Uxmal Govenor's Palace and the SA (after Sharer)
Diagram 10.8

Three power-generating devices, once placed at its doorways, could have projected megalights to the masonry posts and lintels for power. Uxmal possesses a quantity of phallic sculpture. Such motifs are found on the rear façade of the North Building of the Nunnery, platform of the Governor's Palace, and of course, the façade of the so-called Temple of the Phallus (Sharer 1994). These cylindrical objects are probably the new models of the builders' conical devices once placed inside the Neolithic powerhouses in Europe 2,000 years ago (diagrams 10.99 and 10.100).

The Governor's Palace of Uxmal became the builders' powerhouse after A.D. 300, explaining why its whole upper façade is decorated extensively with S-shaped scrolls—probably the builders' sign of the special duty of the monument (diagram 10.9). Similar spiral carvings are commonly found in the Neolithic Europe, especially in the Boyne Valley of Ireland. A stone altar—the Jaguar Throne—lies in the middle of the complex and was probably the refueling platform for the builders' vehicles. Most importantly, the Pyramid of the Magician and the South Pyramid form a perfect SA with the stone altar of the Palace. One can imagine two rows of megalights being produced by the builders' vehicle to connect the two gigantic powerhouses nearby for recharging (diagram 10.7). This magical moment is permanently captured in the sculpture of a double-headed jaguar on top of the Throne (diagram 10.10). Its secret is clearly described by a famous relic of the period (diagram 10.14).

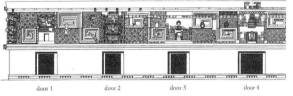

door 1   door 2   door 3   door 4

S-Shaped Scrolls of the Governor's Palace, Uxmal
(after Schele and Mathews)
Diagram 10.9

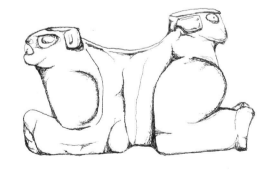

**"Chariot of the God":
Two-headed Jaguar on the Platform
of the Governor's Palace**
Diagram 10.10

Located north of the Governor's Palace is another famous structure, the Nunnery Quadrangle. It is probably the most impressive and mysterious structure in the city. The whole complex is a large open courtyard measuring 76m by 61m framed by long buildings on its four sides. The North Building, which surmounts a 5.5m-high terrace, is the most important unit on the Quadrangle (Sharer 1994) and is constructed with medial staircases. The upper façades of all these quadrangle houses, especially their lintel doorways, are famous for their mosaic-sculptured patterns and symbols—three-dimensional plaster decorations called stucco reliefs. Examples of these are flower lattice, S-shaped scrolls, double-headed serpents, and jaguar masks (diagrams 10.11a and 10.11b).

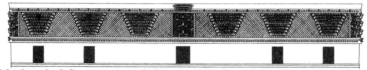

Double-headed Serpents and Jaguar Masks of the Nunnery, Uxmal
(after Schele and Mathews)
Diagram 10.11a

V-shaped Designs Above the Outer Doors of the South Building, Probably Showing the Emission of Energy Generated from the House
(after Schele and Mathews)
Diagram 10.11b

Experts suggest that to the ancient Mayans the vast and heavily decorated open courtyard was the most important sacred precinct, leaving the surrounding buildings with their restricted and undecorated interior space to the priests. The following diagrams show the floor plans of the North, South, and East Buildings. Their doorways of the double-chambered compartments are aligned to the SA (diagram 10.12).

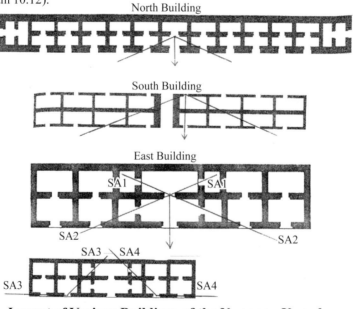

Layout of Various Buildings of the Nunnery, Uxmal
Diagram 10.12

Again, the SA formula suggests that these long and narrow houses were once built for housing the builders' power-generating devices. When the powerhouse was activated, concentric circles of energy would be emitted from the top of their lintel doorways, probably explaining why the doorways are heavily decorated with flowers and scroll spiral patterns (diagram 10.9). The moment and scene of refuelling of the builders' vehicle is depicted by the sculpture of the North Building (diagram 10.13). A cylindrical central figure projects a radiance of light beams to activate the doorway. V-shaped mouldings with three-dimensional double-headed serpents probably represent the energy generated which is then projected above the lintel doorways (diagram 10.11). Once again, the builders' vehicles, always depicted as the gods' masks, were carved above the double-headed serpent mouldings. Behind the Mayan city of Uxmal certainly lies more secrets than we envisage. But the most unexpected finding of the city's thousand-year-old secret is answered by an ancient megalithic carving, an all-time iconic stone of the whole Mesoamerican culture.

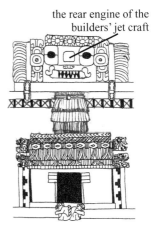

the rear engine of the builders' jet craft

**Builders' Message:
A Jet Craft Refuelling
on Top of a Mayan
Powerhouse**
Diagram 10.13

The Aztec Calendar Stone

"A wheel like the sun, as big as a cartwheel, with many sorts of pictures on it, the whole of fine gold and a wonderful thing to behold…"

—Sitchin (1990)

The Calendar Stone, also known as the Sun Stone, is perhaps the most famous and important prehistoric artifacts of the Aztecs, another mysterious culture that succeeded the Mayans (diagram 10.14). The Stone is a massive disk of carved basalt, 3.6m in diameter and weighing almost twenty-five tons. It was fortuitously uncovered in the central plaza of Mexico City, in 1790. Originally, the stone set horizontally was probably used for the execution of prisoners, but its primary meaning and purpose is still open to debate. According to local legend, the Stone originated from a gold plate

The Aztec Calendar Stone
(hsp-aztec.com)
Diagram 10.14

and was a gift from their deified wise man who brought laws and knowledge to the Aztecs. Based on the hieroglyphs on the Stone surface, experts regard it as a calendar stone which the priests used for determining important days for agricultural and ceremonial activities. The Stone may offer a graphic representation of the Mexican cosmos. Some even suggest the carvings depict the beginning and end of the Aztec world.

Basically, the Calendar Disk, with an Aztec name Cuauhxicalli Eagle Bowl, contains a set of concentric rings around a central carving of the face of Tonatiuh—the fifth solar god of Aztec or Lord of Heaven. Some suggest he was Xolotl, "the god who fell from heaven" (Sitchin 2004), with his tongue sticking out, symbolizing a sacrificial knife (diagram 10.15a). Others think he is a death god in the Miclantecuhtli complex, or simply the wise man who brought civilization to the Aztecs.

**Xolotl, "Lord of Heaven,"
Wearing a Conical Hat with
Radiant Lines** (Sitchin 2004)
Diagram 10.15a

**"Pointer" of the Aztec Calendar Stone
and the German Gold Cone**
Diagram 10.15b

Set around Tonatiuh are four quadrants or squares called Nahui-Ollin, or Four Movement, which probably represent the preceding four eras of ancient Maya. According to legend, the four eras were respectively destroyed by jaguars, wind, rain, and water. The Aztecs believed that they were living in the fifth and last creation of their world. Two other claw-like figures are placed at two sides of the deity, one between each of two quadrants. Coincidentally, the main axes of the four quadrants form two sets of SAs with their angles bisecting at the two claw-like figures respectively (diagram 10.16).

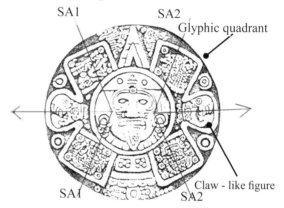

**Innermost Ring of the Calendar Stone
with Four Quadrants Aligned to the SA**
Diagram 10.16

Station Stones of the Calendar Stone

Next to the quadrants are five coordinate circles, known as Nemontemi, which experts speculate represent specific numerical quantities or depict days for sacrifice but no actual meaning is even posed (Wikipedia). However, these circles are strategically laid in the same pattern as the four Station Stones of Stonehenge and form a pair of opposite SAs (diagram 10.17). The fifth coordinate circle, probably similar to the Heel Stone, is precisely at the axis of the angle bisector. Undoubtedly, the Stone carver, like the builders of Stonehenge, was showing the secret of the magic power, on the Stone. It was this sacred angle that determined all the megalithic infrastructures of the prehistoric time and ultimately constituted the mysteries of the ancient world. Most interestingly, a conical device, the calendar pointer as understood by the experts, was placed opposite the fifth coordinate circle. We can identify it from its pointed top and the light holes below. So, where is the sarsen trilithon ring of Stonehenge?

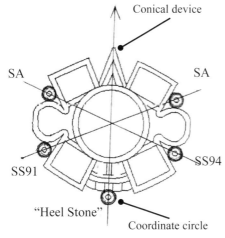

Conical device

SA · SA

SS91 · SS94

"Heel Stone"

Coordinate circle

**Inner Ring of the Aztec Calendar
and Its Station Stones**
Diagram 10.17

Day-Glyph Ring and the Lintel Doorways

The Second Ring from the center, known as the "Day-Glyph Ring," contains twenty named days in a month of the Mayan calendar (Johnson, C). Each glyph is placed between two portals—lintel-doorways. Thus the Ring depicts the setting of the builders' power station formed by a circle of Mayan long houses. The decorations on top of the doorways of the Stone Ring are similar to those on top of a typical Teotihuacan temple (diagram 10.18). The Ring also echoes the architecture of the famous sarsen trilithon circle of Stonehenge with a ring of thirty lintel-portal doorways (diagram 10.19).

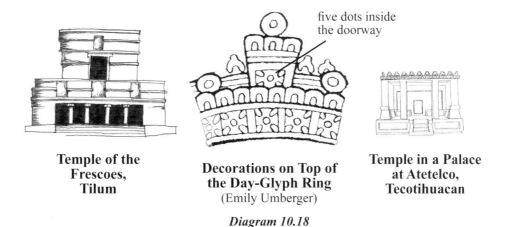

five dots inside
the doorway

**Temple of the
Frescoes,
Tilum**

**Decorations on Top of
the Day-Glyph Ring**
(Emily Umberger)

**Temple in a Palace
at Atetelco,
Tecotihuacan**

Diagram 10.18

On the stone, the secret function of the doorway is further implied by the five dots placed inside it, in the form of a solar-ray motif, probably representing megalights being projected by a conical device. That is why eight mega-sized conical devices are carefully carved between these doorways or on top of the long houses. Needless to say, the builders' conical devices are strategically located to show the SA alignment—the ultimate rule of the powerhouse (diagram 10.19).

On top of the doorways are eight triangular pointers, which were believed to be both solar rays and directional indicators. The four larger pointers indicated the four cardinal directions and served as a symbol for the entire earth (Smith 2003).

2nd and 3rd Rings of the Calendar Stone, Showing a Circle of Lintel Doorways. Conical Devices are Placed According to the SA
Diagram 10.19

As a matter of fact, the Stone Ring design can perfectly apply to the ancient Mayan city of Uxmal, where the "twenty-doorwayed" Ring exactly describes the famous setting of the Nunnery Complex. The diagram below shows the plan of the Nunnery with its central courtyard surrounded by single-storied buildings on four sides. Apart from the North Building, which was constructed in earlier period, the other three long buildings—East, South, and West—have a total of twenty lintel doorways, the same number on the Aztec Stone. A similar setting with twenty doorways is found in the Central Courtyard of the South Group (diagram 10.20).

And on the Stone, an outer ring, next to the second ring, reveals the real function of Uxmal.

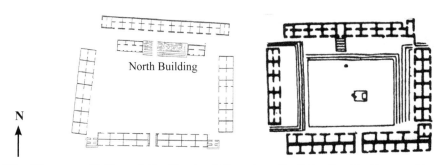

North Building

N

The Nunnery (*left*) and the Central Courtyard of the South Group, Uxmal
Diagram 10.20

Fire Serpents and the Builders' Temple-pyramids

The ultimate secret of the Stone lies in its outermost ring. Many experts see it as two fire serpents, with their scaled bodies divided into ten segments, meeting face to face at the bottom with their tails pointing to each other at the very top. The pointed tail actually represents a typical Mayan temple-pyramid with an extended corbelled roof (diagram 10.21). The temple, built on the top of a four-tiered platform, opens with a single portal-and-lintel doorway and is similar to those on top of the Pyramid of the Magician and the Great Pyramid. A central stairway is carefully carved and a conical object is shown inside its corbelled roof.

The tail has ten body segments, which represent the ten-storied pyramid that forms the foundation of a temple (diagram 10.22). The builders' powerhouse would probably be activated when a device was placed at the doorways. Radiating lines that are projected onto the three sides of the doorway are clearly shown on the body segments. Also, radiating lines of power, probably representing energy waves, are generated from both sides of the triangular corbelled roof at the top of the temple-pyramid. These lines of energy are then connected and projected onto a mega–conical device, as shown at the top of the Calendar Stone (diagram 10.24).

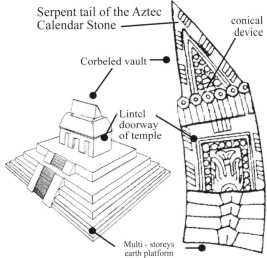

Serpent tail of the Aztec Calendar Stone

conical device

Corbeled vault

Lintel doorway of temple

Multi - storeys earth platform

A Typical Mayan Temple-pyramid with Roof-comb Extension
Diagram 10.21

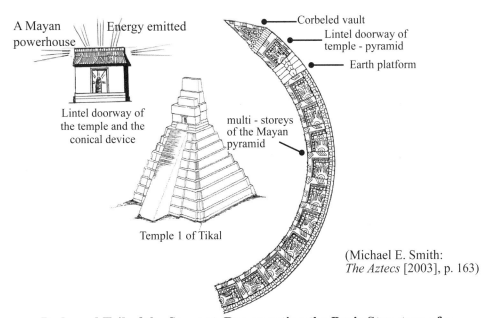

A Mayan powerhouse

Energy emitted

Lintel doorway of the temple and the conical device

Temple 1 of Tikal

Corbeled vault

Lintel doorway of temple - pyramid

Earth platform

multi - storeys of the Mayan pyramid

(Michael E. Smith: *The Aztecs* [2003], p. 163)

Body and Tail of the Serpent, Representing the Basic Structure of a Multistoried Temple-pyramid
Diagram 10.22

The Stone also reveals that another line of energy is projected onto a square glyph at the very top. Many experts interpret and relate the square to "the contemporary Mexican date of 1479" (the date of creation), the year the Mexican king created the Aztec empire. However, it is suggested the square glyph describes the builders' energy mechanism. The square carving can be understood in the following way: a conical device inside a bowl-like container at one side of the courtyard projected megalights onto the other three sides, where cell batteries could be found (diagram 10.23). As further suggested by the Stone, the charged courtyard connects the two corbel-vaulted temple-pyramids at its two sides by lines of energy. This is what once happened in Uxmal (diagram 10.24).

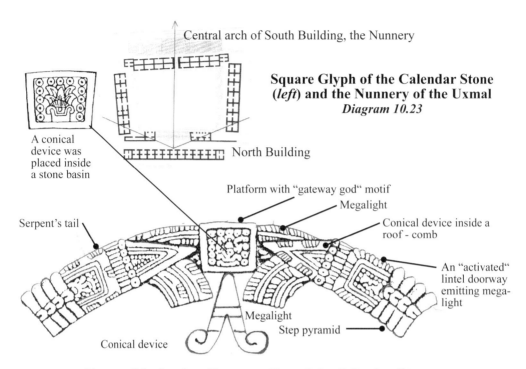

Central arch of South Building, the Nunnery

Square Glyph of the Calendar Stone
(*left*) and the Nunnery of the Uxmal
Diagram 10.23

A conical
device was
placed inside
a stone basin

North Building

Platform with "gateway god" motif

Megalight

Serpent's tail

Conical device inside a
roof - comb

An "activated"
lintel doorway
emitting mega-
light

Megalight

Step pyramid

Conical device

Energy Mechanism Shown on Top of the Calendar Stone
Diagram 10.24

Megalithic Map of Uxmal

The Calendar Stone can be interpreted in the following way: Its core shows the builders' technology: a conical device was once placed inside a courtyard for power. The courtyard is enclosed by long buildings with lintel doorways. A perfect example is the Nunnery Quadrangle of Uxmal. The midst of the central staircase of its North Building forms two sets of SAs with the surrounding tiered pyramids (diagram 10.26a). Today, a restored monument (Stela 17) with an eroded hieroglyphic text is set in the middle of the stairway (Sharer 1994) which probably marks the location of the builders' conical device (diagram 10.25).

SA1 The Pyramid of the North Group and the Pyramid of the South Group,
SA2 The House of the Magician and the Pyramid of the Cemetery Group. Its angle travels through the corbel vault of the South Building of the Nunnery and the main axis of the Ball Court, and finally bisects at the House of the Turtles.

The secret is unfolded by the Calendar Stone: the courtyard of the Nunnery connects the temple-pyramids nearby, constituting a typical power generator in Mesoamerica. Interestingly, the north courtyard of the South Group of Uxmal also forms several sets of SAs with the stairway of its southern long building in the middle (diagram 10.26b):

SA3 Pyramid of the North Group and the Great Pyramid,
SA4 Temple of the Magician and Pyramid of the South Group,
SA5 Pyramid of the Cemetery Group and Pyramid of the Old Woman.

To the Ball Court and
the House of the Turtles

SA2

SA2

To the Temple pyramid
of the Cemetery Group

To the Temple of the
Magician

North Building of the Nunnery

Location of Stela 17

Powerhouse of the North Building, the Nunnery
Diagram 10.25

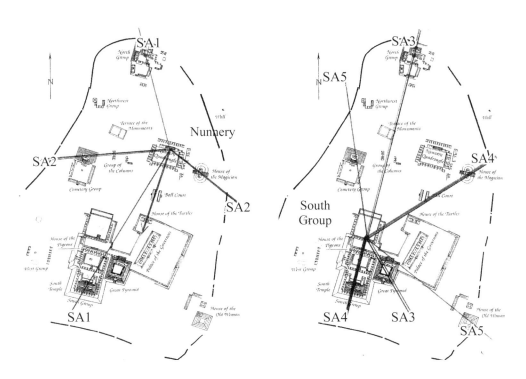

The Nunnery and the SA
Diagram 10.26a

**The Northern Courtyard, South
Group, and the SA**
Diagram 10.26b

The same scene could be found in the North Group (SA6) and the Cemetery Group (SA7) and
the House of the Pigeons (SA8). The stone platform outside the Governor's Palace also forms an
SA with the two famous terraced pyramids nearby. Its angle bisects precisely at the central block
of the Governor's Palace. Again, its secret is revealed in the Calendar Stone. The so-called Aztec
Calendar Stone is actually a megalithic map that describes, explains, and records the builders'
power station of Uxmal. The builders' traveling machines were once parked on the stone platforms inside the courtyards or on the rooftops of the long buildings for refuelling (diagram 10.27).
That is why their vehicles are carved so distinctly on the surfaces of their powerhouses.

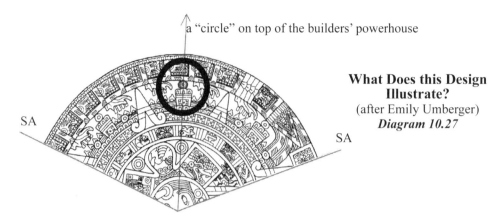

a "circle" on top of the builders' powerhouse

SA

SA

**What Does this Design
Illustrate?**
(after Emily Umberger)
Diagram 10.27

God Chac and the Builders' Jet Engine

The principle of SA is the way to interpret the Mayan architectures and unlock the mystery of how they once supplied power for the advanced builders' vehicles. These flying sedans, which once projected megalights to the lintel doorways of the long houses and temple-pyramids for power, are similar to those of their ancestors who erected dolmens and trilithons in the third millennium B.C. What vehicles were they that could travel effectively in and out of the tropical forestry and could be refuelled simply by megalithic buildings? The question is answered directly by the sculpture on Mayan structures.

God
Chac

Mayan Monster Mask
Diagram 10.28

The lintel doorway is the principal structure of all Mayan buildings. Experts suggest many of them were constructed for ceremonial purposes, as elaborate mosaic friezes of varied forms and figures are found on their external walls. The so-called monster masks are always identified as the ancient gods of Maya, from the rain and lightning god of Chac, to the Earth and Mountain Monsters, Celestial Dragons, and God K. The mask panels with big staring eyes, long curling and hooked noses, fierce teeth in a large open mouth, and huge ear ornaments prevail over the whole Mayan region (diagrams 10.28 and 10.29).

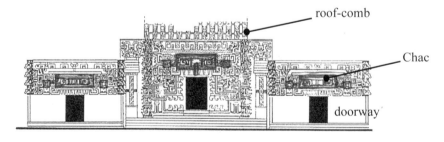

roof-comb

Chac

doorway

Chenes-style Building (Drawing by C. Ramirez)
Diagram 10.29

The stucco mask is actually the back engine of the builders' traveling vehicle. Its two jets are represented by the goggle-eyes, while its two ear ornaments stand for a pair of side jet engines. Functioning like a modern-day jet fighter, the side jets allowed vertical movement of the vehicle. That is why vertical air currents were generated when the engine was activated. It is clearly indicated above and below the two side engines (diagram 10.30a). Similar patterns of air currents are also shown under the main engine (diagram 10.30b and 10.31). There is a remarkable similarity between a Mayan monster mask and an outline of the engine of a modern-day motorbike. What creates the mystery of this Mayan civilization is our disbelief in the existence of an advanced intelligence in Mesoamerica 2,000 years ago.

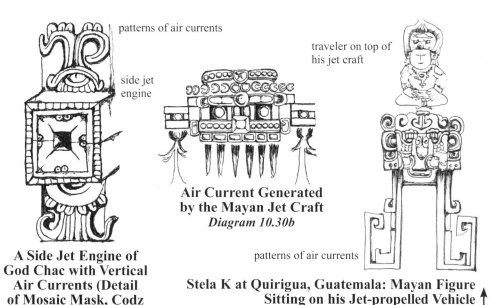

A Side Jet Engine of God Chac with Vertical Air Currents (Detail of Mosaic Mask, Codz Pop, Kabah)
Diagram 10.30a

Air Current Generated by the Mayan Jet Craft
Diagram 10.30b

Stela K at Quirigua, Guatemala: Mayan Figure Sitting on his Jet-propelled Vehicle
(after Stierlin) *Diagram 10.31*

Most of these masks are skillfully carved in three dimensions and, significantly, are located at the sides of the earthen platforms or on top of the long houses, as they actually mark the landing platforms of the builders' jet craft (diagram 10.32). Other masks, surrounded by motifs such as X-shaped lattices and stepped frets, probably depict the energy generated by the builders' powerhouses. In the courtyard of the Governor's Palace at Uxmal, a full-size two-headed stone jaguar sculpture with a saddle in the middle sits on the stone platform. It is another symbol of the builders' jet craft, in which the four limbs of the animal are its engines. Were these

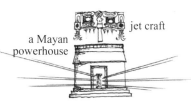

Frieze on Entablature of West Building, the Nunnery, Uxmal, Showing the Builders' Jet Craft on Top of a Mayan Temple
(after Schele and Mathews)
Diagram 10.32

monsters created by the Mesoamericans really objects of deification by superstitious ancients, or are they representing something else? It is nothing extraordinary to find vehicle illustrations and posters in our gas stations. But most people would be surprised to know the builders' jet engines are shown in such detail on Mayan powerhouses. These were the super crafts of the intelligence that traveled in and out of the inaccessible tropical rainforest 2,000 years ago.

a jet craft is refuelling on top of a powerhouse

Sculptures on the upper façade of the North Building

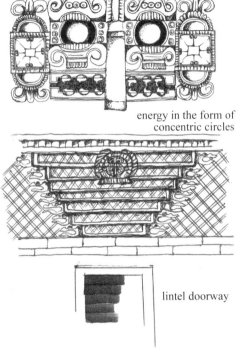

energy in the form of concentric circles

lintel doorway

Stacks of double-headed serpents forming V-shaped designs above the door of the East Building, probably showing energy emitted in the form of microwaves on the powerhouse.

The Nunnery: Power station of the builders' jet crafts

Sculptures on the upper façade of the South Building, with the builders' flying machine parked on top of a powerhouse

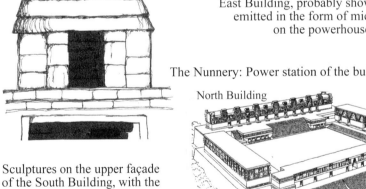

North Building

East Building

West Building

South Building

(diagram: Coe)

Powerhouses of the Nunnery, Uxmal
Diagram 10.32a

Cloud Scrolls or Spirals on the Upper Façade of the West Building of Uxmal Aligned to the SA, Probably Revealing the Real Function of the Different Powerhouses (*bottom diagram*)

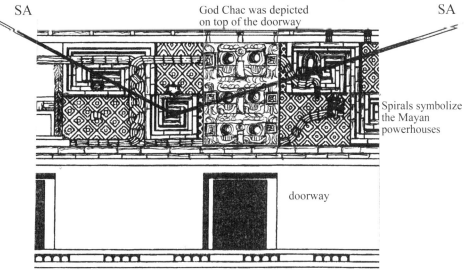

SA

God Chac was depicted
on top of the doorway

SA

Spirals symbolize
the Mayan
powerhouses

doorway

Frieze on the Upper Façade of the West Building, Nunnery
(drawing: Schele and Mathews)

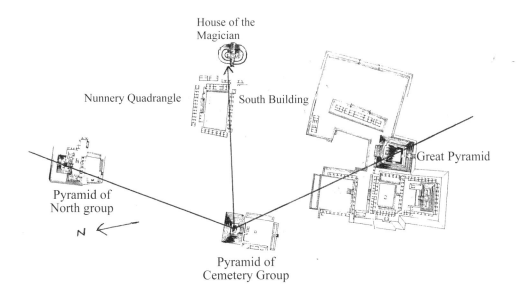

House of the
Magician

Nunnery Quadrangle

South Building

Great Pyramid

Pyramid of
North group

N

Pyramid of
Cemetery Group

Plan of Uxmal: SA Bisecting on the South Building, the Nunnery
(after Coe)
Diagram 10.32b

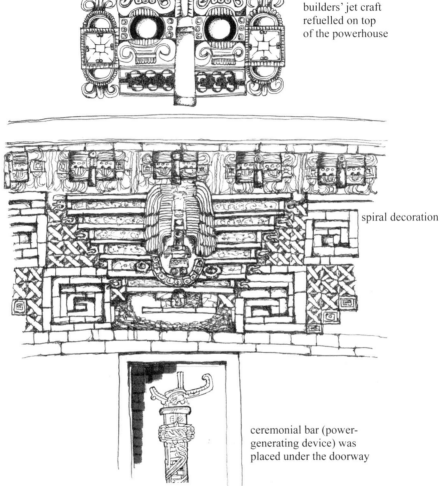

builders' jet craft
refuelled on top
of the powerhouse

spiral decoration

ceremonial bar (power-
generating device) was
placed under the doorway

The True Story of the Governor's Palace
Diagram 10.32c

The Governor's Palace of Uxmal is one of the finest and best examples of the Puuc architectural style—a plain lower section and a richly carved upper façade. Among the depictions on the central sculpture on the palace's façade is a lattice pattern which symbolizes royal power, double-headed serpents with S-shaped ornaments, long-nosed Chac mask panels, and also a central seated god-like figure with a long plumed headdress of quetzel feathers.

Actually, the central sculpture is a detailed description of the work of the powerhouse. The lattice patterns and spirals are energy generated from the building while the V-shaped designs formed by the double-headed serpents are concentric circles of microwaves generated directly above the central doorway where the builders' jet craft is being recharged.

Map of Uxmal

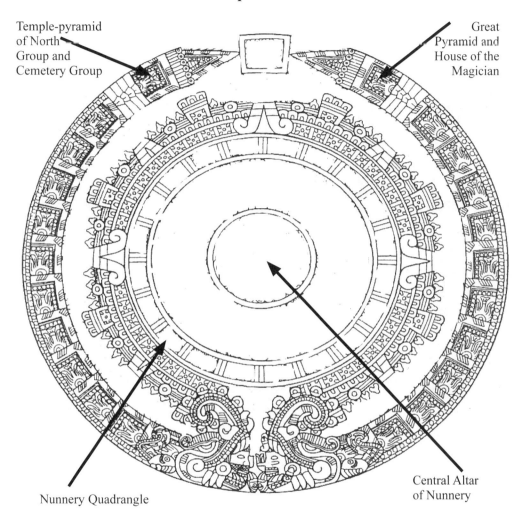

Temple-pyramid of North Group and Cemetery Group

Great Pyramid and House of the Magician

Nunnery Quadrangle

Central Altar of Nunnery

The Power Station of Uxmal, A.D. 850–900
(adapted from a drawing by Emily Umberger in Michael E. Smith, *The Aztecs* [1996])
Diagram 10.32d

Major SAs of Uxmal:
SA1: Temple-pyramid of North Group–The Nunnery–Great Pyramid
SA2: Temple-pyramid of Cemetery Group–The Nunnery–House of the Magician

Palenque and the Temple of the Inscriptions

The ancient city of Palenque is a must-see tourist attraction. Dating back to A.D. 500 and decorated with stucco relief panels, many Palenque buildings have remained intact. The most eye-catching structure is the 24m-high Temple of the Inscriptions. The three internal panels covered with Mayan inscriptions may help to unmask their mystery. In the 1950s, when the deciphering work still had a long way to go, a magnificent burial site hidden within its depth was discovered, further deepening the mystery. The temple itself has five post-and-lintel doorways that link with a long outer chamber where its three doorways open to three inner chambers. Like the builders' other powerhouses, the doorways of the Temple of the Inscription form several sets of SAs (diagram 10.33).

The Temple of Inscriptions is important in Palenque, as it constitutes three sets of SAs with the surrounding pyramids (diagram 10.34):

SA2 the pyramid of the Main Plaza and a pyramid to its right

SA3 Temple of the Sun and the lintel doorway of Temple of the Cross

SA4 Temple X and the Temple of the Count

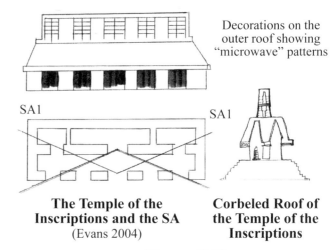

Decorations on the outer roof showing "microwave" patterns

The Temple of the Inscriptions and the SA
(Evans 2004)

Corbeled Roof of the Temple of the Inscriptions

Diagram 10.33

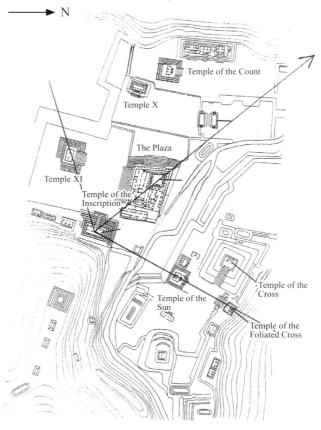

Plan of Palenque
Diagram 10.34

Aztec Calendar Stone and the Palace of Palenque

Another extraordinary infrastructure of Palenque is the Palace. It measures 91m by 73m and is built on a 10m-high platform. Similar to the Nunnery of Uxmal, small interior courtyards are formed by vaulted galleries and rooms. As suggested by the Aztec Calendar Stone, the center of its northwest courtyard forms several sets of SAs with the surrounding terraced pyramids (diagram 10.35). Again, the builders' energy mechanism of Palenque is clearly described on the Calendar Stone.

SA1 Temple of the North Group and Temple of the Foliated Cross
SA2 Great Pyramid and Temple of the Foliated Cross
SA3 Temple of the Count and Temple of the Cross
SA4 Pyramid of Inscription and Temple of the Count

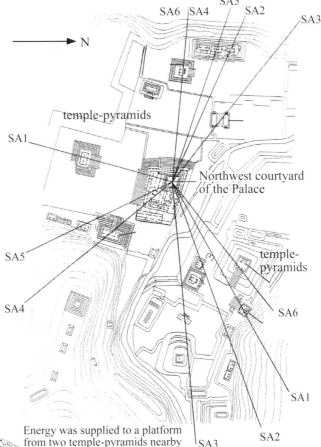

Energy mechanism shown on top of the Calendar Stone

The Palace of Palenque as the Center of Various SAs
Diagram 10.35

The Cross of Palenque and the Jet Craft

The Temple of the Cross and its nearby temples stand on a large, elevated plaza along the eastern side of Palenque. The temple is constructed on top of a thirteen-tier pyramid with its doorways and the rear shrine aligned to the SA (diagram 10.36). It used to be an important powerhouse of the builders, as it is the origin of several sets of SAs (diagram 10.37).

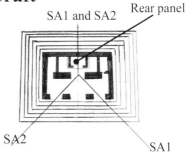

Plan of Temple of the Cross and the SA
Diagram 10.36

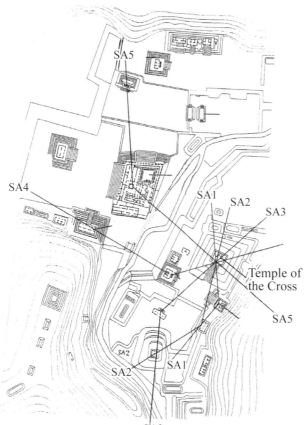

The Temple of the Cross
Diagram 10.37

But what makes the temple superb is its heavily decorated interior, shrines, and doorways. Most of them are framed with hieroglyphic texts and stucco panels. A gigantic monster mask in its full glory is carved predominantly on the lintel of the shrine (the *pib na*) inside the central rear room. The most remarkable carving is a cross-shaped motif decorated on the rear panel of the shrine, which gives the name of the temple. The carved "Cross" represents the center of the universe supporting heaven. Its axis, rising from the mask of the great earth monster below, is the umbilical cord of the world unifying the two poles of the cosmos. Many think that it is a Tree of Life symbolic of an eternal afterworld (diagram 10.38).

Overhead View of
the Builders' Jet Craft

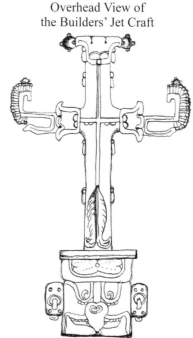

But the Tree can also be interpreted in a "scientific" way. It is a plan of the builders' jet craft. Its rear jet engine is shown at the base of the Cross. The main axis of the Cross is actually the crossbar of a super-bike. There are lights on the front, or head, and brake levers at the ends of the horizontal bar. The vehicle's saddle is clearly carved at the base of the Cross, just above the rear jet engine. The real "soul" of the vehicle—its jet engine—is designed with symmetrical big eyes and huge ear ornaments that center around a big mouth. It is always described and misinterpreted as one of the monster masks found on every Mayan building. The giant mask on the shrine's lintel is actually a representation of a fully charged jet craft (see diagram 10.90 on p. 375, below).

**"Tree of Life" Motif inside the
Temple of the Cross**
Diagram 10.38

A similar design of the so-called Tree of Life is found in the Temple of Inscriptions hundreds of meters west of the Temple of the Cross. The temple is famous both for its fabulous hieroglyphic inscriptions and for the tomb of Pacal, who ruled Palenque in A.D. 615–683. Apart from all the precious burial offerings, the most amazing relic is a mosaic jade mask that covers Pacal's face (diagram 10.39a). The selection of rare stones and the skillful craftsmanship make it the most precious item found inside the tomb. Mask wearing was not a common practice for the ancient Mayans even though there are many carvings and sculptures of Mayan rulers wearing them. But, under what circumstances would a dead person require an air mask in his afterlife? A brand new future world in which he needs to cover his former identity, or high-speed travel that requires wearing an air mask for ventilation?

A Real Space Traveller: The Bearded Jaguar God, Stela 8, Seibal, Wearing a Helmet with Electric Coil Equipment, Goggles, and a Hands-free Communication Device
Diagram 10.39b

"Air Mask" of Pacal
Diagram 10.39a

Most intriguing is the carving on the stone lid of the sarcophagus (diagram 10.40). On top of the lid, there is a tight-suited person, probably the entombed Pacal himself, with his upper body leaning forward like a motorcyclist travelling at speed, as evidenced by his flying hair. Like motorcyclists of this world his left hand seems to be holding a gear while his right hand is operating the clutch. At the same time, his left foot is stepping on some kind of pedal. A Tree of Life is placed behind the leaning cyclist. This cross-like "superbike" is most probably propelled by jet engine at the rear where there would be flame and gas. The jet craft would travel at extremely high speed so the driver would wear a mask for ventilation and protection. Pacal must have imagined the magic of the builders and the power of their vehicle. That is why he is dressed in full gear with his upper body leaning forward, imitating his superior god. However, from the picture on the lid, his driving posture is a mismatch with the travelling vehicle behind. Why? Has he misunderstood something, something he is wanting desperately, something that could take him to the Afterlife? The answer lies in another famous Mayan city, Copan.

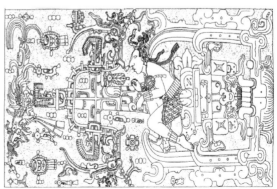

Motifs on the Lid of Pacal's Sarcophagus, Temple of Inscriptions, Palenque
Diagram 10.40

Map of Palenque

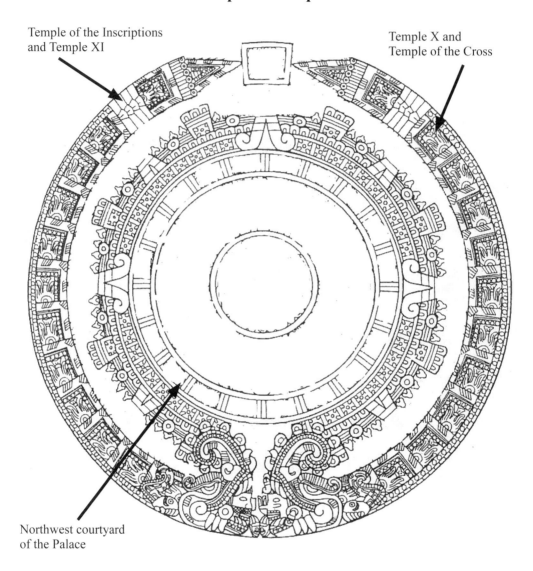

Temple of the Inscriptions
and Temple XI

Temple X and
Temple of the Cross

Northwest courtyard
of the Palace

The Power Station of Palenque, circa A.D. 500
(adapted from a drawing by Emily Umberger in Michael E. Smith, *The Aztecs* [1996])
Diagram 10.40a

Major SAs of Palenque:
SA1: Temple of the Inscriptions–The Palace–Temple X
SA2: Temple XI–The Palace–Temple of the Cross

Copan and Pyramid 16

The ruins of Copan, the most famous ancient city of Maya, are located in what is now Western Honduras of Central America. Archaeologists call Copan the "Athens of the New World," as many impressive and artistic monuments are found on the site. In 1980, Copan was designated a world heritage site by UNESCO (diagram 10.41).

Experts generally believe that the city, originally known as Xukpi, emerged around 1000 B.C. and reached its "golden age" between A.D. 426 and 820. It covered approximately fifty acres and had a population of 20,000. There are some 4,509 buildings. The most important is an artificial acropolis formed and encircled by a group of massive pyramidal structures. Pyramid 16 marks the highest point of Copan. It

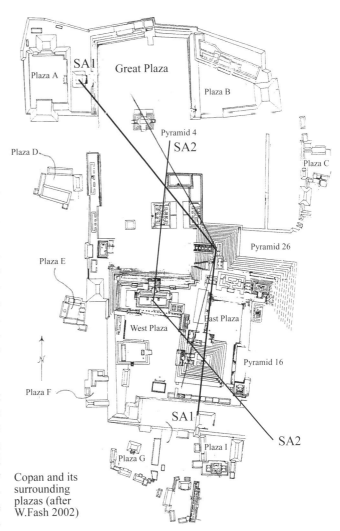

Copan and its surrounding plazas (after W.Fash 2002)

The Great SA of Copan, Formed by North Doorway of Pyramid 4–Lintel Doorway of Pyramid 26–West Platform of Pyramid 16
Diagram 10.41

became notable when the Rosalila Structure, with a giant deity mask, was uncovered. Another tomb of a Mayan ruler was found under the structure. Pyramid 16 is connected with other structures by the SA (diagram 10.42).

Copan is famous for its vast number of hieroglyphic texts, carved not only on a forest of stelae and altars (diagram 10.47a), but also the stairway of its pyramids. The unique Hieroglyphic Stairway of the Temple of the Inscriptions (Pyramid 26 in diagram 10.41) has sixty-three inscribed steps. It seems that their creator, the important king of Copan, "18 Rabbit," was eager to tell his distinctive history and mystery.

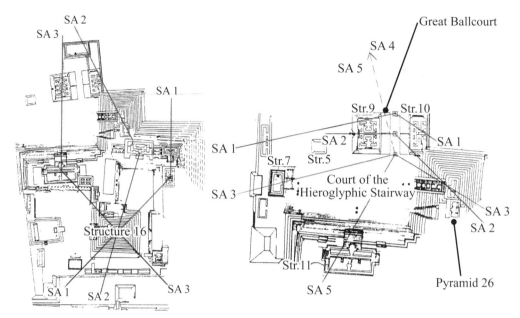

Structure 16 of Copan and the SA
Diagram 10.42

The Great Ballcourt, Copan
Diagram 10.43

Plazas of Copan: The Mayan Stone Circles

Another impressive structure is the Great Plaza, which lies north of the acropolis. It is an expansive, grassy courtyard with Structure 4, a radial pyramid, in the center. As previously mentioned, it forms an SA with two pyramids at its northeast and northwest. The whole city of Copan is surrounded by many smaller plazas or courtyards formed by long buildings and terraced platforms. For example, there are two large additional plazas, at the northeast and northwest corners of the Great Plaza, named Plazas A and B. Several plazas, at the western and southern periphery of Copan, form several SAs with Structure 4 in the middle (diagram 10.44):

SA1: The centers of Plazas A and B form a perfect SA, with the radial pyramid of the Great Plaza in the middle. The angle bisects at Altar A, north of the pyramid.
SA2: Pyramid 4 forms an SA with Plazas C and D.
SA3: Pyramid 4 also forms another SA with Plaza A and the East Plaza of the acropolis.
SA4: Plazas B and E form an SA with Pyramid 4 in the middle.

Probably Pyramid 4, with several projected rows of megalights, once connected different plazas of Copan. Pyramid 26 also forms SA5–8 with its surrounding plazas:

SA5: It forms an SA with the center of the Great Plaza and Plaza G. The angle bisects at altar M to the west of Pyramid 26.
SA6: It forms another SA with the center of Plaza A and the East Plaza, as well as Plaza I to its south. The angle bisects at Plaza E.
SA7: Another SA is formed by Plaza B and the West Plaza with Pyramid 26 in the middle. The angle bisects at Plaza D.
SA8: Plazas C and H form an SA with Pyramid 26.

There is a similar setting at Pyramid 16, located in the center of the artificial acropolis of Copan:

SA9: It forms an SA with the center of Plaza A and the center of the Plaza of El Cementerio.
SA10: Another SA is formed by the centers of the Great Plaza and Plaza G, with Pyramid 16 in the middle.
SA11: Another SA is formed by the center of the East Plaza, the center of Plaza C, and the center of Plaza F. The angle bisects at Temple 11.
SA12: An SA is formed by Plazas C and I with Pyramid 16 in the middle.
SA13: An SA is formed by Plazas D and H with Pyramid 16 in the middle.

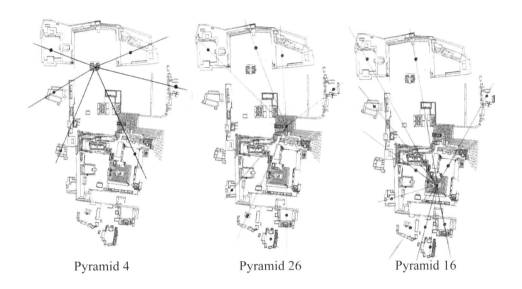

Pyramid 4   Pyramid 26   Pyramid 16

Various Pyramids of Copan and the SA
Diagram 10.44

Altar G1: Superbike of the Builders

"Secrets once safe beneath mountains of rubble have yielded to meticulous excavations and thoughtful interpretation. After decades of archaeological investigation, Copan's royal tombs and amazing sculpture provide us with a glimpse into 'Maya mind.'"

—Turismo de Centroamerica S. de R.L. (2006)

When viewed from above, a plan view of the builders' jet craft with a crossbar and rear jet engines is clearly shown inside the Temple of the Cross at Palenque. Another god-like statue—the Celestial Dragon—on Altar G1 Copan, is an even better depiction of the vehicle (diagrams 10.45a and 10.45b). According to Domenici (2002), "Altar G1 was built by Yax Pac in 800 A.D. in Copan's central square. The altar depicts the two-headed celestial dragon with its open jaws in a representation of the supreme deity Itzamna in animal form. The head on the left is in skeletal form as a symbol of duality. The ball in the middle of the inscription is probably an image of the sun" (diagram 10.45a).

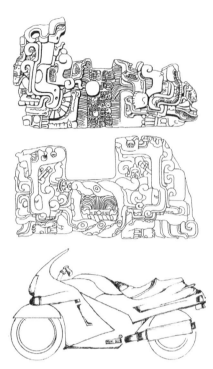

Altar G1
(drawing by C. Ontiveros)
Diagram 10.45a

Altar O
(after Maudslay 1974)
Diagram 10.45a

A Modern-day Motorbike
Diagram 10.45c

Actually, the diagram is a side view of the builders' vehicle. A curved head is connected to a large rear jet engine under a central saddle. A complex of interlocking wire- and tube-like objects are clearly carved in the midsection of the vehicle, which lies just under the seat. The god's two side "legs" carved at the two ends of the vehicle probably represent the jet engines providing propulsion for the vehicle. Most interestingly, if the Mayan ruler Pacal was "removed" from the Tree of Life at Palenque and superimposed on the Celestial Dragon, the jet craft of Copan, it would be a perfect match. An ancient astronaut is on his super-jet (diagrams 10.46a and 10.46b)!

Back view of the builders' jet plane

Pacal Aboard his Celestial Dragon
(Altar GI)
Diagram 10.46a

A Yax-Hal-Witz from Borcampak's Stela I
Diagram 10.46b

It clearly makes sense as the ancient Mayans once depicted their super-advanced deities travelling in their jet crafts with their upper body leaning forward. It might be the most "divine" posture, and probably a prerequisite to the Afterworld, at least in the eyes of the ancient Mesoamericans. And Pacal, the most powerful man at his time, certainly "knew" this secret skill to manipulate his jet monster. That is why this magic moment is captured on his stone sarcophagus. A mask made of jade, a semi-transparent stone, which brought him one step closer to assimilating the real air mask of his god, was probably another basic requirement for high-speed travelling. So, he put it on. Each time he saw the deity's vehicle, it landed vertically on one of these temple-pyramid powerhouses for recharging. And so it became the ideal boarding platform for the Mayan ruler. He knew there was something mysterious and valuable inside these temples that had to be added to the craft before taking off.

Standing Stelae: Dry Cell Batteries

The ancient city of Copan is also famous for its elaborately carved standing monolithic stelae erected on the floor of the Great Plaza and the Plaza of the Hieroglyphic Stairway. They are usually fronting important temples and palaces. Experts suggest that certain stelae are associated with specific structures for unknown reasons. Generally, each stela has a low, round, flat-topped altar placed in front of it. Diagram 10.47a shows that the stelae of the Great Plaza form several sets of SAs, with Altar G1, the builders' jet plane in the middle. The builders captured their power-recharging moment

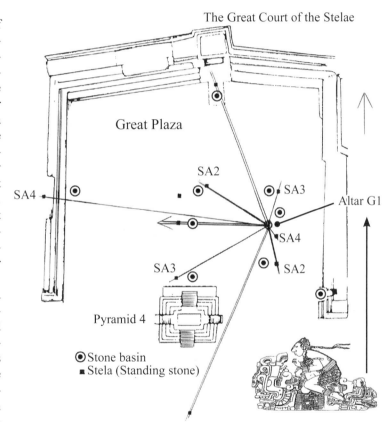

Standing Stones of the Great Plaza, Copan, and the SA
(after Fash 2002)
Diagram 10.47a

by erecting these dry cell batteries and of course, the replica of their jet craft. Later the Mayan rulers carved their portraits onto the stelea so as to show their sovereignty over the intruded lands.

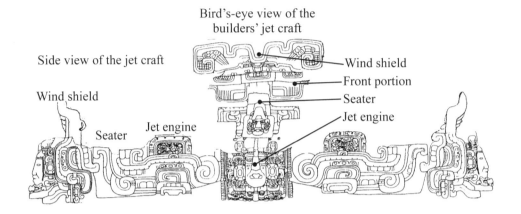

Drawing on the Upper Story of the West Façade of Rosalila Structure, Copan, Showing Views of the Builders' Jet Craft
(drawings by Jose Humberto Espinoza 1991 and Coe 1999, p. 99)
Diagram 10.47b

Temple of Rosalila and the Builders' Jet Craft

An Early Classic structure known as Rosalila is the best-preserved and most stunning temple in all Mayan archaeology with architecture and sculpture intact. It is a two-story temple discovered beneath another temple of Structure 16, the highest building of the Acropolis of Copan—a hieroglyphic step carved, colored, and deliberately preserved by Ruler 10, the Moon Jaguar, who reigned from A.D. 553 to 578.

The Temple of Rosalila consists of three stories with a height of 13m. Experts suggest it represents a deified mountain where double-headed dragons are carved on the lintels of the west and south doorways of the upper story (diagram 10.47b). The carvings also identify Rosalila as a "house of smoke," a place where rulers would reconnect with ancestors of the underworld. To my understanding, the double-headed dragons of Rosalila are identical to the one carved on the Lintel 3 of Temple IV of Tikal. Ruler 10 of Copan is trying to present us with a bird's-eye and side view of his jet craft! It probably explains why many mysterious Copan rulers have weird names such as "Smoke-Serpent" (which might refer to the air currents generated by his jet engine) or "Mirror-Jaguar" (describing the windshield of the vehicle.)

The city, after developing for 2,000 years, established a colossal metropolis of thousands of buildings and inhabitants, with the most well-developed and well-expressed system of hieroglyphics, was mysteriously abandoned in the tenth century A.D. So were several others Mayan city-states. Where did a civilization of ruling elites, artists, astronomers, and mathematicians—who allegedly discovered the zero centuries before the Europeans—go to?

Zoomorphic Altars of Quirigua

The small but important Mayan city of Quirigua is centered on a crossroad between Copan and the major centers of the heartland. A "Sky Dynasty" ruled the city from A.D. 725–748. The city is famous for its public monuments, which are basically divided into tall stelae and round boulders. Many of its standing stones are colossal in size. Some are 8–10m tall and weigh sixty-five tons, with high sculptural quality and striking hieroglyphic texts.

But what makes Quirigua special are its zoomorphic altars—irregular, flat, and animal-shaped boulders. Zoomorph P and its Altar O (monument 23) sit before the stairway of a ruined palace facing the main plaza. The altar is 3.8m long and 5m thick, with its upper surface heavily carved. The lower third of the sculpture depicts a dancing divine figure with his face covered by a jaguar mask. A series of large full-figure glyphs in the form of a T-shaped panel are carved in the center of the altar. It is probably a refuelling platform of the builders, as a jet craft is parked on top of it (diagram 10.47d).

Another zoomorphic altar with a similar design is found on the top of monument 24, opposite Altar O of Quirigua (diagram 10.47e). Another jaguar-masked ruler is carved under a T-shaped panel. As with Altar O, a builders' jet craft is parked on top of the glyphic platform.

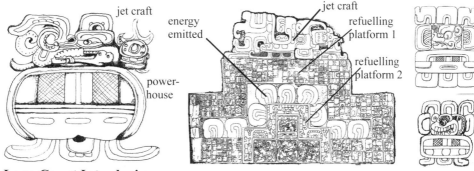

Long Count Introducing Glyph on Stela 63 beneath Structure 10L-26, Copan, Showing the Builders' Jet Craft on Top of a Powerhouse
Diagram 10.47c

Quirigua Monument 23 (partial) with Builders' Jet Craft on Top of a Platform (*left*); Long Count Introducing Glyph of Monuments 6 and 26, Quirigua, Showing the Builders' Jet Craft on Top of a Powerhouse (*right*)
(drawing Sharer)
Diagram 10.47d

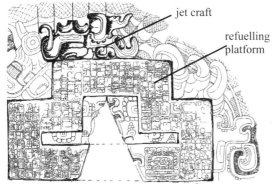

Quiriqua Monument 24, Zoomorph O (partial), Builders' Jet Craft Parked on Top of a Refuelling Platform, with Main Features of the Machine Highlighted by the Author
(after Coe 1999)
Diagram 10.47e

The Pyramid of Castillo of Chichen Itza and the Aztec Calendar Stone

The city of Chichen Itza is famous for its four-sided temple-pyramid named *El Castillo* (Spanish for "castle") (diagram 10.49). It was neither built by the Spanish invaders nor was it a castle with defensive walls. It stands 24m high, the tallest and most dramatic structure on the site. It seems that the builders' energy demand was ever-increasing, as another corbel-vaulted temple was built on the summit of an earth pyramid with four radial stairways. It is interesting to note that the inner and outer doorways of the corbel-vaulted temple form three SAs (diagram 10.50). What was needed was a conical device to activate this powerhouse.

Chacmool—Icon of Mayan Sculptural Style. The Stone Bowl/Dish often Found on the Stomach of the Reclining Figure Is Said to Have Held Sacrificial Offerings
Diagram 10.48

El Castillo with Conical Device at the Northern Entrance
Diagram 10.49

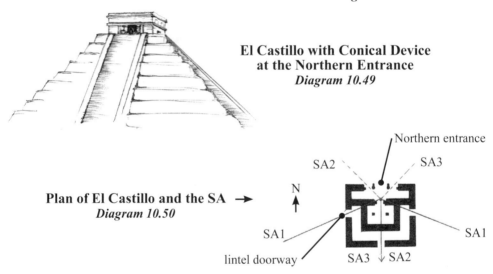

Plan of El Castillo and the SA →
Diagram 10.50

Each of the stairways of El Castillo has ninety-one steps. Including the platform on top, it has a total of 365 steps—probably representing the days of the year. The pyramid also stands for the "Snake Mountain," as giant serpent heads repose at the base of its northern stairways (diagram 10.51). These snakes, known as the *kuxan sum* ("living cord"), were believed to connect the Itza lords with heaven (Schele and Mathews 1998). Today, tourists come to El Castillo at the equinoxes to see its miracle—the interplay of light and shade produced by the decorated balustrades of the stairways gives the impression that the large serpents are sliding down the pyramid. This multi-tier temple-pyramid decorated with serpent heads at its base reflects exactly the outermost "fire serpent" ring of the Aztec Calendar Stone (diagram 10.52).

**Serpent Head at Northern Stairway
of El Castillo, Chichen Itza**
Diagram 10.51

**Fire Serpent of the Aztec
Calendar Stone**
Diagram 10.52

Consequently the Stone might be related to Chichen Itza, or at least to El Castillo and the Tomb of the Great Priest, also known as Osario, another terraced platform decorated with serpents at its balustrades. These two monuments form an SA with the most sacred place of Chichen Itza—the Cenote well of Sacrifice, the home of the Mayan rain god Chac, according to local legend (diagram 10.53). We can see that an SA lies right on the axis of the sacred path—Sacbe no. 1—connecting the well and El Castillo. According to Sharer, "pilgrimages were made to this sacred cenote from all parts of the Mayan area and beyond, so that offerings might be cast into its depth." The Cenote was believed to be inhabited by the gods. It is a great depression with perpendicular walls. It served no utilitarian purpose, as the ancient Mayans obtained water from artificial wells nearby. In addition, the two stairwayed pyramids form an SA with the north facing Nunnery in the south. Most interestingly, its angle bisects at another sacred well—Xtolok Cenote.

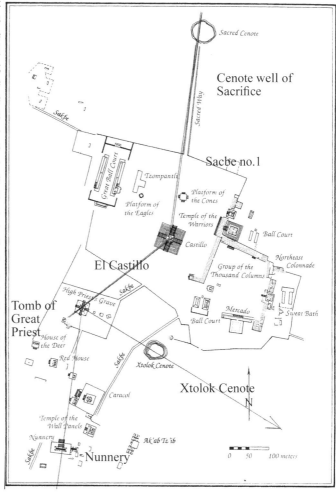

**The Relation between
Two Cenotes and
Major Monuments of
Chichen Itza**
(Coe 1999)
Diagram 10.53

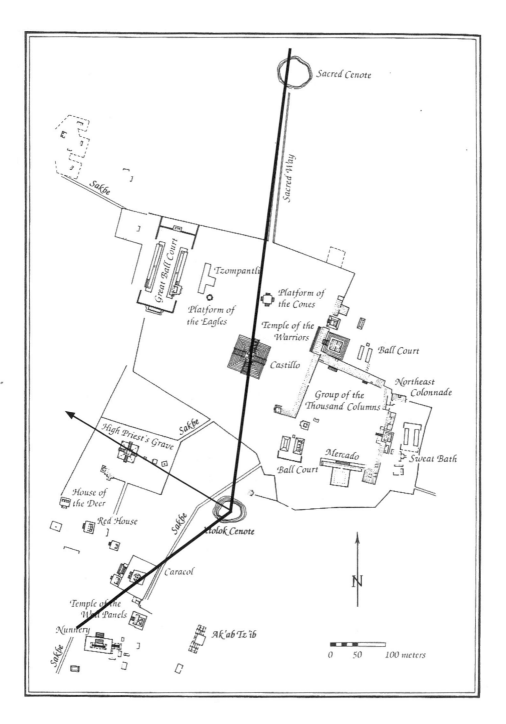

The Perfect Stone Angle of Chichen Itza
Center of the Sacred Lake (Xtolok Cenote) Forms an SA with
Various Important Monuments of the City
(diagram after Coe 1999)

The Platform of the Cones

As shown in diagram 10.54, an SA is derived from the northern lintel doorway of the temple of El Castillo, the only pair of piers heavily decorated with giant serpents, with the west facing the Temple of the Warriors, a double-chambered building constructed on a three-tiered platform, and the east facing the Temple of the Jaguars, another double-chambered temple, with feathered serpents framing its opening. Today, a sculpture-cum-throne in the form of a jaguar at the central lintel doorway of the temple probably marks the location of

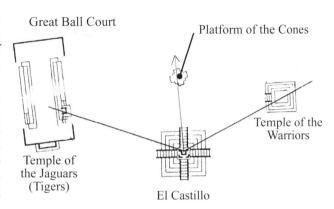

The Power Generator of El Castillo
Diagram 10.54

the builders' conical device. Most interestingly, the SA bisects at the Platform of the Cones, also known as the Venus Platform, after a planet important in the astronomic knowledge of the Mayans. How did the platform get such a name? Does it imply that a conical device was once placed on its top for generating power? Could the microwaves generated by the builders, probably from the sky-high temple-pyramid of Castillo, be transmitted to Venus in A.D. 300? It seems that the real function of the pyramid of Castillo may be "more astronomical" than we think.

Similar layouts can be found in two other ancient Mayan cities—Mayapan and Copan (diagrams 10.55a and 10.55b)—where a radial temple-pyramid stands on the central plaza. The northern doorway of these temples forms an SA with the two temples nearby. Again, the angle bisects at a platform or altar that lies north of the pyramid.

In Chichen Itza, the Temple of the Warriors forms SA2 with the Temple of the Big Tables to its right and another double-chambered temple of the West Colonnade to its left (diagram 10.56). The angle bisects at another platform—the Platform of the Eagles and Jaguars—which lies west of the site (diagram 10.56a).

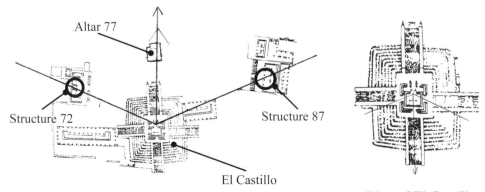

El Castillo of Mayapan and the SA
Diagram 10.55a

Plan of El Castillo, Mayapan
Diagram 10.55b

Mayapan is located in the Yucatan in southeastern Mexico with some of its buildings resembling the buildings in Chichen Itza. The most famous structure is the nine-tiered temple-pyramid again known as El Castillo or "Temple of KuKulcan." It is a smaller version of the El Castillo at Chichen Itza with two serpent columns facing north from the main doorway. It forms an SA with another temple-pyramid (Str. 58) at the north and the sacred cenote Chen Mui at its southeast (diagram 10.55c)

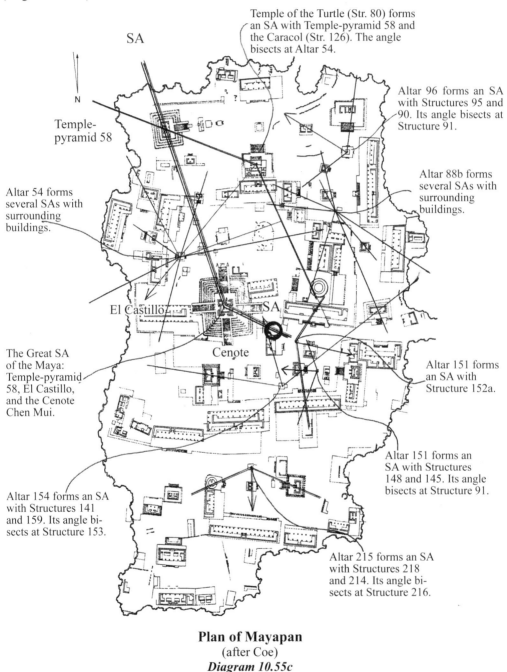

SA

Temple of the Turtle (Str. 80) forms an SA with Temple-pyramid 58 and the Caracol (Str. 126). The angle bisects at Altar 54.

N

Altar 96 forms an SA with Structures 95 and 90. Its angle bisects at Structure 91.

Temple-pyramid 58

Altar 88b forms several SAs with surrounding buildings.

Altar 54 forms several SAs with surrounding buildings.

El Castillo   SA

The Great SA of the Maya: Temple-pyramid 58, El Castillo, and the Cenote Chen Mui.

Cenote

Altar 151 forms an SA with Structure 152a.

Altar 151 forms an SA with Structures 148 and 145. Its angle bisects at Structure 91.

Altar 154 forms an SA with Structures 141 and 159. Its angle bisects at Structure 153.

Altar 215 forms an SA with Structures 218 and 214. Its angle bisects at Structure 216.

Plan of Mayapan
(after Coe)
Diagram 10.55c

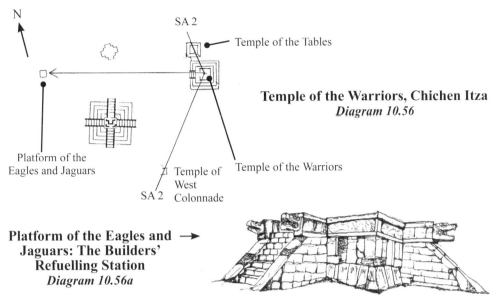

N

SA 2

Temple of the Tables

Temple of the Warriors, Chichen Itza
Diagram 10.56

Platform of the
Eagles and Jaguars

Temple of West Colonnade

SA 2

Temple of the Warriors

Platform of the Eagles and → Jaguars: The Builders' Refuelling Station
Diagram 10.56a

The Platform of the Eagles and Jaguars

Like the Platform of the Cones, the Platform of the Eagles and Jaguars is located at the center of Chichen Itza. As reflected on the Calendar Stone, the platform forms three sets of SAs with the surrounding megalithic structures (diagram 10.57):

SA1 North pavilion of the Great Ball Court–Temple of the Warriors
SA2 Upper Temple of the Jaguar–El Castillo
SA3 North pavilion of the Great Ball Court–the Nunnery

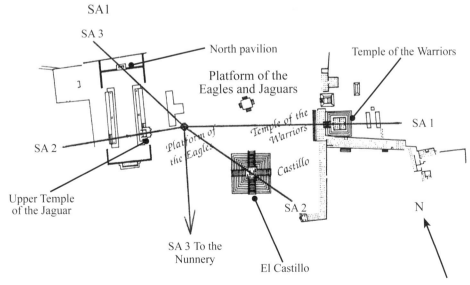

SA1

SA 3

North pavilion

Platform of the
Eagles and Jaguars

Temple of the Warriors

SA 1

SA 2

Upper Temple
of the Jaguar

Temple of the Warriors

Castillo

SA 2

N

SA 3 To the
Nunnery

El Castillo

Platform of the Eagles and the SA
(after Coe)
Diagram 10.57

Another Castillo-like pyramid, smaller in scale, is found southwest of El Castillo. It is called the High Priest's Grave, and its lintel doorway forms an SA with the Platform of the Cones to its left and the mysterious building of Caracol, a two-tiered observatory-like structure with a spiral stairway (diagram 10.58). The angle bisects at a flat, round platform east of the pyramid.

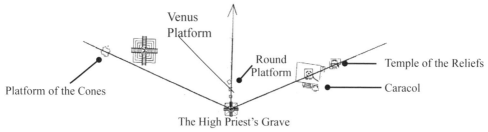

Radial Pyramid of the High Priest's Grave
Diagram 10.58

The building of Caracol has always posed an enigma for archaeologists, as there are numerous niches and doorways along its circular walls. Some suggest these openings were for the observation of constellations. Like those of El Castillo, the lintel doorways of the two-tier building form several sets of SAs (diagram 10.59).

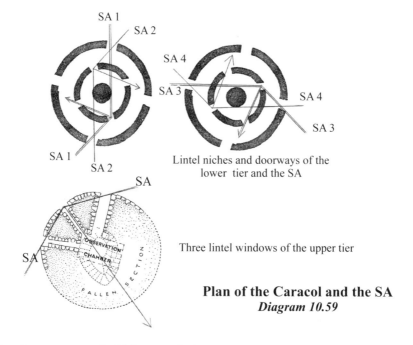

Lintel niches and doorways of the lower tier and the SA

Three lintel windows of the upper tier

Plan of the Caracol and the SA
Diagram 10.59

Another iconic monument of Chichen Itza is its Great Ball court, probably the finest and largest of its kind in the Mayan region. The whole complex lies northwest of the site and covers an area of around 160 by 75m on a north/south axis. It is in the standard I-shape and flanked by two 8m-high banks. The complex contains three main buildings, including a vault-roofed Temple of the Tigers on top of another temple, overlooking the Ball Court at the southern end of the eastern bank. The center of the temple forms an SA with two stands or pavilions that flank the north and south ends of the ball court (diagram 10.60). Temple of the Tigers also forms another SA with the two sacred cenotes.

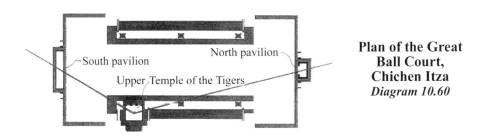

**Plan of the Great
Ball Court,
Chichen Itza**
Diagram 10.60

Stone Circles of Chichen Itza

The huge complex known as the Temple of the Warriors is the most important group in Chichen Itza. It is a square plaza lined by columns of colonnades. Its main structure is a four-tier pyramid that supports a large square cell of solid wall. Its portal entrance, carved with two large rattle-snakes, leads to two bays connected by a narrow doorway. Eight colonnades, either square or round in shape, stand in the inner bay, while there are twelve in its outer bay (diagram 10.61). Interestingly, the middle of the inner doorway forms several sets of SAs with the colonnades in both bays. Similar settings are found in other structures of Chichen Itza (diagram 10.62). Like the Temple of the Tigers in the Great Ball Court, the Temple of the Warriors forms an SA with the two sacred cenotes.

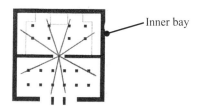

Plan of the Temple of the Warriors
(after Stierlin)

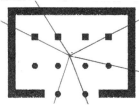

**"Standing Stones" of the Temple of
Tlahuizcalpantecuhtli, Tula**

Diagram 10.61

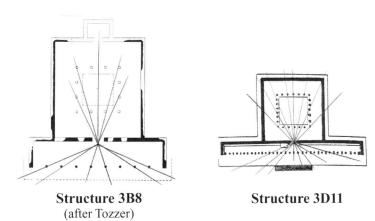

Structure 3B8
(after Tozzer)

Structure 3D11

Diagram 10.62

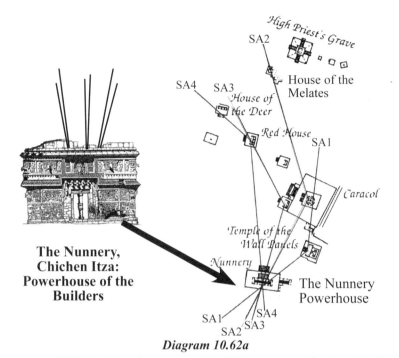

The Nunnery, Chichen Itza: Powerhouse of the Builders

The Nunnery Powerhouse

Diagram 10.62a

The oldest structures of Chichen Itza, the puuc-style buildings, are mainly found in the southern part of the site. They are constructed with the typical mosaic-decorated upper façades. The Nunnery is the most significant monument decorated with large "long-nose" masks. It forms several sets of SAs with the surrounding buildings (diagrams 10.62a and b).

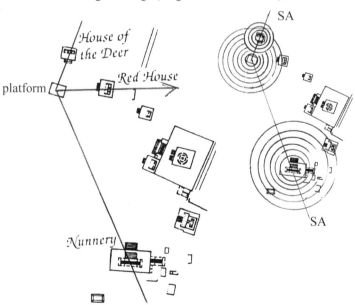

The Powerhouse of the Nunnery, Chichen Itza
Diagram 10.62b

The Builders' Memo

According to the Spanish chronicles, the original Aztec calendar disk, the one the Aztec ruler presented to Hernándo Cortés and his Spanish warriors in the early sixteenth century, was made of gold. This golden sun disk, as described by the Spaniards, was melted down after being shipped back to Spain. Experts have questioned why the ancient Aztecs used gold for their important relics or burial offerings, as it had no practical value in their agricultural society. But Aztec legends believed that gold was the god's metal, a gift of their divine teacher in early times. The divinity—Quetzalcoatl, who brought "civilization," left in his flying machine and promised to return fifty-two years later. Before he took off, he presented the gold sun disk to the Aztecs, probably to remind them of his return. They were told to rebuild and extend all the temples and pyramids every fifty-two years to prepare for his return. Why fifty-two years? Did it take the Aztec divinity fifty-two years to travel to his home planet and then back to Earth? How far away was it for a round trip with his super-advanced space craft?

The Aztec Calendar Stone actually reveals the secret of the builders as it shows the principle of the SA and the work of the energy mechanism. Thus, the genuine gold disk must have been made by that divinity. Why did their divine god leave the disk to the Aztecs and tell them to give it to him on his return? Was the disk, which bore the message from the builders, supposed to be given to other space travellers on their first arrival on Earth, probably once every fifty-two years? Was it some kind of reminder? If the travellers returned every fifty-two years, according to their plan, then Mesoamerica had to be one of the builders' important and favorite places on Earth in the Christian Era. It also explains why the Mesoamerican culture consisted of so many different civilizations that spread over a vast area. Each might have been a culture of the unknown intelligence in different periods of time. Ironically built in the most inaccessible and uninhabited regions, these sophisticated centers came to an end after their "teachers" left them. The Calendar Stone, which the archaeologists describe

The Stone of Tizoc (Evans 2004)
Diagram 10.63

as "the most precious and remarkable monument ever unearthed on the American continent," with the message behind it, reveals the ultimate secret of those lost civilizations (diagram 10.63). It is quite true to say that the Stone is "one of most admirable and perfect achievements" but probably not of our intellect.

Great Plaza of Monte Alban

The spectacular Mayan city of Monte Alban is located in the southeastern area of Mexico. Archaeological evidence suggests that the ancient city was founded about 700 B.C., when the citizens, who claimed to be descendants of the "people of the clouds," built their sacred capital on an artificially levelled mountaintop. Some hieroglyphs refer to it as the "Mountain of the Sacred Stones." One of the earliest structures of the site is known as the Monumento de los Danzantes (the Dancers). The site consists of a vast plaza surrounded by buildings such as the North and South Platforms. The North Platform, known as the Palace, is the largest and probably the most important ceremonial complex in the city. It is a two-part structure with a central staircase. In the upper part are thirteen rooms built around a central sunken patio with an altar at its center. A temple in the center of the plaza has tunnels connecting it to other temples on the site. The South Platform is a large flat structure with two pyramids on top: the central one, Mound III, is the tallest structure on the site (diagram 10.64).

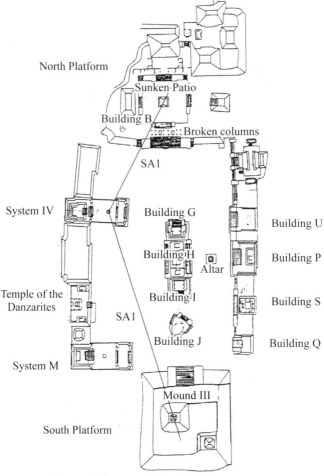

Monte Alban and the SA (Coe 1962)
Diagram 10.64

There are also the Central Buildings, a row of stepped temples designated G, H, and I, constructed in the flat and open central area—the Great Plaza. Central Building H is the largest, with a large staircases and two tombs. Central Building J is unique in that it is the only structure constructed with an orientation to the northwest, built in the shape of an arrow, and believed to have been used as an observatory (surf-mexico.com). Two rows of temples and mounds, some with altar platforms in front, connect the North and South Platforms and frame the central plaza.

Again, the general layout of the megalithic structures in the Great Plaza is aligned to the SA (diagrams 10.65a and 10.65b):

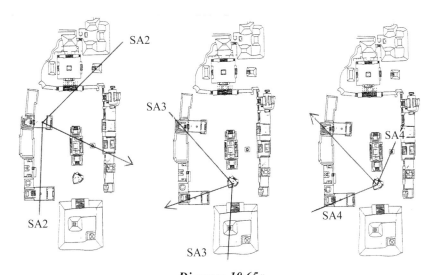

Diagram 10.65a

SA1: The altar of the patio of North Platform and the central pyramid of the South Platform form an SA, with an altar of System IV in the middle.

SA2: The altar of System IV forms another SA with the mound of the North Platform and the altar of System M. The angle bisects at the central altar of the Main Plaza.

SA3: The Observatory forms an SA with the temple of System IV and Mound III of the South Platform. Its angle bisects at the temple of System M.

SA4: The Observatory forms another SA with the central altar of the Main Plaza and the altar of System M, its angle bisecting at the temple of System IV.

SA5: Temple of the Danzantes connects the two altars of System IV and M with another SA.

SA6–SA12: Buildings G and I form several sets of SAs.

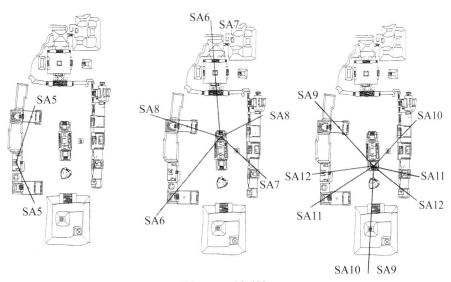

Diagram 10.65b

Plazas, Temples, and Altars of Iximche

The city of Iximche is a ceremonial complex formed by a cluster of plazas and temples. To the left of the complex is Plaza A, formed by three temples; to the west is a typical Mayan Ball Court; while the northern side is enclosed by a long, single-galleried building. Temple 2 is the most impressive and well-preserved monument. It is built on a pyramidal base with stepped-back corners and three doorways leading to a long chamber. The builders set a round firepit in the center of the floor. An extra small chamber, which is probably the "Holy of the Holies," extends from the rear of the chamber. Notably, the pit-and-rear chamber design bears some resemblance to the mysterious temples of Malta, suggesting they might have been used for generating power. The rear chamber of the temple forms SA1 with a low platform at the south corner of the temple, and the round fire pit of the temple chamber in the middle (diagram 10.66a). They mark the exact places for the builders' conical devices. The same setting can be found in the great temple of Tarxien 2,500 years ago.

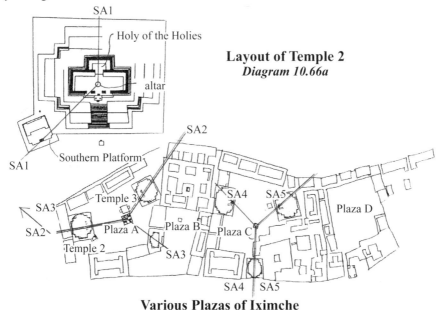

Layout of Temple 2
Diagram 10.66a

Various Plazas of Iximche
Diagram 10.66b

Apart from Temple 2, the Mesoamerican power station, there are two other temples in Plaza A. Temple 3 is located across the court opposite Temple 2. The third one is in the south between Plazas A and B. Two low platforms/altars are found in the middle of the courtyard. With regard to these temple-and-altar structures, experts speculate that Plaza A was an important ceremonial center for the ancient Mayans. But the secret is the central altar of Plaza A forms SA2 and SA3 with the three surrounding temples (diagram 10.66b).

This is no coincidence, as similar structures and layouts are found in Plaza C nearby where, again, the central altar of Plaza C forms SA4 and SA5 with its surrounding temples. Advanced devices were once placed inside these temples, the builders' power stations, for generating energy. When the need arose, the builders would park their jet craft at the stone altar of the plaza, where two rows of megalights were projected into the temples—the powerhouses nearby—for recharging.

Experts further suggest that Plaza B of Iximche with its northern complex was once the palace of the royal family. There is a large court with long buildings opening to several patios. A platform or altar in the center of the northern court forms SA6 with the altars of Plazas A and C. Another central altar inside a small complex southeast of Plaza C forms SA 7 with the central altar of Plaza A and the center of Plaza D (diagram 10.66c).

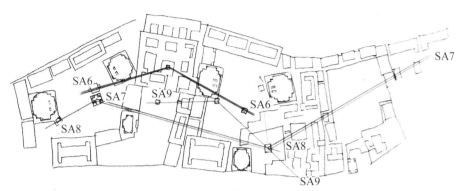

Distribution of Stone Platforms of Iximche
Diagram 10.66c

Similar designs of houses and patios are found in the ancient city of Tula (diagram 10.67). The central altar in the patio of the West House Group and the center of the platform in the East House Group form SA1, with the altar in the patio of the Central House Group in the middle. Another SA (SA2) is formed by the patio altars of the East House Group and the Central House Group, with the platform of the East House Group in the middle.

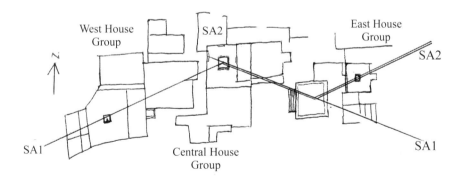

Two House Groups of Tula with Their Patios
and Platforms Aligned to the SA
(Evans 2004)
Diagram 10.67

Great Temple I and II of Tikal

The ancient city of Tikal is located deep inside the tropical forest of Guatemala and is regarded as one of the oldest and largest Mayan sites. The ruins were discovered in mid-nineteenth century and extensively excavated 100 years later. The city, which could date back to 600 B.C., had flourished for more than 1,000 years. There are more than 4,000 structures, including palaces, temple-pyramids, platforms, and plazas on the site. The heart of the city is the Great Plaza, the sacrificial center, which is surrounded by impressive temple-pyramids constructed at great height and reached by a steep slope and gigantic steps (diagram 10.69).

The Great Plaza is flanked by Great Temple I and Temple II, built in the Late Classic period. Temple I, typically Tikal in style and probably the most famous, is a nine-level structure with a corbel-vaulted temple on top. It stands 46m high. Its less-decorated single doorway is constructed with exceptionally thick walls. It seems that the focus of the temple is its height, as reflected in an attempt to place its lintel-doorway and roof-comb high above the tree line (diagram 10.68). Temple II, opposite Temple I, is a three-tier structure with a central stairway. Like Temple I, Temple II has a high decorated roof-comb. Monumental stelae and altars were erected in front of the two temples. Two rows of sculpted stelae and altars were raised at the edges of the stairs leading up to the northern acropolis. Not surprisingly, a single and the largest altar in front of Temple 33 of the northern acropolis forms an SA with the lintel doorways of Temples I and II (diagrams 10.69 and 10.70). Again, the Calendar Stone formula can be applied to Tikal. The story continues as this stone altar forms another SA with the doorway of Temple 33 and the southern temple of Temple II.

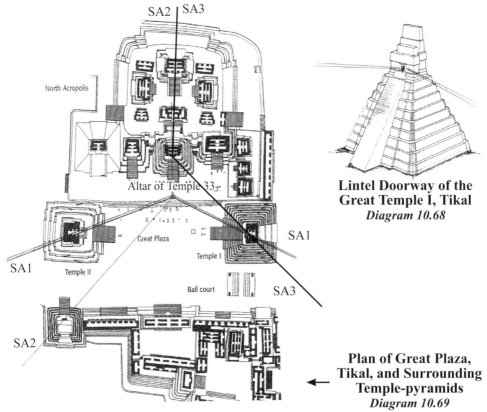

**Lintel Doorway of the
Great Temple I, Tikal**
Diagram 10.68

**Plan of Great Plaza,
Tikal, and Surrounding
Temple-pyramids**
Diagram 10.69

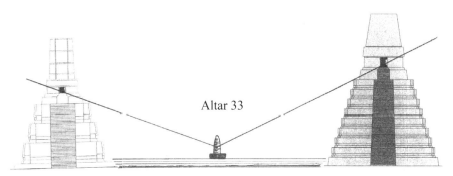

Powerhouse of Temples I (*right*) and II, Tikal
Diagram 10.70

The oldest building in the region is the "Lost World" Pyramid to the southwest of the main complex. In an extensive open plaza, with numerous temples on two sides, the pyramid is designed with steps on four sides. Burke and Halberg recieved "strongest electric currents" by their voltmeter on top of the plateau. They believe the Mayan built the pyramid to "concentrate electric charge in the ground at the top and bunches up the atomsphere's electric field lines at the top." (2005, p. 42). The pyramid and its surrounding structures form several sets of SAs (diagram 10.71).

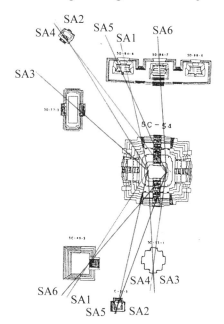

**The Lost World Pyramid
(Structure 5c-54) and Its
Surrounding Temples**
Diagram 10.71

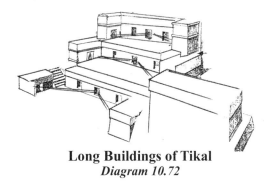

Long Buildings of Tikal
Diagram 10.72

Central Acropolis and the Lintel Buildings

There is a palace-like complex to the south of the Great Plaza. Experts speculate that the Central Acropolis was a complex of palaces and buildings designed for ceremonial and administrative purposes. However, their real function is unknown. These long, low, and multi-roomed buildings are a great contrast to the surrounding pyramids, which are built at an exceptional height. These long rooms have a number of lintel doorways, creating a courtyard in the center. Diagram 10.73 shows the general design of these long buildings and their lintel doorways in Courtyards 3, 4, 5, and 6 of the Central Acropolis. It is interesting that the doorways of these buildings are aligned to the SA. Based on my measurements, the three lintel doorways of Building 56 form three sets of SAs with the single doorway of Building 55 to its right and the doorway of Building 138a, respectively, to its left.

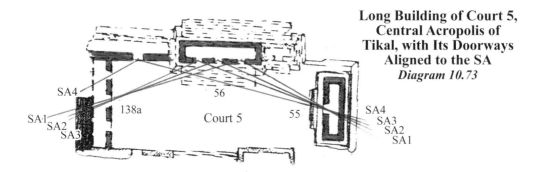

SA4

56

SA1
SA2
SA3

138a

Court 5

55

SA4
SA3
SA2
SA1

Powerhouses of the Northern Acropolis

The Northern Acropolis is the most important complex of Tikal. It contains a royal necropolis with eight funerary temples in the north and four other temple-pyramids in the south. The whole acropolis was built on a terraced platform in A.D. 250–500. Diagram 10.74 shows the general layout and the main axes of the temple-pyramids. Three buildings, namely Temples 22 and 26, and Temple-pyramid 33, form the main axis of the complex. Each of these is constructed with a balcony, a small platform where the ancient Mayans offered their human sacrifices.

Interestingly, these small sacrificial platforms form several sets of SA with the lintel doorways of the temples nearby. For instance, the balcony of structure 22, at the rear of the complex, forms SA1 and SA2, with Temples 20, 21, 22, and 23 respectively. The two angles bisect at the central altar of Temple 22 and Temple 26 respectively.

Temple 26 has its own balcony, which forms SA3 with the rear stone altar of Temples 32 and 34. The angle bisects at the small balcony of Temple-pyramid 33. In addition, the balcony of Temple 33 forms SA4 with the lintel doorways of Temples 25 and 27, the angle bisecting at the balcony of Temple 25. SA5 is formed with the rear altars of Temples 32 and 34.

Temples 23, 24, and 26

In addition, the doorway of Temple 23 forms SA6 with the doorway of Temple 20 and the rear altar of Temple 26, the angle bisecting at the balcony of Temple 22. SA7 is formed by the doorways of Temples 22 and 25, with the doorway of Temple 23 in the middle. The angle bisects at the rear altar of Temple 32 (diagram 10.74).

Similarly the doorway of Temple 24 forms SA8 with the doorway of Temple 21 and the rear altar of Temple 26. Again, the angle bisects at the balcony of Temple 22 (diagram 10.75 and 10.76). SA9 is formed by the doorways of Temple 22 and Temple 27, with the doorway of Temple 24 in the middle. The angle bisects at the rear altar of Temple 26. I believe that more sets of SAs can be derived from the Northern Acropolis, which further suggests that the complex was very important to the builders. But the secret of Tikal is much more than that.

As mentioned above, the Northern Acropolis is probably the core of the whole city. Importantly, the "Holy of the Holies"—Temple 26—marks the real center of Tikal. It forms six sets of SAs with the surrounding structures or complexes (diagram 10.77):

SA1: Temple IV and the temple of Group G form an SA, with Temple 26 in the middle. The angle bisects at the Plaza of the Seven Temples.
SA2: The centers of the plaza of Complex P and the plaza of Group G.
SA3: Temple VI, known as the Temple of the Inscriptions and the center of Complex N, a platform with twin pyramids west of the Northern Acropolis. It forms an SA with Temple 26.
SA4: Great Pyramid of the Lost World and the Plaza of Complex P.
SA5: The center of Complex N and the center of Complex R form another SA with Temple 26.
SA6: The center of Complex Q and the center of the Great Plaza form an SA with Temple 26.

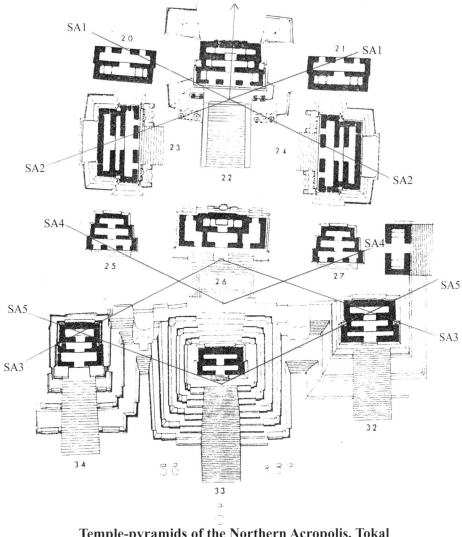

Temple-pyramids of the Northern Acropolis, Tokal
(Coe 1999)
Diagram 10.74

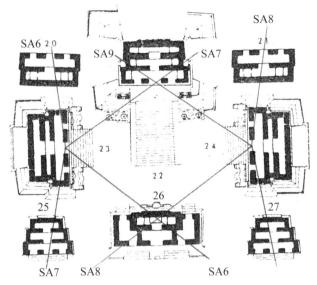

Temple-pyramids of the Northern Acropolis and the SA
(Coe 1999)
Diagram 10.75

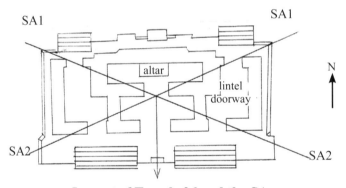

Layout of Temple 26 and the SA
Diagram 10.76

The ancient city of Tikal probably marks the height of the Mayan civilization. However, like all other Mayan cities, it came to an abrupt end about A.D. 900. Experts find no evidence of wars, famine, disease, or natural catastrophes such as changes in climate and water sources that could have caused the demise of the city. The inhabitants of Tikal, as well as their civilization, just disappeared, leaving an empty city gradually absorbed by the surrounding forests.

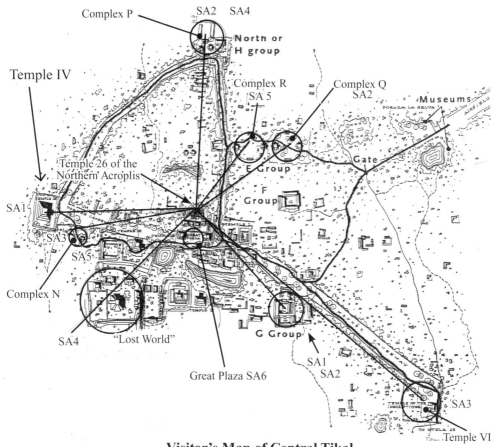

Visitor's Map of Central Tikal
Diagram 10.77

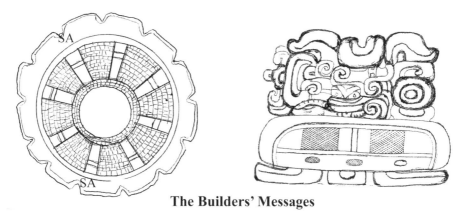

The Builders' Messages

A Turquoise Mosaic Disk Found in Chichen Itza, Probably Showing the Secret of the Ancient City
Diagram 10.78a

The Largest Inscription Carved at the Top of Stela 31, Tikal, Is Probably a Jet Craft Recharging above the Mayan Powerhouse
(after Harrison 1999, p. 72)
Diagram 10.78b

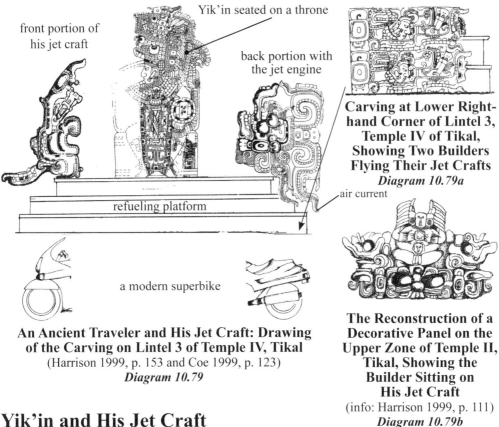

front portion of his jet craft

Yik'in seated on a throne

back portion with the jet engine

refueling platform

a modern superbike

Carving at Lower Right-hand Corner of Lintel 3, Temple IV of Tikal, Showing Two Builders Flying Their Jet Crafts
Diagram 10.79a

air current

An Ancient Traveler and His Jet Craft: Drawing of the Carving on Lintel 3 of Temple IV, Tikal
(Harrison 1999, p. 153 and Coe 1999, p. 123)
Diagram 10.79

The Reconstruction of a Decorative Panel on the Upper Zone of Temple II, Tikal, Showing the Builder Sitting on His Jet Craft
(info: Harrison 1999, p. 111)
Diagram 10.79b

Yik'in and His Jet Craft

Temple IV of Tikal, which is 64.6m high, is the tallest infrastructure remaining in Mesoamerica. It lies on the west end of the main site, the sacred space of the whole city (Harrison). A three-room temple is built on top of a six-terrace pyramid with a central grand stairway, its massive walls up to forty feet thick. A huge roof comb with Maya-style decorations was constructed on top. Experts suggest the temple-pyramid is the largest construction project of Yik'in Chan K'awil, the most important ruler of Tikal. Temple IV connects Temple III and Structure 26—the very center of the Northern Acropolis—by an SA.

Today, Temple IV is famous as a site for observing the sunrise. But it is the two carved wooden lintels decorating the second and third doorways inside the temple that makes it renowned in the archaeological world. The extraordinary carving on Lintel 3, dating back to A.D. 741 (Sharer), shows Yik'in seated on his throne, wearing an enormous serpentine headdress and enveloped by a large two-headed feathered serpent, his divine protector (diagram 10.79; Harrison 1999, illustration 94). It marks the peak of Yik'in's rule in the lowlands.

The carving actually depicts a traveler in ancient times, wearing an air-mask, astride a jet craft parked on a refuelling stepped platform. Images of his riding posture are captured on the steps of the platform (diagram 10.79a).

Other Mayan Sites and the SA

Nakbe is located in the lowlands of northern Guatemala, and is connected with another important center, El Mirador, by a causeway. Experts suggest that Nakbe, which could date back to 1200–450 B.C., was a civic-ceremonial center. The city is divided into eastern and western groups of structures. Diagram 10.80 shows that its major monuments are built according to the SA principle (diagram 10.80)

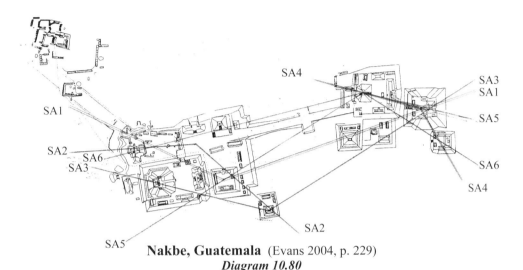

Nakbe, Guatemala (Evans 2004, p. 229)
Diagram 10.80

Edzna is in a remote area in the middle of a wide valley, southeast of Campeche, and could date back to the Middle Preclassic period (600–300 B.C.). The largest structure of the Great Acropolis is known as the Building of the Five Stories, and is a temple sitting on a base measuring 60m × 58m, 31m high and decorated with serpent masks on its comb. Apart from this gigantic structure, the Plaza Central is surrounded by other buildings such as Temple of the Moon, Templo del Norte, the Southwestern Temple, and the Northwestern Temple. Their locations form several SAs with the platform of the Building of the Five Stories in the middle (diagram 10.81). An altar at the center of the plaza probably marks the location where the builders' traveling machine was recharged.

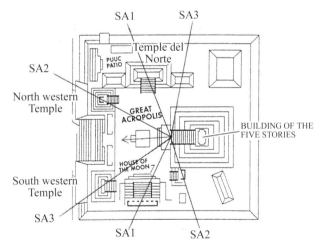

Great Acropolis of Edzna
Diagram 10.81

El Mirador is located between Guatemala and Mexico, north of another great Mayan city—Tikal. The site can date back to the Late Preclassic era, with several groups of triadic pyramids (a central structure flanked by two smaller constructions). The most important example is El Tigre complex, which lies on the western edge of the main group. An SA is derived from the temples surrounding the Tigre plaza, its angle projecting to the great pyramid (diagram 10.82).

According to archaeologists, El Mirador is the largest Mayan site of the Late Preclassic era, when a series of residential sites were formed, each consisting of three or four low and elongated mounds enclosing a central plaza. Several sets of SAs are derived from the great pyramid of Tigre (diagram 10.83).

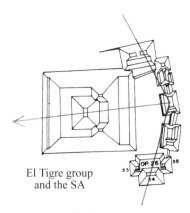

El Tigre group
and the SA

El Mirador
Diagram 10.82

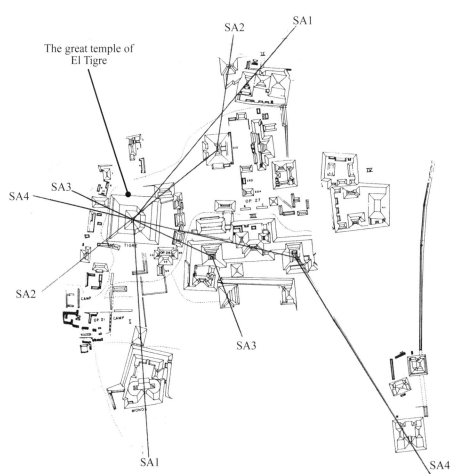

The Western Group of El Mirador: SA Formed by Various Pyramids Centered on the El Tigre Great Temple (Sharer 1994)
Diagram 10.83

The ancient site of Caracol is located on a 500m-high plateau in south-central Belize and could date back to the Late Preclassical era. The core area of the site contains 677 structures arranged in 128 plaza groups. Like El Mirador, several sets of SAs are derived from the largest pyramid of the site (diagram 10.84).

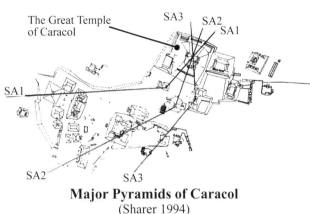

Major Pyramids of Caracol
(Sharer 1994)
Diagram 10.84

Quirigua, a small center in a valley on the southeastern lowlands, could date back to the Early Classic era. The site is divided into several compounds. The main group is the Acropolis and the Ball Court to the west of the site. Several sets of SAs are formed by the buildings of Quirigua (diagram 10.85).

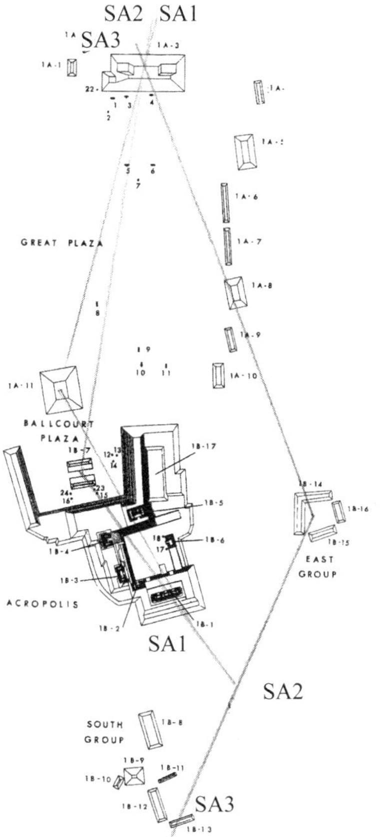

Plan of Quirigua
Diagram 10.85

Yaxchilan, between Mexico and Guatemala, is an extremely important Mayan city of the Classic era. The site is famous for its elaborate stone sculptures with at least thirty-five stelae, sixty carved lintels, twenty-one altars and five stairways, covered with hieroglyhs. Like other major Mayan sites, the structures of Taxchilan are aligned to the SA (diagram 10.86).

Tulum is one of Mexico's best-known archaeological sites because it lies on the east coast of the Yucatan Peninsula, on a cliff 12m above the sea. Experts suggest the site was occupied in the Late Postclassic era, beginning from A.D. 1200. *Tulum* means "wall" in Mayan, the site being enclosed by a stone wall 3 to 5m high, forming a roughly rectangular area of 380 × 165m. Within the wall are sixty well-preserved structures, including masonry platforms and buildings. El Castillo, lying predominantly inside the eastern precinct, is the most impressive building in the region, with a wide staircase leading to a two-chambered temple at the top. On the west side of the temple building is a single doorway supported by two cylindrical columns (Sharer 1994) decorated with feathered serpents. And this doorway provides an answer to Tulum's secret. Several sets of SAs are derived from the major buildings surrounding El Castillo, with its lintel doorway in the middle (diagrams 10.87 and 10.88).

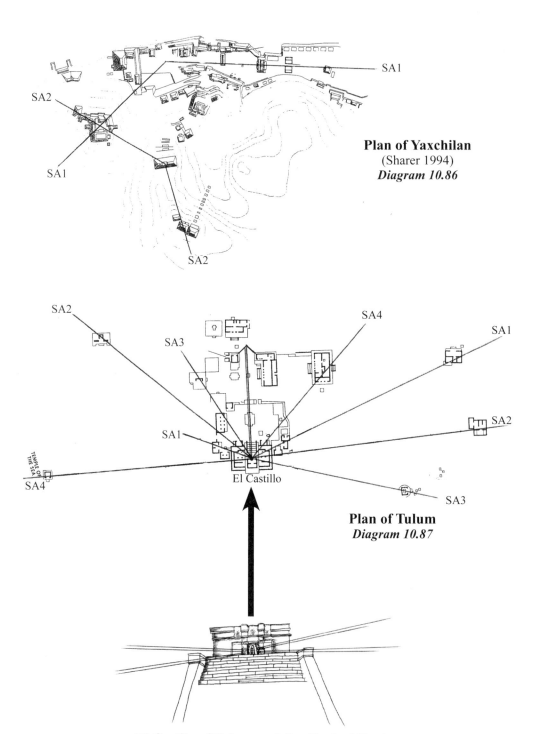

Plan of Yaxchilan
(Sharer 1994)
Diagram 10.86

Plan of Tulum
Diagram 10.87

El Castillo

TEMPLE OF THE SEA

SA1 SA2 SA3 SA4

El Castilo of Tulum and the Conical Device
Diagram 10.88

The Temple of the Frescoes, its walls painted with serpents and gods, is regarded as the gallery of the site. The temple is said to have been used as an observatory for tracking the movements of the sun, as it contains drawings with a solar motif (diagram 10.89). This motif could in fact depict the builders' conical device with radiating lines, probably telling us the real function of these temples.

Drawing on the Interior Wall of Structure 5, Tulum,
Showing Conical Devices with Radiant Lines
Diagram 10.89

Masked Doorways and Corbeled Archways

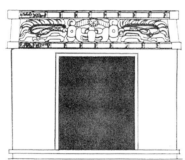

A Fully Charged Jet
Craft, Rear Chamber,
the Temple of the Cross,
Palenque
Diagram 10.90

The heart of the builders' power machines lies in the buildings. Most of them stand on lower and multi platforms with heavily decorated facades. The buildings were usually constructed of solidified lime-based concrete, which results in thick and massive walls. It also gives their plastered rooms relatively little interior space in proportion to their overall size. The corbelled wall surfaces, consisting of a single layer of masonry, are a facing for a rubble hearting. The corbelled arch takes the form of an inverted "V" (Sharer 1994) (diagram 10.91).

Corbeled Vaults:
Dry Cells of the
Builders
(Sharer 1994)
Diagram 10.91

Most of the external walls are decorated with giant monster masks concentrated on the lintel and two sides of the doorway as well as the four corners of the buildings. Thus the building can be recognized in any direction. Its interior walls and galleries are generally plain,but some of the thresholds of doorways connecting two inner bays are decorated with mask motifs. This suggests the relative importance of these masked steps—probably a hint of the installation of the builders' conical devices inside the powerhouse (diagram 10.92).

Chichen Itza: The Puuc-style Buildings in Las Monjas Group
Diagram 10.92

Diagram 10.93 shows one of the most spectacular archways in the Puuc city of Labna. According to Stierlin (2004), the east-facing façade of this monumental structure is decorated with a frieze of duplicated and reversed frets. A series of small vaulted side rooms and shrines is found in its west facing side. Above them is a frieze of huts with a high hatched roof. The arch itself consists of a single bay with a concave intrados.

The midst of the central axis of the arch forms an SA with the "doorways" at its two sides, thus becoming a powerhouse of the builders (diagram 10.94). The lintel of the building is decorated with reversed frets, spiral scrolls and "high thatched roofs," indicating that energy was once emitted from the top of the archway.

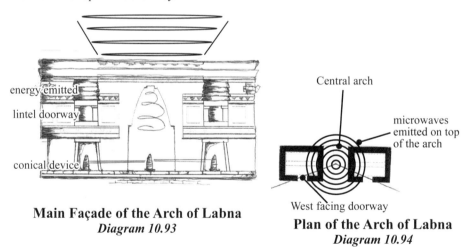

Main Façade of the Arch of Labna
Diagram 10.93

Plan of the Arch of Labna
Diagram 10.94

Many Mayan buildings were constructed with their doorways aligned to the SA (diagrams 10.95a and 10.95b). These portal-lintel doorways are where the secret of their past owners lies. Offerings such as shells, flints, jade and red pigment were found inside the doors of their buildings. Ancient Mayan believed these offerings possessed "soul force" (*kulel*), and one of the aims of the dedication rituals was to transmit the force into the buildings. Schele and Mathews further suggest "this soul-force became even more powerful with usage. The offering plates opened a portal that allowed access to the supernatural world. When the Mayan materialized their gods and ancestors through these portals, the spiritual beings left residual energy in the buildings and the objects that opened the portals. Thus, very old buildings … and the oldest portals contained the most intense kulel of all. The Mayan kept building over these portals for hundreds of years, so that their buildings were like onions—layer after layer accumulating over the sacred core" (pp. 49–50).

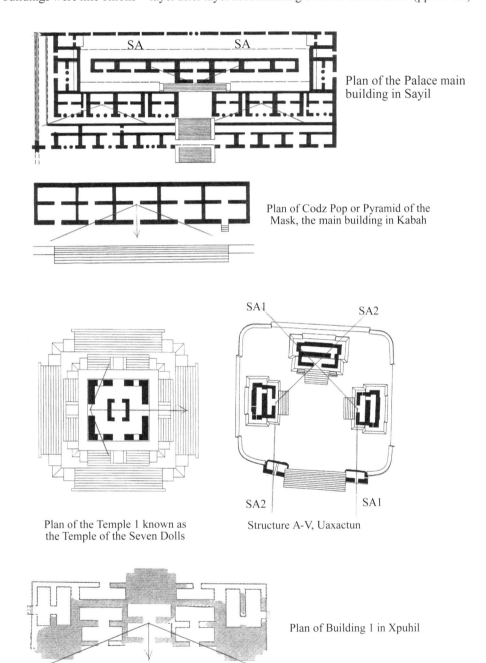

Plan of the Palace main building in Sayil

Plan of Codz Pop or Pyramid of the Mask, the main building in Kabah

Plan of the Temple 1 known as the Temple of the Seven Dolls

Structure A-V, Uaxactun

Plan of Building 1 in Xpuhil

Various Famous Mayan Buildings with Their Doorways Aligned to the SA
Diagram 10.95a

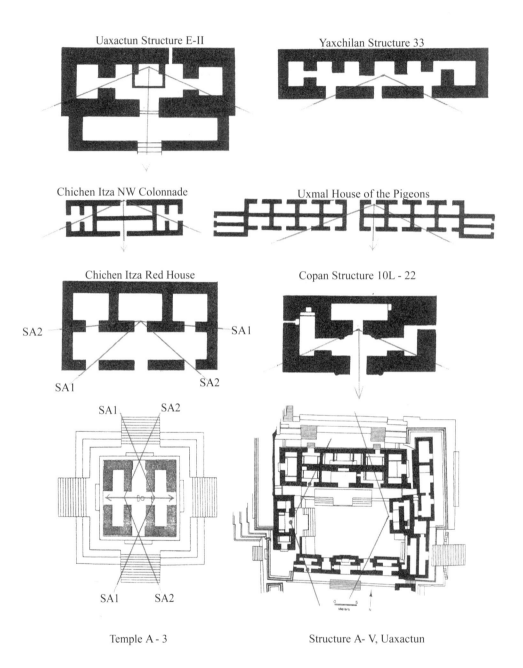

Uaxactun Structure E-II

Yaxchilan Structure 33

Chichen Itza NW Colonnade

Uxmal House of the Pigeons

Chichen Itza Red House

Copan Structure 10L - 22

SA2   SA1

SA1   SA2

SA1   SA2

SA1   SA2

Temple A - 3

Structure A- V, Uaxactun

Various Famous Mayan Buildings with Their Doorways Aligned to the SA
Diagram 10.95b

The above legend or belief becomes a practical fact if we replace the Maya's offerings with the builders' device. It projected megalights (soul force) onto the surrounding doorways (portals), emitting and storing energy inside the corbel buildings. The ancient Maya could only understand it as "putting the soul force into the buildings." When the energy in the corbel-roofed lintel doorway buildings was exhausted after repeated use, another new layer of dry cells would be built on top of the old one. Functioning like the Neolithic powerhouses, the Mayan monuments then needed the builders' devices to activate the energy mechanism. Interestingly, some device-like objects were clearly described by the ancient Maya (diagram 10.96).

**Corbeled Vault of
Copan: The Builders'
Dry Cell Battery**
(info: Henderson 1997)
Diagram 10.96

Ceremonial Bars and the Builders' Power-generating Devices

Apart from the mysterious stucco monster masks, Mayan rulers are the main features on most of the stone sculptures. Representations of different rulers, mostly from the Preclassic era, with their hieroglyphic inscriptions are carved on stone stelae and doorway lintels. Many of them are standing straight like a soldier, with a superbike object in front. Others are seated cross-legged on a monster mask—the builders' jet craft.

In many cases, these Mayan rulers are holding a cylindrical and embellished tube-like object, generally known as a ceremonial bar. These bars, as shown in the sculpture, are usually held horizontally in front of the ruler's chest, as though with great care (diagram 10.97).

Another sculpture shows a helmeted ruler in an eagle costume standing on a feathered serpent. His strange posture suggests he is "feeding" the creature with his ceremonial bar. Another conical object placed on an altar, with a "bird" (refuelling) on top, is clearly shown at the back of the figure (diagram 10.98).

traveller with his energy-generating device

symbol of
builders'
power-
house

builders'
jet craft

Lacamba Lintel 1, Late Classic
(drawing by John Montgomery)
Diagram 10.97

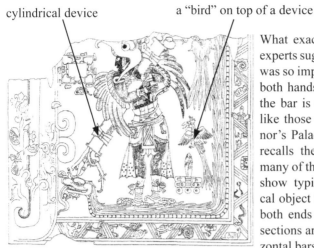

cylindrical device

a "bird" on top of a device

South Mural at Cacaxtla, Puebla
Diagram 10.98

What exactly was this ceremonial bar? Most experts suggest it was a symbol of rulership and was so important that its owner had to hold it in both hands in reverence. On many occasions, the bar is described as a two-headed serpent, like those carved on the lintels of the Governor's Palace of Uxmal. Its cylindrical-shaped recalls the phallic-shaped objects carved on many of the Mayan buildings. Diagrams 99a–d show typical ceremonial bars. The cylindrical object is divided into several sections with both ends flat and rimmed. The three central sections are of equal length, separated by horizontal bars. Small holes between these bars are clearly shown.

The three sections are further decorated with X-shaped lattice-like patterns, like two transverse coils spinning inside a glass cylinder (diagram 10.99a). Sometimes, similar lattice-like markings is added to both ends of the ceremonial bar, which further suggests its importance. In theory, rows of megalights are produced and projected from the light holes of the tube for energy. The spinning transverse coils could be a kind of capacitor. When it was charged, electrons in the form of light beam would be projected from the top end of the ceremonial bar. This specially designed object, its origin or function unknown, was most probably a representation of the builders' device, once placed inside their powerhouses for tapping energy and for recharging their monster-like jets.

energy emitted from two ends

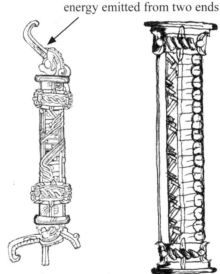

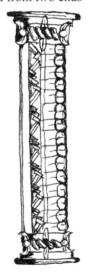

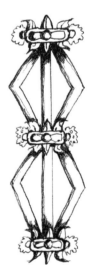

A Ceremonial Bar?
Diagram 10.99a

Drawing of a Ceremonial Bar on Stela 40, Tikal
(by Federico Fahsen, from Harrison 1999)
Diagram 10.99b

Stela 5 and Stela 21, Caracol
Diagram 10.99c

Ceremonial Bar of Ah Cacau, Ruler of Tikal, from Stela 30 of Twin Pyramid Group 3D-1
Diagram 10.99d

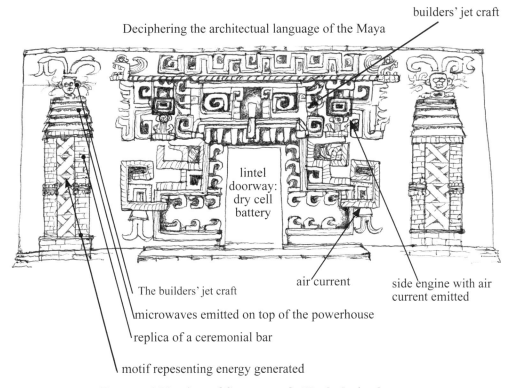

Deciphering the architectual language of the Maya

builders' jet craft

lintel doorway: dry cell battery

air current

side engine with air current emitted

The builders' jet craft

microwaves emitted on top of the powerhouse

replica of a ceremonial bar

motif repesenting energy generated

Restored Version of Structure 2, Hochob, in the Museo Nacional de Antropologia, Mexico City
Diagram 10.100a

A builders' jet craft, decorated with elaborate "air currents" is carved on the lintel doorway. The buildings at the two sides resemble the builders' powerhouses.

ceremonial bar

Labna, Yucatan
Diagram 10.100b

Energy-generating device on the inner doorway of a Mayan temple. Its real function is hinted by the monster decoration and columnar motifs.

Drawing of the Carving of Lintel 3 in Temple I, Tikal, Showing a "Ceremonial Bar" Placed under the Doorway of the Mayan Temple
(after Harrison p.132)
Diagram 10.100c

ceremonial bar: power-generating device under the doorway

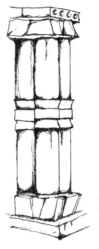

Ceremonial Bar Held by Lord Yax Ain II in the Drawing of Stela 22, Complex Q of Tikal
(after Harrison)

A Cluster of Stone Balusters Bound by a Central Band from the Puuc-style Palace of Chacmultun
Diagram 10.100d

Monolithic Columns on Façade of the Palace at Sayil, with God Mask on top; These Depict the Energy-generating "Ceremonial Bars" of the Builders Placed between Two Doorways
Diagram 10.100e

"Ceremonial Bars" Decoration on the Face of the Arch of Labna
Diagram 10.100f

Four Columns of "Ceremonial Bars" Surrounded by "Energy Patterns" Carved on Top of the Doorway of a Puuc-style Building in Chichen Itza
Diagram 10.100g

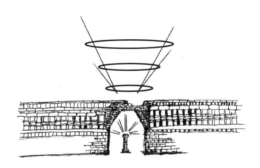

Arch of the Birds Quadrangle, Uxmal (looking east), with "Beremonial Bar" Columns on the Upper Façade, Implying an Energy-generating Device Was Once Placed under the Arch—Dry Cell Battery for Power
Diagram 10.100h

Initial Series of the Maya Hieroglyphs

The Mayan believed in recurring cycles of time, one succeeding another. By counting from a single date in the remote past, the Mayan could use the system to establish absolute chronology (Sharer). According to the Mayan calendar, the current great cycle began on a day in 3114 B.C., the origin date of their calendar and a starting point of their chronology. It is generally known as the Long Count.

The opening date on major monuments is called the Initial Series, an introductory sign reckoned from a fixed point in the distant past, shown by a standardized, oversized glyph, usually four times as large as the following hieroglyphs. The head of the glyph, probably showing a deity, is the only variable element. This standardized, oversized glyph, found on major monuments actually depicts a builders' jet, parked on top of a Mayan powerhouse. A column, the energy-generating device, is clearly shown at the doorway of the powerhouse, probably represented by the ceremonial bar of the Mayan ruler (diagram 10.100i).

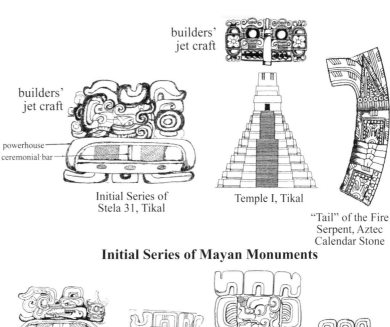

builders' jet craft

builders' jet craft

powerhouse
ceremonial bar

Initial Series of Stela 31, Tikal

Temple I, Tikal

"Tail" of the Fire Serpent, Aztec Calendar Stone

Initial Series of Mayan Monuments

Stela 63, Copan

Stela 17, Copan

Monument 6, Quirigua

Monument 26, Quirigua

Stela 10, Piedras Negras

Lintel 21, Yaxchilan

Lintel 3, Piedras Negras

Glyphs for the Maya Time Period (after Sharer)

"tun"—a typical powerhouse activated by a "column"— ceremonial bar at the doorway

"alautun"—different jet crafts parked on top of powerhouses

Diagram 10.100i

MESOAMERICAN POWERHOUSES AND THE BUILDERS' JET CRAFT

383

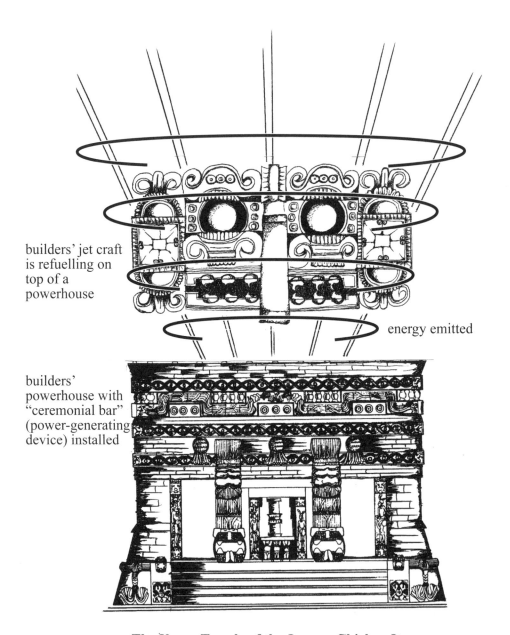

builders' jet craft
is refuelling on
top of a
powerhouse

energy emitted

builders'
powerhouse with
"ceremonial bar"
(power-generating
device) installed

The Upper Temple of the Jaguar, Chichen Itza
(drawing: Schele and Mathews)
Diagram 10.100j

Pyramids and Sunken Plazas of Teotihuacan

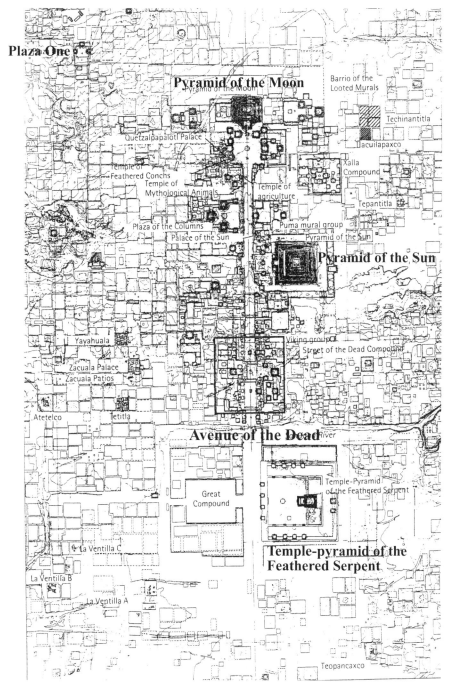

Plaza One

Pyramid of the Moon

Barrio of the Looted Murals

Techinantitla

Tlacuilapaxco

Quetzalpapalotl Palace

Temple of Feathered Conchs

Temple of Mythological Animals

Temple of agriculture

Xalla Compound

Tepantitla

Plaza of the Columns

Palace of the Sun

Puma mural group

Pyramid of the Sun

Pyramid of the Sun

Yayahuala

Viking group

Street of the Dead Compound

Zacuala Palace

Zacuala Patios

Atetelco

Tetitla

Avenue of the Dead River

Great Compound

Temple-Pyramid of the Feathered Serpent

Temple-pyramid of the Feathered Serpent

La Ventilla C

La Ventilla B

La Ventilla A

Teopancaxco

The City of Teotihuacan
(after Evans 2004)
Diagram 10.101

MESOAMERICAN POWERHOUSES AND THE BUILDERS' JET CRAFT

The ancient city of Teotihuacan of Mexico was probably the largest human settlement in the New World between A.D. 450 and 650, which marked the peak of that mysterious civilization. Given the huge size of the city and its importance in Inca history, its origin is still an enigma. No historical writings and records have been found. Not even the name of the city was mentioned. Some experts suggest it is 2,500 years old. Others speculate that the city is much older than expected, probably dating back to 4000 B.C. Teotihuacan, meaning "The City of the Gods" or "Where Men Become Gods," was rediscovered, rehabitated, and renamed by the Stone Age Aztecs in A.D. 750. The complex is formed by more than 2,000 buildings including 600 pyramids of various sizes, temples, plazas, and avenues in an area of 20 square km. But still, about 90% of the city is under the earth. The city is basically divided by the Avenue of the Dead, the main street of Teotihuacan, into two main sections: east and west. It runs from north to south for more than 2.5km (diagram 10.101). Apart from the most famous Pyramids of the Sun and Moon, there are other residential and religious compounds with sunken, open courtyards at the center.

Structurally speaking, the Plaza of the Moon, which lies at the far north of the Avenue, can be classified as one of the sunken courts mentioned above because the central plaza is formed and surrounded by a terraced platform on four sides with a series of satellite step pyramids or pyramidal bases on top. A stepped platform with radial staircases was constructed in the center of this mega sunken court. In addition, the Pyramid of the Moon, the second largest of the site, is located at the extreme northern end of the plaza with an extension built over the southern side of it. Another smaller platform was constructed and placed between the extension and the radial platform of the sunken court. This small platform marks the real center of the whole Moon Pyramid Complex.

Another pyramid, probably the most famous and the largest monument in Teotihuacan, is the Sun Pyramid. It lies on the east of the Avenue of the Dead and southeast of the Plaza of the Moon. It is approximately 225m wide on each side, which only the Great Pyramid of Giza can match, and rises 63m in height and was precisely built inside a square courtyard with an opening to the west. That is to say, the top of the pyramid marks the center of the Sun Pyramid complex.

Temple-pyramid of Feathered Serpent

Further south along the Avenue is another important complex—the Ciudadela, a huge enclosure located at the geographic center of the city. It measures about 400m on one side, and the interior space is surrounded by four large platforms surmounted by satellite pyramids or earthen niches, forming another mega sunken court. The Temple-pyramid of the Feathered Serpent is the central pyramid of this large enclosure. Like the Pyramid of the Moon, an extension known as the Adosada Platfom was added to the western façade of the temple-pyramid to mark the real center of the enclosure (diagram 10.102).

According to Aztec legend, the Temple of Feathered Serpent was for worshipping their ancient sage—Quetzalcoatl, who was believed to have come from the east, and brought knowledge, legislation, and progress to their ancestors, and left in his flying machine. Actually, in Aztec literature, the word "feather" is the quetzal bird, whereas "serpent"—the rattlesnake—represents fertility and regeneration. In other words, it might also be interpreted as the builders' flying machine (the bird) and their power stations (regeneration of energy). It implies that the temple was once a power station of the builders for supplying energy for their crafts. The following diagram is the general layout of the temple with the application of the SA. When the mechanism is activated, the builders will park their plane on the platform for recharging.

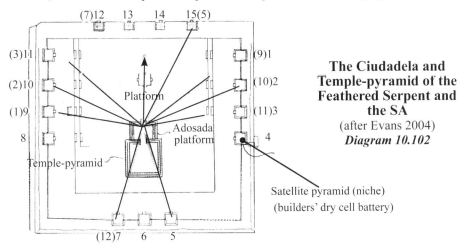

The Ciudadela and
Temple-pyramid of the
Feathered Serpent and
the SA
(after Evans 2004)
Diagram 10.102

Satellite pyramid (niche)
(builders' dry cell battery)

In a recent excavation around the Ciudadela, eighteen cones were found in the temple area (diagram 10.103). They are homogeneous in terms of material and form. They are sharply pointed at one end, and polished and decorated with triangle motifs in a row along the exterior bottom edge. These greenstone cones have never been found elsewhere around the region. Like the European gold hats, the Teotihuacan cones may likely be replicas of the builders' conical devices, and each of them might have once been placed on top of the earthen shrines that surrounded the Temple of Feathered Serpent in order to activate the energy mechanism.

**Greenstone Cone Offerings
at the Feathered Serpent
Pyramid**
(Teotihuacan Home Page)
Diagram 10.103

The Temple is also famous for its mosaic decorations (diagram 10.104). Experts suggest that the motif of a peaceful rain god—Tlaloc with goggle-eyes and big nose rings—was carved and placed next to the feathered serpents. It is actually the rear of the builders' jet craft, in which two propulsive jet engines are clearly shown. The vehicle was probably being recharged as it was "fed" by rows of energy beams generated by the feathered serpent next to it.

As shown in the city map, another complex—the Street of the Dead Compound—is located in the center (the main axis) of the Avenue of the Dead between the Sun Temple and the Temple-pyramid of the Feathered Serpent. There are three platforms or altars constructed separately along the Avenue, which constitutes the main axis of the compound as well. Another tiny plaza (Plaza One) lies northwest of the city. Like other ancient Mayan cities, the sunken courts and plazas of Teotihuacan are aligned to the SA (diagrams 10.105a and 10.105b):

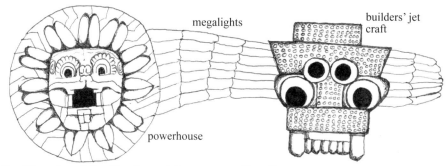

megalights

builders' jet craft

powerhouse

The Temple of the Feathered Serpent at Teotihuacan, Where the Feathered Serpent Carries Mosaic Headdress on His Tail (Schele and Mathewa 1998)
Diagram 10.104

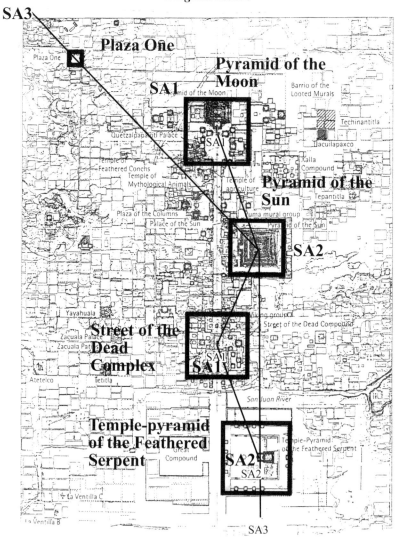

Main Complexes of Teotihuacan
Diagram 10.105a

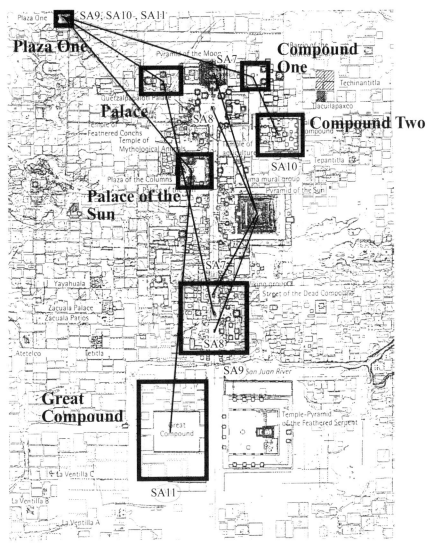

Various SAs of Teotihuacan
Diagram 10.105b

SA1: The central altars of the Plaza of Moon and the Street of the Dead Compound form an SA, with the Pyramid of the Sun in the middle.

SA2: Central altar of the Street of the Dead Compound forms an SA with the Pyramid of the Sun to its left and the Adosada Platform of the Feathered Serpent to its right.

SA3: The Adosada platform of the Temple-pyramid of the Feathered Serpent and Plaza One form another SA, with the Pyramid of the Sun in the middle (diagram 10.105a).

SA4, SA5, and ***SA6:*** The three central platforms of the Dead Compound form three different sets of SAs, with the Pyramid of the Sun to its left and the Adosada platform to its right.

SA7 and ***SA8:*** The northern altar of the Dead Compound forms an SA with the Pyramid of the Moon with the Pyramid of the Sun in the middle, whereas the southern altar of the Dead Compound forms another SA with the central altar of the sunken courtyard of the Pyramid of the Moon, with the Pyramid of the Sun in the middle (diagram 10.105b).

The pyramids of Teotihuacan once served as the builders' power generators during and after the Christian era. According to Sitchin, broad layers of mica, 15mm thick, were excavated from the ceiling and walls of the subterranean chambers inside the Pyramid of the Sun. The source of this mica is an enigma, given that the nearest mica site is 2,000 miles away, in Brazil. Mica is a silicon, the special properties of which make it resistant to water, heat, and electrical currents. It is used as an insulator in electronic and electrical applications such as in nuclear and space technologies (*Lost Realms* [1999], p. 53). Who actually knew the special property of the mineral and deliberately and meticulously covered these rooms with it and for what purpose? Was it essential to generating power? Most mysteriously, the prosperity of the city and even the whole civilization of Teotihuacan suddenly came to an end between the seventh and eighth centuries, when the gigantic city was burned and then abandoned for unknown reason. What kinds of destructive weapon could destroy the largest city of the new world with a population that only Rome could match? How could these 200,000 citizens live without the use of writing and inscriptions? Why did they leave so suddenly, and for where?

Sunken Courts: "Stone circles" of Tiwanaku

The great and ultimate secret of Teoctihuacan lies not in the wide and straight Avenue of the Dead. It is actually kept under the Gateway of the Sun, the most famous monument of Tiwa-naku. Tiwanaku, which the locals believe is the "belly button of the universe," is probably one of the oldest sites, if not the oldest in Mesoamerica. It is located in southern Central Andes. Nobody knows exactly when the culture started, but local legends suggest that it began after the end of the last flooding and was built by a Giant in one night. The complex, which reached its height between A.D. 500 and 900, was a cluster of megalithic sites built over a 1000m × 45m platform and protected by city walls. It consisted of a multi-terraced platform pyramid, a few sunken courts, and several residential ruins. Excavators suggest that there are probably four other cities lying underneath.

The largest and tallest monument is the pyramid of the Akapana, a massive human construction with a roofless sunken court on the summit of the six-terraced pyramid. The centrally located sunken court measures 50m on each side, and it is flanked by vertical pillars joined by ashlar-like masonry. Minerals such as mica and quartz were excavated on the summit of the pyramid. They were probably related to power generation. According to Burke and Halberg, the pyramid was composed of andesite blocks, "a cousin of diorite" (the material of the bluestones of Stonehenge), and they are magnetic (2005, pp. 50–51). They elaborate: "then clay, with all its electrical conductivity, was piled up, followed by a layer of a special type of gravel from the lake. These pebbles were a rich green in color, no doubt because of their high content of copper, the most electrically conductive mineral besides pure gold" (p. 52).

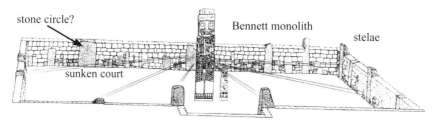

Semisubterranean Temple: "Stone Circle" at Tiwanaku, with Bennett Monolith in the Center Marking the Location of the Conical Device That Projected Mega-lights onto the Surrounding Stelae for Power
Diagram 10.106

Another important structure, the Semisubterranean Temple, lies north of the pyramid of Akapana. The monument is studded with sculptured stone heads set into cut-stone facing walls. Together with a series of sandstone stelae decorated with bas-reliefs, the rectangular wall forms a sunken court in which the famous monolithic Bennett Stela is erected in the middle. This sunken court worked like the stone circles in Neolithic Britain, and was used by the advanced builders for generating power. The Bennett Stela actually marks the location of the conical device. The standing pillars inside the court, acting as dry cells, were used for generating power (diagram 10.106). Most strikingly, the builders had already written their energy mechanism on the Bennett Stela. The famous Gateway God motifs, which dominate the whole iconography of the monolith, actually reveal the secret of Tiwanaku (diagram 10.107).

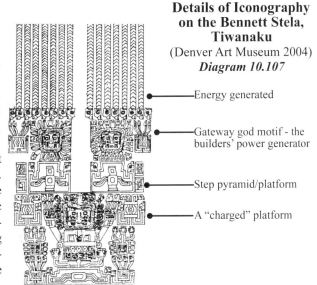

Details of Iconography on the Bennett Stela, Tiwanaku
(Denver Art Museum 2004)
Diagram 10.107

— Energy generated

— Gateway god motif - the builders' power generator

— Step pyramid/platform

— A "charged" platform

Twin-device of Kalasasaya

If the Semisubterranean Temple was once used for generating power, then another setting might be needed for discharging during the energy producing process. Another important enclosure—the Kalasasaya—might take up the job. The structure lies next to the Semisubterranean Temple, forming two "stone circles" side by side. Kalasasaya is a large, slightly rectangular precinct elevated above the ground floor to form a low platform mound. Like other platforms around the region, Kalasasaya is furnished with a central sunken court. Again, Kalasasaya's walls were built of towering vertical sandstone pillars that alternated with sections of smaller blocks of high-quality masonry. It is exactly what "Kalasasaya" means—"The Standing Pillars." An eastern entrance, expressed by a post-and-lintel doorway, connects it with the Semisubterranean Temple. As mentioned above, the central "sunken court" leaning to the east of the enclosure can be regarded as a hollow stage-pyramid—a structure the outer walls of which rise in stages, only to surround a central open-air square courtyard. Most importantly, another sculpture, the Ponce Stela, having similar iconographic content as the Bennett Stela of the Semisubterranean Temple, was erected in the center of the sunken platform. Both stelae are inter-visible (diagram 10.108), with the Ponce stela facing eastward and the Bennett stela oriented with its face toward the Ponce stela. Does it imply that the two stelae were related? Was there any substantial connection, other than that of eye contact, between the two stone figures?

Another similar structure known as the Putuni complex is found west of the Kalasasaya, with an elevated stone platform surrounds a large open courtyard. A monolith, 20cm high, known as the Putuni, was erected in its center.

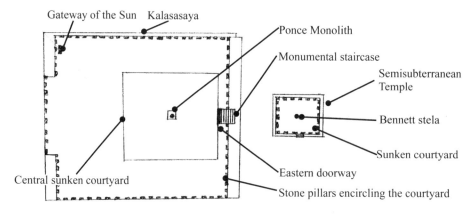

Plan of Kalasasaya (*left*) and the Semisubterranean Temple
Diagram 10.108

For years, the enclosure of Kalasasaya has been regarded as an artronomical-calendrical observatory since its main axis is aligned to the Sun. Arthur Posnansky, the famous European archaeologist of the site, suggests that some of the towering pillars of Kalasasaya mark the precise positions of the equinoxes as well as solstices. However, to me, the enclosure of Kalasasaya is just another model of the builders' power station on our planet. Both the Bennett stela and the Ponce stela mark the location of the builders' devices that were placed inside the courts. Rows of megalights were once projected on to the surfaces of those towering sandstone pillars that framed the whole enclosure, serving the same function as the stone circles of Neolithic Britain (including Stonehenge). Burke and Halberg (2005) even suggest their inside surfaces are smoothed and flattened, and are reminiscent of Stonehenge. The two "stone circles," the Semisubterranean Temple and the Kalasasaya, were linked by a row of megalight 2,000 years ago, forming a typical twin-device mechanism (diagram 10.109).

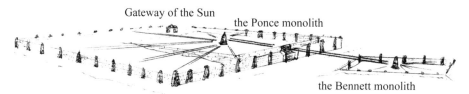

Twin-device Energy Mechanism of Kalasasaya
Diagram 10.109

It is these sunken courts that swung the magic wand. Similar power stations of the builders were constructed with the square walls replaced by a series of mould-top buildings, which were symmetrically arranged to surround the sunken court. For example, in the ancient site of Chiripa, there are sixteen small, rectangular, double-walled buildings with niche-like interior windows (diagram 10.110) constructed around a court. Like those post-and-lintel doorways of the Maya long houses, the doorways and niches of the Chiripa are aligned to the SA as well. It implies that builders' devices were once placed inside these houses to activate the mini power stations that framed the central sunken court of Chiripa. The builders' jet craft was parked in the sunken court and projected a radiance of megalights on the lintel doorways of these houses for power. A similar mechanism, but in a mega size, was found inside the Nunnery at Uxmal. It is repeatedly shown by the Gateway of the Sun in Tiwanaku.

A Reconstruction of Chiripa
(after Moseley 2001)
Diagram 10.110

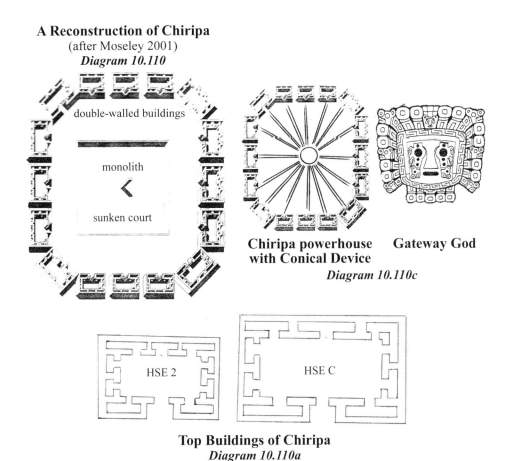

double-walled buildings

monolith

sunken court

**Chiripa powerhouse
with Conical Device**

Gateway God

Diagram 10.110c

HSE 2

HSE C

Top Buildings of Chiripa
Diagram 10.110a

The Tiwanakans built their houses with stones to form tiny rooms which are windowless, with a single small door. The ceiling is covered with large flat stone slabs, like in the rock chambers or dolmens. Some are highly corbelled to assume a beehive-like shape inside. Some even constructed with "magnetic" andesite doorways (Burke and Halberg 2005). They probably represent the builders' dry cell batteries in Tiwanakan style (diagram 10.110b).

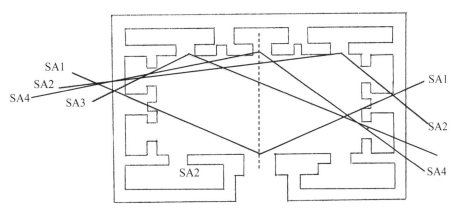

SA1
SA2
SA4
SA3

SA1

SA2

SA2

SA4

Plan of House 2 at Chiripa
Diagram 10.110b

Secret behind the Gate of the Sun

The sunken power generators of the Semi-subterranean Temple of Tiwanaku and the mound-top buildings of Chiripa are well expressed by the Sun God motifs found on the Gateway of the Sun. The massive doorway, like other Mayan lintel doorways, is structurally similar to a Neolithic dolmen. But it stands alone prominently at the northwest corner of the Kalasasaya enclosure. It is 3.05m high and 3.96m wide, and was carved out of a single block of andesite weighing 100 tons (diagram 10.111). It probably came from a quarry a few thousand meters away. It is most misleading to call it a gateway, as it was deliberately placed at the corner of the enclosure with no traces of track leading in or out of it.

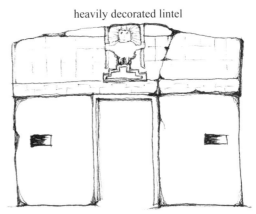

heavily decorated lintel

The Gate of the Sun, with Gateway God Standing atop a Triple-Tiered Platform
Diagram 10.111

The doorway is decorated with the most elaborate and enigmatic Tiwanaku iconography. The upper and probably untouched part of the gateway, the lintel, is heavily carved with a bas-relief of forty-eight winged figures divided in three rows, leaving the two portals undecorated. Like many other Mayan structures, it seems that it is the lintel of the building that is the focus. On the lintel is a large and central pattern, probably Viracocha—the Gateway God, whose face radiates nineteen sun rays in every direction culminating in circles or jaguar heads. Its number is the same as that of the bluestones forming the inner horseshoe of Stonehenge. This "crying god" is standing atop a triple-tiered platform, and his cheeks are lined with tears and his hands are holding two vertical staffs. Similar but simplified motifs of the God, depicting only the central face and framed by a meandering line, were carved along the border of the lintel of the gateway (diagram 10.112).

Gateway God
Diagram 10.112

Disk with Deity Face in Tiwanaku Style
Diagram 10.113

The glyphs or symbols of the gateway are found on other artifacts like pottery, textiles, and standing stones, not only all across Tiwanaku, but also over the entire Andes (diagram 10.113). The motif becomes the icon of the so-called "Tiwanaku Culture." Without any archaeological evidence, experts only speculate that the motif was a calendar to record the lunar and solar cycle.

The Sun God motif is recording and describing a lost advanced technology of the unknown civilization. It is a general layout of the builders' power station, in which a central altar (the head of the god) is encircled by standing pillars (circles surrounding the god's head). The builders' traveling machine, represented by a jaguar under the god's eye, projects a radiance of megalights (sun rays) onto the surrounding pillars (the builders' dry cells) for power. It worked in exactly the same way as the Neolithic stone circles in Europe. In the cases of the Aztecs and the Incas, these dry cells were in the form of standing stelas that encircle the sunken court of Kalasasaya, lintel doorways of mould-top buildings which surround Chiripa, and earthen shrines of the Temple-pyramid of the Feathered Serpent, as well as the pyramidal bases of the Plaza of the Moon!

Gateway God Motif and the Sunken Platform of the Plaza of the Moon

Diagram 10.114b shows the Plaza of the Moon complex of Teotihuacan. It is based on a topographical map of the Japanese archaeologist Saburo Sugiyama. The map is deliberately turned upside-down, with the Pyramid of the Moon in the south of the diagram and a circle of pyramidal bases constructed and framed on the step platform on four sides of the Plaza to form a mega "sunken" court. A platform with radial staircases is located in the middle of the Plaza. As shown in Sugiyama's map, there are at least three pyramidal bases built on each side of the court and two more are strategically placed at the southeast and southwest corners. The structure of the Plaza is a perfect match with the Sun God motif. What it lacks is the builders' chariot to complete the picture (diagrams and 10.114a and 10.114b). A similar setting is found in the Temple-pyramid of the Feathered Serpent, another sunken court surrounded by satellite niches with a platform in the center (diagram 10.115a). The Sun God motif is certainly the answer to the three mysterious Aztec structures.

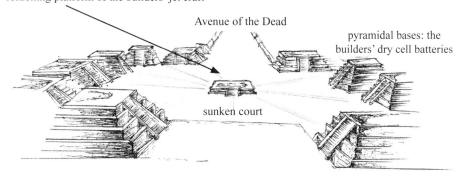

refuelling platform of the builders' jet craft

Avenue of the Dead

pyramidal bases: the builders' dry cell batteries

sunken court

**Power Station of the Plaza of the Moon
(Viewed from Top of the Pyramid of the Moon)**
Diagram 10.114a

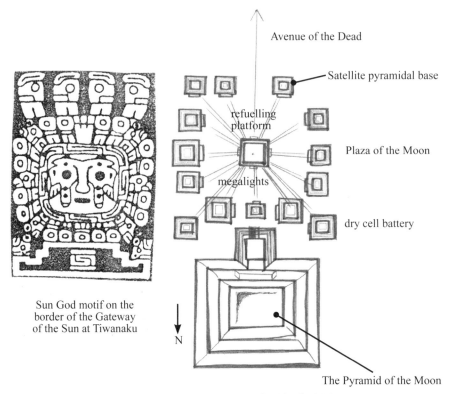

Sun God motif on the
border of the Gateway
of the Sun at Tiwanaku

The Power Generator of the Plaza of the Moon
Diagram 10.114b

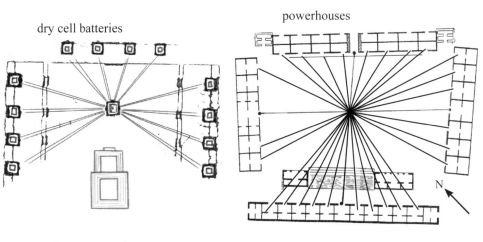

"Sun God of the Ciudadela,"
Teotihuacan
Diagram 10.115a

Long Houses of the Nunnery,
Uxmal, with Inner and Outer
Doorways Aligning to the SA
Diagram 10.115b

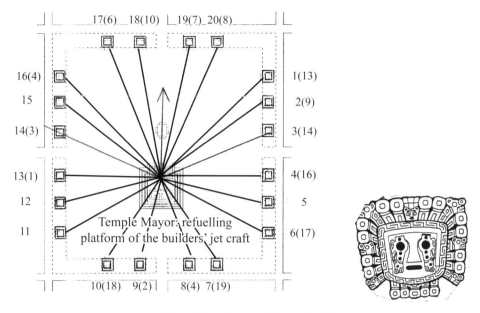

Ritual Precinct of Tenochtitlan
Diagram 10.116

Sacred Precincts of Tenochtitlan

Most Aztec cities had a central religious area, the sacred precinct, where pyramids and temples faced a public plaza in which crowds gathered to watch ceremonies. The most famous and important Aztec ceremonial precinct is the Tempo Mayor, which lies in the heart of Tenochtitlan, the capital of the Aztec civilization. The west-facing temple, which dominates the huge central area, is surrounded by ritual halls and dormitories. Earthen shrines or satellite pyramids are constructed on the four sides of the precinct. Experts suggest that the Tempo Mayor has been enlarged and rebuilt numerous times. The twin temples on the summit were dedicated to the god of war and the god of rain and water. The Aztec priests generally practiced human sacrifices on the small platform outside the twin temples.

Diagram 10.116 shows the layout of the sacred precinct of Tenochtitlan, where the massive Tempo Mayor lies in the middle. With the sacrifice platform of the twin temples as the center, several sets of SAs are formed with the surrounding earthen shrines. The same mechanism once worked inside the Temple of Feathered Serpent in Teotihuacan. Again, it repeatedly recalls the picture of the Sun God motif of Tiwanaku. It is interesting to note that the inner buildings around the Tempo Mayor lie right on the radiant axes of the outer shrines, which obviously explains their purposes.

Diagram 10.117 shows one of the Aztec sites—Cuexcomate—with more than 150 houses, temples and ritual dumps constructed along the mountain ridge extending from north to southeast (Smith 1996, 2003, pp. 74–75, fig. 3.7). Most of these buildings are aligned to the SA, with the public plaza in the middle.

Another important and special ritual precinct of the Aztecs is Malinalco, which is located on the hilltop of a cliff. The site consists of three rock-cut temples or chambers, a series of small shrines and ceremonial platforms. The most impressive structure is the Temple of Eagle-Warrior, which is in the center of the site (Smith 1996, 2003). It is worth pointing out that the stone altar of the temple forms SA1 with the doorway of another rock-cut temple to its right and the doorway of a small circular shrine to its left (diagram 10.118). The jaguar sculpture at the innermost of the temple

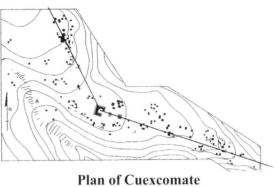

Plan of Cuexcomate
Diagram 10.117

forms another SA with the inner stone altar of the temple to its right and the doorway of the circular shrine to its left. Its angle bisects at the southern ceremonial platform. Finally, a quadrangle rock-cut temple north of the site forms SA2 with the temple and ceremonial platform to its south. The narrow doorways leading to circular chambers with stone altars in the center bear much resemblance to the mysterious temples of the Malta Islands. Even though the main function of this site is still subjected to debate, I do believe that instead of a precinct for rituals and gatherings of the Aztec warriors, they were the power generators of a lost civilization.

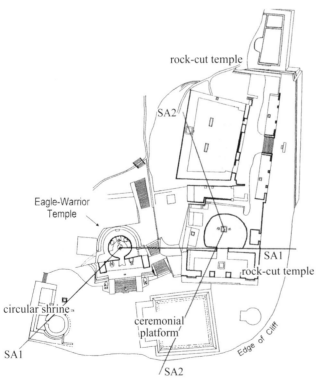

rock-cut temple

SA2

Eagle-Warrior
Temple

circular shrine

SA1

SA1

rock-cut temple

ceremonial
platform

Edge of Cliff

SA2

Map of the Hilltop Ceremonial Precinct of Malinalco (after Marquina 1964)
Diagram 10.118

The Olmecs: America's First Civilization?

La Venta, the most important capital and ritual city of prehistoric Mexico and Central America, stands as one of ancient America's greatest paradoxes. How could this city have flourished in the heart of a vast wetland zone? (Richard Diehl)

La Venta, Tabasco, occupies a ridge of a large alluvial coastal plain near the Tonala River, about 15km from the Gulf of Mexico. Its earliest occupation can date back to 1200 B.C. and it rapidly emerged as the dominant Olmec capital after 900 B.C. The north-south orientation of the site has been interpreted as coinciding with that of the Milky Way (Freidel 1993).

THE GODS' MACHINES

398

The main part of the site itself is in the northern half—a linear complex of pyramids, burial mounds, and clay courts (diagram 10.119a). Among them, the major feature is a huge volcano-shaped pyramid, known as Mound C or the Great Pyramid, which occupies the center point of the city. The clay and limestone monument measures 128m × 114m × 30m.

Complex A, a small group of earth mounds and plazas lying directly north of the Great Pyramid, forms one of the most unusual architectural complexes in the Olmec world (R. Diehl). The complex includes two open-air courts surrounded by earth mounds. The rectangular South Court is formed by two parallel long mounds, Mound 4 and Mound 5. A circular Mound B with Tomb C in the center lies at its northern end.

Three earthen platforms, known as the East, West, and Clay Platforms, lie just north of the South Court, separating it from the North, or Enclosed Court. The platforms are special, as they are formed by adobe bricks, and another mosaic pavement of serpentine blocks in the form of an abstract jaguar mask is discovered below each of them (diagram 10.119d).

Two other platforms are constructed at the two sides of the Enclosed Court. A circular Mound A with three tombs—Tombs A, B, and E—closes the court at the north. A sarcophagus decorated with a were-jaguar is found inside Tomb B, but as with the other tombs, no skeletal remains have been identified (diagram 10.119c).

Experts are puzzled by the fact that the Olmecs imported so many tons of basalt and serpentine to the site to construct such a huge complex while most of them still lived in small villages and huts in the nearby hinterland (R. Diehl). What was the purpose of building the gigantic pyramid and mounds, and paving the dedicated platforms? The diagrams below suggest that the earthen platforms of the Enclosed Court form several sets of SAs with the Great Pyramid and the very centers of the burial mounds, the place where the "tombs" lay (diagram 10.119b). This is why most of the sculpture is carved with the Olmec were-jaguar—an icon of the builders' jet craft.

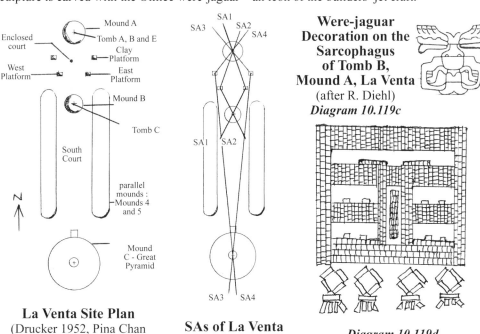

La Venta Site Plan
(Drucker 1952, Pina Chan 1982, and R. Diehl)
Diagram 10.119a

SAs of La Venta
Diagram 10.119b

Were-jaguar Decoration on the Sarcophagus of Tomb B, Mound A, La Venta
(after R. Diehl)
Diagram 10.119c

Diagram 10.119d

Nazca Lines and the SA

"Several centuries before the time of the Incas, the inhabitants of the southern Peruvian coastal region created a monument which being unique in its kind, was intended to transmit an important message to posterity."

—Maria Reiche, *Mystery on the Desert* (1968)
(agutie.homestead.com)

Mesoamerica is certainly one of the capitals of the advanced builders. Several hundreds of years before they constructed their megalithic stations deep inside the tropical forest, the builders had established their first model of power generators on a vast open plain. Today, we can still trace their footprints by studying and understanding those enigmatic lines. The so-called Nazca Lines, stretching across the Nazca Desert, are located in a high arid and flat plateau covering an area of 450 square kilometres. The Lines form animal and plant figures that include spiders and monkeys of more than one hundred meters wide, as well as geoglyphic and geometric forms of straight lines, triangles, spirals, circles, and trapezoids of enormous size (Lee Krystek 1997–2000).

Making these mysterious lines, as suggested by experts, is acheived by simply removing the oxidized pebbles that cover the surface of the desert, and leaving and exposing a lighter-colored subsoil beneath. What puzzles the archaeologists and visitors is that these Lines, probably more than a few centimeters deep, instead of running blindly all over the desert, form dozens of gigantic biomorphs which are only detected from 300m above, in the sky. Besides, those geographs, more than 900 in total, are arrow-straight and run continuously for many kilometers, disappearing in the endless horizon. Most of these Lines radiate from a center, with some Lines intercepting one another. This is why many experts suggest that they were made by the Nazca culture for ritual or astronomical purposes.

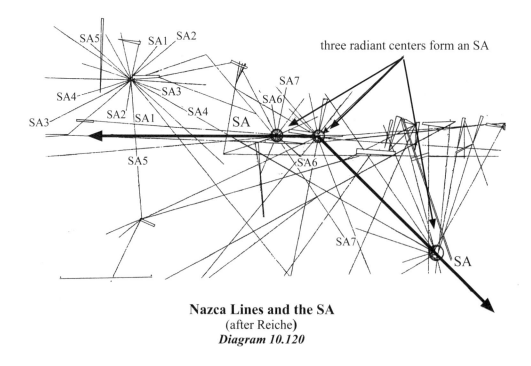

Nazca Lines and the SA
(after Reiche)
Diagram 10.120

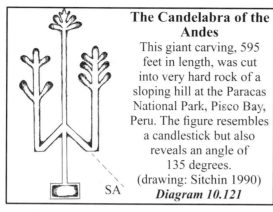

The Candelabra of the Andes

This giant carving, 595 feet in length, was cut into very hard rock of a sloping hill at the Paracas National Park, Pisco Bay, Peru. The figure resembles a candlestick but also reveals an angle of 135 degrees.
(drawing: Sitchin 1990)
Diagram 10.121

Reiche, a famous German mathematician and archaeologist, had been researching the Lines for more than fifty years. The diagram above, based on one of her priceless research around the region, shows Lines radiating from three centers. Interestingly, many of these Lines form several sets of SAs (diagram 10.120). There are stone circles of less than 3m in diameter and stone mounds of less than 1m across found on most of these radiant Lines. With Stonehenge and its Aubrey Holes in mind, I speculate that these mysterious Lines, acting like the Aubrey Holes, once served as indicators for the megalights to connect the stone circles on the vast plateau for power. This might be their earliest generators in Mesoamerica, which could date back to 500 B.C., before they moved and hid them deep inside the tropical jungle.

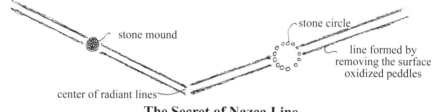

The Secret of Nazca Line
Diagram 10.122

Jong's Nazcan Zodiac: An Answer to the Nazca Mystery

In 1999, a Dutchman, Gilbert de Jong, discovered three Nazca stone circles on the Peruvian coastal plain when he was traveling in the sky above. He personally studied the site and measured these circles by GPS. What is described by Jong as a Zodiac is a geometric design of four concentric circles of small stones and wooden sticks placed inside a square 54.7m in each side (world-mysteries.com).

According to his accurate measurement, there are sixteen lines connecting the very center of the Zodiac with the eight squares nearby (diagram 10.123a). It probably symbolizes the great sun of the natives of the ancient times. But it may also reveal the real secret of the Nazca culture, as these radiant lines are drawn according to the SA, making it no different from the solar motifs inside the Neolithic mounds of the Boyne and of Brittany.

The Nazcan Zodiac makers continued to convey the SA message by deliberately placing the wooden and bamboo sticks in the third and fourth rings of the formation. According to Jong's drawing, each of the sixteen wooden sticks of the third stone circle forms an SA with its two neighboring sticks, and the angle bisects at the center of the Zodiac (diagram 10.123b).

The same pattern repeats itself in the fourth or the outer ring in which each of the thirty-four wooden and bamboo sticks forms an SA with a pair of sticks nearby and the angle bisects at the very center of the formation again (diagram 10.123c). It certainly helps us to have a better understanding of how and why the Zodiac was formed, and it also probably explains the function of those mysterious and endless lines on the Nazca Desert as well.

Besides, Jong's drawing also shows a total of twelve squares, formed by grid lines, lying at the four corners of the square Zodiac. Each of these twelve squares is subdivided into four triangles, each with a pit of small stone dug in the center. Again, these small pits are deliberately placed according to the SA (diagram 10.123d). A similar pattern is found among the eight squares that encircle the center and the smallest stone circle of the Zodiac. The whole formation of the Nazcan Zodiac echoes the enigmatic crop circles that appear mostly in southern Britain two millennia later, which will be discussed in a subsequent chapter.

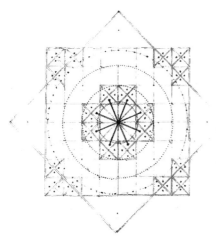

Jong's Nazcan Zodiac
(after Gilbert de Jong; world-mysteries.com)
Diagram 10.123a

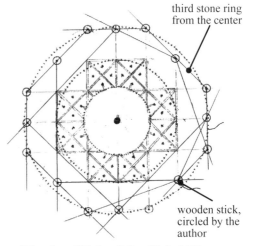

third stone ring
from the center

wooden stick,
circled by the
author

**Wooden Stick of the Third Ring
Forming Various SAs with
Neighboring Sticks**
(diagram: Jong)
Diagram 10.123b

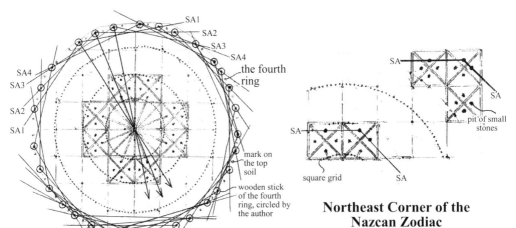

SA1
SA2
SA3
SA4
the fourth
ring
SA4
SA3
SA2
SA1

mark on
the top
soil

wooden stick
of the fourth
ring, circled by
the author

**Wooden Stick of the Fourth Ring
Forming Various SAs**
(diagram: Jong)
Diagram 10.123c

SA
SA
SA
pit of small
stones
square grid
SA

**Northeast Corner of the
Nazcan Zodiac**
(drawing Jong)
Diagram 10.123d

The Builders' Headquarters

The builders definitely turned Mesoamerica into their capital on Earth during the Christian era. It was the time when Europe entered its Iron Age and was troubled by a series of wars and disturbances caused by the aggressive Roman Empire and her surrounding barbarians. The old and rotten stations like Newgrange and Stonehenge were respectively turned into collective tombs for the Irish and a Solar temple of the British Druids. The builders were "forced" to construct their powerhouses in the extreme periphery of the European continent. Mysterious circular infrastructures such as brochs and wheelhouses, protected by high and thick walls, were constructed in the northern islands of Orkney and Shetland for power.

To the builders, the virgin land of America must have been an ideal and probably the last resort since it is far away from the "civilized" Europe and Asia. Besides, the thick and deep rainforest provided a high degree of inaccessibility for intruders, whereas a sea of canopy secured the builders' secret. The local population may have been subjected to "brainwashing" and manipulation before being turned into laborers for constructing those sites or "cities of Gods." As a result, different forms of megalithic power generators were built in different periods of time, from monolithic stelae, earthen platforms, square plazas, and sunken platforms, to sky-catching temple-pyramids. Linking with the corbelled roof-combs, these temple-pyramids, on one hand, served as the builders' powerhouses; on the other hand, they were the communication centers for transmitting microwaves to their destinations. No matter what we call them—the Olmecs and the Aztecs of the South America or the Maya of the Central America—it is the same unknown civilization.

It has always been an enigma how the ancient Mayans, living in a Stone Age society and making a living on simple and primitive farming and hunting, could develop a great understanding of arithmetic and astronomy, the two essential fields of knowledge for space exploration and interplanetary travel. The ancient tales suggest their culture had inherited sophisticated counting systems and knowledge of Venus and Mars from an ancient god. Apart from the so-called "vague year" calendar, which is made up of 365 days—the exact duration of time that our planet needs to revolve around the sun—the ancient Mayans also adopted a 260-day almanac to calculate the important ceremonial events. Why did they choose this special calendar? Is it the revolution of an unknown planet of an unknown solar system somewhere on the other side of our Galaxy, probably the destination for all the Mayan skyscraper microwave communication networks? Venus and Mars had also been their power stations: could we find SA implanted on them? The "cities of Gods" probably mark the end of the builders' megalithic magic shows on Earth. With their technological advancement at rocket speed, a completely new and certainly more efficient and economical way to obtain our Earth energy must have been developed. And we are still puzzled by their new trick *today.*

**Rear View of the Builders' Jet Craft
with a Pair of Gigantic
Power Engines**
Diagram 10.124a

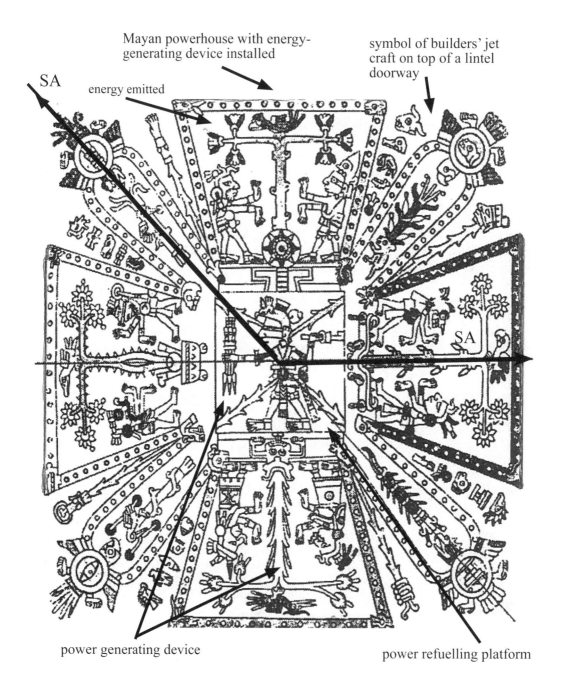

SA

Mayan powerhouse with energy-
generating device installed

symbol of builders' jet
craft on top of a lintel
doorway

energy emitted

SA

power generating device

power refuelling platform

**World Trees Oriented to the Four Directions, Codex Fejervary-Mayer,
Late Postclassic Period, Probably Showing Conical Devices
under Lintel Doorways of the Mayan Powerhouses**
(after Townsend 2000)
Diagram 10.124b

The Piri Reis Map

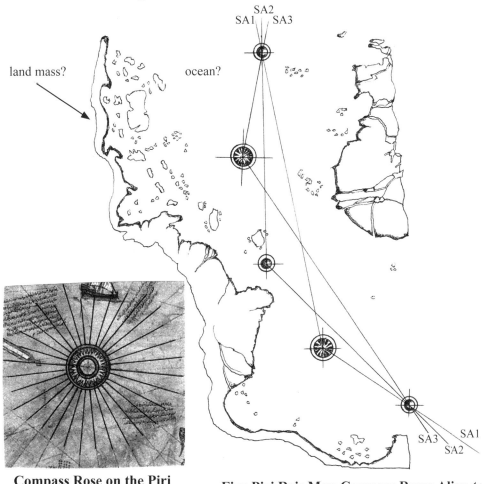

Compass Rose on the Piri Reis Map; Each Pair of Radiating Lines Forms an SA

Five Piri Reis Map Compass Roses Align to the SA (info: world-mysteries.com)

Diagram 10.125

The Piri Reis Map was discovered in 1929 when the Topkapi Palace in Istanbul was being converted into a museum. Generally, the map is believed to have been drawn by the Turkish admiral in 1513, twenty years after Columbus discovered the Caribbean. The map is famous not because of its accuracy and comprehensiveness of the geographical data of the areas, but because of the controversy over when it was made.

A vast ocean that dominates the center of the map is surrounded by two large land masses. Experts identify these coastal lands as South America, West Africa, the Iberian Peninsula—and most importantly, the Queen Maud Land of Antarctica, with a detailed description of its coastal lines, rivers, mountain ranges, deserts, and lakes (not shown in diagram 10.125). This certainly stuns the academics, as these geographical features of the Antarctic are now lying deep under the ice-cap, which is one mile thick. Researchers estimate that the last ice-free period in the region, which would have allowed the making of an accurate map, was 11,000 to 4000 B.C.

Also the accuacy of the Piri Reis Map suggests the use of spheroid trigonometry. According to Hapgood, who brought the map to public attention, it is plotted in plane geometry in great height. The accuracy of the map may even supersedes modern ones, as it can correct some errors in the latter. According to Admiral Reis, twenty ancient maps were used to draw the 1513 map. Someone must have previously charted the coastline of Antarctica, possibly in 4000 B.C.

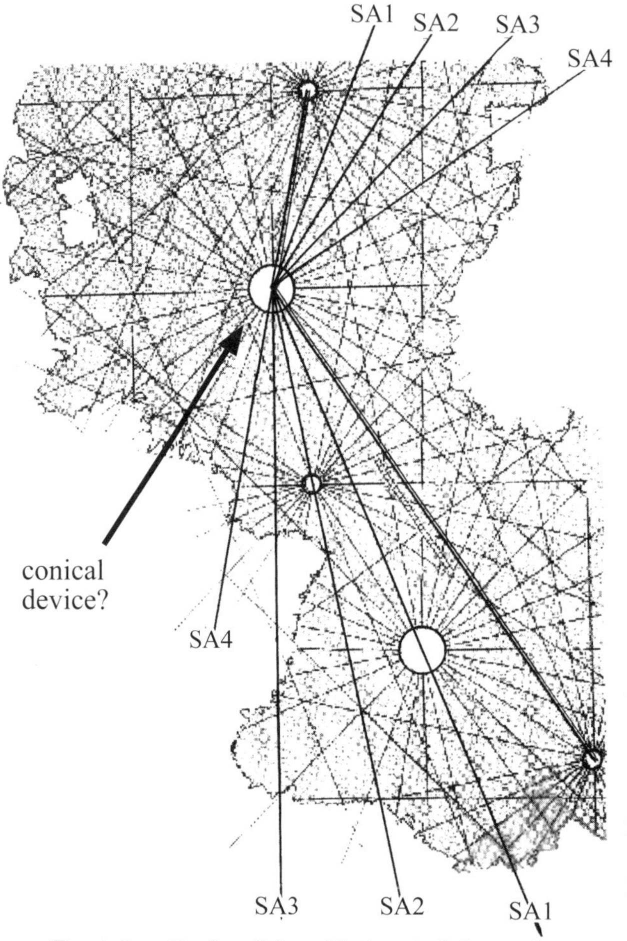

**Portolan Design Lines Extracted from the
Piri Reis Map, Showing the SAs**
Diagram 10.126

What attracts my attention is not the accurate coastal lines, but the vast ocean which is deliberately and predominantly placed in the middle of the map. In this "mysterious ocean" there is a sequence of circles with lines radiating from its center. Experts explain that the map exhibits a network of "rhumb lines," directions radiating in a circular pattern known as the "compass rose."

However, the radiating lines in each of these compass roses also form several sets of SAs (smaller diagram of 10.125 and diagram 10.126). Instead of showing compass directions, they are actually describing circles of radial megalights produced by conical devices. Supporting this assumption is that these five compass roses form three sets of SAs themselves (diagram 10.125). Again, the Piri Reis Map is a depiction of an energy mechanism. Diagram 10.127 echoes this in a crop formation in southern Britain.

**Two "Arms" of the Milk Hill
Crop Circle Formation, 2001**
*Diagram 10.127
(derived from Diagram 12.3)*

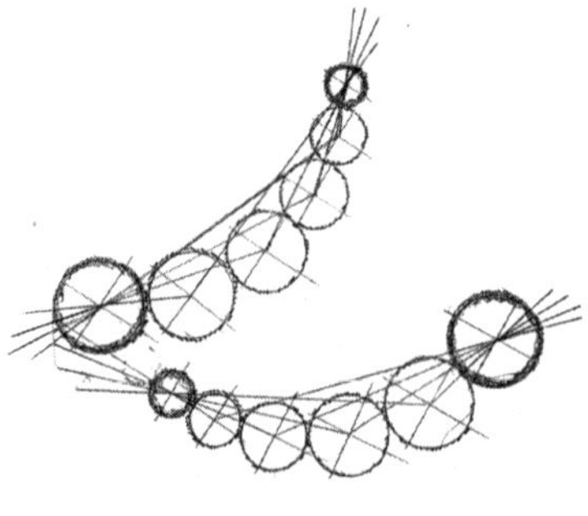

Heel Stone

SS94

SS91

SS93

SS92

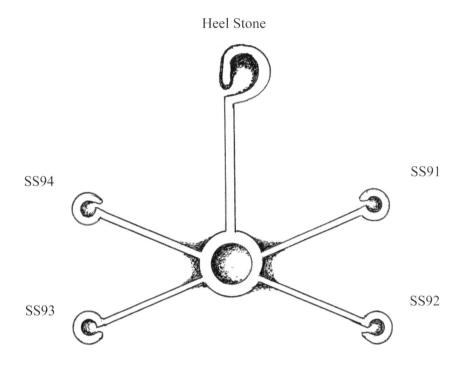

"The Nazcan Stonehenge": Mysterious Carving in the Peruvian Desert
(from world-mysteries.com)
Diagram 10.128

Chapter 11
Angkor Powerhouses and Ancient Indian Aircraft

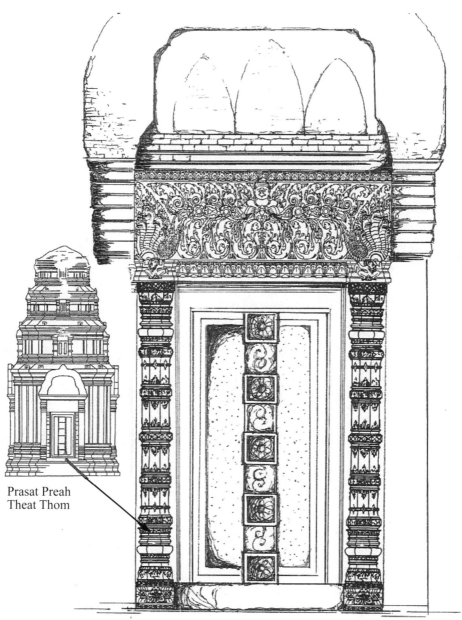

Prasat Preah
Theat Thom

False Door of a Khmer Gopura, Cambodia, circa A.D. 900:
Schematic Representation of Decorative Elements of Lintel, Preah Ko Style—
A Mysterious Elongated Object Was Sculpted and Placed under the Doorway
(after Mazzeo and Antonimi)
Diagram 11.1

Temple-Mountains of Angkor: A Forerunner of Modern-day Crop Circles

"The challenge in reconstructing Cambodia's historical and architectural past, then, lies in an expanded literacy: the ability to 'read' architecture and sculpture for meaning and stylistic development."

—Eleanor Mannıkka, *Angkor Wat: Time, Space and Kingship* (1996)

"There is also an earth-based energy available to human beings, concentrated at specific places all across the planet, which catalyzes and increases this eco-spiritual consciousness. ... That is the deeper meaning and purpose of these magical holy places (in Angkor): they are source points of the power of spiritual illumination."

—Martin Gray (1983)

A recent history of warfare and civil disturbance has not stopped tourists from flocking to Cambodia, where one of world's greatest but least-known civilizations developed. Even aided with modern equipment such as airborne synthetic radar and photogrammetric techniques, we still know little about the ancient city of Angkor, and its lost civilization that appeared and vanished deep inside the rainforest of Cambodia. The only evidence is dozens of complicated structures decorated with imaginative sculptures and undeciphered inscriptions. Probably a total of 900 temples (910 monuments were counted by Lunet de Lajonquiere), approximately the same as the number of mysterious stone circles erected over Northern Europe around 2000 B.C., were identified around the region, the most inaccessible part of the country. Experts suggest that during its heyday, in the twelfth century, 1,000,000 inhabitants lived in the urban complex covering about 1,000 sq km (Coe 2003), and certainly surpassed any European settlements of that period. (For example, London had a population of 50,000 at this time.) The ancient city of Angkor was and is truly a wonder of the world.

Inland Cambodia was not an ideal place for a "world class" civilization to flourish. Experts estimate that over 40% of the land is not suitable for any kind of agriculture and another 30% is covered by high and dense forest (Coe 2003). Water is polluted by the salty soils. Dry rice farming with "slash-and-burn" techniques only guarantees a small and low-yield harvest. Even today, Cambodia is still one of the world's poorest countries. How could it support a huge population with well-nourished workers for all the building jobs? Lying just south of ancient Angkor is the fertile Mekong Delta, covered with nitrogen-rich alluvium and promising highly productive flood-retreat farming. Why did the god-worshipping Khmers decide to build and hide their sacred temple-city in the north, deep inside the forest canopy?

The secret of Angkor, which had "slept" for more than 500 years before it was reawakened by the Spanish and Portuguese missionaries in the sixteenth and seventeenth centuries, was probably the last megalithic mystery to be discovered. With few literary sources and undeciphered inscriptions, its magnificent buildings were once misinterpreted as having been created by Alexander the Great. Local legends said these temples were built by gods or by giants (angkorwat.org). But it was not until the arrival of the French in the mid-nineteenth century that ancient Angkor was really brought to the world and a scientific and systematic study of the region started.

Henri Mouhot, a French explorer and passionate naturalist who knew nothing of architecture and archaeology, accidentally rediscovered Angkor in 1858–60 when he wanted to "contribute to the enrichment of science." Generally speaking, experts believe the civilization was founded by a native minority called Mon-Khmer of Indo-China. According to the inscriptions on a stele dated 1052, the kingdom was founded by Jayavarman II circa A.D. 802, at a time when the political situation there was very unstable (Mazzeo and Antonini). A holy city was built on a high plateau—metaphorically an artificial sacred mountain of the divinity, twenty-five miles northeast of Angkor. And from then on, each capital of the classic Angkorean civilization, from the first half of the ninth century to the end of the twelfth, had its own temple-mountain (Mazzeo and Antonini 1978), turning the area into a veritable country of temples.

Jayavarman II, the "emperor of the world" (Jacques 1990), also introduced the cult of Devaraja to his kingdom, in which a Khmer god—"the king of spirits," with equal status to the king himself—was created. Priests were appointed and temples were built to honor and propitiate the divinity. Even though Jayavarman II was the founder of the great Khmer empire, there is little known about him, as no inscriptions have been found. The king is as mysterious as the empire he created.

Khmer Architecture and Its Ornate Lintel

Like the ancient Egyptians and Mayans, ancient Khmers were prolific temple-builders. They lived in rectangular houses that were raised simply on wooden bases, walled with palm-leaf mats, and protected by bamboo enclosures. Even their palaces were made of wood and could not have survived to the present day. However, they were capable of erecting magnificent megalithic temple complexes, "Temples and Citadels of the Forest," decorated with stylistic sculptures. Their earliest architecture was focused and centered by building a brick tower with thick walls, in which a very small, square inner cell with single entry and three false doorways was constructed (diagram 11.1). The doorway was often made of stone, carved with simple designs. The roof, with its height dominating the whole site, was constructed with superimposing levels decreasing in size (Mazzeo and Antonini 1978). This sacred prasat, the absolute center of the site, was built on top of the terraced platforms and further enclosed by rectangular enclosures which were regularly and concentrically arranged in a precise order.

Between the ninth and thirteenth centuries, such monumental complexes gradually evolved into their mature form—that is, quadrangular towers made of sandstones and laterite built on top of a pyramid of terraces and encircled by concentric vaulted galleries centered with pavilions. Carvings of high quality and detail were made on the lintels of these temple doorways. In order to raise the temple roof, a corbelling technique of piling up large stones on top of one another without mortar was used (angkorwat.org). The best and most famous of its kind is the great temple-mountain of Angkor Wat.

To understand the Khmer temple architecture, their cosmic belief—the cult of the devaraja—should be considered. According to the ancient Khmer inscriptions, Hindu ancestral and regional deities, especially Shiva ("the Lord of the Universe who is king"), were believed to have lived on Mount Meru—the mythical dwelling of the gods. Therefore, the kings of the Khmer began to construct their own "artificial mountains" to honor these gods. These temple-mountains—usually in the form of a step-pyramid composed of four superimposed terraces of earth—became the focal point of the city and the kingdom (John Thomson 1875). Elevated temples were built on the step-pyramid where a lingam—a cylindrical stone replicating the phallus of Shiva, the creator and destroyer of the world—was located. The phallus also symbolized the "life-giving force" of the deity (Mazzeo and Antonini 1978) (diagrams 11.2, 11.3 and 11.4).

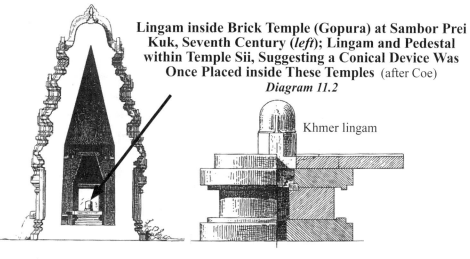

Lingam inside Brick Temple (Gopura) at Sambor Prei Kuk, Seventh Century (*left*); Lingam and Pedestal within Temple Sii, Suggesting a Conical Device Was Once Placed inside These Temples (after Coe)
Diagram 11.2

Khmer lingam

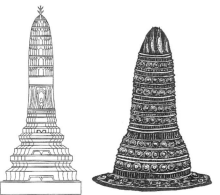

Khmer-style Prang and the Conical Device
(*left:* Colet and Eliot 2002)
Diagram 11.3

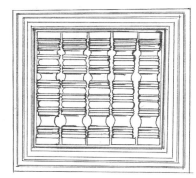

Stone Window with Lathe-turned Balusters, Angkor Wat, Suggesting Cylindrical Devices Were Placed under the Doorways of Khmer Powerhouses
Diagram 11.4

The sculpture on the lintel and the two pedestals of a typical doorway of a Khmer temple is a perfect example to demonstrate and elaborate their beliefs (diagram 11.5). Usually, on the center of each lintel, human figures—probably images of the great gods Shiva and Vishnu—are placed on top of the garuda or the lion, the birdlike monster described by experts as the "vehicle" of the divine (Mazzeo and Antonini). Not surprisingly, pendants surrounded by series of leaves were decorated under their "vehicle." Similar interesting scenes has been described on the Puuc-style lintels of the Nunnery and Governor's House of the Mayan city of Uxmal, as well as on the cylindrical seals of the Sumerians. An old message—the builders' jet craft refuelling on top of their powerhouse—is once again revealed in front of the tourists' eyes, this time in ancient Angkor.

Additionally, the doorway, just under the lintel, is framed by two hexagonal columns, similar to the pair from the Treasury of Atreus in ancient Greece, symbolizing the builders' power-generating device once placed under the lintel doorway. Hence the floral decorations and mythical serpent motifs, symbolizing energy being generated and emitted, that are carved on top of these cylindrical columns, and connected to Vishnu's vehicle. Functioning in exactly the same way as those from contemporary Maya, the Khmer temples were designed to power the builders' vehicles. Their lintel doorways were constructed to house the builders' conical devices, while their towers were built for the installation of all these lintel doorways (diagram 11.6). Only the application of the SA into these mysterious Khmer megalithic temples can best support the power-generating theory.

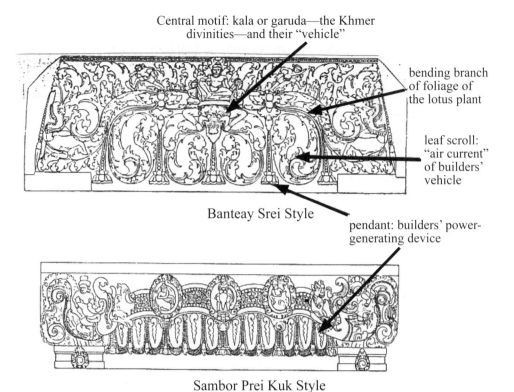

Central motif: kala or garuda—the Khmer divinities—and their "vehicle"

bending branch of foliage of the lotus plant

leaf scroll: "air current" of builders' vehicle

pendant: builders' power-generating device

Banteay Srei Style

Sambor Prei Kuk Style

Carvings on Khmer lintels
Diagram 11.5

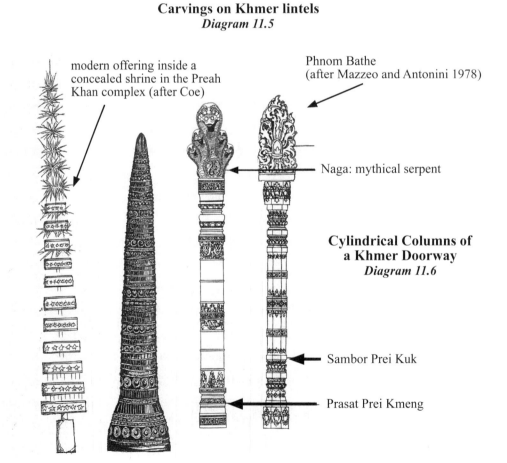

modern offering inside a concealed shrine in the Preah Khan complex (after Coe)

Phnom Bathe (after Mazzeo and Antonini 1978)

Naga: mythical serpent

Cylindrical Columns of a Khmer Doorway
Diagram 11.6

Sambor Prei Kuk

Prasat Prei Kmeng

Sanctuary Towers of the Preclassic Period and the SA

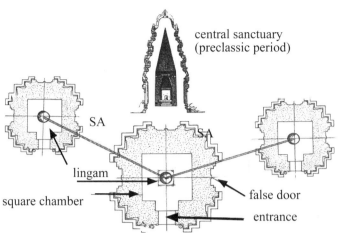

central sanctuary
(preclassic period)

SA

SA

lingam

square chamber

false door

entrance

As mentioned above, the overall design of the temple-mountain is quadrangular. It has the form of an Indian mandala. The mountain is enclosed by sets of concentric walls, which represent the mountains that surround the "square" earth. The outermost moats symbolize the oceans. The multi-tier pyramid—the artificial mountain—is topped with a five-towered sanctuary in a quincunx design.

Khmer Towers Aligned to the SA *Diagram 11.7*

The ancient capital of Bakong, the first significant temple-mountain dating back to the late ninth century, is the best example (diagram 11.8). A single sanctuary temple atop a four-tiered sandstone pyramid was encircled by four enclosures, forming an area 800m by 660m. The central tower, believed to have been rebuilt in the twelfth century, has one real and three false doorways. Another circle of eight large brick towers was constructed encircling the central stepped pyramid, two on each side. These towers all open to the east with four axial stairways. The only sandstone elements are the frames of the openings, with their richly decorated banded cylindrical colonnettes (theangkor.com). Its secret and function is probably revealed by several sets of SAs derived from the towers with the sanctuary in the center.

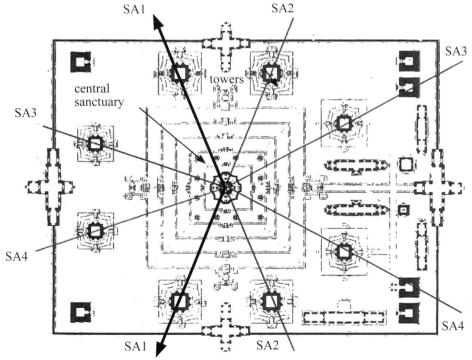

SA1

SA2

SA3

central
sanctuary

towers

SA3

SA4

SA1

SA2

SA4

Plan of Bakong, A.D. 881 (after Freeman and Jacques)
Diagram 11.8

The design of another temple-mountain at Pre Rup further confirms this theory. The structure, built in about A.D. 961, has five sanctuary towers, arranged in a quincunx pattern, constructed on top of a three-tiered, 12m-high pyramid. Its laterite enclosure is divided by four small single-roomed brick gopuras, preceded by a sandstone vestibule (theangkor.com). Several SAs are formed by the four corner towers and the four small gopuras with the central sanctuary in the middle. That is why a lingam—replica of the builders' power-generating device—was erected in its center (diagram 11.9a). Also, twelve small sanctuary towers, each with a lingam inside, standing on the first tier of the pyramid. They were deliberately placed according to the SA (diagram 11.9b).

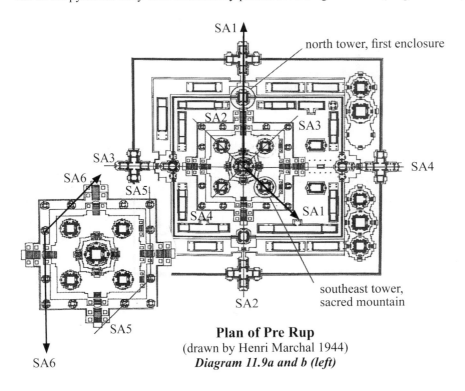

Plan of Pre Rup
(drawn by Henri Marchal 1944)
Diagram 11.9a and b (left)

Phnom Bakheng of the late ninth to early tenth centuries is one of the great monuments of the Khmers. Bakheng is called the "first Angkor," as the original city was larger than Angkor Thom. The temple was cut from the rock that formed the natural hill, 65m high. "Phnom" means "hill" in the Khmer language. Its five sanctuary towers were built on top of a five-tiered pyramid, 13m high. The lingam of the god Shiva was erected within the shrine at the central tower (Coe 2003). The stairways to this central sanctuary are laid out to coincide with the four cardinal directions. A large number of smaller shrines are arranged geometrically on the steps of the pyramid. Another circle of forty-four large towers was constructed encircling the base of the stepped mountain. These towers, together with those in the center, were aligned according to the SA (diagram 11.10).

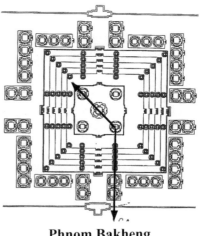

Phnom Bakheng
(after Mazzeo)
Diagram 11.10

East Mebon is a three-tiered temple-mountain on a laterite base, 126m × 121m (Freeman and Jacques 1999). A 3m-high platform supports five brick sanctuary towers. Like those from Bakong and Pre Rup, they form several SAs with four towers of the second platform (diagram 11.11a). In the open space between the inner enclosure wall and the central platform are eight small brick towers in pairs at the cardinal points. They were also sited according to the SA (diagram 11.11b).

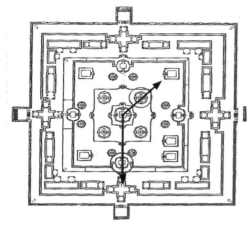 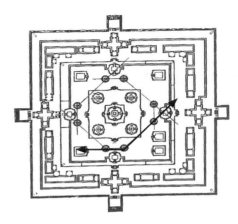

Five central towers and four gopuras
aligned to the SA

Eight minor towers aligned to the SA

Plan of East Mebon
(after Mazzeo)
Diagram 11.11a and b (left)

Double Doorway of the Classic Period and the SA

Banteay Srei (A.D. 967), with the modern name "Citadel of the Women," 20km north of Angkor, is certainly a must-see site. Its small but perfectly proportioned size and impressive carvings earn it the designation "jewel" of the Khmer—the temple of great beauty. The site, 95m × 110m, is arranged in three concentric enclosures. The central sanctuary consists of three towers, built largely of red sandstone on a T-shaped platform. An antechamber connects the central sanctuary with a corridor. Several doorways opened into both the north and south sides of the antechamber. These buildings are heavily decorated all over their external surfaces, but their interiors are bare (Jacques1990).

The pediments of its buildings, especially the tympanum of the east entry pavilion (gopura II), decorated with floral elements, are certainly the most famous of the Khmer art, are the first Khmer architecture. The sandstone relief carvings of its lintels, cut deep and sculpted virtually in three dimensions, are among the finest, showing a near-perfect ornamention technique. It seems that the focus was on these lintel doorways rather than its interior shrines, supposed to be the most sacred place of the building. As shown in diagram 11.12, below, doorway (D1) connecting the antechamber and the central sanctuary forms several SAs with the surrounding doorways. Banteay Srei marked the turning point of the Angkor powerhouses, when lintel doorways replaced brick towers as the cell batteries for the builders' jet vehicles.

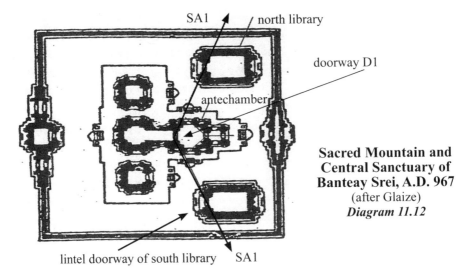

SA1 — north library

doorway D1

antechamber

**Sacred Mountain and
Central Sanctuary of
Banteay Srei, A.D. 967**
(after Glaize)
Diagram 11.12

lintel doorway of south library — SA1

After the successful evolution from Banteay Srei, most of the sanctuary towers of the later classic period are square in plan, with four doors through the four vestibules, each of which has an entrance bay (diagram 11.13). These buildings and their doorways were specially designed to house the builders' power-generating devices. From the Khmer temple-mountain of Ta Keo in around A.D. 975 to the famous complexes of Angkor Wat and Angkor Thom of the twelfth century, their doorways were placed according to the SA.

A Double-doorway Installation of the Classic Period

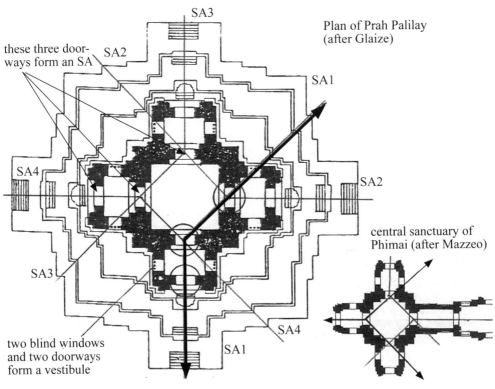

SA3

Plan of Prah Palilay
(after Glaize)

these three door-ways form an SA

SA2

SA1

SA4

SA2

central sanctuary of
Phimai (after Mazzeo)

SA3

two blind windows
and two doorways
form a vestibule

SA4

SA1

Lintel Doorways inside a Classic Tower, Aligned according to the SA
Diagram 11.13

As mentioned, the "golden-tipped mountain" of Ta Keo was built in around A.D. 975. The construction was built entirely of sandstone. Five sanctuary towers in quincunx arrangement were placed on top of a three-tiered pyramid, measuring 122m × 106m at ground level. The pyramid was then surrounded by two platforms, one being encircled by a wall, the other by a vaulted gallery. The five central towers were each open with a door at each side and reached through vestibules, each with an entrance. Structurally, each square chamber was designed and encircled with four sets of "double doorway," each one at its four sides. Such planning allowed the installation of the builders' generating devices, as each pair of its "double doorways" forms an SA with another adjacent doorway (diagram 11.14). It certainly tells the ultimate secret of these towers of the classic period of Angkor.

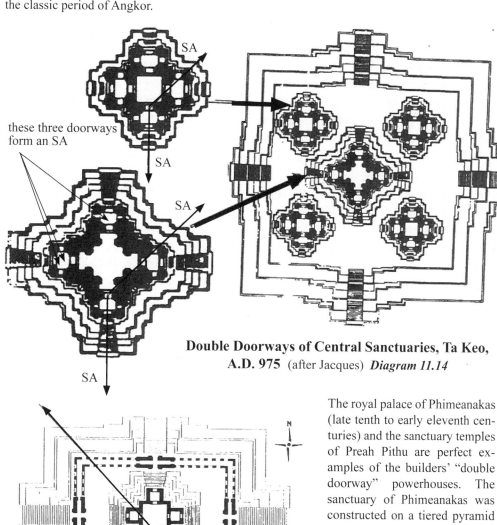

Double Doorways of Central Sanctuaries, Ta Keo,
A.D. 975 (after Jacques) *Diagram 11.14*

Phimeanakas, Late Tenth Century
(after Freeman and Jacques)
Diagram 11.15

The royal palace of Phimeanakas (late tenth to early eleventh centuries) and the sanctuary temples of Preah Pithu are perfect examples of the builders' "double doorway" powerhouses. The sanctuary of Phimeanakas was constructed on a tiered pyramid with radial stairways. Its square chamber is open at four sides, each connected with a bay. A pair of doorways at each side forms an SA with a doorway nearby (diagram 11.15). Similar designs are found inside Temples T, U, V, and X of Preah Pithu (diagram 11.16). They were the typical Khmer powerhouses.

ANGKOR POWERHOUSES AND ANCIENT INDIAN AIRCRAFT

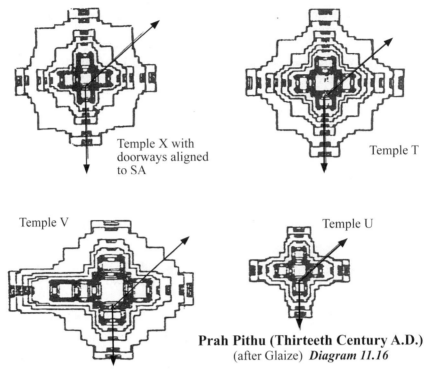

Temple X with
doorways aligned
to SA

Temple T

Temple V

Temple U

Prah Pithu (Thirteeth Century A.D.)
(after Glaize) *Diagram 11.16*

The enormous temple-mountain of Baphuon, one of the finest and most orderly structures, was constructed in mid-eleventh century. A single sandstone tower with bays at four sides was built on top of a massive five-tiered pyramid, protected by a rectangular enclosure of galleries and central gopuras. Four "libraries" were built and placed between the second and third enclosures, probably serving as some kind of shrines. Like those "double doorways" of the central sanctuary, the doorways of its libraries were erected according to the SA (diagram 11.17).

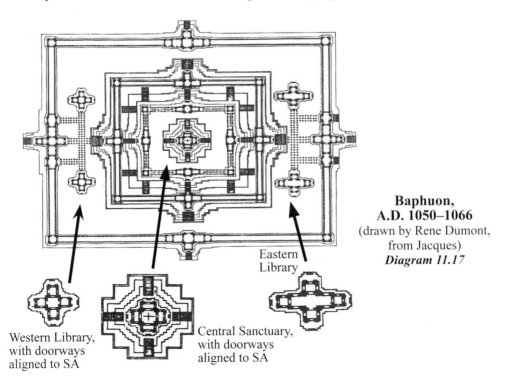

Eastern
Library

**Baphuon,
A.D. 1050–1066**
(drawn by Rene Dumont,
from Jacques)
Diagram 11.17

Western Library,
with doorways
aligned to SA

Central Sanctuary,
with doorways
aligned to SA

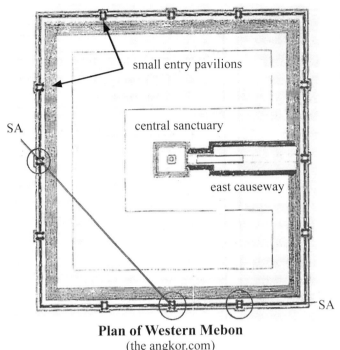

Plan of Western Mebon
(the angkor.com)
Diagram 11.18

The 100-sq-m temple of West Mebon was constructed on an artificial island in the middle of the western baray (pond). The central sanctuary is raised by a sandstone platform, measuring 12m each side, and connected by an eastern laterite causeway (diagram 11.18). Its surrounding enclosure has three small entry pavilions on each side; each with two opposite doors. These single-tiered and square towers are made of sandstone with large eight-petaled lotus crowns. They are further linked to one another by a sandstone enclosure wall (theangkor.com). As expected, these small towers are aligned according to the SA.

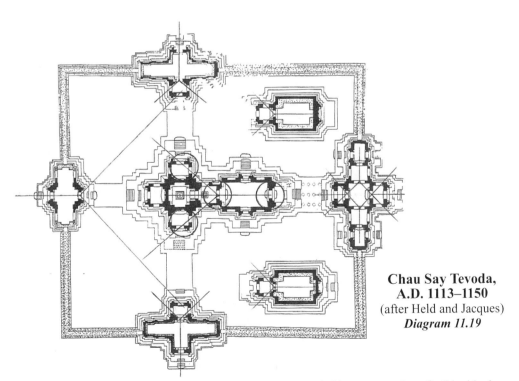

**Chau Say Tevoda,
A.D. 1113–1150**
(after Held and Jacques)
Diagram 11.19

Chao Say Tevoda of the mid-twelfth century was most probably an extension of a "double doorways" powerhouse. As diagram 11.19 below shows, its central sanctuary has an antechamber to the east. The north and south doorways of this extended chamber form several SAs with the surrounding structures. The various doorways of its four gopuras also constitute several sets of SAs.

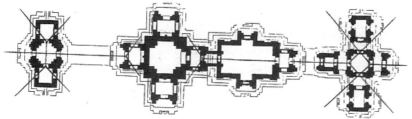

Thommanon (Twelfth Century A.D.) (after Freeman and Jacques) *Diagram 11.20*

The same pattern is repeated in the central tower, antechamber and gopuras of Thommanon and Banteay Samre of the early twelfth century (diagrams 11.20 and 11.21).

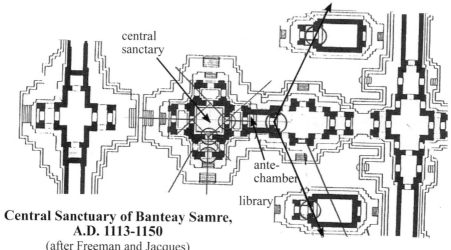

central
sanctary

ante-
chamber

library

Central Sanctuary of Banteay Samre,
A.D. 1113-1150
(after Freeman and Jacques)
Diagram 11.21

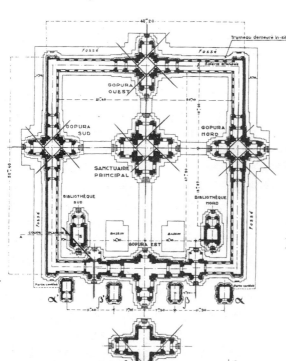

Plan of the First Enclosure,
Preah Khan, with Doorways
Aligned to SA
(from Mauger)
Diagram 11.22

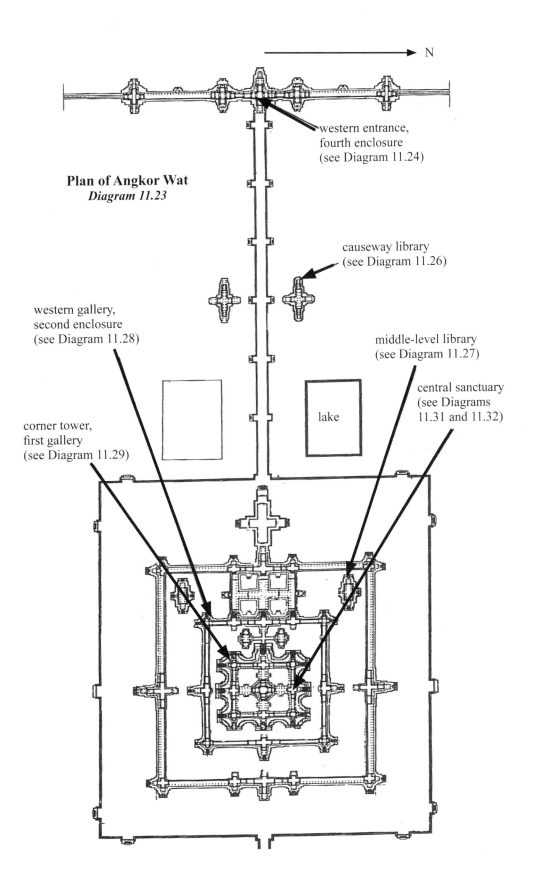

N

Plan of Angkor Wat
Diagram 11.23

western entrance,
fourth enclosure
(see Diagram 11.24)

causeway library
(see Diagram 11.26)

western gallery,
second enclosure
(see Diagram 11.28)

middle-level library
(see Diagram 11.27)

central sanctuary
(see Diagrams
11.31 and 11.32)

corner tower,
first gallery
(see Diagram 11.29)

lake

"Angkor Wat has remained a historical enigma for one good reason: no inscriptions bear any known reference to the monument. Why one of the most imposing temples in Khmer history did not merit more notice in stone steles is indeed a mystery."

—E. Mannikka, *Angkor Wat: Time, Space, and Kingship* (1996), p. 24

"(Under the central shrine of Angkor Wat) … archaeologists discovered a laterite slab with a cavity containing two pieces of crystal and two gold leaves far beneath where the Vishnu statue must have been—here as elsewhere it was deposits such as these that spiritually 'energized' a temple, much as a battery will provide power to a portable electronic device."

—Michael D. Coe, *Angkor and the Khmer Civilization* (2003), p. 118

Angkor Wat, the grandest of all the Khmer temples, is definitely the largest religious complex in the world. The temple is part of the Angkor World Heritage Site, listed in 1992, and attracts over a million visitors each year. Some see it as a "city of pagodas," "beautiful houses built of stone," a "former royal palace," a "great unfinished temple with five peaks," a "tomb to the kings who built it," and even a "walled city" (Dagens 1995). But experts generally suggest this twelfth-century edifice was once the capital and State Temple dedicated to the Khmer divinity. Its sacred artificial mountain is enclosed by a broad moat around an area 1300m by 1500m (diagram 11.23). Inside it has an outer enclosure (fourth) bounded by a laterite wall with gopuras, each at its cardinal points. The west gopura known as the Western Gateways consists of three towers and is the largest among the four, serving as the main entrance to the site. Without doubt, the doorways inside the four outer gopuras were constructed according to the SA (diagrams 11.24 and 11.25).

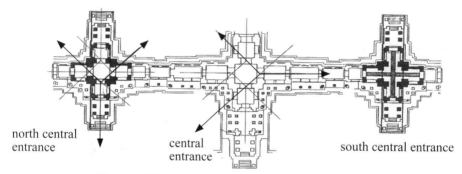

north central
entrance

central
entrance

south central entrance

Western Entrances, Fourth Enclosure, Angkor Wat
(after Mannikka)
Diagram 11.24

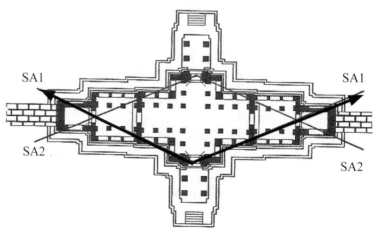

**Three Identical
Entrances
(Northern,
Southern, and
Eastern)
Fourth Enclosure,
Angkor Wat**
(after Mannikka)
Diagram 11.25

SA1

SA1

SA2

SA2

A 350m paved causeway connects the Western Gateways to the temple-mountain at the center of Angkor Wat. Interestingly, the causeway leads to a pair of libraries at its midway point. Sharing a similar design as the outer gopuras, these two identical libraries have four doorways at the cardinal points, and they are aligned to the SA (diagram 11.26).

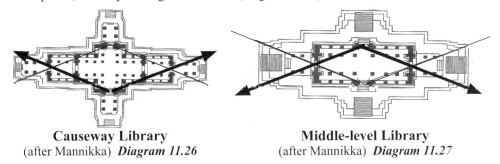

Causeway Library
(after Mannikka) *Diagram 11.26*

Middle-level Library
(after Mannikka) *Diagram 11.27*

The west causeway leads to the western part of the third enclosure which is bounded by a vaulted gallery with gopuras at the four cardinal points and square towers at four corners. A series of covered flights of stairs, generally known as the cruciform cloister, connect the third enclosure with the second. Two other libraries with doorways at the four cardinal points flank these covered stairs. These doorways, like the two flanking the west causeway, are positioned according to the SA (diagram 11.27).

Further east of the western cruciform cloister is the second enclosure of the temple-mountain. Sanctuary towers were constructed at four corners with another four gopuras at its four cardinal points. Doorways of these buildings are aligned to the SA (diagram 11.28).

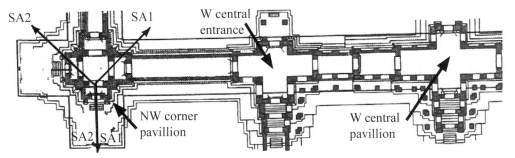

Second Gallery (after Mannikka) *Diagram 11.28*

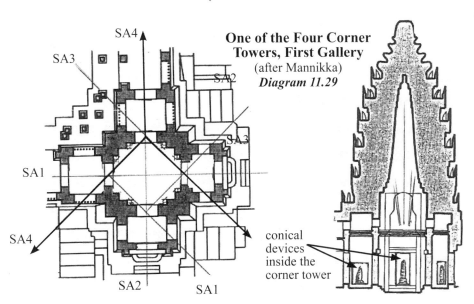

One of the Four Corner Towers, First Gallery
(after Mannikka)
Diagram 11.29

conical devices inside the corner tower

In the most sacred area, five central towers stand on the uppermost level of the temple, forming and connecting by the first gallery. The central sanctuary tower marks the summit of the whole complex with four towers rising from four corners, linked by vaulted galleries. The double-doorways of these corner towers form several SAs (diagram 11.29).

Four pavilions were constructed between these corner towers, at the four cardinal points of the mountain. Their doorways form an SA with a doorway from the central sanctuary, respectively (diagram 11.30).

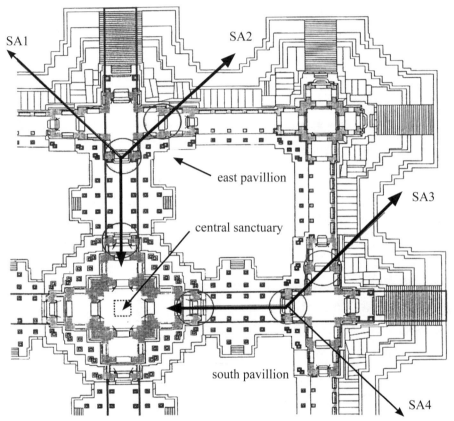

Pavillions Connect the Central Sanctuary with the SA
(after Mannikka) *Diagram 11.30*

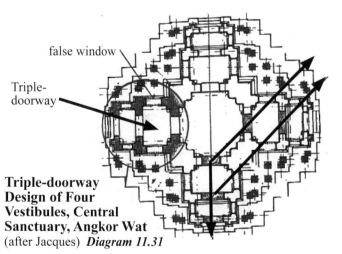

**Triple-doorway
Design of Four
Vestibules, Central
Sanctuary, Angkor Wat**
(after Jacques) *Diagram 11.31*

The central sanctuary has four doorways, one at each side, each opening to two bays or vestibules, one after the other and connected by a doorway. Structurally, the sanctuary of Angkor Wat was an advanced version of a typical double-doorway powerhouse, as more sets of SAs are derived from its triple-doorway design (diagram 11.31).

ANGKOR POWERHOUSES AND ANCIENT INDIAN AIRCRAFT

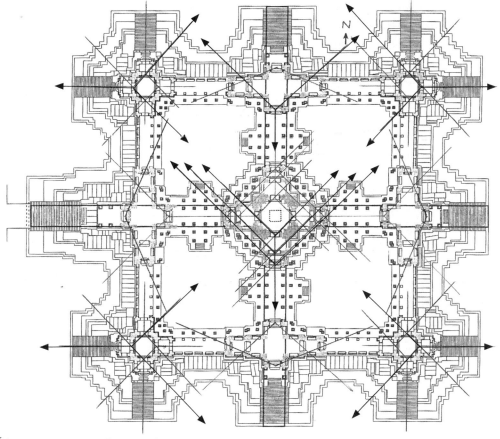

Central Sanctuary of Angkor Wat and Its SAs (after Mannikka)
Diagram 11.32

**Sculptured Pinnacle on Top
of a Khmer Powerhouse,
Symbolizing Energy
Being Emitted**
(after Stratten and Scott 1961)
Diagram 11.33

antefixes

arches

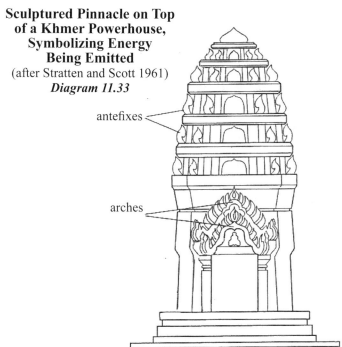

The real function of the sanctuary towers was revealed by the builders, not through ancient inscriptions but explicitly sculptured on top of these powerhouses. Their famous cornices are usually carved with multi-tiers, decreasing in size towards the top and crowned with a motif consisting of three layers of lotus petals (Jacques 1990). These crowning motifs, usually decorated in a uniform theme, symbolize the energy emitted on top of a powerhouse (diagrams 11.33 and 11.35). What is lacking today are the builders' power-generating devices.

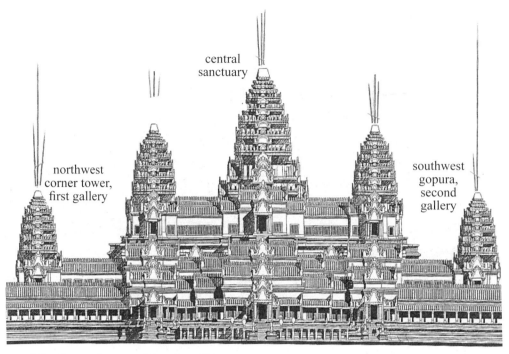

The Powerhouse of Angkor Wat (after Suzanne Held and Claude Jacques 1997)
Diagram 11.34

central
sanctuary

northwest
corner tower,
first gallery

southwest
gopura,
second
gallery

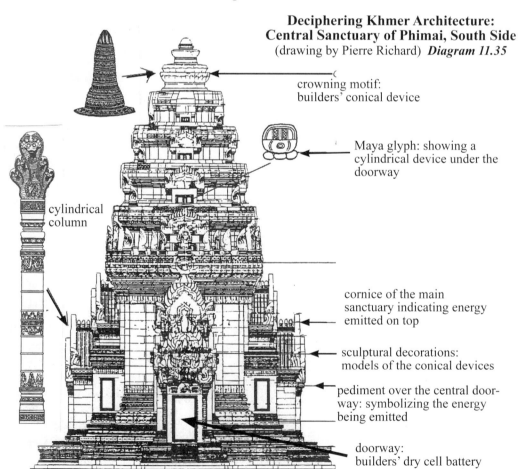

**Deciphering Khmer Architecture:
Central Sanctuary of Phimai, South Side**
(drawing by Pierre Richard) *Diagram 11.35*

crowning motif:
builders' conical device

Maya glyph: showing a
cylindrical device under the
doorway

cylindrical
column

cornice of the main
sanctuary indicating energy
emitted on top

sculptural decorations:
models of the conical devices

pediment over the central doorway: symbolizing the energy
being emitted

doorway:
builders' dry cell battery

The enigmatic temple complex of Bayon with its doorways of gopuras, libraries and central sanctuary aligned to the SA (diagram 11.36).

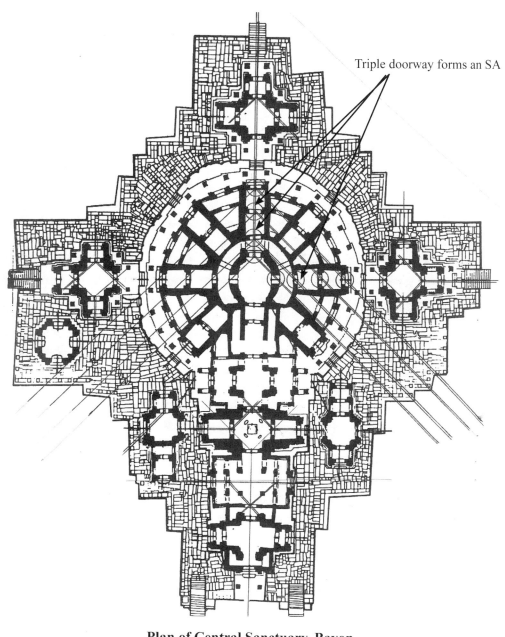

Triple doorway forms an SA

Plan of Central Sanctuary, Bayon
(diagram after Jacques)
Diagram 11.36

The maze of towers and galleries of Angkor Wat and Bayon temple stand as evidence of the peak of achievement of the Khmers, which none of their contemporaries could match. But after Bayon, at the end of A.D. 1200, their 300-year span of temple-building ended. The Khmers began to abandon their city, leaving it to the Thais 200 years later, who left it, finally, to nature. Perhaps, like most of the mysteries explored in this book, it was their deities abandoning their exhausted powerhouses that led to decline of the civilization.

"For, I doubt not, others will follow in my steps, … will gather an abundant harvest where I have but cleared the ground."

—Henri Mouhot: *Travels in the Central Parts of Indo-China, Cambodia and Laos* (1864)

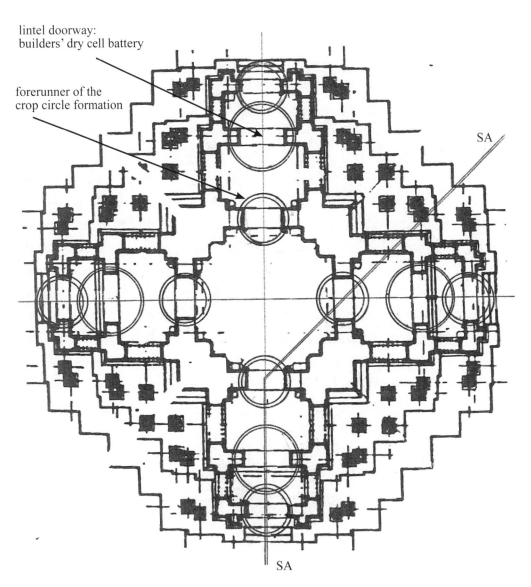

lintel doorway:
builders' dry cell battery

forerunner of the
crop circle formation

SA

SA

Central Sanctuary of Angkor Wat and Its Triple Doorway:
A Formation Mirrored in a Modern-day Crop Circle
Diagram 11.37

Ancient Indian Flying Vehicles

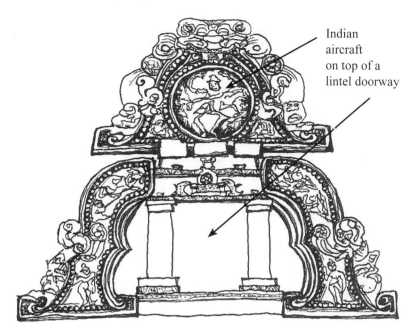

Indian
aircraft
on top of a
lintel doorway

**An Elaborately Arched Decoration of the Tower of the Vaital Deul Temple
in Bhubaneshwar, Orissa, Eighth Century**
(after G. Michell 2000)
Diagram 11.38

"The Hindu temple is designed to bring about contact between man and the gods; it is here that the gods appear to man. ... The center of the sanctuary functions as the focus of other dynamics which is realized through a process of symbolic association. To begin with there is the radiation of energy outwards from the center of the sanctuary in four directions. ... Summit and sacred center (of the sanctuary) are linked together along an axis which is a powerful projection upwards of the forces of energy which radiate from the center of the sanctuary."

—George Michell, *The Hindu Temple* (1977)

People believe that the ancient temples of Khmer are derived from and inspired by those of the Hindus of India of around the fourth century A.D. Even today, Hinduism is so important that about 80% of the people in India, the second-most populated country in the world, are its adherents. According to the experts, this 2,000-year-old religion is a synthesis of many different beliefs and practices, modes of living and thinking, a reconciliation of the cultures of indigenous Indian populations with succeeding invaders (G. Michell 1977).

Hinduism worships personal deities and regional gods or goddesses such as Indra, the greatest Vedic deity, and Brahma, the active creator-god of the Universe. The male god Shiva, expressed in the form of an erect phallus called a lingam, similar to those of ancient Angkor, is worshipped for his essential characteristic of energy that "dominates many aspects appearances of the god" and "is taken to be a direct expression of the inner workings of the universe" (G. Michell 1977). The divine animal or bird "vehicles" (*vahana*), such as the bull Nandi or Garuda of Vishnu, is also worshipped inside the Hindu temple. There are other deities with interesting names meaning "Working Energy" and "Creative Energy" (C. Tadgell 1990, p. 38).

Central Sanctuary and Doorways of the Hindu Temple

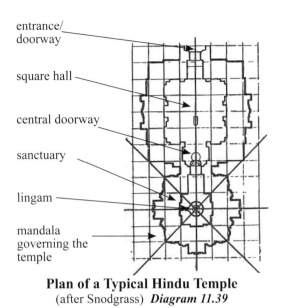

entrance/ doorway

square hall

central doorway

sanctuary

lingam

mandala governing the temple

Plan of a Typical Hindu Temple
(after Snodgrass) *Diagram 11.39*

According to Hinduism, ancient worshippers believed there are "sacred spots" where creative energy are contained and released. They built megalithic structures to tap and store this creative energy. A basic Hindu temple, which consists of a single-opening inner sanctum, the *garbha* or womb-chamber, was built on a sacred geometric diagram known as mandala. Its central sanctuary, a square cell open to a single doorway, is the focal point of the temple and the most sacred part of the whole structure. Here the "image of deity" (a *lingam*) is housed. Sometimes, the sanctuary is encircled with an ambulatory passageway and secured by a series of enclosures with niches and doorways (diagram 11.39). The plan of the temple is strictly oriented to the cardinal directions, usually along an east-west axis.

Planned in exactly the same way as the ancient Khmers, most Hindu temples were once the powerhouses of an unknown civilization because their sanctuaries and doorways are constructed according to the SA (diagrams 11.40–11.43). Power generating devices were once installed inside these superstructures, probably placed inside the sanctuary and under the doorways. An A.D. 600 Hindu temple of India functioned in exactly the same manner as the 5,000-year-old Newgrange and Stonehenge.

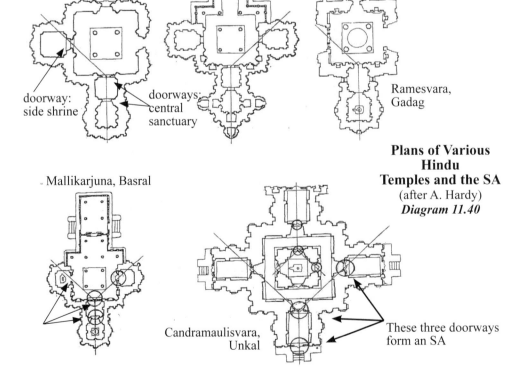

Bettesvara, Agrahara Belguli

Laksmi-Narasimha, Harnahalli

doorway: side shrine

doorways: central sanctuary

Ramesvara, Gadag

Mallikarjuna, Basral

Plans of Various Hindu Temples and the SA
(after A. Hardy)
Diagram 11.40

Candramaulisvara, Unkal

These three doorways form an SA

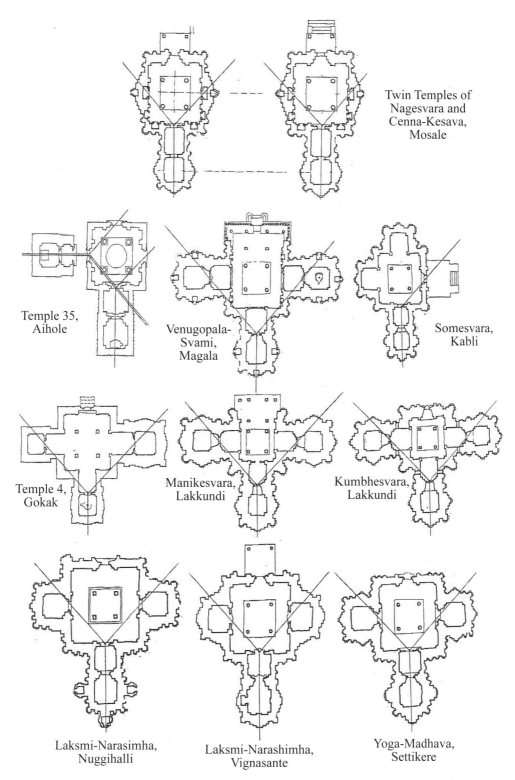

Twin Temples of
Nagesvara and
Cenna-Kesava,
Mosale

Temple 35,
Aihole

Venugopala-
Svami,
Magala

Somesvara,
Kabli

Temple 4,
Gokak

Manikesvara,
Lakkundi

Kumbhesvara,
Lakkundi

Laksmi-Narasimha,
Nuggihalli

Laksmi-Narashimha,
Vignasante

Yoga-Madhava,
Settikere

Plans of Various Hindu Temples and the SA
(after A. Hardy)
Diagram 11.41

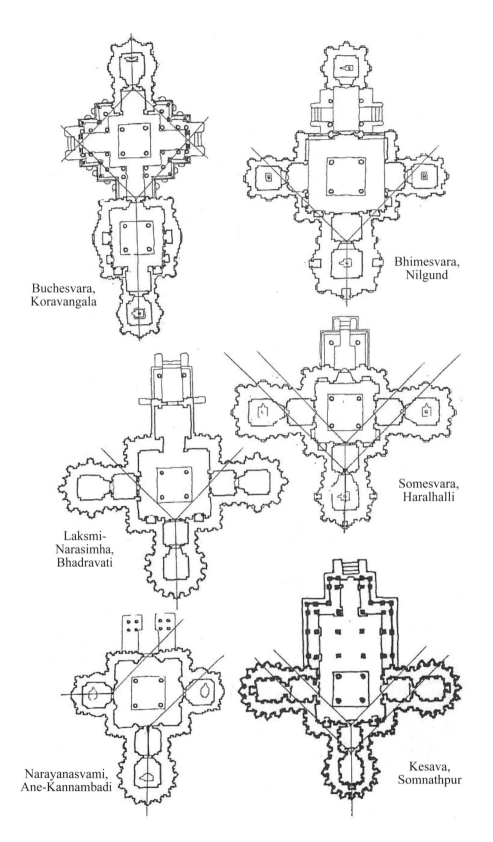

Buchesvara,
Koravangala

Bhimesvara,
Nilgund

Laksmi-
Narasimha,
Bhadravati

Somesvara,
Haralhalli

Narayanasvami,
Ane-Kannambadi

Kesava,
Somnathpur

Plans of Various Hindu Temples and the SA
(after A. Hardy)
Diagram 11.42

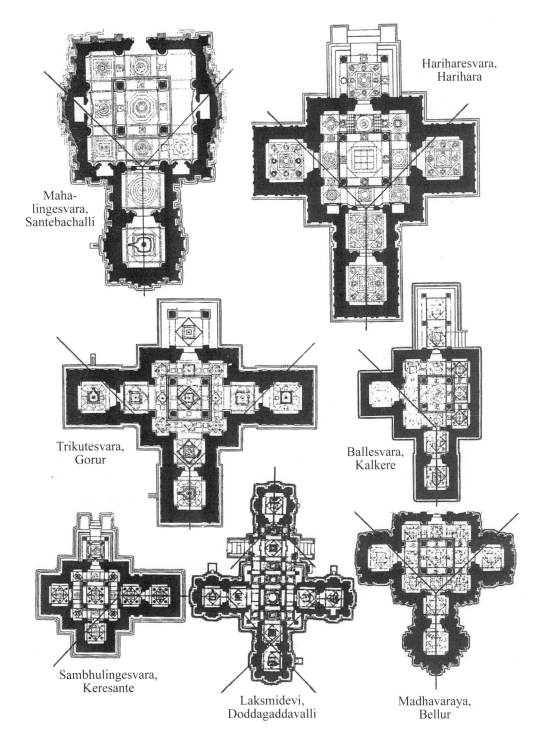

Maha-
lingesvara,
Santebachalli

Hariharesvara,
Harihara

Trikutesvara,
Gorur

Ballesvara,
Kalkere

Sambhulingesvara,
Keresante

Laksmidevi,
Doddagaddavalli

Madhavaraya,
Bellur

Plans of Various Hindu Temples and the SA
(after Settars)
Diagram 11.43

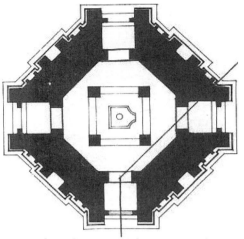

Plan of an Octagonal Sanctuary, Shiva Temple, Mundeshvari Hill, Bihar, A.D. 636
(after G. Michell 2000) *Diagram 11.44*

The diagram at left shows the unusual octagonal plan of some seventh-century temples with their passageways aligned to the SA (diagram 11.44). The finest Hindu temple at Aihole has a circular sanctuary surrounded by an ambulatory passageway. Its apsidal-ended plan is unique. The doorways and ceiling panels of the interior, finely carved with "flying deities," probably unveil the temple's ultimate secret. Without doubt, its doorways are aligned to the SA (diagram 11.46). The temple, like thousands of others, was built to "house" these lintel-doorways: the dry cell batteries of the builders, to be exact.

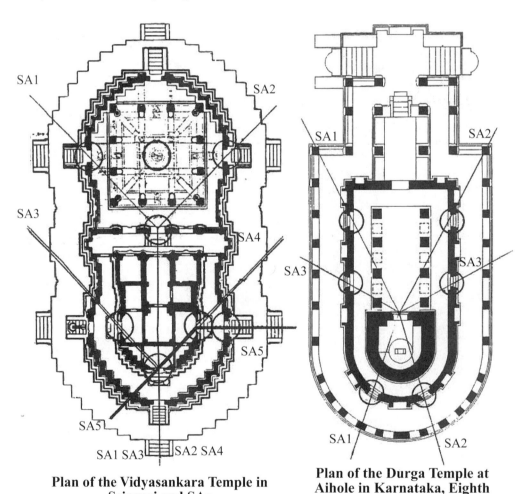

Plan of the Vidyasankara Temple in Sringeri and SAs
(after Ananthalwar and Rea 1980)
Diagram 11.45

Plan of the Durga Temple at Aihole in Karnataka, Eighth Century
(after G. Michell 2000)
Diagram 11.46

Horseshoe-arched Windows

To people's surprise, the innermost sanctuary of a Hindu temple—the most sacred place of the whole structure—is plainly constructed, while the most spectacular craftsmanship, the superb surface ornamentation, is found on its lintel-doorways. The famous doorway of Deogarth temple is expressed in its most precise form. With the central theme working like those false doors of the Khmers, the Hindu builders tried to tell us a similar story. Here the cushion-like capitals of the shallow pilasters that framed the door support a lintel that is created from an overhanging eave furnished with horseshoe-arched windows or niches containing miniature figures (diagrams 11.38 and 11.47). These ornamented doorways form various sets of SA with its central sanctuary and suggest that power-generating devices, probably represented by the pilasters, were once installed. After turning the Hindu temple into a powerhouse, the builders' flying vehicle, described as a horseshoe-arched window, was at once recharged at the top.

Doorway of Deogarth Temple, Framed by Two Pilasters with Five Arched Windows on Top, Surrounded by Scrollwork Decorations
(G. Michell 2000) *Diagram 11.47*

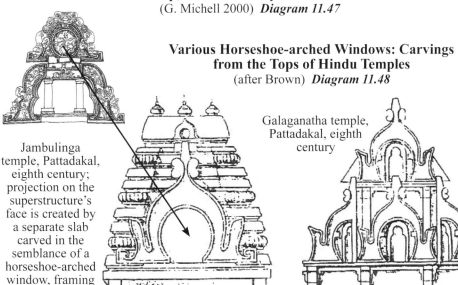

Various Horseshoe-arched Windows: Carvings from the Tops of Hindu Temples
(after Brown) *Diagram 11.48*

Jambulinga temple, Pattadakal, eighth century; projection on the superstructure's face is created by a separate slab carved in the semblance of a horseshoe-arched window, framing Shiva's image (G. Michell 1977)

Galaganatha temple, Pattadakal, eighth century

Hindu Temples: The Builders' Powerhouses

Thousands of Hindu temples are divided into three different forms with distinct architectural styles, because of the geographical and cultural diversities of the Indian subcontinent. They are the *Nagara,* or northern style, the *Dravida,* or southern style, and the *Vesara,* or hybrid style. The most obvious difference between the northern and southern styles is the shape of their superstructures, built on top of the central sanctuary.

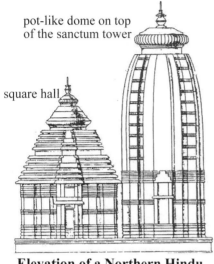

pot-like dome on top of the sanctum tower

square hall

Elevation of a Northern Hindu Temple (after Brown) *Diagram 11.49*

According to Batchelor, the northern style is characterized by a beehive-shaped tower (a *shikhara*) set on a square-walled foundation. This tower, being circular when rising upward, is made up of layers upon layers of architectural elements such as kapotas and gavaksas, featuring slightly curved spires, to assimilate a "mountain peak," all topped by a large round cushion- or pot-like element called an *amalaka* (diagram 11.49).

The southern style has pyramidal towers consisting of progressively smaller storeys of small pavilions (*vimana*), a narrow throat, and a dome on the top. Similar to the Mayan temples, these stone- and brick-built Hindu temples were heavily and skillfully sculptured with motifs on their outer walls, especially on the top of their lintel-doorways, with a unified theme and message.

The Northern Temples

The sanctum tower, *shikhara* ("mountain peak"), of the eighth-century northern-style temple of Parashurameshvara rises in a number of layers created by horizontal mouldings decorated with arched forms, stone windows, or niches. Just above the doorway of its four sides are central bands, presented by a complex series of interlocking horseshoe-arched motifs at different scales, penetrating to the top, where a ribbed-fruit motif and pot finial—a flat circular dome generally known as a *mastaka*—was surmounted (diagram 11.50). The flat dome on top, which was actually a flying-saucer-like object, as mentioned by many ancient Indian Sanskrit texts (mentioned below), represented the builders' flying vehicle that once recharged on top of their powerhouse (diagram 11.51). The same messages were told on the upper façades of the Nunnery of Uxmal, the ancient city of Maya. It explains why the external walls of many Hindu temples were carved and decorated with spaceship-like mouldings (diagram 11.52), which were usually placed on top of power-generating pillars.

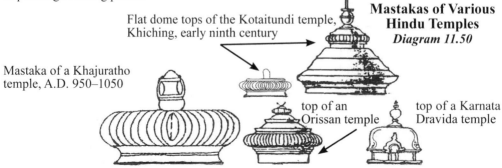

Flat dome tops of the Kotaitundi temple, Khiching, early ninth century

Mastakas of Various Hindu Temples *Diagram 11.50*

Mastaka of a Khajuratho temple, A.D. 950–1050

top of an Orissan temple

top of a Karnata Dravida temple

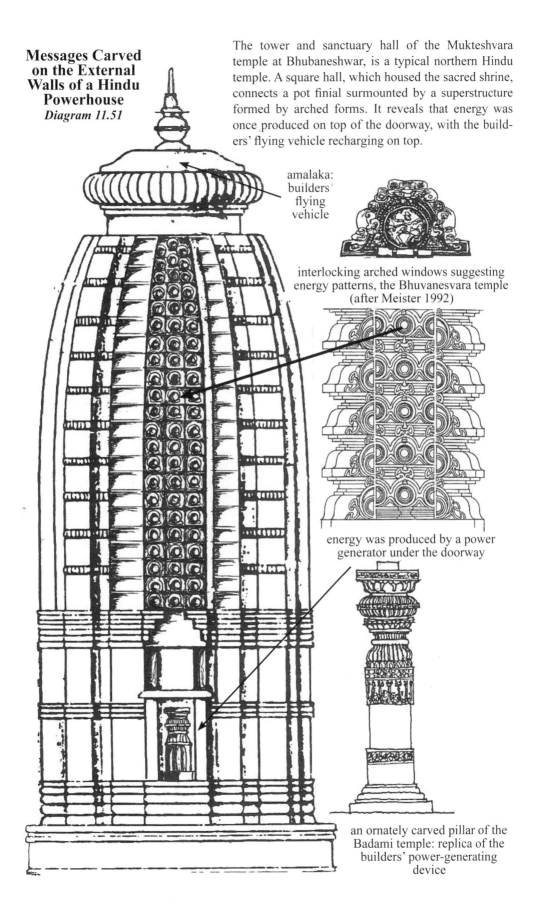

Messages Carved on the External Walls of a Hindu Powerhouse
Diagram 11.51

The tower and sanctuary hall of the Mukteshvara temple at Bhubaneshwar, is a typical northern Hindu temple. A square hall, which housed the sacred shrine, connects a pot finial surmounted by a superstructure formed by arched forms. It reveals that energy was once produced on top of the doorway, with the builders' flying vehicle recharging on top.

amalaka: builders' flying vehicle

interlocking arched windows suggesting energy patterns, the Bhuvanesvara temple (after Meister 1992)

energy was produced by a power generator under the doorway

an ornately carved pillar of the Badami temple: replica of the builders' power-generating device

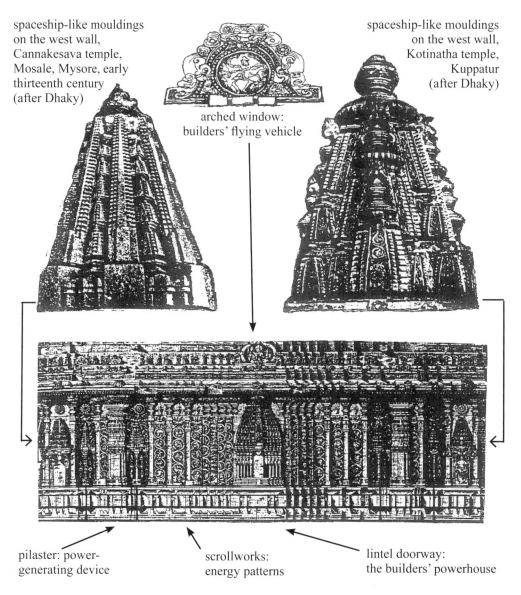

spaceship-like mouldings on the west wall, Cannakesava temple, Mosale, Mysore, early thirteenth century (after Dhaky)

arched window: builders' flying vehicle

spaceship-like mouldings on the west wall, Kotinatha temple, Kuppatur (after Dhaky)

pilaster: power-generating device

scrollworks: energy patterns

lintel doorway: the builders' powerhouse

Messages from the Outer Wall of the Amrtesvara Temple, Amritapura
(bottom after Settars) *Diagram 11.52*

In eastern India, there is a group of distinctive Bengal and Orissa architectural styles of the late eighth century. Bhubaneswar is the capital of Orissa and is famous for its superb Hindu temples. There were once more than 7,000 temples, of which 400 remain. It is believed that these Hindu temples, generally known as Latina mode, were devoted to Saiviam (Ajay Khare 2005), with spires built in the form of tall curvilinear towers on top of single-celled sanctums (diagram 11.53). The tower gradually inclines inward and projections on the substructure are carried up and continue on the superstructure. It is surmounted by a flat and spheroid member ribbed at the edges. The external vertical walls of the square sanctum are decorated with a central shrine flanked by two aedicules (miniature shrines). Its four corners, are each tiered in five or more blumi levels marked by square bhumi amalakas (in the form of flat circular dome). Again, mouldings and carvings of these temples reveal the ultimate secret of the builders.

Telkupi Temple, Bengal
(after Khare 2005)
Diagram 11.54

A Typical Latina Shrine in Bengal
(after Khare 2005)
Diagram 11.53

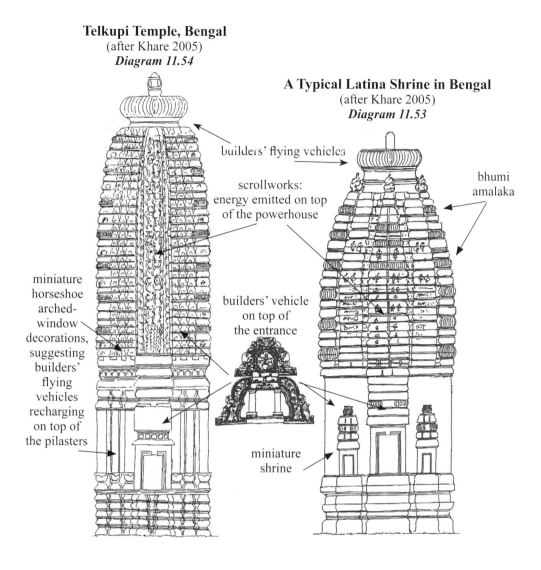

builders' flying vehicles

scrollworks:
energy emitted on top
of the powerhouse

bhumi
amalaka

miniature
horseshoe
arched-
window
decorations,
suggesting
builders'
flying
vehicles
recharging
on top of
the pilasters

builders' vehicle
on top of
the entrance

miniature
shrine

Outer Walls of Latina Shrines in Bengal, Revealing Their Real Function
Diagram 11.53 (right) and 11.54

According to Khare, Telkupi of Bengal is one of the most important temple-building centers in Eastern India. There were once twenty-six sandstone temples, but the whole site was submerged by water in 1963. The exterior of these Latina temples is divided into three parts: a square sanctum with vertical walls, a tall curvilinear spire, and a flattish amalaka with a long diameter. A row of plain pilasters is framed on each of the two sides of the central aedicule (shrine) (diagram 11.54). Each pilaster is crowned by an inverted stepped-pyramid capital supporting the spire above (Khare 2005). The tiers of the tower are composed of miniature arched window mouldings. It shows how energy was once generated by these pilasters—replicas of the builders' power-generating devices.

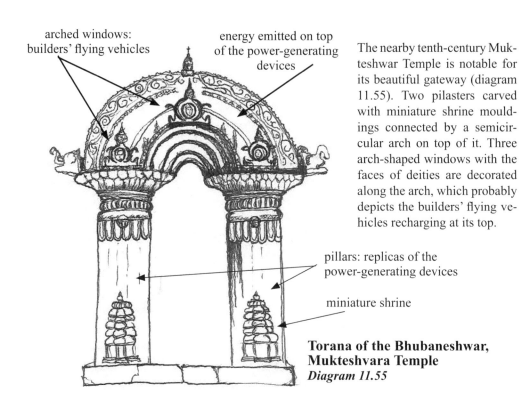

arched windows: builders' flying vehicles

energy emitted on top of the power-generating devices

The nearby tenth-century Mukteshwar Temple is notable for its beautiful gateway (diagram 11.55). Two pilasters carved with miniature shrine mouldings connected by a semicircular arch on top of it. Three arch-shaped windows with the faces of deities are decorated along the arch, which probably depicts the builders' flying vehicles recharging at its top.

pillars: replicas of the power-generating devices

miniature shrine

Torana of the Bhubaneshwar, Mukteshvara Temple
Diagram 11.55

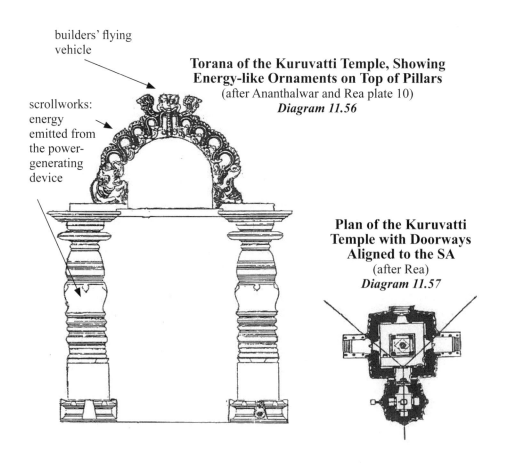

builders' flying vehicle

scrollworks: energy emitted from the power-generating device

Torana of the Kuruvatti Temple, Showing Energy-like Ornaments on Top of Pillars
(after Ananthalwar and Rea plate 10)
Diagram 11.56

Plan of the Kuruvatti Temple with Doorways Aligned to the SA
(after Rea)
Diagram 11.57

The ninth-century temple of Telika Mandir at Gwalior has a rectangular sanctuary with a barrel vault on top. Its doorways and shrines were built according to the SA (diagram 11.58a). Its external walls are decorated with a complex series of interlocking horseshoe-arched motifs—false windows—at different scales. They extend into the horizontal divisions of the tower and function as pediments above the niches and doorways (Michell 1977). These "windows" represent the builders' vehicles, capturing the moment when they were recharging on top of the Hindu powerhouse.

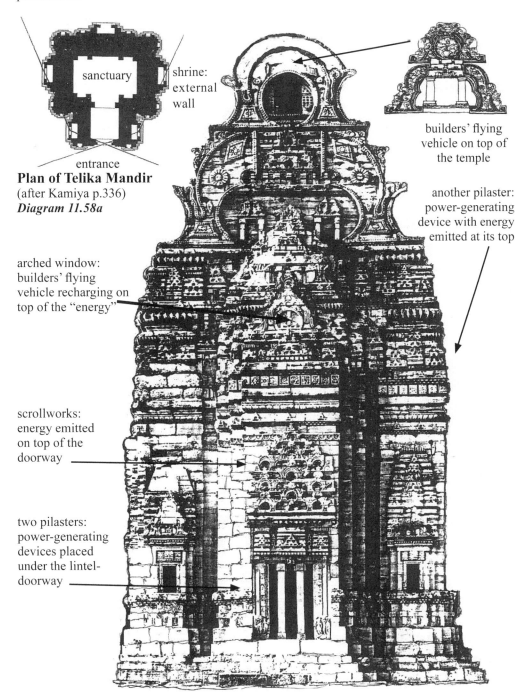

sanctuary

shrine: external wall

entrance

Plan of Telika Mandir
(after Kamiya p.336)
Diagram 11.58a

builders' flying vehicle on top of the temple

another pilaster: power-generating device with energy emitted at its top

arched window: builders' flying vehicle recharging on top of the "energy"

scrollworks: energy emitted on top of the doorway

two pilasters: power-generating devices placed under the lintel-doorway

The Powerhouse of Telika Mandir
(after G. Michell 2000) *Diagram 11.58*

Monuments of Khajuraho, a UNESCO World Heritage Site, are said to be dedicated to the celebration of the "Working Energies" (*yoginis*) of the pantheon (Tadgell 1990, p. 115). There are twenty-five temples (originally eighty-five, according to local tradition), built between the ninth and tenth centuries. These were hidden in a dense forest for 700 years. The Lakshmana temple of the mid-tenth century has a square sanctuary surrounded on three sides by an ambulatory passageway. The doorways of its six open balconies are built according to the SA (diagram 11.59a). Subsidiary shrines, showing the model of the builders' powerhouses, are introduced at the four corners of the platform (diagram 11.59b), rendering the structure a five-shrined complex. Some of its detached pavilions decorated with "images of the vehicles of the gods" (G. Michell 1977).

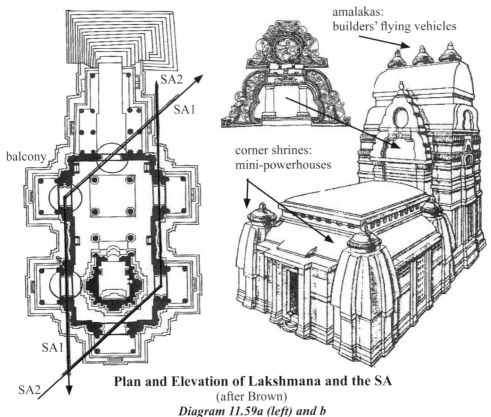

Plan and Elevation of Lakshmana and the SA
(after Brown)
Diagram 11.59a (left) and b

Towers and spires at Khajuraho show the builders' flying vehicles recharging on top. The temple has a pyramidal superstructure employing layers of gavaksha motifs topped with pot-like finials; similar but fewer superstructures rise above the porches (Michell 2000, p. 92).

**Plan of Kandariya-Mahadeo Temple
(A.D. 1050) with Major Doorways
Aligned to the SA**
(after Percy Brown)
Diagram 11.60

central sanctuary surrounded by passageway
with porches projecting on three sides

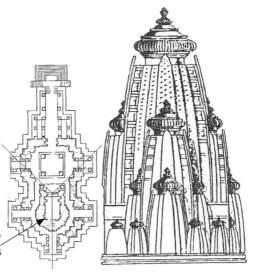

The Visvanatha Temple at Varansi was constructed in the center of a high platform, with four small shrines at the four corners, which make it a five-shrine temple. Like the Lakshmana temple, its six doorways are aligned to the SA. Besides, a large platform extends to the front and a Nandi shrine with a pyramidal tower, has been installed facing the main shrine (Kamiya 2004). The corner shrines of the temple are also built according to the SA (diagram 11.61).

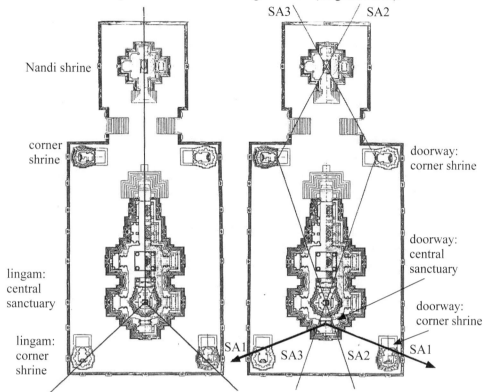

Plan of Visvanatha Temple (A.D. 998) with Main Shrines Aligned to the SA
(after Kamiya) *Diagram 11.61*

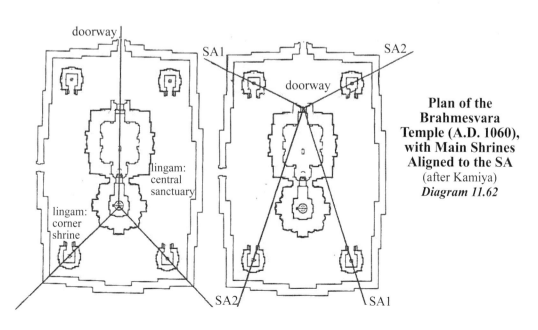

Plan of the Brahmesvara Temple (A.D. 1060), with Main Shrines Aligned to the SA
(after Kamiya)
Diagram 11.62

The eleventh-century Surya temple at Modhera consists of two structures: the columned hall and the sanctuary. Again, its six porches are aligned to the SA. The central sanctuary is open to a single doorway and surrounded by a passageway. A spacious walled mandapa lies just next to the doorway with entrances on four sides. Each of the other three walls of the central sanctuary is constructed with a small shrine. These shrines form SAs with the porches of the walled mandapa (diagram 11.63). The columned hall, which lies east of the temple, has "curved and cusped arches" suspended between its columns. These arches indicate how the builders' energy-generating devices, represented by the columns, are connected, and how energy was produced. It explains why the builders' vehicles were carved on top of these columns (diagram 11.64).

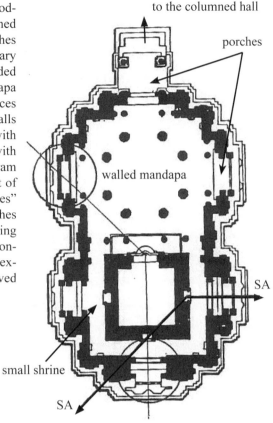

to the columned hall

porches

walled mandapa

SA

small shrine

SA

**Sanctuary of Surya temple,
Modhera, Eleventh Century**
(after Michell 1977)
Diagram 11.63

**Highly Decorated Arches inside
Open-columned Hall, Surya Temple**
(after Michell 1977)
Diagram 11.64

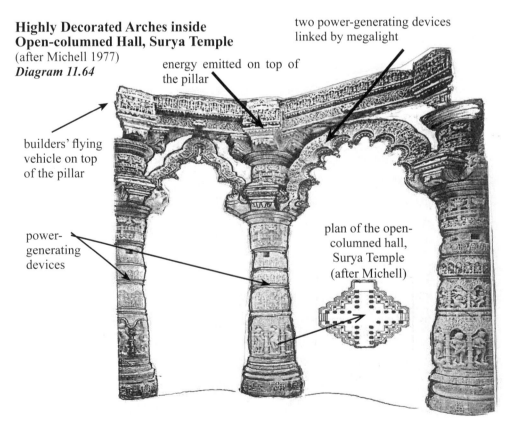

two power-generating devices
linked by megalight

energy emitted on top of
the pillar

builders' flying
vehicle on top
of the pillar

power-
generating
devices

plan of the open-
columned hall,
Surya Temple
(after Michell)

The single temple complex at Konark, a UNESCO World Heritage Site since 1984, is one of India's great architecture achievements. Being conceived as a gigantic chariot, the thirteenth-century temple was dedicated to Surya—the Sun God. The complex, the largest in Orissa, is enclosed within a compound measuring 261m by 164m. Its main structure, the temple of Surya Deul (the sanctum and square hall of the Sun Temple) lies in the middle, with a dance hall at its front and another small temple, Mahagayatri, to its southwest. The sanctum of the Sun temple, believed to have been about 68.5m in height (Donaldson 2003), is no longer there. Its square hall rises to a height of 39m. Its corbelled ceiling consists of huge iron-rich laterite lintels supported by four massive pillars. Are they for power generation?

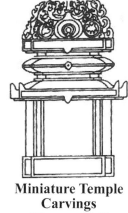

The temple is also famous for its decorations, as it is described as "the most richly ornamented building in the whole world." Miniature temples (the symbolical dry cell batteries) (diagram 11.65) and flanking pillars (power-generating devices) decorated with scrollwork were carved on the vertical walls. They marked the climax of ancient Indian craftsmanship. Twenty-four wheels arranged in pairs, twelve on both the north and south sides, are carved at intervals on the face of the 3.9m-high platform walls. According to Donaldson, "the richly ornamented wheels, 2.9m in diameter, contain eight major spokes and eight tie-rods. A medallion carved on each of the spokes is filled with small images" (2003, p. 37) (diagram 11.66, right).

Miniature Temple Carvings
Diagram 11.65

Similar to the Aztec Calendar Stone, the so-called "Wheel of the Sun temple" is actually a secretive message deliberately left by the same builders to show the real function of the complex. The layout of the Sun temple and Mahagayatri temple nearby reflects an eight-spoked wheel, since their structures are pancha-ratha in plan, with five vertical projecting divisions on each side of their walls (diagram 11.66). Besides, medallions on each pair of spokes of the wheel form an SA with the central medallion, revealing the secret that each pair of the doorways of the temple also forms an SA (diagrams 11.67 and 11.68). Nisha shrines were erected in front of the raha niches. Even though their walls and superstructure are no longer there, they form various sets of SA. Instead of representing the months in a year as suggested by the experts, the Wheel describes how two rows of megalights were once projected from the central shrine of these temples, and connected the doorways nearby in order to refuel the flying chariots of their masters.

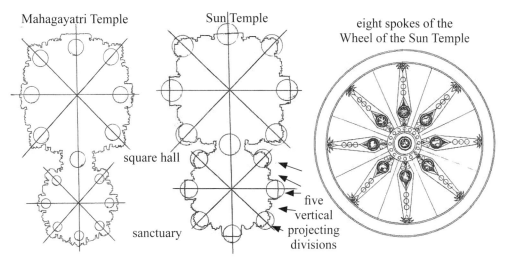

Plans of the Mahagayatri and Sun Temples, and the Wheel
Diagram 11.66

Messages from the Wheel of the Sun Temple
Diagram 11.67

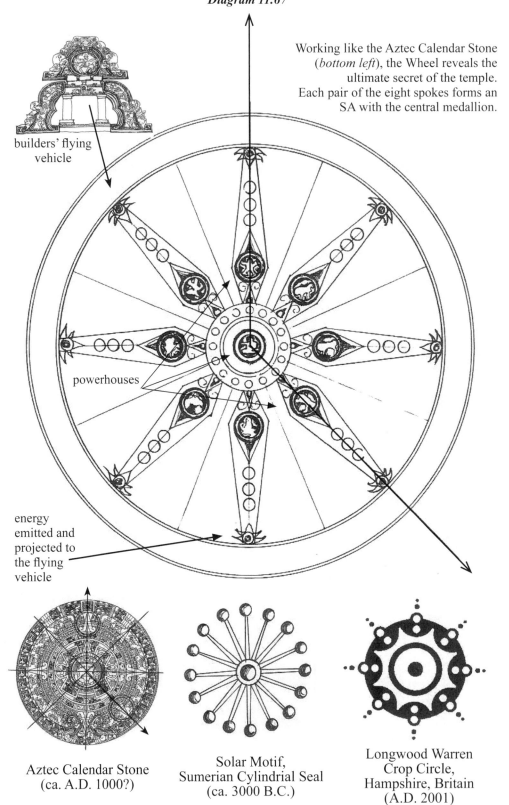

builders' flying
vehicle

Working like the Aztec Calendar Stone
(*bottom left*), the Wheel reveals the
ultimate secret of the temple.
Each pair of the eight spokes forms an
SA with the central medallion.

powerhouses

energy
emitted and
projected to
the flying
vehicle

Aztec Calendar Stone
(ca. A.D. 1000?)

Solar Motif,
Sumerian Cylindrial Seal
(ca. 3000 B.C.)

Longwood Warren
Crop Circle,
Hampshire, Britain
(A.D. 2001)

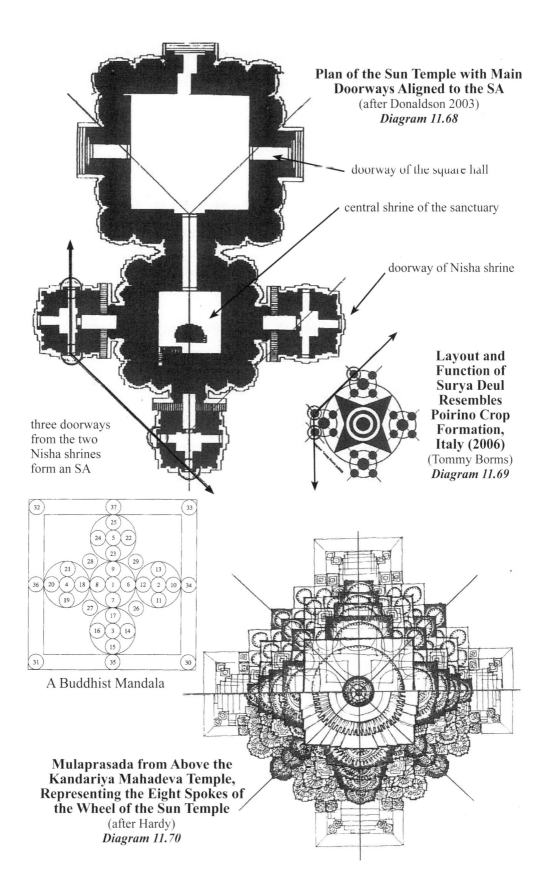

Plan of the Sun Temple with Main
Doorways Aligned to the SA
(after Donaldson 2003)
Diagram 11.68

doorway of the square hall

central shrine of the sanctuary

doorway of Nisha shrine

three doorways
from the two
Nisha shrines
form an SA

**Layout and
Function of
Surya Deul
Resembles
Poirino Crop
Formation,
Italy (2006)**
(Tommy Borms)
Diagram 11.69

A Buddhist Mandala

**Mulaprasada from Above the
Kandariya Mahadeva Temple,
Representing the Eight Spokes of
the Wheel of the Sun Temple**
(after Hardy)
Diagram 11.70

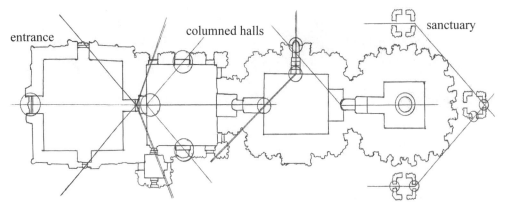

**Plan of the Lingaraja Temple, Bhubaneshwar (Eleventh Century):
A Sequence Columned Halls Leads to the Sanctuary—
the Doorways of Its Nisha Shrines Align to the SA**
(after G. Michell 1977) *Diagram 11.71*

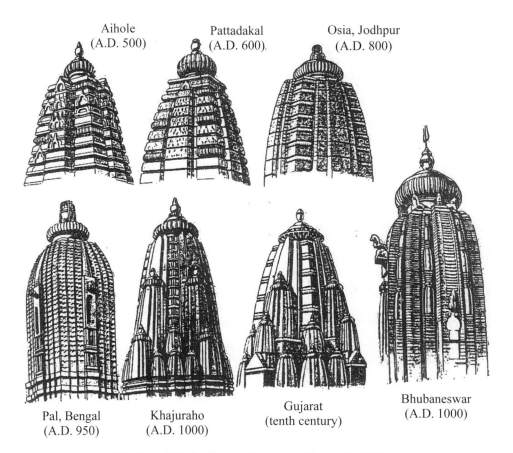

Aihole
(A.D. 500)

Pattadakal
(A.D. 600).

Osia, Jodhpur
(A.D. 800)

Pal, Bengal
(A.D. 950)

Khajuraho
(A.D. 1000)

Gujarat
(tenth century)

Bhubaneswar
(A.D. 1000)

**Various Hindu Powerhouses with the Builders'
Flying Vehicles Recharging on Their Top**
(after Brown)
Diagram 11.72

The Southern Temples

According to the experts, the southern Hindu temples begin with the rock-cut temples of the early seventh century. They each consist of a pillared hall serving as a portico for one or more small sanctuaries (diagram 11.73). A façade is formed by a row of pillars with plain shafts. Its overhanging eave is decorated with horseshoe-arched windows—the builders' flying vehicles.

There are monolithic temples known as *rathas* (meaning "chariots") of the eighth century. The texts of the Rig Veda refer to aerial flying machines as Rathas. They were quadrangular in shape with an inside area of eighty-one square feet and capable of accommodating seven to eight persons (Dr. Kanjilal). According to Michell, the rathas of the southern Hindu temple are "each elevated on a moulded plinth above which the walls divide rhythmically into a number of projections and recesses created by pairs of shallow pilasters. … The curved brackets of the wall pilasters and porch columns support an overhanging eave with carved arched windows. … Above rises a series of mouldings culminating in the parapet—perhaps the most distinctive element of the southern architectural style (diagram 11.74). This is created from a series of ornamental miniature roof forms arranged in rows around the building. … a variety of capping curved roof forms that are either square, rectangular, octagonal, or apsidal-ended" (1977, p. 132).

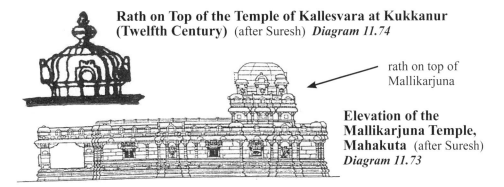

Rath on Top of the Temple of Kallesvara at Kukkanur (Twelfth Century) (after Suresh) *Diagram 11.74*

rath on top of Mallikarjuna

Elevation of the Mallikarjuna Temple, Mahakuta (after Suresh) *Diagram 11.73*

The Vaikunthaperumal temple at Kanchipuram (diagram 11.76) of the eighth century has a square sanctuary surrounded by ambulatory passageways. Again, its doorways are aligned to the SA (diagrams 11.75 to 11.77). Without doubt, the curved roof capping the southern temple, similar to the flat dome of the north, represents the vehicles of the builders.

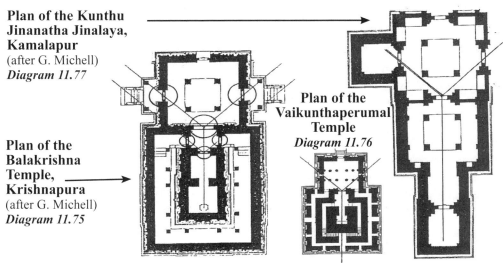

Plan of the Kunthu Jinanatha Jinalaya, Kamalapur (after G. Michell) *Diagram 11.77*

Plan of the Vaikunthaperumal Temple *Diagram 11.76*

Plan of the Balakrishna Temple, Krishnapura (after G. Michell) *Diagram 11.75*

The sixth-century Elephanta cave temples are notable for the deeply carved images of Shiva and Vishnu, some of the greatest masterpieces of Indian sculpture. The structure was chiseled into a rocky cliff. A huge square hall with a northern entrance is supported by two dozen massive columns. These columns are decorated with cushion capitals that employ the northern pot motif. The main sanctuary, housing a rock-cut Shiva lingam, was positioned in the middle of the hall but detached near the rear wall (diagram 11.78). Additional artificial courtyards are excavated and provided with subsidiary shrines. As the diagram suggests, the main entrances and shrines of Elephanta were positioned according to the SA.

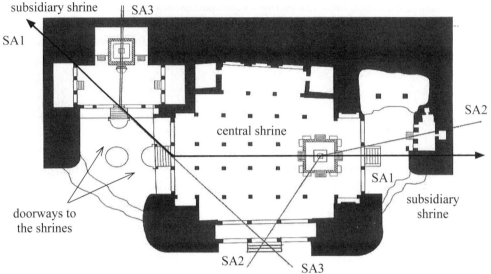

**Plan of the Elephanta Cave Temple, with Its Shrines
and Doorways Aligned to the SA**
(after Bunce 2007 plate 15)
Diagram 11.78

Vimana: The Ancient Indian Aircraft

"O! royal skilled engineer, construct sea-boats, propelled on water by our experts, and airplanes, moving and flying upwards, after the clouds that resides in the mid-region, that fly as the boats move on the sea, that fly high over and below the watery clouds."

—*Yajur-Veda* 10.19

"Behind the veil of legend and scientific truth comes out that three flying-cities were made for and were used by the demons. Of these three, one was in a stationary orbit in the sky, another moving in the sky and one was permanently stationed in the ground. These were docked like modern spaceships in the sky at particular time and at fixed latitude and longitudes."

—Prof. D. K. Kanjilal, *Vimana in Ancient India* (1985)

"There seems to be no doubt that vimanas were powered by some sort of anti-gravity. They took off vertically, and were capable of hovering in the sky, like a modern helicopter. ... Perhaps vimanas had a number of different propulsion sources, including combustion engines and even 'pulse-jet' engines."

—D. Hatcher Childress, *Ancient Indian Aircraft Technology* (1991 and 2004)

Trikutesvara Temple Mouldings, Gadag: Vimana Recharges atop Two Power-generating Devices (after Hardy) *Diagram 11.79*

The term "vimana" is no stranger to alternative historians. It stands for the mysterious ancient flying vehicles of India repeatedly mentioned in classical Indian literature and epics dating back to the fourth century B.C., such as the *Ramayana,* the *Mahabharata,* the *Yajur-Veda,* and the *Rig-Veda.* For example, in the *Ramayana,* these vimanas "navigated at great heights with the aid of quicksilver and a great propulsive wind. They could cover vast distance and could travel forward, upward and downward" (Von Däniken 1970). And "it flew on an enormous ray which was as brilliant as the sun and made a noise like the thunder of a storm" (C. Roy 1899) and is descried as "staying about 4,000 feet above the ground level" (Dr. Kanjilal). "At Rama's behest the magnificent chariot rose up to a mountain of cloud with a tremendous din." (N. Dutt 1891). "One vimana described was shaped like a sphere and moved like a UFO" (Childress).

According to the ancient epics, these aerial vehicles were conical or triangular in shape, made of heat-absorbing and super-light metals (diagram 11.80a). In the *Ramayana,* there were "two storied celestial chariots with windows and they roar like off into the sky until they appear like comets." These flying chariots are "powered by winged lighting. It was a ship that soared into the air, flying to both the solar and stellar regions" (Dr. Vyacheslav Zaitsev). They "possessed very fast speed and moved like a bird in the sky soaring towards the Sun and the Moon and used to come down to the earth with great sound" (Dr. S. Chakravarti). "[It would] stop and hover motionless in the sky" (*Ramayana*), "staying about 4,000 ft above the ground level" (Dr. Kanjilal).

Some vehicles were represented as three-storeyed and piloted by at least three occupants, but some could carry a thousand passengers in the air (G. Kuppuram), described as "aerial flying cities" in the ancient Indian epics. These aerial vehicles were operated and propelled by gas, wind, (white?) liquid fuel (mercury), and even solar energy. And they could "move high up above the region of the clouds and very probably in the exosphere region" (Dr. Kanjilal). The Vedas, the oldest Indian texts, describe vimanas in various shapes and sizes, some with two or more engines (D. Childress). G. R. Josyer of the International Academy of Sanskrit Research suggests that there were five atmospheric regions and 519,800 airways traversed by vimanas in ancient India.

In the Vedic literature of India, vimanas were categorized into those manmade and those "not made by human beings" (Richard L. Thompson). Professor Kanjilal suggests that the vimana was designed and built for the gods Brahma, Vishnu, Yama, Kuvera, and Indra, who came from the remote space in the sky above. He believes that many Hindu temples were designed after the models of the flying machines (1985).

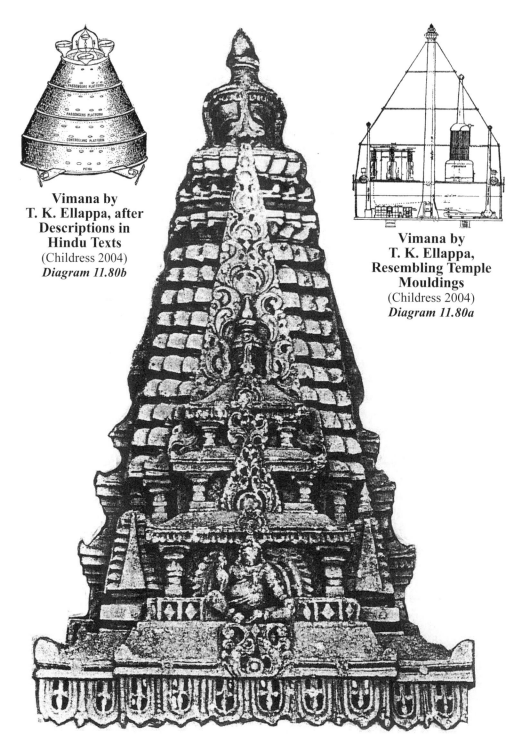

**Vimana by
T. K. Ellappa, after
Descriptions in
Hindu Texts**
(Childress 2004)
Diagram 11.80b

**Vimana by
T. K. Ellappa,
Resembling Temple
Mouldings**
(Childress 2004)
Diagram 11.80a

**Builders' Vimana: Rocket-like Mouldings on the North Wall of the
Canna-kesava Temple, Mosale, Mysole (Early Thirteenth Century):
A Traveller Seated between Two Jet Engines at the Bottom**
(after Dhaky)
Diagram 11.81

The *Vaimanika Sastra* is certainly one of the most important ancient texts on Vimanas. According to Childress, who wrote a book on ancient Indian aircraft in 1991, the text was first reported to have been found in 1918 in the Baroda Royal Sanskrit Library. Mr. G. R. Josyer, Director of the International Academy of Sanskrit Research in Mysore, in 1952 claimed that "the manuscripts were thousands of years old." He suggested that one of the manuscripts "dealt with Aeronautics, construction of various types of aircraft for civil aviation and for warfare" and they were "double and treble-decked aircrafts" capable of "carrying 400 to 500 persons." He came up with some designs, drawings, and plans of these aerial planes based on the directions in the manuscript. These ancient vehicles, according to Josyer's drawings, were usually conical or cylindrical in shape and installed with an air ventilation or electric rotor/generator along their central axes (diagram 11.80a and b) (Childress 1991). Their shape and design resemble a "false window" placed on top of the doorway of a Hindu temple and a flat circular dome (mastaka) surmounted its top.

According to Childress, the Chinese discovered Sanskrit documents in Lhasa, Tibet, which "contain directions for building interstellar spaceships. … And the Chinese announced that they were including certain parts of the data for study in their space program" (*The Anti-Gravity Handbook*). Since 2005, the Chinese government has sent three men to orbit around the Earth in two missions. The latest is a non-human mission to the Moon launched in October, 2007.

Buddha's Lesser and Great Vehicles

The horseshoe false windows carved on the external walls of the Hindu temples were precise description of the builders' flying machines once parked on their tops for recharging energy. The special design of these windows did not actually originate from the Hindus. Experts believe their designs were inspired by and succeeded from the Buddhists, as similar carvings were also found on the façades of many Indian Buddhist cave temples, built several hundreds years before the earliest Hindu temples (diagram 11.82). These Buddhist chaitya halls were rock-cut chambers or caves constructed on the high projections of the chain of hills. The word "chaitya" means sacred spot or the abode of "earth spirits" (Kail 1975). These halls, about 1,200 of them (Mahajan 2004), are divided into two groups: the Hinayana (Lesser Vehicle), and the Mahayana (Great Vehicle).

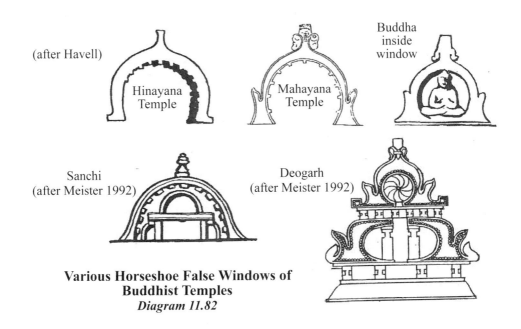

**Various Horseshoe False Windows of
Buddhist Temples**
Diagram 11.82

In general, a chaitya hall of a Buddhist cave temple has a long and large rectangular cell with apsidal or semicircular end. The end is constructed with domical roof. It then contains a stupa or dagoba, the sacred object of worship of the hall. Stone pillars, tapering slightly towards the top, were carved out of the live rock and were arranged in two straight lines meeting in a semicircle at the back of sacred stupa (diagram 11.83). Structurally, and perhaps functionally, the design of a Buddhist chaitya hall resembles and parallels the sarsen and bluestone horseshoes of Stonehenge III. The Karle chaitya hall of Pune and the Ajanta chaitya hall of Aurangabad are the two most famous and well-preserved Buddhist cave temples of the time.

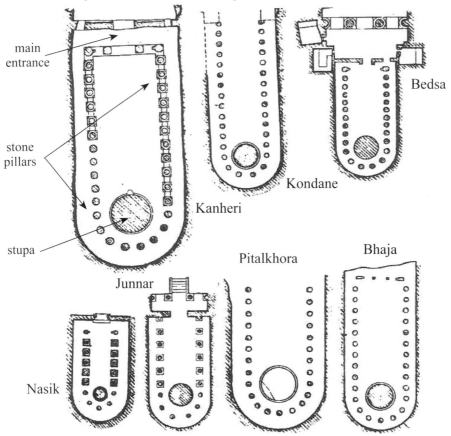

Plans of Chaitya Halls (Second Century B.C.–Second Century A.D.)
(after Brown) *Diagram 11.83*

These chaitya halls are also famous for their ornamented façades. These sculptured façades are horizontally divided into two parts. The lower one is generally provided with three doors in which the central one, being framed by two large and highly carved pillars, leads to the hall. In the center of the upper portion, just above the two carved pillars, there is a large false window in the shape of an arch with projected paws and pointed pinnacle. Besides, the space on either side of this central window is beautifully embellished with mini chaitya windows, rail pattern, and stepped cornice. It definitely suggests the importance of these so-called false windows in the eyes of the ancient Buddhists.

Plan of the Chaitya at Ter, Showing Transition from Buddhist Chaitya Hall to Hindu Temple in the Third Century
(after Ananthalwar and Rea 1980) *Diagram 11.84*

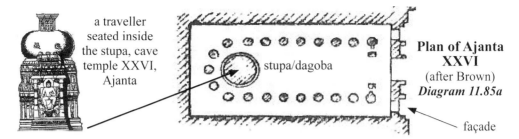

a traveller seated inside the stupa, cave temple XXVI, Ajanta

stupa/dagoba

Plan of Ajanta XXVI
(after Brown)
Diagram 11.85a

façade

The design of this façade is repeatedly telling us an old story—i.e., the ultimate function of all these Buddhist chaitya halls to generate power for the builders' flying vehicles. It explains why the Mahayana Buddhists, the worshippers of the Great Vehicle, believe they had "vehicles" large enough to carry more souls to Salvation or Nirvana—a place of enlightenment, according to the Buddhist texts. On the other hand, there are many small stupas, the Lesser Vehicles of the unknown civilization, each carved with a single-seated figure of Buddha inside.

What actually is Nirvana? According to Kail (1975, p. 14): "Nirvana is described as a glorious state, stainless and undefiled, pure and white, unageing, deathless, secure, calm and happy. It has no definite location, being outside the Universe, yet underlying it but not forming a part of it. It may be realized anywhere and at any time, even while still in the flesh, and the man who finds it never again loses it, and when he dies he passes to this state forever, in his 'parinirvana,' his Final Blowing Out." It seems that Buddha is describing a place anywhere of the Universe but our Earth.

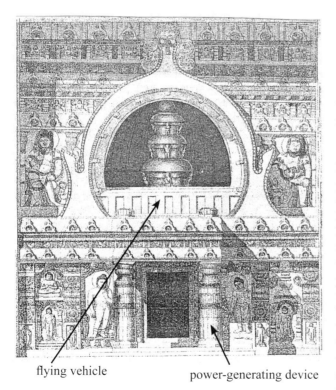

flying vehicle

power-generating device

Façade of Chaitya Hall No. 19, Ajanta
(after Havell 2000)
Diagram 11.85

There were thirty Buddhist cave temples at Ajanta built around the second century B.C. to the sixth century A.D. The site was abandoned in the seventh century and was gradually over-run by the jungle for more than 1,000 years until rediscovered in 1819. The Mahayana chaitya hall no. 19 is one of the most perfect examples of the Buddhist rock-cut architecture with high quality finish. It is a small hall with a façade thirty-eight feet high and thirty-two feet wide. There is a small projected pillared portico with a roof in front of massive entablature. The upper portion just above the pillared portico rises above the big chaiyta arch or window with graceful curves and nicely carved out finial (Malati Mahajan 2004). The side walls of the portico are embellished with a series of mini window arches (diagram 11.85).

The Great Hinayana Chaitya of Karle is the most magnificent example of the rock-cut caves, and marks the climax of Himayan rock-architecture. The single temple was built around the first century B.C., with a high ceiling and deep interior, measuring 37.8m in length, 13.9m in width, and 14m in height. A stupa or dagoba, made up of a two-storied drum with the rail pattern on the upper edge, has been carved out at the center of the circular portion. Fifteen pillars with inverted pot or bell capitals are topped with umbrellas and "male and female riders" (Kail 1975) and join behind the stupa, forming a typical horseshoe. The hall's arched-vaulted roof is fitted with wooden ribs, those in the apsidal end converging at the center. Experts believe these ribs were not used for supporting the roof. If Karle was once a powerhouse of the builders, these ribs probably indicate the energy generated and emitted at the top of the dagoba inside the hall.

A 15m-high gigantic pillar, known as the Lion Pillar, is erected at the main entrance of the cave. It is a plain tapering sixteen-sided pillar standing on a wide cylindrical base, surmounted by a bell-shaped capital on which there are four addorsed lions supporting a wheel. It hints and symbolizes the builders' power-generating device once placed inside the chaitya hall and, interestingly, it forms an SA with the other two pillars that framed the entrance/doorway of the powerhouse (diagram 11.86). Besides, its façade is also decorated with a large horseshoe-arched window representing the builders' flying vehicle. Three smaller ones, perhaps the Lesser Vehicles, were carved on top of the three lintel doorways (diagram 11.87).

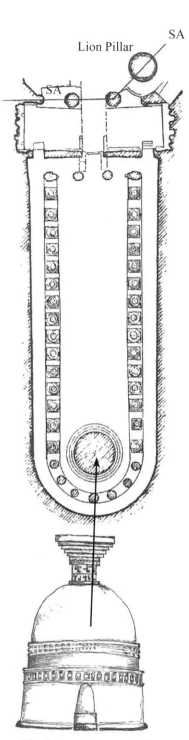

The Stupa—a furnace-like monument—was placed deep inside the elongated hall

Plan of Karle
(after Brown)
Diagram 11.86

Façade of Karle (after Havell)
Diagram 11.87

Mahayana chaitya halls at Ellora, located 30km north-west of Aurangabad district, belong to a much later period. The most famous and important cave is no. 10, also known as Visvakarma. Its hall measures eighty-five feet by forty-four feet and is thirty-four feet in height. In front of the hall there is a large courtyard surrounded by row of pillars. Compartments with single doorways are found on both sides of the central hall and their doorways form two SAs with the central stupa (diagram 11.88).

Like the Ajanta, the lower portion of the façade contains pillared portico. A large chaitya arch/window is carved just above the portico with its two arms brought to form a small opening and then they are extended outwards and turned inside at the end. The whole window here is turned into a shape of trefoil (Malati Mahajan 2004).

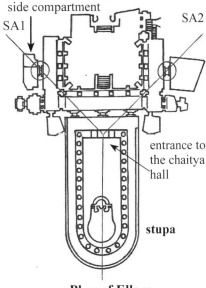

side compartment
SA1
SA2
entrance to the chaitya hall
stupa

Plan of Ellora
(after Kail 1975) *Diagram 11.88*

Stupas of Sanchi

A Buddhist Chaitya hall was built for housing and worshipping the stupa, according to the experts. Before the time of Buddha, people started erecting a low circular funeral mound of earth surrounded by a ring of boulders—the type commonly known as "tumuli." Usually, slabs of granite are placed inside these tumuli. During the Buddha period, a stupa—a simple tomb-like structure—was built, rebuilt, and overbuilt on top of the tumulus. They marked the sacred spots for abiding "earth spirits," according to Buddhism. Stupas were constructed over the bodily remains of Buddha and the objects used by Buddha. Among these objects the golden vessel of Buddha is the most important (Malati Mahajan 2004). Was it the power-generating device? Today, conical-shaped golden offerings are still found inside Buddhist and Hindu temples. According to Mahajan, "For Buddhists the stupa is the symbol of great light that once existed and whose relics were enshrined there. For them it was the mortal body of Buddha that left at the time of Nirvana (p. 29)." Where did this great light come from? And was Nirvana an unearthly destination?

According to Buddhist teachings, there were eight stupas that buried the ashes of Buddha, and the great king Ashoka (272–231 B.C.) further divided and placed them in eighty-four stupas. A stupa is a flat-topped hemispherical dome built on a foundation of stone blocks. A small platform was constructed on its flat top, where an "umbrella" was fixed in its center. Its top platform and stone basement were then protected by a railing. Ornamented doorways carved with images of Buddha in a seating position were erected at the end of the railing. The famous Sanchi lies near Vidisha and is one of centers of Buddhism from around A.D. 1, constructed with many temples, monasteries, and large stupas. Stupa 1 (diagram 11.89), the largest one, was built and rebuilt in brick and stone in the third century B.C. to second century A.D. It is almost in the shape of a semicircular dome with a truncated top fixed with an umbrella. The famous Lion Pillar, a free-standing pillar with inverted bell capital topped by fluted abacus and square harmika above it supporting a group of lion figures bearing a large wheel, was erected in front of one of its doorways. It probably refers to the builders' power-generating device. Working like an European tumulus, Stupa 1 of Sanchi forms several sets of SAs with the surrounding stupas (diagram 11.90). Besides, the two Buddhist temples 18 and 40, of which a number of pillars still stand (each having the chaitya-style design of a semicircular end and a straight and rectangular façade), also form an SA with the great Stupa 1. Considered with the messages carved on the façade of a Buddhist chaitya hall, it is beyond doubt that the Buddhist stupa, before burying Buddha's ashes, was once built for generating and tapping power for the builders' flying vehicles.

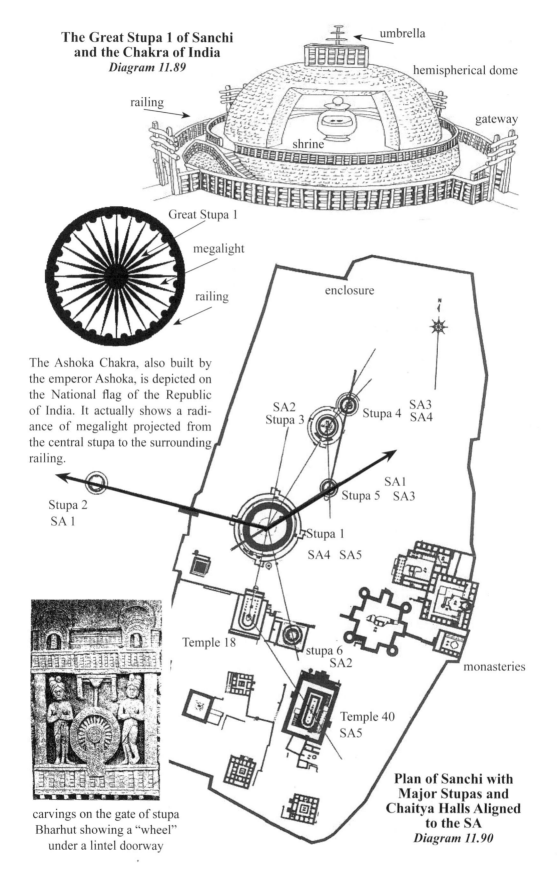

The Great Stupa 1 of Sanchi and the Chakra of India
Diagram 11.89

umbrella

hemispherical dome

railing

gateway

shrine

Great Stupa 1

megalight

railing

The Ashoka Chakra, also built by the emperor Ashoka, is depicted on the National flag of the Republic of India. It actually shows a radiance of megalight projected from the central stupa to the surrounding railing.

enclosure

SA2
Stupa 3

Stupa 4

SA3
SA4

SA1
SA3

Stupa 5

Stupa 2
SA 1

Stupa 1

SA4 SA5

Temple 18

stupa 6
SA2

monasteries

Temple 40
SA5

carvings on the gate of stupa Bharhut showing a "wheel" under a lintel doorway

Plan of Sanchi with Major Stupas and Chaitya Halls Aligned to the SA
Diagram 11.90

Ancient Indian Power-generating Devices

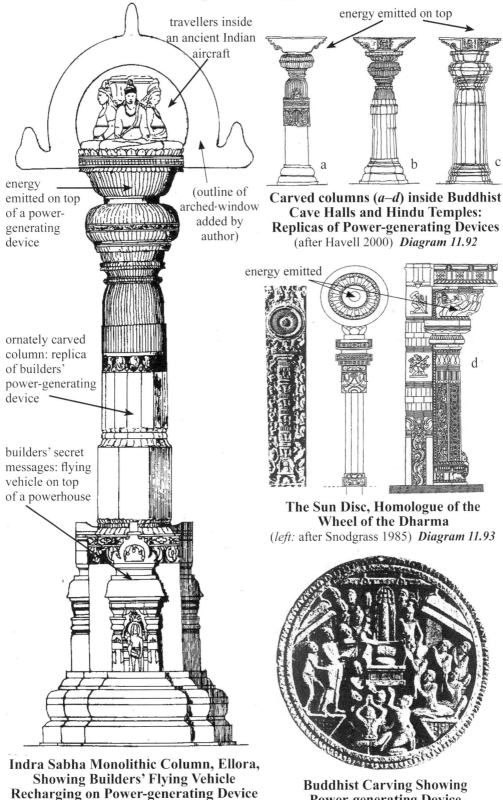

travellers inside an ancient Indian aircraft

energy emitted on top of a power-generating device

(outline of arched-window added by author)

ornately carved column: replica of builders' power-generating device

builders' secret messages: flying vehicle on top of a powerhouse

Indra Sabha Monolithic Column, Ellora, Showing Builders' Flying Vehicle Recharging on Power-generating Device (after Nagar) *Diagram 11.91*

energy emitted on top

Carved columns (*a–d*) inside Buddhist Cave Halls and Hindu Temples: Replicas of Power-generating Devices (after Havell 2000) *Diagram 11.92*

a b c

energy emitted

d

The Sun Disc, Homologue of the Wheel of the Dharma (*left:* after Snodgrass 1985) *Diagram 11.93*

Buddhist Carving Showing Power-generating Device Worshipped by Followers *Diagram 11.94*

Buddha's Mahayana: Buddhist Shrine,
Replica of the Builders' Great Vehicle
(after Benisti) *Diagram 11.95*

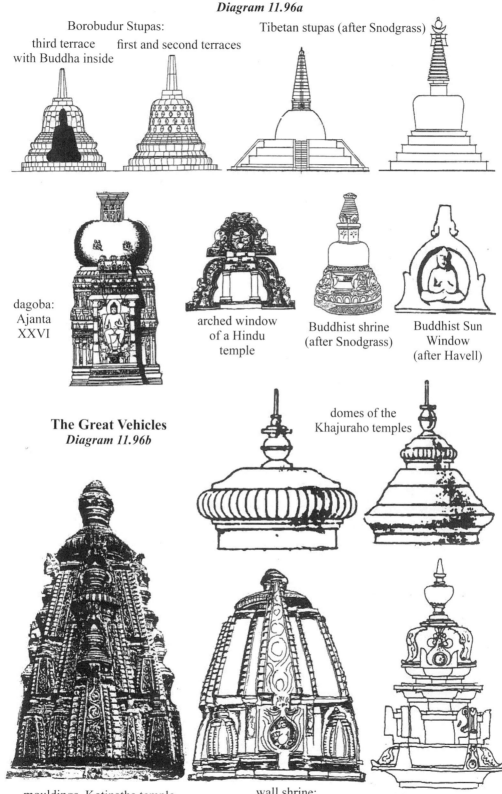

The Lesser Vehicles
Diagram 11.96a

Borobudur Stupas:

third terrace
with Buddha inside

first and second terraces

Tibetan stupas (after Snodgrass)

dagoba:
Ajanta
XXVI

arched window
of a Hindu
temple

Buddhist shrine
(after Snodgrass)

Buddhist Sun
Window
(after Havell)

The Great Vehicles
Diagram 11.96b

domes of the
Khajuraho temples

mouldings, Kotinatha temple,
Kuppatur

wall shrine:
Haveri, Siddhesvara

mouldings, Kuta-aedicule
at Trikutesvara, Gadag

Superstructure of Main Vimana, West Wall, Nilgund, Bhimesvara: Builders' Flying Vehicle Recharging on Top of a Hindu Powerhouse (after Tadgell) *Diagram 11.97*

builders' vimana

"energy" emitted on top of the temple

powerhouse

pillar

A Hindu Powerhouse Placed between Two Power-generating Devices

Wall-shrines in Mandapa, South Wall, Gadag, Sarasuati, Showing Mysterious Energy Emitted on Top of a Hindu Powerhouse (after Hardy plate 124) *Diagram 11.98*

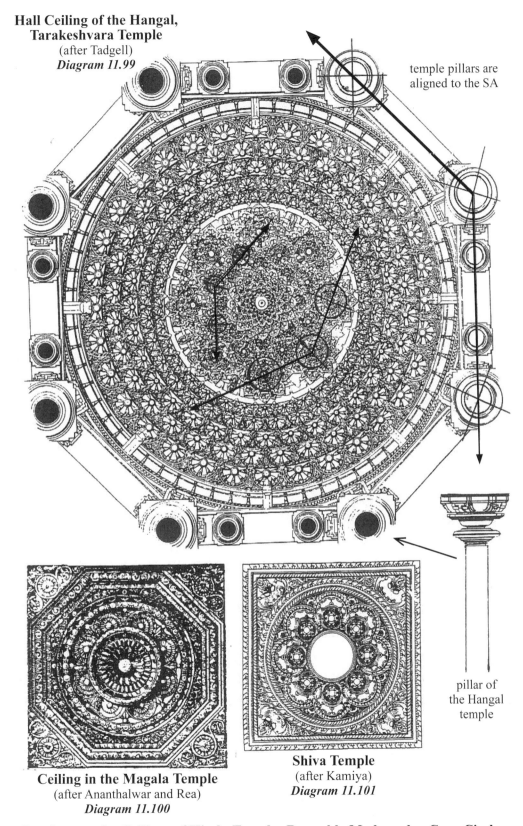

**Hall Ceiling of the Hangal,
Tarakeshvara Temple**
(after Tadgell)
Diagram 11.99

temple pillars are
aligned to the SA

pillar of
the Hangal
temple

Ceiling in the Magala Temple
(after Ananthalwar and Rea)
Diagram 11.100

Shiva Temple
(after Kamiya)
Diagram 11.101

Carvings on the Ceilings of Hindu Temples Resemble Modern-day Crop Circles

Doorways of Angkor and Hindu Temples and Modern-day Crop Circles

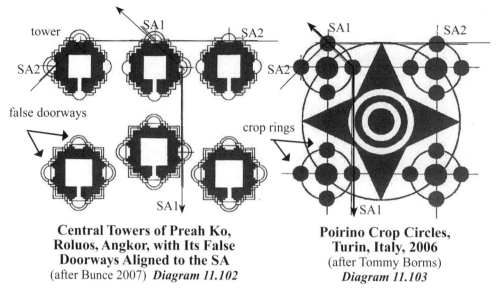

**Central Towers of Preah Ko,
Roluos, Angkor, with Its False
Doorways Aligned to the SA**
(after Bunce 2007) *Diagram 11.102*

**Poirino Crop Circles,
Turin, Italy, 2006**
(after Tommy Borms)
Diagram 11.103

The central area of Preah Ko consists of six brick towers arranged in two rows on a low platform. The towers are square on the lower portion with a porch in each of the cardinal directions. The octagonal columns that framed the false doors are "incontestably the most beautiful of Khmer art" (Rooney 1994). The lintels have a Garuda—the vehicle of the Hindu gods—decorated in the center.

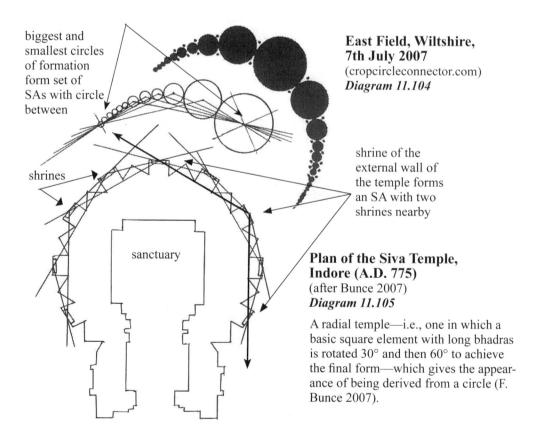

biggest and
smallest circles
of formation
form set of
SAs with circle
between

shrines

**East Field, Wiltshire,
7th July 2007**
(cropcircleconnector.com)
Diagram 11.104

shrine of the
external wall of
the temple forms
an SA with two
shrines nearby

sanctuary

**Plan of the Siva Temple,
Indore (A.D. 775)**
(after Bunce 2007)
Diagram 11.105

A radial temple—i.e., one in which a
basic square element with long bhadras
is rotated 30° and then 60° to achieve
the final form—which gives the appearance of being derived from a circle (F.
Bunce 2007).

An Indian Vimana: Horseshoe Arched Window Carved on the Façade of Karle
(after Havell)

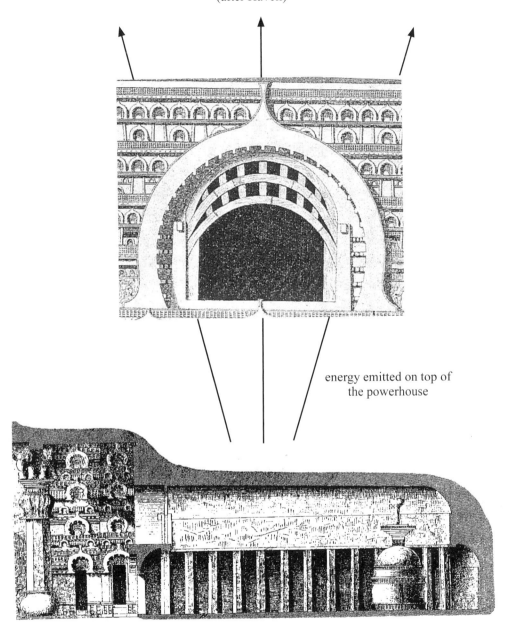

energy emitted on top of
the powerhouse

An Indian Powerhouse: Elevation of the Buddhist Cave Temple of Bedsa
(after Kamiya)

Chapter 12
Crop Circles:
Modern Power Generators

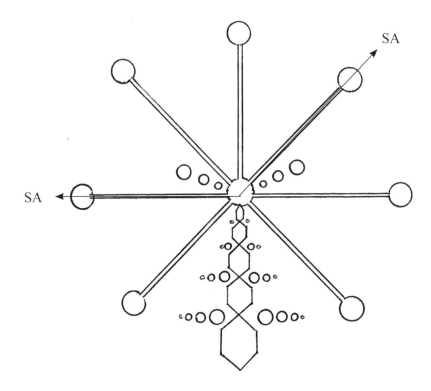

"Solar God" Formation, Milk Hill, Wiltshire, 2005:
Each Pair of Crop-ring "Sun Rays" Forms an SA through the Center
(not to scale; info: kornsirkler.org)
Diagram 12.1

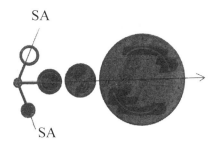

SA

SA

"Cheesefoot Head Punchbowl,"
Hampshire, 1994
(cropcircleresearch.com)
Diagram 12.2a

Like the crop circles themselves, the research of this phenomenon is a source of wonder. It is the collective work of:

Werner Anderhub, Colin Andrews, Allan Brown, Zef Damen, Pat Delgado, Stuart Dike, Mark Fussell, Eltjo Haselhoff, Linda Moulton Howe, Peter Kleinferchner, Jurgen Kronig, William C. Levengood, Andreas Muller, Lucy Pringle, Hans Peter Roth, Wolfgang Schindler, Jan Schwochow, Freddy Silva, Busty Taylor, Andy Thomas, Paul Vigay, Bertold Zugelder, and others.

If without their research and passion, crop formations would still be mere circles of bent vegetation lying insignificantly in the seas of wheat, as well as in our own ignorance.

Crop circle reports and diagrams are courtesy of:

• The Cropcircleconnector web site, which celebrated its 10th Anniversary in June 2005, was the first site on the www to report on the crop circle phenomenon and to share views and experience with the community;

• The Cropcircle-archive, launched in May 2003, is the world's largest archive on crop circle sightings. Its printed edition contains no less than 5200 documented formations worldwide;

• The Crop Circle Research web site, one of its primary aims of which is to help people communicate and share ideas around the world without censorship or prejudice;

• Zefdamen.nl, PTAH homepage, Crop Circle News, CSICOP's Crop Circle Report, lucypringle. co.uk, greatdreams.com, crystalinks crop circles, cropcircleinfo.com, bust-taylor.com, The Crop Circular, Crop Circle Web Ring, Oxfordshire Centre for Crop Circle Studies, Crop Circle Geometry, cicap.org, UKcropcircles.co.uk, German Association for Crop Circle Research.

The Alton Barnes Formation, 1990, with Straight Lines Showing the SA
(after Silva 2002)
Diagram 12.2b

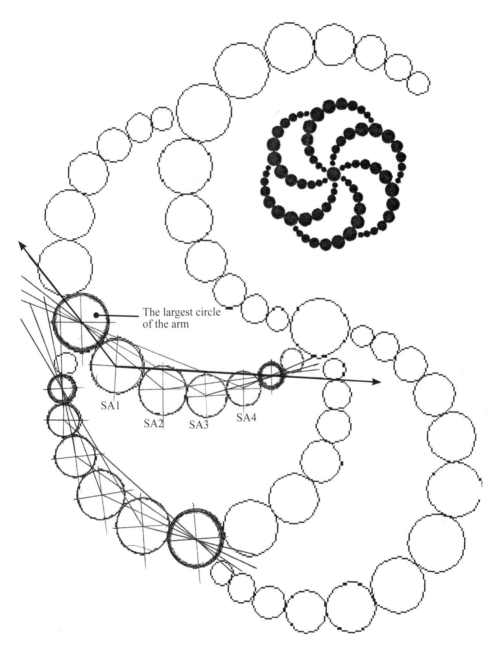

Labels within figure:
The largest circle of the arm
SA1
SA2
SA3
SA4

The Milk Hill Formation, 2001
(after Damen)
Diagram 12.3

This six-armed "fractal" design is the largest single diameter and most elaborate glyph ever to have appeared. It consists of 409 circles covering an area of 800 feet. These crop circles are arranged according to the SA. There was a report of a beam of light from the sky on the night it was formed (A. Thomas 2002).

Crop Circles and the Tube of Light

"The Nature of God is a circle of which the center is everywhere and the circumference is nowhere."

—Empedocles of Agrigentum, fifth century B.C.

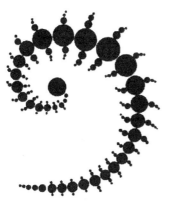

"Julia Set," Salisbury, 1996
Diagram 12.4

The following is the most publicized account of a fascinating crop circle event:

One ordinary Sunday in the summer of 1996, Salisbury Plain once again captured the world's attention, not because of its 5,000-year-old inhabitant—Stonehenge—but due to a circular infrastructure nearby. It was formed by a blanket of wheat in less than an hour (diagram 12.4). A 600-foot centipede-like pattern of 151 circles of different sizes, arranged with superb mathematical and geometrical accuracy, was found undetected, in broad daylight, next to the busiest highway of Wiltshire, and a few hundred meters from Stonehenge, the most visited prehistoric monument in Europe.

The Salisbury Plain is a military exclusion area monitored by satellites. The formation was certainly visible to drivers on Highway A303 where the elevated ground of Stonehenge gives tourists and always-present security guards a panoramic view over the flat plain. How the Circlemakers completed their work perfectly so quickly and unobserved remains a mystery.

The formation was a fractal known as a "Julia Set," formed by swirled and flattened wheat with its stems bent horizontally above the soil. The incredible pattern begins with a circle in the center, spirals away, single-armed, from it with smaller circles that grow in size, first peaking with a large circle, then spiralling down with shrinking ones. Tiny circles orbit each of the spiral circles (Andrews 2003).

As Andy Thomas comments, "rough calculations showed that just to have created random circles would have taken whatever number of bodies making around three every minute or less—without allowing for the many hours which would be needed to lay them out so accurately. To have performed such an incredible feat in full daylight without being seen would be impossible anyhow. … For many, the circumstances surrounding the arrival of the Julia Set provided the final proof that hoaxers were not the answer to the crop circle mystery" (1998, pp. 58–59).

The following diagram shows the center (large) circle of the Julia Set forms several sets of SAs with the surrounding circles (diagram 12.5). That was exactly how Stonehenge worked 4,000 years ago, when its northeastern arc of the bluestone circle formed several SAs with the southwestern bluestone horseshoe and the conical device no. 2 in the center. The Julia Set is most probably a twentieth-century Stonehenge, the most modern powerhouse of the space travellers. Its fractal-styled circles are arranged according to the SA (diagram 12.6).

According to Moore and Lamb, "each circle of the formation had its own energy pattern, as detected by dowsing rods and electronic instrumentation. Each circle was divided into twelve tones, where the energy from the above met the grid energy of the earth (Lyons 1996). The aura of energy immediately outside the formation was also strong" (2001, p. 81).

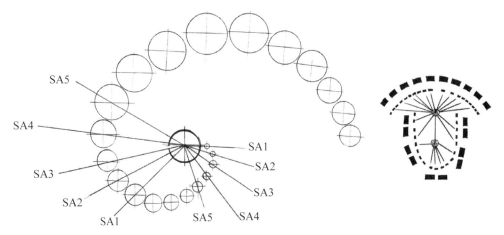

The Twentieth-century Stonehenge
Diagram 12.5

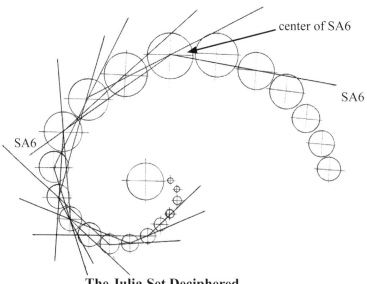

The Julia Set Deciphered
Diagram 12.6

The Incredible "Pointer"

The pictogram below is the most important key to unlock the secret of a crop formation. It was formed at Liddington Castle, Wiltshire, 1996. It is a caterpillar-like fractal with thirty-nine circles squashed together, forming a gigantic letter "C." The circles first increase in size, then spiral down with shrinking ones. The most eye-catching is its central motif—a pointer-like formation, acting like the arm of a clock. Obviously, the arm is pointing at the eighth circle from the left of the crescent pictogram, and it is this very circle that constitutes several sets of SAs, which connect all circles nearby (diagram 12.7). The "Liddington Pointer" shows how the Circlemaker designed his piece of work (i.e., according to the SA again). He even shows his magic in the formation as well! But who does he want to tell?

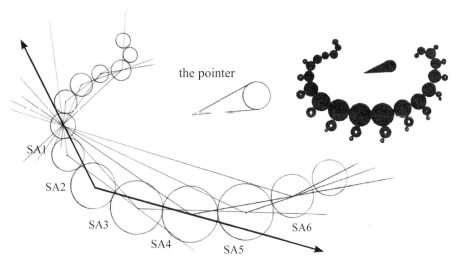

The "Pointer," Liddington, Wiltshire, 1996
Diagram 12.7

A similar style, known as the "Triple Julia Set," is found in Windmill Hill, another famous mega-lithic site. Its early Bronze Age round barrows form several sets of SAs (diagram 6.88b). The pictograph shows it consists of 196 circles of different sizes with three long arms of diminishing circles flowing to a central location. It resembles a huge windmill. The diagram below suggests how the largest circle of each three "arms" is connected with the others by the SA (diagram 12.8). According to the researchers, exceptional mathematical ability is required for each circle of the formation to be completed in every three minutes in a dark crop field.

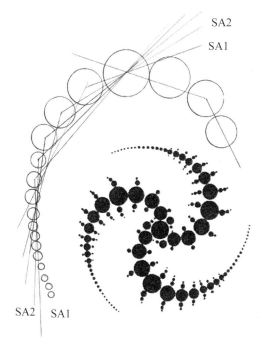

The "Triple Julia Set," Windmill Hill, 1996. It Measures 260 × 260m and Covers a Surface of Over Fifteen Acres; the Circles Are Arranged with Perfect Accuracy
(Anderhub and Roth 2002)
Diagram 12.8

An American surveying company stated that the formation needed three to five days to mark out, with an additional two days for calculation and another three if working at night (A. Thomas 1998).

Crop formations of a similar fractal style - arms with diminishing circles - are illustrated below. Most of these circles are arranged according to the SA (diagrams 12.9 to 12.11).

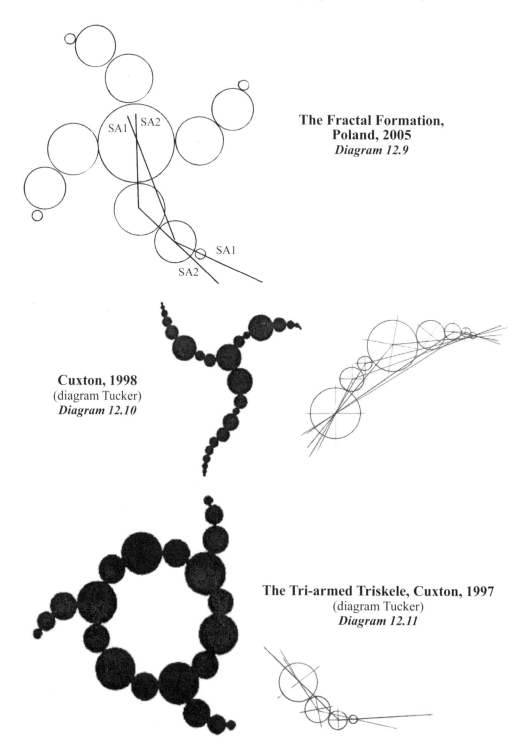

**The Fractal Formation,
Poland, 2005**
Diagram 12.9

Cuxton, 1998
(diagram Tucker)
Diagram 12.10

The Tri-armed Triskele, Cuxton, 1997
(diagram Tucker)
Diagram 12.11

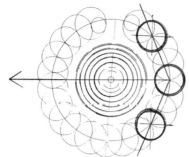

The Labyrinth, Newbury, 1995
(diagram: Hawkins and Silva 1996)
Formation found on a slope directly facing
Highway A303 (Anderhub and Roth).

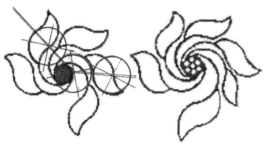

**Heissluftballon mit
Kornkreisformation, Belgium**

the signature

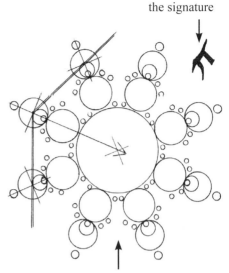

Avebury Manor, Wiltshire, 1999
(after Silva)
A 150-foot formation with eightfold
geometry. There is a "signature" in the
form of the Greek letter Pi, or a trilithon—the builders' dry cell battery.

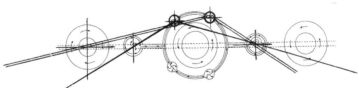

Stanton St. Bernard, Wiltshire, 1999
(diagram: Andreas Muller)

**The Powerhouse of
West Kennet, 1999**

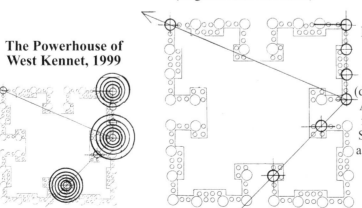

**"Five Pyramids":
Fractal Geometry at
the Long Barrow of
West Kennet,
Wiltshire, 1999**
(diagram: Andreas Muller)
According to Muller, the
formation is 100m long.
Several people witnessed
a strange blue ball of light
moving back and forth
around the long barrow
(Moore and Lamb).

Diagram 12.12a

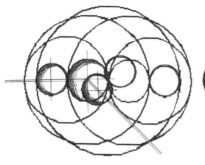 

The "Sun Moon Circle"
Formation, Liddington,
Wiltshire, 1996
(drawing: Bert Janssen,
www.bertjanssen.nl/cropc/)

"The Beltan Wheel," West Kennet Long
Barrow, 1998 (*right;* diagram Silva)
The formation is 72m in diameter and encircled by
thirty-three flame-like elements. According to
Martin Noakes, it is almost impossible to make
in a field (Anderhub and Roth). As shown in
the left diagram, each "flame" is formed
by three circles aligned to the SA.

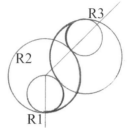 

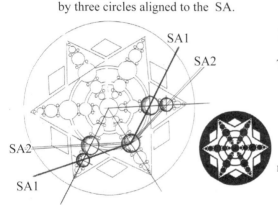

Fyfield Down Formation, Wiltshire,
1999 (diagram: Muller and Howe)
This six-pointed star was found adjacent to
the Devil's Den Neolithic barrow.
Per Howe, two spirals are carved on
the roof of the dolmen. An unexplained
shadowlike beam extending upward
from the formation was photographed by
Bert Janssen and Janet Ossebaard. Some
researchers reported that the batteries were
drained in their cameras, cell phones and
video recorders. Locals had an electric
power failure the night before the circle
was formed (Moore and Lamb 2001).

"The Flower,"
Etchilhampton, 1997
(drawing: Bert Janssen,
www.bertjanssen.nl/cropc/)
According to Silva, the formation
lies on the energy line and its axis
is aligned to magnetic north.

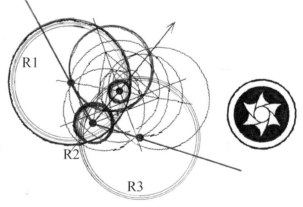

Diagram 12.12b

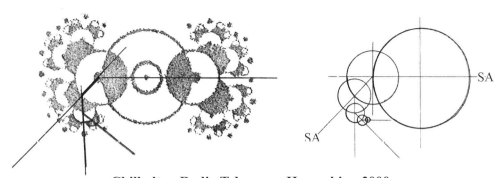

Chilbolton Radio Telescope, Hampshire, 2000
(after Andrews 2003)
Diagram 12.13

Colin Andrews, an electrical engineer turned "cereologist" and a leading crop circle specialist, suggests that "the central circle of the Julia Set is directly aligned with the circle that is formed by the Stonehenge formation, and this invisible line passing through the crop formation and Stonehenge is aligned with the magnetic north, the earth's magnetic pole" (2003). Does it imply that the twin enigmas serve the same function? Or is the appearance of the formation an answer to the indecipherable megalithic rings?

These circle enigmas still attract people's attention, not only in the form of bulky megaliths but now also in organic crop formations. These circles, slightly elliptical, are usually found in barley, oat, or wheat fields in which the vegetation is bent over at right angles and spirals into different patterns. It is due to amplified nodal expansion in the crops, probably caused by rapid evaporation of water vapor inside as a result of an intense burst of heat.

W. C. Levengood's Spinning Plasma Vortice Theory

The BLT Research Team Inc.'s primary focus is crop research—that is, the discovery, scientific documentation, and evaluation of physical changes in plants and soils (bltresearch.com). One of the primary scientific investigators of the team, William C. Levengood, an eminent biophysicist, has discovered that the cell walls of the bent plants inside an authentic crop circle are fractured with starch crystal, which could not be replicated by hoaxers. He further suggests that magnetic material is impregnated in some of the plants and soil of a genuine crop formation, which means that the formation of the crop circles involves energies, such as that generated by microwave radiation from outside our planet, probably in the form of a complex atmospheric plasma energy system that emits heat. Plasmas are collections of electrically charged particles produced when atoms and molecules of matter are heated. Levengood believes that some ion plasma tubes from the upper atmosphere are responsible for the genuine crop formations.

Levengood continues to elaborate, saying that the plasma, an ionized gas which is mostly found in the ionosphere, contains positive and negative charges, making it a good conductor of electricity. He hypothesizes that spinning plasma vortices containing microwaves, magnetic fields, and electric fields produced by charge separation in plasma form the complex energy system that creates crop formations (Howe 2002). Is it the prime media for transferring energy from the crop surface to space? What is this unknown power source that is capable of generating tremendous amounts of heat in a very short period of time and capable of "bending," "crystallizing," and "speeding-up" germination of the plant without damaging it? Dr. Sherwood proposes the possibility of a new and unknown type of energy which is internally hot—probably up to 800 degrees—while externally cold.

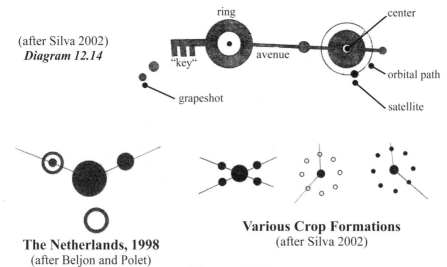

(after Silva 2002)
Diagram 12.14

ring

center

"key"

avenue

grapeshot

orbital path

satellite

The Netherlands, 1998
(after Beljon and Polet)

Various Crop Formations
(after Silva 2002)

Diagram 12.15

Electric and magnetic field anomalies at sacred sites may attract and enable plasma creation. The BLT Team also discovered that tiny magnetized spherical particles of unusually pure iron have been regularly found in soils from the crop circle sites. They concluded that centrifugal force from a spinning vortex or rotating force is distributing these particles to the edges of the formations (the BLT website).

Experts suggest that the designs of these circles have evolved from simple and small ones of the early twentieth century, to three-in-a-line triplets, five-in-a-Celtic-cross quintuples (diagram 12.14 and 12.15), and to much more complicated and elaborate geometric designs with extremely high accuracy, including straight lines, spirals, angles, and the concentric rings of recent years (Andrews 2003) (diagram 12.16). Sometimes, satellite circles termed "grapeshot" are superimposed on the main circle. Besides avenues, connected circles are produced. Some of the sophisticated formations are believed to have been created only with the use of computer.

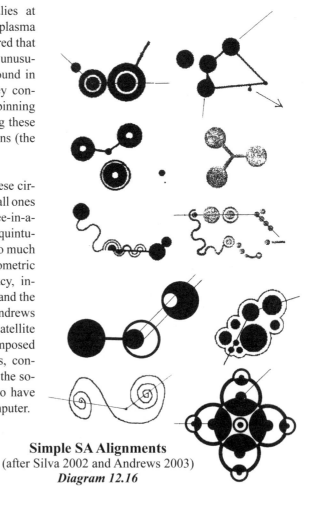

Simple SA Alignments
(after Silva 2002 and Andrews 2003)
Diagram 12.16

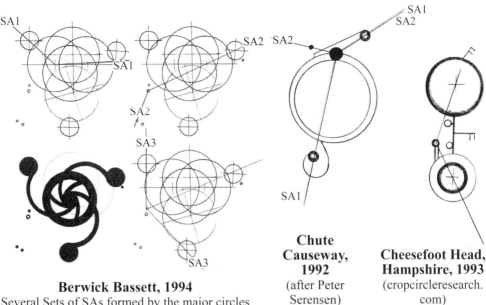

Berwick Bassett, 1994
Several Sets of SAs formed by the major circles
of the formation and surrounding "grapeshot."
(after Silva) *Diagram 12.17a*

**Chute
Causeway,
1992**
(after Peter
Serensen)

**Cheesefoot Head,
Hampshire, 1993**
(cropcircleresearch.
com)

Diagram 12.17b

**The Ogbourne St. George
Formation, 2003**
A complex design of crescents based
on an eightfold geometry (Pringle).
According to Silva, the formation
is strategically aligned to the local
sacred site, and more than 20 golf-
ball-size light balls were filmed in
one afternoon. (after Damen)
Diagram 12.18

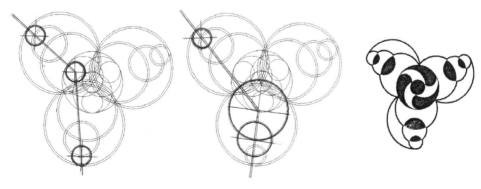

The Ivinghoe Beacon Formation, 2002 (after Damen)
Diagram 12.19

The pictogram below hit the headlines of international news in 1990, silenced most of the sceptics and hoaxers, and introduced crop circle phenomena to the world. A 606-foot long formation formed by circles, rings, boxes, and tridents ("keys") (diagram 12.20a), and connected by two straight avenues, was found close to the old burial mound Adam's Grave in Alton Barnes, heart of Wessex (Silva 2002). It was a new pictogram which puzzled all observers, and was regarded as a message from an higher intelligence. However, it can be deciphered without difficulty. See how generous and explicit the Circlemaker was in showing the principle of the SA in his masterpiece (diagram 12.20b). Several sets of SAs are formed by the oversized tridents which protrude from the centers of the circles.

Diagram 12.20a

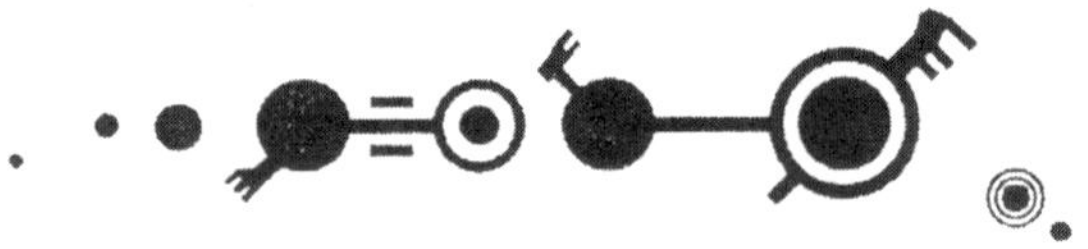

Alton Barnes (1990) and the SA
(after Silva 2002)

Diagram 12.20b

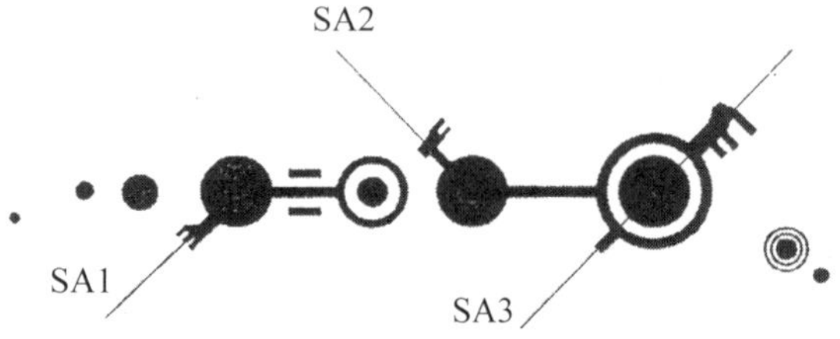

Crop formations of a similar style in which circles are bridged by avenues with "keys" protruding from their centers are shown below and to demonstrate how they are designed according to the SA (diagram 12.21).

There are over 10,000 crop circles recorded, and over ninety percent of them occurred within the old Wessex region and Somerset of southern Britain (Freddy Silva 2002), with Wiltshire County being the acknowledged center of the crop circle phenomenon. They are found near dense archaeological sites such as Stonehenge, Avebury, and Silbury Hill, and more than 100 formations appear around the region each year. The majority of these formations lie within forty miles of Stonehenge (Andrews 2003). Andy Thomas suggests Wiltshire is the focus of the crop circles with Stonehenge roughly at its center. Researchers refer to this area as the "Wessex Triangle."

"These were believed to be powerful, magical locations on which the ancient people grounded and projected energies by building large stone monuments. These energy points appear to attract the making of crop circles. It is

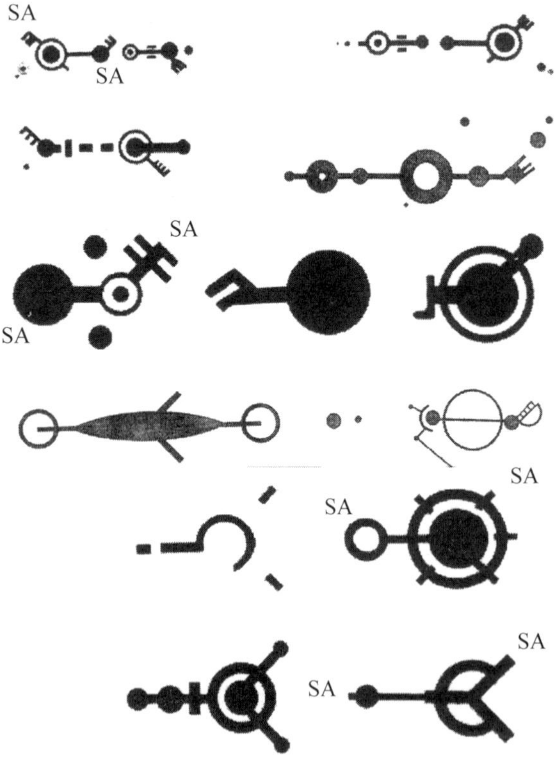

Various Crop Formations and the SA
(after Silva 2002 and Andrews 2003)
Diagram 12.21

hypothesized that the circlemakers need the ley lines and energy vortices to make their formations, or they are trying to infuse or activate latest energy in the earth by adding crop formation there" (Moore and Lamb 2001).

Some people speculate that the prehistoric megalithic circular monuments were built to commemorate and "materialize" mysterious circles created by our prehistoric ancestors. The plan of Stonehenge III, seen from a certain point of view, has a concentric design similar to that of a crop circle. In some cases, microwave radiation readings have been recorded in both Neolithic stone rings and twentieth-century crop circles. Similar crop formations are also found in other parts of the world, including the U.S., Germany, Russia, Australia, and Japan (diagrams 12.22 to 12.26), and interestingly, they are usually in close proximity to ancient sacred sites. For instance, the American Indians described it as "the magic circle in the prairies." American crop circles are typically found near power lines with transformers and often near Indian archeological sites. Researchers found an electrostatic voltmeter "pegged and froze" in front of a dolmen rock chamber in Kent Cliffs, New York, suggesting an electric charge had been recorded in the air (Howe 2002).

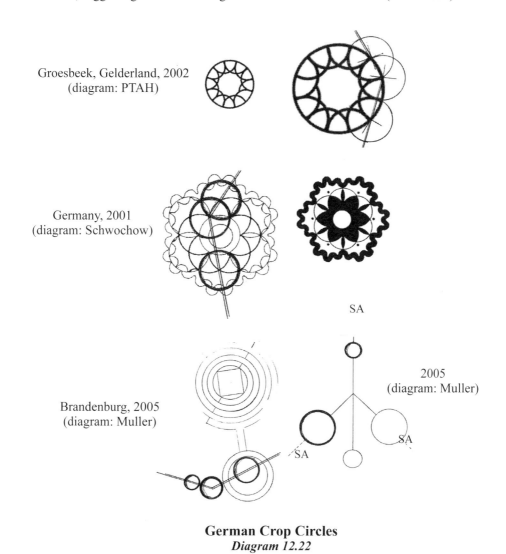

Groesbeek, Gelderland, 2002
(diagram: PTAH)

Germany, 2001
(diagram: Schwochow)

SA

Brandenburg, 2005
(diagram: Muller)

2005
(diagram: Muller)

SA

SA

German Crop Circles
Diagram 12.22

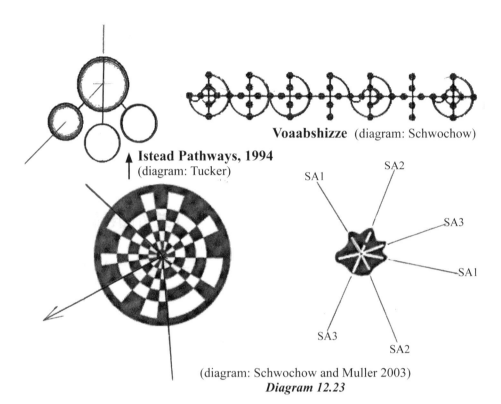

Voaabshizze (diagram: Schwochow)

↑ **Istead Pathways, 1994**
(diagram: Tucker)

SA1 SA2 SA3 SA1 SA3 SA2

(diagram: Schwochow and Muller 2003)
Diagram 12.23

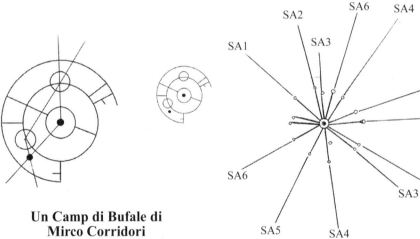

SA2 SA6 SA4
SA3
SA1
SA5
SA1
SA6
SA3 SA2
SA5 SA4

**Un Camp di Bufale di
Mirco Corridori**
(*La Citta Tusolana,* 2003)
Diagram 12.24

**One of the Three Glyphs of the
Laguna Carugon Crop Formation of
1996, Northern California**
(Ed and Kris Sherwood)
Diagram 12.25

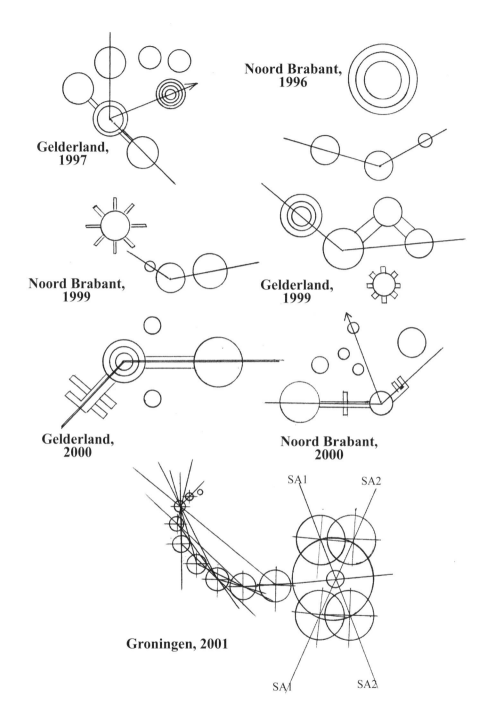

Noord Brabant,
1996

Gelderland,
1997

Noord Brabant,
1999

Gelderland,
1999

Gelderland,
2000

Noord Brabant,
2000

SA1   SA2

Groningen, 2001

SA1   SA2

Dutch Crop Circles (PTAH Foundation)
Diagram 12.26

Andrews (2003) elaborates that "crop circles often appear in or near these [sacred] places is a critical part of the overall meaning of the [crop circle] phenomenon. ... These places manifest an energy that speaks to our inner selves, and crop circles could be serving as living signs identifying and calling our attention to these sacred places." What kind of energy do these crop circles generate, and who is creating them?

The Mayan civilization suddenly vanished entirely in around A.D. 900. Its successor, the Aztecs, who rose from nowhere, continued to flourish until the early sixteenth century and were wiped out bloodily by the Spanish conquistadors. As mentioned before, a deity who once gave laws and knowledge to the Aztecs left in a hurry, leaving behind a gold plate of pictographs, generally known as the Calendar Stone. It is actually a plan of the builders' powerhouse left by the divinity as a token of his return. The same thing might also have happened to the Maya. The repeated revisits of the builders explained why the Mayan cities flourished in different periods of time, one after another. And the powerhouses of each Mayan city had to be rebuilt and extended so as to replace the exhausted ones. That is why old cities were abandoned and declined rapidly when the builders decided to establish a new power site. The Maya could not survive without the blessing of their deities, and so they dispersed.

The earliest account of the crop circle was recorded at roughly the same time as Spain colonized South America. According to the BLT website, in as early as 1686, a chemistry professor described that flattened areas "obtaining three parts of a circle, others being semicircular, some of them quadrants." Another record, entitled *Strange News out of Harford-shire* (1687), describes the appearance of a crop circle being cut by the "Mowing Devil" after a bright light occurred on the field (Haselhoff 2001) (diagram 12.27). The builders might have given up the magical process they had practised for thousands of years for a new method.

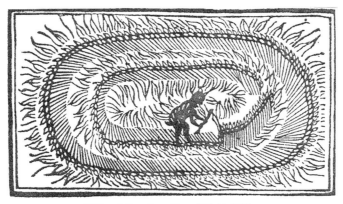

"The Mowing Devil" (1687)
Diagram 12.27

Crop circles can appear throughout the growing season, in the Northern hemisphere from April and continuing until harvest. Midautumn appears to be the peak of the phenomenon, when the crops have grown high enough for formation. Most of the formations are made between midnight and 4:00 a.m.

Some experts suggest that crop circles, like many prehistoric megaliths circles, are located at the intersecting points of the Earth energy lines and major magnetic fields. They tend to alter the local electromagnetic field, thus causing malfunctioning of watches, mobile phones, cameras, recording equipment, and even aircraft electronics.

Freddy Silva, a leading expert of the field, claims that "genuine crop circles appear on the nodes of the Earth's lines of magnetic energy." He further elaborates that "the Circlemakers use aquiferous ground so that the water can balance the tremendous heat generated during the infrasonic circlemaking process. … The Circlemakers also use the spin motion of energy to create an electromagnetic field in water" (2005). Movement of underground water may probably create a static charge that builds up and ultimately discharges at the surface level (Andrews). Therefore, crop circles are created by something tapping this mysterious force. Could it be the builders' energy mechanism?

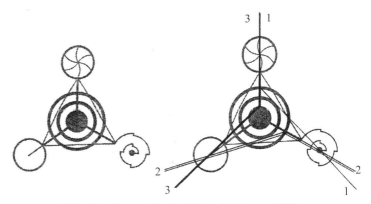

The Barbury Castle Tetrahedron, 1991
(after Silva 2002)
Diagram 12.28

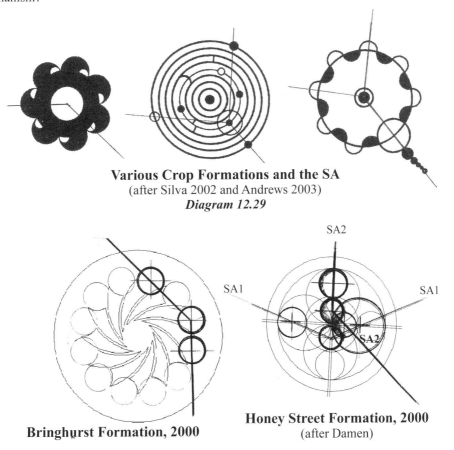

Various Crop Formations and the SA
(after Silva 2002 and Andrews 2003)
Diagram 12.29

Bringhurst Formation, 2000

Honey Street Formation, 2000
(after Damen)

Diagram 12.30

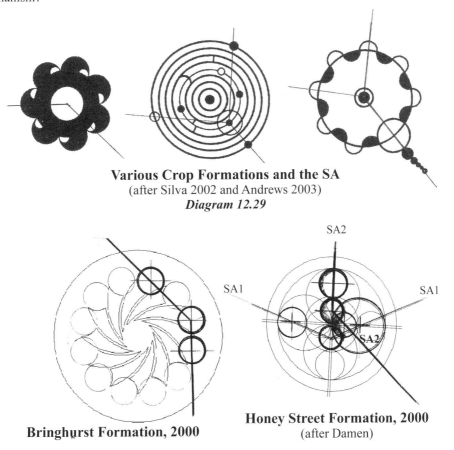

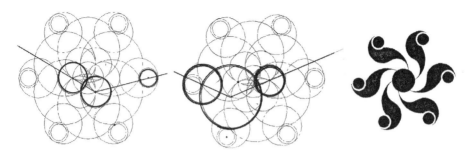

The Honey Street Formation, 2004 (diagram: Damen)
Diagram 12.31

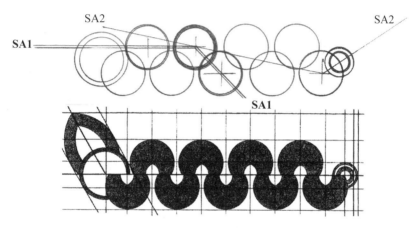

SA2   SA2

SA1

SA1

"Snake" Formation, East Field, 1999 (lower image: Silva 2002)
Diagram 12.32

For decades, experts have offered explantions for the crop circle phenomenon ranging from the work of human pranksters, to results of natural and atmospheric forces probably caused by dust devils or tornadoes, and have even suggested that they are the expression of our despoiled earth. Others suggest they are physical manifestations of an underlying unknown Earth energy, military authority, or extraterrestrials. Even though researchers and scientists of different fields, probably with the involvement of the military, equipped with multimillion-dollar aerial surveillance and instruments such as video recorders, cameras, and image intensifiers, have tried but failed to identify the Circlemakers, or even to catch one. It makes the crop formations a twentieth-century mystery, and one, like Stonehenge, open to different interpretations.

Colin Andrews suggests that these "sacred circles," which incorporate complicated geometry, contain some kind of information and messages from an unknown intelligence. He even established the Andrews Crop Circle Catalogue system in 1983 to document all the crop formations he has knowledge of (2003). Some think that the circles, together with megalithic monuments, acting like hermetic devices, transport people into higher levels of consciousness (Moore and Lamb). "Crop circles are mirrors in which we can polish our souls" (Glickman 2000).

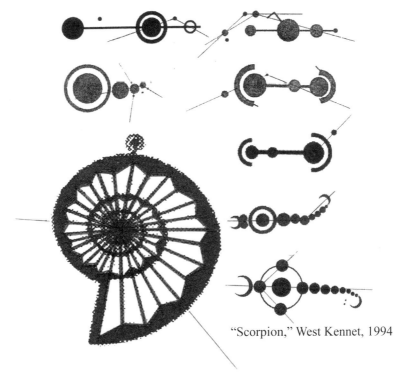

"Scorpion," West Kennet, 1994

Various Crop Formations and the SA (after Silva 2002 and Andrews 2003)
Diagram 12.33

With the application of the SA to the circles, it is logical to conclude that they have resulted from the intelligence's recharging power on the crop surface. Remarkably, the intelligence has continued to use our planet as their way station, from erecting standing monoliths, constructing passage cairns, earthen causeways and stone circles, sky-high pyramids of the Mayan world and finally to the formation of the crop circles. They can all be read and explained by the SA (diagrams 12.34 to 12.39).

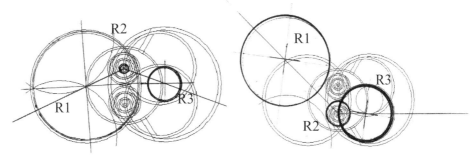

The Milk Hill Formation, 2004 (diagram: Damen)
Diagram 12.34

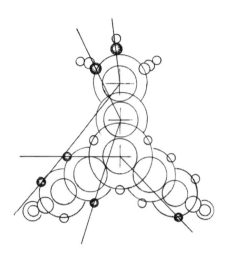

The Borstal Bubble Ring, 2001
(after Tucker)
Diagram 12.35

The Milk Hill Formation, 2004
(after Damen)
A complex arrangement of circles, arcs, and
crescents, it resembles a bee (Pringle).
Diagram 12.36

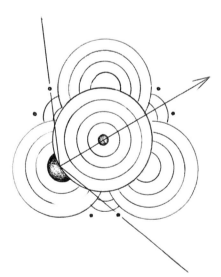

**The Nashenden Farm
Formation, 2004**
(after Tucker)
Diagram 12.37

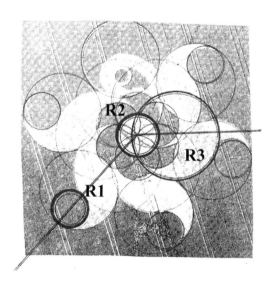

"Lotus," Golden Ball Hill, 2000
(photo by Lucy Pringle,
from Silva 2002)
Diagram 12.38

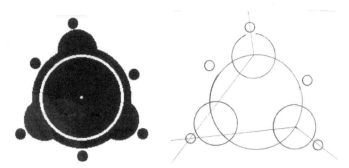

Danebury Ring, 1997 (after John Sayer, cropcircleresearch)
Diagram 12.39

Megalight above the Field

Going back to prehistory, the whole secret of the intelligence lay in the conical device which was capable of projecting the megalights for power. They served as electric wires to heat up the stones nearby, and to tap and transfer the energy in and out of the conical capacitor. Can we find these megalights today?

According to Colin Andrews (2003), "there have been many reports of golden lights seen above the fields in which crop circles later appear." These lights, named the Avebury Lights in his book, are self-luminous and approximately fourteen inches in diameter. Werner Anderhub and Hans Peter Roth, in their book *Crop Circles: Exploring the Designs and Mysteries* (2002), also mention that "people had repeatedly been confronted with strange appearances of light" where crop circles appeared, especially in southern Britain. The authors even "see clearly and plainly a bright, blue-white light beginning to manifest itself… ." They further mention that "within a few seconds after the source of light rises up again from the crop circle, cloudlike, it changes immediately into a three-dimensional rectangular form of enormous size. Now the blue-white light appears to be bundled into a shoebox-shaped body of approximately 6 × 20 × 50cm, shimmering transparently like a jellyfish… ." What they encountered is probably a twentieth-century megalight.

A watcher saw "a bullet-shaped object with rows of colored lights" before the appearance of a crop circle with seven satellites at Bickington, Devon. A column of light came through the clouds near Beckhampton before a crop formation appeared (Silva 2002). According to Nancy Talbott, co-founder of the BLT Research, "three brilliant, intense white columns, or tubes, of light flashed down from the sky to the ground. … The sky had lit up like daylight when each column of light had occurred." (Thomas 1998). In the Netherlands, 2001, Talbott also observed tubes or columns of brilliant white light descended from above with enormous force into a stringbean field just before a new crop formation in the exact location (the BLT website). Residents in Coles County reported unusually bright lights with beams shining downwards in the vicinity of the pattern (Silva 2005). A large orange ball of light dropped from the sky the night before the formation.

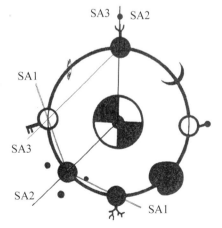

"Charm Bracelet," Silbury Hill, Wiltshire, 1992
(after Wolfgang Schindler)
Diagram 12.40

On many occasions, luminous balls of light, always described as metallic and a few inches in diameter, were seen hovering over crop circles and energy spots, and captured by the watchers' cameras. They often got brighter and then faded out. These balls, enigmatically called Unidentified Flying Objects, floated in circles and "charged" by the Earth energy, a few inches above

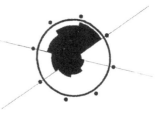

"Hexagon," Cley Hill, Wiltshire, 1997

"Ratchet" Formation Stockbridge Down, 1995

Diagram 12.41

the crop field before the appearance of the crop formation. Howe, after studying all these reports, has identified seven major kinds of anomalous lights: flickering brightness, lights coming from the ground and moving upward or coming from the sky and moving downward, translucent light and white columns, etc (Moore and Lamb 2001).

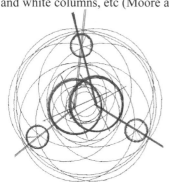

The Beacon Hill Formation, 2004
(after Damen)
Diagram 12.42

The Beckhampton Formation, 2001
(after Damen)
Diagram 12.43

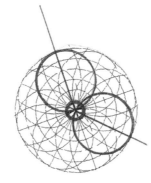

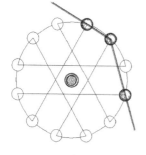

The Wilton Windmill Formation, 2004
(after Damen)
Diagram 12.44

THE GODS' MACHINES

488

Andreas Muller's Accurate Measurement

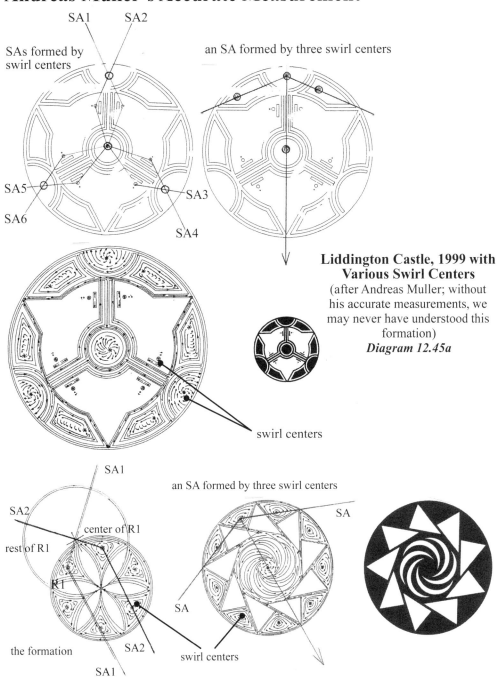

SA1   SA2

SAs formed by
swirl centers

an SA formed by three swirl centers

SA5

SA6

SA3

SA4

**Liddington Castle, 1999 with
Various Swirl Centers**
(after Andreas Muller; without
his accurate measurements, we
may never have understood this
formation)
Diagram 12.45a

swirl centers

SA1

SA2

center of R1

rest of R1

R1

the formation

SA2

SA1

an SA formed by three swirl centers

SA

SA

swirl centers

Avebury Avenue, Wiltshire, 1999
(after Andreas Muller)
Diagram 12.45b

Nine-pointed Star Formation, Cherhill, 1999
(*left:* Andreas Muller, Anderhub and Roth 2002)
Diagram 12.45c

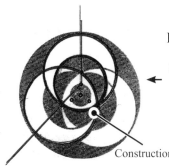

Liddington Castle Formation, 2001
(after Janssen)
In his book *The Hypnotic Power of Crop Circles,* Bert Janssen suggests that they were formed by "construction points" specially placed inside the formation.
Diagram 12.46a

Construction point

Hackpen Hill, Wiltshire, 1997 (*left*), and Milk Hill, Wiltshire, 1997 (*right*) (after John Sayer and Paul Vigay, cropcircle-research.com)
Diagram 12.46b

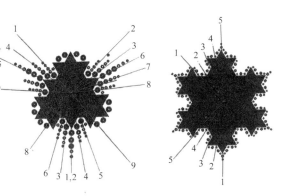

Gog Magog Hills, England, 2001
(after Paul Vigay, cam.net.uk)
Diagram 12.47a

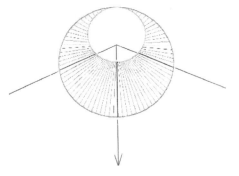

"The Sentence," East Field near Alton Barnes, 1999
The most complex of the key-shaped pictograms, stretching over an area 340m in length (Anderhub and Roth; diagram not to scale). According to Howe, the formation was formed unnoticed within "five hours of darkness" under the eyes of watchers on Knap Hill. According to Moore and Lamb (2001), an orange sphere was photographed over the circle and its energy was strong enough to disable all battery-operated equipment.
Diagram 12.47b

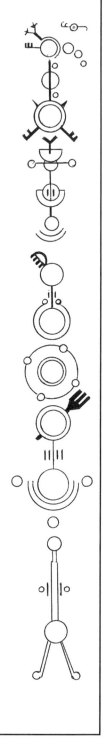

A Technology Too Advanced

Freddy Silva, in his book *Secrets in the Fields,* suggests that an infrasound-generated light tube creates crop circles. High heat is produced by electromagnetism, which helps to transfer electricity through the spiralling tube. He provides an illustration to explain the mechanism (diagram 12.48). Interestingly, his drawing of the tube of light is very similar to the Mayan ceremonial bar embraced with reverence by the ruler on the carved stela.

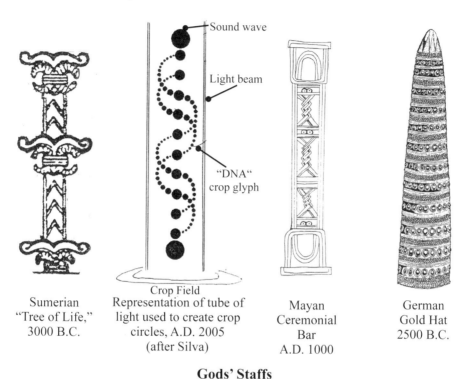

Sumerian "Tree of Life," 3000 B.C.

Crop Field Representation of tube of light used to create crop circles, A.D. 2005 (after Silva)

Mayan Ceremonial Bar A.D. 1000

German Gold Hat 2500 B.C.

Gods' Staffs
Diagram 12.48

As inspired by Silva and the Mayan ceremonial bar, a column of light is projected vertically onto the surface of the crop field. Instead of creating the crop circle, the light tube, probably acting like a Neolithic conical device or a Mayan cylindrical ceremonial bar, aims at tapping Earth energy underneath. Before this tapping, electromagnetically driven metal balls are introduced into the field. These luminous light balls, probably capable of generating tremendous heat, are responsible for "cleaning up" the crop field by heating and bending the crops, and causing starch crystallization inside. These crystals probably function like the crystallized quartz inside a monolith back in prehistoric times, and turn the designated area into the builders' charging fields.

In order to store the energy generated, a "circular wall of crop" is formed by bending the vegetation inside. Similar containers from the Neolithic era are found in megalithic structures such as corbelled-chambered mounds and in earthen henges as well as in Stonehenge, all skillfully constructed. In theory, the crop circles are aligned to the SA, a prerequisite of the builders' energy mechanism for more than five millennia. Earth energy would then be tapped directly from the "tubes of light" and projected from the atmosphere.

After thousands of years of light-speed evolution in space technology, our visitors long ago reached the level where massive solid objects—megaliths—were no longer needed. What they now require are only "laser-like" spinning beams, or the light tubes as described by many watchers. In some cases, experts have found white powdery deposits inside the crop circles, identified as high-purity silicon dioxide, SiO_2 (i.e., quartz: the exact mineral for building their former megalithic powerhouses).

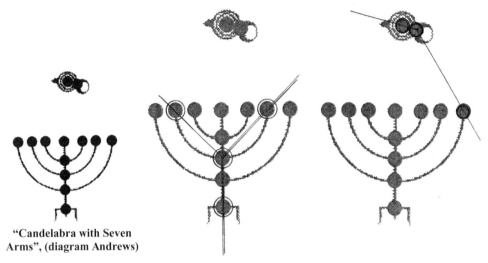

"Candelabra with Seven
Arms", (diagram Andrews)

It Resembled the Jewish Menorah, a Candle-holder with Seven Arms
Diagram 12.49

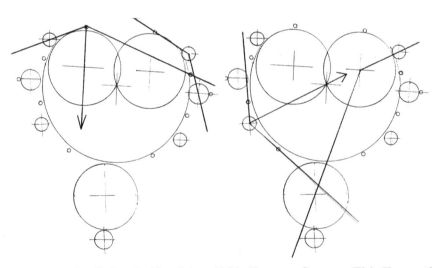

**"Mandelbrot Set," Cambridgeshire, 1991: Experts Suggest This Formation
Could Only Be Created with Computer Assistance**
(after Wolfgang Schindler)
Diagram 12.50

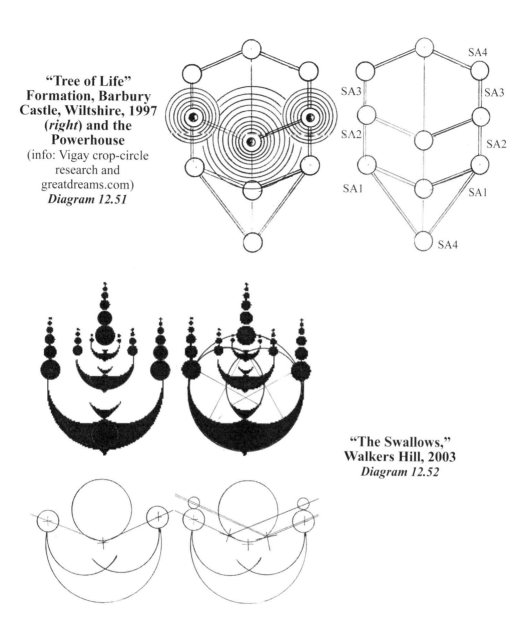

"Tree of Life" Formation, Barbury Castle, Wiltshire, 1997 (*right*) and the Powerhouse
(info: Vigay crop-circle research and greatdreams.com)
Diagram 12.51

"The Swallows," Walkers Hill, 2003
Diagram 12.52

The Magnetic Fields Formations

The crop formation illustrated below recalls the idea of the builders' twin-device energy mechanism. At Avebury Trusloe, Wiltshire, a staggering series of standing and flattened diamond shapes outward in a containing circle was found in 2000. It also reminds some people of "the pattern made by iron filings being moved on a tray by magnets underneath" (Moore and Lamb). There was a controversy whether the formation had been man-made. A series of twenty-nine intersecting lines are created from two central points and they share the axis of the SA (diagram 12.53), which suggests it was not a hoaxer.

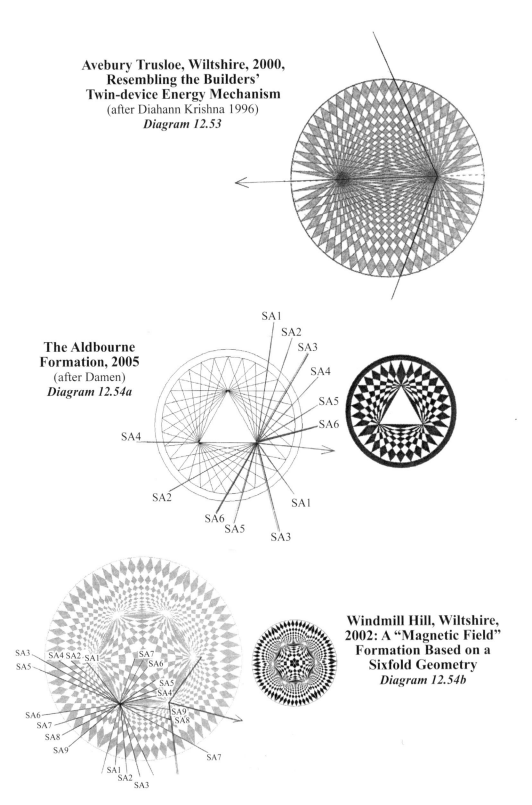

**Avebury Trusloe, Wiltshire, 2000,
Resembling the Builders'
Twin-device Energy Mechanism**
(after Diahann Krishna 1996)
Diagram 12.53

**The Aldbourne
Formation, 2005**
(after Damen)
Diagram 12.54a

SA1
SA2
SA3
SA4
SA5
SA6

SA4

SA2
SA6
SA5
SA1
SA3

**Windmill Hill, Wiltshire,
2002: A "Magnetic Field"
Formation Based on a
Sixfold Geometry**
Diagram 12.54b

SA3
SA5
SA4 SA2 SA1
SA7
SA6
SA5
SA4
SA6
SA7
SA8
SA9
SA9
SA8
SA7
SA1
SA2
SA3

"Solar Motif" Formations

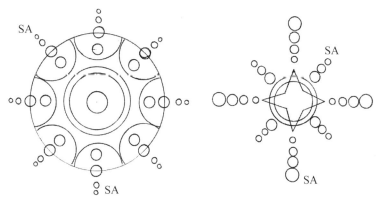

Longwood Warren,
Hampshire, 2001

Silbury Hill,
Wiltshire, 2002

(info: cropcircle-archive) *Diagram 12.54c*

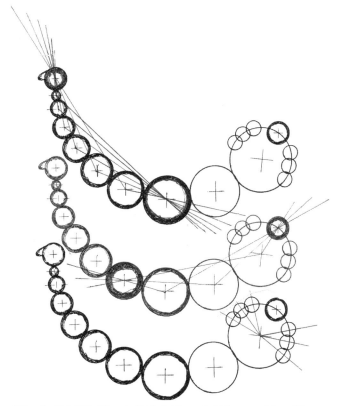

Kits Coy, Bluebell Hill, Kent, 2006: Fractal Formed by Eleven Circles
According to Andy Fowlds, the formation is a hoax and was made by "Team Satan" in Kent
(medwaycropcircle.co.uk)—or is it genuine, as SAs are derived from the formation?
(diagram: cropcircle-archive.com)
Diagram 12.54d

Today, organic vegetation replaces bulky stones as the media for tapping our energy. Crop pictograms, with their complexity, are certainly not intended as calling cards from advanced intelligences. They are simply the by-products of their energy-generating processes. Together with the ancient powerhouses, they bear evidence to the visits of an advanced intelligence here and are a record of their repeated appearances in the history of our civilization.

"Perhaps by focusing on a common mystery, we are creating a unified energy that will ultimately be our salvation," writes Andrews.

2005 and 2006 Crop Circles

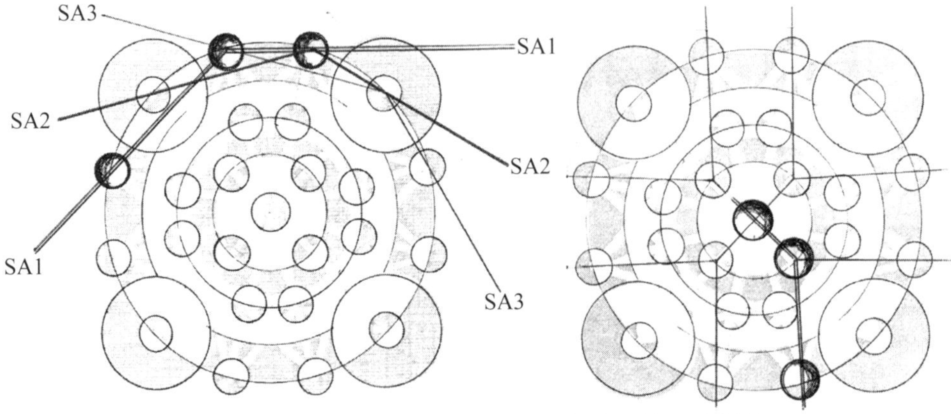

Lurkley Hill, near Lockeridge, Wiltshire, 2005
(Allan Brown, ukcropcircle.co.uk)
Diagram 12.55

Boxley, Kent, 2005
Per Graham Tucker, the formation is a complex trefoil 180 feet across, lying close to the Countless Stones Long Barrow (after Damen, cropcircleconnector.com)
Diagram 12.56

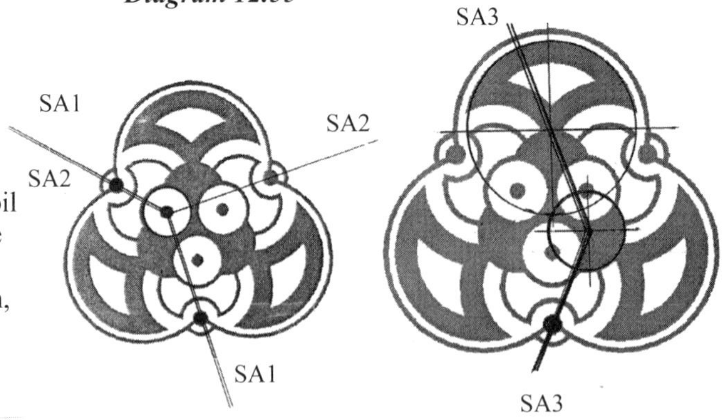

Waden Hill, 2005 (*left*) and Ripley, Dorset, 2005
(Berthold Zugelder, cropcircle-archive.com)
Diagram 12.57

THE GODS' MACHINES

496

Clatford Bottom, 2005
According to cropcircleconnector,
the formation is opposite
"Devil's Den" dolmen.
(after Bertold Zugelder,
cropcircle-archive.com)
Diagram 12.58

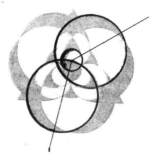

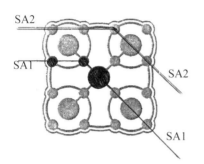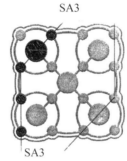

**2005 Avebury
Manor Formation**
(after Zef Damen and Alex,
cropcircleconnector.com)
Diagram 12.59

**Cuxham2 (Cutmill), near Charlgove
Watling, Oxford, 2005**
(diagram: Alex, cropcircle-archive.com)
Diagram 12.60

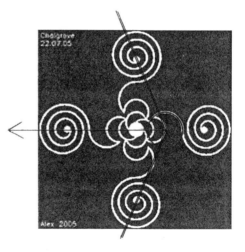

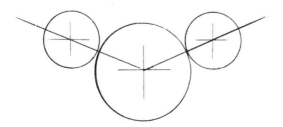

**"Mickey Mouse" Triplets
Crop Formation, Boreham
Wood, Alton Barnes, 1992**
Diagram 12.61

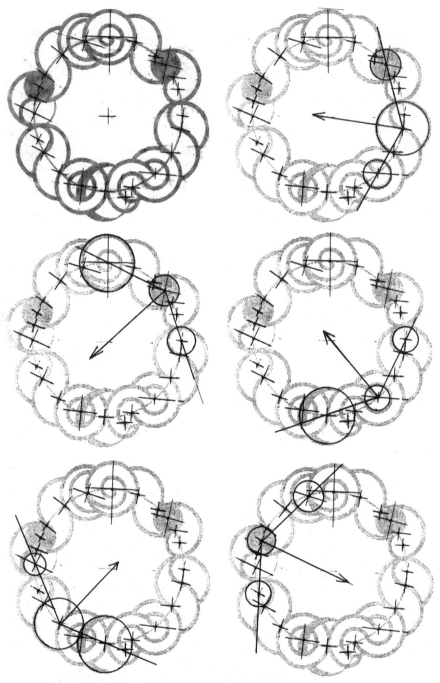

West Overton Formation, 2006
(after Bertold Zugelder, cropcircle-archive.com)
Diagram 12.62

According to the cropcircleconnector, the glyph is an arrangement of twenty-four rings in a cluster spread over approximately 150 feet. To my understanding, these rings are aligned to the SA.

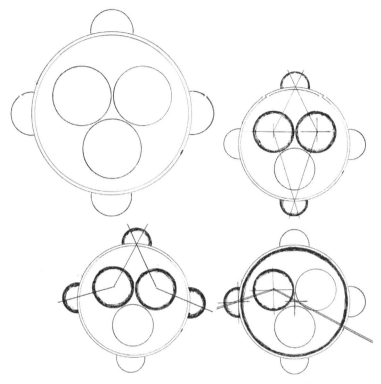

Ceresole d' Alba, Sommariva Bosco, Italy, 2006
(after Federico, cropcircleconnector.com)
Diagram 12.63

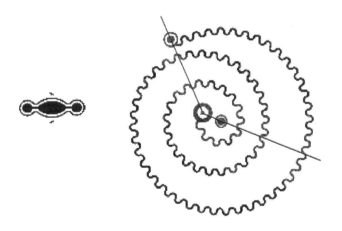

Dornbery, Hessen, Germany, 2006
(cropcircle-archive.com)
Diagram 12.64

CROP CIRCLES: MODERN POWER GENERATORS

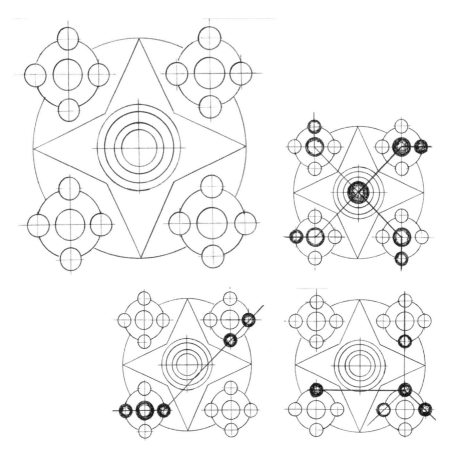

Poirino, Torino, Italy, 2006
(after Tommy Borms, cropcircleconnector.com)
Diagram 12.65

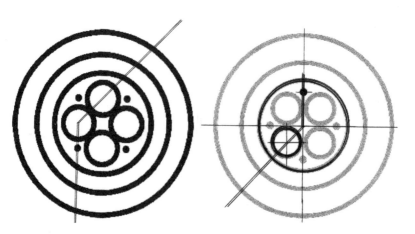

Terzo d'acqui, Alessandria, Italy, 2006
(cropcircle-archive.com)
Diagram 12.66

Rocchino, Alessandria, Italy, 2006
(cropcircle-archive.com)
Diagram 12.67

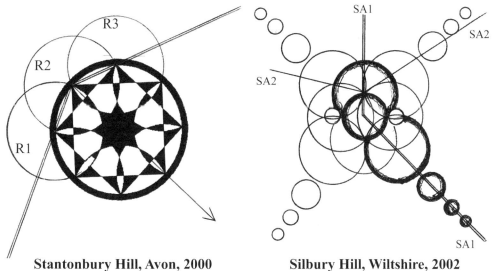

Stantonbury Hill, Avon, 2000
(cropcircle-archive)
Diagram 12.68

Silbury Hill, Wiltshire, 2002
(cropcircle-archive) *Diagram 12.69*

**Toot Baldon,
Oxfordshire, 2005**
(cropcircle-archive)
Diagram 12.70

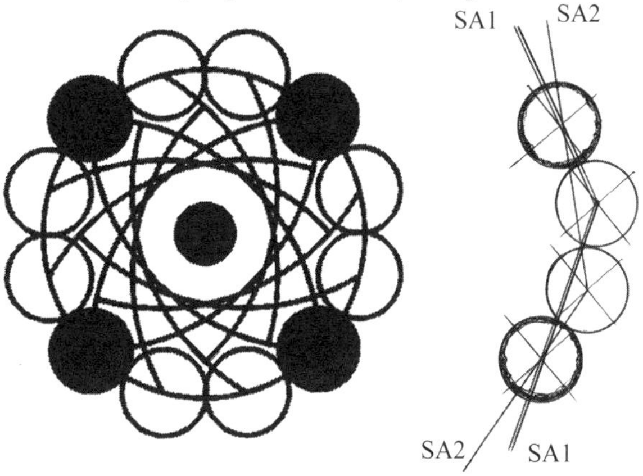

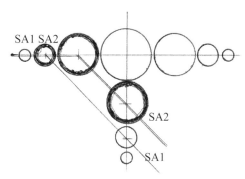

**Bragbury Lane, Datchworth,
Hertfordshire, 2006:
Central Large Circle with Diminishing
Circles on Three Sides**
(cropcircle-archive.com)
Diagram 12.71

**Wejherowie, Pomorskie,
Poland, 2006**
(cropcircle-archive.com)
Diagram 12.72

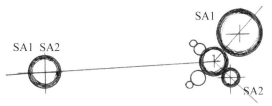

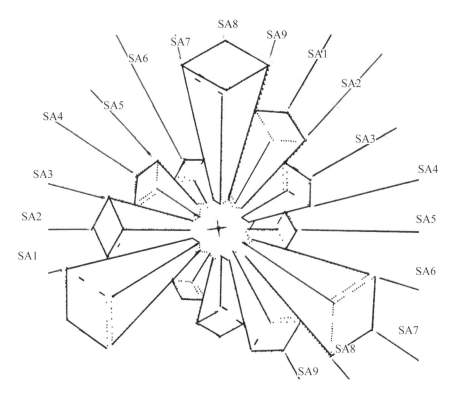

**Wayland Smithy Formation, Oxfordshire, 2006:
According to Andreas Muller, Formation Located
behind Tree-lined Chamber Barrow of Wayland**
(cropcircleconnector.com)
Diagram 12.73

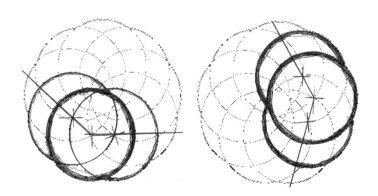

**Rollright Stone Circle Formation, Oxfordshire, 2006:
Formation Comprises Nine Overlapping Rings,
Center of Each Forms an SA with Neighbors**
(after Bertold Zugelder, cropcircle-archive.com)
Diagram 12.74

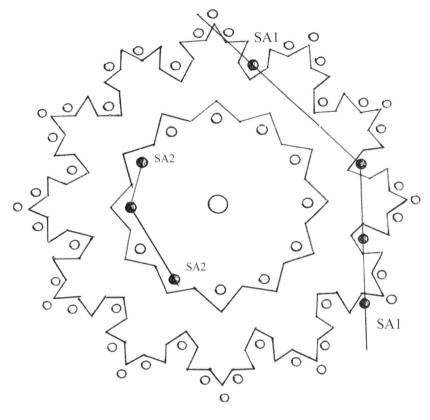

Boxley Formation, Kent, 2006
(Bertold Zugelder, cropcircle-archive.com)
Diagram 12.75

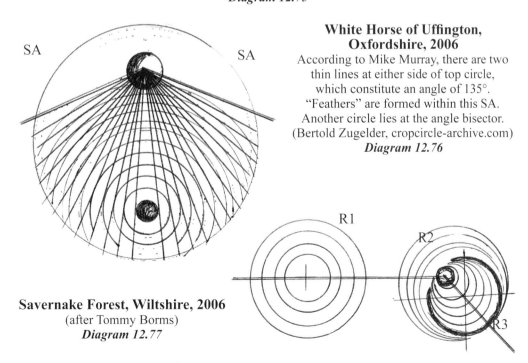

**White Horse of Uffington,
Oxfordshire, 2006**
According to Mike Murray, there are two
thin lines at either side of top circle,
which constitute an angle of 135°.
"Feathers" are formed within this SA.
Another circle lies at the angle bisector.
(Bertold Zugelder, cropcircle-archive.com)
Diagram 12.76

Savernake Forest, Wiltshire, 2006
(after Tommy Borms)
Diagram 12.77

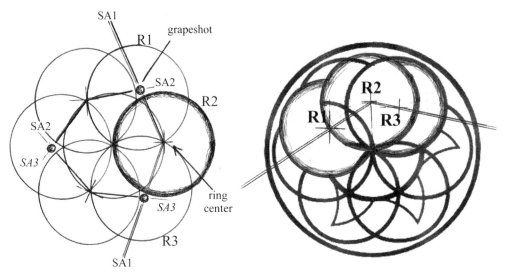

**L'etereo fiore di Calcinaia,
Tuscany, Italy, 2006**
(Tommy Borms, cropcircleconnector.com)
Diagram 12.78

Kessel-Lo, Belgium, 2006
(Tommy Borms, cropcircleconnector.com)
Diagram 12.79

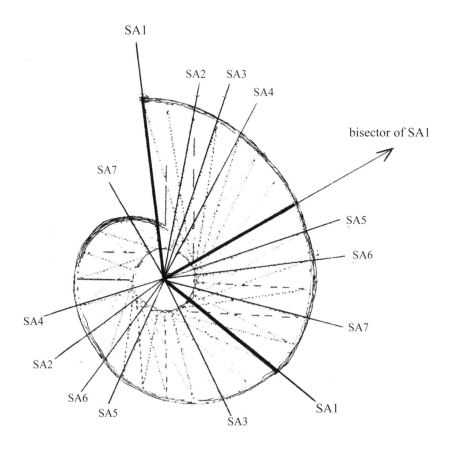

Barbury Castle, Wiltshire, 2006
(Bertold Zugelder, cropcircle-archive.com)
Diagram 12.80

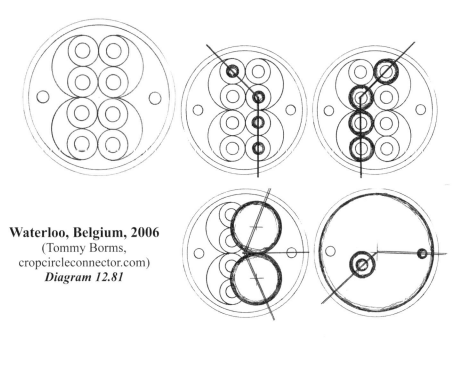

Waterloo, Belgium, 2006
(Tommy Borms,
cropcircleconnector.com)
Diagram 12.81

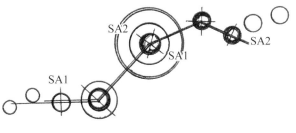

Swibie, Poland, 2006
(cropcircleconnector.com)
Diagram 12.82

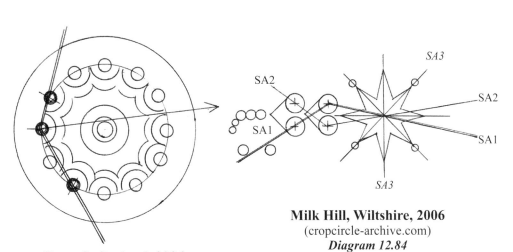

Milk Hill, Wiltshire, 2006
(cropcircle-archive.com)
Diagram 12.84

Bern, Switerland, 2006
(Andreas Muller,
cropcircleconnector.com)
Diagram 12.83

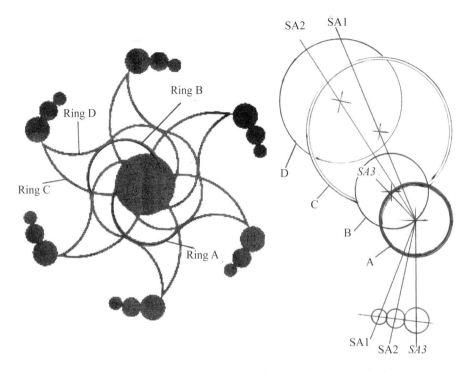

Uberdingen, Baden-Wurttembury, Germany, 2006
(cropcircle-archive.com)
Diagram 12.85

Windmill Hill, Wiltshire, 2006
According to Mike Murray (cropcircleconnector.com),
there is a strong energy line running through the formation.
(diagram: cropcircle-archive.com)
Diagram 12.86

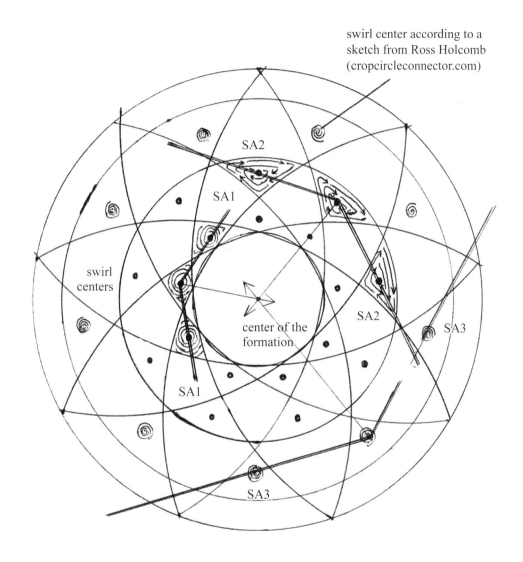

swirl center according to a
sketch from Ross Holcomb
(cropcircleconnector.com)

SA2

SA1

swirl
centers

center of the
formation

SA2

SA3

SA1

SA3

Cheesefoot Head, Hampshire, 2006
(Bertold Zugelder, cropcircle-archive.com)
Diagram 12.87

Crop Circles 2007

(courtesy: cropcirclearchive.com and cropcircleconnector.com)

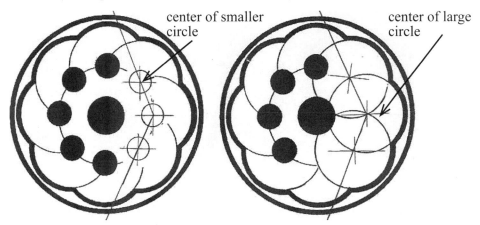

Wilton Water Grid, Wiltshire
(Andreas Muller, cropcircleconnector.com) *Diagram 12.88*

The formation has a central large ring with eight orbiting additional circles, each surrounded by a partial circular arc (information: Ross and Meredith Holcomb).

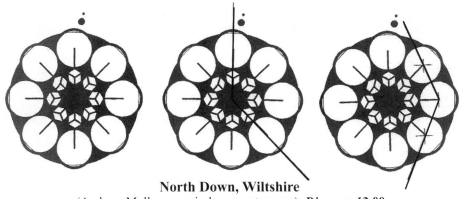

North Down, Wiltshire
(Andreas Muller, cropcircleconnector.com) *Diagram 12.89*

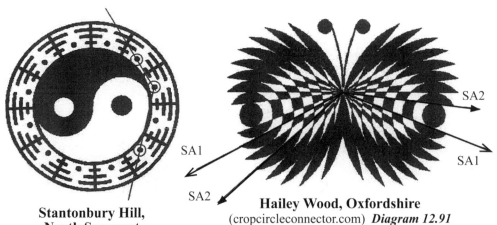

**Stantonbury Hill,
North Somerset**
(cropcirclearchive.com)
Diagram 12.90

Hailey Wood, Oxfordshire
(cropcircleconnector.com) *Diagram 12.91*
The left and right "wings" and "antennae" of the formation are nearly exact mirror-images of each other (Chet Snow).

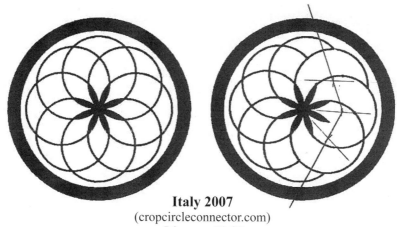

Italy 2007
(cropcircleconnector.com)
Diagram 12.92

According to Mike Murray of cropcircleconnector.com, the East Field formation "dowsed positive." Mark Gareh, a crop circle meditator, reported that he saw a white/yellow bright circular light the night before the formation and it was "bobbing up and down in the treetops while moving from east to west … and it lasted no more than three to four seconds." He witnessed another "bright turquoise" light that "descended slowly in a perfect vertical manner" and "appeared to be progressively tapered towards the top and larger at the base." He was "nearly floored by the energy." (19 September 2007, cropcircleconnector.com)

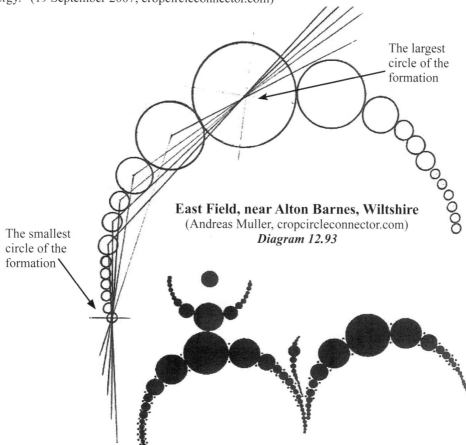

The largest circle of the formation

East Field, near Alton Barnes, Wiltshire
(Andreas Muller, cropcircleconnector.com)
Diagram 12.93

The smallest circle of the formation

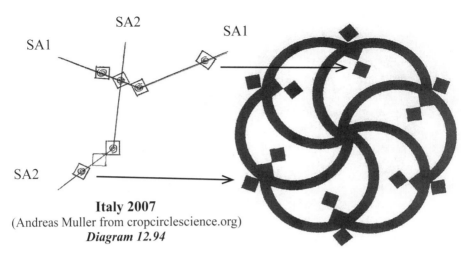

Italy 2007
(Andreas Muller from cropcirclescience.org)
Diagram 12.94

Swirl centers (according to images from cropcircleconnector.com)

According to Ross Hol-
comb, the formation, one
of the two that appeared
in the same night, has a
six-fold geometry built
around six sets of three
truncated vesica pisces
in "propeller" form.

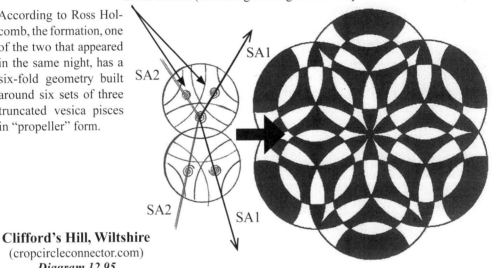

Clifford's Hill, Wiltshire
(cropcircleconnector.com)
Diagram 12.95

swirl centers (according to images from Lucy Pringle, cropcircleconnector.com)

Pewsey White Horse, Wiltshire
(Andreas Muller from cropcirclescience.org)
Diagram 12.96

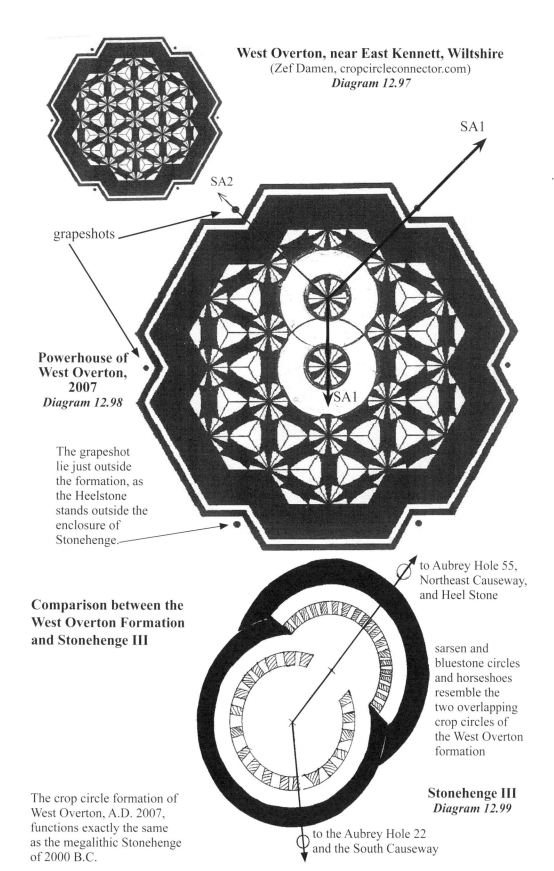

West Overton, near East Kennett, Wiltshire
(Zef Damen, cropcircleconnector.com)
Diagram 12.97

SA1

SA2

grapeshots

**Powerhouse of
West Overton,
2007**
Diagram 12.98

SA1

The grapeshot
lie just outside
the formation, as
the Heelstone
stands outside the
enclosure of
Stonehenge.

**Comparison between the
West Overton Formation
and Stonehenge III**

to Aubrey Hole 55,
Northeast Causeway,
and Heel Stone

sarsen and
bluestone circles
and horseshoes
resemble the
two overlapping
crop circles of
the West Overton
formation

Stonehenge III
Diagram 12.99

The crop circle formation of
West Overton, A.D. 2007,
functions exactly the same
as the megalithic Stonehenge
of 2000 B.C.

to the Aubrey Hole 22
and the South Causeway

CROP CIRCLES: MODERN POWER GENERATORS

How a Fractal Powerhouse is Formed

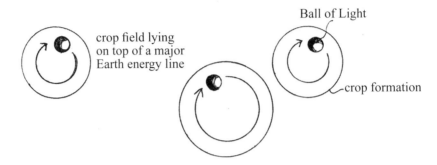

Balls of lights are introduced into the crop field. They spiral over the vegetation to create friction and electrostatic energy. This also helps to tap the Earth energy underneath.

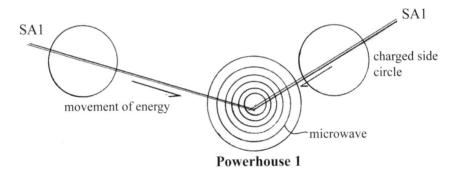

Powerhouse 1

Earth energy is then transferred from the two energy-charged circles to the central powerhouse 1. Tubes of light will project from the atmosphere to recharge the energy of powerhouse 1.

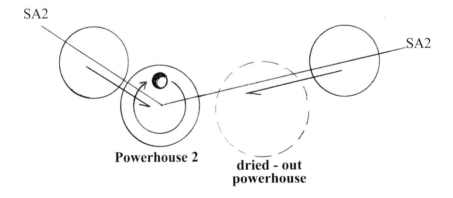

Powerhouse 2   **dried - out powerhouse**

Powerhouse 2 will replace the exhausted powerhouse 1.
Diagram 12.100

Toward a Conclusion

"As long as our past is undiscovered, one entry in the account for the future remains blank. Cannot the past help us to reach technical solutions which will not have to be found for the first time because they already existed in antiquity?"

—Erich Von Däniken, *Chariots of the Gods?* (1970)

God made two great lights (Genesis 1:16)—a step in the creation of life on Earth, which has multiplied and flourished in accordance with the text. In addition to solar energy is that lying deep within the Earth, abundant and powerful. Numerous megalithic infrastructures such as Newgrange and Stonehenge were built to tap and contain this energy, probably before the continuation of the space-traveler/builders' long cosmic journeys. They mark possibly thousands of years of the coming and going of space travelers, and long after these powerhouses were abandoned they have become our prehistoric mysteries.

Expeditions to the extremes of our world certainly require a lot of energy supply and back-up. Professional mountaineers set up their supply camps along the route to the summit. These camps provide sufficient food and shelter for the mountaineers so that their traveling gear can be kept to the minimum, thus facilitating their expeditions. Most importantly, the camp supplies "energy." For instance, an under-cover stove generates sufficient and valuable heat for warming exhausted bodies. A shelter provides a resting place for recovering one's strength, and a sense of security in the midst of a raging snowstorm.

Today, the prospect of interplanetary travel is open to us. Scientists are working on the idea of establishing a base camp on the Moon or Mars in the hope that one day it would serve as our cosmic supply center. In theory, space camps will be established one after another, eventually bringing us to the other side of the Galaxy. It is no longer an unreachable goal, but just a matter of application of resources and time. And it has already been achieved, not in the outer space, but on our planet surface itself. It is exactly what a mysterious intelligence has been doing for 5,000 years.

These visitors from outer space, our "old friends" of this study, dating back to the Stone Age, discovered and established their cosmic supply stations on our earth at the time when our primitive ancestors were still nomadic hunters and gatherers fighting for a precarious existence. They became the future masters of this tiny planet. Back at the dawn of our civilization humans were "tailor-made" for hard manual work. Smarter brains, manual dexterity, and strong bodies have made humans invincible, but ironically, we were first harnessed and developed in building powerhouses for the builders, and their descendants.

That's what we call the start of Neolithic Age and the beginning of human civilization. These evolutionary new men were assembled at selected sites, probably on the junction of underground energy streams, to accomplish advanced projects far beyond their previous experience. The completion of a megalithic monument could have been the day of their salvation, in the knowledge of another world, or Afterworld, as promised by their divine creators.

But these megalithic powerhouses certainly revealed the limits of their designers. They were not gods; they had to rely on energy and fuel for their travel. That's why they came here for supplies. The location of their megalithic generators was restricted to particular areas where there were stones of special properties. Their twin-device energy mechanism was bound by the SA. But still, these now 5,000-year-old megalithic infrastructures were the most advanced machinery ever built on our planet. Today, large amounts of signals and energy are transferred in form of electrons through light beams inside optical fibers. Energy stored and transmitted in the form of microwaves is highly possible in the near future—and it has already been achieved in the distant past.

Experts agree that energy really does exist underground. Some people can even "feel" it. Megaliths do contain minerals, such as iron and mica for electricity conduction. What is missing in this sophisticated energy-generating chain is the builders' conical device, which was capable of projecting power-tapping megalights. There is certainly a lot to learn from our distant past. Fortunately, ancient wisdom has already been unfolded in front of our eyes.

To return to the present, the establishment of a supply camp could be crucial to the survival of stranded mountaineers, with clear indications of the location of essential equipment such as medical kits, a heating stove, and means of ignition. Neolithic carvings such as the Solar God motif of Newgrange, the Dagda Skirt of Loughcrew, and the Conical Motif of Gavrinis, and probably the Aztec Calendar Stone, all serve similar functions—to indicate the builders' power machinery to newcomers. However, human beings, still technologically backward, mistake their buildings for burial tombs and sacred temples. Without the conical device, these powerhouses are just empty functionless monuments, like a nuclear submarine with its nuclear reactor disarmed.

Megalithism can only be understood in this way, a more rational and scientific way. It is no longer just a historical term to describe an outdated period, a blurred and forgotten era gradually fading away from our modern-day history book. Instead, understanding and rediscovering megalithism not only redefines our dim past, it can also reshape our future—a future of power technology and space travel.

We are lucky today, as we live in a world of mysteries but also of their solution. Turning these megaliths into tourist sites would certainly disappoint their original builders in the way our ancestors would have done when they misused them for burial or ritual purposes. That should not continue. The powerhouses of Newgrange and Stonehenge, Mayan cities such as Tikal and Copan, and the crop fields of southern Britain should become sacred precincts for top scientists and physicists. The most glorious days of these prehistoric monuments, together with their primary functions, will be restored. Megalithism is no longer an unanswerable mystery lost in the distant past. In fact, it constitutes the key to our future.

Megalithism deserves a better name.

The Gods' Machines

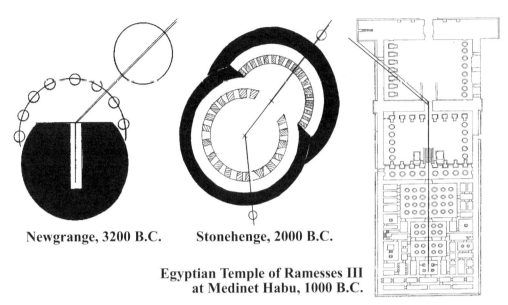

Newgrange, 3200 B.C.

Stonehenge, 2000 B.C.

Egyptian Temple of Ramesses III
at Medinet Habu, 1000 B.C.

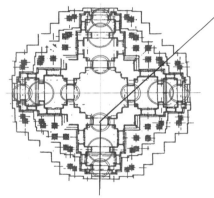

Central Sanctuary of Angkor Wat,
A.D. 1113–1150

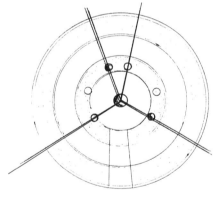

Broch of Mousa, A.D. 200

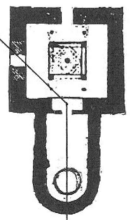

Chaitya at Ter,
A.D. 300

Mayan Temple of
Kukulkan, A.D. 900

Wilton Water Grid Crop Circle
Formation, A.D. 2007

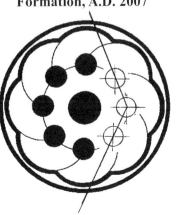

TOWARD A CONCLUSION

The Builders' Power Stations

A. The Boyne Metropolis, ca. 3500–3000 B.C.

B. The Avebury Complex, ca. 3000–2500 B.C.

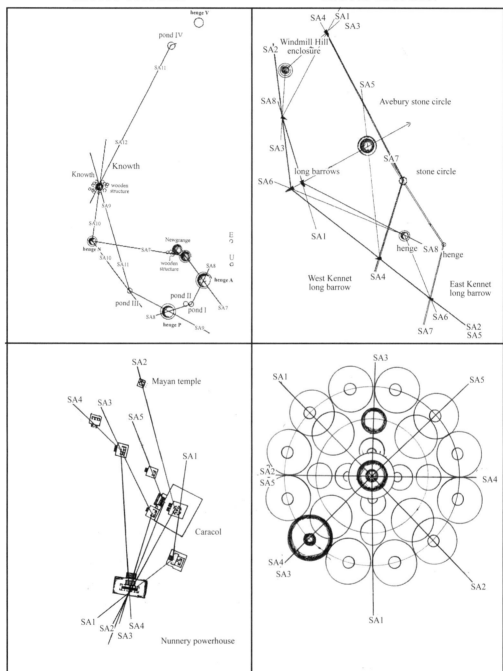

henge V

pond IV

SA11

SA12

Knowth

Knowth   wooden
structure

SA9

SA10

henge N   SA7   Newgrange

SA10   SA11   wooden
structure

SA8

henge A

pond III   pond II

SA8   pond I   SA7

henge P   SA9

E
O
U
O

SA4   SA1
SA3

Windmill Hill
enclosure

SA2

SA5

SA8   Avebury stone circle

SA3

SA7

long barrows   stone circle

SA6

SA1

henge   SA8   henge

West Kennet
long barrow

SA4   East Kennet
long barrow

SA6

SA7   SA2
SA5

SA2

Mayan temple

SA4   SA3

SA5

SA1

Caracol

SA1
SA2   SA4
SA3

Nunnery powerhouse

SA3

SA1   SA5

SA2
SA5   SA4

SA4
SA3

SA2

SA1

C. Oldest Complex of Chichen Itza, ca. A.D. 100

D. Stephen's Castle Crop Formation, Hampshire, A.D. 2000

A Power-generating Device, ca. 3000 B.C.

Bibliography

Adkins, L. and R., *The Handbook of British Archaeology,* St Edmundsbury Press, 1982

Ananthalwar, M. A., and Rea, A. (eds.), *Indian Architecture,* vol. II, Indian Book Gallery, 1980

Anderhub, W., and Roth, H. P., *Crop Circles: Exploring the Designs and Mysteries,* Lark Books, 2002

Andrews, C., *Crop Circles: Signs of Contact,* New Page, 2003

Armit, I., *Towers in the North: The Brochs of Scotland,* Tempus, 2004

Armit, I., and McCartney, M., "Traprain Law: Archaeology from the Ashes," in *Past: The Newsletter of the Prehistoric Society* 49 (April 2005)

Aubrey, B., *Megalithic Brittany,* Thames & Hudson, 1985

————— , *The Stone Circles of Britain, Ireland and Brittany*, Yale, 2003

————— , *The Stonehenge People*, J.M. Dent, 1987

————— , *Great Stone Circles*, Yale University, 1999

Bagens, B., *Angkor: Heart of an Asian Empire,* Thames and Hudson 1995

Balfour, M., *Stonehenge and Its Mysteries,* Macdonald and Jane's, 1979

Balfour, M., and Siering, B., *Megalithic Mysteries,* Dragon's World, 1992

Beckensall, S., *Rock Carvings of Northern Britain,* Hyperion Books, 1989

————— , *Prehistoric Rock Motifs of Northumberland: Ford to Old Bewick,* Stan Beckensall, 1991

————— , *Northumberland's Prehistoric Rock Carvings: Mystery Explained,* Pendulum, 1983

Boujot, C., and Cassen, S., "A Pattern of Evolution for the Neolithic Funerary Structures of the West of France," in *Megaliths from Antiquity,* Antiquity Publications, 2003

Bradley, R., *The Significance of Monuments,* Routledge, 1998

Brown, P., *Indian Architecture: Buddhist and Hindu Periods,* Bombay, 1942 and 1965

Bunce, F. W., *Monuments of India and the Indianized States,* D.K. Printworld, 2007

Burke, J., and Halberg, K., *Seed of Knowledge, Stone of Plenty,* Council Oak, 2005

Burrow, S., "Knowlton Henges Project, Dorset," *School of Conservation Science,* Bournemouth University, 1996

Castleden, R., *The Making of Stonehenge,* Routledge, 1994

Cattaneo, M., and Trifoni, J., *The World Heritage Sites of UNESCO Ancient Civilizations,* White Star, 2004

Childress, D., *Lost Cities of Atlantis Ancient Europe and the Mediterranean,* Adventures Unlimited, 1996

Chippindale, C., *Stonehenge Complete,* Thames & Hudson, 1983

Coe, M., *Angkor and the Khmer Civilization,* Thames and Hudson, 2003

————— , *The Maya,* Thames and Hudson, 1999

————— , *Mexico from the Olmecs to the Aztecs,* Thames and Hudson, 1994

Corliss, W., *Ancient Infrastructure,* The Sourcebook Project, 1999

Cowan, D., and Arnold, C., *Ley Lines and Earth Energies,* Adventures Unlimited, 2003

Cunliffe, B., *The Oxford Illustrated Prehistory of Europe*, Oxford University, 1994

Cunliffe, Barlett, Morrill, Briggs, and Bourke (eds.), *The Penguin Atlas of British and Irish History*

Dames, M., *Mythic Ireland,* 1996

Daniken, E., *Chariots of the Gods?,* Bantam Books, 1970

Darvill, T., *Prehistoric Britain,* Routledge, 1987

Darvill, T., and Malone, C. (eds.), *Megaliths from Antiquity,* Cambridge 2003

Darvill, T., Stamper, P., and Timby, J., *England: An Oxford Archaeological Guide to Sites from Earliest Time to AD 1600,* Oxford University Press, 2002

Devereaux, P., *Secrets of ancient and Sacred Places, the Mysterious World,* Time-Life Books

Dhaky, M. A., *The Indian Temple: Forms in Karnata Inscriptions and Architecture,* Abhinav

DK Eyewitness Travel Guides, *Mexico,* Dorling Kindersley, 1999, 2003

Donaldson, T., *Konark,* Oxford University Press, 2003

Domenici, D., *Mexico: A Guide to the Archaeological Sites,* White Star, 2002

Dunbavin, P., *Atlantis of the West,* Constable and Robinson, 2003

————— , *Secrets of Ancient and Sacred Places*

Dyer, J., *Ancient Britain,* Routledge, 1990

Dyer, J. and Lane, A., *The Penguin Guide to Prehistoric England and Wales,* Penguin, 1983

Edmonds, M., *Stone Tools and Society,* Routledge, 1997

Eltringham, P., Fisher, J., and Stewart, I., *The Maya World,* Rough Guide, 2001

Eogan, G., "Knowth before Knowth," *Antiquity* 72 (1998): 162–172

Evans, S., *Ancient Mexico and Central America,* Thames and Hudson, 2004

Fagan, B., *World Prehistory,* Longman, 1999

Fash, W., *Scribes, Warriors and Kings: The City of Copan and the Ancient Maya,* Thames and Hudson, 2001

Freeman, M., and Jacques, C., *Ancient Angkor,* River Books, 1999

Foster, L., *Handbook to Life in the Ancient Maya World,* Oxford University Press, 2005

Garnham, T., *Lines on the Landscape Circles from the Sky,* Tempus, 2004

Gibson, A., *Stonehenge and Timber Circles,* Tempus, 1998

Gibson, A., and Simpson, D. (eds.), *Prehistoric Ritual and Religion,* Alan Sutton, 1998

Gilbert, A., and Cotterell, M., *The Mayan Prophecies,* Element, 1995

Gimbutas, M., *The Goddesses and Gods of Old Europe,* University of California, 1982

Grude, N. (ed.), *Maya: Divine Kings of the Rain Forest,* Konemann, 2001

Harbison, P., *Pre-Christian Ireland,* Thames and Hudson, 1988

Hardy, A., *Indian Temple Architecture: Form and Transformation,* Abhinav

Hartwell, B., "A Neolithic Ceremonial Timber Complex at Ballynahatty, Co. Down," in *Megaliths from Antiquity*, Antiquity Publications, 2003

————— , "The Prehistory of the Giant's Ring and Ballynahatty Townland"

Harrison, P., *The Lords of Tikal,* Thames and Hudson, 1999

Haselhoff, E. H., *The Deepening Complexity of Crop Circles: Scientific Research and Urban Legends,* Frog, Ltd., 2001

Hasting, J., *Henge Monuments of the British Isles,* Tempus, 2003

Havell, E. B., *Encyclopaedia of Architecture in the Indian Subcontinent,* Aryan Books, 2000

Hawkins, G., *Stonehenge Decoded,* Hippocrene Books, 1988

Henderson, J., *The World of the Ancient Maya,* Cornell University, 1997

Hernandez, Falcon, Fuente, Garza, Cicero and Vera: *The Mayas of the Classical Period,* Java Book, 1999

Howe, L., *Mysterious Lights and Crop Circles,* LMH, 2002

Jacques, C., *Angkor,* Konemann, 1990

James, P., and Thorpe, N., *Ancient Mysteries,* Ballantine Publishing, 1999

Janssen, B., *The Hypnotic Power of Crop Circles,* Frontier Publishing, 2004

Jigourel, T., *Brittany,* White Star, 2004

Kail, O. C., *Buddhist Cave Temples of India,* Taraporevala, 1975

Kamiya, T., *The Guide to the Architecture of the Indian Subcontinent (English Version),* Architecture Autonomous, 2003

Khare, A., *Temple Architecture of Eastern India,* Shubhi, 2005

Kjaerum, P., "Mortuary Houses and Funeral Rites in Denmark," *Megaliths from Antiquity*, Antiquity Publications, 2003

Knight, C., and Lomas, R., *Uriel's Machine,* Arrow Books, 2000

Kolate, A., *The Tiwanaku: Portrait of an Andean Civilization,* Blackwell, 1993

Kvamme, K., *Magnetic Survey at Navan Fort, Northern Ireland*

Lewis, H., French, C., and Green, M., "A Decorated Megalith from Knowlton Henges, Dorset, England"

List, G., *The Secret of the Runes,* Destiny Book, 1988

Mackie, E., "Maeshowe and the Winter Solstice: Ceremonial Aspects of the Orkney Grooved Ware Culture," *Antiquity* 71 (1997): 338–59

Mahajan, M., *A Gate to Ancient Indian Architecture,* Sharada, 2004

Mallan, C., *Moon Handbooks: Yucatan Peninsula,* Avalon Travel, 2002

Mallory, J., and Lynn, C., "Recent Excavations and Speculations on the Navan Complex," *Antiquity* 76 (2002): 532–41

Mannikka, E., *Angkor Wat: Time, Space, and Kingship,* University of Hawaii, 1996

Mazzeo, D., and Antonini, C., *Monuments of Civilization: Ancient Cambodia,* Grosset and Dunlap, 1978

Meister, M., *Essays in Early Indian Architecture,* Oxford University Press, 1992

McGinn, P., and Cunningham, N., *The Gap of the North*

McMann, J., "Forms of Power: Dimensions of an Irish Megalithic Landscape," *Antiquity* 68 (1994): 525–44

Meaden, T., *The Secret of the Avebury Stones: Britain's Greatest Megalithic Temple*, Frog, Ltd., 1999

Michell, G., *Hindu Art and Architecture,* Thames and Hudson, 2000

————— , *The Hindu Temple: An Introduction to Its Meaning and Forms,* Paul Elek London, 1977

Michell, J.,, *A Little History of Astro-Archaeology,* Thames and Hudson, 1989

————— , *Megalithomania,* Thames and Hudson, 1982

Mohen, J.-P., *Standing Stones, Stonehenge, Carnac and the World of Megaliths,* Thames and Hudson, 1998

Mohen, J., and Eluere, C., *The Bronze Age in Europe,* Harry N. Abrams, 1999

Moore, J., and Lamb, B., *Crop Circles Revealed,* Light Technology, 2001

Morrison, T., *Pathways to the Gods, The Mystery of the Andes Lines,* Academy Chicago 1978

Moseley, M., *The Incas and Their Ancestors,* Thames and Hudson, 2001

Noonan, D., *Castles and Ancient Monuments of England,* Aurum Press, 1999

————— , *Castles and Ancient Monuments of Scotland,* Aurum Press, 2000

————— , *Castles and Ancient Monuments of Ireland,* Aurum Press, 2001

O'Kelly, M., *Newgrange, Archaeology, Art and Legend,* Thames & Hudson, 1982

O'Riordain, S., and Daniel, G., N*ewgrange: The Bend of the Boyne,* 1964

Ostfildern, B., *Baedeker's Malta,* Automobile Association, 2000

Pattison, P., Field, D., and Ainsworth, S., *Patterns of the Past,* Oxbow Books, 1999

Pearson, P., and Ramilisonina, "Stonehenge for the Ancestors: The Stone Pass on the Message," *Antiquity* 72 (1998): p.308-326

Pearson, M., Sharples, N., and Mulville, J., "Brochs and Iron Age Society: A Reappraisal," *Antiquity* 70 (1996): 57–67

Pedley, G., *Greek Art and Archaeology,* Laurence King, 1993

Penguin Atlas of British and Irish History, 2002

Piggott, S., "The Tholos Tomb in Iberia," "The Long Barrow in Brittany," and "The Excavations at Cairnpapple Hill, West Lothian 1947–8," in *Megaliths from Antiquity,* Antiquity Publications, 2003

Pitts, Mike., *Hengeworld,* Arrow Books, 2001

Powell, M., "Astronomical Alignments at the Crick Barrow in Gwent, South Wales," *Archaeoastronomy*, vol. 26, no. 20 (1995)

Pringle, L., *Crop Circles,* Thorsons, 1999

Raffaelli, L. (ed.), *Ireland, Everyman Guides,* 1995

Renfrew, C., *Before Civilization: The Radiocarbon Revolution and Prehistoric Europe*, Penguin, 1973

Robins, J., *The World's Greatest Mysteries,* 1989

Rooney, D., *Angkor: An Introduction to the Temples,* Asia Books, 1994

Roughley, C., Sherratt, A., and Shell, C., "Past Records, New Views: Carnac 1830–2000," in *Megaliths from Antiquity,* Antiquity Publications, 2003

Rudgley, R., *Secrets of the Stone Age: A Prehistoric Journey with Richard Rudgley*

Russell, T. (ed.), *The Napoleonic Survey of Egypt,* Ashgate, 2001

Scarre, C., *Exploring Prehistoric Europe,* Oxford, 1999

———, *Monuments and Landscape in Atlantic Europe,* Routledge, 2002

———, "Misleading Images: Stonehenge and Brittany," *Antiquity* 71 (1997): 1016–20

Scarre, C., and Raux, P., "A New Decorated Menhir," *Antiquity* 74 (2000): 757–8

Schele, L., and Mathews, P., *The Code of Kings,* Touchstone, 1998

Schmidt, P., Garza, M., and Nalda, E., *Maya Civilization,* Thames and Hudson, 1998

Schwaller de Lubicz, R. A., *The Temples of Karnak,* Thames and Hudson, 1999

Scoffe, G., and Clare, T., "New Evidence of Ritual Monuments at Long Meg and Her Daughters, Cumbria," in *Megaliths from Antiquity*, Antiquity Publications, 2003

Settar, *The Hoysala Temple*

Sharer, R., *The Ancient Maya,* Stanford University, 1994

Shaw, I., *Exploring Ancient Egypt,* Oxford, 2003

——— (ed.), *The Oxford History of Ancient Egypt,* Oxford University Press, 2000

Silva, F., *Secrets in the Fields: The Science and Mysticism of Crop Circles,* Hampton Roads, 2002

Sitchin, Z., *The 12th Planet,* Avon Books, 1999

———, *The Earth Chronicles,* Bear and Company, 2004

Smith, M., *The Aztec,* Blackwell, 1996

Snodgrass, A., *The Symbolism of the Stupa,* Cornell University, 1985

Strachan, D., "Cropmark Landscape in Three Dimensions"

Stierlin, H., *The Maya: Palaces and Pyramids of the Rainforest,* Taschen, 2004

Souden, D., *Stonehenge Revealed,* Facts on File, 1997

Suresh, K. M., *Temples of Karnataka,* Bharatiya Kala Prakashan

Tadegell, C., *The History of Architecture in India,* Viking, 1990

Taylour, W., *The Mycenaeans*, Thames and Hudson, 1983

Thomas, A., *Vital Signs: A Complete Guide to the Crop Circle Mystery and Why It is NOT a Hoax*, Frog, Ltd., 2002

Thomas, J., *Understanding the Neolithic,* Routledge, 1991

Tilley, C., *The Materiality of Stone,* Berg Publishers, 2004

Wainwright, G., *The Henge Monument,* Thames and Hudson, 1989

Whittle, A., "A Late Neolithic Complex at West Kennet, Wiltshire, England," in *Megaliths from Antiquity*, Antiquity Publications, 2003

Wilkinson, R., *The Complete Temples of Ancient Egypt,* Thames and Hudson 2000

Wilson, C., *The Atlas of Holy Places and Sacred Sites*

Young-Sanchez, M., *Tiwanaku: Ancestors of the Incas,* Denver Art Museum, 2004

Zarmati, L., and Cremin, A., *Experience Archaeology,* Cambridge University, 1998

Internet Resources

Agutie.homestead.com

Ancient Monuments Laboratory of English Heritage

angelfire.com

anima.demon.co.uk

angkorwat.org

arch.soton.ac.uk

archaeology.org

astroarchaeology.org

avebury-web.co.uk

btinternet.com

bust-taylor.com

carrowkeel.com

cicap.org

comp-archaeology.org

countyarmagh.com

cropcircle-archive

cropcircleconnector

Crop Circle Geometry

cropcircleinfo.com

Crop Circle News

cropcircleresearch

Crop Circle Web Ring

Crop Circular

crystalinks.com

CSICOP's Crop Circle Report

easyweb.easynet.cu.ukcropcirclerearch.com

ehsni.gov.uk

emuseum.mnsu.edu

English-heritage.org.uk

Eng-h.gov.uk

German Association for Crop Circle Research

greatdreams.com

hardav.co.uk

Hinduwisdom.com

homestead.com

homeusers.prestel.co.uk

infinito.it

ireland-information.com

irishclans.com

irishmegaliths.org.uk

jahtruth.net

Joussaume, R., "Dolmens for the Dead"

kht.org.uk

Knowth.com

liminae.co.uk

livingarchitecturecentre.com

lovely.clara.net

lucypringle.co.uk

megalithia.com

megalithomania.com

megaliths.co.uk

megalithsites.co.uk

mythicalireland.com

myweb.tiscali.co.uk

NASAexplores.com

Northumberland Rock Art project team

orkneyjar.com

Oxfordshire Centre for Crop Circle Studies

photos.blogger.com

phy.mtu.edu

PTAH homepage

rockart.ncl.ac.uk

romangask.org.uk

sacredsites.com

shetland.museum.org.uk

SPACE.com

stonehenge.co.uk

Stonehenge World Heritage Site

stoneofwonder.com

stonepages.com

surf-mexico.com

Teotihuacan Home Page

theangkor.com

themodernantiquarian.com

touregypt.net

travels-in-time.net

ufoarea.com

UKcropcircles.co.uk

webring.com

wikipedia.org

Wiltshire-web.co.uk

world-mysteries.com

Zefdamen.nl

100megsfree4.com